CURRENT ISSUES IN HIGHER EDUCATION

Research and Reforms

Edited by
Stanley D. Murphy
and
John P. Eddy

Foreword by C. William McKee

University Press of America, Inc.
Lanham • New York • Oxford

University Press of America,® Inc.
4720 Boston Way
Lanham, Maryland 20706

12 Hid's Copse Rd.
Cummor Hill, Oxford OX2 9JJ

Printed in the United States of America
British Library Cataloging in Publication Information Available

Library of Congress Cataloging-in-Publication Data

Murphy, Stanley D.
Current issues in higher education : research and reforms / edited by Stanley D. Murphy and John P. Eddy ; foreword by C. William McKee.
p. cm.
Includes Bibliographical references and index.
1. Education, Higher—United States. 2. Education, Higher—United States—Administration. 3. Education, Higher—China. I. Eddy, John. II. Title.
LA227.4.M87 1998 378.73—dc21 98-34814 CIP

ISBN 0-7618-1218-0 (cloth: alk. ppr.)
ISBN 0-7618-1219-9 (pbk: alk. ppr.)

™ The paper used in this publication meets the minimum requirements of American National Standard for Information Sciences—Permanence of Paper for Printed Library Materials, ANSI Z39.48—1984

Contents

Part III
Student Services in Higher Education

Part IV
Administration, Curriculum and Technology in Higher Education

Part V
Athletics, Diversity and Volunteer Service in Higher Education

Foreword

"Challenges in a Changing Environment"

An often quoted expression that is accepted as truth is "death and taxes will always be with us." In our professional life, the axiom "change will always occur" is equally true. Leaders in American higher education, especially in the area of student development, have both redefined and expanded the policies and practices of the student development profession during the last quarter century. Change is not easy, but necessary. Those entering and continuing in the profession will struggle with new opportunities, approaches and ideas. This struggle makes the practice of student development exciting and meaningful. Each change will result in a new and different challenge.

Student personnel professionals need to understand some of the changing issues in the field. The fifteen items which follow provide a brief statement of the movement of the profession from the past to the present.

- the concept of *in loco parentis* has evolved into the theory that the student is an adult and must be treated accordingly,
- the creation of the office of provost, which has supervisory responsibilities for both academic and student affairs, has negated many chief student affairs officers from reporting to the institutional president/chancellor,
- the enlarging of the student body to include more diverse populations (e.g. women, part-time, evening, minority, returning adults, single parent, etc.) has resulted in the need for new and enlarged personnel services,

- the changing of the legal drinking age from eighteen to twenty-one and the abuse of alcohol and drugs by the student population has created the need for both educational and interdiction programming,
- the emergence of residence halls as "living and learning centers" rather than motels has created new opportunities and obligations for residence professionals,
- the movement to more egalitarian admissions has dictated that special remedial and developmental academic and socialization programs be introduced,
- the opportunity for a larger percentage of students to participate in federally guaranteed grant and loan programs has made financial aid "big business" on a majority of campuses,
- the revival of moral and ethical concerns in the curriculum and in student activities programming has created a need to re-visit the role of the student affairs professional in teaching values and serving as student role models,
- the continuing discussion of the role of students in institutional decision-making is forcing a re-evaluation of the concept of what decisions are and/or should be as part of the student domain,
- the changing role of student health from treating minor emergencies and illnesses to developing programs of wellness, exercise, reproductive education, and determining that mental health must-exist with physical health continues to challenge health service practitioners,
- the emerging idea that a student goes to college to "get a job" versus "get an education" has produced changes in career counseling delivery systems,
- the issues concerning the physical safety and security of individuals on campus and the protection of personal and institutional property have increased the need for professionals in the area of campus police science,
- the defining of the institutional supervisory responsibility for quasi-college sponsored organizations (e.g. fraternities, sororities, honor societies, recognition groups, religious clubs,

etc.) continues to need refinement so that the groups are not abandoned one year and highly regulated the next,

- the enlarging of the scope of student activities to include programming which supports classroom instruction (e.g. lectures, cultural movies, etc.) rather than just providing campus "fun" activities has created the need to redefine the responsibility of student affairs in developing, sponsoring, and supervising the events which define campus ambiance, and
- the broadening of the role of the library, as having both an academic and student development function has forced the institution to expand the thinking and dialogue of student development beyond the "traditional" student personnel functions.

In *Current Issues in Higher Education: Research and Reforms*, the authors Murphy and Eddy have opened new doors of thinking, have discussed opportunities for change, and have encouraged the readers to accept the challenges which always come with learning. Additionally, they have focused on their personal research which codifies many changes in both traditional thinking and current practice. Student Development like all professions will continue to struggle with change. Be encouraged to welcome and embrace change while making a difference in the lives of the next generation of college students.

C. William McKee, Ed.D.
Vice President for Strategic Planning and
Professor of Education
Cumberland University
Lebanon, Tennessee

Preface

It is impossible to separate the problems of higher education from the ills of society. To the student, higher education is a means to employment. To the faculty member, budget cuts, publishing, and obtaining lucrative grants conceal and sometimes obscure the true goal of higher education—educating students. Without the vision that truly makes educating the student foremost, our society will suffer greatly.

Emerging voices are, however, speaking to the problems of higher education. *Current Issues in Higher Education: Research and Reforms* gives a comprehensive analysis through research which addresses various areas of our institutions of higher learning. In this text the authors address leadership, wellness and health programs, student services, administration, curriculum and technology, athletics, diversity, volunteer service and international issues in higher education.

Leaders in higher education must be abreast of the challenges facing the world and their institutions as they enter the 21st century. This book addresses many of those challenges. It is recommended to graduate students studying educational leadership and higher education. It is also recommended as a resource to deans, chairpersons, department heads, and presidents of community colleges and universities who have been delegated the tasks of educational and administrative leadership in their respective areas. The research will challenge your present views, but hopefully, will stimulate your vision for the future of higher education work as you continue to prepare leaders for the 21st century.

Lester G. Pretlow, Ph.D.
United States Army Medical Command
Augusta, Georgia
January, 1998

Acknowledgments

The authors thank their wives for the many hours of sacrifice, encouragement and support throughout the writing of this book. In many ways this work is a tribute to you for your unselfish behind the scenes work. Thank you Saundria and Betty.

Appreciation is also expressed to colleagues and students for their ideas that have contributed to some of the studies in this book. We appreciate greatly your input and feedback. Without you as the primary consumer, we in the higher education profession would not be employed. We hope this small contribution makes a difference in improving the system put in place to educate and prepare men and women like you for leadership in a rapidly changing world.

Moreover, specific colleagues are listed as coauthors in this reference work. We especially thank them for their contributions. We also thank the following editors for their permission to publish these materials:

1. Dr. Russell N. Cassel, Editor of the *Education Journal* and,
2. Dr. George E. Uhlig, Editor of the *College Student Journal* and the *Journal of Instructional Psychology*

Finally, the lead author would like to thank the following people for their many years of love, nurturing, mentoring and support. His personal, educational and career development is directly related to the influence by each of these individuals. This period of influence spans over twenty-four years. Some of these individuals include: William and Alice Murphy, James and Joyce Covington, Agnas Matlock, Chris and Margaret Fentress, Paul and Pat Kurts, Bo and Dottie Culbertson, Roy Duke, Fred Shelton, Mary Jane Wallace, Jackie Reavis, the late Joe E. Nunley, Bob Womack,

Winston Wrenn, Ben Hurt, Ross Spielman, James and Marge Friddle, the late Joseph W. Tkach, Stan and Millicent Bass, Helen Jackson, Ken and Donna Weese, Jeffrey Broadnax, John P. Eddy, Morag B. Harris, C. William McKee, Edward Mauzey, Gilbert Q. Norman, William L. Johnson, Dwayne Robinson, Ron Thomas and Priscilla Drew.

Introduction

The chapters in this book include articles based upon four years of research conducted on various college and university campuses across the country from 1994-1997. The idea for the book came about during one of our weekly telephone conferences to update each other on present professional activities and to share ideas for our next conference presentation. During my doctoral studies at the University of North Texas, Denton, Texas, Dr. Eddy always shared information relating to professional development in order to help students learn the benefits and strengths of collaboration. One of the teaching methods often applied in Dr. Eddy's classes is the dyad concept which emphasizes the "Eddy Wholistic Model of College Student Development" (Martin, Eddy, and Stilson, 1983; Murphy and Eddy, 1995; Murphy, Eddy, and Spaulding, 1997). As a result of this regular professional collaboration, the idea for this book was born.

Current Issues In Higher Education: Research and Reforms is a book which has the following characteristics demonstrating its worth and value:

- All chapters have been published in a number of national refereed journals from 1995 to 1997 on higher education issues.
- All chapters have been presented as subjects at national refereed professional conferences as papers presented from 1995 to 1997 by scholars and students.
- One chapter has been accepted for a new international book published in 1998 by Prentice Hall Publishers of Canada.
- One chapter was selected by the National Association of Academic Affairs Administrators Southeast/South Annual Convention for a keynote annual presentation in New Orleans, Louisiana in 1997.

- One chapter has material that appears in a book published in 1995 by the Adult Development and Aging Counseling Network of the Association of Counselor Educators and Supervisors.
- One chapter relates to an outstanding college orientation program that has a global education approach for college students reaching millions worldwide.
- Two chapters present some of the most comprehensive studies ever done on a college student theory in terms of actual results of a theory being tested.
- One chapter presents a unique new theory for cultural diversity for higher education and society worldwide.
- One chapter covers the internationally famous theory of Dr. Art Chickering on college student development.
- One chapter presents ways graduate students can save money while working on their masters and doctoral degrees.
- One chapter covers one of the most controversial subjects in all of higher education which is intercollegiate scholarship athletics.
- One chapter deals with the tremendously important topic of technology in higher education from computers to other media material.
- One chapter deals with the extremely vital issue of privatization in higher education in America.
- Finally, two chapters deal with the important subjects of college student wellness and health that are seldom mentioned in reference books in American higher education.

Stanley D. Murphy
Norfolk, Virginia

PART I

LEADERSHIP IN HIGHER EDUCATION

Chapter 1

ꕥ

21st Century Leadership Practices Needed for Higher Education

John P. Eddy, Stanley D. Murphy, Donald J. Spaulding, and Kan V. Chandras

Advanced and improved leadership practices for higher education are needed in the 21st Century if universities and colleges are to raise standards, status, and improve the overall campus environment. This article discusses areas in which new leadership practices will be necessary, gives selected examples of current malpractice, and offers recom-mendations for improvement.

Introduction

The effectiveness and efficiency of the university and college campus is an emerging crisis — a crisis directly related to failed practices in certain areas of leadership. The challenge for academe, more specifically leaders in academe, is to initiate and follow new leadership practices that directly confront unethical, failed and out-of-date methods of campus governance. The purpose of this article is to highlight several areas in which enhanced or new leadership practices are necessary, provide selected examples of egregious incidents of executive wrong-doing, and offer recommended leadership practices for the campus of the 21st Century.

Ethical Leadership

The New Era Scam (Eddy and Brubacher, 1996) whereby scores of graduate schools, universities, and colleges were fooled by the investment "Polizing Scheme," is but one example of how higher education leaders and officials (Boards of Regents and Trustees, Presidents, Legal Counsels, Vice Presidents, Business Advisors, etc.) need to commit to a higher level of ethics. This tragedy, the worst financial scam ever in higher education finance, occurred in 1995 when it was discovered that the Foundation for New Era Philanthropy pulled off a Charles Ponzi type financial swindle wherein millions of dollars were lost by scores of seminaries, universities, and colleges. Reflectively, Ponzi's scheme was based on the long chanced theme of huge profits in return for large investments. In repeated articles, higher education journals and periodicals, including the *Chronicle of Higher Education*, relate accounts of "get rich quick" schemes initiated and approved by leaders of academic institutions. Truly, there seems to be an ethical crisis within our campus leaders.

Academic leaders of the 21st Century must re-cast their leadership practice to include the following essential aspects of the ethical dimension:

(1) Leaders set the tone for the ethical climate of their organizations (Kouzes & Posner, 1995). Members of Boards of Regents and Trustees, presidents, vice presidents, deans, and others comprising the academic leadership of the institution must, by deeds, speech, and action, portray their commitment to high ethical standards.

(2) A clearly understandable and set of ethical standards that can be adhered to must be devised and articulated by the campus leadership (Eddy, 1993). An unreachable or idealistic ethical code will be breached in day-to-day or routine business — thus, diluting the components that can be lived up to.

(3) Ethics violations within the leadership hierarchy should be dealt with swiftly, authoritatively, and affirmatively. The results of inquiries and investigations into ethical lapses should be widely publicized.

Team Leadership

Leadership unitage, that is, the quantity of leadership within a particular unit of leadership, is significantly improved when all leaders in the institution are empowered to lead their respective unit — teamwork increases productivity (Spaulding & Eddy, 1996). A shift in organizational leadership is underway according to many experts writing on the subject. Charles Handy has indicated that this evolving leadership should be termed "language of politics" — a process of leadership that includes the concepts of "adhocracy, of federalism, of alliances, teams, empowerment and room for initiative." He identifies the key words as "options not plans, the possible rather than the perfect; and involvement instead of obedience." According to Handy, the title "manager" is being replaced with titles such as lead partner, team leader, facilitator, and project manager (Hesselbein, Goldsmith, & Beckhard, 1996). Critical actions that can be undertaken to improve the institutional climate wherein team leadership can thrive are:

(1) Just as the Boards of Regents and Trustees work as a team so should the academe leadership operating entities. No matter what they are called, problems, challenges, opportunities, or issues, organizational activity requiring leader attention should be pursued via a collaborative or shared effort.
(2) Often, those with new ideas are not considered team players. In the future, team leadership must accommodate the innovative, create, and forward-thinking from team members. Internal procedure must allow for exchanges of creative ideas — sharing a particular new way or another new idea (Spaulding & Eddy, 1996).
(3) Reward joint effort as often as individual effort is recognized.
(4) Instill teamwork through team building and training.

Accountability Leadership

One of the significant new initiatives to impact higher education is the "accountability movement." Legislators, parents, students, government, accrediting bodies, industry, business are all demanding that universities and colleges produce a competent graduate. The Oklahoma State Regents for Higher Education is issuing a degree warranty for selected technical school degrees. Moreover, this Board has established a similar warranty for certain nontechnical and professions degrees awarded by state colleges and universities (Magnuson, 1996).

(1) Exercise visionary and "out-front" leadership in resolving academe's responsibility in arriving at and establishing standards for graduation, guaranteed or warranted degrees, and re-schooling or refresher education for graduates not deemed fully prepared by industry or professions.

Privatization Leadership

The privatization of higher education must be investigated carefully to see if certain services, activities, research and learning can be privatized or "out-sourced." The balance between better services and lower cost must be thoroughly examined in the framework of the mission, scope, and role of the university or college. According to the research of Eddy & Spaulding (1996) some campuses have been successful in their efforts to privatize campus food service and parking while not being successful in other areas of campus activities.

(1) Privatization demands change in the results of the organizational structure. The new paradigm of institution leadership calls for a special ability to wrench out of the traditional bureaucracy an attitude that accepts and thrives on change (Senge, 1996).
(2) Just as public schools are seeking new ways to join with the private sector to fulfill their education mission (Eddy & Spaulding, 1996) so must higher education leaders explore creative paths toward including the private sector in operating the university.

Global Thinking Leadership

The Untied States of America leads the world in the number of other nation or international students studying in U.S. institutions of higher education. Currently, over 400,000 students from outside the U.S. are enrolled in U.S. universities and colleges. These students, many pursuing graduate degrees, return to their country to become influential leaders. Such leaders often take a leading role in policy-making and operational matters affecting world peace, war, and terrorism (Eddy, J.P. 1995). Leadership in this environment requires academic leadership that (1) Understands and projects the global implications of the role of education on the grave matters of peace, war, and the economy (Spaulding & Eddy, 1996). (2) Academic leaders must develop grant contacts in the home countries of international students so as to assist in the retention and graduation of these students (Eddy, McLeod, & Nichols, 1995). Just as business leaders are required to integrate into the economies of other countries so should academic leaders learn to cope with grant challenges in the high student sending countries of China, Russia, Japan, Iran, Germany and others.

Volunteer Leadership

As the age demographics of America change toward an ever increasing older population, many of these citizens are volunteering to assist community institutions. In 1995-1996, the senior author became aware of faculty who were rejected when volunteering services at some colleges while at others these volunteers were warmly received and the best use made of their talents. In 1996 however, this author volunteered to assist several Filipino universities and colleges with the development of their electronic technology and distance education approaches to link over 400 institutions of higher education world-wide. Volunteers will offset the financial retrenchment underway in many higher education institutions. The progressive academic leader of the future must:

(1) Envision the role of and integrate volunteers into the academic institution (Beckhard, 1996).
(2) Develop unique motivational and reward systems to keep volunteers on the job and productive.

Distance Education Leadership

Education is rapidly expanding beyond the physical boundaries of the university and college. The challenges posed by technology assisted education are, as noted by Eddy, Burnett, and Spaulding, and Murphy (1997), (a) balancing the personal contact of classroom professors and the impersonal contact of technology, (b) limitations, such as library access and student services, of not being on-campus, and (c) the benefits of group learning over individual learning. The academic leader in the time that is to come should possess the following leadership skills with regard to distance education:

(1) An appreciation and understanding of the relationship between education, technology, time, distance, location (Eddy & Spaulding, 1996) is essential. Moreover, the goals of education must blend with the technology so as to be the medium rather than the message. Distance education will be commonplace in the future. Just as the home is fast becoming a workplace so might home learning become the central place of learning.
(2) The interaction of communications technology and knowledge dissemination is a rapidly advancing field. Academic executives must rapidly learn to control and harness this process (Mandl & Seti, 1996).

Multicultural Leadership

Leadership in today's society demands recognition of the diversity and difference present in our culture. The effective academic leader of the future must negotiate the multicultural environment by fully recognizing diversity and difference while exercising leadership that unites all toward a common goal. This process of future leadership must include the following:

(1) Successful reformation and change of education can only take place when academic leaders are able to unite disparate and diverse individuals and groups. Envisioning the possible contributions of all persons, regardless of gender, ethnicity, or other measure of difference and diversity, will be a significant challenge to future leaders (Kouzes & Posner, 1995).
(2) Creative means of communicating the accomplishments of diverse and different individuals within our global society must be developed to portray the importance of multiculturalism. In a Texas university, the author or and associates developed a "Gallery of Great Educators" as a permanent visual exhibit, within the education environment, wherein diversity, difference, and internationalism may be studied, understood, and appreciated (Eddy, Cooper, & Spaulding,

1996). A mobile "Multicultural Pictorial Gallery," also established by Eddy and associates, depicts significant contributions of minority women in business, science, and education.

Conclusions

Leadership in American higher education needs to take new directions. Higher education leaders, administrators, and faculty must be more progressive, innovative, and creative to manage the reformation and change that is underway and will occur in the future. This article identifies and makes recommendations critical to the path of future leadership in academe. This new leadership must take new directions in ethics, collaboration, accountability, privatization, international and distance education, volunteerism, and multiculturalism.

References

Beckhard, R. (1996). On future leaders. In Hesselbein, F., Goldsmith, M., & Beckhard, R. (Eds.), *The Leader of the Future* (pp. 125-129). San Francisco: Jossey-Bass Publishers.

Eddy, J.P. (1993). *Higher education perspectives for leaders.* Edina, MN: Burgess International Publishers.

Eddy, J.P. (1995) *International higher education systems.* Denton, TX: Ron Jon Publishers.

Eddy, J.P., Burnett, J., Spaulding, D.J., & Murphy, S.D. (1997). Technology assisted education. *Education.*

Eddy, J.P., McLeod, P., & Nichols, W. (1995). *Grant resources: Theories to writing to funding.* Denton, TX: Ron Jon Publishing.

Eddy, J.P., & Spaulding, D.J, (1996). Internet, computers, distance education and people failures: Research on technology. *Education*, 116(3), 391-392.

Eddy, J.P.. & Spaulding, D.J. (1996). New high tech school opens in Texas. *Reading Improvement* 33(1), 60-62.

Eddy, J.P., Spaulding, D.J., & Murphy, S.D. (1996). Privatization of higher education services: Propositional pros and cons. *Education.*

Hesselbein, F., Goldsmith, M., & Beckhard, B. (1996). *The leaders of the future. New visions, strategies, and practices for the next era.* San Francisco: Jossey-Bass Publishers.

Kouzes, J.M., & Posner, B.Z. (1995). *The leadership challenge.* San Francisco: Jossey-Bass Publishers.

Magnuson, C. (1996, June). Grads for hire, warranty included. *Nation's Business* 84(6), 83.

Mandl, A., & Sethi, D. (1996). In Hesselbein, F., Goldsmith, M., &Beckhard (Eds.), *The Leader of the Future*, (pp. 257-261). San Francisco: Jossey-Bass Publishers.

Senge, P.M. (1996). Leading learning organizations. In Hesselbein, F., Goldsmith, M., & Beckhard, R. (Eds.), *The Leader of the Future* (pp. 41-57). San Francisco: Jossey-Bass Publishers.

Spaulding, D.J., & Eddy, J.P. (1996). *Empowered university and college leadership.* Unpublished manuscript, University of North Texas.

Spaulding, D.J., & Eddy, J.P. (1996). China and Hong Kong: A clash of ideologies. *Journal of Instructional Psychology*, 23(3), 231-233.

PART II

WELLNESS AND HEALTH PROGRAMS IN HIGHER EDUCATION

Chapter 2

ꕥ

Wellness Programming: Does Student Choice Relate to Recognized Development Vectors?

Russell K. Elleven, Donald J. Spaulding, Stanley D. Murphy, and John P. Eddy

Several theories regarding student development and growth during the college years have been developed. The leading theorists, such as Chickering, Astin, and Tinto, seem to focus the development vectors (Chickering's term) toward the practices of the traditional university. The emerging and unique metropolitan university, in its effort to establish a solid reputation in the nonacademic arena of student affairs, is involving the students themselves in the process of selecting and presenting student development programs in the residence halls. This article examines the choices students make in relationship to Chickering's vectors of development.

Introduction

The metropolitan university is a new breed of American university (Lynton, 1995). As such, the metropolitan university is beginning to find a voice in the array of institutional types vying to be heard. Concurrently, the metropolitan university must continue to examine the needs of society and students to ascertain the role a metropolitan university should fulfill (Lynton & Elman, 1987).

Just as the metropolitan university is different so is the student. Nowhere is the student population more recognizably diverse than in the institutions of metropolitan areas (Grobman, 1988). While the student body approaches the characteristics of other universities it is in the metropolitan universities, writes Barnett and Phares (1995), that the needs of the newer older, less affluent, largely minority, commuter student population is being served. Each of these populations, the traditional and the newer, have special needs with regard to scholarship and services (Schlossberg, Lynch, & Chickering, 1989; Cross, 1981; Jacoby, 1995; Coles, 1995).

Chickering, Astin, Tinto, and others have developed theories and models regarding extra-curricular development of students (Upcraft, 1993). These theories are based on the idea that during the college experience students undergo a transition toward an independent identity and values set formation during the college years. Much of this transition takes place outside of the classroom.

University housing is one of the services provided to many students at many metropolitan institutions. Within this housing environment, the metropolitan university typically provides out of classroom learning opportunities. This student development programming component contributes to the overall wellness, growth, change, and development of the student as suggested by Chickering (1969), Astin (1977), Tinto (1975), and others. Wellness, in this case an all inclusive term, has been defined as an integrated method of functioning that is oriented toward maximizing the potential for the individual within his or her environment (Dunn, 1961). Wellness, as one component of student development, is best programmed in the residence or housing programs of the university or college (Leafgren, 1993). However, with the mix of students in residence halls of the metropolitan university the challenge of types of programs can become an issue.

Purpose

This study examines student choice in wellness programming at a regional metropolitan university. The results should portray the diversity within this unique type of university and relate to Chickering's vectors. Resident Assistants (RA's) and students, under the guidance of housing and residence life professionals, at the metropolitan university under study, are afforded the opportunity to select the wellness programs that will be presented in their residence halls. As a result of this process several questions arise. First, when provided a list of potential wellness programs, in what areas do students most often choose? Second, are these programs chosen equally across the different residence halls? Finally, do the programs chosen conform to a recognized theory of development such as the one suggested by Chickering? This article then, examines the choices students make when afforded the opportunity to select residence hall programs designed to contribute to their overall development during their student years.

Student Development

Student development has become an accepted responsibility of the college (Pascarella & Terenzini, 1991). Student development has evolved to theories that charge the university or college with Creating an environment, via policy and programming, that enables the development of the entire or whole person (Andreas, 1993). This holistic approach in student development is usually based on theories of Astin (1977), Tinto (1975), and Chickering (1969) among other pioneers in student development. The residence life program offered at the metropolitan university under study closely parallel the seven vectors of development posited by Chickering (Chickering, 1969; Thomas & Chickering, 1984). The seven program dimensions are combined under a non-academic program termed wellness. From the explanatory and promotional brochure of the metropolitan university the following dimensions are compared with the vectors of Chickering:

Spiritual. Spiritual wellness is defined as searching for meaning in life. It involves questions of the origins and destiny of humanity, learning and developing bases for moral decisions and a philosophy of life. While not directly comparable to Chickering's developing purpose vector this program area helps to answer some of Chickering's questions regarding "Who am I?," "Where am I?," and "Where am I going?" among other meaning of life questions.

Sexual. Sexual wellness involves understanding one's sexual identity. The Chickering managing emotions vector involves development in love, sex, passion, lust, hate, and other powerful emotions. The vector termed establishing identity also places attention on the development of understanding sexual roles and behaviors.

Physical. Developing growth in this dimension allows the student to optimize their level of physical functioning. Specific programs range from diet and exercise to the ills associated with tobacco, alcohol, and drug use. Chickering's first vector, achieving competence, involves a physical and manual skills component.

Intellectual. This dimension is intended to directly supplement academic learning by offering programs that stimulate curiosity and creativity. It intends to stir a desire for learning and the development of responsibility for learning. Achieving competence, as Chickering termed increasing intellectual competence, closely parallels this wellness dimension.

Cultural. This dimension aims at recognition and tolerance of diversity. Chickering's vector freeing interpersonal relationships focuses on tolerance and respect of differences.

Emotional. The acceptance and appropriate expression of personal feelings is deemed an important aspect of development by the metropolitan university under study. This dimension closely conforms to Chickering's managing emotions vector.

Social. Balancing the needs of self and others involves respect and contributions to the common good states the publication on these dimensions. Chickering's theory does not express a vector that is pure in its relationship to this dimension although his vector labeled achieving competence does mention the social development of the college student.

Programming Options

As noted above, the metropolitan university has accepted the responsibility to offer and conduct student development programming. Historically, this programming can be implemented in various ways: (a) university directive, (b) student choice, and (c) a combination of a and b. This study examines the option of combining (a) and (b) to determine whether students, across residence hall types and overall, select programs that focus appropriately on the areas or vectors postulated in certain student development theories.

Methods

A metropolitan university in a large southwestern metroplex was selected for this study. At this university students are provided the opportunity to select, from a list offered by the residence hall staff, the programming they view as most important to their development. The eight halls on this campus, for the purpose of this study are grouped into the four following categories: (a) First year residences, (b) upper class residences, (c) all female residence, and (d) high school residence (a special program that allows talented high school students to finish their last two years of high school while completing their first two years of college).

The data on the number and type of programs was collected at the end of the Spring 1995 semester. The reporters of the data are paid staff who manage the program. Students however, have substantial input as to the number and types of programs. This data is representative of previous semesters. Descriptive statistics are used to analyze the data.

Findings

The data in Table 1 depicts a summary of the wellness programs chosen by the respective categories of students; while Figure 1 represents the total data in percentages. In all cases the social dimension was the top program selection of the students. This selection is 32% of the total 438 programs presented in the residence halls. Intellectual and cultural programs follow as the second or third choice of the students. Combined, these two dimensions represent 34% of the programs. Spiritual programs (26, 6%) represent the dimension least chosen by the students. The emotional (32, 7%) and sexual (33, 8%) dimensions complete the bottom three choices. The bottom three program choices represent 21% of the total programs presented. High School, first year, and upper class residence halls were very similar in priorities of programs chosen. All-female hall choice weighed equally in the social and cultural dimensions whereas this vector was second or third in the other hall categories.

Discussion

Chickering's core vector is identity according to an analysis by Pascarella & Terenzini (1991). Secondly, Chickering's vectors are not a step-by-step or straight line maturation but rather a process whereby growth comes as a result of stimulation throughout the college years. This study reveals that students, when given choice, do select programs that lead to growth in the Chickering establishing identity vector (sub-components of this vector include competence in intellectual, social, physical, and interpersonal relations). The students at this metropolitan university chose most of their programs in the social, cultural, physical, and intellectual dimensions thus locating within Chickering's core vector. Subsequent to developing the vectors Chickering (Thomas & Chickering, 1984) indicated he would sharpen the relationship between the vectors and the older student. He also expressed a desire to increase the interrelationship between the vectors and an aim to strengthen the cultural component. The vectors of development that indicate growth at the higher levels seem virtually ignored by students when given choice in programmatic conception, however. Chickering believes these higher order vectors should naturally be approached by students during the junior and senior years of the traditional college student. There are three ideas that might be developed from this data. First, students at metropolitan universities, because of their diverse background as explained by Grobman (1988), are not only academically behind the traditional college student but developmentally as well. One would expect the programming of the upper class residence halls to incorporate the higher vectors of Chickering if the students were indeed at that developmental level. The data did not lend itself to a conclusion that the developmental level of the juniors and seniors were at the higher levels. A second idea might be that Chickering's model does not incorporate enough dimensions to encompass the student population at a metropolitan university. Chickering has recently acknowledged that there are some gaps in his developmental theory. It might be that Chickering's theory does not serve the students involved in higher learning at metropolitan institutions. The emotional component of emotion was a strong fourth choice in the all-female hall but near the bottom in other halls. Overall, the spiritual, sexual, and emotional dimensions in this metropolitan university were least preferred as a growth vector.

Summary

Students at this metropolitan institution of higher education choose programs that indicate growth among Chickering's developmental model. This growth appears to be most dominant in the four vectors of achieving competence, managing emotions (mostly in the female hall), developing autonomy, and to some extent, establishing identity. Finally, residence hall programming might not be indicative of development in students at metropolitan institutions of higher education. Because these students must often contribute financially to their education, they might not always be the academically best prepared when compared to the rural student population and because they are often transfer students from community colleges, residence hall programming might not be high on the student's priority list.

These ideas should be explored more fully. The housing and residence life administrator of a metropolitan institution of higher education must understand the needs of these students and find ways to encourage them both academically and developmentally.

Table 1
Frequency of Programs by Hall Type

Program Type	F.Y.	U.C.	Female	H.S.	Total
Cultural	44	09	12	08	73
Emotional	17	05	09	01	32
Intellectual	44	13	11	08	76
Physical	37	07	07	06	57
Sexual	19	05	06	03	33
Social	79	29	12	21	141
Spiritual	18	05	03	00	26

Note: F.Y.=First Year; U.C.=Upper Class; Female=All Female Hall; H.S.=High School Programs (n=438)

Figure 1
Program Categories by Percentage

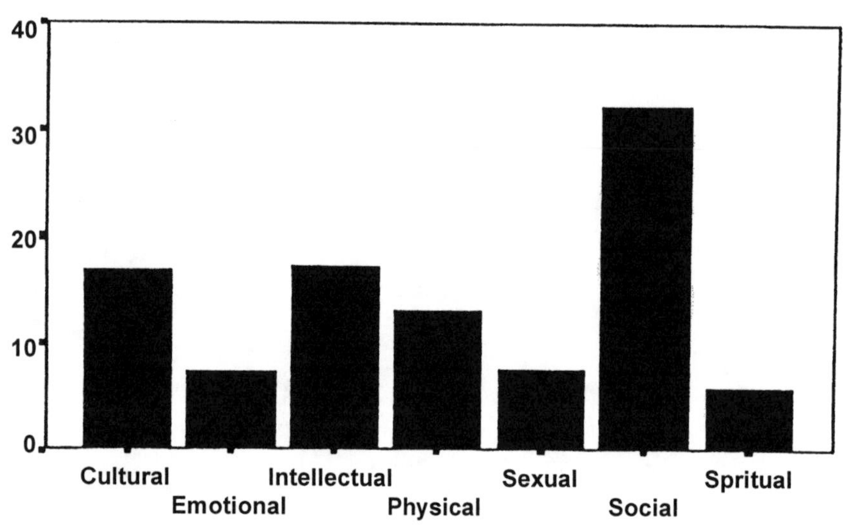

References

Andreas, R.E. (1993). Program planning. In M.J. Barr & Associates (Eds.), *Student Affairs Administration* (pp. 199-215). San Francisco: Jossey-Bass.

Astin, A. (1977). Four critical years. *Effects of college on beliefs, attitudes, and knowledge*. San Francisco: Jossey-Bass.

Barnett, M.R. & Phares, D. (1995). The metropolitan students. In D.M. Johnson & D.A. Bell (Eds.), Metropolitan universities. *An emerging model in American higher education* (pp. 39-50). Denton, TX: University of North Texas Press.

Chickering, A. (1969). *Education and Identity*. San Francisco: Jossey Bars.

Coles, A.S. (1995) Student services at a metropolitan university. In D.M. Johnson & D.A. Bell (Eds.), *Metropolitan Universities. An emerging model in American higher education* (pp. 72-82). Denton, TX: University of North Texas Press.

Cross, K.P. (1981) *Adults as learners*. San Francisco: Jossey-Bass.

Dunn, H.A. (1961) *High level wellness*. Arlington, VA: Betty.

Grobman, A.B. (1988) *Urban state universities. An unfinished national agenda*. New York: Praeger.

Jacoby, B. (1995) Adapting the institution to meet the needs of commuter students. In D.M. Johnson & D.A. Bell (Eds.), *Metropolitan universities: An emerging model in American higher education* (p. 51-62). Denton, TX: University of North Texas Press.

Leafgren, F. (1993) Wellness as a comprehensive student development approach. In R.B. Winston Jr. & S. Anchors (Eds.), *Student housing and residential life* (pp. 443-460). San Francisco: Jossey-Bass.

Lynton, E.A. (1995) Forward: What is a metropolitan university? In D.M. Johnson & D.A. Bell (Eds.), Metropolitan universities: An emerging model in American higher education (p. xi-xxi). Denton, TX: University of North Texas Press.

Lynton, E.A., & Elman, S.E. (1957) *New priorities for the university: Meeting society's need for applied knowledge and competent individuals*. San Francisco: Jossey-Bass.

Pascarella, E.T., & Terenzini, P.T. (1991). *How College Affects Students*. San Francisco: Jossey-Bass.

Schlossberg, N.K., Lynch, A.Q., & Chickering, A.W. (1989) Improving higher education environments for adults. San Francisco: Jossey-Bass.

Thomas, R. & Chickering, A. "Education and identity" revisited. Journal of College Student Personnel, 25, 392-399.

Tinto, V. (1975). Dropout from higher education: A theoretical synthesis of recent research. *Review of Educational Research*, 45, 89-125.

Upcraft, M.L. (1993). Translating theories into practice. In M.J. Barr & Associates (Eds.), *Student Affairs Administration*, (pp. 260-273). San Francisco: Jossey-Bass.

Chapter 3

ꕥ

Gulf War Syndrome: Are Campus Health Officials Prepared to Cope With Persian Gulf Veterans?

DONALD J. SPAULDING, JOHN P. EDDY,
KAN V. CHANDRAS AND STANLEY D. MURPHY

The Department of Defense is undergoing a large reduction-in-force because of the closure of the Cold War. This downsizing, or drawdown as they term it within the defense establishment, is resulting in and will result in an increase in college enrollment as many of these former soldiers, sailors, airmen, marines, coast guardsmen and women head for the college campus. Many of these former military personnel are veterans of the Gulf War. While the evidence is still not fully conclusive, many of these potential students claim to suffer from a mysterious illness termed "Gulf War Syndrome." Are campus health officials — medical and psychological — prepared to treat these veterans? This article surveys these health officials to determine whether student-veterans with Gulf War Syndrome can expect and obtain the health care necessary to enable them to complete their higher education.

The end of the Cold War is causing significant reductions in our military force. According to *Army Times* (1995) the military downsizing, or drawdown as the Department of Defense (DOD) terms it, which began in 1988 and is expected to conclude in 1997, will separate 700,000 servicemen and women. Many of these veterans are entering or returning to college to further their education (Magner, 1988; Myers, 1990). A large number of these student-veterans fought in the Gulf War — a war in which approximately one million American servicemen and women participated (Waldrop, 1993). Like their predecessors from Word War II and the Korean and Vietnam Wars, these veterans are returning to the campus with unique physical and psychological problems. Early Department of Defense and Department of Veterans Affairs (DVA) estimates were that 51,000 Persian Gulf War veterans reported being afflicted with a mysterious illness termed "Gulf War Syndrome" (Spaulding & Eddy, 1995). A more current study quoted in *USA Today* (1996), sponsored and recently released by these same departments, places this number at 75,000. Some on-campus Persian Gulf War veterans may seek treatment from university and college health and counseling clinics for treatment of Gulf War Syndrome. Are Campus health officials prepared to assist these students with their physical and psychological difficulties so that the students can complete their educational goals? Further, are these health entities prepared to assist these student-veterans by referring them to appropriate treatment agencies of the federal government? How many veterans have already sought treatment in normal medical facilities for Persian Gulf War illness related to Gulf War Syndrome?

Purpose

The purpose of this research was to explore the readiness and competence of campus physical and mental health officials to refer or treat veterans with Gulf War Syndrome. This article begins with an overview of Gulf War Syndrome, provides explanations of the research techniques with a discussion of findings, and closes with recommendations on how campuses can improve their readiness to treat and refer Persian Gulf War veterans pursuing higher education.

Significance

This article serves to call attention to an issue that is very important to students suffering from symptoms or a compounding of symptoms of Gulf War Syndrome. In view of the expected large number of perspective students resulting from the Cold War defense drawdown, campus counseling and health officials should be prepared to accommodate these student-veterans.

Gulf War Syndrome (Symptoms & Resources)

Since more than 75,000 Persian Gulf War veterans have reported symptoms of Gulf War Syndrome, speculation on the causes, origins, and treatment regimens vary according to expertise and sources. Cause speculation ranges from (1) chemicals implanted into battle dress uniforms, (2) chemical warfare in the Gulf War region and (3) chemical warfare prevention shots, to (4) extensive gas and diesel fumes (Spaulding & Eddy, 1995). The Department of Defense and Department of Veterans Affairs, while not endorsing a particular cause, have identified thirteen primary symptoms along with seven additional symptoms (Spaulding & Eddy, 1995). These symptoms are listed in Table 1. To date, the government has authorized perhaps as many as twenty-five studies of this mysterious illness (Spaulding & Eddy, 1995). The most recent study by the Department of Veterans Affairs compares a representative sample of 15,000 Persian Gulf War veterans with a control group of 15,000 veterans who did not serve In the Gulf War ("New Study," 1996). This study is not conclusive although preliminary findings confirm the existence of troublesome illnesses among Gulf War Veterans. Recently, as reported widely in the media (for example, *Dallas Morning News*, 1996), the U.S. government revealed the fact that some Gulf War veterans were exposed to chemicals resulting from exploding enemy shells. Meanwhile, until they have published conclusive studies, the Department of Defense and Veterans Affairs have agreed to treat any Persian Gulf veteran who presents symptoms of Gulf War Syndrome. Campus health officials should refer student-veterans to the nearest Department of Defense or Department of Veterans Administration clinic or health facility, and vice versa, prior to admission. Additionally, they should give these students the Persian Gulf Information Center telephone number, 1-800-PGW-VETS (1-800-749-8387). This number puts the student-veteran in contact with U.S. government treatment facilities.

Methodology

Through a national survey, three universities and college in each of the fifty states were asked to respond to questions regarding Gulf War Syndrome. The sample universities and colleges were selected from three categories: (a) one of the two largest (in enrollment) public or private universities in each state, (b) a "second tier" or smaller enrollment public or private university, and (c) a multicampus community college system. Specifically, the inquiry focused on three aspects of the issue by posing the following research questions:

1. Are clinic personnel familiar with the symptoms of Gulf War Syndrome? Respondents were asked to choose one of three responses: "not familiar," "familiar," or "extremely familiar."
2. Are clinic personnel familiar with Veterans Affairs policies regarding treatment of Gulf War Syndrome? The same responses noted above were available to respondents answering this questions.
3. Have students presented themselves to clinics with Gulf War Syndrome? Health clinic officials were asked to give a number response to this query. Health officials were also asked to query counselors regarding this response.

Thus, three surveys were sent to each state for a total of 150 queries. The survey was administered during the period September, 1994 to September, 1995. While the surveys were addressed to the campus health clinic, respondents were asked to consult with mental health or counseling officials. Seventy-four percent, or 111 surveys were returned. Thirteen of these respondents indicated that their university or campus did not operate an on-campus health clinic. Thus, ninety-eight of the returned surveys, or 65% of the total distributed were usable in calculating the data discussed in the findings. Descriptive statistics were used to evaluate the responses of the health officials.

Findings

In response to research question one, about one-half (49%) indicated that clinic personnel were "not familiar" with symptoms of Gulf War Syndrome. The remaining institutions, 51%, indicated "familiar." None of the respondents indicated "extremely familiar" when asked about their level of knowledge regarding the symptoms of Gulf War Syndrome. Several responded, anecdotally, that counselors were also not familiar with the symptoms.

Research question number two asked about health clinic familiarity with federal government policies regarding their (DOD & DVA) treatment of Gulf War Syndrome. In this regard, only nine or 9% indicated familiarity. A review of these nine respondents suggests proximity of the university or college to a military or veterans hospital. Again, several responses indicated that counseling centers were likewise not familiar with government treatment policies.

Research question number three sought to answer the question of how many students had sought assistance for Gulf War Syndrome. At the conclusion of the survey in September, 1995, thirty-one institutions (almost 32%) reported that a total of thirty-seven individuals had sought treatment or information for symptoms related to Gulf War Syndrome. This number combines health clinics and counseling centers contacts. Several respondents indicated that their answers were reflective in nature as precise records of such complaints or treatments were not kept. Again, analysis indicates that 59%, or 22 of the universities or colleges reporting students with symptoms had some proximity to military or veterans medical facilities.

Discussion

Universities and colleges, specifically the health and to some extent counseling services provided by these universities and colleges, seem ill-prepared to treat and refer students who complain or may yet report symptoms associated with Gulf War Syndrome. This finding supports a previous, although preliminary, Spaulding and Eddy (1995) study in which it was suggested that many university and college health officials are not familiar with the symptoms of Gulf War Syndrome nor were they prepared to refer these student-veterans to government-sponsored treatment programs. Speaking in concert with others surveyed, one health official at a large northwestern university stated, "_ we, as a medical and counseling center need information about Gulf War Syndrome as well as leaving the military syndrome." As noted above, the Department of Defense and the Department of Veterans Affairs have published guidance and instructions stating that any veteran sensing symptoms of Gulf War Syndrome can report to the nearest military or Veterans Administration facility for care and treatment. It is apparent from this study that this information is not reaching campus health clinics and counseling centers. Moreover, campuses not near a military or Veterans Administration facility seem to lack awareness of this policy while those with some proximity to military or Veterans Administration facility are more likely to acquire such information. The number of student-veterans reporting symptoms of Gulf War Syndrome demonstrates that veterans of the Gulf War are indeed present on campuses and that many do have some measure of this syndrome. Campus physical and mental health officials can expect more such cases as the military drawdown continues, as Gulf War veterans enter higher education in greater numbers, and as more precise diagnoses are developed.

Limitations

This study is limited in that it did not directly contact campus counseling center health professionals. Recent studies have shown that Gulf War Syndrome may have a psychological base ("Report Urges," 1995). Should this prove to be the basis of the problems suffered by these student-veterans further study should be undertaken to gauge the exact readiness and competence of counseling professionals to treat and refer student-veterans with these symptoms.

Recommendations

As a result of this study the following recommendations are offered.

1. Campus health and counseling officials should seek and obtain current information regarding symptoms and treatment strategies for Gulf War Syndrome.
2. Student Affairs professionals should become familiar with the capabilities of their campus health and counseling entities for treatment of Gulf War Syndrome.
3. Campus health and counseling officials should seek and obtain current referral information to refer student-veterans with Gulf War Syndrome to appropriate treatment facilities.
4. Department of Veterans Affairs officials should initiate and implement a program that distributes appropriate information on Gulf War Syndrome directly to campus health and counseling professionals.

Conclusions

The drawdown of our Cold War force will undoubtedly send many service men and women, most with service acquired college benefits, heading for the college campuses to complete their higher education goals. As this drawdown intensified immediately after the Gulf War some of these new student-veterans have experienced, to varying degrees, some symptoms of Gulf War Syndrome. According to the research results documented in this study, over one-half of our campus health and counseling clinics are not prepared to provide appropriate physical and mental health treatment for Gulf War Syndrome. Moreover, these clinics lack important referral information that would help these students obtain relevant medical assistance in a timely manner. Medical, counseling, and student affairs professionals should immediately become acquainted with referral information and treatment regimens to better enable this group of students to meet their higher education goals.

Table 1
Symptoms of Gulf War Syndrome

Symptoms recognized by Department of Veterans Affairs

- Fatigue
- Skin problems
- Headache
- Muscle pain
- Joint pain
- Neurological problems
- Psychological problems
- Respiratory ailments
- Sleep disturbance
- Stomach/intestinal complaints
- Cardiovascular problems
- Abnormal weight loss
- Menstrual disorders

Additional reported symptoms

- High fever
- Malaise
- Coughs
- Diarrhea
- Anemia
- Leishmaniasis

Note: From Spaulding, D.J., Eddy, J.P., & Chandras, K.V. (1995). Special considerations for counseling older & aging veterans. In K.V. Chandras (Ed.). ACES' Handbook on counseling adolescents, adults and older persons (pp. 61-69). Warner Robins, GA: The H.T.M. Foundations of America, Inc.

Waldrop, J. (1993). 27 million heroes. American Demographics, 11, pp. 4, 56.

References

Fast Track. (1995, December 25). Army Times, p. 23.

Magner, D.K. (1988, November 16). GI Bill drawing veterans to colleges: Influx may offset enrollment losses. The Chronicle of Higher Education, p. A3.

Myers, C. (1990, June 13). Cuts in U.S. Armed Forces may bring an influx of former GI's to Campus. The Chronicle of Higher Education, pp. A17, A20.

Nationaline. (1996, January 5). USA Today, p. 3A.

New study of Gulf veterans. (1996). Disabled American Veterans, 39(1), 12.

Report urges more attention to Gulf War's psychological effects. (1996, January 5). Dallas Morning News, p. 11A.

Spaulding, D.J., Eddy, J.P., & Chandras, K.V. (1995). Special considerations for counseling older & aging veterans. In K.V. Chandras (Ed.). ACES' Handbook on counseling adolescents, adults and older persons (pp. 61-69). Warner Robins, GA: The H.T.M. Foundations of America, Inc.

Spaulding, D.J., & Eddy, J.P. (1995, April). Gulf War syndrome: What counselors can do to counsel affected veterans in society. Paper presented at 44th convention of American Counseling Association, Denver, CO.

Spaulding, D.J., & Eddy, J.P. (1993-1995). Veterans wellness: Reviewing the symptoms and resources for treatment of Gulf War Syndrome. Peace Progress, VI (1, 2, & 3), 54-55.

U.S. revises figure on gulf gas exposure (September 19, 1996). The Dallas Morning News, p. 1A.

PART III

STUDENT SERVICES IN HIGHER EDUCATION

Chapter 4

ꙮ

The Use of the Dyad Concept in Residence Hall Student Development

Stanley D. Murphy and John P. Eddy

This is an article on how the dyad — two college students or two college staff members — work to establish a method of interaction to achieve predetermined goals and objectives. In this case, the dyads worked at Ambassador University, Big Sandy, Texas in a residence life setting. Sixty four resident assistants and 128 students out of a student body of 1150 were involved in this research study. The results of the clinical observations were that improved relations, morale and development of persons were evident. Fewer conflicts and problems were evident to the paraprofessional staff compared to past years.

Introduction

Learning through participation has been a major part of human experiences and the dyad process is presented here with regard to behavioral changes. Dyad may be defined as a mutual association of two individuals who willingly establish a sincere method of interaction to each other to achieve predetermined goals and objectives (Eddy, 1987). The dyad concept in higher education is based on the assumption that social interest/interaction is, and should be an integral part of education, growth and development.

Tinto (1975, 1987), Astin (1975, 1978) and Kemerer, Baldridge and Green (1982) revealed factors that have interacted to bring a higher attrition rate in higher education. Noel, Levitz, and Saluri (1985) have pointed out that effective retention practices focus on improving the campus programs, services, attitudes, and behaviors which results in quality educational experiences for the students and significant increases in retention.

In addition, research conducted by Nwafor (1990) and Pascarella and Terenzini (1991), seem to substantiate the growth emphasis of dyads in student development work in higher education (Nwafor and Eddy, 1993). Through implementation of the "Dyad Concept," the following theories are applied in residence hall living.

Table 1

College Student Retention and Selected Theories

Scholar	Theories
1. A. Astin	1.The more a college student is involved in college activities, the more likely the student is to be retained at the college.
2. R. Pace	2. The greater the quality of the student effort in academic and extracurricular activities, the more likely the student is to be retained at the college.
3. V. Tinto	3. The greater the personal goal commitment of the student to campus social integration, the more likely the student is to be retained at the college.
4. E. T. Pascarella	4. The greater the interaction between the student and the faculty, and the student and the student's peers, the more likely the student is to be retained at the college.

Setting of Ambassador University

Ambassador University in Big Sandy, Texas is a private four-year liberal arts institution. This University, located in East Texas, is on a tract of land of over 347 acres. On this site is an attractive man-made lake, a lovely forest of pine trees, a useful air field, a scenic prairie of wild flowers and a beautiful glade in the center of the campus. Those who enter the campus, pass through a visitor building adorned by blooming bushes. Directly in front of the visitor building on the main road of the campus is the administration building with its flowing fountain with flying geese. Everywhere are new residence halls and modem academic buildings.

Ambassador University has many unique two person apartments. These are unusual student on-campus residence dwellings that individualize a room for [two] students to live in. Students come to Ambassador University from all over the nation and around the world. At one time, Ambassador University had a campus in England and one in California but now all are present [through consolidation] in Texas.

One of the authors of this article has visited over 26 nations of the world and he believes Ambassador University has one of the most beautiful campuses of higher education on earth. This is a good place for the dyad approach for college student development to be actualized.

Table 2
Common Problems in Residence Life Resident Hall Living

1. Curfew violations.
2. Lounge hours violations.
3. Cleanliness (e.g., kitchen, making beds, dorm duties, littering).
4. Stealing (e.g., clothes, food, jewelry, money, etc. . .).
5. Students experiencing frequent episodes of depression.
6. Eating disorders (Anorexia, Bulimia).
7. Personal hygiene.
8. Drinking problems (e.g. underage or overuse).
9. Disrespect for university property.
10. Negative attitudes towards the university.
11. Homesickness.
12. Borrowing things without asking.
13. Romance situations (e.g., appropriateness Vs. inappropriateness).
14. Personal problems resulting from difficult family backgrounds.
15. Unlocked doors.
16. Ignoring requests of other residents.
17. Stress.
18. Developmental issues.
19. Adjustment problems.
20. Roommate conflicts.

Note: The above list was developed by current resident assistants at Ambassador University.

Purpose of the Study

The primary purposes of this study were: (1) to examine the attitudes of college students in the following areas: (a) personal adjustment (b) developmental issues, and (c) student interaction; (2) to enhance the feeling of community and family within residence halls; and (3) to decrease some of the problems common to residence hall living (see Table 1).

Method

Sample: 64 resident assistants who serve as student leaders at Ambassador University participated in this study. In addition, 128 out of 1,150 students were selected through survey method to participate as dyads to a resident assistant in each residence hall. Each residence hall wing consisted of two dyads working together with a resident assistant. The resident assistant in each area maintained the role of group leader to the dyads. Each student leader (RA) was responsible for the following:

1. Meet with his/her group.
2. Explain the dyad program.
3. Introduce the dyads.
4. Develop community group goals within each area.
5. Establish objectives (steps on how to accomplish group goals unique to the area).

The dyad program was implemented spring semester (January, 1994). Volunteers were obtained through our Residence Life Educational Programming Survey administered during the beginning of the fall semester (August, 1993). The definition of the "Dyad Concept" was given on the survey. Volunteers were asked to indicate "Yes" on the survey if they were interested in participating and "No" if they were not interested. Selection of the dyads were made by the director of residence life along with input from the resident assistants. Some of the characteristics we looked for in choosing the dyads included: people orientation, willingness to serve and overall leadership potential for possible future consideration as a resident assistant.

Results

A "Dyad Program Evaluation Survey" was administered to a random sample of 95 students who participated in the study. From this sample, 76 (80%) completed the surveys. In addition, 56 (88%) of the resident assistants liked the idea of having the "Dyad Program." Eighty-eight per cent agreed or strongly agreed that the residence life area was improving in its efforts through the dyad program to assist students in dealing with personal adjustment, student interaction and problems related to residence hall living.

The results of this study seem to indicate that the effectiveness of the dyad concept will be greatly enhanced when it is implemented in the fall semester of the academic year. In an open-ended question seeking additional comments concerning the "Dyad Concept", many of the participants in this study recommended the program to be implemented early on in the fall semester rather than in the spring. This gives the program an additional semester to run its course. Much of the fruit is born sometime near the end of the first three months of the program's implementation.

Conclusion

Enhanced personal growth and development, personal adjustment, fewer roommate conflicts, and a willingness to seek professional help when dealing with deep psychological issues all appear to be an outgrowth of the interaction brought about through the use of the dyad concept in residence hall student development. The dyad concept (Eddy, 1993) is one of the first student development theories with researched evidence of its success. It is based on 'The Eddy Wholistic Model of College Student Development" (Martin, Eddy and Stilson, 1983).

References

Astin, A.W. (1975). *Preventing Students From Dropping Out*. San Francisco: Jossey-Bass.

Astin. A.W. (1978). *Four Critical Years*. San Francisco: Jossey-Bass.

Eddy. J.P. (1987). Student Development and Application: Theory and Dyad Practice. Denton, Texas: University of North Texas unpublished paper.

Eddy. J.P. (1993). *Higher Education Perspectives for Leaders*. Edina, Minnesota: Burgess International Group Publishing, 93-109.

Kemerer, F., Baldridge. J., and Green, K. (1982). *Strategies For Effective Enrollment Management*. Washington. D.C.: American Association of State Colleges and Universities.

Martin, B.E. Eddy, J.P., Stilson, D.C. (1983).*Human Development Education: Principles, Plans and Problems*. Minneapolis, Minnesota: Burgess Publishing Company.

Nwafor, S. (1990). Three-Year Research Study on a Dyad Process in Higher Education. Paper presented to the National Association of Multi-cultural Education Annual Conference, New Orleans, Louisiana.

Nwafor, S. and Eddy, J.P. (1993). Dyad: An empirical examination of a dyad process to higher education courses. *College Student Journal*. 27 (2). 231-233.

Pascarella, E., and Terenzini P. (1901). *How College Affects Students*. San Francisco: Jossey-Bass Publishers.

Tinto, V. (1975). Dropout from higher education: A theoretical synthesis of recent research. *Review of Educational Research*. 45. 89-125.

Tinto, V. (1987). *Leaving College: Re-thinking the Causes and Cure of Student Attrition*. Chicago: The University of Chicago.

Chapter 5

ഇ൦

College Residence Halls Research Study: Student Perceptions of Resident Assistants, Fellow Residents, and Residence Hall Living

STANLEY D. MURPHY, JOHN P. EDDY
AND DONALD J. SPAULDING

This research is a two year follow-up study on student perceptions of resident assistants in college residence halls using the "Dyad Concept". The study was conducted on a small campus environment in a residence life setting. Sixty-three resident assistants were paired with 63 volunteer students to form 63 dyads. A survey analysis assessing three areas of college and university student issues was administered to 1000 students. Results indicated the implementation of the dyad concept provides excellent opportunities for students to work together to accomplish predetermined goals and objectives. In addition, student perceptions toward resident assistants, dyads, other residents, and residence living in general were positively influenced.

Introduction

Providing instruction and training for resident assistants has always been a concern for colleges and universities within the student affairs division. Adequate resident assistant training enables institutions to better serve students. Many institutions in their efforts to assist students in their overall educational growth and development during the undergraduate years struggle with this dilemma. The rapidly changing world: global economy, family structure, information technology, and the emergence of a multicultural society forces leaders in student affairs to create new and effective ways to serve their primary consumers — Students. Colleges and universities throughout the country are attempting to create new and effective ways to enhance the development of students and thus improve student retention.

Resident Assistants and Dyads

Resident assistant training has been categorized into three types: in-service training sessions, retreats, and academic courses (Bowman & Bowman, 1995; Ender, 1983; Upcraft, 1982). At this private liberal arts institution, training consists of in-service instruction and a student leadership retreat for leadership training which is conducted one week prior to the beginning of the fall semester. The retreat lasts for four days and is designed to give resident assistants an orientation to their roles and to build team unity.

Throughout the academic year, resident assistants participate in small group training on a weekly basis. Each group consisted of 10 to 12 RAs. Small group training sessions are excellent in that they provide opportunities for instruction, feedback, and group dialogue on issues of concern within each residence hall complex.

The director of residence life is directly responsible for resident assistant training and development. The major goal is to give RAs adequate training on how to work effectively with residents. A combination of lectures, role plays, and experiential exercises are the teaching modalities used. Topics covered in the instructional content for small group in-service training include: advice from an experienced resident assistant; student emergency management protocol (SEMP) procedures; listening skill development; processes for effective communication; barriers to effective communication; defense mechanisms; Erickson's stages of psychosocial development; Maslow's hierarchy of needs; group leader skills; group stage development; danger signs of suicide potential (conceptions and misconceptions about suicide); major factors that put students at risk; multicultural/ethnic diversity, and how to handle conflict.

Purpose of the Study

This study addresses student perceptions. Specifically, the study examined the following areas: (1) student perceptions of resident assistants and dyads, (2) student perceptions of other residents, and (3) student perceptions of residence hall living.

Method

Sample: 63 students serving as resident assistants participated in this study. An additional 63 students were selected by the director of residence life and resident assistants from a list of volunteers obtained through the "Residence Life Educational Programming Survey." The survey was developed by the Residence Life Department. Each resident assistant was paired with one student selected from the list of volunteers to form 63 dyads. A dyad is defined as a mutual association of two individuals who willingly establish a sincere method of interaction to achieve predetermined goals and objectives (Eddy, 1987).

In each residence hall complex every wing included one resident assistant working with a dyad partner. Each dyad had the responsibility for 20 students. At the beginning of the fall semester each resident assistant maintained the role of group leader and was responsible for the following:

1. Meet with his/her group.
2. Explain the dyad program.
3. Introduce the dyads.
4. Develop residence hall group goals within each area.
5. Establish objectives (steps on how to accomplish group goals).

Results

A "Program Evaluation Survey" was administered to 1000 students living in on-campus housing at the close of the spring semester. The survey was administered by each resident assistant in their respective areas. RAs were given previous instruction on its administration by the director of residence life. The survey consisted of 35 questions utilizing a Liken Scale (1 = strongly agree, 2 = agree, 3 = neutral, 4 = disagree, and 5 = strongly disagree). Seven questions addressed demographic information and the remaining 28 questions addressed student perceptions toward resident assistants and dyads, other residents, and residence hall living.

Of the 1000 surveys administered, 714 were returned for a 71.4% response rate. In regard to leadership (see Table 1), 81.7% of the students surveyed agreed or strongly agreed that resident assistants and their dyads were exhibiting effective leadership. Students agreed or strongly agreed (87.1%) that resident assistants and dyads were approachable. Students also agreed or strongly agreed (85.5%) that resident assistants and dyads were genuinely concerned. In addition, 91.6% agreed or strongly agreed that resident assistants and dyads modeled responsible behavior. The area assessing student perceptions toward resident assistants and dyads received the highest rating. The lowest rating was in the area of scheduling residence hall activities which is a part of the resident assistant's responsibilities.

A total of 72.5% agreed or strongly agreed that resident assistants and their dyads regularly scheduled activities.

The second area examined students' perceptions toward other residents. This area also revealed similar ratings (see Table 2). The topic "Residents overall get along well," received the highest rating. In this area 85.5% agreed or strongly agreed while 8.8% were neutral. The lowest rating was in the area of confronting inappropriate behaviors. A total of 69.6% agreed or strongly agreed that they felt comfortable with confronting inappropriate behavior while 21.7% remained neutral.

The third major area assessed students' perceptions towards residence hall living. Overall, students liked living in the residence ha11(79.7%). The lowest rating was in the area of planned social activities as a valuable part of residence hall living. Only 43.6% agreed or strongly agreed 30.7% remained neutral, while 13.3 % disagreed and 5% strongly disagreed. It appears that one of the greatest challenges for resident assistants in their leadership role is in this area.

Table 1
Student Ratings of Resident Assistants and Dyads

	Strongly Agree	Agree	Neutral	Disagree	Strongly Disagree
Effective Leadership	37.0%	44.7%	10.8%	3.1%	2.0%
Fair and Consistent	39.1%	44.5%	9.9%	3.4%	0.1%
Scheduled Activities	26.8%	45.7%	17.1%	6.7%	2.4%
Inspected Regularly	52.2%	41.3%	3.4%	1.4%	0.3%
Fair in Inspections	45.8%	42.0%	6.4%	3.5%	0.8%
Kept Residents Informed	42.2%	43.6%	9.0%	2.5%	1.3%
Time in Residence Hall	32.4%	42.3%	15.0%	6.3%	2.5%
Were Accessible	37.1%	44.4%	10.6%	4.8%	1.8%
Were Approachable	52.5%	34.6%	6.7%	3.6%	1.1%
Genuinely Concerned	50.3%	35.2%	8.7%	3.5%	1.0%
Were Good Listeners	46.9%	35.4%	13.4%	2.7%	0.8%
Trusted With Confidential Matters	44.4%	30.1%	21.0%	2.5%	0.8%
Set Positive Example	46.9%	40.6%	8.3%	2.8%	0.3%
Modeled Responsible Behavior	51.1%	40.5%	6.0%	1.3%	0.0%
Fostered Community Atmosphere	32.5%	42.2%	16.1%	5.5%	2.2%

(n = 714)

Discussion

The results of the data reported in this research study indicate that perceptions of students are positively enhanced when dyads are implemented in residence hall programming and training (Murphy & Eddy, 1995). Resident assistants play key roles in the student affairs division. The dyad concept places two students in a position to work together to achieve predetermined goals and objectives within each resident hall wing. It should be noted that students who volunteer to serve as a dyad member also receive training which prepares them for possible selection as future resident assistants. This not only assists students in their individual career goals, it also aids the institution's efforts to maintain a steady pool of qualified applicants. In addition, students who live in on-campus housing are better served.

The resident assistant's role becomes even more important when we examine attrition rates and effective retention practices. Tinto (1975, 1987) and Astin (1975, 1978) researched factors which have interacted to bring higher attrition rates in higher education. Student involvement in college activities and campus social integration improves student retention. Kemerer, Baldridge, & Green (1982) conducted research which supports these findings. Pascarella and Terenzini (1991) found that students are more likely to be retained at the college as the interaction between students, faculty, and students' peers are increased.

Implementing the "Dyad Concept" in residence hall programming positively affects student attitudes and perceptions towards many areas of campus life.

Table 2
Student Ratings of Fellow Residents

	Strongly Agree	Agree	Neutral	Disagree	Strongly Disagree
Residents Respect Others Rights	13.3%	59.4%	13.6%	9.7%	1.5%
Residents Respect Right to Study	14.4%	59.2%	12.7%	9.0%	1.0%
Residents Tolerant of Differences	14.6%	60.2%	14.8%	6.9%	0.4%
I Know Most People in My Residence Hall	37.7 %	46.6%	5.9%	5.0%	1.5%
I Get Along Well With My Roommates	48.0%	37.4%	8.8%	2.0%	0.1%
I Confront Inappropriate Behaviors	22.7%	46.9%	21.7%	3.8%	0.6%
Residents Overall Get Along Well	29.1%	56.4%	8.8%	2.0%	0.4%

(n = 714)

Conclusion

As with the original study, enhanced personal growth, development and personal adjustment were reflected in the student ratings. In addition, many areas of campus life, including relationships, psychological and emotional health, and satisfaction with on-campus housing were positively influenced. Further research on a larger college campus is recommended and will help us determine the effectiveness of the dyad concept in a broader setting.

Table 3

Student Ratings of Resident Hall Living

	Strongly Agree	Agree	Neutral	Disagree	Strongly Disagree
Kitchen Appliances/Bath Facilities in Good Condition	10.9%	54.8%	14.6%	10.2%	3.9%
Residence Hall an Attractive Place to Live	15.7%	50.1%	16.1%	8.8%	2.5%
Public Areas are Kept Clean	10.6%	51.0%	15.8%	11.2%	2.9%
Planned Social Activities are a Valuable Part of Residence Hall Living	9.0%	34.6%	30.7%	13.3%	5.0%
No Substance Abuse Exists Within the Residence Hall	27.0%	34.5%	16.9%	11.2%	2.9%
Overall, I Like Living in My Residence Hall	32.2%	47.5%	9.8%	4.5%	1.0%

(n = 714)

References

Astin, A.W. (1975). *Preventing students from dropping out.* San Francisco: Jossey-Bass.

Astin. A.W. (1978). *Four critical years.* San Francisco: Jossey-Bass.

Bowman, R.L., & Bowman, V.E. (1995). Academic courses to train resident assistants. *Journal of College Student Development*, 36 (1), 39-46.

Eddy, J.P., (1987). *Student development and application: Theory and dyad practice.* Denton Texas: University of North Texas unpublished paper.

Ender, S.C. (1983). Students as paraprofessionals. In T.K. Miller, R.E. Winston, JR., & W.R. Mendenhall (Eds.), *Administration and leadership in student affairs: Actualizing student development in higher education* (pp. 323-340). Muncie, IN: Accelerated Development

Kemerer, F., Baldridge, J., & Green, K. (1982). *Strategies for effective enrollment management.* Washington, D.C.: American Association of State Colleges and Universities.

Murphy, S.D., & Eddy, J.P., (1995). The use of the dyad concept in residence hall student development. *College Student Journal.* 29 (1), 53-56.

Pascarella, E., & Terenzini, P. (1991). *How college affects students.* San Francisco: Jossey-Bass.

Tinto, V. (1975). Dropout from higher education: A theoretical synthesis of recent research. Review of Educational Research, 45, 89-125.

Tinto, V. (1987). Leaving college: Re-thinking the cause and cure of student attrition. Chicago: The University of Chicago.

Upcraft, M.L. (1982). *Residence hall assistants in college: A guide to selection training, and supervision.* San Francisco: Jossey-Bass.

Chapter 6

ꙮ

Education Expenses of Graduate Students: Tax Savings Strategies

THOMAS E BRUBAKER, JOHN P. EDDY, KAN V. CHANDRAS AND STANLEY D. MURPHY

Many current and prospective students often overlook a valuable source for financing their graduate education via the income tax laws. In certain situations, graduate students can lower their education costs by deducting the costs of tuition, books, supplies and transportation on their tax returns. This article discusses ways in which students can legally generate tax savings through provisions in the tax code relating to educational expenses, thereby reducing their overall cost of graduate study. The article is not intended to provide legal advice. It is a review of current tax laws that will help many graduate students. If legal advice is required, the reader should seek competent legal counsel.

Introduction

Scholarships, student loans and assistantships are traditional sources of defraying the cost of graduate study. A frequently overlooked source of financing education costs is the section of the tax code which allows students to deduct qualifying education costs on their tax returns, thus lowering their total out-of-pocket costs for graduate study. To assist the graduate student/taxpayer in exploring the possibility of obtaining tax savings through a deduction for education expenses, the authors discuss relevant areas of the tax law and judicial decisions that will be useful in developing tax planning strategies. Furthermore, higher education institutions that offer graduate programs might consider emphasizing the potential tax benefits associated with graduate study and incorporate this into their recruiting strategy.

Educational Costs as Business Expenses

The Internal Revenue Code of 1986 (I.R.C.), as amended, is the extant source of tax law for individual taxpayers, and it contains a provision permitting taxpayers to deduct "all ordinary and reasonable expenses paid or incurred during the taxable year in carrying on any trade or business" (Sec. 162[a]). Educational expenses fall under this general category of business expenses. Treasury Regulations, which are the official interpretations of the I.R.C. issued by the Internal Revenue Service (I.R.S.), state that educational expenses are deductible as business expenses if either of the following are true:

(1) The education maintains or improves skills required by the individual in his employment or other trade or business, or
(2) The education meets the express requirements of the individual's employer, or the requirements of applicable law or regulations, imposed as a condition to the retention by the individual of an established employment relationship, status, or rate of compensation (Treas. Reg. section 1.162-5[a]).

However, the I.R.S. specifically prohibits deducting education costs which "[are] required . . . to meet minimum educational requirements" (Treas. Reg. section 1.162-5[b]). This is why, in most situations, students cannot deduct the costs incurred for their undergraduate degrees.

Treasury Regulations effectively carry the full authority of the I.R.C. statute and are not easily challenged by taxpayers. These regulations have the greatest precedential value of any I.R.S: pronouncement (Raabe, Whittenburg, and Bost, 1987, p.79). In deciding whether or not to deduct educational expenses, graduate students should carefully follow the guidelines above from Treasury Regulation 1.162-5.

Additional Authoritative Guidance

Two other sources provide additional guidance as to the deductibility of educational expenses: Revenue Rulings and judicial decisions. Even within the limited category of education expenses, the number of Revenue Rulings and judicial decisions is extensive. Therefore, only a brief overview of these reference sources is presented here to provide an awareness of the potential for tax savings resulting from education expense deductions.

Revenue Rulings

As official pronouncements of the national office of the I.R.S., Revenue Rulings apply the Internal Revenue Code and Treasury Regulations to specific real-life situations that are usually submitted by taxpayers (the actual names of the taxpayers are not used). A quasi-legal format is used, and each ruling has four major categories: (1) Issues, (2) Facts, (3) Law and Analysis, and (4) Holding (Raabe et al., 1987, pp. 82-84). Graduate students can look to Revenue Rulings to gain insight into how the I.R.S. will treat certain types of taxpayer situations. For example, Revenue Ruling 67-421 held that all reasonable expenses relating to research and typing for a doctoral dissertation are deductible as education expenses, assuming the tuition cost of courses, special fees, and books leading to a doctorate qualify as deductible education expenses under Reg. Section 1.162-5(a). The I.R.S. reasoned that the dissertation is "an integral part of an entire course of study at the graduate level" (Rev. Rul. 67-421, 1967).

In another Revenue Ruling, the I.R.S. allowed a professor who held a masters degree to deduct his educational expenses leading to a doctorate. He was applying for the position of president at the junior college where he taught and incurred the expenses in order to retain his eligibility. Although Treas. Reg. Sec. 1.162-5(b) prohibits deducting educational costs required to meet minimum educational requirements, the I.R.S. stated that ". . . once the taxpayer has met the minimum educational requirements, he is treated as continuing to meet those requirements even though they are changed." Since the professor met the minimum educational requirements at the time of his application for the position of president, all his expenses leading to a doctorate were deductible as business expenses (Rev. Rul. 68-580, 1968).

Graduate students choosing to rely on a specific Revenue Ruling as a basis for an education deduction must be certain that the facts in the ruling are identical to those in their situation. Even a slight variation in facts may result in disallowance of an educational deduction.

Judicial Sources

Federal tax disputes between an individual taxpayer and the I.R.S. are settled in one of the federal trial courts (Tax Courts, Federal District Courts or the U.S. Claims Court) or in a federal appellate court (U.S. Court of Appeals or the Supreme Court) (Raabe et al., 1987, p. 109). Further caution is needed when relying on judicial decisions by the Court of Appeals because of the Golsen rule. In applying the Golsen rule, the Tax Court will follow the Court of Appeals which has direct jurisdiction over the taxpayer, and implies differentiation based solely on geographic area (*Golsen v. Commissioner*, 1970, as cited in Raabe et al., p. 113). The significance of this rule is that contradictory Tax Court decisions are possible, even in situations involving two sets of identical facts. Graduate students should generally follow the holdings of the Court of Appeals for the Circuit in the geographic area in which they work or reside (Raabe et al., 1989, pp. 124-125).

In the case of *King v. Commissioner*, the Tax Court ruled that all of the courses taken by Peggy A. King were related to her duties as a visiting professor and improved her skills in the field of behavioral science. Citing *Carlucci v. Commissioner* (1962), the Tax Court reasoned that earning a degree did not preclude Ms. King from taking a deduction since her education expenses were primarily for maintaining or improving skills required by her employer. The Tax Court also allowed a deduction for Ms. King's previously disallowed travel expenses relating to her education because her out of state stay was determined to be only temporary (*King v. Commissioner*, 1962).

Long absences from a teaching position will usually result in disallowance of education expenses if the point of return to the teaching profession is indefinite. In *Goldstein v. Commissioner* (1981), the Tax Court disallowed a teacher's expenses for graduate education. According to the court, the issue was not whether the taxpayer was a qualified member of the teaching profession, but whether she was engaged in the trade or business of teaching at the time her expenses for a doctorate were claimed. The Tax Court reasoned that membership in a profession does not necessarily imply that one is carrying on a trade or business.

The taxpayer's nonbusiness reasons for leaving teaching and her extended absence from paid teaching were among the reasons the court cited for the decision.

Conclusion

Deducting the costs of graduate study can yield significant savings, but the guidelines set forth in Treasury Regulation 162(a) must be carefully followed. Additional insight may be obtained from the various Revenue Rulings and judicial decisions. Since this is a complex area of the tax law, consultation with a reputable tax advisor such as a Certified Public Accountant or tax attorney, is strongly recommended.

References

Internal Revenue Code, 1986, as amended, Sec. 162 (a).

Goldstein v. Commissioner, 21 T.C.M. (CCH) 1016 (1981).

King v. Commissioner, 21 T.C. M. (CCH) 495 (1962).

Raabe, W.A., Whittenburg, G.E., and Bost, J.C. (1987). West's federal tax research. New York: West.

Rev. Rul. 67-421, 1967-2 C.B. 84.

Treasury Reg. Sec. 1.162-5.

PART IV

ADMINISTRATION, CURRICULUM AND TECHNOLOGY IN HIGHER EDUCATION

Chapter 7

ꙮ

Privatization of Higher Education Services: Propositional Pros and Cons

JOHN P. EDDY, DONALD J. SPAULDING,
AND STANLEY D. MURPHY

The decline in and lack of state and federal monies for public higher education institutions and the limited amount of finances available from private sources, both foundation and individual contributions, has forced many institutions to privatize, or outside connect, many of their services. These services range from college food services (Eddy, 1977) to health clinics and hospitals (Bernstein, 1995), and counseling center (Philips, Halstead, and Carpenter,. 1996). Even the curriculum is becoming sensitive to the privatization strategy; CD ROMS for complete courses are for sale and entire degree programs are offered through on-line education. There are advantages and disadvantages to privatization of higher education services. Are higher education officials proceeding without significant research and analysis of the pros and cons? Certain important propositions relating to these pros and cons are suggested in this article.

The decline in and the lack of state and federal monies for public higher education institutions, combined with the limited amount of finances available from private sources such as foundations and individuals, is forcing many universities and colleges to consider and implement a strategy of privatization of services and curricula as a method of saving money (Goldstein, Kempner, & Rush, 1993). Privatization, or outsourcing of services, ranges from food services (Eddy, 1977) to health clinics and hospitals (Bernstein, 1995), and counseling services (Phillips, Halstead, and Carpenter, 1996). The curriculum is even involved in the sense that some universities and professors are marketing complete courses on CD ROMs while some universities and colleges are considering expanding distance education to the point of offering degrees on-line (Eddy & Buchanon, 1996). Although not exactly a new approach, contracting student affairs services is of such importance that administrators should consider more than just the bottom line. Privatization may save costs, but it has advantages and disadvantages (Drum, 1994). Are administrators aware of and considering some of the more critical aspects of both? This article explores, in the form of propositions, several of the important advantages and disadvantages that should be thoroughly examined prior to implementation of the privatization strategy.

Propositional Advantages of Privatization

University and college officials considering and implementing the privatization of activities on their campuses should weigh the following propositions:

Proposition 1. The contractor or provider will provide the product, service, or operation at a price that will result in clear and long term cost savings, other factors bearing consideration include convenience to students and quality of the service or product. Is cost savings the only bottom line?

Proposition 2. The administration will deflect criticism toward a specific contractor or provider of services should it become necessary to increase revenues as a result of higher costs. Will university or college officials lose cognizance of or ignore cost increases and simply blame a contractor or provider?

Proposition 3. Management skills within the contractor's supervisory hierarchy as well as at the site where a particular service is activated will result in higher quality service. Is the management structure in the private sector likely to be of greater competence than that hired and working within higher education? A reason for this managerial gap, should such exist, may be that universities and colleges internal managers lack capital incentives to make their entity client-friendly.

Proposition 4. The financial resources of a contractor or provider are likely to be greater than those of the university.

Thus, in such a situation, it is likely that the contractor or provider can minimize price by maximizing orders or services — cost savings via volume purchasing. Yet again, is bottom line the sole criterion for judgment of productivity?

Proposition 5. The regulations, rules, and red tape (3 R's for bureaucracy) of state laws controlling expenditures of state monies inhibits the potential of higher education institutions to maximize their dollars. Such restrictions are not imposed on private businesses. State Coordinating Boards of Higher Education may be interfering, through the imposition to supplement state laws, to the point of complicating the process of operating an efficient and effective operation (Eddy, 1995).

Propositional Disadvantages

Just as there are assumed advantages to privatization there are numerous, some directly contrary to the advantages, disadvantages to privatization. The following propositions are offered:

Proposition 6. Will the expected cost savings — the primary argument for privatization — to the institution still be passed on to students, in the form of higher costs, in the long run even though such costs are not passed on to the institution? Thus the question, will costs of operation that would have previously been passed on by the institution to the student still be passed on, albeit by a third party (the contractor or provider).

Proposition 7. The Student development philosophy, accepted and expressed in higher education as a key and primary mission, which calls for the intellectual, moral, physical, social and spiritual growth of students will be compromised by the lack of such intent on the part of contract businesses and services or individuals within the contracted entity or service. Each individual employee of the university or college is imbued with this value and commitment but, will this attitude prevail in the contracted business or service or will this be just an organizational goal for the contractor or provider? Two sub-propositions result from this proportion: (a) the contracted service will be better performed if provided on-campus, and (b) the contracted service can be effectively provided at an off-campus location.

Proposition 8. Privatization contracts will be difficult to change, particularly if this change impacts the bottom line of the contractor or provider. Within contract protocol, the specifications and expectations of delivery of service are considered sacrosanct for the term of the contract. Inexperience on the part of the university or college representative to the contract may not be readily overcome by suggested changes to a contract prior to completion. Moreover, changes in the nuance of the mission, role, or scope of an institution may not be readily implemented through an inflexible contractual system.

Additional Concerns

Beyond the above propositions several other concerns are apparent when considering privatization. These concerns raise questions that include (a) have all of the ways in which privatization will impact students and staff been identified in the literature, and more importantly, at each institution considering privatization, (b) how will privatization impact the student development philosophy and mission of higher education institutions, (c) is the profit motive a healthy concept within the parameters of student development, (d) will all of the personnel in the privatization structure be role models for students, (e) will contractors or providers uphold the high professional and ethical standards expected of higher education personnel, and (f) how will student development professional organizations and associations interact with contractors and providers?

Conclusions

Privatization is taking place throughout the higher education community, especially within student services, but will it overtake the philosophy and mission of student development? Should higher education officials neglect their responsibility to consider all aspects of this shift then, higher education student development may change in ways unacceptable for such institutions. The propositions and concerns offered herein should be of primary concern to higher education administrators so as to not inhibit the mission of the university or college.

References

Bernstein, E.M. (1995, October 25). "Trustees say going private is to save SUNY hospitals." *New York Times*. p. B8Y.

Drum, D. (1994, October). *Changes in the mental health service delivery and finance: Implications for college counseling centers*. Keynote presentation at the Association of University and College Counseling Center Directors 1994 conference, Memphis, TN.

Eddy, J.P. (1977). College student personnel development, administration and counseling. Washington, DC: University Press of America.

Eddy, J.P. (1995, October 31). *Interviews with private college and university administrators on privatization advantages versus public institutions*. Denton, TX: Unpublished paper delivered at the University of North Texas.

Eddy, J.P. and Buchanon, J. (1996), *Privatization in higher education: What is the bottom line?* Paper prepared for American College Personnel Association, Baltimore, MD.

Philips, L., Halstead, R., and Carpenter, W. (1996). The privatization of college counseling services: A preliminary investigation, *Journal of College Student Development*, 32(1), 52-59.

Chapter 8

ജ്ര

Technology Assisted Education (TAE)

John P. Eddy, John Burnett,
Donald J. Spaulding and Stanley D. Murphy

Technology Assisted Education (TAE) has been in existence for over forty years. Pennsylvania State University, an early leader using TAE, began this revolution in education by offering television college credit courses. Since that time programs have evolved to sophisticated distance education using satellites to distributive education using computer systems such as Internet. Many advantages accrue to the university or college that exploits technology. Cost, convenience to professors and students, and the capacity to reach an increased number of students are some advantages to the university or college that exploits technology. Lack of personal contact with a professor role and process training, and equipment failures are disadvantages that follow the introduction of technology. This article explores several of the TAE models in use today, and highlights several advantages and disadvantages to the use of technology in education.

Introduction

Technology Assisted Education (TAE) has been around for over forty years with Pennsylvania State University, an early leader with its television college credit courses. It is important to mention that there are many ways to present a college credit course using technology from television (distance education) and Video Cassette (VCR) film to computer Internet systems (distributive education) (Eddy & Spaulding, 1996; Eddy and Spaulding, 1996). International, national, regional and state-wide video teleconferences use large screen television satellites with telephone outlets in distance learning experiences. The authors have been involved in all of the Technology Assisted Education opportunities.

Purpose

The purpose of this article is to identify the most common TAE models, list general advantages and disadvantages, and offer conclusions regarding TAE.

Models For TAE

Several TAE models have taken hold within the higher education delivery system. The more common methods follow: 1. The "Television Model" is a live television or recorded television college credit course. This model can be interactive or one way. Satellite transmissions are becoming a common mode of dispensing knowledge via this model. 2. The "VCR Model" employs recorded tapes that are used in the classroom or at home. These tapes are used to supplement instruction or as "standalone" courses for college credit. 3. The "Computer Model" uses CD-ROM technology that can be combined with "live" computer transmissions.

All three of these models may use telephone contact during the course or other scheduled time to increase communication between a professor and his or her students. Costs and scheduling may limit the effectiveness of this tool.

Advantages of TAE

Technology Assisted Education can be employed to supplement direct instruction by professors or it can substitute for direct classroom teaching. In such cases some of the advantages are as follows:

1. Costs may be reduced through the use of TAE. These cost reductions can range from overhead (classroom heating, air conditioning, and so forth) to reduced faculty salaries.

2. This type of instruction may be more convenient for many students. Learning can take place in homes for example. In the case of supplementary instruction the time spent preparing and lecturing may be lessened through the use of previously prepared TAE tools.
3. A particular professor's topic can be taught to many more students as the instruction can be proliferated through the use of TAE.

Professors and TAE

Professors in higher education are likely to experience some specific problems with the use of TAE. These include, but are not limited to those listed below:

1. Some TAE require technical experience that may require training time before professors are familiar with its use and employment. Professors do not usually posses the knowledge to effect immediate repair, in the absence of technicians, of technologically advanced equipment.
2. TAE may inhibit the rapport that develops between a professor and that is so important to the learning process. The direct or face-to-face interaction and contact that is so instrumental in human affairs may interrupt or stifle the transmission of knowledge.
3. Relying on technology to carry all the communications between a professor and students leaves out some of the five senses humans are given to experience in a holistic education.

Students and TAE

Students encounter difficulties associated with TAE include the following:

1. Students have expressed a lack of personal emotion in their education. Learning occurs best when there is a whole body experience of interaction between a teacher and a student.
2. Students are usually not able to have direct contact with their professor.

3. Students have expressed a problem of being motivated in situations where there is not substantial direct contact with their professor.

TAE — Myth or Magic?

Higher education leaders need to distinguish the TAE opportunity — is TAE myth or magic? The above advantages and disadvantages should be carefully weighted by higher education administrators before a commitment to TAE is made. While TAE can be magic to some students who cannot participate in the traditional classroom situation it can be a bland process to those who need the inherent advantages of the professor–student relationship.

TAE in Action

Many students from Thailand are seeking advanced education in universities and colleges in the United States. A high number of these students acquired a substantial amount of their undergraduate education through television credit courses. In particular, one Thai university system is providing television credit courses to nearly one million students. Other Asian countries are fast expanding their TAE facilities as TAE is a quick and inexpensive means of transmitting knowledge to students (Spaulding & Eddy, 1995).

In another format, ICI University in Irving, Texas use TAE models in an efficient and low cost manner to offer distance education programs for overseas college credit courses. This university's equipment includes the following:

1. A complete audio and video production studio with three video cameras.
2. Adjacent to the studio is a classroom equipped with six computers enhanced with built-in cameras for two way interaction.
3. Software and communication means provided by American Telephone and Telegraph (AT&T).
4. Internet computer access.
5. The capability to deliver live instruction to students in a distant classroom.
6. CD-ROM and VCR capability.

Conclusions

This article covered various TAE models and how they are designed to work. Several key factors that inhibit learning via TAE, such as cost and operational factors, were offered. Nevertheless, the article points out certain advantages to TAE and shows that TAE is in operation internationally.

A Personal Note

On January 29, 1996, the senior author spoke with Dr. Brian Scott, Senior Research Engineer and Manager of the Allied Speech Technology Laboratory at Stanford University, Palo Alto, California, who is a pioneer in the development of the voice controlled computer. Earlier in the month, the senior author had visited with his father, Mr. Gene Scott — the former owner of the computer company that built one of the first known voice controlled computers. Mr. Gene Scott was involved in World War II in continually breaking the Japanese military code through a computer process that helped win the war. This story demonstrates the values of technology and also illustrates how technology keeps evolving to make it more accessible to more complex and comprehensive human applications for learning world-wide.

References

Cabrales, E.J., & Eddy, J.P. (1992). Developing a simulation model for the development of higher education administrators. *Journal of Research an Computing in Education*, 26(1), 105-112.

Cabrales, E.J., Eddy, J.P., & Richards, T.C. (1992). Staff development using an informatics survey. Administrative Action, 5(2), 1-4.

Cabrales, E.J., & Eddy, J.P. (1992). Evaluation of the actual state of information in Columbia. Acucnoticias Journal, 19(1), 3-60.

Cabrales, E.J., & Eddy, J.P. (1992). Informatics education in Columbia: A study of the present situation and recommendations for the future. *Journal of Information Science*, 19(3), 217-224.

Eddy, J.P., & Spaulding, D.J. (1996). New High tech school opens in Texas. *Reading Improvement*, 33(1), 60-62.

Eddy, J.P., & Spaulding, D.J. (1996). Internet, computers, distance education and people failures: Research on technology. *Education*, 116(3), 391-392.

Eddy, J.P., Spaulding, D.J., & Murphy, S.D. (1996). Privatization of higher education services: Propositional Pros and Cons. *Education*, 116(4), 578-579, 542.

Spaulding, D.J., & Eddy, J.P. (1996). China and Hong Kong: A clash of ideologies. *Journal of Instructional Psychology*, 23(3), 231-233.

PART V

ATHLETICS, DIVERSITY AND VOLUNTEER SERVICE IN HIGHER EDUCATION

Chapter 9

ꟈ

Reform American Intercollegiate Athletics Now: A Fifteen Point Plan to Score Success

DONALD J. SPAULDING, JOHN P. EDDY,
DONALD J. SPAULDING, JR., AND STANLEY D. MURPHY

The already cloudy reputation of intercollegiate athletics, in the face of ineffective leadership from some university and college presidents and governing bodies, continues to darken. Violations of rules and regulations by athletic directors, coaches, players, and those with outside interests abound. Yet, university officials and governing bodies clamber forward with the pace of a snail in an environment that demands and requires the rapid upright action of well trained and prepared athletes. The gradual or incremental steps of the past will not bring the change needed to correct the ills of college athletics. Revolutionary and dramatic change initiated now is needed if the viability and credibility of college sports is to be recovered. This article reviews some of the selected ills of athletics and proposes changes to correct these ills.

Introduction

It is time for the immediate, rather than incremental or gradual, reform of American intercollegiate athletics. The incremental reforms instituted by governing associations and university and college leaders are not lessening or halting the athletic excesses of institutional leadership, coaches, athletes, and alumni. These excesses range from criminal activity to turned-head violations of National Collegiate Athletic Association (NCAA) and National Athletics Intercollegiate Association (NAIA) regulations governing university and college sports in America. Illegal drug use by coaches and players, shootings and thefts by players (Eddy, 1995), the changing and falsification of student player grades by coaches and administrators, and the ignoring of admission standards for outstanding high school athletes by administrators and coaches are specific examples of violations that continue despite rules and regulations against them (Eddy, 1993). The ills seem to go on and on even though there is perfunctory expression of a desire by administrators and coaches to halt such incidents. Thelin (1994), in *Games Colleges Play: Scandal and Reform in Intercollegiate Athletics*, points out the lack of priority in reform by referring to a 1929 Carnegie Foundation report on athletics that concludes that presidents lack the "authority or will" to effect change in sports programs. Collegiate sports must change now so as to preserve the integrity of competition.

Incidents

A review of big or little city newspapers, education newspapers, and journals provides a lengthy litany of violations of NCAA/NAIA rules and regulations. Likewise, examples of university inattention to these matters are ample. A survey of these incidents follows:

1. A star running back for a top collegiate football program has been allowed to return to the program after being found guilty of misdemeanor assault charges against a former girlfriend (Moran, 1995). The athlete has been allowed to return with the provisos of mandatory class attendance, counseling, and community service.
2. Three basketball coaches are convicted of federal conspiracy wire and mail fraud charges and placed on probation for helping recruits cheat to get into school (O'Hanlon, 1995).

3. A head football coach is dismissed after pleading no contest to a disorderly conduct charge associated with his behavior in a bar (Vecsey, 1995).
4. A star wide receiver is arrested for sexual assault on a classmate (Coleman, 1995).
5. An entire university's sports program is viewed, in a national sports magazine, as being the nation's most corrupt athletic program over the last 14 years. This program has been accused of (a) providing improper benefits to athletes, (b) recruiting violations, (c) uncontrolled and unchecked "boosterism," (d) cheating in academics, (e) steroid and drug abuse, (f) ignoring or suppressing positive drug tests, (g) player misconduct involving other students and officials, (h) unruly conduct in football residence halls, (i) various forms of fraud, (j) drunkenness by coaches, (k) players serving alcohol to underage recruits, and (l) unsportsmanlike conduct on the playing field among others (Wolff, 1995).
6. A blue-chip basketball player convicted of felony sex abuse is actively recruited by three prominent universities before public outrage causes them to withdraw their scholarship offers (Leo, 1995).
7. Three players from a prominent football program are accused of receiving payments from an agent who hopes to someday negotiate high figure contracts for the players (Blackstone, 1995).
8. Recent research shows that, at no Division 1-A university or college, have the entrance scores of new football recruits neared the scores of all new students (Sigelman, 1995).

The Problem

College sports is big business. Millions of dollars generated from sports come to universities and colleges each year. The magnitude of this revenue can be seen in one event — the NCAA basketball tournament or, "Final Four." In 1985 this tournament earned revenues of $20.1 million, in 1995, $141 million, and over the next seven tournaments it is expected to average $215.6 million a year (Barnhouse, 1995). This revenue magnitude can also be seen in college football. It has become obvious over the years that the huge amount of revenue generated by college sports can distort the whole that is college athletics. Reform may be slowed as a result of the money.

Collegiate athletics has been the subject of many calls for reform. Reform however, has come in small bits, incremental, or gradual over a long term. Revolutionary reforms are needed in universities, colleges, and regulating bodies if the problems of collegiate athletics are to be corrected. Outside of traditional athletic associations, which include athletic administrators and coaches, it is only recently that university and college administrators in professional associations devoted significant attention to the problems of athletics. The program of the National Association of Student Personnel Administrators in their 1995 convention and the Higher Education Department at the University of North Texas in a singular conference on serious issues in college athletics are examples of non-athletic administrators devoting time and attention to this problem.

The NCAA and NAIA have been slow to make and administer serious reforms and only when external and college and university pressure is exerted have these governing bodies taken action. The big business of college sports overrules speedy reform; athletic reforms may impair the capacity for earnings.

Specific Reforms Needed Now

Certain reforms enacted immediately will steer collegiate athletics toward a two fold goal: (a) a return to the primary purpose of higher learning — academics, and (b) athletic competition among universities and colleges for the sake of pure competition. The following reforms should be promptly initiated to ensure the future viability of intercollegiate athletics:

1. Dramatically restructure the governing body of the NCAA. A plan currently under consideration calls for an executive committee composed 16 college presidents and four ex-officio members. This committee will set the budget and hire, fire, and evaluate the executive director. Each of the three NCAA divisions will have a similarly constructed Board of Directors or Presidents Council. Below each division presidents council will be a body of athletic directors and faculty representatives constituting a management council. This will be the first real change in the governance structure in twenty years and should result in more control and power over athletics by top university officials. This proposed change should be quickly installed.

2. Assign more power to regional accrediting agencies. The six accrediting bodies have little influence over university or college athletic programs. These bodies should draw up common and relevant standards for evaluation of university and college athletic programs. Evaluators from the NCAA and NAIA should accompany accrediting bodies during their visits. The entire accreditation process, from institutional self-study to accrediting body evaluation, should be applied, in the same manner it is applied to academics, to the sports program.
3. Boards of Regents and Trustees should specifically charge Presidents with full responsibility for conduct of athletic programs.
4. Administrators and athletic directors should thoroughly examine the issue of a stipend or scholarship supplement for athletes. University civil rights lecturer and activist Julian Bond is on the same side (D.J. Spaulding & J.P. Eddy, personal communication, August 1, 1994) as former NCAA executive director Walter Byers in calling for compensation for college athletes and the current executive director, Cedric Dempsey, who supports "enhancing benefits" for student-athletes (Barnhouse, 1995). Athletes on nationally ranked teams bring millions of dollars to their university. NCAA athletes are not allowed to hold jobs during the season of their sport whereas other students are free to pursue additional income. This admittedly controversial issue should be thoroughly explored by the appropriate leaders and supervisors of college athletics.
5. Hastening the pace of the currently underway academic reforms affecting athletes will aid the process of restoring credibility to college athletics. Previously implemented reforms of rules such as Proposition 48 have slowly increased the graduation rate of athletes to a point that 1988-1989 freshmen athletes graduated at a rate higher than non-athletes, 58% and 57% respectively (Blum, 1995). Although still not academically "fit" some changes have increased the level of academic preparedness of athletes. Loopholes in academic standards should be closed immediately, not gradually.

6. Establish a commission of high administrators and athletic directors to examine the issues of coaches' multi-year contracts, salaries, stipends, and buyouts. With higher education's limited monies for professors, administrators, student programs, and other university activities coaches salaries appear unrestrained. This commission should also examine the connection of these payments in relationship to increases in student tuition and fees.
7. Get clarification of laws impacting college athletics. The Title IX law for example, is confusing and is difficult to implement. Lawmakers, universities, and sports organizations are currently pressing the Departments of Education, Health and Human Services, and Labor for unity of guidance and directives (Lederman, 1995). Clear guidance will eliminate the vacuum which athletic directors and coaches are now forced to operate in.
8. Eliminate athletes only residence halls. Accounts abound of minor to serious crimes being committed in these dorms.
9. Prompt investigation and resolution of violations should become the operative process for universities, colleges, professional associations, and governing bodies. Years are often spent inquiring into matters because of liberal due process procedures. Vigorous publicizing in the general media of the inquiry and the results may in and of itself reduce violations.
10. Move the sports program disciplinary process into the mainstream process of the institution. Separate disciplinary systems breed suspicion on the part of academics and the student body.
11. Apply equally the rules governing faculty outside income earnings to athletic administrators and coaches.
12. University officials should institute extra-athletic department oversight of various sports programs activities. Fund-raising, monies, recruiting, and so forth should receive outside review.
13. Solidify the reputation of governing bodies at the national and local levels. Restore or elevate the prestige and powers of university athletic councils.

14. Eliminate the influence of civic leaders, community and civic organizations, businesses, alumni, and so forth in the process of disciplining sports programs.
15. Set practice and game times and a schedule of games that will not interfere with the academic progress of the student athlete.

Conclusions

Collegiate sports programs are, in many ways, out of control. The leading mechanism for restitution of control is the principle of firm and effective presidential leadership. Presidents of institutions must, without delay, assert control over their individual program and in concert with other presidents establish effective governing systems and processes over regional and national programs. Closely following this principle should come that of immediate action or immediate reform of mutual governing bodies. Gradualism or incremental reform has not corrected the serious violations perpetuated by athletic directors, coaches, and players. Revolutionary and dramatic action is the only reform that will reestablish the integrity of collegiate sports programs.

References

Barnhouse,. W. (1995). Players want a piece of the action, but don't expect NCAA to change. *Fort Worth Star-Telegram*, pp. B13, B14.

Blackstone, K.B. (1995, October 10). Paying college athletes would lessen agents' influence. *The Dallas Morning News*. p. 5B.

Blum, D.E. (1995, July 7). Athletes' graduation rate. *The Chronicle of Higher Education*. XLI(43), A34.

Coleman, G.R. (1995, September 6). Athletes' violent acts off field show need for less viciousness. *The North Texas Daily*, p. 2.

Eddy, J.P. (1993). *Higher education perspectives for leaders*. Edina, MN: Bugess International Publishers, p. 41.

Eddy, J.P. (1995). *International higher education systems*. Denton, TX: Ron Jon Publishers.

Lederman, D. (1995, October 20). House bill targets enforcement of federal sex-bias law in college sports. *The Chronicle of Higher Education*. XLV(43).

Leo, J. (1995, July 17). Should stars get dunked? *U.S. News & World Report*. 112(17). 18.

Moran, M. (1995, October 25). Osborne allows Phillips to rejoin Husker Team. *The New York Times*, pp. B9, B10.

O'Hanlon, K. (1995. July 8). Baylor coaches slapped with probation. The Denton-Record Chronicle, p. A7.

Sigelman, L. (1995). It's academic — or is it? Admissions standards and big-time college football. *Social Science Quarterly*. 79(2) p. 253.

Thelin, J.R. (1994). Games colleges play: Scandal and reform in intercollegiate athletics. Baltimore, MD: The Johns Hopkins University Press.

Vecsey, G. (1995, September 12). Why can't college champions stay clean? *The New York Times*. p. B12.

Wolff, A. (1995) Beyond repair. Sports Illustrated. 30(7,. pp. 21-26.

Chapter 10

ꕥ

A New Metaphor: Individuals as the Sculptors

KENNETH K. GOODROW, MEE-GAIK LIM, STANLEY D. MURPHY AND JOHN P. EDDY

The authors propose an alternative to the melting pot, tossed salad, and mosaic metaphors for multicultural relations. The new metaphor is of individuals relating as the sculptors while being part of the sculpture of multicultural relations. This is in the sense of metalsmithing and is a more complex and dynamic symbol of human interaction acknowledging the power of relational transformation.

In reflecting on our preparation as multicultural counselors and educators, we see a need for novel metaphors of multicultural relations. Metaphors for relations between diverse peoples have moved from the melting pot to the tossed salad and mosaic concepts, but the meanings held in these terms are limited in their description of current trends. Trends include changes in the construction of ethical codes regarding cultural issues in counseling. For example, the 1988 *Ethical Standards* of the American Association for Counseling & Development promotes guarding against discrimination based on cultural difference (American Counseling Association, 1988). The most recent version of the *ACA Code of Ethics and Standards of Practice* moves further by adding an explicit section on "respecting diversity" which states:

> Counselors will actively attempt to understand the diverse cultural backgrounds of the clients with whom they work. This includes, but is not limited to, learning how the counselor's own cultural/ethnic/racial identity impacts his/her values and beliefs about the counseling process (American Counseling Association, 1995, p. 2).

The trend is toward personal involvement in multicultural matters, rather than merely avoiding discrimination. This leads us to believe a niche for a new metaphor is evolving.

The Meaning of Metaphor

Often, the use of metaphor is not attributed the significance that more "objective" and scientific means of communication are given. Indeed, it is a poetic form important to creative pursuits in art and language, yet in a society where the "objective" and "logical" possess higher value, especially in academic circles, the significance of metaphor is often eschewed. Lakoff and Johnson (1980), though, note that "our ordinary conceptual system, in terms of which we both think and act, is fundamentally metaphorical in nature" (p. 3). These authors also posit that this "conceptual system plays a central role in defining our everyday realities," because "our concepts structure what we perceive...and how we relate to other people" (p. 3). Referring to the influence of metaphor, Embler (1966, p. iv) writes that "words determine the thoughts we have," as well as our behavior. Hayakawa (Embler, 1966, p. i) introduces Embler's work with the strong statement that "we do not use metaphors so much as our metaphors use us." Should these bold statements be true, metaphors are vital to our social world because they not only "always define a relationship between terms," but also define relationships between individuals and cultures (Sapir, 1977, p, 3). This defining of relationships is not purely logical, but contains power and pervasiveness in the arena of meanings (Embler, 1966; Hayakawa, 1990).

As metaphors influence our perceptions of self and others, it is important that we grasp their power and comprehend their pervasiveness. If the concepts which metaphors structure in our minds are not deemed sufficient representations of present or ideal relational realities, they should be changed. Embler (1966) notes that "language is to a great extent responsible for the thoughts we have about phenomena of the world" (p. 134). Due to the power of language, and especially metaphor, in light of ever-changing cultural relations, the authors believe it is time for a transformation of pervasive conceptual realities. It is time to transcend the tossed salad metaphor and to continue to break from the bonds of the melting pot idea.

The Melting Pot

In the past, and in some circles currently, the United States has been spoken of as a melting pot for the peoples that have flocked to its borders for refuge and opportunity. This metaphor was originated by playwright Israel Zangwill (1914). At the time of his play, "The Melting Pot," the nation had been open to unfettered immigration but was becoming increasingly wary of continuance in this direction. The melting pot concept was a romanticized way out of dealing with the impending issues at the time. Fairchild (1926) notes that it "was welcomed as a substitute for both investigation and thought" and "calmed the rising wave of misgiving," but Zangwill's consciousness of facts surrounding immigration affairs was insufficient for his interpretation of social change (pg. 11). Fairchild (1926) believed that the metaphor of Zangwill's drama gained "a significance quite disproportionate to its literary importance" (pg. 9). Indeed, this seems to be the overwhelming opinion on the metaphor today. The melting pot has come to be seen as a concept meant for stripping away cultural individualism (Taitte, 1986; Paradis, 1981; Farrington, 1992).

The Tossed Salad and Mosaic

After a call for awareness of difference within our nation, the popular metaphors have changed to those of a tossed salad (Farrington, 1992) and a mosaic (Savickas, 1992 ·). The new multicultural symbols promote diversity within one nation yet seemingly through "radical separation" on one hand or mere coexistence on the other (Hepburn, 1993; Savickas, 1992). It is with good intentions that these metaphors have been perpetuated, but of course, as all analogies do, these eventually break down. While they emphasize the importance of differences between cultures and individual backgrounds, values, and experiences, they lack a visionary symbolism of our unity, of what the nature of our relationships are. In the pursuit for individual, institutional, and cultural differentiation and autonomy, there has been a lack of emphasis on the nature of what is between us, our commonality and interdependence, and especially on the structure and function of healthy multicultural relationships, which includes those between persons, families, neighborhoods, communities, etc. It seems that dealing with racial crises is often attempted through alleviation of sociopolitical symptoms, while an aggressive study of the nature of productive and successful multicultural relationships is left unbroached or only scantily tended to. We are separate as individuals, but we are together as a nation, or, at least we can be, to one degree or another. In the sense of the tossed salad metaphor, we are basted together in the rich dressing of democracy, but even this picture is passive, lacking detail and vision. The mosaic metaphor also leaves us standing side by side but with little awareness of what this can mean beyond a seeming impersonal coexistence.

New Metaphors Necessary

We believe there is a need for new metaphors and analogies on the nature of the relationships between us in this multicultural nation and world. Now is the time for new ways of thinking about each other, individually, culturally, etc., for the purpose of clarifying objectives to reach a healthy "between-ness." Never should we cling to a figure as if it were reality, which is like seeing through spectacles which transform the beauty and complexity within and between us to something simple, trivial, and unimportant. Thus, we propose a new perspective, a novel metaphor that we hope incorporates important aspects of the old and the new, and as well, encourages us onward to continual speculation and rethinking of what is the nature of the relationship between us — as cultures and most importantly as members of the human race.

As we reflect on our membership and upon our vocations as a clinicians, we see the importance of understanding other cultures, as well as our own. No culture can be fully "understood" by anyone, but figments of experiences of "the others" can be tasted, touched, smelled, felt, and known. A cultural empathy can be increased as experiences of others' worlds resonate with a sense of authenticity between persons.

A New Metaphor

Traversing the road to understanding different cultures, and our own, involves appreciation through consciousness and positive regard of difference. This, of course, is most thoroughly experienced in relationships with people, who by nature have a cultural heritage. As fears are transcended, biases dissolved, and preconceived judgments and notions are abrogated by conscious will through conscious action, then relations with others, who are more "other" than those near oneself, may be melded. Melded, yes, in the sense of the marrying of *distinct* metals in a massive shining sculpture constructed of many beautiful pieces. Under the heat and flame of the torch, which makes joining possible, metals are married, each becoming a part of the other, yet for the most part remaining different and unique. Relating to another human life is always like this, should one wholly commit to the relationship. A mixing of sorts takes place and changes in each person are inevitable, yet individual differences remain.

As clinicians and educators, and even more as human beings, who are sensitive to multicultural issues, we transcend our fears through self-examination and will, driven by the desire to know and be known. It is with this mind that we seek out *marriage* of parts of our lives with others and their cultures, with hope that the marriage results in changes in who we are that are implicit in experiencing difference. Seeking out marriage with different cultures and individuals from diverse backgrounds means experiencing the heat and flame implicit in joining with newness. The heat and flame which, fear says, are reasons to withdraw, and which ignorance says are an infliction of the other, are inevitable. We press on, though, to know and be known, to relate to another who presses on in this same way. We transcend ourselves in appreciation and relationship with the other, and in this become more familiar with ourselves. Together, we create the heat and flame that sculpts life, piece by piece. We are sculptors by the torches of our wills. Should we and the artists within agree to the task, then let the flames and heat we light together torch the papery thinness of ignorance and hate. Let the shiny cores within unite in a marriage of discovery and a unity of distinctness, as continually transforming figures of peace.

Figure 1
Visually represented differences between metaphors

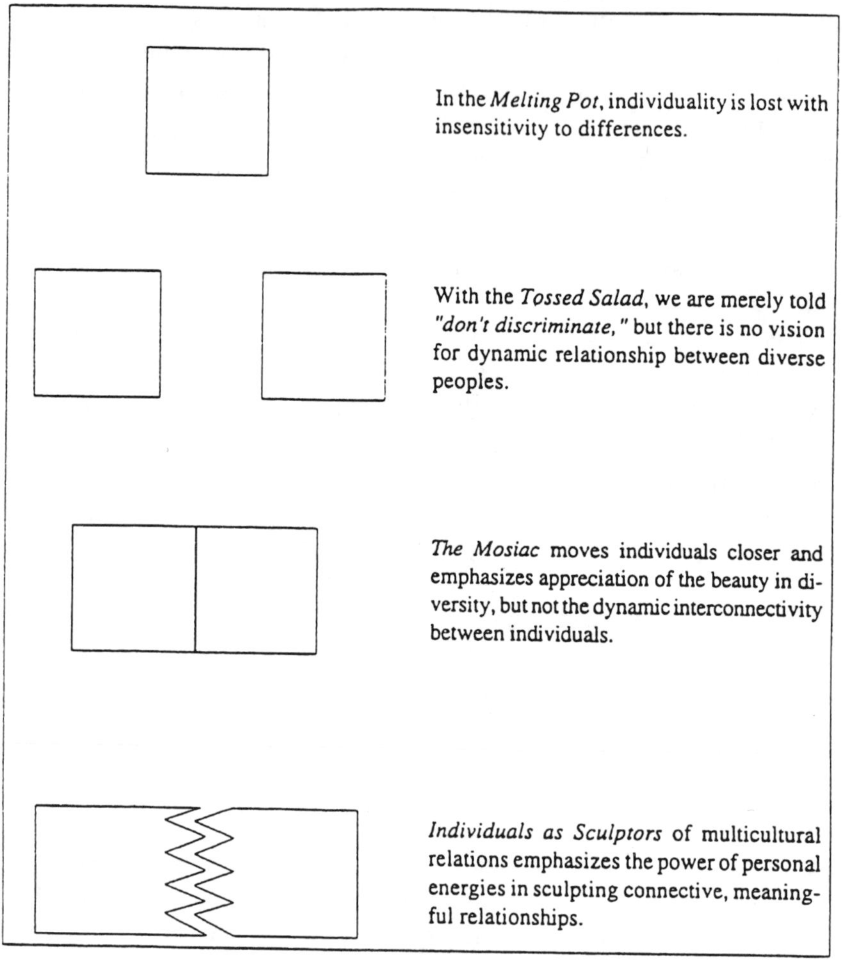

In the *Melting Pot*, individuality is lost with insensitivity to differences.

With the *Tossed Salad*, we are merely told *"don't discriminate,"* but there is no vision for dynamic relationship between diverse peoples.

The Mosiac moves individuals closer and emphasizes appreciation of the beauty in diversity, but not the dynamic interconnectivity between individuals.

Individuals as Sculptors of multicultural relations emphasizes the power of personal energies in sculpting connective, meaningful relationships.

Conclusion

Indeed, through committed relationships, and the challenges and joys implicit in them, we can learn about each other, our uniquenesses, and our cultures. As we ask ourselves, we ask you as well, how open are we to this? How open are we to transcending token appreciation of cultural difference and rising to heights of personal and cultural relationship, the heights and meaning of which we have yet to comprehend? This transcendence and transformation comes from a decision within to make something of what is between. A powerful lobby or appealing political agenda cannot be compared to the value of one personal decision to participate in the sculpting of multicultural relationships between one's self and others. As Martin Buber wrote, "all real living is relating" (Buber, 1947/1968). This is a higher order perception involving a commitment to second-order growth and change. It is a foundational perspective for building multicultural relationships. How will we work on our foundations for multicultural relating, teaching and counseling, that determine our actions in and out of therapeutic and educational settings? What metaphors will we choose to describe our courage and initiative to connect with those different from ourselves? We are the artists and the time is now to commit to creation, to light the torches of our wills and fire the potential of tomorrow.

References

American Association for Counseling and Development. (1988). *Ethical standards*. Alexandria, VA: Author.

American Counseling Association. (1995). Code of Ethics and Standards of Practice. Alexandria, VA: Author.

Buber, M. (1968). *Between man and man* (R. G. Smith, Trans.). New York: Macmillan. (Original work published 1947).

Cecil, A. R. (1986). Introduction. In W. L. Taitte (Ed.)., *A melting pot or a nation of minorities* (pp. 11-30). Austin: University of Texas Press.

Embler, W. (1966). *Metaphor and meaning*. DeLand, FL: Everett Edwards, Inc.

Fairchild, H. P. (1926). *The melting pot mistake*. Boston: Little, Brown, and Co.

Farrington, J. (1992). Goodbye melting pot...hello, tossed salad? *Career World*, 21(1), 4-6.

Hayakawa, S. I. (1990). *Language in thought and action*. San Diego: Harcourt Brace Jovanovich.

Hepburn, M. A. (1993). Concepts of pluralism and the implications for citizenship education. *The Social Studies*. January/February.

Lakoff, G., & Johnson, M. (1980). *Metaphors we live by*. Chicago: University of Chicago Press.

Paradis, F. E. (1981). Themes in the training of culturally effective psychotherapists. *Counselor Education and Supervision,* 21(2), 136-151.

Sapir, D. J., & Crocker, J. C. (Eds.). (1977). *The social use of metaphor: Essays on the anthropology of rhetoric*. Philadelphia: University of Pennsylvania.

Savickas, M. (1992, August). Innovations in counseling for career development. In L. J. Rickmond (Chair), *New perspectives on counseling for the 21st century*. Symposium conducted at the annual convention of the American Psychological Association, Washington, DC.

Taitte, W L,. (Ed.). (1986). *A melting pot or a nation of minorities?* Dallas: University of Texas at Dallas.

Zangwill, I. (1914). *The melting pot: Drama in four acts*. New York: Macmillan.

Chapter 11

ഇൽ

Global Village Education and Volunteer Service: Heifer Project International

JOHN P. EDDY, MICHAEL J. EDDY, DONALD J. SPAULDING, STANLEY D. MURPHY, AND KAN V. CHANDRAS

Hunger, poverty, family planning, livestock, and environmental management are problems that demand the attention of educators and educational institutions world-wide. The Heifer Project International of Perryville, Arkansas is an example of an educational and training effort to combat these seemingly intractable problems. This project, over the past 50 years, has sent over 20 different types of animals to over 110 countries of the world to help over one million needy families and has provided education and training in animal husbandry and sustainable farming methods. Elementary and secondary students, university and college students, teachers and professors, and others have attended a simulation Global Village on how to live on limited food rations and in actual primitive shelter approximating third world conditions. The author and second co-author recently visited this project while the second co-author participated in the educational experience offered by the Global Village simulation.

In the hills of central Arkansas, near the town of Perryville, lies the headquarters of the Heifer Project International. This Project has, in the last half century, provided help to over one million needy families in over 110 countries of the world. The Project teaches families to be self-reliant by training persons in animal husbandry and successful methods in sustainable farming. In over 50 years this Project has sent over 20 different types of animals to over 110 countries along with the requisite animal husbandry and sustainable farming education and training. In 1995, alone there are about 300 current projects operating in 33 countries, including the United States. Over 20 different types of animals are involved from llamas and dairy goats to geese and water buffalo. This Project takes on added importance in view of a recent study released by the United Nations Food and Agriculture Organization. This study strongly suggests that of 3,888 breeds of 28 species of farm animals 873 are at risk for extinction, that is, there are fewer than 1,000 females or 20 males in existence (Many Farm Animal, 1995).

Purpose

The purpose of this article is to survey the intent and accomplishments of Heifer Project International. Primarily however, the authors mean to emphasize the relationship between the project and education

Training in Democracy

While instructing participants in animal husbandry the Project also teaches the importance of democratic ways. Heifer Project International stresses values as follows:

(1) A democratic approach in resolving farming issues; trainers encourage citizens to form a farm cooperative, at the local level, to discuss and find solutions to their own animal program problems.
(2) Special efforts are made to empower men and women in the various animal rearing programs.
(3) Calling on well-documented research that poverty creates and results from overpopulation, family planning training provides positive ways to limit family size in order that associated hunger and health problems might be reduced.
(4) Social responsibility is taught as those receiving animals are required to show environmental improvements on their land; grass and tree planting and the recycling of animal manure to fertilize farm land are examples of these social principles.

Thus, the project teaches visiting students in ways to provide for healthier children, builds greater skills, instructs in better nutrition, teaches means of improving the environment, provides for stronger communities and empowered women and enlightens men to strengthen families.

Simulated Global Village Education

The Project Center offers a simulated Global Village wherein the living conditions in developing countries are set and reenacted for an overnight experience by visiting students. Campers are divided into groups and assigned various resources and sustenance items. Each group, however, lacks some of the components requisite to preparing healthy meals. Working under these deprivations the students must learn to work within and between groups to procure or acquire, usually by barter and trade, the food, water, fire or other resources so that a meal can be prepared. Throughout this process the students are coached on methods of trade, barter, and how to borrow or beg; thus, the skills necessary to avoid hunger are emphasized. Those involved in this learning experience sleep on the ground in huts or shelters similar to the primitive dwellings found in Africa, Asia, or South America. This intense experience intends to teach the cooperation and group-building skills necessary for the sustainment of life.

Summary

Many special programs are offered throughout the year at the education and training center of Heifer Project International. Included among these programs are a Hunger Conference, Harvest Festival, Global Village Day, Heifer Project International University, Hunger Workshop and December Festival. All of the programs intend to educate the public on hunger, poverty, family planning and sustainable development. Study tours are also available world-wide: Africa, Central America, Asia, and Europe. Volunteers are encouraged to join the Heifer International Project International. These volunteers help by completing such tasks as stuffing envelopes, feeding animals, speaking to church groups, answering telephones, writing for a newsletter, leading children in educational programs, and working on farm education and training projects. The Project has educated and trained millions of persons world-wide on how people can help themselves to be more self-reliant. Students in schools and colleges and non-students alike can learn a great deal from their participation in this vital and valuable project.

References

Many farm animal breeds risk extinction, U.N. experts say. (1995, December 7). The New York Times, p. A9.

Suggested Readings

(1995). "Children helping children." Little Rock, AR: Heifer Project International.

(1995). "Helping hungry families feed themselves and care for the earth." Little Rock, AR: Heifer Project International.

(1995). "How your church can share with others." Little Rock, AR: Heifer Project International.

(1995). "Salute to volunteers." Little Rock, AR: Heifer Project International.

(1995). "Small business, big change." Little Rock, AR: Heifer Project International.

(1995). "Project profiles." Little Rock, AR: Heifer Project International.

PART VI

INTERNATIONAL ISSUES IN HIGHER EDUCATION

Chapter 12

ജ്ജ

Cultural Forces that Drive Chinese Education in the People's Republic of China

A.J. Morris, John P. Eddy, Donald J. Spaulding, Stanley D. Murphy, and Eric D. Malmberg

This is a study of cultural forces which influence government decisions that affect Chinese educators, leaders, and students, as discovered during research of college students at Liaoning Normal College of Foreign Language at Liaoyang Province, People's Republic of China.

Purpose of the Study

This article will illuminate selected historical influences that affect decisions of Chinese educators and leaders. It will discuss the planned education system's influence in driving the Chinese of today and tomorrow in an understanding of China.

Basic Assumptions

The article shall discuss how Confucian and Maoist historical influences affect decisions of Chinese educators and leaders. The planned education system serves the strategic plan for China.

Background

The reason for understanding Chinese education planners becomes more critical daily. The forces that imbalance the trade relationships between China and the West are not random, but planned. In 1996, America had a trade deficit of $39.5 billion with China. China is the biggest buyer of U. S. Treasuries and owns over $43 billion of U. S. Treasury debt. This economic power of China can be a threat to America in the future. China has a four pronged strategic industrial plan for distributing through Hong Kong, Taiwan, and Korea. The planners perpetuate cultural forces through economic strategic plans, basic trade alliances, harvesting of world resources, cornering of world capital, and influence as a world supplier. The significance is that China is driven by traditional thinking through education systems.

This finding was the result of research into perceived gains of students from internal contact with faculty at Liaoning Normal College of Foreign Language. Chinese education is designed to move students directly into industry through a Party Record, starting at age 10. Students have a complete record of good or bad behavior to present as credentials for employment (Morris, 1997). This method is used to generate student responsibility and control.

Confucian Cultural Influence

Confucian culture is traditional throughout China despite many historical efforts to destroy it. It is not a religion, nor was Confucius a religious leader, even though some Chinese in about 1920 attempted to make him one. Confucius functioned in government as the national philosopher. The reason for the Confucian influence was the adoption of his teachings in the civil service examinations used in selecting Chinese leaders. This formed the backbone of Chinese education for over 2.000 years and it was discontinued officially in 1905. The teachings established original laws of behavior and values between individuals and governments that cannot be practiced fully today. A visit to the Confucius home by the senior author found he was surrounded by myth. Still, his theories of government were responsible for establishing a system of schools for the young. His theories have been taught at universities and had a profound influence on how the Chinese government made decisions and how the people now cope with conflict. The conflicts of history, the different religions, the prevailing philosophical theories, the reversal of laws by new leaders, the controls of communism within China (Grolier, 1978) serve as reasons why the Chinese people have learned to cope through adapting the "backdoor economy." This offers safety for the network and individuals. Anything that is done officially can be taken away by new leaders or policies, according to Mr. Shi Xu Shu, Instructor, Liaoning Normal College of Foreign Language (personal communication, August 7, 1993). Confucius was a strong advocate that life should not have monetary gain, the worth of a person was in "values." These philosophies pioneered the education system of Hong Kong, Singapore and Taiwan (Kumnuch, 1996). Communism focused on the productivity of "men" not the "man." The backdoor values offered practical survival. Henry Kissinger, who helped open China to American contacts, stated that "power is the ultimate aphrodisiac" and Chinese leaders are applying this dictum in their policies.

Maoist Cultural Influence

The closing of the Chinese schools and colleges from 1966 to 1976 were the effort of Chairman Mao to reorganize the schools to think more Western (Jacobson, 1980). Schools were patterned along the Western curricular and some 80% of the graduating youth read English.

The most important change in the civil service system of China, as result of communism, was the creation of a new position in management called the Party Officer. The purpose of this person was to bring party loyalty to every office. Communism requires loyalty and sincerity of its officers and subjects to be successful. This is a theory that is directly opposed to the Western philosophies of "balance of powers" through controversy, as it is written into democratic constitutions. The Party Officer is the most important position in Chinese administration, and these officers are chosen for their loyalty and communication skills. Party Officers can be identified by Westerners as those persons who attend events, and "don't seem to have a function." In fact, they have the first function that must be settled to "serve the Party."

The Party Officer is influential in selecting company officers and government leaders. According to Mr. Ding Shang Yuan, Former Ministry of Science Officer, people are not allowed to travel outside China without being screened and confirmed to be loyal to the Party (personal communication, April 3, 1993). Not only must company and government leaders be Communist Party members who can be discharged for failing to support Party thinking, but they receive Party training at special schools for leaders. These schools are cornerstones for advancing leaders — Classmates have significance. However, in the West, Chinese are heard to say they are not communist. They know Westerners want to hear this.

All Chinese leaders in business and education must belong to a network that is bound to the Party. The education system perpetuates the Party but the back door rules the people. With Hong Kong becoming a Chinese area on July 1, 1997, the fear of communist policies remains a crucial issue (Spaulding & Eddy, 1996).

Current Concerns

There are many critical concerns about the behavior of China's leaders at this time in history such as:

1. The continued deplorable human rights abuses in China.
2. The continued military weapons buildup in China.
3. The continued Chinese high tariff on American products sold to China.
4. The continued denial of deaths and wrong-doing at Tianamen Square in 1989.
5. The shooting of missiles by China around Taiwan in 1996.
6. The lack of helping feed the starving peoples of neighboring Communist North Korea by China.
7. Military maneuvers around Taiwan in 1996.
8. The sending of thousands of college students overseas by China instead of educating them in China.
9. The continued prejudice against female babies and children in China.
10. The continued selling of military missiles and weapons to nations associated with terrorist activities.
11. The policy of one child per family causes many women to have abortions for their birth control.
12. Unwanted elderly have been known to be cremated before they die of natural causes.

Conclusion

International columnist Georgia Anne Geyer (1997) has written recently of China as follows:

> . . . The Chinese Communist Party, its historical intentions unchanged, still rules supreme. It is using the relaxed restraints on business and investments to build up the country economically so that it can convey its total political, military and strategic power into the resurgence of China as a great power in the 21st Century.

References

Geyer, G. A. (May 17, 1997). Communists doing business as usual. Denton Record Chronicle, p. 12A.

Grolier Incorporated (1978). *The New Book of Knowledge*. New York: Grolier Incorporated Press, 256-264.

Grove, C. L. (1984, March). U. S. schooling through Chinese eyes. *Phi Delta Kappan,* 480-485.

Jacobson, H. W. (1980, May 6). *The education system and academic and technological exchanges of the People's Republic of China. Research report.* Paper presented at the Conference on Communication and China's External Relations, Honolulu, HI.

Kumnuch, E. A. (1996). *A comparison of the higher education systems of Taiwan, Singapore, and Hong Kong as a model for developing nations, 1945-1980.* Unpublished doctoral dissertation, University of North Texas, Denton, Texas.

Morris, Jr., A. J. (1997). *Student perceptions of achievement resulting from informal student-faculty relations at Liaoning Normal College of Foreign Language, Liaoyang, People's Republic of China.* Dissertation, University of North Texas, Denton, Texas.

Spaulding, D. J., & Eddy, J. P. (1996). China and Hong Kong: Clash of ideologies. *Journal of Instructional Psychology,* 23(3), 231-233.

Chapter 13

ꟸ

Examining the Impact of the Chinese Educational System

A.J. Morris, John P. Eddy, Donald J. Spaulding, Stanley D. Murphy, and E.D. Malmberg

The Chinese education system has a greater impact on Chinese industry than Western education systems. This difference affects international industrial competition, the East/West collision of economies, and world stability.

Introduction

Purpose of the Study

China has an education system that connects directly to industry. At age 10, each student joins the Communist Party and begins a record of performance which leads to credentials for a certain job with industry. Each student is responsible for that record and research has found that they take it seriously (Morris; 1997). It has an impact on worker productivity that is more efficient than Western education systems. The difference herein must be explored.

Basic Assumptions

The world trade balance is affected by the quality of labor within each nation, the education system, the work ethic, the ethics of the people, the number of laborers, the technological mixture, and individual values. These are different between the East and West.

Background

China has the world's largest labor base of 1.5-billion people, and almost every Western citizen has bought items made there. Some 80% of the Chinese are Han, a number larger than the total of Caucasian races (Grolier Inc., 1978). This single race of people have veto power at the United Nations. They have centralized planning intended to dominate the world through controlling "the soft underbelly of world manufacturing" (Ding Shang Yuan, Former Ministry of Science, personal interview, March 2, 1992). They already dominate the world in consumer manufacturing of cottons, rayons, silks, leathers, ornaments, toys, and art objects. They defend moralistic values. Behind this production base is an education system which makes youth responsible for their performance and behavior and which ties the industrial complex to the work ethic. Work is not used as a punishment (Jacobson, 1980).

Among the most damaging criticism of the world image makers to China is their human rights record. Dr. Ding Xuhan explained part of the problem stemmed from the Chinese decision to help the United Nations control world populations in the 1960's. China chose to change the law so that government would pay for only one child per family, the family must pay for all others. There is not a law restricting the family to one child as is often reported. China considers this more moral than the free vasectomies or hysterectomies of India and the free abortions or contraception devices of the West (personal interview, May 14, 1993). However, the one child family plan has an ancient conflict, wherein sons inherit the farm, stay home and take care of the old ones, while the daughter, marries and moves away. This tradition has prompted many Chinese fathers to abandon daughters in the hospital, causing an outcry from Chinese mothers and West together. As a result, the sonogram is the fastest growing sales item of technology in China, and promises to place a marriage premium on women as the percentage lowers for future generations. The bottom line is that China could have grown to 3 billion since the 1960s.

The Economic Advantage

China did not accept the John Keynes method of controlling an economy, as Western governments did. As a result, China has had little inflation since the 1950s while Western governments are paying debt with money devalued over 90%. The average college professor and high technical worker each receive about $500 salary per year. The people cannot own automobiles, bank accounts, or incur debt (President Liaon, Liaoning University, personal interview, September 10, 1991). This allowed China to overwhelm the industrial nations and replace the U. S., who once replaced Britain as #1 in consumer manufacturing. Hong Kong, Taiwan and Korea are middlemen for Chinese manufacturing, with favored nation status, and their dynamic Western education systems (Spaulding & Eddy, 1996).

Central planning has given China a nuclear defense plan that mandates every village must provide its own food and shelter (Ding Shang Yuan, personal interview, March 20, 1992). As a result, shelters flourish throughout China and the pedestrian would name China the "greenhouse nation of the world," who provides fresh food year round to its people. The threat of disaster causes neighbors to join together and help one another.

Planned education within China has given industry the strongest labor force in the world in numbers, in work values, and in a system that does not have waste. The Party Record system of controlling students for their best behavior and performance also controls theft and misbehavior on the job. Drug trafficking is not tolerated, and iron clad laws do not allow felons to repeat crime. Only 2.5% of students are allowed to attain college degrees and therein industrial leadership, although many more attend some college classes for professional growth. Since the opening of schools in 1976, the number of students who can read English out of high school is believed nearing 80% (Instructor Shi Xu Shu, Liaoning Normal College of Foreign Language, personal interview, September 3, 1993). The impact of international trade is staggering in China while crippling to Westerners who cannot defend their joint ventures, with some 80% failing (English Professor Ding, Liaoning University). It also opens Western doors to Chinese study and the manufacturing of advanced technology. According to Grove (1984), since Chinese culture does not allow dating, the impact of divided focus from academia is not great. Youth are allowed to help in family businesses. Most important, the government places giving every person a job as the highest priority to the economy (personal interview, July 10, 1993).

China buys more U. S, Treasuries than even the Japanese, so that China owns more than $43 billion of the U. S. Treasury debt. In 1996, the trade deficit with China was at an all-time high at $39.5 billion, allowing them to buy even more U. S. bonds. Is China trying to control our economy via this strategy?

Conclusion

Through central planning, the Chinese education system is tied to industry through a societal structure that is more rigid than those produced by Western education systems. They have overpowered world competition while Western governments have helped their worker through a system of minimum wages, environmental restrictions, and industrial limitations. In China, work is valued before money. Youth and adults both work, sometimes in violation of United Nations Human Rights' documents.

References

Grolier Incorporated (1978). *The New Book of Knowledge*. New York: Grolier Incorporated Press, 256-264.

Grove, C. L. (1984, March). U. S. schooling through Chinese eyes. *Phi Delta Kappan,* 480-485.

Jacobson, H. W. (1980, May 6). *The education system and academic and technological exchanges of the People's Republic of China. Research report*. Paper presented at the Conference on Communication and China's External Relations, Honolulu, HI.

Morris, Jr., A. J. (1997). *Student perceptions of achievement resulting from informal student-faculty relations at Liaoning Normal College of Foreign Language, Liaoning, People's Republic of China.* Dissertation, University of North Texas, Denton.

Spaulding, D. J., & Eddy, J. P (1996). China and Hong Kong: Clash of ideologies. *Journal of Instructional Psychology,* 23(3), 231-233.

References

APPENDICES

Appendix A

Chapter One Discussion Questions

1. Why is it important for higher education leaders to be knowledgeable of current leadership practices and trends in the college and university system?
2. Discuss how ethical leadership relates to personal effectiveness and system effectiveness in the various areas within the college or university structure.
3. Discuss the pros and cons of team leadership compared to individualism and competition.
4. Dialogue from personal experiences on how we can implement and improve accountability systems for leaders m higher education.
5. Discuss how privatization leadership has affected your leadership strategies in your present institution.
6. What is your perspective on global thinking leadership?
7. How will volunteer leadership impact higher education in the 21st century?
8. How will distance education impact the role of leadership m higher education? Identify personnel mostly affected by the growth of distance education.
9. Why will multicultural leadership be important in the 21st century?

Appendix B

Chapter Two Discussion Questions

1. Why are student development issues an important topic of concern for higher education leaders?
2. Based on the holistic approach, discuss the theories of Astin, Tinto, Pascarella, and Terenzini.
3. Discuss Chickering's theory of seven vectors.
4. What could be some advantages to a university education in a metropolitan setting as compared to a rural setting?
5. What aspect of this study did you find most interesting?

Appendix C

Chapter Three Discussion Questions and Activity

1. Discuss some of the challenges of medical and psychological campus officials in rendering services to the student population.
2. Why is Gulf War Syndrome an important concern for campus officials?
3. Discuss the four recommendations made in this study.
4. Name some American universities which may be affected more by Gulf War Syndrome than others.
5. Activity: Develop a set of questions to address Gulf War Syndrome and interview campus health officials (medical and psychological). Report findings to class in a short presentation with handouts followed by a class discussion.

Appendix D

Chapter Four and Five Discussion Questions and Activity

1. Compare and contrast the college student retention theories of Astin, Pace, Tinto and Pascarella listed in Table 1 (RE: The Use of the Dyad Concept in Residence Hall Student Development).
2. Define the dyad concept and discuss its' relevance to college student development.
3. Discuss personal experiences with dyad work or exposure while in undergraduate or graduate school.
4. How can the dyad concept be used in a classroom setting as a student development activity?
5. Activity: Each student will choose a dyad partner, a major class project (e.g. term paper presentation) and work together with their dyad partner for the remainder of the semester to fulfill the assignment.
6. Why is the role of resident assistants so important in the area of student development?
7. In Table I, resident assistants and their dyad partners were rated by fellow students. What values are evident for student development in these student ratings? (RE: College Residence Halls Research Study...).
8. Table 2 lists the results of student ratings of fellow residents. What values are evident for student development in these ratings? (RE: College Residence Halls Research Study...).
9. Reflect and discuss what your on campus undergraduate experiences were like (pros and cons). From a student development perspective, what would have made your on campus experiences more beneficial?
10. Discuss the student ratings of resident hall living given in Table 3. (RE: College Residence Halls Research Study...).
11. What can university student services officials learn from this study?

Appendix E

Chapter Six Discussion Questions and Activity

1. In this chapter discuss the section on Revenue Rulings.
2. How might Revenue Rulings apply to your present situation while you are pursuing your doctoral degree?
3. Share with the class some of your successes in obtaining funding (grants, scholarships, etc…) for graduate study.
4. Share with the class ways in which you have been able to deduct education expenses on your tax return, thus lowering your total out-of-pocket costs for graduate study.
5. Activity: Invite a Certified Public Accountant or Tax Attorney to lead the class in a discussion on the subject of tax saving strategies for graduate students.

Appendix F

Chapter Seven Discussion Questions and Activity

1. Discuss areas most likely to be affected by privatization when an institution begins to consider this alternative strategy.
2. What are some of the pros and cons of privatization?
3. Cite instances where institutions have taken steps to privatize or outsource services.
4. How does the concept of privatization affect the student development philosophy accepted and expressed m higher education as a key and primary mission.
5. What do feel will be the greatest impact on the future of higher education as it relates to privatization?
6. Activity: Invite two or three university presidents, who have recently experienced privatization within their institutions, to lead a panel discussion on this subject.

Appendix G

Chapter Eight Discussion Questions

1. Discuss why technology assisted education is becoming a rapidly accepted mode of educational delivery.
2. What are some of the advantages of technology assisted education?
3. How are professors affected by technology assisted education?
4. How are students affected by technology assisted education?
5. Lead a class discussion on the three most common models which have taken hold within the higher education delivery system.

Appendix H

Chapter Nine Discussion Questions and Activity

1. Discuss your personal reactions on the role of athletics in higher education.
2. What are your personal views towards the incidents cited in this chapter?
3. Discuss the specific reforms stated in the chapter. Do you agree or disagree?
4. What steps would you recommend to speed up the process of correcting a system which has drifted away from its' primary purpose in higher education—academics?
5. Activity: Invite a cross section of college coaches and top level administrators to lead a class discussion on this subject.

Appendix I

Chapter Ten Discussion Questions and Activity

1. Why is the topic of multicultural relations important today for higher education leaders?
2. Discuss personal feelings regarding this topic.
3. As a leader preparing for the 21st century, do you feel you have adequate skills to deal with the various cultural groups?
4. Each of the authors in this chapter are from different cultural groups (Caucasian, Asian, African American, and Indian). Discuss the significance of this to the subject matter.
5. Activity: If the class consists of different cultural groups, lead a class discussion on the importance of the need as professionals to grow in our understanding and appreciation for cultural differences.

Appendix J

Chapter Eleven Discussion Questions

1. What can we learn in higher education from the Global Village Education and Volunteer Service Heifer Project International program?
2. Discuss the section on Training in Democracy.
3. Discuss the section on Simulated Global Village Education where visiting students are given the overnight experience of living conditions in developing countries.
4. Have you ever experienced working in a developing country? If so, please share your experiences with the class.
5. Dialogue on other special programs offered throughout the year at the education and training center of Heifer Project International.

Appendix K

Chapter Twelve and Thirteen Discussion Questions

1. Why is it important to study and examine international education issues?
2. What are some of the political ramifications for understanding the Chinese educational system?
3. Discuss the Confucian influence on the culture of China.
4. Discuss the Maoist influence on the culture of China.
5. Lead a class discussion regarding the current concerns of China's leaders at this time in history.

Bibliography and Chapter Resources

Preface

The bibliography for this book is divided into the subjects of each of the chapters. First, this system enables the reader to turn to the table of contents and select the topic he or she is interested in. Secondly, the reader can turn to the list of references following each chapter and obtain additional resources to investigate further the specific topic chosen. In addition, the following list of references include current research and major published resources used for the writing and development of this book.

Part I Leadership In Higher Education

Chapter 1 Eddy, J.P., Murphy, S.D., Spaulding, D.J., & Chandras, K.V. 21st Century Leadership Practices Needed for Higher Education. *Education*, 1997, 117, 3, 327-331.

Part II Wellness And Health Programs In Higher Education

Chapter 2 Elleven, R.K., Spaulding, D.J., Murphy, S.D., & Eddy, J.P. Wellness Programming: Does Student Choice Relate to Recognized Development Vectors? *College Student Journal*, 1997, 31, 2, 228-234.

Chapter 3 Spaulding, D.J., Eddy, J.P., Chandras, K.V., & Murphy, S.D. Gulf War Syndrome: Are Campus Health Officials Prepared to Cope With Persian Gulf Veterans? *College Student Journal*, 1997, 31, 3, 317-322.

Part III Student Services In Higher Education

Chapter 4 Murphy, S.D., & Eddy, J.P. The Use of the Dyad Concept in Residence Hall Student Development. *College Student Journal*, 1995, 29, i, 53-56.

Chapter 5 Murphy, S.D., Eddy, J.P., & Spaulding, D.J. College Residence Halls Research Study: Student Perceptions of Resident Assistants, Fellow Residents, and Residence Hall Living. *College Student Journal*, 1997, 31, 1, 110-114.

Chapter 6 Brubaker, T.F., Eddy, J.P., Chandras, K.V., & Murphy, S.D. Education Expenses of Graduate Students: Tax Savings Strategies. *College Student Journal*, 1996, 30, 4, 550-552.

Part IV Administration, Curriculum And Technology In Higher Education

Chapter 7 Eddy, J.P., Spaulding, D.J., & Murphy, S.D. Privatization of Higher Education Services: Propositional Pros and Cons. *Education*, 1996, 116, 4, 578-579, 542.

Chapter 8 Eddy, J.P., Burnett, J., Spaulding, D.J., & Murphy, S.D. Technology Assisted Education (TAE). *Education*, 1997, 117, 3, 478-480.

Part V Athletics, Diversity And Volunteer Service In Higher Education

Chapter 9 Spaulding, D.J., Eddy, J.P., Spaulding, D.J. Jr., & Murphy, S.D. Reform American Intercollegiate Athletics Now. A Fifteen Point Plan to Score Success. *College Student Journal*, 1996, 30, 4, 482 485.

Chapter 10 Goodrow, K.G., Lim, M.G., Murphy, S.D., & Eddy, J.P. A New Metaphor: Individuals as the Sculptors. *Journal of Instructional Psychology*, 1997, 2, 3, 191-195.

Chapter 11 Eddy, J.P., Eddy, M., Spaulding, D.J., Murphy, S.D., & Chandras, K.V. Global Village Education and Volunteer Service: Heifer Project International. *Journal of Instructional Psychology*, 1997, 24, 1, 34-36.

Part VI International, Issues In Higher Education

Chapter 12 Morris, A.J., Eddy, J.P., Spaulding, D.J., Murphy, S.D., & Malmberg, E.D. Cultural Forces that Drive Chinese Education in the People's Republic of China. *Journal of Instructional Psychology*, 1997, 24, 4, 219-221.

Chapter 13 Morris, A.J., Eddy, J.P., Spaulding, D.J., Murphy, S.D., & Malmberg, E.D. Examining the Impact of the Chinese Educational System. *Education*, 1997, 118, 2, 210 - 212.

Index

—L—

—M—

—N—

—O—

—P—

—R—

—W—

—Z—

Contributors

Thomas F. Brubaker is a doctoral candidate in higher education at the University of North Texas, where he is the Executive Lecturer and Program Coordinator in the Accounting Programs office. He is a licensed Certified Public Accountant in Texas and a member of the American Institute of Certified Public Accountants. He received his Master of Business Administration in Accounting from the University of Missouri – St. Louis and his Bachelor of Business Administration in Accounting from the University of Texas at Arlington. He is currently serving as Treasurer for the American Association for Wellness Education Counseling and Research and is a member of Phi Delta Kappa.

Reverend John Burnett is Director of Missions for the Assemble of God Church in Johannesburg, South Africa. He is a former Dean of Education of ICI University, Irving, Texas. Reverend Burnett has served the Assembly of God Church overseas in the Philippines and Belgium as well as churches in the United States. He speaks a number of foreign languages and he has a great concern for people wherever he serves.

Kan V. Chandras is a professor of counseling psychology at The Fort Valley State University, Georgia. He received his Ph.D. from Southern Illinois University and did post-doctoral work in psychology at Valdosta State University, Southern Illinois University and University of Georgia. He served on the faculty of McGill University in Canada before moving to Fort Valley State University. He also taught at several universities in India. He has published 9 books and many articles in refereed professional journals. He received several awards for his teaching and research. He serves on the editorial board of the national counseling journal, *Counselor Education and Supervision*. His research areas include diversity, multicultural counseling and education, counseling adolescents and at-risk students.

John P. Eddy, Ph.D. and L.P.C., Professor of Counseling, Development and Higher Education at the University of North Texas, Denton, Texas from 1979 through 1998. Selected background on Dr. Eddy is: 1) He has been a former dean of students at Johnson State College and New Mexico Tech University where he was also a professor of psychology and education respectively. 2) He also taught at Southern Illinois University, Rust College, Mankato State University, Scarrett College, Felician College, Central Y.M.C.A. College, Lake County Community College and Central Mindanao Colleges. 3) He has been a director of counseling at New Mexico Tech University and Johnson State College. 4) He has been a hospital counselor and chaplain at the University of Minnesota Hospitals. 5) He has served over a dozen churches in the inner city, suburbs, cities, small towns, rural areas and on several other college campuses in America and in the Philippines. 6) He has been a counselor in social agencies, in refugee programs and in drug education projects. 7) He has been a volunteer in America and overseas building homes for the poor and buildings for missions projects and programs for needy persons. 8) He has authored or co-authored over 40 books and over 400 articles in refereed national professional journals and other periodicals around the world since 1952. 9) He has authored or co-authored over 60 funded grants worth over $2 million to help numerous educational and humanitarian projects. 10) He has worked in some of the great causes of this country in this century such as: youth religious programs in the 1950s; civil rights work in the 1960s; worldwide peace education in the 1970s; drug education crisis centers and family abuse centers in the 1980s and diversity education and environmental education in the 1990s. 11) He has met and worked with some of the giants of our world for human rights worldwide from Dr. Martin Luther King, Jr. to United Nations Ambassador Eleanor Roosevelt and Reverend Jesse Jackson. 12) He has helped scores of higher education students find thousands of dollars worth of scholarships and grants for their research and social action projects. 13) He has received many awards from national professional organizations for his publications, research service and teaching. 14) He strongly supports his wife who is a Christian religious educator and church librarian, one child in a Christian seminary, one child who is a Christian Psychologist and scientist, one child who is a Christian public school teacher and one child who is a Christian coach and player of professional basketball. 15) He deeply cares for the needs of peoples worldwide as he has an International Computer Project REAL on health related issues that is available to millions of peoples in over 200 nations of the world. 16) He has adopted a Family Day Care Center in Denton, Texas and a public school in Dallas, Texas as a volunteer, to help reach children and youth for a better education in their lives.

Michael J. Eddy is a professional basketball coach and player for the Westman Islands of Iceland. He is a graduate of Hendrix College and a masters graduate student at the University of North Texas. Michael has played professional basketball in Mexico, New Zealand, Australia and Iceland. He was an All-American Honorable Mention NAIA Basketball Player at Letourneau University and an All South Honorable Mention NCAA Basketball Player at Hendrix College. He has served as a youth minister of St. James United Methodist Church in Little Rock, Arkansas and a residence hall assistant at Hendrix College. During his off basketball season, he continues his yard business with lifelong friend and former basketball teammate Judd Holt, Jr. in Denton, Texas. In Iceland, he also coaches youth basketball teams and volunteers as an English teacher in local public schools. Off-season, he also volunteers in a public school where his sister Merri Elizabeth Eddy Blow teaches in Dallas, Texas.

Russell K. Elleven is the former Residence Life Coordinator at the University of North Texas, Denton, Texas. His research interests include student housing, student services, and student activities. In his 1998 position, he is a Health and Wellness Program Specialist for Texas Health Resources, Fort Worth, Texas and an Adjunct Professor for the Department of Technology and Cognition at the University of North Texas, Denton, Texas. He completed his doctorate and has done post-doctoral work at the University of North Texas. He is also published in other refereed journals.

Kenneth K. Goodrow II received his M.S. from Texas A & M University-Commerce, where he was also awarded the Most Outstanding Master's Student. He is a Licensed Professional Counselor, National Certified Counselor, and a Certified Cognitive Behavioral Therapist. He has directed judicial affairs, service-learning, and alcohol & drug education at a private university and is currently directing the treatment program at a regional treatment center for difficult youth. Additionally, he is a part-time faculty member at Adams State College where he teaches on working with difficult youth and supervises graduate counseling students. He has also published in the Journal of Offender Rehabilitation on the application of attachment theory to work with juvenile sex offenders, and in the Journal of Family Psychotherapy on practical uses of Murray Bowen's family system theory in working with young couples. His current research interest include study into the neuropsychological and resulting transgenerational social effects of oppression on diverse populations.

Mee-Gaik Lim is an adjunct professor at Del Mar Junior College in Corpus Christi, Texas. She received her Ph.D. in Marriage and Family Therapy from Texas Woman's University. Her research and publications have focused on marital and family health, ethnic populations, sexual offender issues, and marital case studies. She has received numerous grants to fund her research efforts. She has served as an Associate Editor of Family Perspective and an Ad Hoc Editor of *Journal of Family Psychotherapy*. While teaching at Texas A & M at Commerce from 1993 - 1997, she served as a Faculty Advisor for the Chinese Student Organization and was actively involved in multicultural projects.

Eric D. Malmberg is a doctoral student in Higher Education Administration at the University of North Texas. He is the National President of the American Association of Wellness Education, Counseling and Research; President of the Association of Graduate Students in Higher Education; and by profession an Air Traffic Control Operations Supervisor with the FAA. He received his B.S. and M.Ed. in Education from Oklahoma City University, and an M.B.A. in Management Systems from California Coast University.

A.J. Morris is presently a professor in the department of Economics at the University of Central Arkansas, Conway, Arkansas where he teaches global economics. He has also taught at Northwood University, Richland College in Dallas, Texas, and Hill College in Hillsboro, Texas. He received his Bachelor of Arts from Pittsburg State University, Pittsburg, Kansas, a Master of Business Administration from Dallas Baptist University, and a Ph.D. in Higher Education from the University of North Texas, Denton, Texas. In his doctoral dissertation, he studied how students learn in the Chinese education system. His research interests include international economics and world business and trade relationships.

Stanley D. Murphy is an adjunct professor in the School of Counseling and Human Services at Regent University in Virginia Beach. He received his B.S. and M.A. in Psychology from Middle Tennessee State University and a B.A. in Theology from Ambassador University in Big Sandy, Texas. In addition to his teaching responsibilities, he is also a doctoral student at Regent University's Center for Leadership Studies, where he is pursuing a Ph.D. in Organizational Leadership with an emphasis in Education. He was selected Who's Who Among America's Teachers in 1996. His research and publications have been in the areas of counseling, higher education, and student affairs. Along with his colleagues, he has conducted workshops and presented numerous papers on the local, regional and national level. He is licensed in marriage and family therapy and professional counseling in Tennessee and Texas. He is a clinical member of the American Association for Marriage and Family Therapy. In addition, he holds professional memberships with the American Counseling Association, the Association for Counselor Education and Supervision, the Association for Multicultural Counseling and Development, the American Association of Christian Counselors, the American Association for Wellness Education, Counseling and Research, and the Southern Association of College Student Affairs.

Donald J. Spaulding, Lieutenant Colonel, US Army, Retired, is the former Chair and Professor of Military Science, Eastern New Mexico University, Portales, New Mexico. He is presently completing his dissertation for a Doctorate of Higher Education at the University of North Texas, Denton, Texas. His research and writings are focused on the leadership and processes of higher education. He is currently writing publications for veterans, including a handbook for veterans attending college in Texas.

Donald J. Spaulding, Jr. is currently a physical education teacher and coach in Songes, Texas. He completed his bachelor's degree at Eastern New Mexico University in Portales, New Mexico and is currently working on a graduate degree at Texas Woman's University in Denton, Texas. His research interests include strength conditioning and motivation of young athletes.

Literary Culture in Early New England.

Published in Memory of
Thomas Goddard Wright.

LITERARY CULTURE
IN
EARLY NEW ENGLAND
1620-1730

By Thomas Goddard Wright,

EDITED BY HIS WIFE

NEW YORK / RUSSELL & RUSSELL

1966

FIRST PUBLISHED IN 1920
REISSUED, 1966, BY RUSSELL & RUSSELL
A DIVISION OF ATHENEUM HOUSE, INC.
L.C. CATALOG CARD NO: 66—24771

REPRINTED FROM A COPY IN THE COLLECTIONS OF
THE PRINCETON UNIVERSITY LIBRARY

PRINTED IN THE UNITED STATES OF AMERICA

Contents.

Contents.

PART III

THE NEW CENTURY

APPENDIX

Memorial Note.

THOMAS GODDARD WRIGHT, the author of this book, was born at Fort Ann, New York, the seventeenth of August, 1885. He was the son of the Reverend William Russell Wright and Alma (Boardman) Wright. He was graduated from the Hartford Public High School in 1903, and then entered Yale University, where he received the degree of B.A. in 1907, M.A. in 1908, and Doctor of Philosophy in 1917. On the seventh of June, 1913, he was married to Mabel Hyde Kingsbury, daughter of Dr. and Mrs. Edward N. Kingsbury, of Woonsocket, Rhode Island. From the year 1908 he had served first as Assistant, and later as Instructor in English in the Sheffield Scientific School of Yale University.

This book is in his favourite field of study, and is in part representative of his special research therein covering a period of five or six years. While primarily intended for the use of scholars in history and literature, it is by no means without interest for the general reader.

In the death of Dr. Wright, Yale University suffers a severe loss from the ranks of its scholars and teachers. He was intensely beloved both by his colleagues and by his pupils. His character and personality had an extraordinary charm; he was modest, generous, unselfish, faithful and pure in heart. I never knew a man more free from the meaner vices of self-interest and self-importance. The advancement of his rivals pleased him more than his own achievements. No one could know him without feeling a sense of elevation. His high-minded and unassuming devotion to his work was an example to us all, and his influence will be permanently fruitful.

WILLIAM LYON PHELPS.

Yale University, Tuesday, 3 June, 1919.

Preface.

THE subject of the study which follows was suggested to me by Professor Henry A. Beers, to whom I owe more than I can express for his wise guidance and sympathetic encouragement throughout the preparation of this work. I wish to acknowledge also the assistance of Professor William Lyon Phelps, under whose supervision the work was carried on after the retirement of Professor Beers from active teaching.

I owe much to Professor Keogh and Messrs. Gruener and Ginter of the Yale University Library, and Mr. Sanborn, formerly of the Library, all of whom I have found invariably responsive to any demands which I have made upon them for help in finding material for this work. I wish to acknowledge also the kindness of Mr. Julius H. Tuttle of the Massachusetts Historical Society, Mr. Clarence S. Brigham of the American Antiquarian Society, and Messrs. William C. Lane and Walter B. Briggs of the Harvard University Library, who assisted me in my search for material. To Mr. Albert Matthews of the Colonial Society of Massachusetts and Professor Charles M. Andrews of Yale, who kindly read my manuscript, I am indebted for many valuable suggestions.

Finally to those who, in connection with the various historical and antiquarian societies of New England, have gathered and made accessible a wealth of valuable material I owe an inestimable debt; without the fruits of their labor my task would have been an impossible one.

T. G. W.

Introduction.

MOST students of our colonial literature devote themselves primarily to the appraisal of its value as literature. The pages which follow will not attempt to weigh colonial literature, either to condemn or defend it (although at times they may endeavor to correct impressions which, to the writer, seem erroneous), but rather will attempt to determine that which lies back of any literature, the culture of the people themselves, and to study the relation between their culture and the literature which they produced. In the attempt to determine the culture of the people of New England the writer has made a study of their education, their libraries, their ability to obtain books, their use and appreciation of books, their relations with political and literary life in England, and their literature. In the course of the study certain generally accepted notions of the low estate of colonial culture will be shown to be incorrect or exaggerated. There were in New England as in Old England many people who were without culture and even illiterate; but the general state of culture in the colonies will be shown to be higher than it has usually been rated.

This study has been limited approximately to the first one hundred years of colonial life, and to the New England colonies with Boston as their center. These colonies form a distinct unit, akin to each other, and differing from any other colony, or group of colonies, in both antecedents and interests. That much more is said of those who settled on Massachusetts Bay than of those elsewhere in New England is due partly to the greater comprehensiveness and accessibility of the extant records of that region, and partly to the fact that Boston was the literary and cultural center as well as the chief city of these colonies. It must have a predominant place in this discussion, just as London would in a similar study of the literary culture of England.

It is not easy to divide the first century of colonial life into cultural periods which have definite limits. To attempt to discuss conditions according to generations, first, second, third, is impossible, because of the range of age of the first settlers, and their varying longevity. Brewster, Hooker, and Winthrop all died in the forties; John Norton and John Wilson lived into the sixties, the latter almost outliving the Reverend John Eliot, Jr., who had been born in New England. For convenience the one hundred years will be discussed as if divided into three periods, the first of fifty years, the second of thirty, and the last of twenty. The first, ending about 1670, covers the years during which those who came to America as settlers, men born and educated in England, were in control of the affairs of the colony, and determined its culture. By 1670 practically all of these men had died, and government, education, and culture were in the hands of men reared and trained in the New World. The second period ends with the seventeenth century, partly because the century mark makes a convenient terminal, and partly because there are certain differences in the life of the colonists before and after the opening of the century. The third period covers the rest of the one hundred years. It must be remembered, however, that the limits of the periods are approximate, *not* exact; the last period, for example, instead of stopping absolutely at 1720, includes a discussion of certain events in the half-dozen years immediately following that date.

The writer recognizes that his study is incomplete. It never can be complete because too many of the records have perished. Certain records which are preserved but which have been inaccessible might throw more light upon the subject; but presumably these would merely add detail and in no way affect the main conclusions.

Part I:

The Early Settlers.

1620-1670.

Errata and Notes.

Page 128, l. 12: For "augment [atione]" read "augment [is]."
Page 131, l. 6: For "State of E [urope]" read "State of E [ngland]."
Page 150, ls. 4 and 5: Hornius' "Carthaginian Dream" is a reference to page 129 of Lib. II of "De Originibus Americanis."
Page 185, l. 3: For "Huylin" read "Heylyn."
Page 197, l. 17: For "Edward Calamy" read "Edmund Calamy."

Chapter I: Education.

WITH the exception of the group which settled Plymouth, the founders of New England included in their ranks a remarkably high proportion of university men. The settlers of Plymouth, mostly village and country folk of no particular education,[1] lost rather than gained educationally during the years of their hardships in Holland (which was one reason for their desire to leave), so that when the *Mayflower* crossed the seas it carried but one man of university training, and even he did not have a degree. William Brewster had entered St. Peter's, or Peterhouse, Cambridge, December 3, 1580,[2] and had there spent a year or two before leaving for active life as a private secretary or confidential servant to William Davison, later Secretary of State, and then busy helping to carry out Queen Elizabeth's designs in Scotland and Holland. Until Ralph Smith, the first settled minister of Plymouth, arrived in 1629, Brewster was the only university man in the colony.[3] In the thirty years that followed less than a score of university men came to the colony, and of these only three remained and followed their calling. "Able men, like Norton, Chauncy, Hooke, and Williams, tarried but a short time and went to wider fields."[4] "Prior to 1650 Harvard College neither received from Plymouth nor contributed to that place more than one or two persons."[5] The other settlements presented a striking contrast to Plymouth. Even before Winthrop

[1] "In the main they were plain farmers." H. M. Dexter, The England and Holland of the Pilgrims, p. 379.

[2] *Ibid.*, p. 256.

[3] F. B. Dexter, Massachusetts Historical Society, Proceedings, 1st Series, xvii. 344.

[4] William Bradford, History of Plymouth Plantation, i. 134 note.

[5] *Ibid.*, i. 134 note.

came in 1630, university men had settled on the shores of Massachusetts Bay,[6] and with Winthrop, or following him in the next ten or fifteen years, were Oxford and Cambridge men to the number of nearly one hundred[7] out of a total population of not more than 25,000.[8] Of these at least fifty were the possessors of advanced degrees, and half a dozen had been appointed Fellows. Nearly every college of each university was represented here, and among the colonists were men who had been in Cambridge when Milton was studying there, although no one who was in Christ's College with him. Thomas Shepard, John Norton, Abraham Pierson, John Harvard, Henry Dunster, and Roger Williams may be mentioned among the contemporaries of Milton and Jeremy Taylor, and of these Williams was, at a later period at least, a personal friend of Milton's.[9] The friendship may well have dated back to college days.

Such an unusual proportion of university men gave to the young colony a cultural tone unique in the history of colonization. And if it must be acknowledged that a dozen of the men included in the figures given above left the universities without qualifying for degrees, among them John Winthrop, Harry Vane, Richard Saltonstall, and Giles Firmin, the list may be supplemented by such names as Nathaniel Eaton, who studied at Franeker, Hol-

[6] William Blackstone settled in Boston Bay in 1623 and on the site of Boston in 1625. The Rev. William Morell, author of the Latin and English poem on New England (*Nova Anglia*), with whom Blackstone may have come to these shores, had lived at Weymouth a year and a half (1623 to 1625), then returning to England. In 1629 Francis Higginson, Samuel Skelton, Francis Bright, and Ralph Smith were among the settlers of Salem. Bright soon returned to England; Smith went to Plymouth the same year.

[7] F. B. Dexter, Massachusetts Historical Society, Proceedings, 1st Series, xvii. 340.

[8] Dexter, *ibid.*, p. 344, and Estimates of Population in the American Colonies.

[9] Williams wrote to John Winthrop, Jr., July 12, 1654, "It pleased the Lord to call me for some time and with some persons to practice the Hebrew, the Greeke, Latine, French and Dutch: The Secretarie of the Councell, (M[r] Milton) for my Dutch I read him, read me many more Languages." (Massachusetts Historical Society, Collections, 3rd Series, x. 3.)

land;[10] John Winthrop, Jr., who studied at Dublin, was admitted to the Inner Temple as lawyer in 1625,[11] and later spent fourteen months touring the Continent, spending three months in Constantinople, and visiting practically all the countries of Europe on the way;[12] Henry Whitfield, who studied "at the university, and then at the Inns of Court;"[13] Thomas Parker, who, withdrawing from Oxford on the exile of his father, studied at Dublin under Dr. Usher, and at Leyden under Dr. Ames, and "proceeded master" before the age of twenty-two with "the special esteem of Maccovius, a man renowned in the Belgick universities;"[14] and Dr. Robert Child of Corpus Christi, Cambridge, "a gentleman that hath travelled other parts before hee came to us, namely Italy . . . . he tooke the degree of Doctor in Physick at Padua."[15]

Many of these men were recognized by their contemporaries in England and on the Continent as scholars of ability. That several were elected Fellows at the universities has already been noted. Charles Chauncy, later president of Harvard, was elected professor of Hebrew, and served as professor of Greek, in Trinity College, Cambridge.[16] Thomas Fuller classed Thomas Shepard, Thomas Hooker, Nathaniel Ward, and John Cotton among "the learned writers of Emmanuel College,"[17] and of John Norton's answer to Apollonius he wrote, " . . . . of all the *Authors* I have perused concerning the *opinions* of these *Dissenting Brethren*, none to me was more *informative*, then Mr *John Norton*, (One of no less *learning* then *modesty*) . . . . in his answer to

[10] F. B. Dexter, Massachusetts Historical Society, Proceedings, 1st Series, xvii. 344.

[11] R. C. Winthrop, Life and Letters of John Winthrop, i. 203.

[12] *Ibid.*, i. 263.

[13] Cotton Mather, Magnalia Christi Americana, i. 592.

[14] *Ibid.*, i. 481.

[15] Edward Winslow, New England's Salamander Discovered, Massachusetts Historical Society, Collections, 3rd Series, ii. 117.

[16] Magnalia, i. 465.

[17] Fuller, History of Cambridge University, p. 147.

Apollonius."[18] Henry Dunster was an Oriental scholar of reputation, as is shown by his correspondence with Ravius.[19] The esteem in which many of the colonists were held is further shown by the fact that three New England ministers, John Davenport, John Cotton, and Thomas Hooker, were invited to sit in the Westminster Assembly,[20] and that several were recalled to high positions in England, as was Hugh Peter, who became Cromwell's chaplain. Of this more will be said later.[21]

It is not surprising that a colony comprising so many educated men should take an active interest in the problem of the training of the young men whom they brought with them. Some were trained, as was Thomas Thacher, by residing with and studying under some minister of scholarly repute. Thacher, the son of a minister of Salisbury, England, had been offered his choice of either university, but had preferred the more congenial atmosphere of New England, where he came in 1635. He "was now cast into the family and under the tuition of that reverend man, Mr. Charles Chancey; . . . . Under the conduct of that eminent scholar, he became such an one himself."[22] But such methods did not satisfy the colony, and in 1636 the General Court voted £400 for the establishing of a college. When John Harvard, the first minister in the colony to die without leaving dependents, bequeathed to the college in 1638 his

[18] Magnalia, i. 290. Fuller, Church-History of Britain, xvii Century, xi Book, p. 213.

[19] Chaplin, Life of Henry Dunster, p. 86. Ravius (Christian Rau) after travel and study in the Orient was professor of Oriental languages successively at Gresham College and the Universities of Utrecht, Oxford, and Upsala.

[20] Winthrop's Journal, i. 223 note; ii. 71.

[21] See Chapter III, below.

[22] Magnalia, i. 490. Mather mentions thirteen others who were educated in this manner: Samuel Arnold of Marshfield, John Bishop of Stamford, Edward Bulkly of Concord, Thomas Carter of Woburn, Francis Dean of Andover, James Fitch of Norwich, Thomas Hunford of Norwalk, John Higginson of Salem, Samuel Hough of Reading, Thomas James of Easthampton, Roger Newton of Milford, John Sherman of Watertown, and John Woodbridge of Newberry." (Magnalia, i. 237.)

library and one half of his estate,[23] the beginning of college education in America was made possible. The first teacher appointed, Nathaniel Eaton, had been educated in Holland, at Franeker. When he proved unsatisfactory for reasons other than scholastic,[24] Henry Dunster was appointed in his place, and under him the first class of nine completed its course in 1642. For a colony only twelve years old this was no small achievement.

The course of studies was similar to that of the English universities, including Logic, Physics, Ethics, Politics, Arithmetic, Geometry, Astronomy, Greek, Hebrew, Chaldee, and Syriac, with especial emphasis on Rhetoric, it being required that "every scholler . . . . declaime once a moneth."[25] Much Latin and some Greek were required for admission,[26] and the college rules stipulated the use of Latin for all conversation in the college. Under such scholars as Dunster and Chauncy the standards were undoubtedly as high here as in England.[27] On both sides of the water the chief purpose of the universities was to train men in divinity, and

[23] The college received by this bequest £779.17.02. College Record Book III. 1.

[24] Nathaniel Eaton went from Massachusetts to Virginia and thence, after some years, to Italy, where he received the degrees of Doctor of Philosophy and of Medicine at Padua in 1647. The rest of his life was spent in England. (Littlefield, Early Massachusetts Press, i. 70.)

[25] New England's First Fruits, (1643), Massachusetts Historical Society, Collections, 1st Series, i. 245.

[26] *Ibid.*, i. 243. "When any schollar is able to understand Tully, or such like classicall Latine author extempore, and make and speake true Latine in verse and prose, ... and decline . . . . the paradigim's of nounes and verbes in the Greek tongue: Let him then . . . . be capable of admission."

[27] The endeavor of those interested in the college to ensure good teaching is shown by the following item from the Magnalia, ii. 14: "That brave old man Johannes Amos Commenius, the *fame* of whose worth hath been *trumpetted* as far as more than *three* languages (whereof every one is indebted unto his *Janua*) could carry it, was indeed agreed withal, by our Mr. Winthrop [the younger] in his travels through the *low countries*, to come over into New-England, and illuminate this Colledge and *country*, in the quality of a President: But the solicitations of the Swedish Ambassador, diverting him another way, that incomparable Moravian became not an American." *Cf.* Albert Matthews, Comenius and Harvard College, Publications of the Colonial Society of Massachusetts, xxi. 146-190.

liberal learning suffered common neglect.[28] Harvard at least attempted to give as much culture as the English universities, for, in the study of Greek, for example, the requirements were: Etymologie, Syntax, Prosodia and Dialects, Grammar, Poesy, Nonnus, Duport, Style, Composition, Imitation, Epitome, both verse and prose.[29] One form of literary activity practised at the English universities, the writing and production of plays, was, of course, totally missing at Harvard.

That the education to be gained at Harvard even in its earliest days was the equivalent of that of Cambridge and

[28] Of Cambridge about 1600 J. B. Mullinger writes (History of the University of Cambridge, p. 134), "Such are the chief features in the history of the university in the reign of Elizabeth. It had been decided that Cambridge should be mainly a school of divinity. . . . . The main interest having centred in the discussion of theological questions, whatever was taught of liberal learning sank to an almost lifeless tradition." Of Cambridge in the first half of the 17th century he writes elsewhere (Cambridge Characteristics in the Seventeenth Century, p. 55 ff.), "An attempt which he [Barrow] made to introduce the Greek tragedians to the attention of his scanty auditory met with so little encouragement that he was compelled to fall back on Aristotle. . . . . No mention appears to be made of Thucydides as a college subject during this period. . . . . Æschylus is rarely quoted, and Pindar . . . . still less. I find no instance of the employment of Lucretius as a class-book. . . . . Of the inimitable beauties of the Latin poets of the præ-Augustan school there is not a glimpse of anything like adequate recognition. . . . . Indeed, if we except the names of Meric Casaubon, Milton, Herbert, Barrow, and Duport, it is doubtful whether we could point to any scholar in England during the earlier part of the century, who possessed that refined form of scholarship represented in the present day by so nice a sense of the beauties and delicacies of Greek and Latin verse. . . . . Milton, indeed, stands in almost painful contrast to his University from his superiority in this as in more important traits." Of the latter Mullinger writes further (*Ibid.*, p. 76), "In the case of Milton, for instance, beyond the culture of his classical taste, there is little reason for supposing that Cambridge did much toward moulding his character, or, if so, it would appear to be quite as much by the development of antagonistic as of sympathetic feelings. . . . . [p. 78.] However reluctantly, it would seem, therefore, that we must forego that thrill of pride with which we should delight to trace, in the productions of the genius of John Milton, the fostering and guiding influence of his university career." G. C. Brodrick, in his History of Oxford, p. 94, says, "Spenser and other Elizabethan poets had received an University education; but such men derived their inspiration from no academical source; their literary powers were matured in a very different school."

[29] New England's First Fruits, Massachusetts Historical Society, Collections, 1st Series, i. 244.

Oxford is best shown by the careers of some of its earliest graduates. Sir George Downing, of the first class, rose to distinction under Cromwell, acting as his minister at The Hague, a position which he retained under Charles II, who knighted him in 1660, and made him a baronet three years later.[30] Benjamin Woodbridge of the same class became one of the chaplains in ordinary to Charles II after the Restoration, and was given the choice of being canon of Windsor if he would conform,—which he refused to do.[31] Henry Saltonstall, also of the first class at Harvard, was given recognition at Oxford. Among the incorporations of 1652, according to the record in Wood's "Athenæ Oxoniensis," appears, "June 24, Henr. Saltonstal, a Knight's Son, Fellow of New Coll. by the favor of the Visitors, and Doct. of Phys. of Padua, was then incorporated. The said degree he took at Padua in Oct., 1649." Samuel Mather, the first graduate to be made a Fellow of Harvard, became chaplain to Thomas Andrews, Lord Mayor of London, about 1650. He was admitted by Cambridge, Oxford, and Trinity, Dublin, "ad eundem," and by the latter was offered a "baccalaureatus in theologia" which he declined, although he accepted an election as Senior Fellow. He also served as chaplain in Magdalen, Oxford, preaching sometimes in St. Mary's.[32] Increase Mather became a Master of Arts at Trinity, Dublin, and was well received by the scholars there, being offered a fellowship which he declined.[33] Before returning to Boston at the age of twenty-two,[34] he served for a time as chaplain at Guernsey.[33]

With the graduates of Cambridge and Oxford who returned to England when the Puritans came into power, went a number of Harvard men other than those mentioned above, all of whom seem to have been equipped to succeed

[30] Winthrop Papers, i. 536 note.

[31] Massachusetts Historical Society, Collections, 1st Series, x. 32 note.

[32] Magnalia, ii. 43.

[33] Wendell, Cotton Mather, p. 19.

[34] Magnalia, ii. 18.

in England. One of them, Nathaniel Mather, wrote back to his relatives in New England, in 1651, "Tis incredible what an advantage to preferm^t it is to have been a New English man."[35] It is with natural pride that Cotton Mather remarks, "From that hour [the time of the founding of Harvard] *Old* England had more ministers from *New*, than our New-England had since *then* from Old."[36]

The satisfactory condition of scholarship at Harvard is further shown by the fact that "in several instances youth of opulent families in the parent country were sent over to receive their education in New England."[37]

Colonial interest in education was not limited to the higher education of the college, as is shown by the law passed in Massachusetts in 1647:[38]

> . . . . every township in this jurisdiction, after the Lord hath increased them to the number of fifty householders, shall then forthwith appoint one within their town to teach all such children as shall resort to him to write and read, whose wages shall be paid either by the parents or masters of such children, or by the inhabitants in general . . . . where any town shall increase to the number of 100 families or householders they shall set up a grammar

[35] Massachusetts Historical Society, Collections, 4th Series, viii. 5. He reports receiving, within three hours of landing in England, two offers of churches, one worth £140 per annum.

[36] Magnalia, i. 237. In addition to those mentioned above, the following Harvard men took advanced degrees: Benjamin Woodbridge (A.M., Oxford, 1648), James Ward (A.M., Oxford, 1648, M.B., 1649), William Stoughton (A.M., Oxford, 1653), John Glover (M.D., Aberdeen, 1654), Leonard Hoar (M.D., Cambridge, 1671), Isaac Chauncy (M.D.), Ichabod Chauncy (M.D.), Joshua Ambrose (A.M., Oxford, 1656), and John Haynes (A.M., Cambridge, 1660). Publications of the Colonial Society of Massachusetts, xviii. 210.

[37] Palfrey, History of New England, ii. 49. Palfrey gives Johnson's Wonder-Working Providence as authority. Johnson writes, ". . . . some Gentlemen have sent their sons hither from England, who are to be commended for their care of them, as the judicious and godly Doctor Ames, and divers others." (p. 202, Jameson ed.) Among the "divers others" was Sir Henry Mildmay, who "sent his Son *William Mildmay*, Esq; the Elder Brother of *Henry Mildmay*, Esq; of *Shawford* in *Hampshire*, to study here [Harvard]." (Neal, History of New England, i. 206, 2d ed.) Richard Lyon, who helped Dunster with the revision of the Bay Psalm-Book, was the tutor of Mildmay. (*Ibid.*, p. 207).

[38] Littlefield, Early New England Schools, p. 77.

school, the master thereof being able to instruct youth so far as they may be fitted for the university. . . . .

Before this law was passed many towns had made provision for grammar schools.[39] Just how zealously the law was enforced it is impossible to determine, but there are records of towns being fined for failure to provide schools, as well as records of towns fining men for not teaching their children or apprentices to read and write.[40] The grammar schools were supplemented, as in England, by dame schools. The established endowed grammar schools of England were probably superior to the colonial schools, but not as numerous in proportion to the population, for England had no compulsory school law until two hundred years later, and illiteracy was common.[41]

Before 1645, also, two books for school use had been printed at Cambridge. One of these, of which no copy has survived,[42] is referred to as "The Spelling Books," printed by Stephen Day between 1642 and 1645. The other is John Cotton's catechism entitled "Spiritual Milk for Boston Babes in either England Drawn out of the Breasts of both Testaments for their soul's nourishment."[43] Such catechisms,

[39] Small, Early New England Schools, p. 30, gives the following dates for the founding of grammar schools:

Boston	1635–6	Braintree	1645–6
Charlestown	1636	Watertown	1650
Salem	1637	Ipswich	1651
Dorchester	1639	Dedham	1653
New Haven	1639	Newbury	1658
Hartford	1639	Northampton	1667
Cambridge	1640–3	Hadley	1667
Roxbury	1645	Hingham	1670

[40] *Ibid.*, pp. 346 ff. Sometimes the towns escaped the fine upon the plea of inability to obtain a schoolmaster.

[41] In 1847 there were official statistics in England that one-third of the men and half the women who presented themselves for marriage were unable to sign their names. In 1856 it was reported that there were 700 teachers of the dame school type who could not write. De Montmorency, The Progress of Education in England, pp. 90, 94.

[42] Littlefield, Early New England Schools, p. 118.

[43] *Ibid.*, p. 107. Printed before 1646.

it must be remembered, were commonly used as primers or first readers in day schools in both Old and New England in the seventeenth and eighteenth centuries. The shifting of religious education to Sunday and the Sunday-school was the work of the nineteenth century.

All the above evidence would seem to indicate that, as far as the possibilities and benefits of a satisfactory education were concerned, the early colonists and their children were under no serious disadvantage in comparison with those whom they had left behind in England.

Chapter II: Libraries and the Circulation of Books.

ALTHOUGH the Pilgrims, as has been said, came from the lower ranks of society, and although they endured years of hardship from their first interrupted attempt to leave England until they were finally established in Plymouth nearly twenty years after, they were not without books. William Brewster, for example, left at his death in 1643 a library of nearly four hundred books,[1] and the old soldier, Miles Standish, left about fifty.[2] Among the latter are such interesting items as:

The History of the World
Turkish History
A Chronicle of England
The History of Queen Elizabeth
The State of Europe
Bariff's Artillery
Caesar's Commentaries
Homer's Iliad
The Swedish Intelligencer
The French Academy
The Country Farmer
Calvin's Institutions

Brewster's library is more interesting as well as larger. The fact that many of the books were published after 1620 shows that the cares of colonial life and the distance from book-stalls did not prevent the continued acquisition of books,—the steady acquisition, if we may be allowed to draw any conclusion from the fact that in his library every

[1] Massachusetts Historical Society, Proceedings, 2d Series, v. 37.
[2] New England Historical and Genealogical Register, v. 337.

year from 1620 to that of his death, with the exceptions of 1639 and 1641, is represented.[3] The following partial list will show the more literary tone of this collection:

Camden,	Britain
Camden,	Remains
Smith, J.,	Description of New England
Bacon,	Advancement of Learning
Bacon,	Declaration of Treasons of the Earl of Essex
Raleigh,	Prerogative of Parliament
Machiavelli,	Princeps
Richardson,	On the State of Europe
	The Swedish Intelligencer 1632
Cornwallis,	Essays of Certain Paradoxes
Prynne,	Anti-Arminianism
Prynne,	Looking-Glasse for all Lordly Prelates
Rainolds,	The Overthrow of Stage Plays
Hakluyt,	Principal Navigations
Wither, G.,	Works
Dekker, T.,	Magnificent Entertainment given to King James, March, 1603, with speeches and songs delivered
[?]	Adventure of Don Sebastian
[?]	Messelina (perhaps Nathaniel Richard's The Tragedy of Messalina,) acted by the company of His Majesty's Revels, 1640[4]
Herring,	Latin poem in honor of James I
Hornby,	Scourge of Drunkenness (verse)
Rich, R.,	Newes from Virginia, 1607 (verse)
Johnson, R.,	Golden Garland of Princely Pleasures
Brathwait,	The Description of a Good Wife (verse)
Smith,	Commonwealth of England and Government Thereof
Lodge, T.,	Translation of the works of Seneca
Cawdrey,	Treasurie of Similies
Keckerman,	Systema Geographicum

[3] Massachusetts Historical Society, Proceedings, 2d Series, v. 37.

[4] *Ibid.*, v. 37. If the identification of *Messalina* is correct, this and Dekker's *Magnificent Entertainment* are the earliest evidences we have of the existence of the drama in New England libraries. Another play, *Roxana Tragedia*, is mentioned in the John Harvard library.

Rathbone,	Surveyor
Norden,	Surveyors Dialogue
Standish,	New Directions . . . . for Increasing Timber

Governor Bradford left a library of about eighty volumes, including, in part, the following.[5] It is regrettable that so many were uncatalogued.

The ffrench acaddamey
The Guiciardin
The history of the Church
The history of the Netherlands
Speeds generall Description of the world
The method of phiscicke
Taylers libertie of Phrophecye
Gouges Domesticall Dutyes
three and fifty smale bookes
Calvine on the epistles in Duch with Divers other Duch bookes

Very few of the Pilgrims were without books. The inventories of estates filed among the Wills in the Plymouth Colony Records give proof of this. Of over seventy inventories examined in the first two volumes of the Wills, only a dozen failed to make specific mention of books, and among these were some whose entire estates, including house and land, clothes and tools, amounted to only twenty-five or thirty pounds. Such people, among them single men who had evidently come to the new colony with almost nothing, probably uneducated, would not be likely to possess books in a frontier town even today. In many cases the books mentioned are very few, the exact number being hidden under such phrases as: "bookes," "all his bookes," "3 bibles and other books." Inasmuch as "all his bookes" were valued at only eighteen shillings,[6] and "3 bibles and

[5] Mayflower Descendant, ii. 232.

[6] Plymouth Colony Records, Wills, i. 31. Estate of John Bryant. In these volumes the numbers refer to sheets, not pages. Up to one hundred, and in a few cases beyond that, the sheets are numbered 11, 21, 31, or 651, 661, 671, when

other books" at six pounds,[7] the phrases are of little value in estimating the possible number. That even so small a collection as "1 bible, 1 book catechism, 1 book Practice of Christianity" was itemized[8] would seem to show their respect for the mere presence of a book. The valuation helps little to estimate the number where only value is given. Brewster's library of 400 volumes was appraised at £42.19.11,[9] which would give an average of ten books to the pound; but William Gibson's "1 bible and 10 other books" at £00.06.00,[10] and Thomas Pryor's "1 great bible 1 smale bible and 50 other bookes" at £01.10.00,[11] give a different ratio.

It is not possible, then, outside of a few lists in addition to those given, to estimate the number of books in the homes of the Pilgrims; but the following details will give some indication.

Name	Year	Total Inventory	Books
Steven Deans	1634	£ 87.19.06	£ 01.00.00
Thomas Pryor	1639	22.07.06	01.10.00
Nathaniel Tilden	1641	200.00.00	05.00.00
John Atwood	1643	186.14.00	09.00.00
John Jenney	1644	108.03.03	01.03.06
William Brewster	1644	150.00.07	42.19.11
Edward Foster	1644	42.03.00	06.00.00
Love Brewster	1650	97.09.01	05.12.04
Nicolas Robbins	1650	38.19.09	02.14.00
Henry Smith	1651	149.16.00	01.00.00
William Thomas	1651	375.07.00	08.05.00
John Hazell	1651	165.19.00	04.06.00
William Hatch	1652	95.03.04	01.10.00
Judith Smith	1650	120.06.00	01.00.00
Henry Andrews	1653	330.16.00	02.00.00

we would use 1, 2, 3, or 65, 66, 67. I have changed uniformly to the modern system.

[7] *Ibid.*, i. 60. Estate of Edward Foster.

[8] *Ibid.*, i. 29. Estate of William Palmer.

[9] *Ibid.*, i. 53–59.

[10] *Ibid.*, i. 35.

[11] *Ibid.*, i. 34.

Robert Waterman	1653	£ 78.00.00	£ 01.04.00
John Lothrop (Rev.)	1653	72.16.06	05.00.00
Ann Atwood	1654	24.00.03	07.00.00
William Phillips	1654	78.08.00	01.00.00
William [torn]	1654	157.09.00	01.10.00
James Pilbeame	1655	48.05.10	01.10.00
Elizabeth Pole	1656	188.11.07	02.00.00
Miles Standish	1656	358.07.00	11.13.00
John Gilbert	1657	200.00.00	02.00.00
William Bradford	1657	not given	15.00.00
Park Chittenden	1676	156.08.05	01.14.00
John Miles (Rev.)	1683	260.00.00	50.00.00

Where titles are itemized they are in most cases devotional or theological. In the inventory of Samuel Fuller, 1633, of the twenty-six given by title, but three are non-religious: a book on government, one on husbandry, and a "dixionary;" a volume of "notable things" might belong to either class.[12] There are also "other bookes" to the value of one pound. The inventory of John Atwood includes "Acts and Monuments" in three volumes, a history, Prynne's "Historio [*sic*] Mastix," and divers other books to the value of three pounds.[13] Ann Atwood possessed two of Prynne's works, unnamed, two French books and a French Testament, and "four and fifty smale bookes at 6^d the piece."[14] John Hazell had Josephus and two history books.[15] Governor Thomas Prince owned, among books to the number of 187, valued at £13.18.08 in a total estate of £422.00.00, Laud's "Conference with Fisher the Jesuit," Prynne's "Account of Laud's Trail," Morton's "New England's Memorial," and the "Essays" of Sir William Cornwallis.[16]

Books and libraries were much more common among those who settled in the neighborhood of Boston and in

[12] *Ibid.*, i. 22.
[13] *Ibid.*, i. 47.
[14] *Ibid.*, i. 124.
[15] *Ibid.*, i. 101.
[16] F. B. Dexter, Proceedings of the American Antiquarian Society, xviii. 143.

Connecticut. Each minister had at least a small library, and some who were not ministers had excellent collections of books, as, for example, John Winthrop, Jr., who, according to his father's Journal, had in New England, in the year 1640, a library of over 1000 volumes.[17] Two years later the father, Governor Winthrop, was probably one of the magistrates who collectively gave to Harvard books to the value of £200;[18] and about 1660 he gave to Harvard's library some forty volumes more.[19] The best example of the kind of library which the colonists brought with them is John Harvard's, which made a substantial part of his bequest in 1638 to the college then being built in Cambridge. As Harvard had been in the colony but a year, he could not have added many books to those he had with him upon arrival. Although naturally largely theological or expository, this collection contained a considerable number of books of a literary nature, as the following selected list will demonstrate:[20]

Anglorū prælia
Aquinatis Opa. Conclusiones
Aynsworts [Henry Ainsworth] workes
Alstedij Physica Harmonia
Aschamj Epistolæ
Æsopi fabulæ
Academia Gallica

[17] Journal, ii. 18. "Mr. Winthrop the younger, one of the magistrates, having many books in a chamber where there was corn of divers sorts, had among them one wherein the Greek testament, the psalms and the common prayer were bound together. He found the common prayer eaten with mice, every leaf of it, and not any of the two other touched, nor any other of his books, though there were above a thousand." It seems probable that these represented only a part of the library of John Winthrop, Jr. It does not seem likely that a man who prized books as he did would have left valuable books in a storeroom in which grain was kept.

[18] Chaplin, Life of Henry Dunster, p. 78. See pp. 40 and 41, below.

[19] Life and Letters of John Winthrop, ii. 438. College Book III, 32.

[20] Harvard Library, Bibliographical Contributions, No. 27, 1888, p.7. [Revised by A. C. Potter, Catalogue of John Harvard's Library, Publications of the Colonial Society of Massachusetts, XXI: 190-230. 1919. *Ed.*] His library contained over 300 volumes.

βασίλικον δῶρον
Bacons advancem^t. Essayes
Camdens remaines
Calliopæia [rich store-house of . . . phrases.]
Duns Scotus in 8 Libros Arist. Phys.
Erasmj Colloquia
Epictetj Enchyridion
Elegant Phrases
Garden of Eloquence
Essayes morall & Theol.
Felthoms resolues
Homers workes in English[21]
Haylins Geography
Juvenalis
Isocratis Orat: Græc & Latin
Lightfoots Miscelanes
Lucanus
Londons complaint
Nichols mirrour for Magistrates
Plautus
Plutarchj [North's Translation] Vitæ Angl.
Porcensis orationes
Persij Satyræ
Poetarū flores
Quarles Poems
Roxanæ Tragedia[22]
Salustius
Terentius
Thesaurus poeticus
Tullij, opa in 2 Tomis. de officijs
Withers [Title not given]

The colonists, then, were not unfurnished with books when they arrived; and there is much evidence that their libraries were constantly increased by shipments from Eng-

[21] This may be Chapman's translation, a copy of which was in the Harvard Library in 1723. Bibliographical Contributions, No. 27, p. 10.

[22] By W. Alabaster. In five acts and verse. Given at Cambridge. Published 1632.

land. Isaac Johnson was scarcely in New England before John Humfrey wrote to him from England,

> I have sent you those new bookes that are lately come out, Dr. Ames' Cases to Mr. Governor[23] which I purpose to send you by the next, & now Dr. Sibs' Bruised Reede & Mr. Dike of Scandals to you.[24]

Henry Jacie wrote to John Winthrop, Jr., in January, 1631,

> A book of the Northern Star (by Dr. Goad) was sent you to go herewith.[25]

Edward Howes wrote to John Winthrop, Jr., November 9, 1631,

> The bookes Mr. Gurdon hath fetcht away, and the *Luna* is at your service; soe is [*sic*] both the books & *Sol*, & *quodcunque sub sole habet*, *vel habebit me*, *tuum*.[26]

The next year he wrote:

> I havinge sent some bookes to James Downinge . . . . beinge incited thereunto by his father; . . . . I sent your honored father a booke of bookes among those to J. D.[27]
>
> . . . & that your worthy father, with all my louinge frinds may reead at large the workinge of our God in these latter dayes, here I haue sent you the Swedish Intelligencer which speakes wonder to the world; withall I haue sent you your Archymedes and an Almenack, with a booke or two of other newes besides.[28]
>
> Here in closed you shall find a booke of the probabilities of the North West passage.[29]
>
> I have sent Mr Samford the Instrument and sight ruler the Germaine bespoke for him, together with a booke to teach the

[23] Mr. Governor is John Winthrop, Sr.

[24] Winthrop Papers, i. 4. December 9, 1630.

[25] Massachusetts Historical Society, Collections, 3rd Series, i. 241.

[26] Winthrop Papers, i. 472.

[27] Massachusetts Historical Society, Collections, 3rd Series, ix. 243. April 3, 1632.

[28] Winthrop Papers, i. 477. 1632.

[29] *Ibid.*, p. 480. November 23, 1632. This book was by Howes himself. The copy inscribed by him is in the collection of the Massachusetts Historical Society.

use thereof, namely Smyths Arte of Gunnery at folio 58 there the same Instrument is to be seene; I have likewise sent him Nortons Practise of Artillerie chosen by the Germaine for him; and alsoe diverse platformes of the latest invented forts and fortifications: For new bookes I writt to you of D[r] Fludds works and sent you a cattalogue of them by M[r] Hetherley; there is a booke lately come out of mathematicall conclusion and recreations, which I bought purposely for you, but M[r] Saltonstall hath borrowed it . . . . albeit I have sent you two other bookes viz[t] Malthus Fireworks, and the Horizontall Quadrant full of new devices; which I present to your kind acceptance.[30]

The same year F. Kirby wrote to the younger Winthrop at various times:

For the Catalogue of bookes from Frankfort I have sent you that of the Autumnall mart 1631. the next is not to be had the third not yet come by reason of Contrary wind, but I shall send it God willinge by the next ship. . . . . I have now received all your mony of Edward Howes which maketh in all 4li. 12sh. for the bookes and carriage of them.[31]

With this I enclose the Catalogue of the last vernall mart, the last autumnall is not yet to be had.[32]

I have sent you heer inclosed the Catalogue of the Autumnall mart 1632. all the former I have sent before.[33]

In the years that follow Edward Howes continued to send books.

. . . . in a bundle of clothes for your cosen Mary . . . . you shall find from him a cattalogue of the last marte bookes; and from your poore frind an exact and large and the latest discouery of the North West passage, made by a painfull and industrious gent., Capt. James, as a remembrance of my obliged loue.[34]

I haue bin held in hand at Mr. Fetherston's shop by his men,

[30] Massachusetts Historical Society, Collections, 3rd Series, ix. 255. March 18, 1632–3.

[31] *Ibid.*, p. 249. November 25, 1632.

[32] *Ibid.*, p. 252. December 3, 1632.

[33] *Ibid.*, p. 260. March 26, 1633.

[34] Winthrop Papers, i. 487. June 22, 1633.

euer since 8ber,[35] to be furnished with all those bookes you writt for, and now am forced to buy them where I can find them.[36]

The bookes I haue sent you, March, 1634.

2 Catalogues of printed bookes.

	li.	*s.*	*d.*
Dr. Fludds Macrocosme in 2 volumes	1	10	0
Isagoge Phisico Magico &c.	0	1	6
Petrus Galatinus de Arcanis Catholicæ veritatis	0	10	0
Phillippi Grulingij Florilegium	0	2	0

These are parte of them you writt for.

I haue here alsoe sent you a few others, which if you like not, I pray send them againe, or any of them.

Mercurius Rediuiuus per Norton	0	2	6
The Rarities of Cochin China	0	1	0
Wingates Logarithmes	0	4	6
An English Grammer	0	1	0
The Gunners Dialogue	0	2	0
Bedwells Messolabium	0	1	0

. . . .

The rest I cast in to the bargaine, for you and your fancie to make merry withall.[37]

The bookes you writt for, I haue not mett with them as yet at the shopps where I haue bin.[38]

One consignment of books to the elder Winthrop may have failed to reach Boston. Robert Ryece wrote to him, January 17, 1636,

I wrotte vnto you the 17 of Maye laste, accompanied with a boxe of boocks, which I sente by my brother Samuell Appleton, to be convayed to hym for you. . . . . I do feare . . . . that the schippe with the passengers, mooche stuffe & goods, are all perished by the waye.[39]

There is no further record of this.

35 October.
36 Winthrop Papers, i. 496. March 29, 1634.
37 *Ibid.*, i. 497.
38 *Ibid.*, i. 506. April 14, 1639.
39 *Ibid.*, i. 394.

The London Port Books give other evidence of the shipment of books to Boston.

xvj Februar 1633[-34] In le Mary and John of London . . . .

j chest bookes.

Quinto Aprilis 1634 . . . . In le Elizabeth and Dorcas . . . .
ij packes made clothes and bookes vj trunckes apparell and bookes for prouision for the passengers.[40]

Others than the Winthrops were receiving books from England, although unfortunately most of the records of these shipments have been lost. President Dunster's father wrote to him, March 20, 1640–1, "Your brother Thomas remembers his love, and hath sent you two dozen of almanacks."[41] Henry Jacie wrote March 6, 1647–8, "I have sent to Mr. Cotton or Mr. Wilson a book for the Governors, of the present proceeds between the King & Parliament."[42] The colonists seem to have been able to get books fresh from the English presses. Roger Williams wrote in a letter which, although undated, undoubtedly belongs to the year 1650, "The Portraicture [Eikon Basilike], I guesse is Bp. Halls, the stile is pious & acute, very like his, & J. H. subscribes the Epitaph."[43] And on February 15, 1654–5, he wrote of two books published in 1653, "We also here that 2 of Mr. Dells bookes were lately burnt at the Massachusetts, (possibly) containing some sharpe things against the Presbyterians & Academians, of which I brought ouer one cald the Triall of Spirits."[44]

At least one comprehensive library was brought over for

[40] Massachusetts Historical Society, Proceedings, xlvii. 179, 183. Both shipments were consigned to John Winthrop, Sr.

[41] Chaplin, Life of Dunster, p. 22. It must be remembered in connection with this item that the almanac was in better esteem then than now, being the sole convenient handbook of scientific information, often containing useful tables of varied information besides the usual astronomical calculations and astrological prophecies, the latter often rhymed.

[42] Winthrop Papers, i. 465.

[43] *Ibid.*, i. 282 and note.

[44] *Ibid.*, i. 291. He returned from England in the summer of 1654.

sale in the early days, for Cotton Mather records with pride the fact that although the learned Dr. William Ames was prevented by death from coming in person to America, his library did come.[45] A later historian says,

> Harvard College being built, a Foundation was laid for a *Publick Library* . . . . The first Furniture of this Library was the Books of Dr. *William Ames*, the famous Professor of Divinity at *Franequer*.[46]

The return to England of a number of ministers during the Puritan régime undoubtedly deprived the colony of several libraries, but in some cases the libraries were retained in New England. Samuel Eaton, returning in 1640, gave to New Haven his library of over 100 volumes, including the following books:[47]

Plutarch (perhaps North's translation)
Virgil
Sandys' metrical translation of Ovid[48]
Dionysius of Halicarnassus
More's Utopia
Erasmus' Proverbs
Raleigh's History of the World
Foxe's Book of Martyrs
Heylyn's Cosmography

A few years later John Eliot wrote,

> And for my self I have this request (who also am short enough

[45] Magnalia, i. 236.

[46] Neal, History of New England, i. 202. It is not quite clear whether the historian means to imply that this purchase was made before Harvard left his library to the college, or was the first addition after that. If the gratuity granted to Mrs. Ames by the Colony in 1637 was a partial return for the library of her husband, that library preceded the books from Harvard's estate and formed the foundation of the Harvard library. See Publications of the Colonial Society of Massachusetts, xvii. 210, and page 40 note 62, below. The Ames library was almost entirely theological or philosophical.

[47] Proceedings of the American Antiquarian Society, xviii. 138.

[48] It is interesting to note that this product of the Virginia colony, and the finest piece of literary work which the first century of colonization produced, reached the northern colony within fifteen years, if Eaton had the complete edition.

in books) that I might be helped to purchase my brother *Weld* his books, the summe of the purchase (34 li.) I am loth they should come back to *England* when we have so much need of them here.[49]

The books were purchased for him in 1651 by the Corporation for New England.[50] Herbert Pelham, who returned to England in 1649, mentioned in his will (he died in 1676) "all other Brass, Beding, and Linnin with all my Books and other Utensills and moveables which I have in the Massachusetts Bay."[51] The Rev. Thomas Jenner, returning to England about 1650 because of trouble with the churches, was "compelled by poverty to sell his library, which seems to have been bought for Harvard College."[52]

Libraries were not limited to the studies of ministers, for Lion Gardiner wrote to John Winthrop, Jr., in 1650, in reference to the obtaining of a pastor for the small settlement of which he was leader,

> Att present wee ar willing to giue this man you writ of 20*li.* a year, with such diat as I myself eat, til we see what the Lord will do with vs; and being he is but a yong man, hapily he hath not manie books, thearfore let him know what I have. First, the 3 Books of Martters, Erasmus, moste of Perkins, Wilsons Dixtionare, a large Concordiance, Mayor on the new Tstement; Some of theas, with othar that I have, may be vcefull to him.[53]

When William Tyng, merchant, died in 1653, leaving the largest estate recorded up to that time (totaling £2774.14.04), part of the estate comprised, according to the inventory, "Books as per schedule valued at 010 00 00."[54] The schedule

49 Massachusetts Historical Society, Collections, 3rd Series, iv. 128.

50 New England Historical and Genealogical Register, xxxvi. 371.

51 *Ibid.*, xviii. 175.

52 *Ibid.*, xix. 247, and Maine Historical Society, Collections and Proceedings, 2d Series, iii. 293 ff.

53 Winthrop Papers, ii. 59.

54 Publications of the Colonial Society of Massachusetts, xiii. 289.

lists nearly one hundred books, mostly in quarto, including the following:[55]

Bookes of Martyrs in 3 volumes
Books of Statutes at Large
The Survey of London
Speeds Chronicle
Camdens Britannia
Marchants Accompts
Gecords Herball[56]
Treatise of Magistracy—two
Enonimous Tresure
Apeale to Parliament
Janua Linguarum
a Duch Worke
Circkle of Comerse
abridgm^t of Camden
Singin Psalemes
office of executors
Imposts & customes
logick & Rethoricke
16 Ciceroas orations
Interest States & kingdomes

The will of Nicholas Busby, September 10, 1657, bequeathed

vnto my two Sonns *John Busby* & *Abraham*, my printed bookes, in manner following;
to *John*

all my Phisicke bookes, as
Glendall practice,
Barrowes method,
Dutch Phisicke & garden of health
Mr *Coggans* treatis, and
the Dialogue of Phisicke Surgery, with
Plinnys Naturall Hystory

[55] New England Historical and Genealogical Register, xxx. 432.
[56] Probably an error for Gerarde's.

Vnto *Abraham*,

my bookes of Divinitie, vizt.
Mr *Perkins*
Mr *Willet* sinops and Comentary on the Romans, &
Mr [*sic*] *Hieroms* two bookes;

as for the rest of my bookes of divinities, or Hystory, my desire is, they may Loveingly & Brotherly devide them betweene except the three Bibles.[57]

Governor Thomas Dudley, dying the same year, left a small but interesting collection of books, including in part:[58]

General History of Netherlands
Turkish History
Livius
Camden: Annale Regnante Eliza
Commentaries of the wars in France
Buchanan: Scot Hystory
Abstract of Penal Statutes
Vision of Pierc Plowman[59]
Apology of ye Prince of Orange
Baynes: Letters
Swedish Intelligencer
Mantuanii Bucolica ~~[Virgil]~~
The book of Laws
8 French books
Several pamphlets
New books
Smalle writings[60]

While individual libraries were slowly growing by importations and gifts from England and, from as early as 1647,

[57] New England Historical and Genealogical Register, viii. 279.

[58] *Ibid.*, xii. 355.

[59] This is perhaps the most curious item in all the lists of colonial books. It would cast much light upon colonial culture if we could know how he came to own such a volume, and whether he ever read it. The latest edition he could have had is that of 1561.

[60] The last three items are typical of the vagueness of many of the comparatively few book records preserved. Complete lists would add much to our knowledge.

by purchase in the shop of Hezekiah Usher,[61] the Harvard College library was also growing from its beginning in the Ames library and the 320 volumes left by John Harvard.[62] Roger Harlakenden, dying in 1638, willed "to the librarye ten pownds & all my books wch are not usefull for my wife."[63] The first notable increase was the gift by the magistrates in 1642 of books from their own libraries to the value of £200.[64] If the appraisal of William Tyng's library of nearly 100 volumes at £10 were any criterion,[65] this must have meant a great addition; but doubtless a majority of these books were large and expensive theological folios, which would proportionately lessen the number of books added. There was still need for many more books, for we find President Dunster writing in 1645,

> Seeing the public library in the College is yet defective in all manner of books, specially in law, physics, philosophy, and mathematics, the furnishing whereof would be both honorable and profitable to the country in general and in special to the scholars, whose various inclinations to all professions might thereby be encouraged and furthered; we therefore humbly entreat to use such means as your wisdom shall think meet for supply of the same.[66]

I have found no record of any results from this plea.

[61] In 1647 Usher is referred to in Aspinwall's Notarial Book as "Hezekiah Usher of Boston, bookseller." (Littlefield, Early Boston Booksellers, p. 67.) Samuel Danforth's Almanac for 1647 bears the imprint, "Cambridge printed by Mathew Daye; and to be sold by Hezekiah Usher, at Boston." (Thomas, History of Printing, i. 48 note.)

[62] Mr. Julius H. Tuttle, of the Massachusetts Historical Society, thinks that it may be inferred that the gratuity to Mrs. Ames from the General Court was in recognition of the use of the Ames library by the students of Harvard, and that a somewhat similar grant to the widow of the Rev. Jose Glover may indicate that his library was also used by the college just as his printing press was established in connection with it. (Publications of the Colonial Society of Massachusetts, xiv. 65, 66 note.)

[63] New England Historical and Genealogical Register, ii. 182.

[64] Chaplin, Life of Dunster, p. 78.

[65] See p. 37, above.

[66] Chaplin, Life of Dunster, p. 80. The letter was addressed to the Commissioners of the United Colonies of New England.

But books were being added by gifts both at home and from England. Joshua Scottow, of Boston, presented "Henry Stephen his Thesaurus in foure volumes in folio" with a curious proviso.[67] Sir Kenelme Digby, scientist and man of letters, in spite of his leanings toward Catholicism, twice sent books to the young Puritan college,[68] perhaps in-

[67] Chaplin, Life of Dunster, p. 79. The proviso follows. "Thes p^{r}sents witness^{e}, that wheras Joshuah Scottow, of Bostō, march^{t}, hath of his owne free accord procured for the library of Harvard Colle[ge] Henry Stephen his Thesaurus, in foure volumes in folio, and bestowe[d] the same thereon: it is on this condic̄on, and wth this p[ro]mise following that if ever the said Joshuah, during his life shall have occasion to use the said booke, or any parcell thereof, he shall have free liberty thereof, and accesee thereto: and if God shall blesee the said Joshuah wth any child or childrē that shal be students of the Greeke tongue, thē the said bookes above specifyed shalbee unto them delivered, in case that they will not otherwise be satisfyed wthout it." Dated October 28, 1649. Thus were books esteemed! It might be assumed from this that Scottow, although there is no record that he was a university man, read Greek; if not, why should he reserve such a privilege? He certainly knew French, for he translated The Rise, Spring and Foundation of the Anabaptists, or Re-baptized of our Time. Written in French by Guy de Brez, 1565. . . . . And Translated for the use of his Countrymen, by J. S. [Joshua Scottow] Cambridge: Printed, and to be Sold by Marmaduke Johnson. 1668. (Green, Early American Imprints in Massachusetts Historical Society, Proceedings, 2d Series, ix. 424.)

A later item, undated, in the College Records shows that he availed himself of his reserved privilege. (College Book I, 260.)

"Recev^{d} of Mr Vryan Oakes p^{r}s[ident] ye above Expressed Thesaurus in foure volumes acc^{r}ding to Condition above: upon the demand of my sonn Thomas Scottow I say received p^{r} me this 30th of August

Josh: Scottow"

Urian Oakes was president, acting or official, from 1675 to 1681. As in 1682 Cotton Mather includes a copy of this Thesaurus in a list of books which he had purchased from the duplicates in the Harvard Library, either the Scottows soon returned their set, or two others were presented to the library. (Ms. list in Mather's handwriting in possession of the American Antiquarian Society.) Thomas Scottow graduated from Harvard in 1677.

[68] Winslow, New England's Salamander Discovered. 1647. Massachusetts Historical Society, Collections, 3rd Series, ii. 117. "As for Doctor Childe hee is a gentleman that hath travelled other parts before hee came to us, namely Italy; . . . . he tooke the degree of Doctor in Physick at Padua. . . . . Hee comes [to New England] a second time, and not onely bestoweth some bookes on the Colledge, as Sir Kenelme Digby and many others commendably did. . . . ."

In 1654 Hugh Peter wrote from London to John Winthrop, Jr., "I haue sent you 2 peeces of black stuffe . . . . all by the hand of Mr. Norton of Boston, in a great chest of bookes sent agayne by Sir Kenelme Digby, who longs for you here." (Winthrop Papers, i. 116.)

fluenced by his acquaintance with John Winthrop, Jr.[69] There are two references in the College Records to Sir Kenelme's gifts. In College Book I there is a list of seventeen titles, mostly church fathers, given by him in 1655.[70] In College Book III, p. 31, under the date 1659, are mentioned several gifts to the college, the first item being "Sr Kenelme Digby gave to s^{d} Colledges Library, as many books as were vallued at Sixty pound." It is impossible to tell whether this refers to both gifts together, or to the more recent.

The other gifts recorded with Sir Kenelme's are:

> Sr Thomas Temple Knight. gave two Globes a Caelestiall & Terrestriall to s^{d} Colledge.
>
> Mr Thomas Graves gave some Mathematicall Books tow^{ds} the furnishing of the Library.
>
> Mr Ralfe ffreck gave to s^{d} Library Biblia Polyglotta.
>
> Mr John ffrecks gave some Books to the vallue of ten pounds.
>
> Mr John Winthrop gave toward ye furnishing s^{d} Library many choice books to the vallue of twenty pounds.
>
> Sr Richard Daniel Knight gave many books to the Library.

Two undated book-lists in College Book I record other gifts.[71] One is a list of twenty titles given by Richard Bellingham. The other is a list of thirty-five titles given by Peter Bulkeley, perhaps at his death in 1658, but probably earlier, as it is not mentioned, as one might expect it would be, in the 1659 list with Sir Kenelme Digby's. Two other men are known to have contributed during this period,

[69] See end of note 68, above. Sir Kenelme wrote to John Winthrop, Jr., from Paris, January 26, 1656 n. s., "I beseech you present my most humble thankes to the President and fellowes of y^{r} college for the obliging Letter they haue bin pleased to send me. So small a present as j presumed to make them, deserued not so large a returne." (Massachusetts Historical Society, Collections, 3rd Series, x. 16.) Other letters among the Winthrop Papers testify to the correspondence between the two. See i. 116, ii. 588, 593; Massachusetts Historical Society, Collections, 3rd Series, i. 183. See also p. 66 ff., below.

[70] Harvard Library, Bibliographical Contributions, No. 27, p. 13.

[71] *Ibid.*, pp. 13, 14.

Dr. Robert Child[72] and Ezekiel Rogers.[73] In the inventory of college property made December 10, 1654, at the time the college was settling accounts with Dunster, who had just resigned as president, the "library & Books therin" were "vallued at" £400.[74]

Before the Harvard library was a quarter century old it had a rival in a public library in Boston. Robert Keayne, merchant, suggested in his will, dated August 1, 1653, the erection of a town-house (apparently a combination of a town hall and a neighborhood house) which should contain a market, a library and a gallery, rooms for divines and scholars, for merchants, for strangers, and so on, should his estate prove large enough to provide sufficient funds above his bequests to his family. Of his own books, "all English none Lattine or Greeke," his son and wife were to take their choice "whether Divinitie, Hystory, or Milletary;" the rest were to be looked over by John Wilson and John Norton, who were to choose out for his town-house library all fit books, selling any others. The will further provided that if the town-house was not built the books were to go to Harvard.[75] As the estate was not quite large enough, a sum of £300 was raised by subscription and the building begun in 1657.[76] Unfortunately there are no more records of this library for fifteen years, either in regard to nature, size, or growth; but it is an indication of the culture of the place that such an institution was in existence thus early in the history of the colony, and partly built by the people themselves. Of its subsequent history more will be said later.[77]

During these years there were some losses of books by

[72] See p. 41 note 68, above.

[73] New England Historical and Genealogical Register, v. 125, and p. 44, below.

[74] College Book III, p. 41.

[75] New England Historical and Genealogical Register, vi. 90. The will, the abstract of which covers eleven pages of the Register, the will itself covering 158 pages of the original record of Suffolk County Wills, gives striking evidence of the originality and individuality often found among the dissenters and Puritans.

[76] Publications of the Colonial Society of Massachusetts, xii. 120.

[77] See pp. 132 ff. and 179 ff., below.

fire. Stephen Bachiler wrote to John Winthrop, May 18, 1644, "I haue had great losse by fire, well knowne, to the vallue of 200*li.*, with my whole studdy of bookes."[78] In 1651, on the evening of his third wedding, Ezekiel Rogers lost his house and entire library by fire.[79] In 1666 the Bradstreet house at Andover was burned. Simon Bradstreet thus records the loss in his diary:

> July 12, 1666. Whilst I was at N. London my fathers house at Andover was burnt, where I lost my books. . . . . Tho: my own losse of books (and papers espec.) was great and my fathers far more being about 800, yet ye Lord was pleased . . . . to make up ye same to us.[80]

There may have been other losses of which record is lost;[81] but in general there was a steady increase in the number of books in New England. Simon Bradstreet's reference above to the making up of the lost books, and the fact that Ezekiel Rogers, having lost his entire library in 1651, at his death in 1660 was able to bestow upon Harvard College "his books wherewith he had recruited his library, after the fire, which consumed the good library that he had brought out of England,"[82] including Latin books valued at

[78] Winthrop Papers, ii. 107. The phrase "whole studdy of bookes" would seem to imply a considerable library.

[79] Winthrop Papers, ii. 205 note. New England Historical and Genealogical Register, v. 124.

[80] Ellis, Works of Anne Bradstreet, lxi.

[81] The house of Herbert Pelham, first treasurer of Harvard, was burned in December, 1640. Mr. Downing's house was burned in April, 1645, with a loss of household goods to the value of £200. The same week the house of John Johnson of Roxbury was totally wrecked by a fire and the explosion of gunpowder stored therein. (Winthrop's Journal, *passim.*) At the burning of Springfield by the Indians in 1674, "thirty-two houses, and amongst the rest, the minister's with his well-furnished library, were consumed." (Magnalia, ii. 565.) The library of William Blackstone, formerly of Boston, was destroyed during King Philip's War, when his house at Lonsdale, R. I., was burned by the Indians, shortly after his death. There were some 160 books in the collection. The house of Increase Mather was burned on November 27, 1676. (Massachusetts Historical Society, Proceedings, 2d Series, xiii. 373-374.)

[82] Magnalia, i. 412.

£47 and some of his English books to the value of £26,[83] demonstrate both the possibility and the fact of considerable book-buying within forty years of the founding of Boston. Although John Johnson's house was wrecked by fire and explosion in 1645, in 1647 he possessed books which Richard Mather was glad to borrow.[84] The church in Hartford, inviting Jonathan Mitchel to succeed Thomas Hooker, who died in 1647, as pastor, promised that they would "immediately upon his acceptance of their invitation, advance a considerable sum of money, to assist him in furnishing himself with a library."[85] The books were evidently to be procured in Boston before he left for Hartford. Thomas Mayhew, writing to John Winthrop, Jr., of his son, Thomas Mayhew, missionary to the Indians of Martha's Vineyard and Nantucket, who was lost at sea in 1657 while on his way to England, said, "He allso hath had of the Commissioners in all, besides his books, 160*li.*, his bookes were 37*li.*, as I take it."[86] It is not clear whether books to that value had been sent from England, or whether the money had been sent to buy books in Boston. In either case there is evidence that the colonists found it possible to procure books in considerable numbers.[87]

Books, largely gifts, continued to come from friends in England. John Winthrop, Jr., wrote to Robert Child, March 23, 1648–9,

> I am glad to heare of those bookes coming forth, Paullin and

83 Publications of the Colonial Society of Massachusetts, xii. 49.

84 See p. 44 note 81, above, and p. 57, below.

85 Magnalia, ii. 88.

86 Winthrop Papers, ii. 35.

87 Although Hezekiah Gay, who died in 1669, seems to have had but two books to will ("give my mother, Mr. Burrowes' Book and my sister Whiting that new book concerning Thomas Savage," New England Historical and Genealogical Register, xlviii, 324,) one of them had been published within a year: Gods Justice Against Murther, or the bloudy Apprentice executed. Being an exact . . . . relation of a bloudy murther committed by one T. Savage . . . . in Ratcliffe upon the maid of the house his fellow servant. London, 1668. *Cf.* Publications of the Colonial Society of Massachusetts, xx. 237-239.

Propugnaculi Fabri, and Helmonts workes, but how to be certaine to procure thẽ I know not, except you please to doe me the favour to send for thẽ where they are to be had, and desire Mr Peters, or my brother in my name to lay out the price for me. . . . . I desire also y^{t} in high Duch, Glauberus, if you approve of it, and one more I desire you earnestly to procure for me; that is Vigineere des Cyphres wch you know is to be had at Paris; . . . . I would have one in this country before the impression be quite worn out.[88]

Stephen Winthrop wrote from England in 1649 to his brother, John Winthrop,

. . . . ye rest voted the triall of the King, who is since beheaded, ... but I canot inlarg to pticuler, passingers & bookes will informe best. I shall send my father some."[89]

Richard Saltonstall wrote to President Dunster from England where he was visiting,

This enclosed booke I must entreate you to accept insteade of such lines as I should have added.[90]

Roger Williams wrote, February 21, 1656,

Sir Henry Vane being retired to his owne private in Lincolnshire hath now published his observations as to religion, he hath sent me one of his books.[91]

John Eliot wrote to Mr. Hord, October 8, 1657,

. . . likewise I did receive a smal packet of books from Mr. Jessy according to Mr. Jessy's appointment.[92]

John Davenport wrote to the younger John Winthrop, August 19, 1659,

[88] Winthrop Papers, iv. 41. "Vigineere des Cyphres" is the *Traité des Chiffres* of Blaise de Vigenère.

[89] *Ibid.*, p. 209.

[90] Massachusetts Historical Society, Collections, 4th Series, ii. 194. The letter is undated, but marked as received May 15, 1651.

[91] *Ibid.*, 3rd Series, x. 19.

[92] Massachusetts Historical Society, Proceedings, xvii. 246. Mr. Hord was treasurer of the Corporation for Spreading the Gospel among the Indians. Mr. Jessy was a minister in Southwark, England.

I have received letters & bookes, & written papers from my ancient & honored freinds Mr. Hartlib, & Mr. Durie, wherein I finde sundry rarities of inventions . . . . which I long for an opportunitie to communicate to your selfe . . . . They are too many to be transmitted unto you by passengers.[93]

The next year he wrote, July 20,

Sir, I humbly thanck you for the Intelligence I received in your letters, and for the 2 weekly Intelligences, which Brother Myles brought me.[94]

A few days later he wrote again (August 11),

Mr Hartlib . . . . hath sent also sundry wrightings, and bookes, some to your selfe, some to me . . . . Mr Drury also hath sent some papers and bookes to the 2 Teaching Elders at Boston, and to me.[95]

Samuel Hartlib wrote to John Winthrop, Jr., in 1661,

. . . . Mr. Davinport, to whom I cannot write for the present, but have sent him by these ships a smal Packet directed to his name with a Book or two of the Bohemian Ch-Government, & some Prophetical Papers. . . . . Some weekes agoe I sent you the Systeme of Saturne with all the Cuts, being Mr. Brereton's gift . . . . Hevelii Selenographia in fol. with excellent Cuts is no more to bee had . . . . Mr. Morian promised to send mee for you all the Glauberian Tracts with some other wch are counted truer Adepts.[96]

In the same letter in which he urged John Winthrop, Jr., to write a "philosophical letter" to the Royal Society,[97] Henry Oldenburg, Secretary of the Society, wrote,

The Bearer hereof will doubtlesse give you the use of ye printed

93 Winthrop Papers, ii. 504. For Mr. Hartlib see p. 70, below.

94 Massachusetts Historical Society, Collections, 3rd Series, x. 36.

95 *Ibid.*, p. 38.

96 Massachusetts Historical Society, Proceedings, 1st Series, xvi. 212. It should be noted that this one letter mentions three different people as sending books to New England.

97 See p. 72, below.

History of yᵉ R. Society;[98] by wᶜʰ you will find what progres they have made hitherto . . . . I presume to transmit you some of the Transactions I monthly publish.[99]

He wrote again in 1669,

> My letter, recommended to yᵉ sᵈ Stuyvesand [Peter] for you, was accompanied wᵗʰ an Exemplar of the History of yᵉ R. Society, and wᵗʰ some of the Philosophicall Transactions. . . . . I send you herewᵗʰ a Printed paper, wᶜʰ contains yᵉ predictions of Mʳ Bond for the variations of yᵉ Needle for several years to come . . . you will take notice . . . how the variation varies in New England.[100]

John Eliot wrote in 1670 to Robert Boyle of "that worthy gift, which your honour is pleased to bestow upon me, viz. Pool's Synopsis, or Critica Sacra."[101] Presumably these are but chance records saved and indicate what must have been a general custom.

Books constantly came in with visitors or settlers from England, sometimes against the will of the government of the Colony. Upon the introduction of certain Quaker books, the General Court voted, August 22, 1654:

> It is ordred, that all & euery the inhabitants of this jurisdiction that haue any of the bookes in their custody that haue lately bin brought out of England vnder the names of John Reeues & Lodowick Muggleton . . . . & shall not bring or send in all such bookes now in their custody, to the next magistr̃, shall forfeit the sume of ten pounds for euery such booke that shalbe found. . . . [102]

William Baker, brought before the Middlesex Court in 1657, denied the possession of any Quaker books, saying that he disliked those which he had seen and had burned

[98] By Bishop Sprat.

[99] Massachusetts Historical Society, Proceedings, 1st Series, xvi. 230. Dated October 13, 1667.

[100] *Ibid.*, p. 239. Received May 6, 1669.

[101] Massachusetts Historical Society, Collections, 1st Series, iii. 177.

[102] Massachusetts Records, iii. 356.

them.[103] In 1662 action was brought against Captain Robert Lord for bringing in Ann Coleman of the "cursed sect," who "came furnished wth many blasphemous & hæretticall bookes, which she had spread abroad."[104]

Reference to the wills and inventories of the time (some of which have already been quoted) shows not only the presence of many collections of books, large and small (chiefly the latter), but a keen appreciation of their value. Edward Tench, of New Haven, died in 1640, leaving a library of 53 volumes, appraised at £12.10.00 out of a total estate of £400.[105] John Tey, in 1641, ordered his books to be kept for his son in the hands of "Mr. Eliote, Teacher of Roxburye."[106] John Oliver, the same year, mentioned among his possessions books and geometrical instruments.[107] In 1644 Israel Stoughton willed

> to sonne *Israel* one fourth part of smale Library, & vnto *John* another fourth pt, & unto *W^m* the other halfe, for his incouragm^t to apply himself to studies . . . . Provided also, concerning the Bookes, that my wife retaine to her vse during life what she pleaseth, & that my daughters chose each of them one for theire owne, that all may haue something they may call theire ffathers.[108]

George Phillips, minister of the church at Watertown, died July 1, 1644, leaving a "study of bookes" valued at £71.9.9.[109] William Brinsmade, in 1647, left to his son all his books.[110] In the same year Thomas Hooker left books appraised at £300.[111] John Cotton's will, dated November 9, 1652, states,

103 Middlesex Court Records, i. 145. Quoted in Duniway, Freedom of the Press, p. 37 note.

104 Massachusetts Records, iv. part 2, 55. Duniway, Freedom of the Press, p. 37 note.

105 Proceedings of the American Antiquarian Society, xviii. 137.

106 New England Historical and Genealogical Register, ii. 105.

107 *Ibid.*, iii. 266.

108 *Ibid.*, iv. 51.

109 Mullinger, The University of Cambridge, iii. 176 note 3.

110 New England Historical and Genealogical Register, iii. 266, 267.

111 Palfrey, History of New England, ii. 45.

My books I estimate to ye value of 150 l. (though they cost me much more) and because they are of vse only to my two sonnes, *Seaborne & John*, therefore I giue them unto them both, to be devided by equal portions.[112]

John Ward wrote in his will, December 28, 1652,

My bookes I doe give to Thomas Andrews of Ipswich, and allso my chirurgery chest and all that is now in it.[113]

John Lothrop, of Barnstable, who died August 10, 1653, left his books to his children, in order of age, as they might choose, the rest to "bee sold to any honest man whoe can tell how to make use of them."[114] Books were mentioned in the will of Thomas Rucke, Jr., about 1653.[115] Daniel Maud, of Dover, N. H., wrote in his will, January 17, 1654,

what few books I have I leave [to my successor] for the use and benefit of such a one as may be fit to have improvement, especially of those in the Hebrew tongue; but in case such a one be not had, to let them go to som of the next congregation as York or Hampton: except one boke titled "Dei [illegible] wch I woul have left for Cambridge library, and my little Hebrew bible for Mr. *Brock*.[116]

In the inventory of the estate of Nathaniel Rogers, pastor at Ipswich, taken August 16, 1655, books were listed at £100 out of a total estate of £1497.[117] Peter Bulkeley bequeathed the following books, April 14, 1658:[118]

to Sonne John, Mr. Cartwright upon the Rhemish testament
& Willets Sinopsis
to Sonne Joseph, Mr. Hildersham upon the one & fiftieth psalme
History of the Councell of Trent in English
Cornelius Tacitry [!] in English
Mr. Bolton on Gen. 6

112 New England Historical and Genealogical Register, v. 240.
113 *Ibid.*, xxii. 32.
114 *Ibid.*, v. 260.
115 *Ibid.*, v. 295.
116 New England Historical and Genealogical Register, v. 241.
117 Records and Files of the Quarterly Courts of Essex County, iii. 232.
118 New England Historical and Genealogical Register, x. 167.

[to others] Dr. Twisse against the Arminians
Mr. Rutherfords treatise upon the woman of Canaan
Mr. Rutherfords upon the dying of Christ
Rutherford upon John 12
Mr. Cooper on the 8th chapter to the Romans
Mr. Dike on Jeremiah 17th
to Sonne Edward, All Piscators Commentaries on the bible
Dr. Willett on Exod. & Levitt. on Sam. 1. 2. & on Daniell
Tarnovius in 2 vollūms upon prophetas minores
Dr. Owen, against the Arminians . . . .
One part of the English anotations upon the bible, the other part to be to my Son Gershom
Mr. Aynsworth notes upon the 5 books of Moses & upon the psalmes.

Bulkeley's library was appraised at £123.[119] In 1658 Ralph Partridge left a collection of 420 volumes valued in his inventory at £32.09.00.[120] The library of John Norton, according to the inventory of April 24, 1663, contained 159 books in folio, valued at £187.19, and 570 smaller books valued at £112.1, or a total value of £300.[121] The same year Samuel Stone left books valued at £127.[122] John Wilson, in 1667, wrote in his will,

> To my son, *John Wilson*, I give all my old Bookes and my new Bookes lately bought of *Mr. Usher* or of any others in New England.[123]

[119] Proceedings of the American Antiquarian Society, xviii. 140.

[120] *Ibid.*, p. 141.

[121] New England Historical and Genealogical Register, xi. 344.

[122] Palfrey, History of New England, ii. 45.

[123] New England Historical and Genealogical Register, xvii. 343. Other wills might be quoted in this connection, from Edward Holyoke's, 1658, referring to a considerable library, "As for my books and wrightings, I giue my sonn *Holyoke* all the books that are at Linn . . . . and the bookes I haue in my study that are *Mr Beanghans* works I giue him . . . . and my dixinary . . . . and A part of the New testament in Folio, with wast paper betwin euery leafe, and the greate mapps of geneolagy," (*Ibid.*, ix. 345), to such as John Coggan's careful bestowal of his single book: "My booke of Martires I giue vnto my sonne *Caleb*, my dau. *Robinson* & my dau. *Rocke*, the Longest Liuer of them, to enjoy the

The library of John Davenport was inventoried in 1670 at £233.[124]

One excellent indication of the kind of library to be found in the colonies toward the end of this period is given in a manuscript list of his books made out by Increase Mather in 1664, from which the following titles are selected:[125]

Milton	Defence of Smectymnuus
Milton	defensio Populi Anglicani
Fuller	Lives of Fathers
Fuller	Lives of Englands Worthyes
Herbert	Poems[126]
Camden	[No title given; probably Britannia]
Camden	Remaynes
Verulamus	de Augmentis scientiarum
Februn [?]	Body of Chymistry
Alstedii	encyclopædia
Child	History of Waldenses
Prideux	Introduction to History
de Laet	America descriptio
Sands	his Traveles
Purchases	Pilgrimage
. . . . .	Rerum Anglicarum Scriptores post Bedam
Bacon	Natural History
Howes	History of England
Mortons	History of New England
Raleigh	The Prerogative of Parliaments
Burtons	Pryns and Bastwicks Trial
. . . . .	Sr. H. V[ane's] Trial

same wholly"—in the meantime they were to divide it as they best could. (*Ibid.*, ix. 36). Many wills simply mention books, from which no deductions as to size can be made; but the almost general reference to books in the wills emphasizes the reverence in which they were held.

[124] Palfrey, History of New England, ii. 45.

[125] Proceedings of the American Antiquarian Society, xx. 280.

[126] In the New England Historical and Genealogical Register, xxvii. 347, A. E. Cutler records his ownership of the third edition of Herbert's "Priest to the Temple; or, the Country Parson," London, 1675, which contains the dated Latin autograph of Increase Mather: Crescentius Matherus, 1683. This cannot be the same volume as the one in the 1664 list; evidently he had two volumes of Herbert's poems in 1683, or had given away the earlier one.

. . . . .	Against Actors showing of stage plays
Josephus	His works
{ Juvenal et Persius	cum Lvbini Commentar.
Plautus	
Senecæ	Tragæd.
Sophocles	Tragæd.
Poetæ Minores	
Demosthenes	Orat.
Horatius	
Ovidii	Amorum Libri
Æsopi	Fabulæ
Lucani	dialog.
Grotius	de imperio Majestatis
Verstegan	English Antiquities

Another interesting list of books is that given in the inventory of the estate of Thomas Grocer, "stranger," who died in Roxbury February 2, 1665. Grocer was a London trader who had dealt with Barbados. The books may have been his private library but were more likely brought as a venture, even though the lack of duplicates among the itemized books might seem to support the first theory. The books mentioned by title number 202; 384 books of various sizes are given as a single item, with a value of £28.16.00, and similarly "120 sticht bookes" are valued at £1. Among the titles given the following are of interest:[127]

Burtons Melancholy
Journey of Fraunce
a Booke of Jests
Character of King Charles
4 uolumes of poems *at* 4*s*.
Mountignes Assayes
Purchase right ordering of the Bees
Bancrofts epigrammes
Lilly anatomye of witt
Golden remaines

[127] Ford, The Boston Book Market, p. 71 ff.

Epicures Morals
greens farewell to Follye
Relation of a Uoyage to Guiana
9 paper Bookes of Manuscripts
Heywood [The Hierarchie] of Angells
German Dyet
Treatise of Fruit trees

It is impossible to prove that the colonists had as large libraries as their contemporaries in England, or as they themselves would have had if they had remained in England; but the evidence given above would seem to show that the early settlers did not suffer for books, either old or new, since the good libraries they brought with them were constantly increased by importations. Furthermore, the comparative nearness of the various settlements made it possible for the colonists to increase their range of reading by borrowing, or to assist their friends by lending. Such libraries as that of John Winthrop, Jr., were almost circulating libraries. The following extracts from colonial letters are characteristic.

I vmblie pray you that when you haue perused the followinge treatise, that you will restore it to mee againe.[128]

Lent to Mr Williams, 18. 8, my blew manuscr̃., my relac̃on, the brev^t of Cambridge, Nath. Wiggins Reasons, & the printed relation of the Martyrs.[129]

I have therefore bene bold to send you the Medulla and the Magnalia Dei.[130]

By this bearer . . . . I received your booke, & had by the same returned it, but that I desire to reade it ouer once more, finding it pleasant & profitable, & craue the sight of any other of that subiect at your leasure, kindly thancking you for this inclosed.[131]

[128] John Blackleach to John Winthrop, 1637. Winthrop Papers, ii. 149.

[129] Thomas Lechford, Note-Book, p. 4. 1638. Mr. Williams is probably Roger Williams. The numbers give the date, October 18th.

[130] Roger Williams to John Winthrop, Jr., 1645. Massachusetts Historical Society, Collections, 3rd Series, ix. 268.

[131] Roger Williams to John Winthrop, Jr., 1649. Winthrop Papers, i. 267.

He [Mr. Caukin] tells me of a booke lately come ouer in Mr. Pynchon's name, wherein is some derogation to the blood of Christ. The booke was therefore burnt in the Market place at Boston, & Mr. Pynchon to be cited to the Court. If it come to your hand, I may hope to see it.[132]

Dr. Choyse hath none of the bookes mentioned in your note.[133]

I pray you to read & returne this Jew. I haue allso an answere to him by a good plaine man, expounding all which the Jew takes literally, in a spirituall way: & I haue (in a discourse of a Knight (L'Estrange) proving Americans no Jewes) another touch against him . . . . [134]

My deere Frend,—I had yours, and truly doe loue you hartily, though I haue bin some tymes troubled at my busines having no returnes, & you selling my house for 20*l*, & lending out my bookes & things & sending home nothing to mee.[135]

I send you, by this bearer, such books of Intelligence, as were sent me.[136]

I would now (with very many thanks) have returned you youre Jesuits maxims but I was loath to trust them in so wild a hand, nor some tidings which I have from England.[137]

Deare S[r],—I have herewith sent you two of a sort of those bookes I promised you; to the intent you may reserve one by you, and yet pleasure your freinds either by loane or gifte with the other. I have also sent you the dementions of a furnace hearth. But I can not at present find the booke it is in, it being packed away in some trunke amongst other things. I shall mynd it, and send it to you by the first opportunity . . . . [138]

[132] Roger Williams to John Winthrop, Jr., 1650. *Ibid.*, i. 285.

[133] John Davenport to John Winthrop, Jr., evidently in reply to a request for certain books. 1654. *Ibid.*, ii. 488.

[134] Roger Williams to John Winthrop, Jr., 1654–5. *Ibid.*, i. 291.

[135] From Hugh Peter, then living in England, to Charles Gott, deacon of Salem, evidently his agent. This library was circulating too freely to satisfy its owner! 1654. Winthrop Papers, i. 116.

[136] John Davenport to John Winthrop, Jr., 1654–5. Massachusetts Historical Society, Collections, 3rd Series, x. 7.

[137] Roger Williams to John Winthrop, Jr., 1655–6. *Ibid.*, p. 11. The "wild hand" indicates that an Indian was the bearer.

[138] Richard Leader of Piscataway to John Winthrop, Jr., 1655. Massachusetts Historical Society, Proceedings, 2d Series, iii. 192.

Sir) I thanck you for the 2 bookes you sent me to peruse, which I am reading dilligently.[139]

I am much obliged vnto your Worshipp that at last you were myndfull of me, & sent the boke soe much desyred by goodman Staythrop, by which I haue gott much satisfaction.[140]

More workes of the same, I would gladly see . . . . I pray you parte not with my booke.[141]

. . . . many thancks for . . . . the Almanack, which I had not seene before, though, since my receite of yours, the president of the Colledge sent me one.[142]

The booke concerning bees, which you desired, I now send you, by John Palmer, & with it 3 others, viz., 1. An Office of Address, 2. An Invention of Engines of Motion, 3. A Discourse for divisions & setting out of Landes. . . . . I shall add unto them a 4th booke in 8°, called Chymical, Medicinal, & Chirurgical Addresses. These are a few of many more which are sent to me. I hoped for an opportunity of shewing them to you here, & shall reserve them for you til a good opportunity.[143]

Sir, I humbly thanck you for the Intelligence I received in your letters, and for the 2 weekly Intelligences, which Brother Myles brought me.[144]

I shall send the an answer to John Nortons booke . . . . if I cann procuer it.[145]

I make bold wth you to transmitt by your hand to Colonell Temple those books [*illegible*] wch you will receive heerwth (want of fitt artists heere must be my excuse that they appeare in that dessolate forme); they were sent me before winter, from the great intelligence of Europe, Mr Samuell Hartleb, a Germã

[139] John Davenport to John Winthrop, Jr., 1655. Massachusetts Historical Society, Collections, 3rd Series, x. 14.

[140] Jonathan Brewster to John Winthrop, Jr., 1656. Winthrop Papers, ii. 72. The book referred to is one on alchemy.

[141] Jonathan Brewster to John Winthrop, Jr., 1656. *Ibid.*, ii. 78, 81.

[142] John Davenport to John Winthrop, Jr., 1659. Massachusetts Historical Society, Collections, 3rd Series, x. 23.

[143] John Davenport to John Winthrop, Jr., 1659. Winthrop Papers, ii. 509.

[144] John Davenport to John Winthrop, Jr., 1660. Massachusetts Historical Society, Collections, 3rd Series, x. 36. The *Intelligence* is probably the *London Intelligencer.*

[145] William Coddington to John Winthrop, Jr., 1660. Winthrop Papers, ii. 287.

gentlemã, as conteinig something of novelty. That they are yet in sheets may have this convenience, that, being divers distinct relations, the Govern^r^, Mr Wilson, & Mr Norton (if there be any thing worth their notice), or any other friends he please, may have the pvsall of some p̃ts [*illegible*] whiles the other parts are reading.[146]

I humbly thank your Worship for your last present, vizt those printed papers of Intelligence referring to the philosophical transactions of the Royall Society of the Virtuosi: I did according to your order to me acquaint Mr Danforth of Roxbury and others with them; the communication thereof renders us all, but especially myself greatly indebted unto your Honour.[147]

In connection with this, mention must be made of the list in his own handwriting of 90 books borrowed by Richard Mather from John Johnson and William Parks of "Rocksbury," January 10, 1647–8. These are all theological except "Seneca his works."[148]

Additional information in regard to books owned or read by the early settlers may be gained from a study of their references to or quotations from books. Ezekiel Rogers, in his epitaph on Thomas Hooker, written about 1647, wrote the following:[149]

> America, although she do not boast
> Of all the *gold* and *silver* from that coast,
> *Lent* to her sister Europe's need or pride;
> (For that repaid her, with much gain beside,
> In one *rich pearl*, which Heaven did thence afford,
> As pious Herbert gave his honest word;) . . . .

The reference is evidently to the passage in Herbert's

[146] John Winthrop, Jr., to Thomas Lake, 1661. *Ibid.*, iv. 73.

[147] Thomas Shepard to John Winthrop, Jr., 1669. Massachusetts Historical Society, Collections, 3rd Series, x. 71.

[148] Massachusetts Historical Society, Collections, 4th Series, viii. 76. Johnson and Parks were both laymen, and yet had libraries of theological books, at least, from which as prominent a minister as Richard Mather found it worth while to borrow books in considerable numbers! See p. 45, above.

[149] Magnalia, i. 351.

"Church Militant" beginning at line 235, which refers to the Puritan movement toward America.[150]

Governor Bradford, in his polemical writings, quotes authorities freely, and sometimes cites authors or volumes which are not mentioned in the extant lists of his own library or any contemporary Plymouth library. Such names may furnish a clue to the identity of some of the uncatalogued books in his library. The following are quoted, some more than once.

[Whittingham?]	A Brieff discours off the troubles begonne at Frankford . . . . 1554.[151]
Baylie, R.	A Dissuasive from the Errors of the Time, 1645.
Cotton,	Answer to Mr. Baylie
Eusebius,	Ecclesiastical History
Fulke,	On Romans the xi.
Robinson, J.,	Apology
Robinson, J.,	A Justification of Separation
Speed,	Cloud of Witnesses
Taylor,	The Liberty of Prophesying, 1647.[152]
Anderton, L.,	The Triple Cord, or a Treatise proving the Truth of the Roman Religion, 1633.
Bale, John,	Acts of English Votaries
Barnes, R.,	On the Keyes
Beza,	Confessions
Bullinger,	Not stated
Burton, H.,	A Vindication of Churches commonly called Independent, 1644
Calvin,	Not stated
. . . . .	Centuries of Madgeburg
Fox,	Abridgment of Acts and Monuments
Gillespie, G.,	Aaron's Rod Blossoming, 1646
Grosthead, R.,	Not stated

[150] See p. 137, below.

[151] Quoted in the Introduction to the Ecclesiastical History of the Church at Plymouth.

[152] The references in this group are quoted in "A Dialogue, or the sum of a Conference between some Young Men born in New England and sundry ancient men that came out of Holland and Old England, Anno Domini 1648."

Gualter, R.	On Acts
Guicciardini,	History of the Wars of Italy
[?]	An Harmony of the Confessions of Faith, 1643
Jacob, H.,	Attestation
Jewell, J.,	Not stated
Mantuanus,	Quotes poetry
Peter Martyr,	Commonplaces
Mornay, Philip,	Mysterie of Iniquity
Mornay, Philip,	Fowre Books of the Institutions
Pareus,	Commentary on Revelation, 1644
[?]	The Reasons presented by the Dissenting Brethren against certain Propositions, 1648
Serres, J.,	Generall Historie of France, 1624 [English edition]
Socrates,	Church History
Symson, P.,	Historie of the Church
Tindall, W.,	Not stated
Vives, Lud.,	Edition of Augustine's De Civitate Dei
Whetenhall,	Discourse on the Abuses in the Church of Rome
Whitgift,	An Answere to a certain Libell
Whittaker,	Not stated
Willett, A.,	Commentary on Jude.[153]

Richard Mather quoted the following:[154]

Bullinger,	Decad. 5, Serm. 9.
Ames,	Cases of Conscience, 1. 4, C. 28. Q. 1.
Alsted,	Encyclopædia, p. 25
Alsted,	de Casibus, c. 8. reg. 3, memb. 12
Calvin,	Institutions, (Several)
Martin,	Loci Communes, Clas. 4, c. ii. Q. 14

[153] References in this group are quoted in "A Dialogue or 3d Conference, between some yonge-men borne in New-England; and some Ancient-men, which came out of Holand and Old England concerning the church." This was probably written in 1652. It is noticeable that many of these books, the dates of which I have added in the list, were published after the Pilgrims came to America, and that some were used by Bradford within a year or two of the time of publication. It is evident that even in Plymouth, which had no bookseller, and was in general far behind Boston in culture, books fresh from the press were not unknown. See pp. 25 and 26, above.

[154] Mather Papers, p. 74.

Musculus,	Loci Communes, de Cœna
Mead,	Inst. Loc.
Pareus,	On 2 Corinthians, 11: 26
Zepper,	de Polit. Eccles. L. 1, c. 14

Anne Bradstreet in her poems referred to various writers:

> To whom the old *Berosus*[155] (so much fam'd)
> His Book of Assurs monarchs dedicates.
>
> No *Phoenix* pen, nor *Spencers* poetry,
> Nor *Speed's* nor *Cambden's* learned History[156]
>
> If *Curtius* be true in his report[157]
>
> He that at large would satisfie his mind,
> In *Plutarch's* Lives his history may find.[158]
>
> Which makes me now with *Sylvester* confess,
> But *Sidney's* Muse can sing his worthiness.[159]

References to DuBartas, author of the "Divine Week," and to Sylvester, who turned DuBartas' poems into English, are frequent in her poems, one of which is "In Honour of DuBartas." According to J. H. Ellis, who edited her poems, much of her historical material was taken from Raleigh's "History of the World"; his evidence is satisfactory.[160]

Nathaniel Morton, in his "New England's Memorial," occasionally drew upon history for illustrations, giving in each case his authority and generally the page reference. Authors cited include Carion, Languet, Peter Martyr, Pliny, Purchas, and Socrates.

155 The Works of Anne Bradstreet in Prose and Verse, edited by J. H. Ellis, p. 317. Berosus, a Babylonian historian of about 260 B. C., was probably met by Mrs. Bradstreet in the pages of Raleigh's History.

156 *Ibid.*, p. 358. Camden's Annales Rerum Anglicarum . . . . Regnante Elizabetha was published in 1615. English versions appeared in 1625 and 1635. Speed's History of Great Britain was published in 1623.

157 *Ibid.*, pp. 257, 265. Quintus Curtius, Roman Historian.

158 *Ibid.*, p. 297.

159 *Ibid.*, p. 349. In An Elegie upon that Honourable and renowned Knight, Sir Philip Sidney, she has much to say of his work as a poet.

160 *Ibid.*, pp. xlvii–xlix.

It would seem, then, from the foregoing evidence, that, as the colonists brought with them many good libraries, constantly added new books, and supplemented their own libraries by borrowing freely from their neighbors near and remote, they were not without the means of culture and had access to a moderate amount of real literature. It must be remembered that we possess only fragmentary records of private life in the colonies; more comprehensive records would almost certainly give added proof of the possession of books and libraries. It seems fair to assume that, although the colonists were at a disadvantage in this respect compared with their English contemporaries who lived in or near London or either university, they were under no greater handicap than if they had been living in some remote place in the north or west of England.

Chapter III: Intercourse with England and English Literary Men.

IT is a mistake to think of New England colonists as practically cut off from the outside world, dwellers in a lonely desert place. Our popular histories have created this impression by their over-emphasis on the dramatic elements of the hardships of the first years of settlement, especially at Plymouth. The settlers of Plymouth had few friends in England and were, perhaps, isolated from the world until the Massachusetts Bay settlements were established. The latter, however, were always in close touch with England. John Josselyn, coming to Boston in 1638, presented his "respects to Mr. *Winthorpe* [*sic*] the Governour, and to Mr. *Cotton* the Teacher of *Boston* Church, to whom I delivered from Mr. *Francis Quarles* the poet, the Translation of the 16, 25, 51, 88, 113, and 137. Psalms into *English* Meeter, for his approbation."[1] Mention has already been made of early graduates of Harvard who returned to England to engage in public life there.[2] Twenty-seven of the ministers who came to the colony in the early years returned to England, some of whom became colonists again at the Restoration.[3] Business trips to England were such ordinary affairs as to call for no comment; in all of my reading I have found no reference to them either as difficult or as unusual.[4] The colonists thought of themselves as Englishmen, further

[1] Josselyn, Two Voyages to New England, p. 20. The last phrase is interesting.

[2] See p. 18, above. Others not Harvard men also returned to active life in England, such as Giles Firmin, who, born in England, accompanied his father to New England, was educated and married here, but later returned to England to spend his life. Such people were a bond between the old and the new.

[3] Magnalia, i. 588.

[4] John Wilson went to England in 1631 and again in 1635. (Winthrop's Journal, i. 80, 145.) Edward Winslow went to England in 1635 as agent for Plymouth,

away from London, the heart of England, than if they had stayed in Old England, but still living in a part of England, New England. Edward Johnson, in his "Wonder-Working Providence," used the phrase "our Countreymen" to refer to people in England,[5] and seemed eager to have his readers think of himself and his colonial neighbors as interested essentially in the welfare of England.[6] The affection felt by New England for Old England is also shown in Anne Bradstreet's poem, "A Dialogue between Old England, and New England," and by a statement of John Dunton in one of his letters. He spoke of his own love for England, adding, "And 'twas thus with the first Planters of this Country, who were, even to their 80th year, still pleasing themselves with hopes of their Returning to England."[7]

During the period of the Commonwealth they felt perhaps even more strongly their ties to the mother country, for their friends, and in many cases their neighbors or members of their families, were taking an active part in English affairs. Dr. Palfrey writes,

Hugh Peter and Thomas Welde, sent over by Massachusetts to look after its affairs, both rose to influence with Cromwell, and

and in 1646 as agent for Massachusetts. (Magnalia, i. 115.) William Hibbens of Boston accompanied Hugh Peter and Thomas Welde to England in 1641, returning the next year alone. (Winthrop's Journal, ii. 32, 71.) In 1646 Samuel Gorton and two of his followers went to England to complain of their persecutions at the hands of the Massachusetts authorities. (*Ibid.*, ii. 282.) John Wheelwright visited England during the Protectorate and was well received by his old friend the Protector. (*Ibid.*, i. 197 note.) John Winthrop, Jr., made three trips to England; his brother Stephen also made repeated visits to the mother country. (Winthrop Papers, iv. 199 note.) Daniel Gookin went to England in 1650, 1654, and 1657. (Gookin, Life of Daniel Gookin, p. 81 ff.). Henry Wolcott of Windsor, Connecticut, crossed the ocean for business in 1654, 1663, and about 1671. (Wolcott, Memorial of Henry Wolcott, pp. 36–38.)

[5] "the learned labours of this Souldier of Christ [John Norton] are obvious to our Countreymen." (p. 103.) "Many pamphlets have come from our Countreymen of late, to this purpose." (p. 173.)

[6] "for Englands sake they are going from England to pray without ceasing for England. O England! thou shalt finde New England prayers prevailing with their God for thee." (p. 53.)

[7] Letters, p. 62.

the former, as his chaplain, walked by the Protector's Secretary, John Milton, at his funeral.[8]

Hugh Peter married Mrs. Reade, the mother of the wife of John Winthrop, Jr.;[9] her first husband, Edmund Reade, had been a colonel in the parliamentary army.[10] Stephen Winthrop, brother of John Winthrop, Jr., and Fitz-John, the latter's son, both served in that army. Stephen Winthrop, on a visit to England in 1646, accepted a commission in the Parliamentary army. He rose rapidly to the rank of colonel. Roger Williams, writing from England to John Winthrop, Jr., in 1656, mentioned the fact that "Your brother Stephen succeeds Major-General Harrison." In this same year he represented Banff and Aberdeen in Parliament. He married one sister of Colonel Rainsborough of the Parliamentary army, another becoming the fourth wife of his father, Governor Winthrop.[11] Fitz-John Winthrop went to England in 1657, having been offered commissions by two of his uncles, Stephen Winthrop and Thomas Reade. He accepted a lieutenancy in Reade's regiment of foot, rose to a captaincy, and at one time was governor of Cardross in Scotland.[12] Samuel Desborough, the first magistrate of Guilford, Connecticut, returned to England and became, under Cromwell, Lord Keeper of the Great Seal of Scotland. His brother John had married Cromwell's sister Jane.[13] John Hoadley, also of Guilford, became one of Cromwell's chaplains at Edinburgh, and afterwards chaplain to General Monck.[14] Samuel Mather, brother of Increase, was chaplain to Thomas Andrews, Lord Mayor of

[8] History of New England, i. 586.

[9] Dictionary of National Biography; Massachusetts Historical Society, Proceedings, xlii. 169.

[10] Dictionary of National Biography.

[11] Winthrop Papers, iv. 199 note; Dictionary of National Biography.

[12] Massachusetts Historical Society, Proceedings, 2d Series, i. 118 ff.; Winthrop Papers, ii. 203; iv. 266 note.

[13] Dictionary of National Biography.

[14] Steiner, History of Guilford and Madison, p. 43.

London, and later was chosen to accompany the English Commissioners to Scotland. Still later Henry Cromwell took him as one of his chaplains on his Irish expedition.[15] Francis Higginson, second son of the Reverend Francis Higginson of Salem, studied at Leyden, conformed to the Church of England, and spent his life as a vicar in Westmoreland.[16] The two sons of Governor John Haynes by his first wife had stayed in England when he emigrated; both are said to have drawn "their swords in the great Civil War,—the elder for the King, the younger for the Parliament."[17] John Haynes, Jr., son of Governor Haynes by his second wife, after graduating from Harvard in 1656, went to England in 1657 with Fitz-John Winthrop. Instead of going into the army, he went to Cambridge, where he took the Master's degree in 1660. He remained in England and, having conformed, spent his life as rector of the Church of England in Suffolk and Essex.[18]

Several others returned to enter the Parliamentary army. Major Robert Sedgwick of Charlestown rose to the rank of Major-General, and was employed by Cromwell in the expedition against the West Indies, succeeding General Fortescue as Governor of Jamaica.[19] Captain George Cook, who had been active in the Massachusetts militia, became a colonel in Cromwell's army.[20] Israel Stoughton, whose son William was lieutenant-governor under William and Mary, became a lieutenant-colonel among the Ironsides.[21] Captain John Mason, hero of the Mystic fight, was urged by Sir Thomas Fairfax, his old comrade in arms, to join the army of Parliament, but he did not return to England.[22]

[15] Massachusetts Historical Society, Collections, 1st Series, x. 26 note.

[16] Dictionary of National Biography. See p. 153, below.

[17] Massachusetts Historical Society, Proceedings, 2d Series, i. 118.

[18] *Ibid.*, i. 118 ff.

[19] John Hull's Public Diary, p. 174 note.

[20] Winthrop's Journal, ii. 140 note.

[21] *Ibid.*, i. 147 note.

[22] *Ibid.*, i. 218 note.

John Collins, Harvard 1649, was a chaplain in Monck's army;[23] and William Hooke, of New Haven, was one of Cromwell's chaplains, his wife, a sister of General Whalley, being a cousin of the Protector.[24] He was also probably Master of the Savoy.[25] Edward Hopkins, of New Haven, was active in public life during Cromwell's régime.[26] Edward Winslow, having gone to England as agent of Massachusetts in 1646, remained in England and later became one of the Grand Commissioners of Cromwell's expedition against Hispaniola.[27] Daniel Gookin, on his third visit to England, served for a time (1658–1659) as collector of customs at Dunkirk, being appointed later Deputy Treasurer of War there. He was acquainted with Cromwell, and it was through him that Cromwell gave his invitation to the New Englanders to remove to the balmier climate of Jamaica. On his return to Boston in 1660 he was accompanied by Goffe and Whalley, the regicides.[28]

Mention has already been made of the friendship between John Winthrop, Jr., and Sir Kenelme Digby.[29] There are several references to this in letters to Winthrop from William Hooke, then in London. He wrote, April 13, 1657, "For Sir Kenelme Digby is in France, and when he will return I hear not.[30]" Again, April 16, 1658, "Sir Kenelme Digby is not, as yet, returned, & therefore I can give you no account of him."[31] And again, March 30, 1659, "As for Sir Kenelme Digby, I have not heard of him a long time. He is not (for ought I heare) in England. He is a greate schollar, but I

[23] John Hull's Diary, p. 159 note 3.

[24] Dictionary of National Biography.

[25] *Cf.* Massachusetts Historical Society, Proceedings, xli. 304.

[26] Winthrop's Journal, i. 223 note. He was successively First Warden of the Fleet and a Commissioner of the army and navy.

[27] Magnalia, i. 115.

[28] Gookin, Life of Daniel Gookin, *passim*. Tyler, History of American Literature, i. 152.

[29] See pp. 41 and 42, above.

[30] Massachusetts Historical Society, Collections, 3rd Series, i. 183.

[31] Winthrop Papers, ii. 588.

heare no good of him by any."[32] One letter from Sir Kenelme himself gives further evidence of a friendship which would seem to have been close, to judge both by the eagerness with which Winthrop was making inquiry for Sir Kenelme through his London correspondent, and by Sir Kenelme's evident desire to serve Winthrop. The opening sentences refer to his second gift to the Harvard Library.

Paris 26. *Jan.*,1656. *new stile.*

. . . . . I beseech you present my most humble thankes to the President and fellowes of y[r] college for the obliging Letter they haue bin pleased to send me. So small a present as j presumed to make them, deserued not so large a returne. . . . . I haue searched all Paris for Blaise Viginere des Chiffres. I had it in my library in England: But att the plundering of my house, j lost it wth many other good bookes. I haue layed out in all places for it: and when j gett it, it shall be for you by the first conueniency of sending it to you.[33]

John Winthrop, F. R. S., grandson of John Winthrop, Jr., in a letter to Cotton Mather written in 1718, referred as follows to this friendship:

The famous & learned S[r] Kenelme Digby (then at Paris) earnestly solicited my hon[rd] granfather to returne back to England, urging that America was too scanty for so great a philosopher to stay long in. My good ancestor modestly answered, '*Res angusta domi*, my duty to a numerous family, will not permitt it.'[34]

Hugh Peter would seem to have been acquainted with Sir Kenelme also, for it is he who first sent word to Winthrop that the knight was sending a great chest of books to Harvard.[35]

Cromwell had a college mate in the colonies, John Wheelwright, B. A. of Sidney Sussex in 1614, and M. A. in 1618. Of him he later said,

[32] *Ibid.*, ii. 593.

[33] Massachusetts Historical Society, Collections, 3rd Series, x. 15.

[34] Winthrop Papers, vi. 384 note.

[35] *Ibid.*, i. 116. See p. 41 note 68, above.

> I remember the time when I was more afraid of meeting Wheelwright at foot-ball, than I have been since of meeting an army in the field, for I was infallibly sure of being tripped up by him.[36]

Cromwell was also well acquainted with John Cotton, if we may judge from the friendly tone of a letter which has been preserved.[37] John Oxenbridge was another colonial friend of Cromwell, and of Milton and Marvell as well.[38] If conditions in England had differed upon one occasion, Cromwell himself would have come to New England. He told Lord Falkland in 1641 that if the Remonstrance had not passed, "he would have sold all he had the next morning, and never have seen England more."[39] Cotton Mather mentions Cromwell, with "Mr. Hambden, and Sir Arthur Haselrig," among those who were forcibly detained from coming.[40] This legend lacks satisfactory proof; in fact, at the time they were supposed to have been stopped, Hampden was in the midst of his legal contest against the ship-money, and it is hardly believable that he would have deserted in the heat of the fight. But that it was believed by the next generation and has been accepted quite generally ever since gives evidence of its truth in probability, if not in fact. New England did not seem far away to those who desired asylum from political oppression in England; nor, as we have seen, did England seem far away, when political conditions changed, to those on this side of the water who desired a larger field for action than the colonies seemed to afford. Chance, or beliefs, or both, had much more to do with determining who came than ability. The men who

[36] Memoir of John Wheelwright, p. 2.

[37] New Hampshire Historical Society, Collections, i. 258.

[38] Publications of the Colonial Society of Massachusetts, xii. 121. When Marvell was tutoring William Dutton, Cromwell's ward, he went to live, upon Cromwell's advice, with Oxenbridge, then a fellow at Eton. Marvell wrote the epitaph upon the first wife of Oxenbridge. Marvell's poem "Bermudas" was probably suggested by Oxenbridge, who had lived there for a time. (Dictionary of National Biography, and Poems of Andrew Marvell, Muses' Library edition.)

[39] Clarendon, Rebellion, Book IV. §52.

[40] Magnalia, i. 79.

settled New England, it must be remembered, were not an inferior class.

The feeling of unity between New and Old England at the time of the Commonwealth is well illustrated by the behavior of the authorities of Massachusetts in the case of the burning, in 1650, of William Pynchon's "The Meritorious Price of our Redemption." When the General Court found it to be "erronyous and hereticale," and ordered it to be burned, it was careful to issue a "Declaration" of its detestation of the heresy.

The "Declaration" was immediately sent to England to be printed and circulated there, in order that the Court might set itself right with its Christian brethren, while John Norton was entreated to answer Mr. Pynchon's book with all convenient speed, and his answer was also to be sent to England to be printed.[41]

At the Restoration New England once more became the place of refuge for exiles from England. Cotton Mather mentions fourteen ministers who came to avoid persecution at this time,[42] and refers also to "some eminent persons of a New-English *original*, which were driven back out of Europe into their own country again, by that storm."[43] Among these exiles were some who, as the highest judges of England, had tried even a king. It is interesting at this point to speculate upon the possibility that, had he been accorded harsher treatment, Milton himself might have followed the Regicides to America, in which case "Paradise Lost" would have been written in New England,—or not at all. Which is the more probable of these two possibilities will be discussed elsewhere.[44] At least he would have found friends here; Roger Williams seems to have been on intimate

[41] Duniway, Freedom of the Press in Massachusetts, p. 32.

[42] Magnalia, i. 237. The ministers are James Allen, John Bailey, Thomas Baily, Thomas Barnet, James Brown, Thomas Gilbert, James Keith, Samuel Lee, Charles Morton, Charles Nicholet, John Oxenbridge, Thomas Thornton, Thomas Walley, and William Woodrop.

[43] *Ibid.*, i. 238.

[44] See pp. 93 and 94, below.

terms with him during his visit to England from 1651 to 1654,[45] as was also the Reverend John Clarke of Newport, R. I.;[46] and Milton knew and corresponded with John Winthrop, Jr.[47] Winthrop probably became acquainted with Milton through their mutual friend, Samuel Hartlib, author of many works on agriculture and natural history, to whom Milton addressed his tract "Of Education" with every evidence of close acquaintance, and with whom Winthrop had an extensive correspondence.[48] Theodore Haak, said to have been the founder of the "London Club, or Invisible College of Natural Philosophers," from which the Royal Society developed, and Henry Oldenburg, for several years Secretary of the Royal Society, were also friends and correspondents of Winthrop, and friends of Milton.[48]

It was through these friends that Winthrop became one of the early fellows of the Royal Society, being nominated as fellow in 1662,[48] when the Society was less than two years old.[49] Winthrop's interest in science was evidently strong before he came to New England, as a reference to

45 Williams wrote to John Winthrop, Jr., July 12, 1654, having just returned from England, "It pleased the Lord to call me for some time and with some persons to practice the Hebrew, the Greeke, Latine, French and Dutch: The Secretarie of the Councell, (Mr Milton) for my Dutch I read him, read me many more Languages." It is probably in this way that Milton became acquainted with the Dutch Lucifer by Vondel. Williams seems to have discussed education with Milton, for he says further in this letter, "Grammar rules begin to be esteemd a Tyrannie. I taught 2 young Gentlemen a Parliament mans sons (as we teach our children English) by words phrazes and constant talke &c. I have begun with mine owne 3 boys." (Massachusetts Historical Society, Collections, 3rd Series, x.3.) See Milton's criticism of the time wasted in the study of grammar, in Of Education.

46 Clarke lived in England from 1651 to 1663. He was also acquainted with Sir Henry Vane and the Earl of Clarendon. It was through the latter that he obtained from Charles II the remarkable Rhode Island Charter of 1663, granting religious freedom. (Early Religious Leaders of Newport, p. 16.)

47 Philosophical Transactions of the Royal Society of London, xl. 1741. Dedication.

48 Massachusetts Historical Society, Proceedings, 1st Series, xvi. 207. See p. 47, above.

49 The Society was founded in 1660, and incorporated in 1662. Encyclopedia Britannica.

the titles of books sent him by his friends in England shows.[50] That theology was not the all-exclusive factor in colonial life that it is often pictured as being is shown by the fact that a busy colonial governor found the time to keep up his study of science after the experimental method newly discovered by Bacon, and was considered by English scientific men worthy to become their associate in research, and even to serve on two committees of the Royal Society in 1664.[51] His friendship with Sir Kenelme Digby may easily have resulted from their common interest in alchemy. The letter of Sir Kenelme from which quotation has already been made was largely made up of explanations and discussions of wondrous liquids, potent medicines, and especially Digby's favorite sympathetic powder.

Winthrop's correspondence with scientific and literary men in England and on the Continent was extensive. Dr. Cromwell Mortimer, Secretary of the Royal Society, in dedicating the fortieth volume of the Transactions of the Society to John Winthrop, F. R. S., grandson of John Winthrop, Jr., referred to "the great Treasure of curious Letters on various learned Subjects" written to the earlier Winthrop and then in the possession of the younger, and listed over eighty of the writers of these letters.[52]

[50] See pp. 32–34, above.

[51] Massachusetts Historical Society, Proceedings, 1st Series, xvi. 206 ff.

[52] The following names are characteristic of the list:

Earl of Anglesey
Earl of Arundel
Elias Ashmole
Robert Boyle
Tycho Brahe
Lord Brounker
Dr. Browne [probably Sir Thomas]
Jo. Camden
Lord Clarendon
Comenius
Charles II
O. Cromwell
Ernestus Coloniæ, Episc.
Robert Hooke
Ch. Howard, Duke of Norfolk
Joh. Keppler
Dr. Lovell, Oxon.
Earl of Manchester
John Milton
Sir Rob. Moray
Lord Napier
Isaac Newton
Dr. Pell
Earl of Pembroke
Pet. Peregrinus, Romæ
Alb. Peterson, Amstel.

His friends of the Royal Society expected from him valuable contributions to knowledge, and were not disappointed. Henry Oldenburg, Secretary of the Society, wrote in 1667:

SIR,—So good an opportunity as this I could not let passe w^t^hout putting you in mind of y^r^ being a member of ye Royall Society, though you are in New-England; and that even at so great a distance you may doe that Illustrious Company great service. . . . . We know y^r^ ingenuity, experience, and veracity, ye best qualities of a man and a Philosopher; . . . . And, since you have now been from us severall years, give us at last a visit by a Philosophicall letter.[53]

In a postscript he discussed the value of the experimental method of searching "the works of God themselves." Early in 1669 he wrote again in regard to scientific equipment in America, and requested certain experiments performed:

Giue me leaue . . . . to inquire . . . . Whether you haue any good Telescopes, to compare the Phænomena from that Coast wth the Accompts of Hevelius, Ricciolo, Cassini, etc. What advance of Harverd Coll. in y^r^ Cambridge? Whether you are furnisht wth the modern books of ye most Ingenious and famous Philosophers and Mathematicians [of whom he gives a list] . . . .

I send you herew^th^ a Printed paper, wch contains ye predictions of Mr Bond for the variations of ye Needle for several years to

Joh. Espagnet
Dr. Everard
Gal. Galileo
J. R. Glauber
Dr. Goddard
Princeps Gothar
Dr. Grew
J. B. van Helmont
J. F. Helvetius
Lord Herbert [of Cherbury?]
Hans Albrecht, Dominus Herberstein
Joh. Hevelius
Sir Jo. Heydon
Frederick Princeps Holsatiæ et Dominus Slesvic
Conrad Roves, Dominus Rosenstein, Margrav. in Croatia
Prince Rupert
Dr. Sackville
Earl of Sandwich
J. Slegelius
Sir Rob. Southwell
Bishop Sprat
Princeps Sultsbergensis
Dr. Tanckmarus
J. Tradescant
Dr. Wilkins
Dr. Willis
Dr. Witherly
Sir Henry Wotton
Sir Christopher Wren

[53] Massachusetts Historical Society, Proceedings, 1st Series, xvi. 229, 230.

come. . . . . you will take notice . . . . how the variation varies in New England . . . [54]

The next year Oldenburg wrote to thank Winthrop for a collection of curiosities sent to the Society with a written account of them:

SIR,—Y^r^ Kinsman, Mr. Adam Winthrop, hath acquitted himself faithfully of ye trust you had reposed in him, in delivering into my hands both y^r^ letter and ye American Curiosities accompanying the same. . . . . His Maj^ty^ himselfe, hearing of some of ye rarer things, would see y^m^, and accordingly the Extraordinary Fish, the dwarf-oaks, ye gummy fragrant Barke, wth knobbs, ye silken podds, ye baggs wth litle shells in them, etc., were carried to Whitehall, ... [55]

Winthrop's account of these things was published soon after in the Transactions of the Society, with drawings of some of the curiosities including the "extraordinary fish," which was a starfish.

In a letter to Henry Oldenburg written November 12, 1668, Winthrop mentioned sending seeds, roots, and such things to Robert Boyle, Lord Brereton, Charles Howard, Dr. Goddard, Dr. Merret, Dr. Whistler, Dr. Benjamin Worsley, and Dr. Keffler.[56]

John Davenport also seems to have been interested in science, for he too was corresponding with Hartlib, receiving from him "bookes, & written papers . . . . wherein I finde sundry rarities of inventions. . . . . you [Winthrop] will finde some particularities among them, which may be advantagious to your private proffit, in the improvement of your Fishers Island."[57] The last clause would indicate that some of these books and papers were on Hartlib's favorite subject, scientific farming. In another letter to Winthrop,

54 *Ibid.*, xvi. 239, 242. The undated letter was received May 6, 1669. See p. 48, n. 100, above.

55 *Ibid.*, xvi. 244. Letter dated March 26, 1670.

56 Winthrop Papers, iv. 129.

57 *Ibid.*, ii. 504. See p. 47, above.

given on page 56, above, Davenport mentions four scientific books as "a few of many more which are sent to me." These may have been from Hartlib.

Thomas Shepard thanked Winthrop for copies of the Transactions of the Royal Society, which he had passed on to others to enjoy,[58] and in the same letter reported some astronomical observations.

Besides all these who had a true interest in science (and the list could be extended, did more data survive), Connecticut boasted one genuine alchemist. Jonathan Brewster, who was glad to borrow books on chemistry from Winthrop, and willing to lend his own in return,[59] was searching to find the true elixir. He reported to Winthrop that the latter's books had been of great service to him, enabling him to understand some operations "which before I understode not, ... as the head of the Crowe, Vergines milke, &c." With this help he felt sure that his elixir, already well started, would be perfected in five years, provided that the Indians did not burn down his house or otherwise interfere with his work.[60] If the statement of Secretary Mortimer is accurate, it was only chance which prevented the founding of a colony of experimental scientists in Connecticut, to keep Winthrop and Brewster company. He writes:[61]

In Concert with these [Boyle, Wilkins, Oldenburg] and other learned Friends, (as he often revisited *England*) he was one of those, who first form'd the Plan of the *Royal Society;* and had not the Civil Wars happily ended as they did, Mr. *Boyle* and Dr. *Wilkins*, with several other learned Men, would have left *England*, and, out of Esteem for the most excellent and valuable Governor, JOHN WINTHROP, the younger, would have retir'd to his new-born Colony, and there have establish'd that *Society for promoting Natural Knowledge*, which these Gentlemen had formed, as it were, in *Embryo* among themselves; but which after-

[58] See letter on p. 57, above.
[59] See letter on p. 56, above.
[60] Winthrop Papers, ii. 79.
[61] Philosophical Transactions of the Royal Society of London, xl. Dedication.

wards receiving the Protection of King CHARLES II. obtain'd the style of ROYAL . . . .

Robert Boyle, member of the Royal Society and at one time its president, and, with the possible exception of Sir Isaac Newton, the most representative English scientist of his day, also had considerable correspondence with the leading men of New England. This was not primarily scientific, however, but rather missionary in character, Boyle being for years Governor of the Corporation for the Spread of the Gospel in New England.[62]

There were other links between the colonists and the men in active life in England. Sir Thomas Temple, proprietor of Nova Scotia (together with Colonel William Crowne), resided here for several years during the Interregnum, acquiring property and business interests, part of which he sold in 1653 for £5500.[63] At about this time John Crowne, "Starch Johnny" Crowne (son of Colonel William), poet and dramatist of the Restoration period, was living in Boston. He resided for a time, at least, (about 1660) with the Reverend John Norton, and studied at Harvard.[64]

It would seem certain, then, that the inhabitants of New England, during the first half century of their colonization, were able, as far as they desired, to keep in touch with political, scientific, and literary men and activities in England; and that, beyond any other of England's colonies, at any time in her history, during the period of colonization, they felt a desire for these things. Their life may have been simple, or even rough; luxuries or comforts may have been lacking; but there is no evidence of any lack of intellectual eagerness or of the means to satisfy such eagerness.

62 Dictionary of National Biography.

63 Massachusetts Historical Society, Collections, 1st Series, vii. 229, and manuscript copy of the deed in the Ewer MSS., in the library of the New England Historical and Genealogical Society. It is Sir Thomas who is said to have told Charles II that the tree on the pine-tree shilling was the royal oak which had preserved His Majesty's life at Worcester, thereby turning away the King's anger at the colonists for daring to coin money without the King's consent.

64 Calendar of State Papers, Colonial Series, America and West Indies. 1661–1668. No. 161, p. 54.

Chapter IV: Other Phases of Culture.

THE early settlers of New England were not only well educated and furnished with libraries, but in many cases came from families of distinction and even of title, and brought with them considerable wealth. Among those who came with John Winthrop in 1630 were Isaac Johnson and his wife, the Lady Arbella, sister to the Earl of Lincoln. These two did not live long enough to influence the life of the colony, but that they desired to come is significant. Three years later the Lady Arbella's sister, Lady Susan, and her husband, John Humfrey, joined the colonists.[1] Lady Alice Apsley Boteler, widow of Lord John Boteler and daughter of Sir Edward Apsley of Sussex, married Mr. George Fenwick just before he embarked for America, and accompanied him to Connecticut.[2] Sir Richard Saltonstall also boasted a title, and was the son of a Lord Mayor of London.[3] John Winthrop had been a magistrate and man of affairs in England, and his father, Adam Winthrop, was also a magistrate and, for a number of years, auditor of Trinity College, Cambridge.[4] Edward Johnson, town clerk of Woburn and author of "The Wonder-Working Providence," was the son of the parish clerk of St. George's, Canterbury, and possessed a considerable estate in Canterbury and elsewhere in Kent.[5] Thomas Dudley had been steward for the Earl of Lincoln and managed the large estate successfully.[6] Simon Bradstreet, Dudley's son-in-law, had succeeded him in the management of the

[1] Winthrop's Journal, i. 127.

[2] Steiner, History of Guilford and Madison, p. 22.

[3] Winthrop's Journal, i. 25 note.

[4] Diary of Adam Winthrop, in the Life and Letters of John Winthrop, i. 405 ff.

[5] Jameson, Johnson's Wonder-Working Providence, p. 5.

[6] Magnalia, i. 133.

affairs of the Earl of Lincoln, and later had been steward for the Countess of Warwick.[7] Governor William Leet of Connecticut was by education a lawyer, and by employment a register in the Bishop's court.[8] John Wilson was a grandnephew of Edmund Grindal, Archbishop of Canterbury.[9] Mrs. Anne Hutchinson was second cousin to the poet Dryden.[10] President Chauncy's wife was granddaughter of Bishop Still.[11] President Hoar married a daughter of Lord Lisle, one of the Judges of Charles I.[12] Theophilus Eaton had been employed by the King of England as envoy to the King of Denmark, and had been successful in business as a member of the East Land Company.[13] The list might be extended to considerable length, but one quotation will perhaps be sufficient to show the type of people who helped to settle New England. Speaking of one town, and that not one of the largest, Scituate, Deane writes:

> Many of the fathers were men of good education and easy fortune, who had left homes altogether enviable, save in the single circumstance of the abridgment of their religious liberty. In 1639, this town contained more men of distinguished talents and fair fortune than it has at any period since. They were "the men of Kent," celebrated in English history as men of gallantry, loyalty and courtly manners. Gilson, Vassall, Hatherly, Cudworth, Tilden, Hoar, Foster, Stedman, Saffin, Hinckley, and others had been accustomed to the elegancies of life of England.[14]

There are numerous evidences of wealth among the pioneers. John Winthrop had sufficient property so that the mismanagement and defalcation of his steward to the amount of over £2000 did not ruin him, although it was a

[7] Ellis edition, The Works of Anne Bradstreet, p. xxii.
[8] Magnalia, i. 156.
[9] Winthrop's Journal, i. 51 note 3.
[10] New England Historical and Genealogical Register, xx. 366.
[11] *Ibid.*, x. 253.
[12] Massachusetts Historical Society, Collections, 1st Series, vi. 100 note.
[13] Magnalia, i. 151; Winthrop's Journal, i. 223 note.
[14] Quoted by Chaplin, Life of Henry Dunster, p. 205.

great loss.[15] John Harvard left an estate of £1600, besides his books.[16] Thomas Flint brought with him an estate of £2000.[17] Peter Bulkeley brought £6000.[18] William Tyng, dying in 1653, left a property inventoried at £2774.14.04.[19] The estate of Henry Webb, inventoried September 25, 1660, amounted to £7819.[20] Edward Breck "died in the year 1662, leaving an estate, the value of which ran into hundreds of pounds sterling, a large sum for his day."[21] The

[15] Life and Letters, ii. 253; also Massachusetts Historical Society, Collections, 4th Series, vii. 224 ff. In considering the question of wealth in the colonies, the difference in the value or purchasing power of money must be kept in mind. The highest salary paid to any minister around Boston in 1657, according to a report made by a special committee to the General Court, was £100, and the average of the twelve listed in the report was £65, only three out of the twelve receiving over £60. The families to be supported on these salaries averaged seven in number. Some had farms in addition to the salary, but they could hope for no other income, as marriages they considered a civil function, to be performed only by the magistrates. The cost of labor also illustrates the high value of money at that time. A report to the General Court of Connecticut in 1680, signed by William Leet, Governor, and John Allen, Secretary of the Colony, complains that "labour is dear, being from 2*s* to 2*s*6 a day for a labourer." (Massachusetts Historical Society, Collections, 1st Series, iv. 222.) Evidently labor had been cheaper in the early days of the colony; but accepting this figure, and comparing it with present (1916 pre-war) prices of from $1.50 to $2.50 for unskilled labor, we get a ratio of about four to one. An estate of £1000 then would thus be equivalent to one of $20,000 today, and John Eliot's £60 salary as pastor of the church at Roxbury would amount to $1200. As the Connecticut report also quotes pork at 3d a pound, beef at 2¼d, and butter at 6d, the ratio of four to one does not seem too high. F. B. Dexter (Proceedings of the American Antiquarian Society, xviii. 137) calls £300 equivalent to perhaps six or seven thousand dollars with us.

[16] Thomas Shepard's Autobiography, p. 63.

[17] Peter Bulkeley wrote (to whom is not known, as the name is missing from the letter), "I . . . . do further entreat you would please, both of you, to take into consideration the condition of Mrs. Flint, the widow of worthy Mr. Flint deceased, who served in the same office of magistrate many years, and never received of the country any recompense. . . . . And some things there are which may persuade on this side more effectually, both in regard of a great family of children, and the great decay of his estate which he brought into this country, (being about £2000,). . . . " (Massachusetts Historical Society, Collections, 3rd Series, i. 47.)

[18] New England Historical and Genealogical Register, xxxi. 155.

[19] *Ibid.*, xxx. 432.

[20] *Ibid.*, x. 180.

[21] Dr. Edward Breck in Publications of the Colonial Society of Massachusetts, xiv. 49 ff. He adds, "It is significant of the degree of refinement obtaining among

Reverend John Norton's estate was appraised, April 24, 1663, at £2095.[22] The Reverend John Wilson left £419 in addition to a farm valued at £1300.[23] John Endicott's estate, 1665, totalled £2269.[24] John Bracket was worth £1021, according to inventory of February 22, 1666;[25] and the same year Henry Shrimpton, brasier, left assets of £11,979, and debts to the amount of £5743.[26] The estate of Hezekiah Usher, who died in 1676, was appraised at £15,358.[27] These are just some of the larger estates, and the Suffolk and Essex Probate Records contain many inventories of estates appraised between £500 and £1000.

There is further interesting testimony in regard to the existence of men of wealth in New England in the sarcastic reference to them made by John Josselyn, an English merchant, in his account of his two voyages to New England:

> The grose *Goddons*, or great masters, as also some of their Merchants are damnable rich; generally all of their judgement, inexplicably covetous and proud.[28]

Elsewhere he wrote of Boston as it was in 1663:

> The buildings are handsome, joyning one to the other as in London; with many large streets, most of them paved with pebble stone. In the high street towards the Common, there are fair buildings, some of stone; and, at the east end of the town, one amongst the rest, built by the shore by Mr. Gibs, a merchant,

even the earliest pioneers of New England [Breck came in 1635], that in the inventory of Edward Breck's estate occurs the mention of a bath-tub."

[22] New England Historical and Genealogical Register, xi. 344.

[23] *Ibid.*, xvii. 344.

[24] *Ibid.*, xv. 128. This inventory, as perhaps some of the others, includes farm lands; but as one farm of 550 acres is appraised at just £550, I do not think the inventories are "padded" with undeveloped land.

[25] *Ibid.*, xv. 250.

[26] *Ibid.*, xv. 78. The expenditure for his funeral amounted to £134.05.06 ($2500.00 in modern equivalent). It must have been an elaborate ceremonial to have cost that much!

[27] Littlefield, Early Boston Booksellers, p. 68.

[28] Josselyn, Two Voyages to New England, p. 180.

being a stately edifice, which it is thought will stand him in little less than £3,000 before it be fully finished.[29]

In the matter of wealth, as in other things already noted, Plymouth was far behind the rest of New England. Estates above £500 were rare, and £200–£300 was the usual figure, as will be seen by reference to pages 28 and 29, above.

The settlers of New England, then, were not without some wealth, just as they were not without either libraries or means of education. And they possessed one other element of culture at a surprisingly early period in their history: a printing-press was brought over and set up at Cambridge in 1638, before Boston was ten years old.[30] This may not seem at all remarkable until we compare Cambridge with other cities both in England and in other colonies. Printing was begun in Glasgow one year later than in Cambridge. It was first practiced in Rochester in 1648, or ten years later, and at Exeter in 1668, thirty years later. There was no printing in Manchester until 1732, and none in Liverpool until after 1750.[31] The first press in Pennsylvania[32] was William Bradford's, established about 1686. Bradford moved to New York in 1693 to establish the first press there.[33] A press was running in Virginia in 1682, but was quickly suppressed, there being no further printing in that colony until 1729.[34] There was no press in Canada until 1751, when Bartholomew Green, Jr., brought one from Boston to Halifax.[35] Another was es-

[29] Josselyn, New England's Rarities Discovered, p. 1. $60,000 (in modern equivalent) for a house!

[30] Massachusetts Historical Society, Collections, 4th Series, vi. 99.

[31] Truebner, Bibliographical Guide to American Literature, p. ix.

[32] Thomas, History of Printing, i. 208. The Quakers, like the Puritans, showed their interest in books by the early establishment of a press, within five years of the granting of the charter.

[33] *Ibid.*, i. 291.

[34] *Ibid.*, i. 331. In 1671 Governor Berkeley remarked, "I thank God we have not free schools nor printing." (*Ibid.*, i. 330.)

[35] *Ibid.*, i. 357.

tablished in Quebec in 1764, and one in Montreal in 1775.[36] One press did not satisfy New England long, for a second press was established in 1674, in Boston, followed by several others before 1700, and one was set up at New London in 1709.[37] Some of the productions of the New England presses will be discussed in the following and later chapters.

[36] *Ibid.*, i. 362; Truebner, Bibliographical Guide, p. viii.
[37] Thomas, History of Printing, i. 184.

Chapter V: The Production of Literature.

AS the preceding chapters have shown that the culture of New England in its earlier years did not differ greatly from that of England during the same period, it is necessary to discuss and explain the seeming inferiority of New England's literature to contemporary English literature. To do this it will be necessary not only to consider the literary production of the colonists,—its kind, its extent, and its quality,—but also to compare it with that of the English Puritans and account for such actual differences as are found.

An indication of the nature of the literary activity during this period may be obtained from the following tabulation of the output of the press at Cambridge from its establishment through the year 1670.[1]

Total number of publications	157
Almanacs (many contained verse)	26
Books in the Indian language	19
Religious books (prose)	58
Religious books (verse)	5
Lists of Harvard theses	12
Laws and official publications	22
School books	3
Poetry	4
History, Biography, etc.	8

This list, however, fails to give an accurate impression of the extent of their production of books. It must be remembered that the colonists thought of themselves as Englishmen primarily,[2] and in any important book would wish to

[1] These figures are based upon the list of publications given in Evans' American Bibliography.

[2] See pp. 62, 63, above.

address their countrymen who still lived in England as much as, if not more than, their New England neighbors. All books before the press was established at Cambridge in 1638, and the more important books after that time, were sent to London for publication. Roger Williams' "The Bloody Tenet of Persecution for Cause of Conscience," written by Williams while visiting in London, was published there in 1644. A copy soon reached the library of John Cotton in Boston, who saw fit to reply to it. The reply, "The Bloody Tenet washed and made white in the Blood of the Lamb," was sent to London, where it appeared in 1647. When this reached Williams in Rhode Island he wrote a second book to reply to Cotton's argument, "The Bloody Tenet yet more Bloody, by Mr. Cotton's Endeavor to wash it white in the Blood of the Lamb." This also crossed the ocean for publication in 1652. Thus did men living within fifty miles of each other argue over a range of six thousand miles because they were writing for all Englishmen to read. Similarly, elegies and books of religious verse for local use, such as "The Bay Psalm Book," were printed at Cambridge; but the first volume of poetry written with literary intent, Anne Bradstreet's "The Tenth Muse, lately sprung up in America," was sent to London for publication in 1650.

To the productions of the press at Cambridge, then, must be added the many books published abroad. These were fewer in number, but really amounted to more, since many of the Cambridge volumes were merely sermons, or thin pamphlets, whereas the books sent to England were generally full-fledged books.

Religious books were numerous among those printed in England, but were perhaps exceeded by a class of books almost unknown to the Cambridge press, descriptions of America or of life in America. These range from such discussions of the natural history of the region as Wood's "New England's Prospect" and Josselyn's "New England's Rarities Discovered," to such defenses against those who published unfavorable reports of conditions, either physical, political, or religious, in New England as Winslow's "Good News from New England" and Johnson's "Wonder-Working Providence."

To the products of the presses on both sides of the ocean certain other writings must be added if we are to get a fair estimate of the activity of New England pens during these years. Several books, among them some which rank highest in modern estimates of the period, were not printed until years or even centuries had passed. Such are Bradford's "History of Plymouth Plantations," Winthrop's "Journal,"[3] and Mason's account of his fight with the Pequots at Mystic. Considerable verse also escaped publication, some until Cotton Mather wrote his "Magnalia Christi," and more until antiquarian interest set people to hunting through ancestral records.

In quantity, it is evident, the literary output of the early colonists was considerable. Its quality is less marked, how much less depending upon the standards by which it is tested. Tested in comparison with the best which England produced in the seventeenth century, it is certainly deficient. Tested in comparison with the bulk of the writings of English Puritans during the same period, its deficiency is not very marked. Surely the latter test is the fairer one, and William Prynne a more typical author with whom to compare the New Englander than John Milton.

If we eliminate poetry from the discussion, the best that New England produced is not greatly inferior to Milton's work. In Governor Winthrop's "Journal" there are many eloquent passages, in spite of the fact that much of it was evidently written in great haste at odd moments. Governor Bradford's style in his "History" is remarkably simple and direct, and the same may be said of Winslow's in his narratives.[4] Roger Williams and John Winthrop, Jr., also wrote

[3] Sometimes called Winthrop's History of New England. This was first printed in part in 1790, and as a whole in 1825. Bradford's History was printed in 1856.

[4] It must be remembered that Dryden was the first to write a prose which can

effective prose. As for religious literature, it is impossible to distinguish between that produced in the colony and in the mother country, partly because so many of the leading divines preached and published their sermons with equal satisfaction to hearers and readers in either country. That so many books written in New England were published in London is further evidence that a voyage to America did not affect either the ability or the popularity of a writer. If no great literature was produced by the Puritans in New England, it may be not because they were in New England, but because little great literature was produced by the Puritans anywhere.

It is only when we turn to conscious literature, to belles-lettres and especially to poetry, that we find any decided inferiority in New England. Milton, Marvell, and Wither have no rivals there, although the worst of Wither has perhaps nothing to distinguish it from the better colonial poems. But we must not forget that to compare Anne Bradstreet with Milton may be unfair; it would seem more just to compare her with Mrs. Katharine Philips (Orinda), her English contemporary. If it is true that Mrs. Bradstreet is remembered only as a curiosity of American literature, it seems just as true that Mrs. Philips is not remembered at all. This is not to imply that the poetry of Mrs. Bradstreet or of her neighbors is good poetry, but to warn the reader against the common tendency to rate it lower than it deserves in comparison with the general output of Puritan poetry in England at the same time.

Funeral elegies were a custom of the time, a custom faithfully observed in both New and Old England.[5] Of English

be called modern, that is, which does not seem somewhat strange to a modern ear, and that his first separate prose publication, the Essay of Dramatic Poesy, did not appear until 1668, practically at the end of the period under discussion.

[5] Samuel Stone of Hartford wrote to Thomas Shepard of Cambridge, July 19, 1647, "If I have the whole winter, you may think whether it may not be comely for you & myselfe & some other Elders to make a few verses for Mr. Hooker & inscribe them in the begin[g] of his book, as if they had been his funerall verses." (Mather Papers, p. 546.)

elegies of the period most of us know only "Lycidas" and perhaps Marvell's "Poem upon the Death of his Late Highness the Lord Protector," and when we read the colonial elegies we compare them with these, forgetting that these are quite exceptional. And the fact that the colonial elegies (because so many of them were preserved for us by Morton in his "New England's Memorial" and by Cotton Mather in his "Magnalia Christi," whereas much fugitive poetry undoubtedly perished) form an abnormally large part of the whole body of colonial poetry gives us a false impression of the whole. It might be fairer to disregard them entirely in our estimates of colonial poetry, as we practically do disregard the English elegies of the same period when we consider English poetry of the seventeenth century.[6] But if we must consider them, let us compare them with similar elegies produced in England. The colonial ministers wrote elegies not because they felt themselves to be poets, but because it was the fitting way to pay tribute. English ministers did the same for the same reason. Did they succeed any better? To get some answer to this question, I examined the works of an English Puritan divine, well known and popular both as a preacher and as a writer and perhaps typical, to see whether he ever attempted verse or not. I discovered that Richard Baxter had not only written but published a volume of verse which went through three editions in the seventeenth century, and was reprinted in 1821. One of the first poems I read was an elegy, part of which I venture to copy here for comparison with one of the colonial elegies which Professor Tyler[7] used as an example of the "elaborate

[6] Who ever reads the other elegies to Edward King published with Lycidas? No criticism of colonial verse is more severe than Professor Masson's remark (Globe ed. Milton, p. 432), "All the more striking must it have been for a reader who had toiled through the trash of the preceding twelve pieces (I have read them one and all, and will vouch that they *are* trash) to come at length upon this opening of a true poem:—

'Yet once more, O ye laurels . . . . '"

[7] A History of American Literature, i. 269.

and painful jests" and the "ingenuities of allusion" which characterized them.

Upon the Sight of Mr. VINES his Posthumous Treatise on the Sacrament, Octob. 18, 1656. who dyed a little before.

While thou grew'st here, thy fruit made glad
The hearts that sin and death made sad:
Lest we would surfeit of thy fruit,
Thy Life retired to the root.
Desiring with us first to keep,
A Passover before thy sleep:*
Weary of Earth, thou took'st thine Ease,
Passing into the land of Peace:
The threatned Evil we foresee,
But hope to hide our selves with Thee.
Though thou art gone, while we must fight,
We'll call it *Victory*, not *Fight.*
When God hath taken up this VINE,
We thought no more to taste its Wine,
Till in the Land of *Salem's* King,
We drink it new, even from the Spring:
But unexpectedly we find,
Some Clusters which are left behind:
This Mantle from thy Chariot fell;
We know it by the pleasant smell:
Who knows but from this little seed
Some more such fruitful *Vines* may breed?
The *Tree of Death* bears precious Fruit,
Though in the Earth it have no Root.

. . . . . .

The Soul imboided [imbodied] in those Lines,
Doth make us say, that, This is VINES:
And if our Hearts with you could be;
Our Lord would say, that there are we.
But as according to desert,
The Heavens have got thy better part;

* He dyed suddenly on the Lords Day at night, after he had Preacht and Administred the Sacrament. [Author's note.]

And left us but some of the Wine,
Whilst they have taken up the *Vine:*
So we look up, and wait, and pray,
And yet still feel, we live in Clay.
Here we are keeping sin's account,
While some small sparks do upward mount,
Crying "How long, Holy and True."
Till we are taken up to you.
Thus also we must follow LOVE*,
To find our HEAD and LIFE above.
He that is made by the New-Birth,
A *Burges* of the Church on Earth,
And then by Faith can rise so high,
In Divine LOVE to live and die,
Shall be translated to your soil,
Remov'd from sin, and fear, and toil;
And from this House of Worms & Moles
Unto that Element of Souls.
Where every Branch becomes a VINE;
And where these clods like stars will shine
God is not there known by the Book!
You need not there the pruning-hook:
There you have Wine without the Press;
And God his praise without distress.

. . . . .

A Threnodia upon our churches second dark eclipse, happening July 20, 1663, by death's interposition between us and that great light and divine plant, Mr. Samuel Stone, late of Hartford, in New England.[8]

Last spring this summer may be autumn styl'd,
Sad withering fall our beauties which despoil'd;
Two choicest plants, our Norton and our Stone,

* Mr. A. *Burgesse* was Minister at *Lawrence* Church: Mr. *Love* succeeded him, and was beheaded by the Remnant of the Long Parliament, which cut off the K. for sending Money to some about the present King. Mr. *Vines* succeeded him. [Author's note.]

[8] Chronicles of the Pilgrim Fathers, p. 197.

Your justs threw down; remov'd, away are gone.
One year brought Stone and Norton to their mother,
In one year, April, July, them did smother.
Dame Cambridge, mother to this darling son;
Emanuel, Northampt' that heard this one,
Essex, our bay, Hartford, in sable clad,
Come bear your parts in this Threnodia sad.
In losing one, church many lost: O then
Many for one come be sad singing men.
May nature, grace and art be found in one
So high, as to be found in few or none.
In him these three with full fraught hand contested,
With which by each he should be most invested.
The largest of the three, it was so great
On him, the stone was held a light compleat,
A stone more than the Ebenezer fam'd;
Stone splendent diamond, right orient nam'd;
A cordial stone, that often cheered hearts
With pleasant wit, with Gospel rich imparts;
Whetstone, that edgify'd th' obtusest mind;
Loadstone, that drew the iron heart unkind;
A pond'rous stone, that would the bottom sound
Of Scripture depths, and bring out Arcan's found;
A stone for kingly David's use so fit,
As would not fail Goliah's front to hit;
A stone, an antidote, that brake the course
Of gangrene error, by convincing force;
A stone acute, fit to divide and square;
A squared stone became Christ's building rare.
A Peter's living, lively stone (so reared)
As 'live was Hartford's life; dead, death is fear'd.
In Hartford old, Stone first drew infant breath,
In New, effused his last; O there beneath
His corps are laid, near to his darling brother,[9]
Of whom dead oft he sighed, Not such another.
Heaven is the more desirable, said he,
For Hooker, Shepard, and Hayne's company.

E. B.*

[9] Thomas Hooker, Stone's colleague, had died in 1647.
* Supposed to be Edward Bulkley.

Both poems are unquestionably bad, and for the same chief cause, the tendency to overdo the fantastic. Of the two, I do not feel that the colonial poem is the worse, for it seems to me that it has more form and that the playing upon the word *stone* is better managed and more effective than that upon the word *vine*.

In another and even humbler form of verse, that which appeared in the almanacs of the day, a form generally, and perhaps deservedly, neglected by students of literature, the colonial writers were also not inferior to those of the mother country. A comparison of the incomplete file of seventeenth century British almanacs in the Massachusetts Historical Society library with the almanacs published in Massachusetts during the period under discussion, shows that more colonial almanacs in proportion contain verse, that they average more lines of verse per almanac, and that in general this verse exhibits more originality. No New England almanac maker found it necessary to repeat, with slight changes, the verses which he had used the year before, as Edward Pond did in his almanac for 1611, nor to reprint verse which he had used over twenty years before, as Ralph Partridge in 1705 drew upon his own "Merlinus Redivivus" of 1684. Most of the verse on both sides of the water is mechanical rhyming upon the trite topics of the changing seasons, the influence of signs of the zodiac, astrological advice, or the possibilities of the coming year. Three of the American almanacs, however, show some originality. Samuel Danforth's "An Almanack for the Year of our Lord 1649" contains an eighty-eight line poem followed by an eight line prognostication, the whole planned to fit the almanac with eight lines at the head of each month. The poem is an elaborate and not ineffective (though not very poetical) allegorical account of the settlement of New England and the trials of the colonists. Hurricanes, Indian uprisings, the "antinomian" errors of Mrs. Hutchinson, plagues of pigeons and army worms, and even echoes of the troubles in England, are brought into this account of the "Orphan" driven from "England's armes" into the wilderness. Josiah Flint's "Almanack" for 1666 contains a history of the Jews in rhyme. John Richardson's "Almanack" for 1670 furnishes an example of a quality generally lacking in colonial literature —humor. "The Countryman's Apocrypha," as the main poem is called, is a satire upon the vulgar belief in and love of marvels. The satire is exaggerated and the humor is blunt;[10] but there is nothing trite or conventional about the poem. Neither English nor colonial almanacs printed selections from real poetry at this time; that custom was not established until the second quarter of the eighteenth century. Those who depended upon the annual almanac for their literature had meager fare; but they were at no disadvantage if they lived in New England.

In attempting to determine the quality of the literature produced by the people of New England it must not be forgotten that in so far as they were consciously writing, they were writing for their contemporaries, and that, in consequence, it should be judged by their standards. To us

[10] The following lines are characteristic:

The Moon is habitable, some averre;
And that some Creatures have their Dwelling there;
Judge what you please; but yet 'tis very true,
This year the Moon a Pair of Horns *will shew.*

The satire at the expense of the ignorant aroused the ire of Samuel Bailey of Little Compton, who wrote in reply The College Ferula, the almanac, printed at Cambridge, being considered a college product. Bailey's poem, sent to John Whipple, town clerk of Providence, lay hidden in manuscript among the town records until 1840. It is a better poem than the other. It concludes:

These are grave sophisters, that are in schools
So wise they think their aged fathers, fools
That plough and cart; and such they are indeed
Or else they would not work so hard, to breed
Their boys to flout them; but I cannot stay
Foddering of asses thus; I must away
And give my sheep their breakfast, who, I fear,
Wait at the stack, while I write verses here.

The entire poem is printed in the New England Historical and Genealogical Register, ix. 356.

much that they wrote seems absurd, and such effusions as "The Bay Psalm Book" and Wigglesworth's "The Day of Doom" are held up for ridicule in almost every history or collection of American literature. Yet contemporary England found nothing absurd in them. "The Day of Doom" was twice reprinted in England,[11] and "The Bay Psalm Book" passed through eighteen editions in England, the last in 1754, and twenty-two editions in Scotland, the last in 1759.[12] The latter was popular in the mother country long after Tate and Brady's version had supplanted it in some of the New England churches.[13] Perhaps New England taste was not abnormal or even peculiar; perhaps it is only the popular taste of seventeenth century England on either side of the water which seems so strange, and which, met almost solely in the poetry of New England (since few read the equivalent poetry written in England, there being so much that is better), gives us a false impression of colonial taste and literary culture.

We expect too much of early New England literature, then, if we attempt to compare it solely with the best of contemporary literature; and we are also unfair to New England when we compare its production with that of all England—the colony in its earliest years with the mother country. It would be fairer to compare the colonies with some district of England,—to compare Boston in New Eng-

[11] At London in 1673, and at Newcastle in 1711.

[12] Truebner, Bibliographical Guide to American Literature, p. viii. Thomas Prince wrote in the preface to the version of 1758, "I found in England it was by some eminent Congregations prefer'd to all Others in their Publick Worship, even down to 1717, when I last left that Part of the British Kingdom." (Sewall's Diary, iii. 16 note.)

[13] "A sing lecture att y[e] north Brick. Mr. Coleman preached from those words "They sung a new song" . . . Sung Tate & Brady 4 psalms . . ." (Diary of Jeremiah Bumstead, September 21, 1722, in the New England Historical and Genealogical Register, xv. 196.) An edition of Tate and Brady's Psalms, "for the use of her Majesty's Chapel in America," was published at Boston in 1713. (Thomas, History of Printing, ii. 367.) Copies of the English version were on sale in Boston as early as 1700, five copies being listed in the inventory of the estate of Michael Perry, Bookseller. (Ford, The Boston Book Market, p. 176.)

land and the district around it with Boston in Old England and the surrounding county of Lincolnshire. Thomas Fuller in his Lincolnshire section of "The Worthies of England" mentions the following as writers since the Reformation: Edmund Sheffeild, Peter Morwing, Anthony Gilby, John Fox, Dr. Thomas Sparks, Dr. Tighe, and Fines Morison. The editor of the 1840 edition of the "Worthies" adds a list of writers since Fuller's time. The only names in that list which come within the period of the entire first century of colonial life are Susannah Centlivre and Sir Charles Cotterell, the translator of "Cassandra." Such limited literary activity as these names represent would not indicate that New England was, by comparison, sterile soil for literature.

The preceding attempt to determine a fair standard by which to judge of the quality of colonial writings partly explains why the early colonists did not produce a finer literature than they did; they were producing the literature which, in general, their class in England produced. The earlier chapters have shown that their education and literary culture were not greatly affected by their removal to a new land. For just that reason their literary activity was little affected by their change. If no fine poetry was produced, it was because the Puritans had few poets of ability and of them none chose to come to New England. Poets of little ability seem to have been uninfluenced by emigration. John Wilson wrote much poor poetry in New England; but there seems to be no evidence that the volume which he published in England in 1626 before he came contained any better poetry. If a poet of real ability had come to Boston, he would not have ceased to be a poet. If John Milton, for instance, had been driven over by the Restoration, I see no reason why he could not have developed "Paradise Lost" as well as in England. There is a possibility that the busy life of a young colony might in some cases have militated somewhat against the production of poetry, but that would not have affected Milton, whose blindness would have ensured to him the leisure necessary for his work.

The really remarkable thing about the literature of New England in its earliest days is that there is as much of it as there is, and that it is as good as it is. There were certainly many things which might have hampered and probably did hamper literary work. The lack of leisure time, already mentioned, might have hindered some, although the ministers and some of the wealthier men would have been free from this handicap. The necessity of sending all material, at first, to England for publication, and of sending much even after a press was established at Cambridge, may have been a restraining influence. Still another was the rigid censorship of the colonial press, little used during this period, as far as the records show, but nevertheless always in existence, as shown by the fining of Marmaduke Johnson for printing without authority in 1668,[14] and by the stopping of a partially printed edition of Thomas à Kempis in 1669.[15] The narrowness of some of the leaders may have had a repressing influence upon freedom of expression.[16] There was no literary circle for the mutual encouragement of those who might be interested in the production of literature, and no

[14] Johnson, associated with Bartholomew Green at the Cambridge Press, printed without authority The Isle of Pines, a pamphlet of the Baron Munchausen order, already popular in England. For this offence he was fined £5. (Massachusetts Historical Society, Proceedings, 2d Series, xi. 247–249.)

[15] "The Court, being informed that there is now in the presse, reprinting, a booke, tit̃ Imitac̃ons of Christ, or to y[t] purpose, written by Thomas a Kempis, a Popish minister, wherein is conteyned some things that are less safe to be infused among the people of this place, doe comend it to the licensers of the press, the more full revisall thereof, & that in the meane tjme there be no further progresse in that worke." (Massachusetts Colony Records, iv. Part II, p. 424.) As no copy of an Imitatio Christi printed in New England at this time has ever been discovered, the licensers evidently decided that suppression was preferable to revision. (Diary of Cotton Mather, ii. 582 note.)

[16] Thomas Shepard found it necessary to write to Governor Winthrop, "Your apprehensions agaynst reading & learning heathen authors, I perswade myselfe were suddenly suggested, & will easily be answered by B: Dunstar, if yow should impart them to him." (Winthrop Papers, ii. 272.)

sufficient home market for any work of a purely artistic nature. In spite of all this, a great deal was written, and a large part of what was written was in the form of verse. Professor Tyler remarks,[17] with perhaps unnecessary sarcasm, upon the almost universal tendency to attempt to write verse. If they did not succeed in writing much good verse, it was not for lack of effort. That they wrote some real poetry must be acknowledged.[18]

It seems safe to conclude that the early New England colonists wrote more than they would have written had they remained in England, and that the quality of their work was not lowered by their removal, or by any lack of opportunities for culture in the new home.

[17] History of American Literature, i. 267.

[18] Anne Bradstreet's Contemplations and some of her shorter pieces, Wigglesworth's Vanity of Vanities and certain stanzas of The Day of Doom, Edward Johnson's From Silent Night, True Register of Moans, are instances of poems which have poetic merit.

Part II:

The End of the Seventeenth Century.

1670-1700.

Chapter VI: Education.

WHEN President Charles Chauncy of Harvard died in 1672, the college ceased to be in the control of those who had been educated in England, and was managed thereafter by its own graduates. Leonard Hoar, his successor, had taken his first degree at Harvard in 1650, and his three successors, Urian Oakes, John Rogers, and Increase Mather, had graduated there, the first two in 1649, and the third in 1656.[1] The change seems to have had little effect upon the quality of the work done in the college, partly, perhaps, because even before this Harvard graduates, as tutors, had done much of the teaching.[2] Another reason for the slight effect of the change may have been that three of the four successors of President Chauncy had either studied or lived in England after finishing their courses at Harvard. Leonard Hoar went to England in 1653 and preached for some time at Wanstead. He later studied medicine at Cambridge, taking the degree of Doctor of Medicine in 1671.[3] While living in England he married the daughter of Lord Lisle.[4] Urian Oakes went to England soon after graduating, and there became pastor of a church at Titchfield. Being silenced at the Restoration, he accepted the call of the church at Cambridge, Massachusetts, and was soon after chosen President.[5] Increase Mather studied at Trinity College, Dublin, gaining the Master's

[1] Magnalia, ii. 30.

[2] *Ibid., passim.* George Downing and John Bulkly, Harvard 1642, had been the first tutors.

[3] Massachusetts Historical Society, Collections, 1st Series, vi. 100 note; Magnalia, ii. 14.

[4] *Ibid.* Mrs. Hoar's mother was the unfortunate Lady Alice Lisle, cruelly beheaded at Winchester in 1685 for giving refuge to fugitives from Monmouth's defeated forces.

[5] *Ibid.*, ii. 115, 116.

degree, and being offered a fellowship which he declined. He also preached in the island of Guernsey before returning to New England.[6]

The arrival of Charles Morton in 1686 and his appointment in 1692 as fellow and in 1697 as vice president of Harvard brought to the colony and the college a valuable cultural influence, for Morton had been a fellow of Wadham College, Oxford, and for years a successful teacher in London. When he was appointed vice president it was planned that in time he should succeed to the presidency,[7] but he died in 1698 while Increase Mather was still president. Upon his arrival he read lectures on philosophy at his own home; but the lectures attracted so many from the college that he was requested to abandon them.[8]

Such contact with England and English scholastic life must have had considerable effect in keeping the college from becoming too provincial. Its standing was still sufficiently good to attract at least one student from England. Nathaniel Mather of Dublin wrote to his brother Increase, then newly chosen president, December 31, 1684:

> . . . one Mr. Rich. Lob, merchant in London, who marryed my sister Thompson, desyres me to write in behalf of this gentleman, the bearer, his kinsman Mr. Penhallow of Falmouth in Cornwall, who designs to spend a year or two in New England, in the Colledg, for the perfecting of his learning, hee having lived 3 or 4 years under the instructions of one Mr. Morton . . . who is constreyned to withdraw by reason of Capias's upon an Excommunicac̃on.[9]

One unfavorable picture of Harvard during this period

[6] See p. 21, above.

[7] Massachusetts Historical Society, Collections, 2d Series, i. 158 ff; Eggleston, Transit of Civilization, p. 45; Dictionary of National Biography. One of his pupils in England had been Daniel Defoe. He brought two students with him. At his death Morton left a sum of £50 to Harvard, and his funeral was attended by the officers and students of Harvard in a body.

[8] See Mather Papers, pp. 111, 112, for the letter requesting him not to compete with the college.

[9] Mather Papers, p. 59.

exists in the account of the visit to it of Jasper Danckaerts, a Dutch scholar, in 1680. In reading this it must be remembered that when the visit occurred Harvard had been four years without a president, and had not recovered from the disturbances and quarrels which led to the resignation and death of President Hoar. Urian Oakes, referred to at the end of the account, had been chosen president, but was not yet installed. The graduates of 1680 were but five, and in 1682 none took degrees.[10]

We reached Cambridge about eight o'clock. It is not a large village, and the houses stand very much apart. The college building is the most conspicuous among them. We went to it, expecting to see something unusual, as it is the only college, or would-be academy of the Protestants in all America, but we found ourselves mistaken. In approaching the house we neither heard nor saw anything mentionable; but, going to the other side of the building, we heard noise enough in an upper room to lead my comrade to say, "I believe they are engaged in disputation." We entered and went upstairs, when a person met us, and requested us to walk in, which we did. We found there eight or ten young fellows, sitting around, smoking tobacco, with the smoke of which the room was so full, that you could hardly see; and the whole house smelt so strong of it that when I was going upstairs I said, "It certainly must be also a tavern." We excused ourselves, that we could speak English only a little, but understood Dutch or French well, which they did not. However, we spoke as well as we could. We inquired how many professors there were, and they replied not one, that there was not enough money to support one. We asked how many students there were. They said at first, thirty, and then came down to twenty; I afterwards understood there are probably not ten.[11] They knew hardly a word of Latin, not one of them, so that my comrade could not converse with them. They took us to the library where there was nothing particular. We looked over it a little. They pre-

[10] Magnalia, ii. 31.

[11] The number was exactly thirty, seventeen undergraduates and thirteen graduates, according to Cotton Mather's lists of the graduates of the classes then in Harvard, Urian Oakes of the class of 1678 having died in 1679. (Magnalia, ii. 31).

sented us with a glass of wine. This is all we ascertained there. The minister of the place goes over there morning and evening to make prayer, and has charge over them; besides him, the students are under tutors or masters.[12]

As for the inadequacy of the Harvard Latin so severely criticized by Danckaerts, the fault may have been in Dutch ears, in different methods of pronunciation, or in youthful shyness in the presence of strangers. Cotton Mather, who had taken his first degree at sixteen just two years before this, and at this time was pursuing advanced studies, states that pupils were required to speak true Latin, and to write it in verse as well as prose, before they could enter Harvard; and he boasts that commencement orations were delivered in Latin, Greek, and Hebrew, and even in verse of all three.[13] No one familiar with his writings can doubt Mather's fluency—at least in quoting Latin.

It is worth mention here that two members of the class which was to have degrees conferred upon it in a few days after this visit, William Brattle and John Leverett, later became tutors of Harvard and, during Increase Mather's three and one-half years' absence in England, had complete charge of the teaching. Among the men whom they taught in those years were Paul Dudley, later Attorney General of the Colony, Samuel Mather, who became pastor of a church in England, Benjamin Wadsworth, later president of the college, and Benjamin Colman, leader in the religious and literary activities of Boston during the next two generations. The students whom Danckaerts pictured so unfavorably were capable of training men of ability, and Leverett himself was later chosen president of Harvard; both Lever-

[12] Journal of Jasper Danckaerts, p. 266, under date of July 9. Danckaerts' whole account of conditions in and around Boston is marked by an evident lack of sympathy and a willingness, if not an eagerness, to find faults.

[13] Magnalia, ii. 12. More than half of the students who were in Harvard at this time became clergymen, and as such they would have to have some fluency in speaking Latin.

ett and Brattle were honored by election as Fellows of the Royal Society.[14]

The following criticism of Cambridge University, England, in 1710—forty years later—also by a foreigner, one Uffenbach, a German savant, as given by Mullinger, should be taken into consideration when attempting to judge of conditions at Harvard.

> [This] keen-eyed traveller, in visiting the other colleges [besides Trinity, whose hall he found dirty and "smelly"], could not but be struck by the indifference evinced for the higher interests of learning. At Caius College he found the manuscripts placed in "a miserable garret under the roof," and lying "thick with dust" on the floor. At Magdalene all the books were "entirely overgrown with mould." . . . At Trinity Hall, the library appeared to him "very mean, consisting only of a few law books." At Emmanuel, the books, though "respectable in number," stood "in entire confusion." At Peterhouse, the manuscripts were "buried in dust" and in the greatest disorder. At the University Library, a rare codex of Josephus being "torn at the end," the library-keeper obligingly presented him with a leaf![15]

Nathaniel Mather, of Dublin, writing in 1686, seems well satisfied with the scholarship of Harvard, although he criticizes some details:

> The method of these, & the last years Theses is in my judgm̃t better than an[y] I have seen formerly. But the grammar of some of [them] might bee mended, *e. g.*, in Thes. 2, . . . it should have been *producant*, not *producerent;* . . . But I perceive the Cartesian philosophy begins to obteyn in New England, & if I conjecture aright the Copernican System too. There should also in a thing coming out from scholars in an university, have been more care taken of orthography. *e. g.* Thes. Phys. 28, *nitrolis* for *nitrosis;* and *Phillipsius* should not bee with a double p.[16]

There is little evidence in this period of the attitude of

[14] Publications of the Colonial Society of Massachusetts, xiv. 291; Sibley, Harvard Graduates, iii. 183.

[15] Mullinger, History of Cambridge, p. 168.

[16] Mather Papers, p. 63.

the English universities toward Harvard; for after the Restoration few Harvard men were tempted to England either for study or to seek for churches. Cotton Mather and Thomas Brattle, like William Brattle and John Leverett, were honored by being chosen Fellows of the Royal Society;[17] the former was given the degree of Doctor of Divinity by the University of Glasgow in 1710;[18] and Jeremiah Dummer, Harvard 1699, was given the degree of Doctor of Philosophy at Utrecht in 1703.[19] Benjamin Colman, Harvard 1692, was also given the degree of Doctor of Divinity by the University of Glasgow in 1731.[20] Samuel Myles, Harvard 1684, and William Vesey, Harvard 1693, received the degree of Master of Arts from Oxford in 1693 and 1697.[21] One other possible evidence of Harvard's standing in the world of scholarship is found in a statement of Increase Mather writing of the college in 1689:

> . . . the Learned Men there have a corresponding communication with other Learned Men in divers parts of the World, where the Reformed Religion is professed, and by them [are] highly reverenced for their Learning and Sobriety.[22]

In this period, then, Harvard had come to hold a much less important place in the English speaking world than it had held in the first period, and to that extent had become provincial; but this change had not greatly affected the quality of scholarship, and had, if anything, increased the influence of the college in the colonies. There were few Oxford or

[17] Publications of the Colonial Society of Massachusetts, xiv. 81 ff; Narratives of the Witchcraft Cases, p. 167.

[18] Sibley, Harvard Graduates, iii. 39.

[19] Sewall, Letter-Book, i. 302.

[20] Turell, Life of Benjamin Colman, p. 157.

[21] Publications of the Colonial Society of Massachusetts, xviii. 210, n. 1. The last two degrees were awards to men who had adopted Episcopalianism, and that to Colman was given at the request of Governor Belcher. If they were not always rewards for scholastic ability solely, at least they showed that the British universities were willing to recognize Harvard officially through such honors to her graduates.

[22] A Brief Relation of the State of New England, Andros Tracts, ii. 162.

Cambridge men to compete with the Harvard men. Cotton Mather, speaking of the influence of Harvard in 1696, states that of 87 ministers in Massachusetts, 76 were Harvard graduates, and of 35 in Connecticut, 31 were from Harvard.[23]

As to the quality of the scholarship, one or two more illustrations may be given. Nathaniel Mather, brother of Cotton Mather, graduating from Harvard in 1685 at the age of sixteen, was sufficiently skilled in mathematics and astronomy to figure out the statistics and calculations of almanacs for the years 1685 and 1686, which he published.[24] Samuel Sewall, Harvard 1671, seems to have had a sound classical training. Dr. William Everett, in referring to Sewall's original English and Latin poems, says,

> . . . in the latter, at least, the metre is irreproachable, according to the rules of quantity as recognized by the scholars of his time. An exhaustive examination of the verses in the Diary leaves no doubt on this subject.[25]

Sewall also shows his scholarship elsewhere. In a letter he writes:

> There is mention made of a new Translation of the Bible: If it go forward, I would propound One Word of amendment: John, 10. 16. The Word (Fold) in the latter part of the verse ought to be changed for the word(Flock).[26] The new French Translation has it (*Un seul tropeau*) I have a Latin Testament printed *Parisijs ex officina Rob. Stephani typographi Regij M. D. XLV*. He seems to be scrupulous in departing from the Vulgar Latin; yet has this Marginal Reading (*ut fiat unus grex*) Beza in his latter edition, has (*grex*) Tremellius his Translation of the Syriack, runs thus (*fietq*[*u*]*e totus grex unus*) In reading Austin

[23] Magnalia, i. 86.

[24] The Boston Ephemeris, an Almanack for the year 1685 [and the same for 1686]. Many of the Boston almanacs of the seventeenth century were compiled by the graduates of Harvard who were continuing their studies in residence after graduation. Such resident bachelors specialized in astronomy and mathematics.

[25] Massachusetts Historical Society, Proceedings, 2d Series, iv. 80.

[26] This change was made in the revised version of 1881, as the editors of the Letter-Book pointed out.

upon the Psalms, I have often met with, (*Unus grex, unus pastor*) Psal. 71. Col. 780. Psal. 77. Col. 852. Psal. 78. Col. 878. *ter legitur*. I do not see that the word is any where else translated (Fold). In Act. 20. 28, 29, and 1 Pet. 5. 2, 3, the word is of the same Origination, though of the Neuter Gender, and is still rendred (Flock).[27]

On one occasion he reports that he and a friend spent the evening reading Latin verse to each other.[28] In another letter he discusses the "enetymology" of the word "Lordane, by Corruption, Lurdane; . . . . Though your English Dictionary carrys it another way."[29] The following memorandum in his "Letter-Book" also indicates his interest in study:

To Mr. Stretton, to buy Bellarmine, two volumes, polemical works, fair print. Some Spanish Books; Barthol. de las Casas in Spanish, and in English too; Gramar and Dictionary, if to be had; and what else you shall see convenient for my purpose of getting a Smattering of the Spanish tongue.[30]

Somewhat later Cotton Mather also became interested in Spanish, as is shown by his own account:

About this Time, understanding that the way for our Communication with the *Spanish Indies*, opens more and more, I sett myself to learn the *Spanish Language*. The Lord wonderfully prospered mee in this Undertaking; a few liesure Minutes in the Evening of every Day, in about a Fortnight, or three weeks Time, so accomplished mee, I could write very good Spanish. Accordingly, I composed a little Body of the *Protestant Religion*, in certain Articles . . . This I turn'd into the Spanish Tongue.[31]

[27] Letter-Book, i. 297.

[28] "Mr. Bradstreet read to me Chrysostom's going out of Constantinople into Banishment; and I read his Return; both in Latin, very entertaining. 'Twas occasion'd by my mentioning the two folios I had given him. I offered to give Dr. Mather's Church History for them and put them into the Library. It seems Mr. Bradstreet has all the Eton Edition." (Diary, iii. 163.)

[29] Letter-Book, i. 18.

[30] *Ibid.*, i. 123. In the year 1691.

[31] Diary, i. 284. January, 1698–9. He confessed in the Diary that the task gave him a terrible headache!

In the "Magnalia" he quoted one proverb in Spanish.[32] He also wrote at least one tract in French.[33] In a day in which the education of woman was neglected, he taught his daughter Katherine both Latin and Hebrew.[34] Evidently the scholarly spirit was not lacking in this period of the colonial life.

Nor was the period without scientific spirit. Nathaniel Mather's letter, given on page 103, refers to the growing influence of the Cartesian philosophy in the Colonies. Thomas Brattle also refers to this in a letter which he wrote at the time of the witchcraft troubles.

> The Salem justices . . . are so well instructed in the Cartesian philosophy, and in the doctrine of *effluvia*, that they undertake to give a demonstration how this touch does cure the afflicted persons.[35]

It had become established at Cambridge not long before this.[36] The Reverend Deodat Lawson, whose lecture at Salem Village, March 24, 1692, was largely responsible for the beginning of the witchcraft persecutions, had been educated in England, where he had spent six years at the English universities, whence he had brought the current beliefs of English scholars.[37] The Copernican theory was accepted with some hesitation, but slowly gained way. It was stated and explained as early as 1659 in Zechariah Brigden's "Almanack" for that year. Alexander Nowell in his "Almanack" for 1665 defended it. In 1665 Samuel Danforth published "An Astronomical Description of the late Comet, or Blaz-

[32] Magnalia, ii. 581.

[33] Diary, ii. 651. It was entitled *Grande Voix du Ciel à la* France *sous La Verge de Dieu.*

[34] Wendell, Cotton Mather, p. 257.

[35] Massachusetts Historical Society, Collections, 1st Series, v. 63.

[36] Mullinger in his History of Cambridge, *ca.* p. 158, speaks of it as attracting great attention and interest around 1660.

[37] Littlefield, Early Boston Booksellers, p. 164. It must be remembered that the colonists in their beliefs in witchcraft were not behind the times, but rather accepting the latest ideas as expressed by Joseph Glanvil and Henry More of Cambridge. See p. 142 and p. 160, below.

ing Star," in which he maintained that the orbit of the comet was elliptical, and that its center was not the earth.[38] In 1675 John Foster's "Almanack" advanced strong arguments for the theory. In Nathaniel Mather's "Almanack" for 1686, already referred to, Robert Hook's discovery of a sensible parallax of the earth's orbit among the fixed stars was cited as proof of the truth of the new system.[39]

The influence of Harvard in this period, then, may have been more provincial; but there seems to be no proof that this change was attended by any appreciable decline in scholarship. Harvard was still training men satisfactorily for the ministry; its graduates were achieving distinction in political life, Samuel Sewall, Paul Dudley, Benjamin Lynde, and Gurdon Saltonstall, for example; and two other graduates of this period, Cotton Mather and Thomas Brattle, received recognition for their scientific writings by the publication of their articles in the Transactions of the Royal Society as well as by election to that Society.[40]

Of common school education during this period there is no detailed information. School books were imported in large numbers,[41] and some were printed in the colony. Marmaduke Johnson testified in 1668 that he had printed a primer;[42] and before or by 1690 Benjamin Harris had pub-

[38] Eggleston, Transit of Civilization, p. 35. This was reprinted in England.

[39] Sewall, for all of his classical learning, was somewhat skeptical of the new science. As late as 1714 he wrote in his Diary (iii. 31), "Dr. C. Mather preaches excellently from Ps. 37. Trust in the Lord &c. only spake of the Sun being in the centre of our System. I think it inconvenient to assert such Problems." Sewall's earlier credulity in accepting the spectral evidence in the witchcraft cases reacted upon him to make him cautious of things not too evident.

[40] Thomas Brattle was recognised for his ability as a mathematician and astronomer, Mather for his writings reporting natural (and sometimes, in the eyes of the modern reader, unnatural and absurd) phenomena. The seeming absurdity of some of these articles must not blind us to the fact that they did not seem absurd at the time and were not at all out of place in the most learned periodical of the time. "The Relation," commented the astronomer Halley, as editor, writing of one of the most absurd, "seems to be well attested." (Publications of the Colonial Society of Massachusetts, xiv. 82.)

[41] See book lists in the following chapter.

[42] Massachusetts Historical Society, Proceedings, 2d Series, xi. 247.

lished the famous "New England Primer."[43] That primers such as these and catechisms like Cotton's "Spiritual Milk for Boston Babes"[44] sufficed for a primary education equivalent to that obtainable in old England is shown by the statement of John Locke in his "Thoughts Concerning Education," written in 1690, that the method of teaching children at that time in England "was the ordinary road of Hornbook, Primer, Psalter, Testament, and Bible."[45] Mr. Littlefield's statement seems to sum up the situation accurately: "The writer is very strongly of the opinion that the facilities for instruction in the colonial and provincial periods were greater than is generally supposed."[46]

43 Littlefield, Early New England Schools, p. 148; Ford, Boston Book Market, p. 29.

44 See p. 23, above.

45 Littlefield, Early New England Schools, p. 92.

46 *Ibid.*, p. 328. That Massachusetts was interested in the enforcement of her public school law is shown by the fact that when she assumed authority over the province of Maine she applied to that territory the school law, and in 1675 the towns of Kittery, Cape Porpus, Scarboro, and Falmouth were all presented because they did not as towns take care to have their youth taught their catechism and educated according to the law. Maine Historical Society, Proceedings, 2d Series, iv. 192.

Chapter VII: Books and Libraries.

THE flow of books to the New England colonies increased rather than diminished during the second period. Gifts and shipments to individuals continued to come from England; booksellers became numerous; and both the Public Library and the Harvard Library grew in size.

As in the earlier period, John Winthrop, Jr., was one of the chief recipients of books. In 1670 Henry Oldenburg, returning to Winthrop the thanks of the Royal Society for curiosities which he had sent, wrote,[1]

And y^t this returne may not be altogether verbal, you are to receiue wth it some few books lately printed here by several Fellows of ye Society, viz.:

1. Mr. Boyles Continuation of ye Experimts concerning the Spring and weight of the Aire.
2. Dr. Holders Philosophy of Speech.
3. Dr. Thurston *de Respirationis usu primario.*
4. The Transactions of the last year.

In 1671 he wrote,

I herewith send you a few philosophical Books, lately printed here; viz.:—

1. M^r. Boyl's New Tracts about ye wonderful rarefaction and Condensation of the Air, etc.
2. Monsr Charas's New Experiments vpon Vipers.
3. The Transactions of 1670.

To these I adde a small discourse . . . . against y^t great Sorbonist, Monsr Arnaud, touching ye Perpetuity of ye Romish Faith about the Eucharist.[2]

[1] Massachusetts Historical Society, Proceedings, 1st Series, xvi. 244.
[2] *Ibid.*, xvi. 251.

A year later he wrote,

I cannot but thank you for the particulars contained in y^r^ letter; for wch I have nothing to return . . . . but the Transactions of ye last year. . . . . The Discourse of Mr. Boyle concerning the Origine and Vertue of Gems is not yet printed off: when it is, you shall not faile, God permitting, of hauing a Copy of it sent you by ye first ship y^t^ shall goe for y^r^ parts after its publication.[3]

Similarly Samuel Petto of Suffolk, England, wrote to Increase Mather in 1677,

I also intend to send with it [his letter], Dr Owen of the reason of faith.[4]

and again in 1678,

I have herewith sent you three books *Christianismus Christianandus*, and M^r^ Ny's paper, of a question which is much debated here, . . . also Mr Troughton of Divine Providence, ... If I knew what other such bookes would be acceptable to you, I would send them.[5]

Four years later he wrote,

I did also direct a few lines to you, with Mr Stockton's book entituled Consolation in Life & Death. . . . . I intend to send you another of Mr Stockton, entituled The best Interest when it is finished.[6]

Others were sending books, too. T. Jollie of England wrote in 1679,

I have sent you herewith 2 treatises, which severall yeares agoe I drew up when I was a prisoner.[7]

Abraham Kick of Amsterdam wrote in 1683 to Increase Mather,

I hope the bookes sent by Mr. John Pecke came safe to your hand . . . .[8]

[3] *Ibid.*, xvi. 248.
[4] Mather Papers, p. 341.
[5] *Ibid.*, p. 343.
[6] *Ibid.*, p. 348.
[7] *Ibid.*, p. 325.
[8] *Ibid.*, p. 598.

Samuel Baker of England wrote, September 2, 1684,

I have given Mr. Epps order to send you,

1. An Acc° of the present state of the Prot. Religion, supposed by Dr. O[wen], though I guess you have it, for which reason I do not send you his Meditations of Glory.
2. A defence of his 12 arguments in answer to Baxter.
3. The Dr's Escot reprinted, with a Catalogue at the end, of all the Dr's books.
4. A little book against Health-drinking.
5. The life of one Mr. Henry Dorney . . . .[9]

He wrote again later,

I . . . return my acknowledgm[t] for the books I haue rec[d]. . . . I know not what return to make in this kind more acceptable than of Dr. Burnett's L[rs],[10] herewith sent.[11]

Jonathan Tuckney of Hackney, England, sent books to Increase Mather from time to time, as the following letters indicate.

I wrote to you about two months since & therewith sent you two bookes of my father's labo[r]s, one English sermons, the other Latin Prelections & Determinations (as also two for my Cous. Whiting and two for my Cous. your Br. John Cotton), which I hope may be come to hand.[12]

. . . . your kind letter of May 8, together with your new peece of Illustrious Providences . . . . whereas you desire to see Dr. Spencer of Prodigies, I have procured it you, & herewith send it. . . . .[13]

. . . I have thought (since my writing that letter of August 29, (wherein I inclose this) myself, to read over Spencer of Prodigies before I part with it from me. . . . . And I desire you to accept from me in Exchange (which (you know the old saying is) that it is no robbery) another Latin piece

[9] *Ibid.*, p. 513.

[10] Rev. Gilbert Burnet's Travels through Switzerland, Italy, and some parts of Germany.

[11] Mather Papers, p. 513.

[12] *Ibid.*, p. 352. September 9, 1679.

[13] *Ibid.*, p. 354. August 29, 1684.

of the same author's concerning *Urim & Thummim:* what they were.[14]

The following letter to Increase Mather from John Leusden, Professor of Hebrew and Jewish Antiquities at Utrecht, January 1688–9, is an example of the correspondence with learned men abroad to which Mather referred in the passage quoted on page 104.

Most Reverend, Much to bee Respected S^r.,—I sought you in America,[15] and thither on the 30th of March I sent some books, vizt a New Lexicon, a Compendium of the Greek New Testament, two Psalters in Hebrew and English, and one in Hebrew & Latine. The Psalmes in Hebrew & English, I dedicated to M^r. Eliot, & those four and twenty Preachers, lately heathens, now christians.[16] The Psalmes in Hebrew & Latine I have inscribed to your Rev^d. name. . . . I lately received moreover two American[17] Bibles, two American Grammars, & other American books, as also the Indian's A.B.C. and some others, . . . You now desyre fifty Hebrew Psalters for the use of the students in Harvard Colledge; which I would now have sent, but because you doe not express what kind of Psalters it is which you desyre, whether Hebrew & Latine, or Hebrew & English . . . .[18]

Increase Mather sent home books from London during his residence there. His nephew, Warham Mather, wrote to him in 1688,

I delivered the Books I received from yourself according to order. . . . I am yet made a greater debter, by those for me.[19]

Cotton Mather recorded in his diary, January 7, 1698, "Arrives to mee, a Book in *Folio*, this year published in *London* . . . . a Collection of *Remarkable Providences*;"[20] and again, " . . . . some such Thing as to read a little

[14] *Ibid.*, p. 355. September 3, 1684.
[15] At this time Increase Mather was in London.
[16] Indian converts.
[17] *American* seems to be used here as equivalent to *Indian*.
[18] Mather Papers, p. 678.
[19] *Ibid.*, p. 671.
[20] Diary, i. 246.

Book, *De Satana Colaphizante*, which I received from *Holland*, the day after I was taken sick."[21]

Such items give some indication of the way in which books constantly came to America through private gifts. Even more striking is the increased importation of books through the regular channel of the booksellers' shops. Before this period opened there was at least one well-established bookseller in Boston, Hezekiah Usher, who died in 1676, "leaving a goodly fortune and two sons to quarrel over it and evoke the aid of the law."[22] His son, John Usher, carried on the business, but not without considerable competition. When John Dunton, a London bookseller, arrived in Boston in 1686 for the double purpose of collecting bad debts[23] from New Englanders who had bought books of him and of disposing of surplus stock, he found several booksellers established here, and three others soon followed him. He speaks of some of them thus:

This Trader [Mr. Usher] makes the best Figure in *Boston*, he's very Rich, adventures much to Sea; but has got his Estate by BOOKSELLING; he proposed to me the buying my whole Venture, but wou'd not agree to my Terms. . . . Mr. *Philips, my old Correspondent* . . . I'll say that for SAM (*after dealing with him for some Hundred Pounds*) he's very just, and (as an Effect of that) very Thriving. . . . I rambled next to visit *Minheer Brunning*,[24] he's a *Dutch* Bookseller from *Holland*. . . . *Brunning* is vers'd in the Knowledge of all sorts of Books, and may well be stil'd *a Compleat Bookseller*. . . . From the DUTCH, I went to the SCOTCH Bookseller, one *Duncan Cambel*. . . . The next I'll mention shall be *Andrew Thorncomb*, Bookseller from *London* . . . ,[25]

. . . tho' I have first broke the Ice, in bringing hither a Cargo of Books; yet by some Letters I receiv'd by the Rose Frigot [*sic*] . . . I perceive I shall not be the last. [He proceeds to report

[21] *Ibid.*, i. 365.

[22] Days and Ways in Old Boston, p. 95. See pp. 40 and 79, above.

[23] To the amount of £500. Dunton, Life and Errors, p. 101.

[24] Otherwise known as Joseph Browning.

[25] Dunton, Life and Errors, p. 127 ff.

the coming of Benjamin Harris and the How brothers, Job and John.][26]

The following list will give an idea of the number of men who engaged in the book business in Boston up to the year 1700, besides the Ushers and Dunton, who have already been mentioned.[27]

1672. John Tappin published at least one book. Books were incidental to his business in general merchandise as is shown by the inventory of his estate in 1678: Books, £16.00.00, other stock, £4777.07.07.

1673. Edmund Ranger established himself as bookseller, bookbinder, and stationer. He did little bookselling, his name appearing in three books, but was called bookseller in a legal document.

1675. John Foster took over Marmaduke Johnson's press when the latter died. He combined bookselling with printing until his death in 1681, when Samuel Sewall succeeded him.

1677. Henry Phillips, after seven years' apprenticeship with Usher, opened a bookshop in the Town House. Upon his death in

1680. Samuel Phillips, his brother, succeeded to the business. Although his shop was burned down in the great fire of 1711 and he did not resume business, he died wealthy in 1720.

——. Duncan Campbell. Date of arrival unknown; probably before 1679.

1679. William Avery married the widow of John Tappin and took over the bookshop which she and her son, Joseph, had carried on after her husband's death. When Avery died in 1687, the widow continued the business. She died in 1707.

[26] Dunton, Letters, p. 144.
[27] The list is summarized from Littlefield, Early Boston Booksellers.

1679. John Griffin's name first appeared as publisher of a book. He died in 1686. Benjamin Harris may have taken over his shop when he arrived that same year.

1681. Samuel Sewall succeeded John Foster. He gave up the press and shop in 1684.

1681–2. John Ratcliff, who came over to work on the Indian Bible, published some books.

1682. Joseph Browning arrived from Amsterdam. He died in 1691.

1684. Richard Wilkins arrived from Limerick, where he had sold books. He opened a shop opposite the west end of the Town House. Dunton used his shop as headquarters and upon leaving put in his hands his collections amounting to £300. Wilkins retired in 1704.

1684–5. James Cowes opened a shop. He returned to England three years later.

1685. Andrew Thorncomb arrived. After the reference to him by Dunton, quoted above, there are no records. He may have returned to London.

1686. Job How arrived. Further detail is lacking except his name in one book as publisher.

1686. Benjamin Harris, a London bookseller, driven out of London because of anti-Catholic publications, set up a shop in Boston. He visited London in 1687 and again in 1688. In 1695 he closed his business in Boston and returned to London.

1690. Nicholas Buttolph opened a bookshop. His shop was burned down in 1711, but he continued the business.

1694. Michael Perry began business in Samuel Phillip's old shop when the latter moved to a new location. Upon Perry's death in 1700 his widow continued the business.

1698–9. Benjamin Eliot began a business which was very successful. He died in 1741.

Two others who carried books with other merchandise were

Elkanah Pembroke, who opened a shop in 1689 at the Head of the Dock, and Joseph Wheeler, who had a shop in Dock Square, and published one book in 1697.

Samuel Sewall, even after he disposed of the printing and book shop, continued to do business in books. During his visit to England, 1688–1689, he recorded at different times payments for books which total over £30; and an invoice records that, among other freight:

Samuel Sewall hath aboard the America, Wm. Clark, Commander:

Punchin Books
Barrel of Books
A Map of England and London.[28]

His "Letter-Book" under date of April 25, 1698, contains a memorandum of an order per Capt. Thos. Carter to Amsterdam which includes a "Ream of Marbled paper, Spanish Bible of Cypriano Valero, Deodats Italian Bible."[29] In his diary, in 1700, he recorded:

The President[30] desires me to send for the above mentioned Books [which are here written below]:

1. A Narrative of the Portsmouth Disputation between Presbyterians and Baptists at Mr. Williams's Meeting-house.
2. B[isho]p of Norwich's Sermon of Religious Melancholy.
3. Amintor, a defence of Milton with Reasons for abolishing the 30th Jan.y; [Two of them.]
4. An Account of the first Voyages into America by Barthol de las Casas 4s. [Two of them].
5. Account of a Jew lately converted . . . at the Meeting near Ave Mary-Lane [Four of them].[31]

[28] Sewall, Diary, i. 288. At about the same time he recorded in his diary (i. 284), "Mr. Matthew Wotton, Bookseller, sends me by his Servant a parcell of Englands Duty, which are 25, the Sale of which in N[ew]. E[ngland]. I am to warrant. . . . . [They] Are sent to Mr. Joseph Brañing [Browning], at Boston."

[29] Sewall, Letter-Book, i. 199.

[30] Presumably the president of Harvard.

[31] Sewall, Diary, ii. 13; Letter-Book, i. 239.

At the same time he copied into his letter-book the following:

The books I would have bought are

Ars Cogitandi. 2.
Le Grands Philosophy, Latin.
Heerboordi Meletomata. 3.
Dr. Charletons Physiologia.
Dr. Moors Im̄ortality of the Soul.
Metaphysicks, Ethicks
Glanvils Sceptis Scientifica
Dr. Wilkins's nattural Principles, and Duties. His World in the Moon.
Stallius his Regulæ Phylosophicæ
Stierij Questiones Physicæ cum Praeceptis Philosophiæ.
Burgerdicius, Logick with Heerebords Notes.
The great Hist. Geographical, and Poetical Dictionary being a curious Misscellany of Sacred and Prophane History printed at London for Henry Rhodes. If there be an Edition since 1694, Send the best Two of them.
Francis Turretini Institutio Theologiæ Elencticæ . . .
Turretini Disputationes de satisfactione Christi.
Poles Synopsis criticorum . . . if [you] light on them a peniwoth.
A K[ing] Edward 6th, his Common Prayer Book
Queen Eliz[abeth] [her Common Prayer Book]
Queens Bible, If . . . reasonable.[32]

He added to this order:

If the Money doe more than hold out, send in School Books;
Esops Eng[lish] and Lat[in],
Corderius Eng[lish] and Lat[in],
Terrence Eng[lish] and Lat[in],
Ovid de Tristibus,
Metamorphosis,
Virgil,
Tullies de Officijs,
Grammars,
constr[u]ing Books.[33]

[32] Sewall, Letter-Book, i. 237. June 10, 1700.
[33] *Ibid.*, i. 238.

Later in the year he ordered:[34]

Pole's Synopsis Criticorum if to be had under five pounds: as much cheaper as you can,
A Ream of good Marble Paper.
A gross of Horn-books.
Two Cambridge Concordances.
Octavo Bibles.

and a few days later:[35]

Duz. of Dr. Bates's Harmony of the divine Attributes,
6. Flavels mental errors,
2 Mordeus Geographie rectified,
12. Colsons Seamans Kalendar.
6. Wakely's Compass rectifier.
6. Norwoods Epitome of Navigation.
One great Histor. Geograph. and Poetical Dictionary of the newest Edition . . . .[36]

There were, evidently, plenty of channels through which the people of Boston and vicinity could obtain the latest books; and they made good use of their opportunities. With all the competition from the established bookshops Dunton seems to have found a good market; he wrote with satisfaction,

> . . . having stock'd the Town of Boston with my Books; (some having bought more, I'm afraid, than they intend to pay for)[37] and having still a Considerable Quantity left, Several Gentlemen have given me great Encouragement . . . to send a Venture to Salem . . . .[38]

and there also he had success.

It is a mistake to think of these booksellers as carrying only theological or devotional works. No doubt such books

[34] *Ibid.*, i. 248.
[35] *Ibid.*, i. 247, 248.
[36] See list on page 118, above.
[37] His sale of books on credit alone amounted to £300. See p. 116, above, under Richard Wilkins.
[38] Dunton, Letters, p. 248.

were an important part of their stock in trade, perhaps even the larger part; but this would have been just as much so in England. We do not know, unfortunately, just what books Dunton brought with him from England, or what he took back with him unsold; but one item in his "Letters" may throw some light on the matter. He wrote of one customer,

> The chief Books she bought were Plays[39] and Romances; which to set off the better, she wou'd ask for Books of *Gallantry*.[40]

Plays and romances are hardly in keeping with the common notion of Puritan life in 1686, and it might seem necessary to reject this statement as one of the many untruths in Dunton's very unreliable "Letters"[41] were it not for the fact that recently discovered invoices of book shipments to New England show that such books were on sale in Boston even before Dunton came. In 1682 Robert Boulter, a London bookseller, sent to John Usher as a venture, "without ordre," a shipment of nearly 800 volumes under about 125 titles. As Mr. Usher in October, 1680, was owing Mr. Boulter £370, he evidently had traded with him for some time, and therefore Boulter's consignment was not a blind venture but a shipment of books to a market with which he was familiar.[42] For that reason the items included in the list are of value as an indication of the probable taste of Boston readers. Some of the more interesting titles follow.[43]

3 faramond [*Pharamond*, Or The History of *France*. A Fam'd Romance . . .]
2 last part of the english rogue
2 parismus [The most Famous . . . History of *Parismus*, the most renowned Prince of *Bohemia*]

[39] A dancing master had set up in Boston in 1681, and a fencing master in 1686. See p. 155, below.

[40] Dunton, Letters, p. 116.

[41] See C. N. Greenough's account of the plagiarisms in the Letters and his evidence of their untrustworthiness as historical material: Publications of the Colonial Society of Massachusetts, xiv. 213 ff.

[42] Ford, The Boston Book Market, p. 9 ff.

[43] *Ibid.*, p. 88 ff. Fuller lists of the items in these invoices are given in the Appendix.

1 destruction of troy
1 Valentyn and orson [The Famous History of *Valentine* and *Orson*, the two sons of the Emperour of *Greece*]
4 esops in english
2 felthams resolves
16 Cap of gray haires [A Cap of Gray hairs for a Green head, or The Father's Counsel to his Son, an Apprentice in *London*]
2 Clelias [A four volume translation from Scudery]
9 argalus and parthenia [The pleasant and delightful History of *Argalus* and *Parthenia*,]
1 pembrooks arcadia [Sir Philip Sidney's *Arcadia*]
2 reynolds on Murther [The Triumphs of God's Revenge against the . . . Sin of Murther, Expressed in Thirty several Tragical Histories.]
2 perfect politician [or A . . . Life . . . of *O. Cromwell.*]
2 temples miscellanea [By Sir William Temple]
1 Bacons works
1 Cambdens Elizabeth
1 Miltons history [The History of *Britain*]
6 Guy of Warwick
6 Reynard fox
12 dr Faustus [The History of . . . Dr. *John Faustus*]
12 Joviall Garland [. . . containing a Collection of all the newest Songs and Sonnets used in Court and Country]
12 Crown Garland
6 Garland of delight
6 fortunatus [The right pleasant, and variable Tragical, History of *Fortunatus*]
6 royall arbours [A Royall Arbor of Loyall Poesie, consisting of Poems and Songes, digested into Triumph, Elegie, Satyr, Love, and Drollerie]
8 Soggins jests [Scoggings Jests]
4 Mandevills travells
4 pack cards

The four other invoices, all of ordered books, show no such proportion of the light reading of that day, but do show that some real literature was imported into Boston. In connection with these items it must be remembered that these invoices report only the purchases of one Boston bookseller through a single ship captain (excepting those listed above sent by Boulter without order) in a period of less than two years.

Invoice of September 5, 1683.[44]

1 Hacklutes Uoyages
1 Mori Utopia
1 Felthams Resolues
7 Accademy Compliments [. . . with many new Additions of Songs and Catches à la mode]
1 Shaftsburys Life
1 Poeticall History [a mythology]
7 Accademy Compliments, another sorte.
30 History of Dr. Faustus

Invoice of March 3, 1683–4.[45]

2 Erle of Rochesters Poems
4 Miltons Paradise Lost
6 Lestranges Erasmus in English
1 Baker's Chronicle [of the Kings of England]
1 Pembrooks Arcadia
3 Accademy of Compliments
6 Nuga Uenales [. . . being new Jests . . .]
3 Present State of England
18 Dr. Faustus
6 Wilds Poems
6 Argulus and Parthenia
5 Oxford Jests

Invoice of May 29, 1684.[46]

4 State of England
3 Markhams way to get wealth
2 History of Parismus

[44] *Ibid.*, p. 108 ff. In this and in the next list it is reported that certain volumes ordered could not be supplied. Some of the items are designated for individuals not booksellers.

[45] *Ibid.*, p. 121 ff.

[46] *Ibid.*, p. 133 ff.

20 Gentle Craft [. . . with Pictures, and Variety of Wit and Mirth]
2 Wonders of the Femall world [. . . or A general History of Women]
1 Her and His [*Haec et Hic*, or The Feminine Gender more worthy than the Masculine.]
10 Second Part of the Pilgrims Progress.
2 Two Journeys to Jerusalem
2 London Bully [or The Prodigal Son; displaying the principal Cheats of our Modern Debauchees]
2 Informers Doome [. . . with the Discovery of the Knavery and Cheats of most Trades in *London*]
3 Uenus in the Cloyster

Invoice of April 13, 1685.[47]

2 Glissons Common Law Epitomized
8 Jure Maritimo
2 Terms of the Law
3 Daltons Justice [The Country Justice]
2 Keebles Statutes
2 Cooks Reports Engl. [By Sir Edward Coke]
3 Blounts Law Dictionary
1 Sheppards Grand Abridgement [of the Common and Statute Law of England]
1 Hobbarts Reports [law]
3 Miltons Logick
6 History of Dr. Faustus
2 Rochesters Life [Burnet's Life of the Earl of Rochester]
2 Pulton of the Common Pleas Engls.
5 Sheppards Sure Guide [for his Majesties Justices of Peace]
10 Wonderful Prodogies

From these invoices and certain references to bills and indebtedness Mr. Ford estimates that in the years 1679–1685, inclusive, John Usher imported books to a value of £567. Such a figure is a minimum rather than a maximum; he bought that much and he may have bought more through

[47] *Ibid.*, p. 140 ff.

other captains and of other London booksellers, record of the transactions having disappeared, even as these invoices vanished for centuries. One other invoice of the period has survived, together with a letter from the shipper to Increase Mather. The shipper was Richard Chiswell of London, whom Dunton calls "the Metropolitan Bookseller of England." He seems to have had a large trade in New England; the last four invoices above were of consignments from him. The letter and invoice follow; unfortunately the latter is not complete, including only the books sent to Dr. Mather, and not those to Usher which accompanied them.

S^r^,—I rec'^d^ yours of July 19th, & have in Mr Vsher's Cask p^r^ Anderson, in the Ship Blessing, sent you all the books you wrote for, & have returned 8 of your Principles, which I cannot sell . . .

I have added a few new things of good note which I hope you will be pleased with, the first of them is an answer to a Pamphlet I sent you in the last ꝑcell, & which makes no small stir here at present. Hales of Eaton, & Stillingfleet are very famous. Walker of Baptism is said to be very learned & exceedingly well done. The two books of Contemplations were writ by the Lord Cheif Justice Hales, a person who for all kind of learning, Philosophy, Physick, Mathematicks, &c., as well as Law, (his proper profession,) and for most exemplary piety . . . has not le[ft] his fellow, . . . the whole nation mournes for the loss of him. That Great audit or Good Steward's account, in the first vollume, is a most lively & exact character of his life. . . . I know not any two books have come forth these 20 yeares, that have sold so great a number in so short a time, as these two vollumes of his,[48] . . . I have sent a few books to Mr Vsher without order, which I put in to fill up the Cask. You may see them at his shop, & I hope may help some of them off his hands, by recoṁending them to your publick Library, especially the new ones, which cannot be there already, ꝑticularly Dr Caves Lives of the Fathers,

[48] This letter has been given so fully because of its interesting testimony to the fact that the colonists were not entirely dependent upon their own tastes, or their knowledge of contemporary books. Their London correspondents tried to keep them abreast of current works.

& Dr Cary's Chronologicall account of ancient time, which are both exceeding well esteemed by the most learned & ingenious men here.[49]

A Coppy.

	£ s. d.
Postage . . . Letters . . .	0. 1. 0
Dr Tuckneys Sermons, 4°	0. 8. 0
Straight gate to heaven, 12° bound,	0. 0. 8
Hotchkis reformation or ruine, 8°	0. 2. 0
Discovery of Pigmies, 8°	0. 1. 0
Horologicall Dialogues, 8°	0. 1. 0
Hornes Cause of Infants maintained, 4°	0. 1. 0
Whiston on Baptism, all 3 parts, 8°	0. 5. 6
State of Northampton, 4°	0. 0. 3
Tozer's Directions to a godly life, 12°	0. 1. 0
Barbets Chirurgery, 8°	0. 6. 0
Leybournes Dialling, 4°	0. 3. 0
Hook's Motion of the Earth, 4°	0. 1. 0
Stephenson's mathemat. compendium, 12°	0. 2. 6
8 First principles of New England, 4° returnd[50].	0. 8. 0
ADDED.—	
Pacquet of advices to the men of Shaftsbury, 4°	0. 1. 6
King & Ld Chancellor's Speeches.	0. 0. 6
Dr Stillingfleet's Letter to a Deist, 8°	0. 2. 6
Mr Hales (of Eaton) his Tracts, 8°	0. 2. 6
Hornecks Law of Consideration, 8°	0. 3. 6
Walker of Baptism, 12°	0. 3. 6
Rules of Health, 12°	0. 1. 0
Family Physitian, 12°	0. 1. 0
Judge Hale's Contemplations, 2 Vol. 8°	0.10. 0
24 Warrs of New England, 4°[51]	———
Catalogue No. 7. 8. 9. 10, fol.	———

[49] Mather Papers, p. 575. The letter was written in February, 1677.

[50] This was a book by Increase Mather which proved to be a poor seller, and so the left over copies are returned.

[51] Chiswell had reprinted this book by Increase Mather, and is sending these copies as a gift to the author, although he has been disappointed at not selling more than 500.

Besides the regular booksellers, there were hawkers of books whose influence cannot be estimated for lack of information. Ballads, broadsides, popular books such as "Pilgrim's Progress" and Wigglesworth's "Day of Doom," and almanacs doubtless made up much of the hawker's stock in trade. Cotton Mather's busy brain saw opportunity for good here, for he recorded in his diary in 1683, "There is an old *Hawker* who will fill this Countrey with devout and useful Books, if I will direct him."[52]

There were, evidently, sufficient opportunities for the growth of private libraries. A letter from Increase Mather to Joseph Dudley, November 10, 1684, gives additional testimony of this fact. Writing of a letter containing defamatory matter to which his name had been forged to discredit him (probably by Edward Randolph),[53] he says:

He pretends as if I sent to Amsterdam for the New Covenant of Scotland, Carill upon Job, and Mr. Owen's last works. Now herein he has so grossly played the fool, soe as to discover the letter to be a meer peece of forgery. As for the new Covenant of Scotland, I never heard of such a thing, . . . Carill have been in my study this fiveteen years, & if I had him not, it is likely that I should send to Amsterdam, for Mr. Carill & Doct. Owen's works, which are here sould in Boston.[54]

The best of the private libraries of New England were undoubtedly those owned by the Mathers, father and son. Of the latter's Dunton wrote in 1686, when Cotton Mather was but eight years out of college:

. . . he shew'd me his Study: And I do think he has one of the best (for a Private Library) that I ever saw: Nay, I may go farther, and affirm, That as the Famous Bodleian Library at Oxford, is the Glory of that University, if not of all Europe, . . . so I may say, That Mr. Mather's Library is the Glory of New-

[52] Diary, i. 65. For later importance of hawkers of books see pp. 191-193, below.

[53] This is a part of the long quarrel between the Mathers and Randolph.

[54] Mather Papers, p. 101.

England, if not of all America. I am sure it was the best sight that I had in Boston.[55]

Of this library Cotton Mather wrote in his diary, October 16, 1700:

> [A widow] had a Parcel of Books, which once belong'd unto the Library of our famous old Mr. *Chancey;* and if I would please to take them, she should count herself highly gratified, in their being so well bestowed. I singled out, about *forty Books*, and some of them large Ones, which were now added unto my Library, that has already between two and three thousand in it.[56]

An extensive private library was brought to New England in 1686 by Samuel Lee, pastor of the church at Bristol from that year to 1691. Returning to England in 1691 he was taken prisoner by the French and died in France. The books which he left in Bristol were put on sale in Boston in 1693 at the shop of Duncan Campbell. The catalogue of these books, printed by Campbell, contains, besides pages of theological titles, the following titles:[57]

Subject	*Number*	
Physics	124	
Philosophy	83	
Mathematics and Astronomy	48	(in Latin)
	13	(in English)
History	112	(in Latin)
	45	(in English)
School authors	60	
Law books	8	
Unclassified	327	

The following partial list will give an idea of the range of this library:

Paracelsi	Opera
Paracelsi	de Vita Longa

[55] Dunton, Letters, p. 75.
[56] Diary, i. 368.
[57] *Titles*, not volumes.

Reolani	Anatomia
Willis	Anatomia cerebri
Helmontii	Opera
Helmont[ii]	dies Aurora rubra
Roger Bacon	perspect. per Combas.
————	Theatrum Chemicum vols. 1–4
Platonis	Opera
Seneca	Opera
Luciani Phylosoph:	Opera
Xenophon	Philosoph.
Aristotilis	[several]
Bacon	de augment [atione] Scientiarum
Cartesii	Metaphisica
Petri Rami	prælectiones
Archemedis	omnia opera
Tychobrachy	opera omnia
Joan: Stadii	Ephimeridis
Evevautii	Ephimerid.
Newtons	Trigonometry
Newtons	Astronomy
Dugdal.	Monast. angl.
Duckdales	Antiquities of Warwickshire
Stout's	Survey of London
Hollinshead's	Chronicles of Scotland
————	England & Ireland in 3 vols.
Fox's	Acts and Monuments
Rawleigh's	History of the World
Eabran's	Cronicles
Crackinthorp's	Councils
Everard's	Collections
Philpot's	Survey of Kent
Sayndy's	History of China
Wilson's	History of Great Britain
Crossel's	History of England
————	The Union of the Houses of York and Lancaster
Jones's	Antiquity of Great Britain
Burlons	description of Leichester
Delaval's	Travels

Howel's	History of London
Isaacson's	Chronology
Brughton's	Ecclesiastical History of Great Britain
Evebins [Evelin]	Discourse of Trees
Morison's	Travels
Summer's	Antiquity of Canterbury
Isaac's	Rarities of Exeter
Langhorn's	Introduction to the History of England
Ailan's	History of King Henry VII
Pitit's	ancient Right of the Commons of England
———	The History of Mary Queen of Scotland
———	The History of the Navy of Great Britain
———	The Life of Merlin
———	The History of Scanderberg
Prin's [Prynne]	new Discovery of the Prelates Tyranny
Bacon's	Natural History
Bacon	Hist[oria] Naturalis
Baconi	Hist[ory of] Hen[ry] 7th
Demosthen[es]	Oration[es] &c.
Homeri	Iliad (3 copies)
Homeri	Odysse[y] (5 copies)
Lucan	cum notis
Ashylii	Tragediæ
Terentii	Tragediæ
Hesiodi	opera cum Scholiis
Pindari	Odes
Persii	Satyr[æ]
Sophaclis	Antigone
Sophaclis	traged[iæ] cum Scholiis
Horatius	(3 copies)
Aristophanis	(3 copies)
Euripidis	Hecuba Græca
Salust	———
Martialæ	Epigram
Tascitus	———
Macrobius	———
Boetius	de Gemmis
Plutarchi	vitæ
Caesaris	Comment. (2)

Ceneca [*sic*]	Tragicus
Erasmi	Colloqui
Beda venerab.	de natura rerum (2)
————	Marmora Arundeliana

As another example of the variety to be found in colonial libraries, the following list of titles from a library of only thirty volumes in all is of interest.[58]

London Despencettory
Dixonarey
Norwood's Trigonometry
Gervase Markham's Gentleman Jocky
Lambarde's Perambulation of Kent
Morton's New England's Memorial
Sir Matthew Hale's Contemplations
The Effect of Warr
11 books on law

Some idea of Increase Mather's library may be gained from the statements as to his reading which are found in his fragmentary diary for the years 1675 and 1676.[59] The authors read, with the titles of the books when given, are listed here. It should be noted that this list contains almost no duplicates of the titles found in the lists given on pages 52 and 53 and on pages 237–242.[60]

Albaspinus	De Ritibus Ecclesiæ
Alsted	[not stated]
[Alwaerden?]	History of Severitus [Servetus?]
Autores	De Sinceritate
Bates	Vocatio
Bell	[not stated]
Boreman	"de swearing"
Bownd	"of Sabbath"

[58] Proceedings of the American Antiquarian Society, xviii. 136.

[59] Massachusetts Historical Society, Proceedings, 2d Series, xiii. 339 ff.

[60] The lack of duplication in these three different lists is typical in that the writer has found it almost invariably true that every new source of information in regard to colonial libraries has added details entirely new. Our knowledge of most of the colonial libraries is at best fragmentary.

Bridges	On Luke 17: 37
Buxtorf	Lex. Thalmud
Camel	not stated
Carter	On Hebrews 1: 1
Caryl	[not stated]
Chamberlain	State of E[urope]
Cicero	Orations
Clark	Vanity of Earthly Things
Clark	Examples
Elias Levita	[not stated]
Fenner	Alarm
Firmin	Real Christian
Franklin	Of Antichrist
Franzius	History of Brutes
Aul. Gellius	[not stated]
Goclenii	Logicæ
Goodwin	Sermons
Hall	On Timothy 3: 2
Herbert	Country Parson
Hubbard	History of Pequot War
Jerome, St.	Of Pliny
Johnson	[not stated]
Leigh	Of Colledges
May	History of War in E[ngland]
Morton	History of New England
Moxon	Of Globes
Owen	[various]
Paget	Chronography
Pareus	Orationes
Powell	[not stated]
Purchase [*sic*]	"of America"
Revius	de Capillitio
Reynolds	[not stated]
Rivet	[not stated]
Rutherford	"de drawing to Ct [Christ]"
Schindler	de Moseroth
Sibs	On Hosea 14
Smith, C.	Experiences
Stoughton	Of Covetousness

Twisse	[various]
Voetius	[not stated]
Ward, R.	Politick Strategy
Willisius	de Memoria

Other books are mentioned without sufficient detail for identification. A few of these items follow.

Discourse of Witchcraft
Help to discourse
Cabinet of Mirth
Autores de Conviction
Tollis^{n} of ye Jews
de doctoribus Misnicis
Coma Berenices
Capell Hall
Life of Richard 3
History of Formosa.

The Public Libraries as well as private ones continued to grow. There are unfortunately few references to the Boston Public Library in the town-house during this period. Sir Thomas Temple, in a will drawn up and filed October 14, 1671, before he sailed for England, inserted the following clause:

> . . . . as also all my Bookes which I estimate at £150 &c in case of sd Nelsons death before he receive them then I doe give & bequeath . . . . the Bookes above sd. at the select men of Bostons dispose viz: such as are fit for the Towne Lybrary unto that; and the rest to be sold & given to the poor of this Towne.

Before he died he drew up another will in London, in which there was no mention of the Library.[61] In a will dated March 12, 1673–4, John Oxenbridge made the following bequest:

> To the Public Library in Boston or elsewhere, as my executors

[61] Suffolk Probate Files No. 697, quoted in Publications of the Colonial Society of Massachusetts, xii. 122.

and overseers shall judge best, Augustine's Works in six volumes, the Century's in three volumes; the catalogue of Oxford Library.[62]

The Boston Athenæum owns a copy of Samuel Mather's "Testimony against Idolatry and Superstition," inscribed "ffor the Publike Library at Boston, 1674."[63] On August 2, 1683, the Selectmen gave an order to David Edwards

to receaue of Elder John Wiswall & Doct^{r} Elisha Cooke £34.4s. in mony for severall things he brought from England for ye vse of the Library, by order of Captain Brattle. . . .[64]

In 1686 the Town Records mentioned "the library room at the east end of the town house;"[63] and the same year Andros met the ministers "in the Library" at the town-house.[65] At a town meeting March 11, 1694–5, it was voted

. . . . that all Bookes or Other things belonging to the Library . . . . be demanded and Taken care of by the Selectmen.[66]

At a meeting of the Selectmen January 1, 1701–2, it was

Ordered that whereas Samuell Clough did formerly borrow the Towns Globes that he do now return them unto the Town Treasurer.[67]

In Chiswell's letter already given on pages 124 and 125 there is also a reference to this Library which would seem to indicate that Chiswell was accustomed to having many books of his sending bought by or for it:

I hope may help some of them off his hands by recommending

62 Winsor, Memorial History of Boston, i. 501.

63 *Ibid.*, iv. 279.

64 Boston Record Commissioners' Reports, vii. 162, quoted in Publications of the Colonial Society of Massachusetts, xii. 124.

65 Sewall, Diary, i. 162.

66 Boston Record Commissioners' Reports, vii. 220, quoted in the Publications of the Colonial Society of Massachusetts, xii. 125.

67 Boston Record Commissioners' Reports, xi. 13, quoted in the Publications of the Colonial Society of Massachusetts, xii. 126.

them to your publick Library, *especially the new ones, which cannot be there already.*[68]

The last phrase sounds as though any books but the newest might be expected to be found there.

The Harvard Library during this period received many important accessions. Under date of May 1, 1675, John Knowles wrote to John Leverett,

> Alderman Ashurst hath about 50 books of history for the College from Mr. Baxter.[69]

The same year John Lightfoot bequeathed his library, containing "the Targums, Talmuds, Rabbins, Polyglot, and other valuable tracts relative to Oriental literature."[70] In 1677 the Reverend Theophilus Gale left to it all his books, consisting chiefly of patristic and controversial theology.[71] In 1682 Sir John Maynard, sergeant-at-law, gave to the Library eight chests of books, valued at £400.[72] The last two gifts brought in so many duplicates that the Fellows of the College ordered "that the double Books in the Colledge Library be prized & sold & ye money improved for the buying other books y^t^ are wanting."[73]

There exists in the collections of the Massachusetts Historical Society a manuscript "Catalogue of such books as are double in ye Colledge Library," and with it what purports to be a record of volumes sold, with the amounts paid. The second list, containing 396 items, is more extensive than

[68] The italics are mine.

[69] North American Review, cvii. 572. Richard Baxter, fearing that his library would be seized to pay a fine, planned to give most of it to Harvard, but learned that Sir Kenelme Digby had given them "the Fathers, Councils, and Schoolmen, and that it was history and commentators which they wanted. Whereupon I sent them some of my commentators, and some historians, among which were Freherus', Reuberus', and Pistorius' collections."

[70] *Ibid.*, cvii. 572.

[71] *Ibid.*, cvii. 573. Neal, History of New England, i. 202, called Gale's "a large and Valuable Collection of Books."

[72] North American Review, cvii. 573.

[73] Harvard Library, Bibliographical Contributions, lii. 10.

the "catalogue," which lists 99 in folio, 36 in quarto, and 37 in octavo and smaller. There are no dates on either. The record of sales is partly in Increase Mather's hand. It may be that the second list covers a longer period of time, including later additions of duplicates. At any rate, about 400 titles of duplicates were sold, adding to the Library's funds about £98.10.00. Among the duplicates sold were:

Bacon's Essays (2 copies sold, one at 2s, one at 1s.)
Bacon's Advancement of Learning
Feltham's Resolves
Hackluit's Voyages
Herodotus
Aristophanes
Gassendi
Keckermann
Plutarch in English[74]

John Dunton's visit also added books to the Harvard Library, and gives us a glimpse of it through London eyes. He wrote home,

> I was invited hither [to Harvard] by Mr. Cotton[75] . . . by his means I sold many of my Books to the Colledge.[76]

Elsewhere he wrote,

> The *Library* of this *Colledge* is very considerable, being well furnish'd both with Books, and *Mathematical Instruments*.[77]

With the increased importation of books and with the growth of libraries there seems to have been an increase rather than a decrease in the borrowing and lending of

[74] Cotton Mather took advantage of this sale of duplicates to the extent of 96 titles, for which he paid £43.19.00 in installments. (Ms. list in possession of the American Antiquarian Society. See Publications of the Colonial Society of Massachusetts, xviii. 407 ff., for a photographic reproduction of this list and a catalogue of the books included.)

[75] John Cotton was Library-keeper at Harvard 1681–1690.

[76] Dunton, Letters, p. 156.

[77] Dunton, Life and Errors, p. 157. Neal, History of New England, i. 202, estimated it at between three and four thousand volumes before 1700.

books. Of this the following extracts from letters written during this time are indicative. More letters illustrating this tendency are given in the Appendix.

G. F.[78] hath sent the a booke of his by Jere: Bull, & two more now, which thou mayest communecatte to thy Counsell & officers.

Allso I remember before thy last being in England, I sent the a booke, written by Francis Howgall againest persecution, ... which booke thou loueingly accepted. . . .[79]

My last to thee was of the 29 D. 4. 72,[80] which Richard & Ester Smyth informed me they sent it to thee, so that they made noe doubt of thee safe convaience of it, with George Ffox bookes to thee, to which I shall refere thee. I haue other writings of G. F. not yet copied, which, if thou desireth, when I heare from thee, I may convaie them vnto thee; . . .[81]

May these few hasty lines salute you acceptably though only to certify the receiving of yours of the 18 of the former, & to thank you for that kindnesse, & that little volume of poetry therewith.[82]

Thinking it might be acceptable, I have sent you a verse-book; and desire you would send the other to Mr. Walley.[83]

It is evident from the details given in this chapter that the colonists did not lack for books, and that those which deserve the term literature were on their shelves in a fair proportion for the time. Evidence of the possession of still other books, and of their familiarity with and use of them, is to be found in the quotations with which they embellished their own writings.

[78] George Fox, then visiting New England.

[79] William Coddington to John Winthrop, Jr., 1672. Winthrop Papers, ii. 289.

[80] June 29, 1672. "My last" refers to the letter just quoted.

[81] William Coddington to John Winthrop, Jr. Winthrop Papers, ii. 291. The reference to copying books by hand demonstrates another method of supplementing libraries. Edward Taylor of Westfield had a considerable library of books which he had himself copied and bound.

[82] John Winthrop, Jr., to Roger Williams, January 6, 1675. Winthrop Papers, i. 306. If only he had mentioned the title!

[83] Samuel Angier to Governor Hinckley of Plymouth, January 29, 1677. Mr. Walley was preacher at Barnstable. Massachusetts Historical Society, Collections, 4th Series, v. 13. Governor Hinckley was a writer of verse.

Chapter VIII: Quotations by New England Writers.

AS a large part of the published writings of the New Englanders consisted of sermons, and as it seems to have been against their custom to use in their sermons any quotations except from Scripture or rarely from some of the Fathers, the field for quotations is somewhat limited. It is still further limited by the fact that few of the writers of narrative embellish their narratives with borrowed ornaments, either of prose or of poetry. From such books as do not belong to these two classes, from letters, and from a few narratives, the quotations to be included are taken.

Daniel Gookin, in his "Historical Collections of the Indians," Chapter IV, referred to "that seraphick prediction of holy Herbert, that excellent poet, ... which he elegantly declared in that poem: Herbert, Church Militant, 190, 191 page." He proceeds to quote twenty-four lines, from

> Religion stands on tiptoe in our land
> Ready to pass to the American strand

to

> But lends to us, shall be our desolation.

From his reference to the paging, which is the same in the fifth edition as in the first, it is evident that he had a copy of Herbert's "The Temple" before him. There are two or three errors in the quotation which he may have made in copying, but which are more likely typesetters' mistakes.

In a letter to Increase Mather, Nathaniel Morton wrote,

> . . . . and in some sort comply with our Englis Poett, George Withers; (saith hee) Alas that I was borne soe late, or else soe

soone; to see soe cleare, soe bright a morne, soe darke an afternoone.[1]

Thomas Shepard, writing to his son, then entering Harvard, in regard to his studies, echoed Bacon's essay, "Of Studies":

Lett your studies be so ordered as to have variety of Studies before you, that when you are weary of one book, you may take pleasure (through this variety) in another: and for this End read some Histories often, which (they Say) make men wise, as Poets make witty; both which are pleasant things in the midst of more difficult studies.[2]

The witchcraft controversies naturally called forth much citing of authorities. John Hale, in his "Modest Enquiry," referred to or quoted the following:

Bernard[3]
Baxter and R. Burton, their Histories about witches.[4]
Finch: Common Law[5]
Keeble of the Common Law[6]
St. Germans: Abridgment of Common Law
Wierus: De Præstigiis Demonum[7]

He also quoted a story by "my Lord Cook," evidently

[1] Written August 8, 1679. Mather Papers, p. 594.

[2] Publications of the Colonial Society of Massachusetts, xiv. 194. Probably written in 1672, as Thomas Shepard, third of that name, was of the class of 1676. Bacon's phrase is "*Histories* make Men Wise; *Poets* Witty." Shepard may have acquired this phrase at second hand; but, as several copies of the "Essays" have already been noted in the comparatively few libraries of which record remains, presumably he took it from its source.

[3] Bernard, "Guide to Grand-Jury men . . . in cases of Witchcraft," 1627.

[4] Baxter, "The Certainty of the Worlds of Spirits fully evinced by unquestionable Histories of Apparitions and Witchcrafts," 1691. R. Burton, or R. B., was the pseudonym of Nathaniel Crouch, publisher of London, who wrote many chapbooks. The reference may be to "The Kingdom of Darkness," 1688.

[5] Sir Henry Finch, "Treatise of Common Law," 1627, 1638, 1678; or "Summary of Common Law," 1673.

[6] Joseph Keeble wrote "Statutes," 1676, and "An Assistance to Justices of the Peace," 1683, 1689.

[7] Johann Weyer, a Rhenish physician, 1515–1588; quoted by the Mathers, and also by Burton in "The Anatomy of Melancholy."

Sir Edward Coke. A phrase which he used, "A dwarf upon a giants shoulders can see farther than a giant," may have been taken from Burton's "Anatomy of Melancholy," where it is found;[8] it may, however, have been a current phrase.

Robert Calef, merchant of Boston, in his attack on the Mathers which he called "More Wonders of the Invisible World" in mockery of Cotton Mather's "Wonders of the Invisible World," also showed familiarity with the literature of demonology, from which he freely quoted:

> And in the Mercury for the month of February, 1695, there is this account[9] [from which he quotes]
>
> . . . . the indians' adorations, which agrees well with what A. Ross sets forth, in his Mistag. Poetic. p. 116,[10] that . . . .
>
> Bernard's work on witches[11]
> Mr. Gaule's book on witches[12]
> Perkins' work on witches[13]
> Bodin[14]
> . . . . the fancies of Trithemius[15]

Calef was not content, however, with recent authors on the subject, but went back to the lives of Justin Martyr, Apollonius Tyaneus, and Julian the Apostate, and to the works of Josephus; he even quoted Ovid and Virgil. He has two quotations from Sandys' metrical translation of the "Metamorphoses": eighteen lines from Liber 7, and nine from Liber 14; and two passages from a metrical translation of Virgil's "Bucolics" which I have been unable to identify:

[8] Democritus to the Reader, p. 8, Chatto & Windus edition, 1907.

[9] P. xv. Calef's book was written in 1697.

[10] P. 129. Alexander Ross, "Mystagogus Poeticus, or the Muses Interpreter," London, 1647.

[11] See p. 138 note 3, above.

[12] John Gaule, "Select Cases of Conscience touching Witches and Witchcrafts," London, 1646.

[13] "Discourse of the Damned Art of Witchcraft," 1608.

[14] Jean Bodin, "Demonology."

[15] Johann Trithemius, 1462–1516.

two lines from Eclogue 13, and eleven lines from Eclogue 8. Although Calef complained that he was not an educated man, in contrast to the Mathers whom he was opposing, he knew both his Virgil and his Ovid, in English at least, sufficiently well to recall passages which very effectively illustrated his point that the current notions of witchcraft came from paganism and had no authority from the Bible.

The Mathers, especially Cotton, with his vast learning and a willingness to exhibit it, are very helpful to this study because they did quote so freely as to give some idea of the books with which they were familiar. Increase Mather quoted or cited (giving page or chapter reference) at least one hundred and thirty different authors, not including anonymous works quoted or cited, such as "The History of Sham Plots" or the "German Ephemerides." Besides these there are over thirty authors to whom he referred familiarly, but did not directly use. Cotton Mather quoted or cited over three hundred authors, and referred without direct use to nearly two hundred others. As it would be tedious to comment on all of these, only a few will be discussed, the rest being merely listed.

The most interesting quotation by Increase Mather is one from Burton's "Anatomy of Melancholy." Mather wrote:[16]

> . . . . There is in special, a sort of melancholy madness, which is called *lycanthropia* or *lupina insania*, *h. e.*, when men imagine themselves to be turned into wolves or other beasts. Hippocrates relates concerning the daughters of king Prætus, that they thought themselves kine. Wierus (*de Præstigiis Dæmonum*, l. iii. c. 21) speaketh of one in Padua, that would not believe to the contrary but that he was a wolf; and of a Spaniard, who thought himself a bear. Euwichius (and from him Horstius) writeth of a man that was found in a barn under the hay, howling and saying he was a wolf. The foolish rusticks, who surprized him, began to flay him, that so they might see if he had not hair growing on the

[16] Remarkable Providences, p. 122.

inside of his skin. Forestus has many instances to this purpose. Heurnius saith, that it is a disease frequent in Bohemia and Hungaria. No doubt but this disease gave occasion to Pliny's assertion, that some men in his time were turned into wolves, and from wolves into men again. Hence was Ovid's fable of Lycaon, and the tale of Pausanius being ten years a wolf, and then a man again. He that would see more instances, may read Austin, *de Civ. Dei.* l. xviii, c. 5; Burton of *Melancholly*, page 9. They that are subject unto this malady, for the most part lye hid all the day, and go abroad in the night, barking and howling at graves and in desarts. We may suppose that Nebuchadnezzar was troubled with this disease.

From Mather's brief reference to Burton in the above no one would imagine his real indebtedness to him for almost every detail in the passage. An idea of his wholesale borrowing in this instance will be obtained by a comparison of this with the parallel passage in Burton which follows:

Lycanthropia, which Avicenna calls Cucubuth, others Lupinam insaniam, or Wolf-madness, when men run howling about graves and fields in the night, and will not be persuaded but that they are wolves, or some such beasts. Ætius and Paulus call it a kind of melancholy; but I should rather refer it to madness, as most do. Some make a doubt of it whether there be any such disease. Donat ab Altomari saith, that he saw two of them in his time: Wierus tells a story of such a one at Padua 1541, that would not believe to the contrary, but that he was a wolf. He hath another instance of a Spaniard, who thought himself a bear; Forrestus confirms as much by many examples; one amongst the rest of which he was an eye-witness, at Alcmaer in Holland, a poor husbandman that still hunted about graves, and kept in churchyards, of a pale, black, ugly, and fearful look. Such belike, or little better, were King Prætus' daughters, that thought themselves kine. And Nebuchadnezzar in Daniel, as some interpreters hold, was only troubled with this kind of madness. This disease perhaps gave occasion to that bold assertion of Pliny, "some men were turned into wolves in his time, and from wolves to men again:" and to that fable of Pausanias, of a man that was ten years a wolf, and afterwards turned to his former shape: to

Ovid's tale of Lycaon, &c. He that is desirous to hear of this disease, or more examples, let him read Austin in his 18th book *de Civitate Dei*, *cap.* 5. *Mizaldus*, *cent.* 5. 77. *Sckenkius*, *lib.* 1. *Hildesheim*, ... [names several others]. This malady, saith Avicenna, troubleth men most in February, and is now-a-days frequent in Bohemia and Hungary, according to Heurnius. Schernitzius will have it common in Livonia. They lie hid most part all day, and go abroad in the night, barking, howling, at graves and deserts; . . . .[17]

There are one or two original items in Mather's, but nearly everything is borrowed, even to the phraseology, except the order. Was Mather the first of the many who have borrowed from the "Anatomy" without giving due credit?

Increase Mather knew Sir Thomas Browne as well as Burton, and quoted three times from his "Pseudodoxia Epidemica,"[18] citing the page once. He also cited Sir Kenelme Digby's "Discourse of Bodies," pp. 409, 410.[19] Thomas Fuller he cited and quoted;[20] and of course Joseph Glanvil, whose writings were the chief stronghold of those who believed in the necessity of witch-hunting.[21] His acceptance of the absurdities of the witchcraft delusions was not, however, due to any lack of access to or familiarity with the best scientific writings of his time. He took illustrations from five numbers of the Philosophical Transactions of the Royal So-

[17] Pp. 88, 89, Chatto & Windus edition, 1907.

[18] "Johnston (and from him Dr. Browne in his *Vulgar Errors*) hath truly asserted the contrary." (Remarkable Providences, p. 73.) "Dr. Browne, in his *Pseudodoxia Epidemica*, p. 63, does rationally suppose . . ." (*Ibid.*, p. 74.) There is also a reference on p. 76.

[19] *Ibid*, p. 72.

[20] "Such persons do (as Fuller speaks) fence themselves . . ." (*Ibid.*, p. 180.) "The like is reported by Dr. Fuller, in his *Church History*," (*Ibid.*, p. 261.) "Fuller's History of the Church p. 424." (Prayer, Early History of New England, p. 269.)

[21] He quotes or cites from the "Sadducismus Triumphatus or the Collection of Modern Relations," on pages 112, 127, 133, 149, 156, 158, 166, 170, 171, of Remarkable Providences.

ciety,[22] from two volumes of the Philosophical Conferences of the Virtuosi of France,[23] and from half a dozen volumes of the "German Ephemerides;"[24] he also quoted Robert Hooke[25] and Robert Boyle.[26] Of the latter he remarked in the Preface to "Remarkable Providences," "I have often wished that the Natural History of New-England might be written and published to the world; the rules and method described by that learned and excellent person Robert Boyle, Esq., being duely observed therein."

The list of the other books or writers made use of by Increase Mather, given in the Appendix, will show the variety of his reading, and, with the lists already given on pages 130 and 131, will throw light upon the content of his library.

The quotations by Cotton Mather are not only more in number than his father's, but have a more literary tone at times, partly because they include more poetry. He was familiar with "Paradise Lost," as is shown by three well chosen passages from that poem which he used in the "Magnalia." Charles Francis Adams, although he quotes these passages, makes the inference that we have no positive record of any copy of Milton's poems in New England before 1720;[27] a study of Mather's treatment of the passages he quotes will, however, I think, convince the reader that there must have been at least one copy of "Paradise Lost" in New England before 1698, lying open on Cotton Mather's table as he wrote his greatest book. Speaking of the diffi-

[22] Numbers cited are for 1665, 1666, 1670, 1672, and 1676. Remarkable Providences, pp. 83, 226, 213, 216, and 219, respectively.

[23] Vols. i and ii. Remarkable Providences, pp. 212, 82.

[24] Also called the "Observations of the Imperial Academy." The years quoted are 1670, 1671, 1675, 1679, 1687, 1689.

[25] "the late *Philosophical Collections*, published by Mr. Robert Hook, page 9."

[26] "The truly noble and honourable Robert Boyle, Esq., . . . in his book of the *Usefulness of Natural Philosophy*, p. 15."

[27] Massachusetts Historical Society, Proceedings, xlii. 154 ff. See, however, p. 123, above, and p. 181, below.

culties met by the colonists in their wars with the Indians, he wrote:[28]

> . . . . they found that they were like to make no weapons reach their enswamped adversaries, except Mr. Milton could have shown them how
>
> To have pluckt up the hills with all their load—
> Rocks, waters, woods—and by their shaggy tops,
> Up-lifting, bore them in their hands, therewith
> The rebel host to 've over-whelm'd.—

A comparison of this with the original, "Paradise Lost," VI, 643–647, 650–651, shows that Mather's changes are not misquotations from memory, but careful changes, evidently with the original before him, to preserve the rhythm and at the same time fit the new context.

> From their foundations, loosening to and fro,
> They plucked the seated hills, with all their load,
> Rocks, waters, woods, and, by the shaggy tops
> Uplifting, bore them in their hands. Amaze,
> Be sure, and terror, seized the rebel host,
>
> . . . .
>
> Till on those cursed engines' triple row
> They saw them whelmed, ...

The great impression made upon Mather by the details of the contest between the rebel host and the forces of the Almighty is shown by his own statement and by the two other paraphrases on the poem:

> . . . . but we who felt ourselves assaulted by unknown numbers of *devils in flesh* on every side of us, and knew that our minute numbers employ'd in the service against them, were proportionably more to *us* than mighty *legions* are to nations that have existed as many centuries as our colonies have years in the world, can scarce forbear taking the colours in the Sixth Book of Milton to describe our story:[29]

[28] Magnalia, i. 183.
[29] *Ibid.* ii. 566.

For after this, the *Auri sacra Fames*, that "cursed hunger of lucre," in the diverse nations of Europeans here, in diverse colonies bordering upon one another, soon furnished the salvages with *tools* to destroy those that furnish'd them:

—Tools, pregnant with infernal flame,
Which into hollow engines, long and round,
Thick ramm'd at the other bore, with touch of fire
Dilated and infuriate, doth send forth
From far with thund'ring noise among their foes
Such implements of mischief, as to dash
To pieces and o'erwhelm whatever stands
Adverse.—[30]

Milton, "Paradise Lost," VI, 482–491, wrote:

These in their dark nativity the Deep
Shall yield us, pregnant with infernal flame;
Which, into hollow engines long and round
Thick-rammed, at the other bore with touch of fire
Dilated and infuriate, shall send forth
From far, with thundering noise, among our foes
Such implements of mischief as shall dash
To pieces and o'erwhelm whatever stands
Adverse, that they shall fear we have disarmed
The Thunderer of his only dreaded bolt.

Mather, "Magnalia," ii. 568.

And now, *sic magnis componere parva!* Reader,

And now their mightiest quell'd, the battel swerved,
With many an inrode gor'd; deformed rout
Enter'd, and foul disorder; all the ground
With shiver'd armour strown, and on a heap,
Salvage and Sagamore lay overturn'd,
And fiery, foaming blacks: what stood, recoil'd,
O'er wearied, and with panick fear surpris'd.

"Paradise Lost," VI, 386–393.

And now, their mightiest quelled, the battle swerved,
With many an inroad gored; deformed rout

[30] *Ibid.*, ii. 557.

Entered, and foul disorder; all the ground
With shivered armour strown, and on a heap
Chariot and charioter lay overturned,
And fiery foaming steeds; what stood recoiled,
O'er-wearied, through the faint Satanic host,
Defensive scarce, or with pale fear surprised—

Chaucer, too, Mather evidently knew, for he hoped "that saying of old Chaucer [might] be remembred, 'To do the genteel deeds, that makes the gentleman.' "[31] Presumably this is a recollection of a passage in the "Wife of Bath's Tale."

Loke who that is most vertuous alway,
Privee and apert, and most entendeth ay
To do the gentil dedes that he can,
And tak him for the grettest gentil man.[32]

If the phrase had come to Mather as a current saying it would hardly have had Chaucer's name attached; at least it is hardly to be expected that people in general in New England would be so careful to preserve the name of a poet of whom Pope could write so slightingly, within ten years,

Now length of fame (our second life) is lost,
And bare threescore is all e'en that can boast;
Our sons their fathers' failing language see,
And such as Chaucer is, shall Dryden be.

Presumably Mather had a copy of Chaucer, or had used the Harvard Library copy.[33] He made one other reference to Chaucer, speaking of "the famous old Chaucer's motto:

[31] *Ibid.* i. 107.

[32] Chaucer, D. 1113–1116 (Skeat's Oxford edition).

[33] As the copy of Chaucer listed in the 1723 catalogue of the Harvard Library is reported as having no title page (see p. 273, below), it is probably not the Urry edition of 1721, which would hardly be so mutilated in a little more than a year, the catalogue being compiled largely in 1722; it is then either one of the Speght editions of 1598, 1602, or 1687, or some earlier edition. In any case it might easily have been in the college library for several years before the "Magnalia" was written.

Mors mihi ærumnarum requies."[34] On Chaucer's tomb in Westminster Abbey this is given as *Ærumnarum requies mors.*

Other quotations by Cotton Mather are from Cowley's Latin poems,[35] Fuller's "Church History" and other writings,[36] James Howel's "Familiar Letters,"[37] Dr. Burnet's "History of the Reformation,"[38] Wood's "Athenæ Oxoniensis,"[39] and so on. From Sir Richard Blackmore's "Prince Arthur," published in 1695, while the "Magnalia" was being written, he quoted two passages, one of 26 lines.[40] Besides these quotations he has references to "Hudibras,"[41] to Tom Tusser's lines on the harshness of Nicholas Udall, master of Eton,[42] to Ronsard's comment on DuBartas,[43] to Rabelais' "Pantagruel,"[44] and to the legend of the Pied Piper.[45] He seems, also, to have

[34] Magnalia, ii. 613. The phrase really belongs to Sallust (Catiline, 51.20). It is not found in any edition of Chaucer previous to Urry's of 1721. Mather probably became acquainted with it through the account of Chaucer's tomb given in Cambden's "Reges, Reginæ, Nobiles, et Alij in Ecclesia Collegiata B. Petri Westmonasterij Sepulti," London, 1606, pp. 66, 67.

[35] On the title page of the 4th Book are three lines from the "Plantarum," Lib. 5, end.

[36] In Magnalia, i. 290, he quotes from the "Church History," Cent. xvii, Book xi. 213; in Magnalia, ii. 15, from the "History of Cambridge University," in Magnalia, i. 76, from his "Comment on Ruth."

[37] Magnalia, i. 27, 35; ii. 27, 46.

[38] *Ibid.*, i. 441.

[39] *Ibid.*, *passim.* He sometimes vents his spleen at this anti-Puritan writer: "as a certain *woodden* historian . . . has reported," (Magnalia, i. 321).

[40] *Ibid.*, i. 65, "Prince Arthur," Book I, 552–567; 569–579. *Ibid.*, Title page to Book IV, "Prince Arthur," Book II, 101–103. See p. 198, below, for correspondence between Mather and Blackmore.

[41] Magnalia, i. 58, tells of use of Weymouth episode in *Hudibras.*

[42] *Ibid.*, i. 303, "whom now we may venture, after poor *Tom Tusser*, to call, 'the severest of men.'"

[43] *Ibid.*, ii. 28.

[44] *Ibid.*, ii. 645: "Let us now leave our friend Maule's works as a fit volume to be an appendix unto the famous '*Tartaretus*,' and worthy of a room in Pantagruel's library."

[45] This he might have found in Burton's "Anatomy of Melancholy" or Howel's "Letters;" but he seems to have taken it from Richard Verstegan's "Restitution of Decayed Intelligence in Antiquities," p. 92 (edition of 1673). Mather speaks of "the Transylvanian children;" there is no mention of Transylvania in either

been familiar with "Don Quixote," for he speaks of "romances of *Don Quixote* and the *Seven Champions*,"[46] and elsewhere[47] speaks of the "quixotism" of Roger Williams. It would be interesting to know whether Mather "coined" that term for himself; the "New English Dictionary" records but one use of it earlier than this, in a book or tract, "Pulpit Popery, True Popery," 1688, and quotes the next example from *The Briton*, No. 20, 1723. Certainly Cotton Mather, before the end of the century, had considerable literary background. The other books which he quoted or cited are listed in the Appendix.

In addition to all these, Cotton Mather was fond of using such phrases as "a saying of the Jews," "the Arabian proverb," "an account of a certain bishop of Rome," "the Italian proverb," "a certain proverb in Asia," "the witty epigrammatist hath told us," "as he that writes the life of holy Mr. Bains expresses it," "the author of the life of Belgic Wallæus," "the famous judge's motto," etc. In the "Magnalia"[48] occur two lines from Herbert, which, however, are not quoted by Mather, but in a prefatory epistle written by Matthew Mead of London. Presumably Mather could have quoted Herbert had he cared to, as a copy of Herbert's poems was in his father's library as early as 1664.[49]

Samuel Sewall's "Diary" and "Letter-Book" contain a few references to his reading. On his voyage to England in 1688 he carried with him a volume by Dr. Preston, Manton's "Exposition of James," and Erasmus.[50] At another time he recorded saying to Benjamin Colman, "Philomela would have

Burton or Howel, but Verstegan tells the tale in connection with his account of the Transylvanian Saxons, giving the location of the episode, however, as do the others, in Brunswick, at Hamel. Mather's memory was inaccurate here. A copy of Verstegan's book was in his father's library; see p. 53, above.

46 Magnalia, i. 208.

47 *Ibid.*, ii. 497.

48 *Ibid.*, ii. 153.

49 See p. 52, above.

50 "my Erasmus was quite loosened out of the Binding by the breaking of the water into Cabbin." (Diary, i. 238.)

found out some words . . . .,"[51] Philomela being the *nom de plume* of Elizabeth Singer Rowe, a popular English poetess of the day. On the cover of his journal he copied in full "An Elegie on Mrs. Alicia Lisle, which for high Treason was beheaded at Winchester, September the 2d 1685," evidently taken from an English broadside.[52] This is followed by letters dated 1686, and therefore was copied not long after publication. Sewall was no doubt especially interested in this poem because one of the daughters of the unfortunate Lady Alice Lisle was living in Boston, the wife of Hezekiah Usher, and formerly wife of President Hoar of Harvard.[53] The following item shows his interest in reading, and his taste. He was trying a case at Bristol at the time.

Rain hinder'd our setting out that day. So after diñer at Mr. Saffin's, Not knowing better how to bestow my time, Look'd on Mr. Saffin's Books, and lit on Dr. Fullers History of the Worthies of England, and in p. 116. 117. found mention made of the Inundation at Coventry, on Friday April, 17. in the Maioralty of Henry Sewall my Father's Grandfather. Mention is made p. 134. of Wm Dugdale's Illustrations of Warwickshire.[54]

Sewall did not need to go to Bristol to read Fuller, however, for two passages in his "Letter-Book" would indicate that he had more than one volume of Fuller in his own library, and was familiar with their contents.

I transcribe the following passage out of Dr. Fuller's Engl[ish] Worthies in London, p. 202[55] . . . .

Transcribed the passages of George Abbot Archb[ishop] out of Fuller's Ch[urch] History; knew not what better to write.[56]

[51] *Ibid.*, i. 507.
[52] *Ibid.*, ii. 8.
[53] See note 4, p. 99, above.
[54] Diary, i. 484. *Ca.* 1695.
[55] Letter-Book, i. 369.
[56] *Ibid.*, i. 374. Although Sewall wrote that "he knew not what better to write," the quotation was not a mere spacefiller but recorded a close parallel to a recent event in the life of the man to whom he was writing. Sewall knew his Fuller well enough to draw upon it for illustrations.

Other authors or books which he quoted, or to which he referred, are: Augustine's Psalms,[57] Baxter's "Glorious Kingdom of Christ Described,"[58] Calvin's "Institutions,"[59] Calamy's "Life of Baxter,"[60] Horn's "De Originibus Americanis,"[61] Hornius' "Carthaginian Dream,"[62] Pareus' "Commentaries,"[63] Thorowgood's "Jews in America,"[64] and *The London Gazette* of June 27, 1700.[65]

If the anonymous lines to Cotton Mather, written about 1700,[66]

> For *Grace* and *Act* and an Illustrious *Fame*
> Who would not look from such an *Ominous Name*,
> Where *Two Great Names* their Sanctuary take,
> And in a *Third* combined, a *Greater* make!

are, as Barrett Wendell very reasonably suggests,[67] in imitation of Dryden's lines "Under Milton's Picture"

> Three poets, in three distant ages born,
> Greece, Italy, and England, did adorn.
> The first, in loftiness of thought surpassed;
> The next, in majesty; in both, the last.
> The force of nature could no further go;
> To make a third, she joined the former two.

then we have another evidence of acquaintance with Milton's

[57] *Ibid.*, i. 199.

[58] *Ibid.*, ii. 202.

[59] *Ibid.*, i. 260.

[60] *Ibid.*, i. 294. He wrote to Calamy to correct statements in the latter's abridgment of Baxter's Life.

[61] *Ibid.*, i. 23. See Publications of the Colonial Society of Massachusetts, xiv. 167.

[62] Letter-Book, i. 289.

[63] Diary, i. 115.

[64] Letter-Book, i. 22.

[65] *Ibid.*, i. 16.

[66] Mather copied these lines in his diary on February 12, 1700, under the title *Ab Amico Satis Adulatore on Cotton Mather*, with the comment "Too gross Flattery for me to Transcribe; (tho' the Poetry be good." According to the editor of the Diary the lines are struck out in the manuscript—but in such a manner that they may still be read easily.

[67] Cotton Mather, p. 182 note.

poems, or at least with "Paradise Lost," in the 1688 edition of which these lines first appeared.

The foregoing quotations not only add many items to the book lists of the preceding chapter, but also give some idea of the familiarity of the colonists with the books which they possessed. They certainly were not as lacking in books as has been generally believed; and it seems equally true that they read and appreciated such literary books as they possessed to an extent for which they have never been given due credit.

Chapter IX: Relations with England and Other Phases of Culture.

THE close and sympathetic interest between the colonists and the government of England, as described in Chapter III, naturally came to an end at the Restoration. In its place a mutual suspicion developed, fostered on the one side by the colonists' disloyal protection of the Regicides, and on the other by the loss of colonial independence and the fear of possible religious coercion. At the same time a generation was growing up which knew not England; in fact it was almost a second generation from England, since in many cases the parents had left England when mere children. Those who had grown to maturity in England and had personal friends there were passing away; the death of John Winthrop, Jr., in 1676 broke one of the chief links that kept the best of the new world in touch with the best of the old. Social intercourse between New England and Old England seems to have reached, during the last quarter of the century, a lower ebb than at any time before or since.

It would be a mistake, however, to think of the colonies as isolated from the outside world even during this period. As has been shown in Chapter VII, the gifts of friends in England and the establishment of several booksellers made it possible for both the college and the colony to keep in touch with current thought. Settlers continued to come, too, even if in smaller groups than during the first period; and among them were occasionally men of high scholastic attainments, such as Samuel Lee,[1] who settled in Bristol, and Charles Morton[2], who settled in Charlestown. Occasionally,

[1] See p. 127, above.
[2] See p. 100, above.

too, young colonists went back to England to try their fortunes there, and not without success, as, for example, three sons of the Reverend John Higginson, of Salem. Thomas Higginson became a goldsmith in England; Francis went to live with his uncle Francis in England[3] and was educated at the University of Cambridge; and Nathaniel was first steward of Lord Wharton, and later went to the East Indies, where he succeeded Elihu Yale as Governor of Madras, and, like him, grew rich.[4] His letters, both from India and from England after his return,[5] show that he was interested in New England and had tentative plans for returning thither, as his father so earnestly urged him to do; but he never came. The Reverend Warham Mather had thoughts of going to England, for he wrote to his uncle, Increase Mather, then in London, as follows:

> S^r, we expect not your return before winter. It will be profitable for me to know what advice you think it will be best for me to follow, relating to a remove for England, before that time, for it is not likely I should sell what estate I have here for the worth thereof at short warning.[6]

He did not go, however.

New Englanders continued to visit England for both business and pleasure. Increase Mather went twice as agent of Massachusetts. Of his second trip a modern historian writes:

> During Andros's administration some of the prominent men of the colony, dissatisfied with the curtailment of their former privileges, determined to appeal to England for relief. Increase Mather, the influential pastor of the Old North Church, was selected to bear to the king, James II., the complaints of the colony,

[3] See p. 65, above.

[4] Massachusetts Historical Society, Collections, 3rd Series, vii. 196; F. B. Dexter, Publications of the New Haven Historical Society, iii. 238.

[5] Massachusetts Historical Society, Collections, 3rd Series, vii. 198 ff. The eagerness with which his father urged him not to forget his native place is quite pathetic.

[6] Mather Papers, p. 671. July 6, 1688.

and to obtain, if possible, a restoration of the charter. He was admirably adapted to the task, having served as agent in England only a few years before, while his pleasing address and familiarity with the men and ways of the court at Whitehall were certain to stand him in good stead in the work to be done.[7]

It is worth noting that on this errand he was well received by the courts both of James II and of William and Mary.

In 1688 Samuel Sewall, accompanied by his brother Stephen and two others, went to England on a trip which combined the pleasure of a visit to his birthplace in England with considerable buying of commodities, presumably upon commission.

Joseph Dudley went to England in 1682 as an agent of Massachusetts.[8] In 1693 he again went to England and there resided for nine years, taking an active part in English affairs, even serving in Parliament.[9] Another who spent several years in England was Benjamin Colman, who went to London in 1695. He was well received by the Dissenting clergy there, once being sent by a committee of them to preach at Cambridge, and later, after preaching at Ipswich, being chosen by the London Presbytery to take an important church at Bath, where he remained two years. He left only to accept a call to a new church in Boston.[10]

Benjamin Lynde, Harvard 1686, went to London to study for the bar at the Middle Temple. His wife accompanied him either at that time or on some later trip, for her portrait was painted in England by Sir Godfrey Kneller.[11]

During this period there is practically no evidence of any intercourse or friendship between any one in New England and the literary men of England, if such writers of religious literature as Richard Baxter be excluded.[12] Anthony à

[7] C. M. Andrews, Narratives of the Insurrections, p. 271.

[8] Kimball, Public Life of Joseph Dudley, p. 13.

[9] *Ibid.* pp. 65, 208.

[10] Turell, Life of Colman, *passim.*

[11] Massachusetts Historical Society, Proceedings, 1st Series, xvi. 396.

[12] See p. 134, above, for details of Baxter's gift to Harvard.

Wood turned to Increase Mather, when the latter was in London, for information in regard to the Oxford graduates who had emigrated to New England;[13] but the "Athenæ Oxoniensis" can hardly be classed as pure literature.

In spite of all this lessening of intercourse, the colonists continued to feel a keen interest in England and conditions there, as their constant eagerness for gazettes and news-letters shows;[14] and this sometimes found definite expression, as in the following passage from John Higginson's "Attestation" to the "Magnalia."

> That the little daughter of New-England in America, may bow down herself to her mother England, in Europe, presenting this *memorial* unto her; assuring her, that though by some of her *angry brethren* she was forced to make a *local secession*, yet not a *separation*, but hath always retained a dutiful respect to the *Church of God* in England; and giving some account to her, how graciously the Lord has dealt with herself in a *remote wilderness*, and what she has been doing all this while; giving her thanks for all the *supplies* she has received from her; and because she is yet in her *minority*, she craves her farther *blessing* and *favour* as the case may require; being glad if what is now presented to her, may be of any use, to help forward the *union* and *agreement* of her *brethren*, which would be some satisfaction to her for her undesired local distance from her dear England; and finally promising all that reverence and obedience which is due to her good *mother*, by virtue of the *fifth* commandment.[15]

If the colonists did not go to England as much as at an earlier period, certain elements of English life, formerly absent, were introduced, especially under Governor Andros. A dancing-master set up in Boston,[16] and a fencing master

[13] Massachusetts Historical Society, Collections, 2d Series, vii. 187.

[14] See pp. 222 and 223, above.

[15] Magnalia, i. 16. Dated 1697.

[16] Wendell, Cotton Mather, p. 44. The first dancing master of whom there is record was one Henry Sharlot or Sherlot, who is described both as Irish and as French. On September 6, 1681, the Court of Assistants decided that "Henry Sherlot a frenchman, that is newly come into this Towne as he sajth, a Dancing master and a person very Insolent and of ill fame, that Raves and scoffes at Religion

as well.[17] Public fencing bouts were held, and a maypole was erected.[18] Just previous to this John Dunton and other booksellers had brought over plays and romances and playing cards.[19] In connection with the latter the following passage in Sewall's "Diary" is of interest.

> Wednesday, June 21 [1699]. A Pack of Cards are found strawed over my fore-yard, which, tis supōsed, some might throw there to mock me, in spite of [for] what I did at the Exchange Tavern last Satterday night.[20]

Boston was losing its former character of a city devoted to religion, and was becoming a worldly commercial seaport. This was felt strongly by the critical Dutch traveler, Jasper Danckaerts, who wrote of Boston in 1680:

> Nevertheless you discover little difference between this and other places. Drinking and fighting occur there not less than elsewhere; and as to truth and true godliness, you must not expect more of them than of others. When we were there, four ministers' sons were learning the silversmith's trade.[21]

. . ." be ordered away. It is unfortunately not clear whether his personality or his profession was chiefly responsible for the Court's action. (Massachusetts Historical Society, Proceedings, xlix. 99 ff.) His successors had better fortune. To meet this new evil, Increase Mather considered it necessary to prepare "An Arrow against Profane and Promiscuous Dancing. Drawn out of the Quiver of the Scriptures," published in 1684 by Joseph Brunning. (Sibley, Harvard Graduates, i. 445.)

[17] The Council granted, September 15, 1686, the following petition: "The humble petition of Richard Crisp, humbly sheweth, That whereas there are several gentlemen in this town, that are desirous your petitioner should instruct them in the use of weapons, and whereas there is a law, that forbiddeth the building of any edifice with wood, above such a bigness as the said law permits, I humbly pray . . . liberty to build a low, slight house for that purpose . . ." (Massachusetts Historical Society, Collections, 3rd Series, vii. 157.)

[18] Increase Mather recorded in his diary in 1687: (April 27.) "Sword playing was this day openly practised on a Stage in Boston & that immediately after ye Lecture, so y^t^ the Devil has begun a Lecture in Boston on a Lecture-Day wh was set up for Christ . . ." (May 1.) "A May pole was set up in Charlestown." (Massachusetts Historical Society, Proceedings, 2d Series, xiii. 411.)

[19] See p. 120 ff., above.

[20] Diary, i. 498. Unfortunately there is no further report of the affair at the Exchange Tavern.

[21] Journal of Jasper Danckaerts, pp. 274, 275.

In connection with Danckaerts' last remark it must be remembered that there were nearly a score of silversmiths working at their craft in Boston before the end of the century. Many of the things which they wrought were necessary articles; but the rapid growth in their numbers toward the end of this period, as well as examples of their work which have been preserved, indicates that Boston afforded a good market for luxuries.[22] That four ministers' sons at once were turning to this lucrative work instead of preparing to follow in the footsteps of their fathers shows the tendency of the time.

The wealthy men of the first period had been those who brought fortunes with them. In the second period we find men who had made their own fortunes in the new land, such men as John Hull, silversmith and mint-master, whose wealth is a tradition with us.[23] Hezekiah Usher, bookseller, dying in 1676, left a fortune of over £15,000 for his two sons to quarrel over.[24] John Dunton speaks of the wealth acquired by John Usher[25] who succeeded his father. Wait Winthrop in Boston and Fitz-John Winthrop at New London were living in a style resembling that of the landed gentry of England, whom they were planning to imitate in the establishing of an estate practically in entail.[26] Even in Plymouth there was an increase in wealth, according to

[22] Bigelow's "Historic Silver of the Colonies and its Makers" gives interesting details of the lives of these silversmiths and contains illustrations showing the beauty of their work. His record is not complete, however, for he does not mention the Dutch silversmith, Willem Ros, from Wesel, whom Jasper Danckaerts found carrying on his trade in Boston in 1680. (Journal of Jasper Danckaerts, p. 260.)

[23] There seems to be no satisfactory estimate of his wealth, but he was unquestionably wealthy for his day. His gift to his daughter upon her marriage to Samuel Sewall is estimated at £500 ($10,000 in modern equivalent). (Hull's Diary, p. 275.)

[24] See pp. 79 and 114, above.

[25] See p. 114, above.

[26] John Winthrop, F. R. S., won his suit against the other heirs of his uncle, Fitz-John, and his father, Wait, by showing that the two brothers had planned to leave their vast holdings of land to a single heir that they might be handed down intact from generation to generation, and not to be broken up and soon dissipated by division among group after group of heirs. (Winthrop Papers, vi. *passim.*)

Governor Josiah Winslow's statement that "most men there are freeholders, few tenants; incomes of 2000*l.* are rare among them."[27] They may have been few, but the interesting thing is that there were any. Twenty-five years earlier estates totaling one-quarter of that sum were unknown.[28] Comprehensive lists of men of wealth and their estates seem unnecessary here, for the very fact that so many booksellers and silversmiths set up shop in Boston[29] is in itself evidence that there was a considerable public which could afford the luxuries of books and silver plate. Even portrait painters were beginning to cater to the vanity of the colonists. Before 1667 the Reverend John Wilson refused to have his portrait painted for his friends, although Edward Rawson brought to him a "limner, with all things ready."[30] Portraits of Henry and Margaret Gibbs bearing the date of 1670 are still in existence.[31] In 1679 or 1680 Increase Mather sat for a portrait which he sent to his brother Nathaniel, of Dublin.[32] In 1684 Joseph Allen came from Dublin bearing letters from Nathaniel to Increase Mather in which he was described as skilled in "graving" and "limning."[33] Wait Winthrop wrote in 1691 of a man who could copy miniatures.[34] Evidently as far as Boston and the older settlements were concerned, the pioneer days of hardship were over.

[27] Calendar of State Papers, Colonial Series, America and West Indies, 1677–1680, p. 522, no. 1349.

[28] See pp. 28 and 29, above.

[29] See pp. 114–117 and 157, above.

[30] Magnalia, i. 320.

[31] Massachusetts Historical Society, Proceedings, 1st Series, x. 41 ff.

[32] Mather Papers, p. 28.

[33] *Ibid.*, p. 52.

[34] Winthrop Papers, iv. 500. Under date of October 31 he wrote to Fitz-John Winthrop, "If you could by a very carefull hand, send the litle picture of my grandfather, put carefully up in som litle box, here is one would copy it for my cousin Adam . . ."

Chapter X: The Production of Literature.

AS the previous chapters have shown, New England grew provincial after the middle of the century, and especially after the Restoration. This is shown most strikingly in the literature produced during this period. Literary movements in England had practically no influence across the sea. Of course the most important element in the English literature of the time, the dramatic, because of its very nature, could in no way stimulate literary activity where the drama was tabooed. Furthermore, most non-dramatic literature was written by Tories and Royalists, many of them courtiers, in whose writings New England Puritans could take little interest. It is not so easy to explain why Milton aroused no echo in New England; but it is evident to any student of the period that the chief writer of Boston, Cotton Mather, although he evidently knew "Paradise Lost" well,[1] made no attempt to imitate the grandeur of its style, preferring the elaborate conceits and puns characteristic of the style which the earliest settlers brought over with them. In England there had been great changes; in New England the literary style, like the language, tended to remain fixed. The leaders of thought in Boston were generally as conservative in their writing as in their religious thinking, looking to the past rather than to the present or the future.

Where the influence of the earlier colonial verse-writers is not evident, as in Peter Folger's "A Looking-Glass for the Times," in some of Benjamin Tompson's poems, and elsewhere, as in some of the poetry of the almanacs, the style seems either original, or else derived from ballads or hymns, the metres especially resembling those of the ballad or short

[1] See p. 143 ff., above.

or common metre hymn. There is absolutely no suggestion of contemporary English poetry of the better kind here.

Very much the same thing is true of the prose of the period. The style of Cotton Mather in the "Magnalia," written in the last decade of the seventeenth century, resembles, as does his father's style, the prose writings of such Englishmen as Robert Burton and Thomas Fuller, who belong to the earlier part of the century.[2]

It is necessary to distinguish here between literary influences and influences of a political or even intellectual nature. Unresponsive as the people of New England were to literary movements, they were in close touch not only with English politics, but with certain philosophical movements. Their interest in politics was natural, as they were personally affected by what happened in London. Their familiarity with the scientific movement of the time has been noted.[3] Their reaction to the writings of the Cambridge Platonists is more striking. The attempts of such writers as Joseph Glanvil and Henry More to prove the reality of the spiritual world culminated in "Sadducismus Triumphatus," begun by Glanvil and finished by More in 1681. Three years later Increase Mather published his "Remarkable Providences" as a contribution to the growing body of material which sought to support the teachings of Glanvil and More. Within ten years New England had reacted to the belief in demons in

[2] Cotton Mather's love of quoting Latin and Greek, and even Hebrew, is a relic of the tendency which led Lord Coke, who died in 1633, to illustrate the knotty points and subtle distinctions of the law with 300 extracts from Virgil—and then boast of his achievement. (Mullinger, Cambridge in the Seventeenth Century, p. 64, note.) Before Cotton Mather was born, Samuel Butler had ridiculed this style of writing, calling it (Hudibras, Canto I, 93–98)

A Babylonish dialect,
Which learned pedants much affect:
It was a parti-colour'd dress
Of patch'd and piebald languages;
'Twas English *cut on* Greek *and* Latin,
Like fustian heretofore on satin.

[3] See above, pp. 107 ff. and 142–3.

an even more striking way, by the persecution of witches, especially at Salem. Witch-hunting did not begin in the colonies at that time, but the extent and violence of the Salem persecutions in contrast with the sporadic witchcraft cases in New England previous to 1680 would seem to be the result of a direct reaction to the Cambridge philosophers. The fact that Deodat Lawson, whose lecture at Salem Village, March 24, 1692, marked the beginning of the worst persecutions, had studied at Cambridge gave weight to his words and was largely responsible for the severity of the frenzy.

The provincialism of the period is nowhere better shown than in the growing preponderance of sermons in the publications of the local presses. In the eight years including 1682 and 1689, of the 133 books published in Boston, 56 were sermons, 39 more were of a religious nature, and of the remaining 38, 12 were almanacs, and 17 were proclamations or political pamphlets arising from the revolt against Andros in 1689.[4] The lowest ebb of American literature was reached at this time; the only poetical items are Cotton Mather's "A Poem Dedicated to the Memory of . . . . Mr. Urian Oakes" and "An Elegy on . . . . Rev. Mr. Nathanael Collins," Richard Steere's "A Monumental Memorial of Marine Mercy," and reprints of Wigglesworth's "Meat out of the Eater" and "The Day of Doom."

The dearth of literature is not relieved to any great extent, as in the first period, by publications abroad. Some colonial writings were published in England, but most of these, as Increase Mather's accounts of the Indian wars, were reprints of books already printed in New England. One book, and that undoubtedly the most important book of the period,[5] Cotton Mather's "Magnalia Christi Americana," was considered by its author sufficiently important to be sent

[4] These figures are compiled from Evans' American Bibliography, and include books printed in Cambridge.

[5] Although not published until 1702, it was written about 1697.

to England for its original publication; but this is rather the exception.

Some poetry of the period escaped publication at the time, and should be added in estimating the amount of literature produced; but this is much less in quantity than in the earlier period. Edward Taylor of Westfield filled a notebook with verse, none of which has ever been published, as the writer forbade publication. Many elegies, such as those preserved in Blake's "Annals of Dorchester" and others passed on from generation to generation in family records, waited until later times for their appearance in public. But even these are not sufficient either in amount or in merit to bring the production of this period to the level of either the earlier or the later periods.

All this does not mean that there were no writings of literary value during these years, for that would not be true. The most interesting and important of the writings of the two Mathers belong to this period: "Remarkable Providences," "The Wonders of the Invisible World," and the "Magnalia Christi Americana." To these must be added the four clever political fables which Cotton Mather wrote in defence of his father's activities as agent of the Colony.[6] Robert Calef's "More Wonders of the Invisible World" also deserves mention here for its rationality, which gives it, in contrast with the Mather witchbooks, a surprisingly modern tone. Another modern seeming book is Sewall's anti-slavery pamphlet, "The Selling of Joseph."

The poetry of the period was inferior to the prose; there was, however, some verse with poetic merit. One example of a poem which is at least natural, and not without humor, has been printed in part on page 91, Samuel Bailey's "The College Ferula." Of the conceits which marred much of the colonial poetry perhaps the most effective and fitting is the one used by Joseph Capen at the end of his elegy upon John Foster, printer and almanac maker:

[6] Printed in the Prince Society Andros Tracts, ii. 325 ff.

Thy Body which no activeness did lack
Now's laid aside like an old Almanack
But for the present only's out of date;
Twil have at length a far more active State.
Yea, though with dust thy body Soiled be,
Yet at the Resurrection we Shall See
A fair Edition & of matchless worth,
Free from Errata, new in Heav'n Set forth:
Tis but a word from God the great Creatour,
It Shall be Done when he Saith IMPRIMATUR.[7]

The concluding stanzas of Urian Oakes' lament for Thomas Shepard are worth quoting, although the greater part of this elegy exhibits the usual faults of New England poetry.

In vain we build the prophets' sepulchers,
In vain bedew their tombs with tears, when dead;

7 "It has been thought," writes Samuel A. Green, in his study of John Foster (page 35), "that the closing lines of Capen's Elegy suggested to Franklin the quaint epitaph which he wrote for himself." The parallel is so interesting that the epitaph is given here for comparison:

The body of Benjamin Franklin, printer, (like the cover of an old book, its contents torn out, and stript of its lettering and gilding) lies here food for worms; yet the work itself shall not be lost, for it will (as he believed) appear once more in a new and more beautiful edition, corrected and amended by the author.

The parallel becomes more interesting when we carry it back a generation to Benjamin Woodbridge's elegy upon John Cotton, who died in 1652. Presumably the elegy was written soon after that date.

A living, breathing Bible; tables where
Both covenants, *at large, engraven were;*
Gospel *and* law, *in's heart, had each its column;*
His head an index to the sacred volume;
His very name a title-page; *and next,*
His life a commentary *on the text.*
O, what a monument of glorious worth,
When, in a new edition, *he comes forth,*
Without erratas, *may we think he'll be*
In leaves *and* covers *of eternity!*

It would be remarkable if Woodbridge's figure of speech should have recurred twice unconsciously; if it was used consciously, it forms a curious link between the seventeenth and eighteenth centuries in American literature.

In vain bewail the deaths of ministers,
Whilest prophet-killing sins are harboured.
Those that these murtherous traitors favour, hide;
Are with the blood of Prophets deeply dy'd.

New-England! know thy heart-plague: feel this blow;
A blow that sorely wounds both head and heart,
A blow that reaches all, both high and low,
A blow that may be felt in every part.
Mourn that this great man's faln in Israel:
Let it be said, "with him New-England fell!"

Farewell, dear Shepard! Thou art gone before,
Made free of Heaven, where thou shalt sing loud hymns
Of high triumphant praises ever more,
In the sweet quire of saints and seraphims.
Lord! look on us here, clogg'd with sin and clay,
And we, through grace, shall be as happy as they.

My dearest, inmost, bosome-friend is gone!
Gone is my sweet companion, soul's delight!
Now in an hud'ling croud I'm all alone,
And almost could bid all the world "Goodnight."
Blest be my Rock! God lives: O let him be,
As He is All, so All in All to me!

Whereas literary production during the first period of colonial life was in keeping with the culture of the people, during the second period literature lagged behind culture. The chief reason for this, provincialism, has already been discussed. While the culture, although not as low as it has often been pictured, had grown somewhat provincial, the literature had become entirely divorced from English literary movements. The colonists did have London books; but their ears could not catch the note of the literary activity which centered in London. There were other reasons for this than the width of the Atlantic. The Restoration had in time brought about the loss of charter and privileges; and thus began that long struggle between colonist and crown which was to monopolize the interest and energy of the people of New England for over a century. Cotton Mather was eager to peruse any books which his father might bring from England; but he was vastly more interested in the charter which his father might bring back for the colony and indirectly for the college. Whether the ministerial party headed by himself and his father would be able to control the colony; whether the orthodox element in New England could continue to guide the college;—these matters were vastly more important than the fact that a new period in English literature was developing. Even if this had not been the case, the tremendously busy life which Cotton Mather led was enough to make careful literary work impossible. As Barrett Wendell writes,

> Until one actually inspects the documents, it seems incredible that in forty-five years any single human being could have penned so many words as we thus see to have come from the hand of one of the busiest ministers, one of the most insatiable scholars and readers, and one of the most active politicians whom America has ever known.[8]

Cotton Mather himself referred to the difficulties of literary work in the face of his other activities:

> . . . . I have been forced . . . . to throw by the work [the "Magnalia"] whole months together, and then resume it, but by a stolen hour or two in the day, not without some hazard of incurring the *title* which Coryat put upon his History of his Travels, "*Crudities hastily gobbled up in five months*."[9]

> If I could redeem the Time, now and then to dress up sublime Thoughts in an agreeable Metre, I might in Time, have a Collection, which may prove a profitable and an acceptable Entertainment, unto the Church of God.[10]

Two extracts from his diary show his hasty manner of writing.

[8] Literary History of America, p. 47.
[9] Magnalia, i. 32.
[10] Diary, ii. 335.

> The Printer, wanting something to fill the last Leaf of his Almanack, for the year, 1699, came unto mee, to furnish him. . . . . I took my Opportunity, and wrote a few pungent Lines, concerning the Changes, which may bee coming as *a Snare upon the Earth*. . . .[11]

> There is printing a new Edition of our *Psalm-book*. In every former Edition, that excellent Portion of Scripture, the 36TH CHAPTER OF ISAIAH, was in such a metre, that few of our Churches could sing it. Wherefore I this day, took a few Minutes, to turn it into another Metre, with perhaps, a smoother and sweeter Version. So tis published in the *Psalm book;* . . . [12]

As, in spite of the unfavorable circumstances under which they were composed, Cotton Mather's productions taken all in all are not without literary merit, it is interesting to surmise what he might have done in literature had he not been so distracted by other things, including the constant abuse of his health by vigils and fasts.[13] The one man in New England who had the greatest familiarity with English literature, whose mind was a veritable storehouse of learning of every kind, never gave what literary ability he may have had an opportunity to develop.

What is true of Cotton Mather is true in less degree of all New England. Life was too full of other interests to allow much energy to be devoted to literary work. During the seventies the colonists were carrying on a bitter war with the Indians, a war which cost the United Colonies over £100,000 and many lives. During the eighties public interest was absorbed by the struggle to maintain colonial rights against the encroachments of Randolph and Andros. In the last decade of the century began the struggle between the ministerial party, headed by the Mathers, and the more liberal party for the control of the government and the college.

[11] *Ibid.*, i. 276. The article appeared in Tulley's Almanack for 1699.

[12] *Ibid.*, i. 300.

[13] Tyler, in his History of American Literature, ii. 76, says, ". . . it was computed that, in the course of his life, the number of his special fast-days amounted to four hundred and fifty."

The censorship still added its restraint to the other influences which retarded literary production. According to their instructions, provincial governors held complete control of the press. Before Andros came, Randolph, as secretary of the province, had appointed an official printer and had sent the following notice to the other printers:

> I am comanded by M[r] Secretary Randolph, to give you notice that you doe not proceed to print any Almanack whatever without haveing his approbation for y[e] same.
>
> Yo[rs] Ben: Bullivant
>
> Boston: 29 Novemb[r] 1686.[14]

Soon after the installation of Governor Andros the proceedings of his Council contained this entry:

> The Councill being met His Ex[ce] acquainted them that it was his Maj[ties] express commands that the printing Presses in the Towns of Boston and Cambridge in New England should be effectuall [*sic*] taken care of. Upon which an order passed in Councill, that no Papers, Bookes Pamphlets &c should be printed in New England untill Licensed according to Law. . . [15]

Andros' loss of power did not end the censorship, for the House of Representatives in November, 1689, passed orders to control the press.[16] The first newspaper in America, *Publick Occurrences, both Foreign and Domestick*, was suppressed immediately upon the appearance of its first number, unlicensed, on September 25, 1690.[16] In 1695 action was brought against Thomas Maule of Salem for circulating a book of his which he had had published in New York.[16] He was acquitted by jury, but the fact that action was brought against him shows that the censorship was active.

The final reason for the low estate of literature during this period was the lack of any sympathetic support by either the reading public or any literary coterie. Enough litera-

[14] Duniway, Freedom of the Press in Massachusetts, p. 64.
[15] *Ibid.*, p. 65.
[16] *Ibid.*, p. 67 ff.

ture from England was available through the booksellers for those who were interested in literature, and from the local presses only books of purely local interest were expected, such as contemporary sermons, almanacs, and political pamphlets. It is true that "Pilgrim's Progress" was reprinted on one of the New England presses,[17] but this was exceptional for the period, and is counterbalanced by the fact that such a local book as the "New England Primer" seems to have been printed first in England.[18]

Group interest in literature as literature, or any mutual encouragement toward the production of literature, is not in evidence until the very end of the period. The influx of books through the many booksellers who came to Boston after 1685[19] could not but have some effect upon literary production in New England; but results are not evident until the very end of the period, and are more noticeable in the opening years of the eighteenth century. The earliest indication of any group interest in literature is found in the literary friendship between Samuel Sewall and Richard Henchman, schoolmaster, which probably began before the year 1700, the first evidence of it being given in Henchman's poem to Sewall under date of January 1, 1700–1. There is more evidence of their mutual interest in poetry during the years that follow, as will be shown in Chapter XIV.

In conclusion, then, it may be said that although this period marks the nadir of American literature, at the end of the period, thanks to the activities of the Boston booksellers and to renewed intercourse with England, there was beginning a literary movement in New England which was to develop rapidly in the opening years of the new century.

[17] Bunyan's prefatory verses to the second part of Pilgrim's Progress, published in 1684, refer to an edition of the first part printed in New England. This was printed in 1681 by Samuel Green for Samuel Sewall. A copy of this edition is in the Boston Public Library.

[18] At least a New England Primer was printed in England by John Gaine in 1683. As all copies have disappeared, it is impossible to ascertain to what extent it resembled the New England Primer printed by Benjamin Harris about 1690. (See the letter by Worthington C. Ford in *The Nation*, January 11, 1917, p. 46.)

[19] See p. 116 ff, above.

Part III:

The New Century.

1700-1727.

Chapter XI: Education.

THE new century brought no changes into the educational work carried on at Cambridge. The growing liberality of the Harvard theology caused certain of the conservatives in the colonies to become disaffected and resulted in a contest for the control of the college in which the liberals were victorious;[1] but the contest, although it affected the political life of the community, seems to have made little if any change in the value of the instruction given to the students. The old system continued under the same men, or under men similarly trained; and it was not until the end of the period under consideration that the benefactions of Thomas Hollis, and especially the establishment by him of two professorships, one of Divinity and one of Mathematics and Natural Philosophy, gave the college a new impetus.[2]

If, during these years, no change in educational methods took place, at least increased opportunity for education was offered through the establishment of a new college in Connecticut in the very first year of the century. The "Collegiate School" at Saybrook, later moved to New Haven and re-named "Yale College," was modeled after Harvard, the founders and teachers being Harvard graduates. The young college benefited by the support of the Mathers, Judge Sewall, and others who, disliking the liberal tendencies at Harvard, turned to the younger school as the last refuge of New England orthodoxy. They enlisted the aid of their friends in England with such success that Yale soon had a fair endowment and a library which, if not as large as

[1] See Quincy, History of Harvard University, i. chaps. x–xiv.

[2] *Ibid.* i. The first gift from Hollis arrived in 1719. The Professorship of Divinity was offered in 1721, and the Professorship of Mathematics and Natural Philosophy in 1727.

Harvard's, was well chosen and contained a larger proportion of current literature.[3]

The education given in the new college seems to have been equivalent to that at Harvard. The graduates were fitted to hold high positions in the community, and two members of early classes were honored by recognition by the English Universities. Samuel Johnson, of the class of 1714, was given the honorary degree of Master of Arts in 1723 by both Cambridge and Oxford, and was made a Doctor of Divinity by the latter in 1743.[4] Jonathan Arnold, of the class of 1723, was granted the honorary Master's degree at Oxford in 1736.[5]

Outside of the formal education of the college there was a growing interest in science. Thomas and William Brattle, Cotton Mather, Paul Dudley, Thomas Robie, and the younger John Winthrop were all members or correspondents of the Royal Society, and nearly all had papers published in the Society's Transactions.[6] Others, like Dr. William Douglass,[7] were making observations and keeping in touch with contemporary science. Increasing intercourse with England, and the temporary residence in Boston of Englishmen who came over to take part in the government of the colonies, were further educational and liberalizing influences.

Thus we find in the colonies, by the end of the first century of colonial life, a large and steadily growing body of educated men. The proportion of college men has never been as great as it was during the first years of the colonies, when conditions were abnormal,[8] but it was much greater in the third period than in the second, when the college as well as the colonies showed the most provinciality, and it had de-

[3] See p. 184 ff., below.
[4] Dexter, Biographical Sketches of the Graduates of Yale College, i. 124.
[5] *Ibid.*, p. 275.
[6] See p. 108, above, and pp. 199 and 200, below.
[7] See pp. 200 and 201, below.
[8] See Chapter 1, above.

veloped under more liberal surroundings.[9] That this growth in numbers and the changing environment resulted in an increasing literary productivity will be shown below.[10]

[9] See Chapter XIII, below.
[10] See Chapter XIV, below.

Chapter XII: Books and Libraries.

DURING the early years of the new century the flow of books to New England continued. Judge Sewall constantly imported, as the records of his "Diary" and "Letter-Book" show. In 1701 he ordered

Dr. Nehemiah Grew: Cosmologia Sacra (two copies)
Dr. Holder: Time
Dr. Holder: Natural Grounds of Harmony
The Assembly Confession of Faith and Catechisms in Latin.[1]

The same year he recorded in a letter to John Love, his London agent,

> I have received the Box of Books . . . . Mr. Colman has deliverd me my Dictionary . . . . I was very desirous of the new Edition of the Dictionary. But Mr. Collier has mard and not mended it by his alterations.[2]

He inquired in the same letter about a book by Sir William Petty on the greatness of London, and about another showing that London is bigger than imperial Rome was, ordering one of the first, and three or four of the second.

In 1705 he bought "the two Folios of Mr. Flavell's works for £3.10,"[3] and sent the following order to London:

> Buy for me all the statutes at large made since Mr. Keeble's Edition 1684. Let them be well Bound in one or two Covers as shall be most convenient:
>
> The Register[4]

[1] Letter-Book, i. 261.

[2] *Ibid.*, i. 259. Jeremy Collier edited the 1701 edition of "The Great Historical, Geographical, and Poetical Dictionary . . . . printed for Henry Rhodes." See p. 118, above.

[3] Diary, ii. 122.

[4] Crompton, Richard: L'Authoritie et Jurisdiction des Courts. Bracton, Henricus de: De Legibus et Consuetudinibus Angliæ. Britton, Joannes: On the Laws of England.

Crompton[4]
Bracton[4]
Britton[4]
Fleta
Mirror[5]

as many of them as you can get in Latin or English;

Heath's Pleadings
Sir Edward Coke's Reports.[6]

In 1711 he "sent to Mr. Love for the Books following; viz.

Pole's English Annotations, two Setts.
Mr. Henry's Añotations
Dutch Annotations.
Cambridge Concordance;
Preaching Bible.
Junius and Tremellius, a fair Print to carry to Church.
Pareus, his Adversaria on the Bible.
Dr. Lightfoot's Works in two volumns
Harris's Lexicon Tecnicum.
Alcuinus;
Tigurine Bible.
Pauli Freheri theatrum vivorum Eruditione claror.
Rushworth's Collections Abridgd and Improvd.
Dr. Preston's Works.
Ray of the Wisdom of GOD in the Creation.
All Calvin's Comentaries.
Dr. Owen on 6–13. of the Hebrs.
Dr. Saunderson's Sermons.
Stillingfleet's Origines Sacrae.
Irenicum, Ch. Rome.
Pearson on the Creeds[7]."

This list was sent again a few months later with the exception of the "preaching Bible," Saunderson's Sermons, and Pearson on the Creeds, and with the following addenda:

[4] See p. 174, note 4 above.
[5] Horn's Miroir des Justices.
[6] Letter-Book, i. 310.
[7] *Ibid.*, i. 411.

Supplement to the great Historical Dictionary.
Dr. Edwards his Tracts.
Two Herbert's Poems.
Mr. Watts's Hymns.
Virgil in usum Delphini. I have Ovid's Metamorphosis; if there be anything else of Ovid in Usum Delphini, let me have it.
Dr. Arrowsmith's Armilla.
If any of the Old Books be so scarce, that they are very dear; forbear buying them; and acquaint me with the Price.[8]

A year later he recorded

I by him presented his Excellency the Governour with Dr. Calamy's Abridgment of Mr. Baxter's Life &c. in Two Volumes, Cost me 30^s . . . [9]

In 1704 a Madam Rebecca Overton of London considered Boston a sufficiently good market to send over by Mr. Anthony Young "to be by him disposed of for her Most advantage" a consignment of nearly fifty books, mostly theological.[10]

Wait Winthrop, like Sewall, was sending to London for old books. Samuel Reade wrote to him in 1708,

Y^e person you mention that did collect those bookes hath been dead many yeares, & none hath succeeded him in that curiosity; ye bookes almost out of printe, & upon inquiry of severall booksellers cannot heare of but very few. . . . [11]

That Sewall and Winthrop sent to London for certain books is not to be construed as an indication that books were difficult to obtain in Boston. The opposite is rather the case. New book shops were opened in addition to all those established before 1700,[12] and these were supplemented by auction sales of imported consignments of books, generally at some coffee-house. Catalogues of these collections

[8] *Ibid.*, ii. 10.
[9] Diary, iii. 154.
[10] Publications of the Colonial Society of Massachusetts, xiii. 291.
[11] Winthrop Papers, vi. 171.
[12] See p. 115 ff, above, and Littlefield, Early Boston Booksellers.

were printed for free distribution, and the sales were well advertised in the Boston papers. New importations for the regular book trade were also advertised. Boston evidently furnished a good market for the bookseller and sufficient opportunity for the book buyer.[13]

The most zealous and successful book collector of this period was Cotton Mather, who constantly recorded in his diary his joy at the steady growth of his library.[14] The following quotations will give an idea of some of the ways in which it grew.

. . . . I have a mighty Thirst after the Sight of Books, now and then published in *Holland:* which may upon sending you the *Titles* be transmitted with the Goods that you may send hither, and I pay here . . . . There is one *Thomas Crenius*, who had published . . . .[15]

I have had of late Years, many great and strange Accessions to my *Library* . . . . I will not have unmention'd, a Present of

[13] The following are typical advertisements:

"*Corderius Americanus* . . . . sold by Nicholas Boone . . . . As also a large parcel of choice English Books of Divinity, Poetry, History, &c. In the last Vessel from England." (*News-Letter*, October 11–18, 1708.)

"And many other New Books from England in the last Ship . . . . B. Eliot, at his shop in King Street." (*Ibid.*, March 23–30, 1713.)

"A valuable Collection of Books, consisting of Divinity, Physick, Mathematicks, History, Classicks, Belles Lettres, in Latin, English and French, to be sold by Publick Vendue or Auction, at the Crown Coffee-House in Boston . . . . Printed Catalogues may be had *gratis*." (*Ibid.*, February 6–13, 1715/6.)

"A Collection of choice Books, Ancient and Modern, in several Languages, upon most of the Arts and Sciences, few of them to be had at the Stationers, the Books very neatly Bound, to be sold by way of Auction . . . . at Mr. *Sibly's* Coffee-House . . . . King-Street, Boston." (*Ibid.*, August 20–27, 1716.)

"A Fine & Large Collection of BOOKS, lately Imported from London, is to be Exposed to Sale by RETAIL . . . . By *Samuel Gerrish* Bookseller in *Corn-Hill* near the Town-house. The Sale to begin at 10 of the Clock. The Catalogue is Printed, and may be had gratis. The Number of Books contained in it is as follows, Folios, 154. Quartos. 596. Octavos, 712." (*Boston Gazette*, September 23–30, 1723.)

[14] He frequently mentions among other favors of God or answers to prayer his "convenient study with a well-furnished Library;" "my exceedingly-well-furnished Library;" "a Library, exceeding any man's in all this land;" "my extraordinary *Library*, and the Possession of several thousands of Books." (Diary, *passim.*)

[15] Diary, ii. 421. Crenius is an error for Crusius.

Books made me this Winter, from the united Library of our three famous *Shepards;* which enriched me, not only with printed Books, which very low prized, might be counted worth more than 12 lb. but also with *Manuscripts* of each of those three worthy Men, which are vastly more valuable than all the other Books. . . . [16]

Within these Few Days, I have received packetts from *Gresham-Colledge;* by which I am sensible, That some former packetts from them hither, have unhappily miscarried. . . . . [17]

I have newly received large packetts from *Tranquebar* in the *East-Indies;* with a New Testament & some little Books of piety, printed in the *Damulic* Language & character; which are the first things that ever were printed in those parts of the world.. . . . [18]

Mather's eagerness for books resulted in the gathering of a library of probably four thousand volumes.[19]

Unfortunately no comprehensive list of the books in this greatest of colonial private libraries exists. Nearly a century ago descendants of the Mathers gave to the American Antiquarian Society such books of Cotton Mather's as were still in their possession. From this collection and from books containing Mather's autograph in various other libraries, Julius H. Tuttle of the Massachusetts Historical Society has compiled a list of books known to have been in his library.[20] The following are a few of the titles in that list:

	Collectanea Chymica: [10 tracts]
Hakluyt	Principal Navigations
Hatton	A New Treatise of Geography
Howel, Wm.	An Institution of General History

[16] Diary, i. 532.

[17] Letter to John Winthrop, July 15, 1720. Mather Papers, p. 440.

[18] Letter to John Winthrop, December 26, 1720. Mather Papers, p. 445.

[19] In 1700 it was approaching 3000. See p. 127, above. Mr. C. S. Brigham, Librarian of the American Antiquarian Society, estimates the library at 4000 volumes. (Publications of the Colonial Society of Massachusetts, xviii. 408.) W. H. Whitmore's note on page 75 of John Dunton's Letters is incorrect in ascribing to Cotton Mather the 7000–8000 volumes which composed the library of his son. See Drake: Mather's "King Philip's War," p. xxiii.

[20] Proceedings of the American Antiquarian Society, xx. 301. See also chapters VII and VIII, above.

Purchas	his Pilgrimage
Boyle, R.	6 vols. of science
Browne, T.	Religio Medici
Digby, K.	Observations upon Religio Medici
Hayward, J.	Life and raigne of King Henrie the IIII
Hayward, J.	Life and Raigne of King Edward the Sixt
Hooke, R.	Several volumes of science
Laet, Jean de	Several volumes of descriptions of countries
———	Judicial Astrologie judicially condemned
Machiavelli	Princeps
Milton	Eikonoklastes
———	Overthrow of Stage Playes, 1600
Plautus	Comœdiæ XX
Prynne	Histrio-Mastix and others
Rawlinson	New Method of . . . History and Geography
Roberts	Merchants Mappe of Commerce
Stubbes	Anatomie of Abvses
Withers	Grateful Acknowledgment of a late Trimming Regulator
Osborn, F.	Miscellany of sundry Essayes
Fletcher, G.	Israel Redux
Delamer, H.	Works

It was during the latter part of this period that the Reverend Thomas Prince began to collect his splendid library of colonial books. It is impossible to determine what books he gathered during these years; but some idea of the number may be gained from the following single item in the manuscript account-book of Daniel Henchman, bookseller, preserved, curiously enough, in the Prince Collection of the Boston Public Library.

Dec. 20, 1726.

Rev[d] Tho[s] Prince, Dr.

To 56 octavos 2[d] hand	7.00.00
8 Quartos 5/	2.00.00
3 Folios	2.00.00

During these years the Boston Public Library both grew and suffered loss. On August 31, 1702, the Selectmen ordered "that Mr John Barnard jun^r^ be desired to make a Cattalogue of all the bookes belonging to the Towns Liberary and to Lodge the Same in ye s^d^ Liberary."[21] On February 28, 1704, they further ordered that "Mr. John Barnard Junr having at the request of the selectmen Set the Towne Liberary in good order he is allowed for s^d^ Service two of those bookes of wch there are in ye s^d^ Liberary two of a Sort."[21] The fire of 1711 damaged the Town-House, and Judge Sewall made the following note in his letter-book:

> In our Boston Library several valuable Books were lost, as the Polyglott Bible, the London Criticks, Thuanus's History, a Manuscript in two Folios left by Capt: Reyn [Keyn] the Founder; &c.[22]

After the fire an attempt was made to recover as many as possible of the books mislaid at the time of the fire, as the following advertisement in *The Boston News-Letter* of June 8, 1713, shows.

> All Persons that have in their Keeping, or can give Notice of any of the Town Library; or other things belonging to the Town-House in *Boston*, before the late Fire: are desired to Inform the Treasurer of the said Town thereof, in order to their being returned.
>
> The first Volumn of *Pool*'s Annotations was carryed away in the late Fire in *Boston;* any Person that has it, or any other Books, carry'd away at that time, or any other Goods, are desired to bring them to the Post Office, that the true Owners may have them again.[23]

Of the Harvard Library at this time there are more records, though for a time there seem to have been few gifts. The following are from the records of meetings of the Harvard Corporation.

> Voted that the Library keeper within the Space of one month

[21] Publications of the Colonial Society of Massachusetts, xii. 126.

[22] Letter-Book, i. 422.

[23] Publications of the Colonial Society of Massachusetts, xii. 128.

next coming, take an Inventory, of all Books, mathematicall Instruments, & other things of value committed to his Custody, & Give receipt for them to the praesident, to be accompted for by him at the Expiration of his Year annually, or at his leaving his place, before he receive his salary.[24]

Voted

2. That Mr Edward Holyoke be Library keeper for this year & that Six pounds be allowd him for the said Service.

3. That fifty shillings be allowed and paid to Mr Gookin for his taking a Catalogue of the books in the Library.[25]

Voted, that Mr. Presidt and the Residt Fellows agree with Mr Brattle for what Books may be in the late Treasurers Library, they think proper for the College Library.[26]

Voted, that Sr Welsted be Library Keeper for the Year Ensuing, and that £8 be allow'd him for that Service, and that he be directed to take Speciall Care that the Library and Books be kept in a better and more decent Condition than heretofore.[27]

On the second of February, 1721–2, Thomas Hollis, who was then just beginning to take an interest in Harvard, wrote to Benjamin Colman that he had two volumes of Milton's "Works," the new edition, to send to the college. He also asked for a catalogue of the books in the college library that he might know what to send them.[28] This letter resulted in the following actions of the Corporation of Harvard:

The worthy Mr Hollis having Sent Over a new & fair Edicon of Milton's Poetical Works, directing, That if the College have Such like already, the sd Books are at Mr Colmans Service either to dispose of or keep, Now Mr Colman being desirous that the College shd Have these new, fair and Well-bound Books intire, thô part of the Like be in the Library, Voted that what of Milton's Poetical Works heretofore belonged to the Library be de-

[24] Meeting of August 6, 1707. Harvard College Book IV, p. 27.

[25] Meeting of September 5, 1709. *Ibid.*, p. 36.

[26] Meeting of October 27, 1713. *Ibid.*, p. 52. The late Treasurer was Thomas Brattle, who died in 1713.

[27] Meeting of September 24, 1718. *Ibid.*, p. 63.

[28] Manuscript letter.

liver'd to the Revd Mr Colman to be disposed of as he sees meet.[29]

Upon the Intimation lately made by M^r^. Hollis, and formerly by Mr Neal, that it may be of great Advantage to the College Library, that a Catalogue of the Books in the s^d^ Library be printed and Sent abroad, Voted, that forthwith the Library-keep^r^ take an exact Catalogue of the Books in the Library, and that the same be printed in Order to transmitt to friends abroad.[29]

. . . . The Treasurer is directed to pay the Printer afores^d^ the Sum̃ of £22.5^s^ out of the College Treasury from [*sic*] printing the s^d^ Catalogue containing 13½ sheets.

2. Voted, That Mr Treasurer pay Mr Saml Gerrish the sum of £12.14^s^ upon the delivery of 300 of the Printed Catalogues.

3. Voted, That Mr Gee be paid out of the College-Treasury £20. for his Service in preparing the Catalogue . . . .

4. Voted, that One hundred of the afores^d^ Catalogues be sent to England, & that 30 of them be deliver'd to Mr Hollis. . . .[30]

This catalogue of 1723 contained about 3100 *titles*, almost equally divided among folios, quartos, and octavos (including all smaller), the library being catalogued according to size. A selected list of the literary, historical, and scientific books will be found in the Appendix, pp. 272 to 293. Reference to this list will show that Harvard had a satisfactory collection of books, including, outside the field of theology, representative works and authors in philosophy, science, and literature. It is weakest in English literature, but even there some of the best poets, such as Milton and Shakespeare, are found, and many lesser poets from Herbert to Wither. Such prose works as the seventeenth century produced are well represented from Hakluyt to Sir William Temple.

Upon the distribution of the 1723 Catalogue, interest in the Harvard Library greatly increased, especially in England under the stimulus of the interest of Thomas Hollis, himself

[29] Meeting of April 30, 1722. College Book IV, p. 75. It is unfortunate that we cannot know how long the Harvard Library had possessed part of the poetical works of Milton, or just what part it was.

[30] Meeting of December 25, 1723. College Book IV, p. 93.

the chief benefactor of the library throughout his life,[31] and of Henry Newman, at one time "Library-keeper" at Harvard, and from 1709 to 1741 agent of the College in England.[32] In 1723 Newman wrote from the Middle Temple to Henry Flint reporting that he was sending copies of the statutes of Cambridge and Oxford, the third and fourth volumes of Brandt's "History of the Reformation," and the first volume of Saurin's "Dissertation on the Old and New Testaments" as presents to the College Library.[33] In 1724 came a gift of books from Isaac Watts.[34] Gifts were also received from interested friends at home, as shown by the vote of thanks of the Corporation to Samuel Gerrish "for his bounty to College Library, he having presented to the College sundry Books to the Value of Ten pounds."[35]

The Library grew so rapidly after the publication of the 1723 Catalogue that the Corporation saw fit to order, at the meeting of June 2, 1725, the printing of three hundred supplements to the Catalogue, one hundred of which were to be sent to Thomas Hollis for distribution in England.[36] This supplement listed 61 *titles* in folio, 25 in quarto, and 80 in octavo and smaller, a good growth for less than two calendar years. A selected list of these additions will be found in the Appendix, pp. 293 to 295.

[31] Harvard College Book IV, p. 112, in the records of the Corporation reports a "Box of Books, N? 10, from M$^{r.}$ Hollis." See also pp. 181, 182, above.

[32] The sketch of Newman in "The Librarians of Harvard College," p. 11, states that "during the whole of his life in England, Newman was active in furthering the interests of the College in that country, and procured for it many gifts both of money and of books." An example of his work is given in a vote of the Harvard Corporation passed April 6, 1741, as follows: "That the Pres^{dt} be desir'd to give the Thanks of the Corporation to Henry Newman of London, Esq., for the information he gives us by Dr Colman of some Prospect there is, of our obtaining a part of the Library of Sr Richard Gyles Bar. which he is about to bestow upon Dissenters, & pray him to continue his good Offices to the College, and particularly in that affair." (Harvard Library, Bibliographical Contributions, No. 52.)

[33] Massachusetts Historical Society, Collections, 1st Series, vi. 118.

[34] Harvard College Book IV, p. 97.

[35] Meeting of December 25, 1723. *Ibid.*, p. 94.

[36] Meeting of June 2, 1725. *Ibid.*, p. 102.

During these years another college library had been established in Connecticut, first at Saybrook and later at New Haven. The library of Yale began with books donated from the ministerial libraries of the colony and grew by means of gifts at home and abroad. Sir Henry Ashurst, for many years the London agent of Connecticut, wrote to Gurdon Saltonstall in 1709 offering to send "Mr Baxter's practicall volumes" if they would be acceptable to him for the young college.[37] Sir John Davie, a graduate of Harvard in 1681, and a farmer at New London when he unexpectedly succeeded to an English title and wealth, sent nearly 200 volumes to Yale in its early days.[38] In 1714 there arrived over 700 volumes sent by Jeremiah Dummer, one-fifth given by himself, the rest contributed by various English gentlemen, including Sir Richard Steele, Sir Isaac Newton, Bishop Kennett of Peterborough, Sir Edmund Andros, Francis Nicholson, Sir Richard Blackmore, Dr. John Woodward of the Royal Society, Richard Bentley, Dr. William Whiston, Edmund Halley, the astronomer, and Elihu Yale.[39] In many cases these men contributed volumes of their own works, Steele contributing, for instance, "all the Tatlers and Spectators being eleven Volumns." Besides many theological books, the collection included practically all of the important current books on medicine and philosophy, and representative works on science and in history and literature. Some idea of the books in the latter classes may be gained from the selected lists which follow:

Science

Boyle	Complete works, philosophical and moral
Wilkins	Mathematical works
Woodward	Natural History of the Earth

37 Winthrop Papers, vi. 196.

38 The year in which these books arrived is not known; they are recorded in Clap's catalogue before the Dummer books.

39 The details in regard to these books are taken from President Clap's manuscript catalogue of early accessions to the library of Yale.

Locke	Upon Education
Locke	Essay on Human Understanding
Huylin	Cosmographia
———	Sea Chart of the Mediterranean
———	Guide to the Practical Gauger
———	Miscellanea Curiosa . . . . Discourses read to the Royal Society
———	Musaeum Regalis Societatis
von Helmont	Works
Newton	Principia Mathematica Naturalis Philosophiæ
Newton	Optics
Glauber	Works
Whiston	Astronomical Lectures
Whiston	Theory of the Earth
Gregory	Elements of Astronomy
Halley	Synopsis of Comets
Gassendi	Metaphisica
Hugenius	Discovery of Coelestial Worlds
Pemberton	View of Sir Isaac Newton's Philosophy

History and Literature

Raleigh	History of World
Clarendon	History of the Rebellion and Civil Wars
———	Complete History of England to the Reign of William III
Ricaut	History of the Ottoman Empire
Herbert	Memoirs of Charles I
———	Annals of Queen Anne for 1710–1711
Steele, etc.	Tatler
Steele, etc.	Spectator
Blackmore	King Arthur
Blackmore	Prince Arthur
Blackmore	Eliza
Blackmore	A Paraphrase on Job
Blackmore	Creation
Browne	Religio Medici
Browne	Vulgar Errors
Cowley	Works
Chaucer	Works and Life

Cleveland	"Works of Mr. Cleveland the poet"
Milton	Paradise Lost and all Poetical Works
Milton	Complete Collection of Prose Works
Jonson	Works
Spenser	Works
Wotton	Works
Bacon	Advancement of Learning
Bacon	Natural History
Barclai	Argenis
Buchanani	Poemata
Butler	Hudibras
Temple, Wm.	Miscellany
Glanvil	Sadducismus Triumphatus
Hale	Contemplations
Feltham	Resolves
———	The Turkish Spy
———	The Athenian Oracle
———	A Defence of Dramatic Poetry in Answer to Collier
Collier	Essays
Shaftesbury	Works

In 1718 over four hundred volumes more arrived, the gift of Elihu Yale. These added many classical books, many historical books, and some current literature. Other gifts followed, of which detail is lacking, but the library evidently continued to grow, as is indicated by the following vote of the trustees of Yale at the meeting of September 8, 1731:

Whereas there are several Books in the Library that are duplicates we resolve that one Book or Sett of each duplicate be sold by the Rector & Tutors & the money improved in purchasing of other Books that the Library at present is not furnished with.[40]

An attempt was made to interest Thomas Hollis in Yale, but the attempt failed as the following letter shows:

I have now another letter—anonimous—about Yale College—I know not the man, but supose him to be urged unto it by your

[40] Dexter, Documentary History of Yale, p. 290.

agent Dummer—I inclose it you. I have no inclination to be diverted from my projected design—if you know the Author, pray let him know so—I have told Dummer the same.[41]

The failure to interest Hollis was compensated by the interest which Bishop Berkeley took in the young college, which resulted in his gift, shortly after the close of this period, of over one thousand volumes, including the best of English literature from Shakespeare and Bacon to Pope, Gay, and Swift, with several volumes of plays—even Wycherley.[42]

Besides these public libraries, at least one semi-public library was established during the latter part of this period in connection with Franklin's *New England Courant*, the first issue of which appeared August 7, 1721. In No. 48 of the *Courant*, published July 2, 1722, is given a list of the books kept in the office of the paper for the use of writers. It includes the following:[43]

Shakespeare's Works
Virgil
Aristotle's Politicks
Hudibras
Milton
The Spectator, 8 volumes
The Guardian, 2 volumes
The Turkish Spy
The Athenian Oracle
The British Apollo
The Art of Thinking
The Art of Speaking
The Reader
The Lover
Cowley's Works
Burnet's History of the Reformation

[41] Letter of Hollis to John White, Treasurer of Harvard, July 12, 1721. From copy in the files of the Librarian of Harvard University.

[42] President Clap's manuscript catalogue.

[43] Cook, Literary Influences in Colonial Newspapers, p. 20.

Burnet's Theory of the Earth
Oldham's Works
The Tale of the Tub
St. Augustine's Works
Tillotson's Works
Dr. Bates' Works
Dr. South's Works
Mr. Flavel's Works
Mr. Charnock's Works
Many pamphlets.

Of interest in connection with the lists already given are the lists of the books which William Adams, Yale 1730, packed to carry to college with him at the beginning of his Freshman and Sophomore years:

Acc[t] of Books y[t] William Adams put up to carry to College, Nov 5. 1726.

Elisha Coles Dictionary,
A Latin Grammar,
A Greek "
Tully's Offices,
" Orations,
Virgil's Works,
Horace,
English Virgil,
Greek Testament,
Latin "
Catechisms, and Confessio Fidei,
Latin Bible,
Septuagint,
Florilegium Phraseωn,
Phraseologia Anglolatina,
Pasor's Lexicon,
Lucius Florus,
An English Bible,
A Call to Backsliders,
English Exercises,
Ovid de Tristibus,
Corderius' Colloquies,

Terence,
Ramus,
Mr. Willard's Penitent Prodigal,
An English Dictionary,
Observations on the Present State of Turkey,
The Strong Helper,
The Everlasting Gospel,
The life of Mr. Edmund French,
The Songs of the Redeemed,
Nomenclator, Singing Book,
Catechism,
Some of his father's Sermons.[44]

The next year he carried the following, October 23:[45]

Locke of the Human Understanding,
Locke of Education,
Hebrew Bible, with Greek Testament at the end,
Hebrew Grammar,
Amesii Medulla Theologiæ,
Burgersdicii Logica,
Buxtorf's Lexicon,
Clark's Formulæ,
Allin's Alarm,
Mr. Coleman of Mirth,
Mr. Williams' Redeemed Captive,
Flemming's Rod or Sword,
Mr. Penhallow's Hist: of ye Indian War,
Mr. Flavel's Divine Conduct, or Mystery of Providence.
Kennet's Roman Antiquities,
Gordon's Geographical Grammar,
Hist. of ye House of Orange.
Pope's Homer, Vol. 2.
Homer's Iliad,
Dugard's Rhetorick,
Grotius, De jure Belli et Pacis,
Sanderson, De Conscientiâ,
" De juramento.

[44] Massachusetts Historical Society, Collections, 4th Series, i. 43.
[45] *Ibid.*, p. 44.

With all the growth of libraries and the means to acquire books, the old custom of borrowing and lending continued, and those who lived near the booksellers sent gifts of books to those who were at a distance. As in the early days of the colonies, the name of Winthrop is most prominent in this exchange of books; but this may be partly because we have more records of the Winthrops than of any other family. Wait Winthrop wrote to his son,

> I want Buckstone's Lexicon for one of the words . . . [46]

Again he wrote,

> I likewise send an Almanack and the Importance of Duncark, which is worth reading if you go through; it is M[r] Lechmers[47] brothers, and must be sent again, and then you may haue more.[48]

John Winthrop wrote to Cotton Mather,

> I thank you heartily for yo[r] very agreeable and entertaining communications from y[e] Royall Society, and especially for y[e] sight of D[r] Woodwards *Naturalis Historia Telluris*.[49]

Cotton Mather wrote to him January 11, 1718–9,

> I have begun with sending you, that peece of my dear S[r] *Richard*,[50] which will prepare you for the rest.[51]

November 30 of the same year he wrote,

> When shall S[r] *Richard* return! some of my Neighbours dun me for him.[52]

Again the next February he wrote,

> My dear,—Hast thou not yett with thee one of S[r] *Richards* volumes, His "*Essayes*," in prose? Examine thy Library.[53]

[46] Winthrop Papers, vi. 225. Dated October, 1710.

[47] This is probably the Thomas Lechmere who married Wait Winthrop's only daughter, Anne, in 1709.

[48] Winthrop Papers, vi. 280. October 28, 1713.

[49] *Ibid.*, p. 332. November 5, 1716. Dr. Woodward's book was published in 1714.

[50] This is Sir Richard Blackmore. See p. 198, below.

[51] Mather Papers, p. 433.

[52] *Ibid.*, p. 435.

[53] *Ibid.*, p. 437.

In spite of Winthrop's tardiness in returning books, Mather continued to send them:

I hope, you have received the packetts which I sent you a few weeks ago: Both a Number of COHELETH;[54] And also D[r] *Woodward's* pamphletts.[55]

As a borrower Mather wrote to Thomas Prince, April 16, 1718, to ask,

. . . . if you'l favour me, by this Bearer, with the Book of Poetry, you bought the last week at your Booksellers.[56]

Samuel Sewall, writing to John Williams, of Deerfield, added,

Inclosed the Non-Conformists Letter, this weeks News-Letter, Half Duz. Mr. Hobart's verses, with the occasion; They are chiefly hortatory, and therefore I might honestly print them.[57]

Many similar quotations might be given as further evidence of this custom, but it seems unnecessary to add more than the following statement of Cotton Mather's which shows how far the practice was carried:

Seldome any *new Book* of Consequence finds the way from beyond-Sea, to these Parts of *America*, but I bestow the Perusal upon it.[58]

In the meantime the popular distribution[59] of books, pamphlets, and broadsides had increased, for Mather recorded in his diary, in 1713,

I am informed. that the Minds and Manners of many People about the Countrey are much corrupted, by foolish Songs and Ballads, which the Hawkers and Pedlars carry into all parts of the Countrey. By way of Antidote, I would procure poetical Com-

[54] Coheleth: A Soul upon Recollection. Written by a Fellow of the Royal Society. Cotton Mather. 1720.

[55] Mather Papers, p. 442.

[56] Proceedings of the American Antiquarian Society, xx. 295.

[57] Letter-Book, ii. 8.

[58] Diary, i. 548.

[59] See p. 126, above.

posures full of Piety, and such as may have a Tendency to advance Truth and Goodness, to be published, and scattered into all Corners of the Land. There may be an Extract of some, from the excellent *Watts's* Hymns.[60]

When, in the latter part of that year, the Assembly passed laws restricting pedlars,[61] Mather feared lest its provisions might interfere with his plan, for he noted in his diary:

I must also assist the Booksellers, in addressing the Assembly, that their late Act against Pedlers, may not hinder their Hawkers from carrying Books of Piety about the Countrey.[62]

From the last sentence of the above it would seem that the booksellers made regular use of such hawkers in extending their business; this may have been the case for many years, for Mather planned to have books of piety so distributed as early as 1683.[63] Of course it cannot be presumed that these hawkers carried much or, perhaps, any real literature, their stock being made up chiefly of broadside ballads, chapbooks, and almanacs; but if there were so many pedlars selling so many questionable books that a law was necessary to regulate them, evidently there was a public demand for interesting narrative in either prose or verse, if not for real poetry. Most of their ballads and chapbooks were probably imported from England, but such homemade productions as Wigglesworth's "The Day of Doom," "The New England Primer," and Cotton Mather's "Life of Sir William Phipps" would be among the best sellers.

If James Gray, the only book hawker of whom there seems to be any extant record, may be considered typical, these pedlars found their business profitable. Upon his death the following notice appeared in *The Boston News-Letter* of April 9–16, 1705:

On Thursday last Dyed at Boston, James Gray, That used to

[60] Diary, ii. 242.
[61] Province Laws, i. 720. Published November 14, 1713.
[62] Diary, ii. 283.
[63] See p. 126, above.

go up and down the Country Selling of Books, who left some considerable Estate behind him, and 'tis confidently affirmed that he made a Will, which he left in some honest persons hand, with some other Papers, which have not yet been found: And any person in Town or Country who have said Will or Papers, are desired to bring them unto the Office of Probates in Boston.

Judge Sewall was sufficiently interested in either the man or the case to make a note of the amount of the estate in the margin of his copy of the *News-Letter*. Edward Bromfield and Paul Dudley were appointed administrators of the estate. According to their final accounting, the value of the estate was £712.11.3, of which £699.06. was in cash, eight bags of coin of all kinds and denominations being listed in the inventory.[64] "James Gray, Bookseller *als*. Pedler," as he is entitled in the Probate Record, had evidently found the country folk of New England ready and eager to purchase his books.

Other information in regard to books owned or read during these years is found in quotations from or references to them. Samuel Sewall, for instance, recorded in his diary,

. . . set out [from Bristol] . . . . for Narraganset. Din'd at Bright's: while Diñer was getting ready I read in Ben Johnson, a Folio . . . [65]

From the folio he copied some dozen lines into his diary. At other times he recorded:

I gave the President and him the reading of Mr. Sewell's Answer to the Bp. Salisbury's new preface. . . .[66] Gave each of them Maroll's Martyrdom, Marbled.[67]

Inclosed . . . . Dr. Edwards's Answer to Sacheverell.[68]

Inclosed Mr. Prior's Epitaph (which Govr Saltonstall had not seen before):

[64] Suffolk Probate Records, xvi. 289 and 620, 621.

[65] Diary, ii. 167.

[66] *Ibid.*, ii. 391.

[67] *Ibid.*, ii. 391. This was published in 1712.

[68] Letter-Book, i. 398.

"Monarchs, and Herauldds, by your leave
"Here ly the bones of Matthew Prior;
"The Son of Adam and of Eve:
"Let Bourbon, or Nassau, goe higher!"[69]

This last quotation is very interesting because it seems to have reached New England before it was published in England. Austin Dobson writes,[70] "This epitaph does not appear to have been published during Prior's lifetime." Prior died in September, 1721, and Sewall quoted the poem January 15, 1721–2. It was probably first published in "A New Collection of Poems," 1725. It may have circulated in manuscript or even by word of mouth; in either case its reaching America so soon would indicate that some of the colonists were in close touch with English letters. This is also indicated by the following "good device" jotted down by Cotton Mather in August, 1713:

Perhaps, by sending some agreeable Things, to the Author of, *The Spectator*, and, *The Guardian*, there may be brought forward some Services to the best Interests in the Nation.[71]

Anything he might have sent would probably have been too late for publication, as *The Guardian* ceased with the issue of September 22, 1713; on the other hand, as it began publication May 28, 1713, Mather was not slow to realize its value. At the end of his printed sermon or "essay," "A New Year Well Begun," which bears the date of January 1, 1718–9, Mather added *New-Years-Day*, "From Sir Richard Blackmore's Collection of Poems, Printed at London, Anno 1718." Still another example of colonial interest in English literature is the item published in *The New England Courant* No. 22, January 1, 1722, "a noble Duke is about to erect a Monument in Westminster Abby to the Memory of Milton, the Poet."[72]

[69] *Ibid.*, ii. 142.
[70] Selected Poems of Matthew Prior, p. 233.
[71] Diary, ii. 227.
[72] Albert Matthews in *The Nation*, December 24, 1908. (Vol. 87, p. 624.)

That James Franklin was interested in Milton as a poet is shown by the presence of a copy of Milton in the *Courant* library,[73] and by his twice quoting from "Paradise Lost," once with the introductory remark, "Hear how the lofty *Milton* sings of this in his own inimitable Strain."[74]

Another who was interested in Milton was the Reverend Thomas Buckingham of Hartford, who carried with him on the expedition against Crown Point in 1711, along with a Bible and Psalm-book, "Milton on Comus," as he called it in his journal.[75]

Speaking of the reprinting of "George Barnwell" in *The New England Weekly Journal*, beginning February 14, 1732, Miss Cook remarks:[76]

> One of the most noteworthy realistic tragedies of the eighteenth century was thus reprinted in the Puritan stronghold of America, within a surprisingly short time of its first appearance.[77] This fact seems to have escaped observation until now. Probably a stray copy of the play had found its way into Kneeland's book-shop. We cannot suppose that it had a place in the Prince or Byles libraries! Evidently Boston readers were rather more liberal in their tastes than we have been accustomed to think.

If we recall the interest in contemporary literature which has been shown in this chapter, as well as the possibility that John Dunton sold plays and romances in Boston nearly fifty years earlier,[78] it will not seem so strange that such a play as "George Barnwell," with its sturdy Puritan morality, should be reprinted in Boston. On the contrary, such reprinting is just what we might expect when we take into consideration the evidences of the growing liberality of life in Boston which will be presented in the next chapter, as well as the constantly increasing accessibility and appre-

[73] See p. 187, above.

[74] Massachusetts Historical Society, Proceedings, xlii. 164.

[75] The Journals of Madam Knight, and Rev. Mr. Buckingham, p. 106.

[76] Literary Influences in Colonial Newspapers, p. 55.

[77] The play was produced in 1730, two years earlier.

[78] See p. 120, above.

ciation of books and literature of all kinds during the last forty, and especially the last twenty, years of the first century of colonial life. At the close of its first century New England was in touch with and responding to the literary movements of England.[79]

[79] See Chapter XIV, below.

Chapter XIII: Other Phases of Culture.

IN the opening years of the new century there seems to have been a revival of intercourse between New Englanders and representative men in England. Joseph Dudley, who returned to Boston in 1702 as Governor, after a nine years' residence in England,[1] had during those years become a close friend of Sir Richard Steele, who was private secretary to Lord Cutts, Governor of the Isle of Wight, when Dudley was Lieutenant-Governor. The following extract from a letter written by Steele to Dudley shows their intimacy.

S^{r},— I have your kind raillery of the 4th and shall not pretend to answer it: you may excuse my not doing that in your observation of the losse of my brains, ...[2]

Benjamin Colman's four years in England[3] gave him the opportunity to form many friendships which he continued by correspondence. Among his correspondents were Thomas Hollis, Isaac Watts, Daniel Neal,[4] Edward Calamy, Bishop White Kennett of Peterborough,[5] Sir Richard Blackmore[6] and Mrs. Elizabeth Singer Rowe ("Philomela").[7]

Cotton Mather established a correspondence with men

[1] See p. 152, above.

[2] Massachusetts Historical Society, Proceedings, 2d Series, iii. 201. The letter bears the date of June 25, 1700.

[3] See p. 152, above.

[4] Colman contributed much material to Neal's History of New England. (Turell, Life of Colman, p. 150.)

[5] Jeremiah Dummer wrote to Colman from England, January 15, 1714, "I pray your acceptance of the prints inclosed. . . . . I have committed to captain Willard, a book presented you by your good friend the dean [later the bishop] of Peterborough." Massachusetts Historical Society, Collections, 1st Series, v. 199.

[6] Blackmore sent him copies of his poems. (Turell, Life of Colman, p. 150.)

[7] *Ibid., passim.* See p. 149, above.

not only in England but on the Continent. On May 23, 1711, he made the following entry in his diary:[8]

> Having some epistolar Conversation with Mr. *De Foe*, I would in my Letters unto him, excite him to apply himself unto the work of collecting and publishing an History of the Persecutions which the Dissenters have undergone from the Ch[urch] of E[ngland].

In September of the same year he named Sir Richard Blackmore among the "eminent Persons beyond-sea" who "take notice of me, and such as I myself never have written unto, send me their Letters and their Presents."[9] In December he recorded an idea:

> I would write unto Sir *Richard Blackmore*, my Desires, that His incomparable Pen may make its furthest Efforts, in paying an Homage to our admirable JESUS; in celebrating His Beauties, before which those of the whole Creation languish and vanish; in uttering the awakened Songs of His Love to the Children of Men; in describing the illustrious Exemple of all Goodness, which He has given us; in asserting His Government over the Works of God; and Painting out the Grandeurs wherein He shall come to raise the Dead and judge the World, and the Delights of the new Heavens and the new Earth, which shall succeed the Resurrection.[10]

Mather also corresponded with Dr. Franckius, in Lower Saxony,[11] with Anthony W. Boehm of Halle, who had written to him in regard to a copy of the "Magnalia" which had come into his hands,[12] and with certain other professors at the University of Halle.[13]

In 1713 Mather's paper on "Curiosa Americana" was read before the Royal Society and he was proposed for membership. Soon after he was elected, but his name did not appear

[8] Diary, ii. 74.
[9] *Ibid.*, ii. 105.
[10] *Ibid.*, ii. 141.
[11] *Ibid.*, ii. 74.
[12] *Ibid.*, ii. 411.
[13] *Ibid.*, ii. 150.

upon the rolls of the society for a decade because at the time members had to qualify in person, which he was unable to do as he did not visit England. In 1723 arrangements were made whereby his name appeared upon the rolls as a regular member.[14]

William Brattle was elected a Fellow of the Royal Society March 11, 1714.[15] Paul Dudley, many of whose articles were published in the Transactions of the Society, was elected a Fellow on November 2, 1721.[15] Dr. Zabdiel Boylston, who was the first in America to experiment with inoculation for smallpox, was invited by Sir Hans Sloane, the court physician, to visit London. He received flattering attention from the scientists of England, being elected a Fellow of the Royal Society, before which he read a paper on the subject of inoculation. This paper was published in London in the year 1726, being dedicated by permission to the Princess of Wales.[16]

John Winthrop, son of Wait Winthrop, generally referred to as John Winthrop, F.R.S., to distinguish him from the other John Winthrops, also corresponded with the members of the Royal Society. He wrote to Cotton Mather in April, 1721,

> W^t is become of the Doct^r at Gresham?[17] I am making an other sett of rarieties & curiositys for the Royall Society, wch I am thinking to present wth my owne hands.

In 1726 he did go to England, and there became an active member of the Royal Society, the 40th volume of the So-

[14] Publications of the Colonial Society of Massachusetts, xiv. 81 ff. Criticism has often been directed against Mather for using the initials F.R.S. after his name many years before 1723. As he had been officially notified of his election in 1713, and as No. 339 of the Philosophical Transactions, issued in 1714, gave him this title, such criticism is unjust.

[15] Publications of the Colonial Society of Massachusetts, xiv. 291.

[16] Green, History of Medicine in Massachusetts, p. 67.

[17] Winthrop Papers, vi. 399 note. The Doctor referred to is presumably Dr. John Woodward, Secretary of the Royal Society, who continued to reside at Gresham College, London, after the Royal Society moved to other quarters.

ciety's Transactions being dedicated to him.[18] Winthrop enjoyed English life so much that he never returned to New England.

Thomas Robie, Harvard 1708, later a tutor and Fellow of the Corporation, had several papers on mathematical and physical subjects published in the Transactions of the Royal Society, but does not seem to have been a member.[19] He died in 1729 at the age of forty-one; had he lived longer he might have been chosen a Fellow. Dr. William Douglass, a Scotch physician (best known perhaps because of his strong opposition to the practice of inoculation and its sponsor, Cotton Mather,) accepted Robie's observations of eclipses, latitude, longitude, etc.[20]

Others than Winthrop went to England to reside during this period. Henry Newman, Harvard 1687, went about 1707. For a time he lived in the family of the Duke of Somerset, in what capacity is not known, and later acted as the agent of Harvard College, from 1709 to 1741, and also as agent of New Hampshire.[21] Jeremiah Dummer, Harvard 1699, after studying at Utrecht,[22] settled in England, where he acted for a time as the agent of Connecticut.[23]

While such Americans living in England formed a bond between the old and the new, other links were formed by the Governors sent out from England and their trains, and by those who still turned to the new world to better their fortunes. The latter included such men as Dr. William Douglass, who, in spite of his very conservative attitude toward smallpox inoculation, was interested in science. In a letter to Dr. Cadwallader Colden of New York he sent a complete report of the weather for the year past—that is, as complete as he could keep it with "no other instru-

[18] *Ibid.*, iv. 571 note.
[19] Librarians of Harvard College, p. 16.
[20] Massachusetts Historical Society, Collections, 4th Series, ii. 185.
[21] See p. 183, above.
[22] See p. 104, above.
[23] Winthrop Papers, vi. *passim.*

ments than the naked eye, pen, ink, and paper, I know of no Thermometer nor Barometer in this place."[24] He added that there was a "good Quadrant and Telescope in the College about four miles from this," whereby he hoped to take observations of the sun, study eclipses, and so on. Some time after this he was one of the organizers of the Boston Medical Society.[25]

Another who came in search of a fortune was Thomas Lechmere, younger son of Edmund Lechmere, Esq., and grandson of Sir Nicholas Lechmere, a distinguished judge. Thomas Lechmere's older brother, Nicholas, became the Attorney-General of England and was raised to the peerage as Lord Lechmere in 1721. Lechmere brought with him money with which to trade, and soon added to it by marriage with Anne Winthrop, sister of John Winthrop, F.R.S.[26]

Of wealth and luxury in New England at this time one illustration will perhaps be sufficient. The expenditure at the time of the funeral of Fitz-John Winthrop, in 1707, amounted to over £600, the modern equivalent for which would be somewhat over $10,000.00. The single item of sugar for the burnt wine was £2.09.06, or about $50.00![27]

There are evidences that the "worldliness" noticed in the second period[28] was increasing. In 1714 Samuel Sewall found it necessary to write to Isaac Addington:

There is a Rumor, as if some design'd to have a Play acted in

[24] Massachusetts Historical Society, Collections, 4th Series, ii. 165. Letter dated Feb. 20, 1720–1. In connection with the lack of such instruments it must be remembered that the Fahrenheit thermometer had been invented only in 1714, and that the barometer, although devised earlier, was but slowly coming into use. There had been a barometer in Boston many years before this, for in the inventory of the estate of John Foster, the printer, occurs the item "wether glasses," which was the seventeenth century term for barometer. The inventory was taken in 1681. (Green, John Foster, p. 52.)

[25] This was formed about 1735; it published some papers. Massachusetts Historical Society, Collections, 4th Series, ii. 188.

[26] Winthrop Papers, vi. 367 note.

[27] *Ibid.*, v. 412. When Mrs. Katherine Eyre married Wait Winthrop in 1707, the inventory of her property totaled £5,328.12.2. (Winthrop Papers, vi. 158–9.)

[28] See p. 156 ff., above.

the Council-Chamber, next Monday; which much surprises me: And as much as in me lyes, I do forbid it. The Romans were very fond of their Plays: but I never heard they were so far set upon them, as to turn their Senat-House into a Play-House. Our Town-House was built at great Cost and Charge, for the sake of very serious and important Business; . . . . Let it not be abused with Dances, or other Scenical divertisements . . . . Ovid himself offers invincible Arguments against publick Plays.[29]

The next year Wait Winthrop, writing to his son John, mentioned the fact that "Molle . . . . is well and brisk, and goes to dancing."[30] *The Boston News-Letter* for August 22–29, 1715, published the following notice:

This is to give Notice that at Cambridge on Wednesday the 21st day of September next, will be Run for, a Twenty Pound Plate, by any Horse, Mare or Gelding not exceeding Fourteen and an half hands high, carrying 11 Stone Weight, and any Person or Persons shall be welcome to Run his Horse &c, entering the same with Mr. *Pattoun* at the Green Dragon in Boston, any of the six days preceding the Day of Runing, & paying Twenty Shillings Entrance.[31]

For Tuesday night, January 7, 1717–8, Judge Sewall recorded, "The Gov[r] has a Ball at his own House that lasts to 3 in the Morn."[32] Such items show the tendency of the time, as do also the growing popularity of the taverns and coffee-houses, the increase in numbers and wealth of the silversmiths, and the laments of such men as Cotton Mather over the degeneracy from the better days of old.

These years saw also the establishment and development of the newspaper upon English models. A single issue of a paper called *Publick Occurrences* had appeared before the end of the previous century, but the paper was promptly suppressed by the authorities. On Monday, April 24, 1704,

[29] Letter-Book, ii. 29. Sewall quotes passages from Ovid to illustrate.

[30] Winthrop Papers, vi. 310.

[31] A notice of another horse race at Cambridge is reprinted in Publications of the Colonial Society of Massachusetts, xiv. 408.

[32] Diary, iii. 158. Samuel Shute was governor at this time.

appeared the first number of *The Boston News-Letter*, published by John Campbell, postmaster. When William Brooker succeeded Campbell as postmaster, one of his first acts was to establish a new weekly, *The Boston Gazette*, begun December 21, 1719. These were poor enough as newspapers, printing little but news items taken from London papers whenever the latter were accessible, and at other times filling in with local news, reports of speeches in provincial legislatures, or anything available.[33]

James Franklin was the printer of Brooker's *Gazette*. After forty numbers Brooker sold the paper to Philip Musgrave, who succeeded him as postmaster. When Musgrave employed Samuel Kneeland as printer instead of Franklin, the latter, "encouraged by a number of respectable characters, who were desirous of having a paper of a different cast from those then published . . . . began the publication, at his own risk, of a third newspaper, entitled, *The New England Courant*."[34] This paper was not founded just to furnish news; its purpose was to provide readable essays on the order of those which had made the *Spectator* and its successors popular. Franklin had served his apprenticeship in London previous to the year 1717, when he set up his press in Boston, and thus had come in touch with the English journalism and literature of the day. The nature of the articles published in the *Courant* must be left until the next chapter for discussion. The point that should be emphasized here, as the last evidence of the culture reached at this time in New England, is the fact that Franklin felt that there was sufficient interest in literature, as apart from news, in the neighborhood of Boston, to warrant the establishment of a paper without news, and in competition with two established newspapers. The success of his paper proved that he was right. Thus we find within a year after

[33] For details in regard to colonial newspapers see Elizabeth C. Cook's "Literary Influences in Colonial Newspapers," from which much of the material in these paragraphs is taken.

[34] Thomas, History of Printing, i. 110.

the close of the first century of New England, if we reckon from the founding of Plymouth, and several years before the end of the first century of Boston's existence, a deliberate and recognized literary organ which reflected the growing literary culture of the colonists, even if it did not, as we shall see, accurately mirror contemporary literary taste.

Chapter XIV: The Production of Literature.

THE literary movement which was beginning in and around Boston at the end of the seventeenth century[1] developed more rapidly after the new century opened. The central figure in this movement was Samuel Sewall, who, although he has no fame as a writer of poetry,[2] wrote considerable verse, both Latin and English. His Latin verses were sufficiently well known in Boston in the first year of the century to call forth a burlesque.[3] Sewall was less interested in English poetry,[4] and yet some of his verses in English are not without merit. His penchant was epigrammatic verse, the following lines on the death of Tom Child, the painter, being perhaps the best example of his art.

> Tom Child had often painted Death,
> But never to the Life, before:
> Doing it now, he's out of Breath;
> He paints it once, and paints no more.[5]

Others who were interested with Sewall in the writing of poetry were Richard Henchman, Nicholas Noyes, Nehemiah Hobart, Experience Mayhew, and a Mr. Bayly. It is not

[1] See p. 168, above.

[2] He is not mentioned as a writer of poetry by such historians of American poetry as Moses Coit Tyler and William B. Otis, or in the Cambridge History of American Literature. This is true also of the literary friends of Sewall mentioned in the text (see above), with the exception of Noyes.

[3] Sewall recorded in his diary, May 29, 1701, "This day a Burlesqe comes out upon Hull-street, in a Travestie construing my Latin verses." (Diary, ii. 35.)

[4] In one of his letters to Richard Henchman, Sewall wrote, "It is convenient to sing the Downfall of Babylon, in verses that will stand." As the accompanying verses are in Latin, it is evident that Sewall chose that rather than English for work which he considered important and desired to have endure. (Letter-Book, i. 318.)

[5] Diary, ii. 170. November 10, 1706. The verses are prefaced by the statement, "This morning Tom Child, the Painter, died."

possible to determine whether these men ever came together as a group for mutual encouragement in literary work; but it is evident that Sewall kept in touch with the literary work which all of them were doing, encouraged them, and both criticized their verses and sent his own to them for criticism.[6] This group did not produce any body of good verse, because none of its members had any real talent for poetry; but that they made the effort to produce, and that they encouraged each other's efforts, shows that literary culture in New England had reached the creative stage.

There were still many things to handicap literary development. The most important of these was the lack of suitable means of publishing short or occasional poems, such as these men usually wrote. If we may judge by the poems that have survived, or of which we have record, no one of these men produced enough for a volume of poems. The newspapers of Boston printed practically no poetry until after 1720.[7] Therefore the only means of publication was the

[6] Sewall's Verses upon the New Century, bearing the date of January 1, 1700–01, brought immediate response from Henchman in a long and effusive poem in praise of Sewall, dated January 2, 1700–01. To Henchman, Sewall wrote, February 24, 1703–04, "Sir,—I send home your Verses with Thanks. There are many good strokes in them: but in my mind, the English excell. I think—*dominantur undiq[u]e fraudes*, does not well end a verse; the last syllable in [*Dominantur*] is short by Rule." (Letter-Book, i. 293.) He wrote to Henchman in 1705, "It is convenient to sing the Downfall of Babylon, in verses that will stand: let me therefore have your Examination and censure of the following Distich . . . . " (Letter-Book, i. 318.) At about the same time he wrote to Nicholas Noyes, "Sir, —How am I ready to sink down into ingratitude on a sudden, and unawares! My Brother in a Letter had raised my Expectation of receiving a distich or 2 from you; and the disapointment puts me out of Tune." [He adds an apposite quotation from Ovid.] (Letter-Book, i. 315.) On March 27, 1712, Nehemiah Hobart addressed a Latin poem of thirty-seven lines to Sewall, who sent to Hobart in acknowledgement of the compliment a copy of Virgil: "I give him Virgil on account of the Poem he has gratify'd me with." (Diary, ii. 346.) This was soon turned into English verse by Henchman. (Letter-Book, i. 314 note 2, which gives both Latin and English versions.) Evidence of his interest in the poetry of Bayly and Mayhew is given in note 8 on page 207, below.

[7] A very few times the *News-Letter* reprinted from English papers articles which included lines of verse. One four line Latin epigram by Sewall, published in the *News-Letter* in 1705, is the only original poem which I have been able to find in

broadside, and in this form some of the verses of these men appeared. Other poems that circulated did so in manuscript. Sewall seems to have been as interested in the circulation of these poems as in their production, and therefore in a double sense was the center of this literary movement.[8]

One poem by Richard Henchman may indicate the existence of literary patronage in Boston at this time. This poem, entitled "Vox Oppressi,"[9] was addressed to the Lady

the papers before 1720, and we have Sewall's testimony (Diary, ii. 149) that it was with difficulty that he persuaded John Campbell to print it.

[8] The following quotations show Sewall's custom of enclosing poetry in his letters. It should be noted that some of the poems were evidently printed as broadsides. "This day I made this Distich . . . . [omitted]. Gave them and two more to Mr. Phips at Charlestown." (Diary, ii. 140. October, 1705.) "In my Letter I inclosed a News-Letter, two Copies of Mr. Bayly's Verses, Babylon is fallen." (Letter-Book, i. 351. August, 1707.) "Writ . . . . to Mr. Moodey . . . . [enclosed] this day's News-Letter; Two Setts of Verses; Libels, and proceeding thereupon. Vindicated Glascow. Sent ꝑ Capt. Lyon to whom I gave Mr. Danforth, and Mayhew's Verses." (Letter-Book, i. 408. December, 1710.) "To Sir Charles Hobby . . . . inclosing . . . . 2 of Mr. Mayhew's Poems on daughter Gerrish." (Letter-Book, i. 412. 1711. Sewall's daughter, Mrs. Gerrish, died in 1710.) "To Mr. Joseph Lord . . . . Sent him . . . . One Consolations, Frenches Verses, My verses on the Taking of Port-Royal. 4. Mr. Mayhew's verses; 1 Mr. Danforth on Daughter Gerrishes Death." (Letter-Book, i. 408. February, 1710–11.) "I visit Mr. Wadsworth . . . . Give a verse to him and to Mr. Pemberton." (Diary, ii. 359. August, 1712.) "Left the Gov[r] two of Mr. Hobart's verses . . . . Gave Mr. Colman one of Mr. Hobart's verses." (Diary, ii. 360–1. August, 1712. These would seem to be printed copies of the Latin poem to Sewall to which reference has been made on page 206, note 6.) "Writ to Mr. Williams of Derefield, inclosed . . . my Verses on Merrimak River finish'd yesterday." (Diary, iii. 240. January 16, 1719–20.) "Inclosed *Merrimak* dry'd up, with the occasion of it . . . . Inclosed 6. of Mr. Hobart's printed verses." (To Timothy Woodbridge, February 1, 1719–20. Letter-Book, ii. 104.) "Merrymak is printed off, about 300. I give Sam. Mather two of them." (Diary, iii. 279. February, 1720–21. This poem is printed in the Proceedings of the Massachusetts Historical Society, 2d Series, ix. 8.) "Sent . . . . Mr. Hobart's Verses—*Nocte viator*." (To Edward Taylor, February 16, 1719–20. Letter-Book, ii. 105.) "Mr. Prince and I go next the Relations. I gave him Merrimack; he desired me to give him copies of all my performances." (Diary, iii. 283. March 7, 1720–21.) "Having only one *Renatus* by me, I have inclos'd it, & a copy or two of Judge Lynde's verses." (To John Winthrop, January 8, 1725–6. Winthrop Papers, vi. 422.)

[9] Preserved in manuscript in the Boston Public Library.

Phipps, the wealthy widow of the former governor to express the poet's gratitude for a gift of money. As further evidence is lacking, it is impossible to say whether the gift was to encourage Henchman's poetical efforts, or to reward him for some poem in Lady Phipps' honor or in honor of her husband, or merely charity; but the tone of the poem seems to be that of poet to patron.

Outside of the group of Sewall's friends there were several who were writing verse, some for their own amusement, others for publication. Of the first class, the most interesting is Sarah Kemble Knight, whose journal of her trip from Boston to New York in 1704 owes much of its charm to the rhymes which furnished her a means to express privately the feelings which she could not express in public.[10] Her satirical humor is matched by that of other poets of the day, of varying merit as poets, but deliberately satirical.[11] Such

[10] "But I could get no sleep, because of the Clamor of some of the Town tope-ers in next Room, ... I set my Candle on a Chest by the bed side, and setting [*sic*] up, fell to my old way of composing my Resentments, in the following manner:

I ask thy Aid, O Potent Rum!
To Charm these wrangling Topers Dum.
Thou hast their Giddy Brains possest—
The man confounded wth the Beast—
And I, poor I, can get no rest.
Intoxicate them with thy fumes:
O still their Tongues till morning comes!"

(The Journal of Madam Knight, p. 38.)

Being refused accommodation at the house of a Mr. Devill, she wrote the following warning to other travelers:

"*May all that dread the cruel feind of night*
Keep on, and not at this curs't Mansion light.
'Tis Hell; 'tis Hell! and Devills here do dwell:
Here dwells the Devill—surely this's Hell.
Nothing but Wants: a drop to cool yo'r Tongue
Cant be procur'd these cruel Feinds among.
Plenty of horrid Grins and looks sevear,
Hunger and thirst, But pitty's bannish'd here—
The Right hand keep, if Hell on Earth you fear!

(*Ibid.*, p. 40.)

[11] Sewall recorded in his Letter-Book (i. 255) a satire upon "The Gospel Order Revived" (an answer by Benjamin Colman and his friends to Increase

satire may reflect the growth of English satirical poetry during the latter part of the seventeenth century and at the opening of the eighteenth. John Danforth, who had written some verses for his own almanacs at an earlier date, printed a poem a page in length at the end of his published lecture

Mather's "The Order of the Gospel") which was being circulated at Plymouth (March 1701). Part of the poem follows:

. . . .

The old strait Gate is now out of Date,
The street it must be broad;
And the Bridge must be wood, thô not half so good
As firm Stone in the Road.

. . . .

Saints Cotton & Hooker, o look down, & look here
Where's Platform, Way & the Keys?
O Torey what story of Brattle Church Twattle,
To have things as they please

Our Merchants cum Mico do stand Sacro Vico;
Our Churches turn genteel:
Parsons grow trim and trigg with wealth wine & wigg
And their crowns are coverd with meal.

A better satire is John Banister's on Cotton Mather's degree of Doctor of Divinity from Glasgow University, also found in Sewall's Letter-Book (i. 407. November, 1710), Increase Mather having loaned him a copy of it.

ON C. Mr's DIPLOMA.

The mad enthusiast, thirsting after fame,
By endless volum'ns [sic] *thought to raise a name.*
With undigested trash he throngs the Press;
Thus striving to be greater, he's the less,
But he, in spight of infamy, writes on,
And draws new Cullies in to be undone.
Warm'd with paternal vanity, he trys
For new Suscriptions, while the Embryo lyes*
Neglected—Parkhurst† says, Satis fecisti,
My belly's full of your Magnalia Christi.
Your crude Divinity, and History
Will not with a censorious age agree.

* His 2 volumus [*sic*]—Sewall's note. The reference is undoubtedly to Mather's Biblia Americana, which Mather several times vainly endeavored to publish by subscription. It is still in existence—unprinted.

† Parkhurst was the London bookseller who published the Magnalia.

"The Right Christian Temper in every Condition."[12] Cotton Mather wrote several poems, found in his diary and elsewhere, most of which show more poetical feeling and expression than do the poems which he published in the "Magnalia."[13] Samuel Wigglesworth, son of the author of "The Day of Doom," wrote one long poem, "A Funeral Song,"[14] which, in spite of its title, in no way resembles the elegies of the earlier periods, but on the contrary shows

Daz'd with the stol'n title of his Sire‡
To be a Doctor he is all on fire;
Would after him, the Sacrilege commit
But that the Keeper's care doth him affright.§
To Britain's northern Clime in haste he sends,
And begs an Independent boon from Presbyterian friends;
Rather than be without, he'd beg it of the Fiends.
Facetious George brought him this Libertie
To write C. Mather first, and then D. D.

Another satire, less poetical but very bold, appeared in 1717. To quote Sewall, ". . . . a virulent Libel was starch'd on upon the Three Doors of the Meeting House [the New South], containing the following Words;

TO ALL TRUE-HEARTED CHRISTIANS.

Good people, within this House, this very day,
A Canting Crew will meet to fast, and pray.
Just as the miser fasts with greedy mind, to spare;
So the glutton fasts, to eat a greater share.
But the sower-headed Presbyterians fast to seem more holy,
And their Canting Ministers to punish sinfull foley."

(Diary, iii. 116.)

Still another satirical poem, which has disappeared, is mentioned in Thomas' list for 1714 (History of Printing, ii. 372) under the title "Origin of the Whalebone petticoat." A Satyr (In Verse). Boston, August 2d, 1714.

‡ Increase Mather's degree of Doctor of Divinity had been conferred upon him through his own influence at a time when it is questionable whether Harvard had the right to confer such a degree. His enemies criticized him for accepting it.

§ Leverett—Sewall's note. President Leverett belonged to the party unfriendly to the Mathers.

[12] Published at Boston, 1702. He also wrote a poem upon the death of Elder Hopestill, of Dorchester, in 1719. See Memoirs of Roger Clap, p. v.

[13] See his Diary, i. 450; ii. 138, 786; and Kettell, Specimens of American Poetry, i. 14.

[14] Printed in full in the New England Historical and Genealogical Register, iv. 89, and in part in Tyler, History of American Literature, ii. 36 ff.

greater poetical imagination than do his father's poems. In 1713 Richard Steere of Connecticut and Long Island brought out at Boston a ninety-page volume of verse under the title of "The Daniel Catcher."[15]

The last named volume deserves especial attention, not for the fifty-three page biblical poem in rhymed couplets, of the familiar colonial type, from which the volume gets its title, but for three of the shorter poems included in the volume. The first of these is a nineteen page poem in blank verse. The blank verse is not very good, but unique in the colonial poetry of the period, and unusual in any English poetry of the time, there being practically no non-dramatic blank verse from Milton to Thompson. The second, a poem on the visit of the angels to Bethlehem at the birth of the Saviour, is interesting for its echo of Milton's "Hymn" in "On the Morning of Christ's Nativity." The theme is the same, although treated differently, and the metre resembles Milton's in its regular stanza form with the Alexandrine at the end of each stanza; it differs in having an added line instead of the longer third and sixth lines of Milton's. The resemblance is not remarkable, but it is difficult to believe that the writer was not influenced, even if not inspired, by Milton. If so, this is the first colonial poem which shows such influence. The third poem deserves quotation here as showing more poetic feeling than most of the contemporary poetry, and even more as an instance of an appreciation of nature at a time when sincere appreciation of nature was practically unknown in English poetry on either side of the ocean.

ON A SEASTORM NIGH THE COAST.

All round the Horizon black Clouds appear
A Storm is near:
Darkness Eclipseth the Sereener Sky,
The Winds are high,

[15] Printed in full in Littlefield, Early Massachusetts Press, ii. This was his second volume of verse. His first, A Monumental Memorial of Marine Mercy, was published in Boston, 1684.

Making the Surface of the Ocean Show
Like mountains Lofty, and like Vallies Low.

The weighty Seas are rowled from the Deeps
In mighty heaps,
And from the Rocks Foundations do arise
To Kiss the Skies:
Wave after Wave in Hills each other Crowds,
As if the Deeps resolv'd to Storm the Clouds.

How did the Surging Billows Fome and Rore
Against the Shore
Threatning to bring the Land under their power
And it Devour:
Those Liquid Mountains on the Clifts were hurld
As to a Chaos they would shake the World.

The Earth did Interpose the Prince of Light
Twas Sable nigh[t]
All Darkness was but when the Lightnings fly
And Light the Sky,
Night, Thunder, Lightning, Rain, & *raging* Wind,
To make a Storm had all their forces joyn'd.

Such verse writers as these were responsible for the increased interest in literature during the early years of the century, and prepared the way for the even greater activity to follow when the influence of *The Spectator* and similar papers and of Pope and his contemporaries should be felt in New England. That the colonists so soon reacted to the literary movements in England may have been because of the work of these people, poor as it was in itself. As early as 1714 Cotton Mather was ready to attempt essays of the *Spectator* type;[16] and as soon as a vehicle was provided in *The New England Courant* there were many who were eager to contribute.[17] The essays in the *Courant* were the work

[16] See p. 194, above.

[17] An indication of the eagerness to contribute either to the *Courant*, or, for the more conservative, to the *News-Letter* or *Gazette*, is shown by the fact that one of

of a group of men sufficiently organized so that John Campbell, publisher of *The Boston News-Letter*, disgruntled at the success of a new rival, and perhaps offended by the atheistic or deistic tone of the essays, gave them the name by which they have ever since been known, the Hell-Fire Club, that being the name of a London atheist club of unsavory repute. Isaiah Thomas speaks of the group as "a society of gentlemen."[18] The essays in the *Courant* were quickly answered by essays in the *News-Letter* and *Gazette;* and for several years public questions of the day, such as inoculation, were debated. Several months after the *Courant* ceased publication in 1726, *The New England Weekly Journal* was begun. This, like the *Courant*, was the organ of a group of men whose purposes were definitely literary. This group included such young writers as Mather Byles, Thomas Prince, Judge Danforth,[19] and probably Matthew Adams, formerly associated with the *Courant.*[20] The name "Proteus Echo" was assumed for the editor, as "Old Janus" had been used in the *Courant*, both in obvious imitation of the *Spectator*. Both journals printed verse as well as prose, and both frequently lightened the work of their writers by reprinting from English periodicals.[21] The chief poet of the *Journal* was Mather Byles, whose style bears witness to his admiration of Pope's poetry.[21]

Another illustration of the colonial response to English literary movements, as well as an illustration of increasing interest in the production of literature, is found in a manu-

the several verse contributions which Sewall sent to the *News-Letter* was an adaptation of a poem which he had written in 1676. It was published in the *News-Letter* for March 28, 1723, having waited nearly fifty years for a suitable medium for publication. It was evidently recalled by Sewall when he was seeking material to contribute. (Diary, i. 27; iii. 320 note.)

[18] History of Printing, ii. 31.

[19] *Ibid.*, ii. 41, 42.

[20] Massachusetts Historical Society, Collections, v. 211 note.

[21] Cook, Literary Influences in Colonial Newspapers, Chapters I and II, where much detail is given.

script volume recently acquired by the Harvard Library.[22] This volume, in the handwriting of Ebenezer Turell, contains thirteen numbers of a student periodical, modeled after the *Spectator*, which evidently circulated in manuscript. The periodical is called *The Telltale*, and most of its papers are signed by Telltale. One paper gives an account of the "Telltale alias Spy Club—wch consists of these Six members: Telltale, Blablonge, Sharpsights, Courage, Intelligence, Quick." Verse is found in one of the papers. Of this volume Mr. Lane writes, "It is the earliest college production of the kind of which I have any information." That Harvard preceded any English college in attempting periodical literature is striking evidence of the awakening to literary activity in New England in the first quarter of the eighteenth century.

There are other indications of the literary tendency of the time. In 1724 T. Fleet published "The Indictment and Tryal of Sir Richard Rum," a clever temperance tract with literary merit. In 1725 Nathaniel Ames began his "Almanac," which differed from the earlier almanacs both in its use of the best English poetry (whereas earlier almanacs printed third rate original verse), and in its blending of wit and wisdom in effective phrases, wherein Ames anticipated Franklin's "Poor Richard." From now on the almanac yearly carried real literature into every home.

It must be admitted that most of the literature produced during this period is unsatisfactory. The imitations of the *Spectator* do not measure up to their model. The imitators of Pope may have caught the trick of his verse, but they lack both his brilliant wit and his poetic power. That the colonists did not succeed in their attempts is much less important, however, than the fact that they made the effort, and that at the end of the first century of colonization the effort was a general one, not limited to a few ministers or to the edu-

[22] This volume is described in detail in a paper by William C. Lane, Librarian of Harvard, read before the Colonial Society of Massachusetts. (Publications of the Colonial Society of Massachusetts, xii. 220.)

cated class. The leaders in the movement to establish literary journalism had been James Franklin, whose education had been merely that of a printer's apprentice, and Matthew Adams, whom Benjamin Franklin describes as "an ingenious tradesman."[23] Benjamin Franklin himself was only a self-educated printer's apprentice, and a mere boy as well, yet he also came under the influence of the *Spectator* and attempted essays with such success that the Dogood papers, begun in the *Courant* early in 1722, when Franklin was hardly sixteen, were among the most literary essays which that periodical published. Unquestionably we owe the writings of the greatest American writer of the eighteenth century to the literary movement which developed in New England and centered in Boston about the year 1720, as if to commemorate the one-hundredth anniversary of the establishment of English civilization in New England.

[23] Autobiography, p. 22.

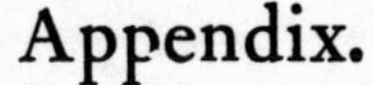

Appendix.

THE *Appendix had not been completed by the author and as it stands now does not include, by any means, all of the material which he had gathered for possible publication in this volume. Owing to lack of space the editor has omitted the catalogues of libraries belonging to William Bradford, Thomas Dudley, Samuel Eaton, Cotton Mather, Increase Mather, Thomas Prince, Miles Standish, William Tyng, John Winthrop, Jr. These lists may be found in Mr. Wright's manuscript at the Yale University Library.*

Appendix.

Items Illustrating the Movement of Books to and among New Englanders.

HERE is the Young Clerks Guide, with the Banquet of Jests.[1]

Nov. 30. I was at Boston, bought Diodati's Annotations.[2]

Also I have desired & obtained of Major Bradford, a Booke in folio written by his father, which I shall send by the first opportunity by water; if I cannot send it by land. The Journall of Plimouth beginnings[3] I could send you, but I thinke it needs not, for you told me some passages in it; whence I conclude you have that booke. Major Bradford hath another printed Booke, which he thinks would well contribute to you. Its title is Good Newes from P. in N: E:[4] But he cannot finde it.[5] [A postscript reports it found.]

I can only tell you that I have sent yo[r] book (this being the first since I wrote to you last) & returne you a thousand thancks for y[e] use of y[e] same.[6]

Mr. Shove was this day at my house; as he passed along to Barnstable, (for your booke he thankes you) . . . .

Yours I received & the bookes, 7 of those which came first are sold at Bridgewater; I will endeavour to sell as fast as I can.[8]

[1] Thomas Johnson of London to Marmaduke Johnson, the printer, April 23, 1663. Littlefield, Early Massachusetts Press, i. 225.

[2] Diary of Rev. William Adams of Dedham, 1670. Massachusetts Historical Society, Collections, 4th Series, i. 15.

[3] The *Journall* is probably the so-called *Mourt's Relation.* The "Booke in folio" is Bradford's famous History of Plymouth. Mather is borrowing these as material for his own history of New England.

[4] Good News from New England, 1624, by Edward Winslow.

[5] John Cotton to Increase Mather, from Plymouth, November 24, 1676. Mather Papers, p. 229.

[6] Giles Sylvester, Jr., of South-ton, to Fitz-John Winthrop, March 9, 1677. Massachusetts Historical Society, Proceedings, 2d Series, iv. 286. In another letter (August 19, 1677) he refers to a book, evidently on heraldry, by Gwillim, which he has had and returned.

[7] John Cotton to Increase Mather, June 25, 1677. Mather Papers, p. 239.

[8] John Cotton to Increase Mather, October 20, 1677. *Ibid.*, p. 239. The books referred to are probably Mather's account of the troubles with the Indians (1677),

If you have Gorsius works by you, doe so much as send out a discours which is as I remember about a quarter or 3 part of the book in containing Exhortations to young people . . . .[9]

Tell him wee thanke him heartily for our Almanacks.[10]

I perceive you have come in the way of sundry pieces of the *Virtuosi.*[11] . . . . I would earnestly entreat you, out of a pitty to a famished man, to send me such treatises historical or philosophical as you have by you, especially that concerning the designes of a French Government in England. I shall carefully return you. And as a pledge of my care, at last I now send you your Hudson. I have kept it long . . . . I did some years agone see papers of weekly edition after the manner of the Gazets, under the name of Philosophical Observations by John[12] Oldenburgh, Felow of the Society. Those of them that I saw contained relations and passages exceeding worthy the knowledge.[13] . . . I have latly seen a smal treatise in verse, such as it is, not over Heliconian, yet honest, printed at Boston, against the Quakers, by one B. K. whose name I cannot unridle. . . . .[14]

I also haueing lately rec^d^ from Mr Whiteing's hand another booke & token of respect, viz: *Diatriba de Signo ffilii Hominis:* I know not what further returne to make, but thanks, &c., unlesse to adde some Apology for my owne indesert of a Lattin booke, being growne so rusty in that *lingua*, with wishing it might be reprinted in English for the benefit of N: E: Towards the charge whereof I shall willingly be a subscriber; haueing had a tast of what you so printed about the Calling of the Jewes; which I borrowed & red, tho: I haue it not by me now:[15]

Yours I received, what sent by Capt. Selleck to myself & freinds, Mr Wakeman & Mr Chauncey, of your own & M^r^

[9] Joseph Eliot to Increase Mather. 1678. *Ibid.*, p. 377.

[10] John Cotton to Increase Mather, March 12, 1679. *Ibid.*, p. 251.

[11] Probably the Philosophical Conferences of the Virtuosi of France.

[12] Really Henry Oldenburg.

[13] Joseph Eliot of Guilford, Conn., to Increase Mather, July 17, 1678. Mather Papers, p. 376. He goes on to urge Mather to send for these collections, not knowing that the Mathers had many volumes of them. See p. 143, below.

[14] B. K. was Benjamin Keach, an English Non-Conformist, whose "The Grand Impostor Discovered: or, the Quakers Doctrine weighed in the Ballance and found wanting" was printed in Boston by John Foster, 1678.

[15] William Leete of Guilford to Increase Mather, July 5, 1682. Mather Papers, pp. 621–623.

Hookes good labo^rs^. What was belonging to me I kindly accept; & what to others, I have conveyed according to your mind.[16]

I unfeynedly thank you for your kindnes to my wife,—sending her one of your last books . . . .[17]

Yours I have received, with that further expression of your love to me, the book of Remarkable Providences,[18] for which I thank you . . . . The booke you sent me last before this was Mr. Torrey his sermon, with your epistle before it. I received three of them; one for Mr. Hanford, one for Mr. Chauncey, ... & the other to myself . . . .[19]

I Received the Booke you sent, which is profitable & of very good use, for which I return you hearty thankes . . . .[20]

Mr. Saltonstall hath a printed book in vindication of the Protestants, and Captain Thomas hath many printed pieces of news. Could I obtain them, I would soon transmit them to your honor.[21]

S^r^, I return you many thanks, as for the many good books which you have sent me, so I giue many thanks to you & to good Mr Willard . . . . for this booke.[22]

Yours of the 2^d^ of this instant I received, & with it your good booke upon occasion of the sore persecution of the Saints in France . . . .[23]

Mr. Willard here, I returned Alsop of Scandal.[24]

To the Rev^nd^ & his estemed ffriend Mr Increase Mather, at his house in Boston, in New England, these, together with a booke.

[16] John Bishop of Stamford, Conn., to Increase Mather, August 3, 1682. Mather Papers, p. 309. Mr. Wakeman was pastor at Fairfield, and Mr. Chauncey at Stratford.

[17] John Higginson to Increase Mather, February 5, 1683. Mather Papers, p. 283.

[18] By Increase Mather, published 1684.

[19] John Bishop to Increase Mather, June 10, 1684. Mather Papers, p. 312. Mr. Hanford, or Hunford, was pastor at Norwalk.

[20] Solomon Stoddard of Northampton to Increase Mather. Mather Papers, p. 586. Undated; probably about 1680.

[21] John Cotton to Governor Hinckley, January 13, 1681. Massachusetts Historical Society, Collections, 4th Series, v. 57.

[22] Thomas Cobbet of Ipswich to Increase Mather, December 13, 1681. Mather Papers, p. 292.

[23] Thomas Cobbet of Ipswich to Increase Mather, May 18, 1682. Mather Papers, p. 293.

[24] Sewall, Diary, i. 109. About 1685.

. . . . Be pleased to lend the litle book to my brother to [peruse] if he desires it.[25]

I received your letter in winter, with an almanack and some verses, for all which I thank you.[26]

I received the verses & Almanacks you sent . . . .[27]

I take the freedom to present thee with a Book.[28]

S^r^, I dare beg no more books, but if you have any newes . . . .[29]

Cous. Greenleaf sups with Mother. I give him the Catechise, Day of Doom, &c bound together in a good Cover . . . .[30]

[Mr. Noyce] greatly desires to see Potter on the number 666. It lyes on my study Table. I should bee glad if you would bee pleased to send it by Mr Grafton.[31]

I must again desire of you to send mee a Book, viz. my Ames' Medulla. It stands in my second shelfe. . . . . Dr. Swinnerton desires to read that volume of the Transactions that treats of Volatile Alcalies. The Book, as I remember, had on it, before the Title, those words *Laudanum Helmontii Junioris*, written by yourselfe. It is about the 100th No. Mr Higginson earnestly desires to see Knoxes History of the Island Ceylon (which lyes on my Father's Table) and Taverniers Travels. Now as for the former of them, If you will send it you will oblige him. Butt as for the latter, it being so Choice a Book and so well bound, that I should bee almost sorry to have it exposed to any Dam̃ages. Butt if you will send it, I'le take what Care I can about it.[32]

There is also som gazetts in the pocket.[33]

[25] Ichabod Chauncy of Bristol, England, to Increase Mather, February 17, 1681–2. Mather Papers, pp. 617–619.

[26] Joseph Eliot to Increase Mather, 1683. *Ibid.*, p. 378.

[27] Simon Bradstreet of Medford to Increase Mather, 1683. *Ibid.*, p. 479.

[28] William Penn of Pennsylvania to Governor Hinckley, 1683. Massachusetts Historical Society, Collections, 2d Series, vii. 185, 186.

[29] Timothy Woodbridge of Hartford to Cotton Mather, April 14, 1684. Mather Papers, p. 639.

[30] Sewall's Diary, i. 223. August 14, 1688.

[31] Nathaniel Mather to his brother Cotton, August, 1688, from Salem, whither he had gone for medical treatment at the home of Dr. Swinerton. He died there in October. Mr. Noyes (Noyce) was one of the Salem preachers. Mather Papers, p. 672.

[32] Nathaniel Mather to his brother Cotton, August 31, 1688. Mather Papers, p. 673. Mr. Higginson was a preacher in Salem.

[33] Wait Winthrop to Fitz-John Winthrop, July 7, 1682. Winthrop Papers, iv. 427.

Pray send or bring 50 ℔ of very fine salt peter; and Glaubers Works translated, and reprinted since the first edition in English.[34] I haue som of his works in Latin, but not halfe, I think.[35]

Pray send ye Gazets, &c., to Mr Saltonstall, & then to Hartford.[36]

Send me by the next post a little booke bound called the Devout Soul's dayly Exercise, in prayers, ... etc: by R. P: D. D. for a friend, as also the verses made about the queenes death.[37]

If you haue not Mr Josh. Moodyes Artillery Election Sermon, June, 1674, I would advise your Honour as a Christian & good souldier to give a look vpon my Annalls of God's Blessing of N. E. in ye yeare 1674, where you'l finde som passages of it recorded. I suppose if you haue never seen those my scripts Mr Cotton Mather may accommodate your Honour wth y^m^. Those my Chronilogicall Decads haue rings or loops by wch they may be fastened together or hang'd vp, to preserve from mice or rats.[38]

For ye gent^m^ of the Council at Hartford I have sent a Gazet, wch I desire you to returne.[39]

I carryed home to Mr. Pierpont 2 books, and borrowed Ward on Mathew.[40]

The Obligations under which you lay me are many and lasting. And these Books, with which you last favoured me, have heaped *Pelion* upon *Ossa*.

For so many fatt Birds, I now return you a Feather; and I pray you to Accept one of the Enclosed, and convey the other.[41]

[34] The same to the same, then in London. November 1, 1694. *Ibid.*, iv. 503.

[35] The same to the same, October 28, 1695. *Ibid.*, iv. 511.

[36] Fitz-John Winthrop, then in London, to Wait Winthrop, July 13, 1695. *Ibid.*, iv. 325.

[37] John Tulley of Saybrook to Mr. Harris, the printer, of Boston, July 17, 1695. He also orders a London "Ephemeris," complaining that the Boston one sent him is poorer than he himself can work out unaided. Massachusetts Historical Society, Proceedings, I. 76.

[38] Samuel Stow of Middletown to Wait Winthrop, 1696. Winthrop Papers, vi. 35. The last sentence may explain the disappearance of many valued colonial books!

[39] Fitz-John Winthrop to the Council at Hartford, February 15, 1700. Winthrop Papers, iv. 374.

[40] Diary of Rev. Joseph Green of Danvers, April 10, 1700. Historical Collections of Essex Institute.

[41] Cotton Mather to Major Stephen Sewall, October 15, 1701. New England Historical and Genealogical Register, xxiv. 110.

Send me Psalmanaazaar again in a month. I think that is time enough,—if not, six weeks.[42]

A Certain Person has Lent Fuller's Holy War, his name is on the Frontice Leaf of it: Whosoever has borrowed the said Book, or into whose hands it may come, are desired to return it unto John Campbell . . . . that the true Owner may have it again.[43]

Stolen or Lost in September last, out of Samuel Dogger of Marshfield his Sloop then in Boston, the first part of Purchasses Pilgrims a History in Folio . . . . [44]

A Certain Person some time since, Lent *Dryden's* Virgil in Folio with Cuts, but has forgot to whom . . . . [45]

A Valuable Collection of Books & Pamphlets, Consisting of Divinity, History, Classicks, Physick, Poetry, Mathematicks, &c., in several Languages: To be sold by Public Vendue or Auction at the House of Mr. *Rowland Dyke* at the Sign of the Royal Exchange in King-Street, Boston: Beginning on Tuesday the 29th Instant . . . . Printed Catalogues may be had gratis.[46]

The Books and other Things of Mr. *Edward Weaver*, Deceas'd, is to be Sold on Thursday the 28th of this Instant February . . . . at the Crown Coffee house in King Street.[47]

Invoice.

BOOKS sent to John Usher of Boston without order by Robert Boulter of London.[48]

12 Terrences
38 Bonds horrace
13 erasmus Colloquies

[42] Cotton Mather to Major Stephen Sewall, May 2, 1706. New England Historical and Genealogical Register, xxiv. 111.

[43] Advertisement in the Boston News-Letter, September 2–9, 1706.

[44] *Ibid.*, December 30–January 6, 1706–7.

[45] *Ibid.*, March 12–19, 1715–6.

[46] *Ibid.*, May 7–14, 1716.

[47] *Ibid.*, February 18–25, 1717.

[48] Sent about 1682. Ford, Boston Book Market, pp. 12, 88–107. The collection was valued at £75.2.9.

13 dyers worcks
22 apples of Gould
3 Calamys ark
6 meads almost a Christian
10 foxes end of tyme
3 faramond
4 brooks ark
9 norwoods epitomy
15 bybles
12 Cocker Cockers tutours
4 Glasson of law
2 last part of the english rogue
22 turky skins
2 parismus
1 destruction of troy
1 Valentyn and orson
4 Goulmans dictionarys
15 dugarts Rhetorique
10 Complete modelist
4 Johnson arithmatick
4 ovid metamorphosis
4 esops in english
2 burroughs on matthew
5 Carmicheal on mortification
5 mitchells sermons
8 alleins allarm
3 remains [of Joseph Alleine]
2 lyfe and death [of Joseph Alleine]
5 sincere Convert
9 sound beleevers
1 owen on the sperit
1 ——— on the hebrews
4 person of Christ
16 boatswains art
2 felthams resolves
1 Cooks marrow [of chirurgery]
8 Cotton on the Covenant
3 queens Closet
4 winchester phrasis

16 Cap of gray haires
2 rarlerys remains
2 Clelias
13 sellers navigation
12 seamans Companion
6 brooks remedies
9 argalus and parthenia
1 Assemblys annotations
7 Clarks tutours
2 Compleat Clark
6 burrougs Contentment
2 Collins on providence
2 Everards workes
6 Baxters Call
6 Doctrin of the byble
10 Wills Commonwealth
2 reynolds on Murther
1 pembrooks arcadia
3 Colliers divinity
2 Flavell on providence
3 touchstones [by John Flavell]
12 smiths narrative
12 Clarks formula
24 testaments
6 senecas
3 Doolitles Catechis
2 Coles soveranity
3 Januas works
5 Culpepers dispensatory
6 phisitian
2 perfect politician
6 ashwoods trade
3 rythers plat [for mariners]
1 baxter of Concord
1 tanners art of physick
2 temples miscellanea
6 pearse of death
3 douting Christian
2 Vertuous woman

4 help to discours
18 flavell on the sacrement
24 vincents Catechis
6 alleins Catt
6 leis Catt
6 Janewais life
4 Johnsons Deus Nobiscum
3 watsons Contentment
6 pooles nullity [of the Romish Faith]
12 ——— Dialogues
100 testaments
1 Bacons works
1 Cloud witnesses
1 phillips dictionary
1 Caesars Commentary
2 leighs Caesars
6 wise masters
2 Erastus
2 Vnlucky Citicen
2 Rich Cabinet
1 Senecas moralls
9 Gentle Craft
1 Cambdens Elizabeth
1 Miltons history
6 Guy of Warwick
6 Reynard fox
3 war with the Jews
1 Parys Narative
12 dr Faustus
6 tom reading
6 [Tom A] Lincolns
12 Joviall Garland
12 Crown Garland
6 Jack Newberry
4 absolute accoumpt
6 Garland of delight
6 fortunatus
6 royall arbours
8 S[c]oggins jests

6 history of Joseph
6 Devill & Dives
6 Booke of knowledg
4 Mandevills travells
6 wise masters
3 wakemans tryalls
2 Langhams
3 dugdalls
12 Processions
4 pack cards

Invoice.

BOOKS delivered by Richard Chiswell of London to Mr. John Ive, September 5, 1683, for shipment to New England.[49]

For Mr. Wise

1 Poolls Critticks 5 vol.
1 Carryl on Job. 2 vol.
1 Hacklutes Uoyages
1 Mori Utopia
1 Zanchii Opera 2 vol
1 Boltons Instructions
1 Greenhill on Ezekiel Compl in 3 vol
1 Culpepers English Physitian
1 Wilson's Christian Dictionary
4 Markhams Works
2 Sure Guide to Justices
8 Allens Allarme
3 Bridges Remaines
7 Gouges Young mans guide with word to Sts and Sinners and Xtian Housholder
12 Doz of White Clasps
10 Hodders Arithmetick
5 Janeways Heauen on Earth

[49] *Ibid.*, pp. 108–120. Value about £50.

1 Uenns Military Discipline
3 Barriffs Military Discipline
4 Little peace Maker
4 Baxters family book
20 Flauells Saint Indeed
20 ——— Token for Mourners
10 ——— on the Sacrement
8 ——— Touchstone
5 ——— on Providence
10 ——— Seamans Compas
4 ——— Husbandry
20 ——— 2 Treatises
20 Baxters Call
10 ——— Now or Neuer
5 Brooks String of Perles
6 ——— Apples of gold
4 ——— Ark for Gods Noah
1 Baxters Saints Rest
10 Brooks Mute Xtian
12 Ayres Copy books
1 Flauells Fountaine Life
12 Cockers Tutor to Writing and Arithmetick
30 Strongs Spelling book
6 Uernons Compting house
1 Felthams Resolues
20 Fox of Time
10 Dyers workes
10 Norwoods Epittomy
10 Oxford Bibles
50 Oxford Testaments
4 Skins of Blew Turkey Leather
7 Janeways Life
6 Julian
6 Allens Remaines
5 ——— Life.
7 Accademy Compliments

For Mr. Mather

3 Chamberlins Geography

1 Haworth of Consumption
1 Bens Sermons.
1 Baxters how to doe good to many.
1 Womans Aduocate
1 Miracles no uiolat. Laws Nature.
1 Shaftsburys Life
2 London gilt.

For Mr. Shepard

1 Mordens Geography
1 Piety the best Rule of Orthodoxie
1 Poeticall History
1 Owen on the Hebrews.
2 ——— of the Person of Christ
2 ——— on the 130th psalme
10 Burtons Wonderful Prodogies
20 Doolittle on the Sacriment 1st p[art]
15 ——— on the Lds Sufferings
50 New England psalms
50 Idem
30 History of Dr. Faustus
1 Teats Map of the Wilderness Sin
Terme cattallouge No. 11. 12

. . . .

7 Accademy Compliments, another sorte.

. . . .

The order not mentioning which Accademy of Compliments you would haue, both sorts are sentt.

Hookers doubting Christian, Allens Rebuke, Owen of Comunion } out of print and not to be had

Burtons Wares of England, ——— Amicable Curiositys } out of print and doing againe.

Eltons Military Discipline—uery scarce and sold for 12*s*.
Moxons Monthly Exercises—Not to be had compl.

Invoice.

BOOKS sold by Richard Chiswell of London to Mr. John Ive for John Usher of Boston, March 3, 1683–4.[50]

3 Virtuous Woman found.
2 Erle of Rochesters Poems.
30 Hoolls Corderius.
6 Greek Testaments.
3 Rauerius Practice of Physick.
6 Sellers Epittomie of Astronomical Systems.
4 Miltons Paradise Lost.
40 Strongs Spelling booke.
5 Sheppards Sincere Conuert.
50 New England Psalmes.
1 Bible 4° Oxon with Common prayer and Apockchryphia.
100 Sententiae Pueriles.
50 Latine Catos.
40 Ouid de Tristibus.
6 Meads Almost Christian.
12 Erasmus Colloquies Latin.
6 Lestranges Erasmus in English.
1 Baker's Chronicle.
3 Doz. Brass Compasses largest sorte
3 Wilsons Christian Dictionary.
20 Foxes End of Time.
8 Pounds of Vermillion with Box.
1 Dutch Annotations in 2 Vol.
2 Supplement to the Morning Exercise.
1 Pembrooks Arcadia.
1 Keebles Statutes last Edit.
2 Queuedos Visions Compl. both parts.
3 Cambridge Concordance.
30 Nomen Claturas
10 Dugards Rhetorick.
10 Smiths Rhetorick.
4 Ames Cases of Contience in Lat.
10 Hookers Doubting Christian.
1 Gutberleths Physick.

50 *Ibid.*, pp. 121–132. The entire collection was valued at £61.5.6.

10 Lattine Testaments.
18 Greek Grammars.
3 Wollebeus Compendium in Lat.
30 Token for Children Compl.
2 Burroughs Gospel worship.
12 Norwoods Epittomy.
12 Gouges Youngmans Guide with Safe way of Thriueing.
12 ——— Directions.
3 Accademy of Compliments.
5 Janeways Life.
6 Nuga Uenales.
3 Cotton on the Couenant.
12 Warr with the Deuill.
2 Burroughs Gospel worship.
3 Present State of England. Comp. all parts
4 Jure Maritimo.
2 Clarks Liues of the Fathers.
2 Sturmies Mariners Magazine.
18 Dr. Faustus. 1st and 2d pt.
18 Calamys Godlymans Arke
6 Brookes Arke.
6 Wilds Poems.
6 Argulus and Parthenia.
3 Tanners Art of Physick.
4 Littletons Dictionary.
2 Gassendus Astronimy.
12 Sturmies Epistles.
2 Bythner on the Psalmes.
2 Leusdens Hol. Bible.
6 Oxford Grammars.
5 Oxford Jests.
13 Rami Logica.
16 Culpepers English Physitian.
16 ——— Dispensatorys.
4 Dauenports Saints Anchorhold
2 Zouche Jurisdiction of Courts of Admiralty.
10 Englishmens Liberties.
1 Hebrew Bible of Mannasseth Ben Israel
1 ——— Idem of Uenice Edition.

1 ——— Idem of Plantins Edition.
Terme Catalogue No. 13. 14

1. All the books are sent that could be procured.
2. Some few are raised by reason of the scarcity.

Invoice.

BOOKS sold by Richard Chiswell of London to Mr. John Ive for John Usher of Boston, May 29, 1684.[51]

2 Bibles 24 Ruled Turkey gilt back
30 Greek Grammers
3 Bythner on the Psalms
6 SincereConvert
10 Flauel on the Sacriment
10 Cattechise
2 Cambridge Concordance
2 Sellers Practical Nauigation
2 Wilsons Christian Dictionary
5 Clarks Tutor
4 Burroughs Gospel Remission
4 State of England in 2 vol both parts
3 Markhams way to get wealth
2 Eltons Military Discipline
6 Oxon Bibles large
5 Hesiod
2 Blounts Law Dictionary
2 Daltons Iustice
50 Lattine Grammers.
50 Construing books
20 Smiths Great Assize
2 History of Parismus
20 Gentle Craft
10 Gentlemans Jockey
5 Uernons Compting House.
2 Flauels Fountaine of Life
2 ——— Method of Peace.

[51] *Ibid.*, pp. 133–139. Value, £25.6.10.

7 ——— Treaty of Sufferings.
3 Norwoods Doctrine of Triangles.
6 ——— Epittomy.
8 Gellibrands Epittomy.
2 Erly Religion a Sermon.
1 Showers Ser[mon] at Mrs. Ann Barnardiston funl.
1 Dorringtons Ser[mon] of the Right use of an Estate.
1 Demaris Pearses Remaines.
1 Memoires of the Fam. of the Stuarts.
2 Wonders of the Femall world.
1 Her and His.
10 Second Part of the Pilgrims Progress.
2 Two Journeys to Jerusalem
200 Pare of Clasps for writeing books
2 London Bully 1st and 2d p[art]
3 A Ramble to Hackney.
1 Popes Life.
2 Informers Doome.
2 Melius Inquirendum.
2 Sherlocismus Eneruatus.
3 Uenus in the Cloyster.
2 Womans Aduocate.

London Gilt is out of print and not to be had.

Invoice.

BOOKS sold by Richard Chiswell to Mr. John Ive for John Usher, April 13, 1685.[52]

1 Goodwins Works in 2 vol.
1 Rogers on Peter
1 ——— Parable of the Prodigal
20 Smith's Great Assize
20 Flauels Compas
15 ——— Token for Mourners
30 ——— Saint Indeed
10 Erasmus Colloquies 8° English Lestrange

[52] *Ibid.*, pp. 140–151. Value, £61.19.01/2.

20 Doolittle on the Sacrament
15 Hookers Doubting Christian
100 Hoolls Sententia
60 ——— Cases
30 Fox of Time
20 Baxters Call
10 ——— Now or Neuer
22 Farnabys Ouid
12 Hoolls Terrence
6 Booke of Rates
30 Warr with the Deuill
4 Duty of Man
12 Aristotle's Problems
8 Hebrew Psalters
30 Token for Children Complt.
10 Flauel on the Sacrement
2 Norton's Orthodox Euangelist
3 Office of Executors
30 Lillys Rules
10 Calamys Godlymans Arke
12 Lattine Justins
18 Tullys Offices
1 Dutch Annotations in 2 vol
10 Gollibrands Epittomy
6 Woollebius Compend: Lat.
4 Lattine Bible
8 Flauels Touchstone
8 Winchester Phrases
2 Glissons Common Law Epitomized
8 Jure Maritimo.
2 Eltons Millitary Discipline.
3 Barriffs Millit. Discipline with Horse.
40 Marriners New Kallender
4 Ittallian Conuert
1 Dells Sermons.
2 Terms of the Law
3 Daltons Justice
2 Keebles Statutes.
2 Cooks Reports Engl.

3 Blounts Law Dictionary.
1 Sheppards Grand Abridgement
1 Hobbarts Reports.
3 Culpepers English Physitian.
3 ——— Dispensatory.
5 Midwifery per Culpeper.
10 Greek Gramers
20 New England Psalmes
3 Miltons Logick.
2 Wingates Arithmattick.
2 Records Arithmattick.
4 Johnsons Arithmattick.
3 Hodders Arithmattick.
10 Strongs Spelling book.
6 History of Dr. Faustus.
2 Rochesters Life.
2 Owen on the 3d p[ar]t [of Hebrews]
12 Lattine Terrence.
3 Amesii Medulla.
3 ——— de Conscientia.
3 Littletons Dictionary.
2 Pulton of the Common Pleas Engls.
5 Sheppards Sure Guide.
10 Wonderful Prodogies.
20 Accidencies.
10 Dugards Rhetorick.
15 Nomen Claturas.
6 Bonds Horrace.
3 Greek Testaments
20 Protestant Tutors.
3 Clarkes Phrases.
2 Poolls Annotations on the Bible in English.
6 Siluanus his Theocritus.
1 ——— Lucian.
1 ——— Isocratis.
1 ——— Essopi Fabula.
1 ——— Plutarck.
Term Cattalouge No. 15. 16. 17. 18.

. . . . The 4 books of Syluanus are sent as a present to the Chief

Schoolmaster in New England being a New Praxis upon some Greek Authors which is well entertained in our Schooles here and much used.

Book References in Increase Mather's Writings.

A. Books Cited or Quoted.[53]

Author	Title
———	The History of Sham Plotts
———	Acta Eruditorum, Leipsic
Adam, Melchior	Vita Melancthonis
Adam, Melchior	Vita Myconii
Agricola, Georg	
Agrippa, C.	de Occulta Philosophia
Agrippa, C.	The Vanity of Sciences
Alting	Loci Communes
Ambrose	Treatise of Angels
Ames	Cases of Conscience
Augustine	de Civitate Dei
Avicenna	
Balduinus	Cases of Conscience
Baldusius	In 2 Corinthians
Bartholinus	
Baxter, R.	Book about Witchcrafts
Baxter, R.	Church History
Beard	Theater of Gods Judgements
Bernard	66 Sermones in Cantica
Bernard	A Guide to Grand Jurymen in Cases of Witchcraft
Beza	Life of Calvin
Beza	Commentaries

53 These are in addition to those mentioned in Chapter VIII. Where no title is given, the reference in Mather was to the author only.

Binsfield	de Confessionibus sagarum
Bodin	Dæmonomania
Boissardus	de Secretis Mag.
Bootius	de Gemmis
Bovet	Pandemonium
Brockmand	Theol. de Angelis
Bromhall	History of Apparitions
———	The Bucuneers of America
Burnet	Life of Rochester
Burroughs	On Matthew 11, 28
Burton	Miracles of Nature[54]
Burton	Prodigies of Mercies
Burton	History of Dæmons
Cambden	Britannia
Camerarius	Horæ Subsecivæ
Camerarius	Centuriæ Quattuor Symbolorum
Cardano	de Rerum Varietate
Cardano	de Subtilitate
Casaubon	Of Spirits
Childrey	Britannia Baconica
Chiverius	Historiarum totius Mundi Epitome
Chytræus	
Clark, Samuel	Examples
Clark, Samuel	Lives of English Worthies
Clark, Samuel	Martyrology
Clark, William	Natural History of Nitre
Cooper, Thomas	Mystery of Witchcraft
Cotta	The Tryal of Witchcraft
Darrel	Seven Possessed Persons in Lancashire
Delrio	Disquis. Magicarum
Dubravius	Historia Bohemiæ
Eusebius	in Vita Constantii
Fernelius	de Abditis Rerum Causis
Forestus	
Gaul	Select Cases of Conscience concerning Witches and Witch-craft
Gerhard	Loci Communes
Gesner	

[54] See note 4, p. 138, above.

Gnaccius	Compend. Malefic.
Godelmannus	de Lamiis
Goodwin	Doctrine of Saints Perseverance
Gorges, F.	Narration
Goulartius	Select History
Hale, Matthew	The Account of Tryals of Witches at Bury, Suffolk
Hall, Bishop	Autobiography
Hall, Bishop	"Psalm 82"
Heinsius	in Matthew viii, 16
Hemming	de Superstitione Magica
Henkelius	de Obsessis
———	History of Lapland
Holder	"book about the natural production of letters"[55]
Honsdorsius	Historical Theater
Horace	Various
Horneck, A.	History of the Witches in Sweden
Horstius	Inst. Med.
Javellus	Medicinæ Compendium
King James	Discourse of Witchcraft
Janeway	Remarkable Sea Deliverances
Johnston	Thaumatograph
Josephus	History of Wars with the Jews
Josephus	Antiquities
Jovius, P.	History
deLaet, J.	Description of America
deLaet, J.	de Gemmis
Lavater	de Spectris
Lecus	Compend. Hist.
Lemnius	
Lewiston	Of Fulfilling the Scriptures
Malderus	de Magia
Mandelslo	Travels
Martinii	Lexicon Philologico-Etymologicum
Martyr, P.	Commentary of 1 Samuel
Mede	Works

[55] This book was a treatise on lip-reading; a very modern seeming book for the company it is in!

Mede	Discourse on John x, 20
Melanchthon	Consilia
Menna	de Purgatione Vulgari
Merden	Geographia Physica
Meurerius	Comment. Meteorolog.
Meurtius	Athenæ Batavæ
Morland	Hist. Waldenses
Munster	Notes on Leviticus xvii
Owen	Work of the Spirit in Prayer
Pensingius	de Pulvere Sympathetico
Perkins	Discourse of Witchcraft
Polydore, Vergil	
Pontano, G.	
Porta, Bapt.	
Proclus	de Sacrificio et Magia
Rainolds	de Libris Apocryphis
Remigius	
Ricaut	History of the Present State of the Ottoman Empire
Roberts	Narrative of Witches in Suffolk
Rulandus	
Schotten	Physic. Curios.
Selden	de Diis Syriis
Sennertus	Practica Medicinæ
Sennertus	Med. Precl.
Sinclare, G.	Satan's Visible World Discovered
Smetius	Miscellanies
Socrate	History
Spotswood	History of Scotland
Sprenger	Malleo Malleficarum
Sympson	Ecclesiastical History
de Thou	Historiarum sui Temporis
Thyræus	de Obsessis
Thyræus	de Apparitionibus Spirituum
Thyræus	Disput. de Dæmoniacis
laTorr	Disputationes
Tostatus	in Matthew 8
Vairus de Fascino	
Valerius Maximus	

Verstegan	Antiquities
Voetius	de Emergumenis
Voetius	de Spectris
Voetius	de Operationibus Dæmonum
Voetius	de Magia
Voetius	Disputat. Select.
Wanly	Of the Wonders of the Worldous, 1680
Webster	Book of Witchcraft
———	Weekly Memorials for the Ingeni
White	Relation
Wierus	de Præstigiis Dæmonum
Willet	Commentaries
Wm. of Malmsbury	Lib. ii
Zacchias, P.	Questionibus Medicis
Zanchy	Epistol. 2
Zuinger	Theatrum Vit. Human.

B. Books Referred to Without Quotation or Citation.

Bannosius	Life of Ramus
Burgensis	
Cabeus	On the Loadstone
Caussin	Holy Court
Chassalion	Histories of the Judgements of God
Codronchus	
Conring	
Cornelius à Lapide	
Cumanus	Lucerna Inquisitorium
Epiphanius	
Freherus, Paulus	Theatrum Vivorum Eruditione Claru
Gassendi	Essays
Gennadius	
Gilbert	De Magnete
Hakluyt	Voyages
Henningus Witten	Memoria Theologorum nostri seculi
Isidore	
Jerome	
Kepler	On the Loadstone
Kircher	On the Loadstone
Kommannus	

Linschoten	Voyages
Mendozo	
Molianus	
Pomponatius	
Prochorus	
Schopfius	Academia Christi
Serrarius	
Spineus	
Sulpitius Severus	In Vita Martini
Verheiden	Elogia Theologorum
Ward	On the Loadstone
Windet	

Book References in Cotton Mather's Writings.

A. Books Cited or Quoted.[56]

Aben Ezra	
Acosta, J.	History of the Indies
Adam, Mel.	Lives
Ady, T.	Perfect Discovery of Witches
Agapetus	
Agathius	
Algazel	
Alphonsus of Arragon	
Alsted, J. H.	
Altenburg	
Ambrose	
Amyraldus	
Angellius	
Anselm	
Antiochus Syracusanus	

[56] These are in addition to those mentioned in Chapter VIII. A few quotations which really belong to the third period (after 1700) are included here in order to give a complete list of Mather's borrowings.

Antoninus	
————	Aphor. Polit.
Aquinas	
Aristotle	
Arnobius	
Arrianus	
Arrowsmith	
Athanasius	Life of Antonius
Athenæus	
Augustine	Several
Avril	Travels
Baily, R.	
Baker, R.	
Bartholinus	
Barton, W.	(quotes a hymn)
Basil	
Bates, W.	
Baxter, R.	Several
Bede	Ecclesiastical History of England
Bellarmine	
Bernard	
Beroaldus	
Besoldus	Axiomatæ Philosophiæ Christianæ
Bethel, S.	The Interest of Euroipe
Beverly	
Beverovicius	
Beza	Life of Calvin, Psalms
Blackerby	
Blahoslius	History of Johannes Cronu
Boccalini	
Bodin	
Bolsecus	Life of Calvin, etc.
Borellus	
Brahe, Tycho	
Bradwardine	
Brownrig	
Bucer	Scripta Anglicana and others
Bucholtzer	
Bullinger	

Burnett	History of his Times
Burroughs, J.	
R. B.[urton]	History of Dæmons
Calamy	Sermon on Earl of Warwick, etc.
Calvin	
Camerarius	
Canus. Melch.	
Carthagena	
Carthusian	
Caryl	
Casaubon	
Cassianus	
Castel	
Cato	
Chamier	
Chemnitius	
Chrysostom	De Deo Orando and others
Cicero	De Natura Rerum
Cicero	Orat. pro Plancio, De Senectute, & others
Clark, S.	Examples, etc.
Claude	
Claudian	
Clemens Alexandrinus	
Clemens Romanus	
Cocceius	
Colerus	
Contzen	
Coryat	
Cranmer	
Cranzius	
Crespin	Histoire des Martyrs
Cudworth	Intellectual System
Curtius	History of Alexander the Great
Cyprian	
Demosthenes	
Denys, N.	Description of Coasts of North America
Diodorus Siculus	History
Dionysius Halic.	
Eccles, S.	The Quaker's Challenge

————	Ephemerides Medico-physicæ
Epiphanius	
Erasmus	Epistolæ, and other works
Eusebius	
Eutyches	History of Nicene Synod
Festus	de Verborum Significatione
Firmin	The Real Christian
Fisher the Quaker	Pamphlets
Flavel	
Fox, George	Great Mystery
Fox, J.	Book of Martyrs, Acts and Monuments
Fuller, Nich.	
Fuller, T.	Church History
Gaule, J.	Select Cases . . . . Touching Witches
Gerhard	Meditationes Sacræ, etc.
Gerson	
Gesner	
Gildas	
Glanvil	Collections of Sundry Trials
Gregory the Great	
Gregory Nazienzen	
Gregory of Nyssa	
Grotius, H.	
Grynæus	
Guitton	
Gulielmus Parisiensis	
Gustavus Adolphus	
Hale, Matthew	Tryal of Witches
Hall, J.	
Heinsius	
Helvicus	Epitaph
Helwigius	
Hemming, N.	Admonitio de Superstitionibus Magicis
Hesychias	
Heylin	
Holland	
Homer	Iliad
Horace	Various
Horneck	

Hornius	
Hottinger	
Hoyl, J.	
Ignatius	Various
Inghiramius	
Isidore	
Isocrates	
Jermyn	
Jerome	
Josephus	
Junius	
Jurieu	Traite de L'Unite de L'Eglise
Justin	
Justin Martyr	
Keeble	Common Law
Kimchi, Rabbi	
Lactantius	
LeClerk	
Leigh	Critica Sacra
Libingus	
Lipsius	
Livy	
Lucian	
Lucretius	
Ludovicus Molinæus	
Lupichius	
Luther	Various
Lysimachus	
Machiavelli	
Madgeburgensian Centuriators	
Maimonides	
Manethon	
Marbeck	Concordance
Martin of Tours	
Martyr, Peter	Commonplaces, etc.
Maurier	
Mede, J.	
Melanchthon	

Mersennus	
Mohammed	Alcoran
More, Henry	Glanvil's Sadducismus, etc.
Morland	History of Waldenses
Murtadi	Egyptian History
Musculus	(verse)
Musonius	
Myconius	
Newton	
Nieremberg	
Norton	Answer to the Sylloge Quæstionum
Oecolampadius	
Origen	Various
Osiander	
Ovid	Metamorphoses
Owen, J.	Various
Panormitan	
Parker	
Parliamentary	Speeches
Patin	Travels
Penn	
Perkins	Witchcraft, etc.
Philo Judaeus	
Philostratus	
Philpot	
Photius	
Plato	
Plautus	Amphitruo, etc.
Pliny	
Plot, R.	Natural History of Oxfordshire
Plutarch	
Pœdianus	
Poiret	L'Œconomy Divine[57]
Polybius	
Polycarp	
Polydore Vergil	
Porphyrius	
Portugal, King of	Translation of Psalm

[57] English translation not published until 1773; therefore read in the original.

Posidonius	Life of Augustine
Potts, T.	Discoverie of Witches in Lancashire
Powel, V.	
Prudentius	
Purchas	Pilgrims
Quercetanus	
———	Quest. et Resp.
Quintilian	
Raleigh	
Ramus	
Randolph, N.	Letters
Rivet, A.	
Rodiginus	
Romanus	
———	Roman Law, XII Tables of
Row	
Ruffinus	
Rushworth	Collections, 1629
Rushworth	Collections, 1640
Rycaut	History of Turks
Ryther	A Plot for Mariners
Sadoletus	
Salmasius	
Salomon, Rabbi	
Salvian	
Sanbert	
Sarracius	
Saumer	
Scaliger	
Scribonius	Physiologia Sagarum
Seneca	
Sigonius	
Simeon Metaphrast	
Sobinus	
Soulinge	
Stenius	
Strabo	
Streitbergerus	
Stupius	

Suidas	
Symmachus	
Symons, E.	Discourse, 1637
Synesius	
———	The Taanith
Tacitus	
———	The Talmud
Tertullian	Apology, etc.
Theodoret	
Theophylact	
deThou	
Tillotson	On Family Worship
Tolner	
Turretin	
VanHeer	Observations
Vegetius	
Vincent	True Touchstone
Virgil	Various
Voetius	
Vossius	
Waller, W.	Meditations
Weinrichius	
Wendover	
Whitaker	
Widerus	
Wierus	de Præstigiis Dæmonum
Wigandus	
Wilkinson	Conciones Sex ad Academicos Oxon.
Wotton	
Zanchy	
Zeira, Rabbi	
Zepperus	

B. Books Referred to without Quotation or Citation.

Abericus	
Alting	
Ames, William	Medulla Theologiæ, etc.
Archilochus	
Archimelus	

———	Life of J. Angier
Arndt	Verus Christianismus
Bacon	Advancement of Learning
Baldwin	
Bannosius	Life of Ramus
Baronius	
Barrow, I.	
Basnagian	
Bekker	
Bennet	Concordance
Bernard	Guide to Grandjurymen
Bilson	
Binsfield	
Blondel	
Bochart	Curiosities
Boehm	Recapitulation, etc.
Bolton	Sermons
Bovet	
Boyle	
Brombal	
Bucan	
Burnett	Essay on Scripture Prophecies
Cambden	
Carbilius	Æneidomastix
Castalio	Sacred Dialogues
Cochlæus	
Cole, T.	Discourse of Regeneration
Corbet	Self-Employment
Corinna	
Cornelius à Lapide	
Cotton	Concordance
Davenport, C.	
Defoe	The Storm
Delrio	
Descartes	
Didymus	
Dietericus	Antiquitates Biblicæ
Diodati	
Dorney	Divine Contemplations

Dorotheus	Collections
Downham	Concordance
Edwards	Preacher
Empress Eudocia	Poems
Eunapius	
Fabius	Life of Beza
Faustinus	
Fenner	Treatise on Impenitency
Ficinus, Marcil.	Several
Florus, Luc.	
Franke	Manuductio, etc.
Gassendi	
Genebard	
Gennes	Relation of Voyage
Godefridus de Valle	De Arte Nihil Credendi
Gualteb	
Guicciardine	
Hardy	Guide to Heaven
Hevelius	Selenography
Herennius	
Herodian	
Herodotus	
Hilary	
Hildersham	
Hobbes	
Hooker, R.	
Hornius	De Origine Gentium Americanarum
Hortensius	
Hospinian	
Howe, J.	On Blessedness of Righteousness
Irenæus	
Janeway	Treatises; Token for Children
———	The Oxford Jests; Cambridge Jests
Juvian	
La Placette	La Morale Chrétienne Abregée
Laertius	
Langius	Medecina Mentis
Leontius	
Lightfoot	Curiosities

Lubbertus	
Lukins	Interest in Spirit of Prayer
Lycophron	
Lyra	
Maccovius	
Macrobius	
Marot, C.	Psalms in Metre
Marshall	Gospel Mystery of Sanctification
———	Mass-books
Mathesius	
Meddendorpius	
Mendoza	
Nathans, Rabbi	Concordance
Neal	History of New England
Neander	
Norcott	
Oldmixon	English Empire in America
Oppian	
Pagius	
Palladius	Dialogus de Vita Chrysostomi
Pamphilia	
Pancirollus	Res Deperditæ
Paterculus	
Peter Crinitus	
Pezelius	
Pictet, B.	Saintes Conversationes
Platerus	
Pocock	
Pole, M.	Annotations
Posselius	
Ravanellus	
Reynolds	
Ricciolus	Almagestum Novum
Roswitha	Chronicles
Rowe, J.	Saints' Temptation
Saleius	
Sallust	
Sandford	De Descensu Christi
Sarocchia	

Schlusselbergius	
Schurman	
Scribanius, C.	
Selden	
Servius	
———	The Seven Champions
Simeon Metaph.	
Simplicius Verinus	
Sleidan	
Socrates	
Spencer	Discourse Concerning Prodigies
Stapelton	De Tribus Thomis
Stegmannus	Studii Pietatis Icon; De Vero Christianismo
Strato	
Suetonius	
Swinnock	Discourses
Theophylact	
Thucydides	
Torniellus	
Tympius	
Usher	Body of Divinity
Victor	
Wallis	
Weigel	
Whiston	Apostolical Constitutions
White	The Power of Godliness
Wickens	
Wilkins	
Wise, J.	Vindication
Witten	Memoriæ Theologorum
Woodward	Natural History of the Earth
Xenophon	Hellenica
Xenophon	Cyropædia
Zosimus	
Zuinglius	

Inventory of the Library of William Brewster.[58]

2 little chatachismes
1 Lambeth on the Will of man [by François Lambert.]
1 morrall discourse
Discouery of Spanish Inquisition [by Gonsalvius Montanus.]
Johnson on 18th Math. [by Francis Johnson.]
Remaynes of Brittaine [by Wm. Camden.]
Description of New England [by John Smith.]
Nova Testamenti Malarato [by Avg. Marloratus.]
Tromelius & Junius Biblia Sacra [by I. Tremellius and F. Junius.]
Beza noua testament, lat. & gre.
Centuria Selecta
Calvin duodecim pphet [Prælectiones in Dvodecim Prophetas]
Clauis Scriptura flacio Illirico [by Flacius Illyricus.]
Peter Martyr Com[mentarii]. prior ad Corinthos
Musculus ad Isaiam & Romanos [by Wolfgang Moesel.]
Regneri prandinī
Œcolumnadī in Ieremia [by J. Œcolampadius.]
Crisostm, Mattias & Ioannes [by J. Chrysostom.]
Musculus Psalmos David [by W. Moesel.]
Calvī at Daniel [Calvin: Prælectiones in Librum Prophetiarum Danielis.]
Calvī on Isā [Calvin: Commentarii in Isaiam.]
Musculus ambos Epist ad Corinthos [by W. Moesel.]
Molleri ad Psalmos
Lanaterus Esequeh [L. Lavaterus: Ecclesiastes Salomonis.]
Zanchī ad Ephe[sios]
Syntagma amudo polo Syntagmatis Theologia Christian [Amandus Polanus: Syntagma Theologiæ.]
Sulteti Isaiam [Abraham Scultetus: Annotata in Proph. Esaiam.]

58 Massachusetts Historical Society, Proceedings, 2d Series, v. 37 ff. Explanatory notes in brackets are condensed from Dr. H. M. Dexter's.

Purei Hoseam [David Pareus: In Hoseam.]
Gualterin Deluerin, nou. testa. [Rodolph Gualther: Archetypi Homiliarum in quatuor Evang, etc.]
Psalm Pagnii [S. Pagnini.]
Pareus in Genosa [in Genesin Mosis.]
Piscator in Nova Testament
Pareus ad Romanos
Pareus ad Priorem Corinthis
Caluin Eze[chielis] vigint prima
Tabula Analytice Stephano
Cartwright harm[oni]ā 4 Euangl
Pascillia Hemnigm [N. Hemmingius: Postilla Evangeliorum.]
De Vera Ies. Chr. Religione [P. Duplessis-Mornay: De veritate Religionis Christianæ liber.]
Erasmus in Marcin [Marcum]
Parkerius politica Eccle [R. Parker: De Politeia Ecclesiastica Christi.]
Piscator in Genesn̄
Kykermano Systema Phisica [Bart. Keckerman.]
Beza Confess. Christ
Rollock in Dany [R. Rollici: In Librum Danielis Prophetæ.]
Dauen in priō Juni [L. Danæus: Commentarium in priorem ad Ioannem Epistolam.]
Thom Thomaseus Dix [Dictionarium, etc.]
Bastwick Apologeticus [1636]
Machauelii princeps
Elenchus papistice Bastwick [J. Bastwick: Elenchus Religionis Papisticae. 1633.]
Rollock at Psalmos
Rainoldi de Romana Eccles
Caluin in Josua
Syntagma Vigandus [Jo. Wigandus: Syntagma..]
Epistola Apologetica
Paraphrasa Erasmus in Luke
Latina Grammatica
Hebrew gramat
Camden Brittan [Britannia]
Rollock ad Romanos Ephes[ios]
Dictio. Triglott

Buxtorff Lexicon
Cartwright prouerbīa
Iunii ad Ecclām Dei [F. Iunius: Ecclesiastici . . . .]
Tyrocinia [J. Prideaux: Tyrocinium ad syllogismum . . . .]
Poemata Heringii [Fr. Herring: In fœlicissimum . . . . Iacobi primi, Angliæ . . . . Regis, etc. Poema Gratulatorium.]
Ad Reverend. patres Eccles. Anglican [Remonstrance agt ye. treatt of Puritans. 1625.]
Amesii contra Grevin. Co. [against Nic. Grevinchovius.]
Hypomneses [Prideaux: Hypomnemata Logica, Rhetorica, etc.?]
Antichristus prognostica
Harmonia Evangelia [by M. Chemnitius and Polycarpus Lyserus.]
1 English bible lattin letter
1 English bible
A new Testament
Mr. Ainsworths Psalms in prose & meter
1 new testament
Major Coment new testament [J. Mayor: A Commentarie . . . .]
Hexapla vpon Daniell [by A. Willet.]
2 volumes of Mr. Perkins
Mr. Hernes works [?Samuel Hieron 1624.]
Babingtons works [by Gervase Babington.]
Cartwright against Remisc [A Confutation of the Rhemists translation . . . .]
Byfield on Coloss
Dodoner Herball [by Rembert Dodoens.]
Mr Rogers on Judges [by Richard Rogers.]
Mr Richardson on ye state of Eur[ope]. [by Gabriel Richardson. 1627.]
Knights Concord[ance] [by Wm. Knight.]
Calvin on Isay
Willet on Romans
Greusames works [Richard Greenham?]
Bodens Comon weale [by Jean Bodin.]
Willet on the 1st Samuel
Surveyor by Ratbone [Aaron Rathbone: The Surveyor. . . . .]
Willit on Genesis
Seneca Workes
Wilcocks on Psalmes [T. Wilcox.]

Cottons Concordance 2 volumes [1631.]
Scholastical discourse about the crosse [by R. Parker.]
Taylor upon Tytus
Hill upon Life Euer[lasting].
Wilsons Dixonor [Thos. Wilson: A Christian Dictionary. . .]
Waimes Christiā Synagogue [by Jo. Weemes.]
Gibbines question & disputacons [by Nich. Gibbens.]
Caluin Harmon Evan[gelists].
Defence of Synod of Dort by Robin [by Jo. Robinson.]
Messelina [?Nath. Richards: The Tragedy of Messalina, 1640.]
Downams Warfare 2 pt [J. Downame: The Christian Warfare.]
Barlow on 2 Tymothy [1625.]
Cartwright ag^st Whitgift 2 pt
Jackson ag^s. Misbeliefe [1625.]
Granger on Eccl[esiastes]. [1621.]
Brightman on Reuel[ation].
Birdag Anti [?Tho. Beard: Antichrist the Pope of Rome. 1625.]
Byfield on 1 Peter [1623.]
Weymes on Image of God in Man [J. Weemes. 1627.]
Parr on Romans [1631].
Robinsons Observacons [J. Robinson. 1625.]
Right way to go to worke [1622.].
Byfields sermons on 1 Peter
Dod on Commandm^ts
Mayor on Catholick Epistles [Jo. Mayer. 1627.]
Taylor parable on the Sower [Tho. Taylor. 1621.]
Narme of Chr. Strarr. [W. Narne: Christs Starre . . . . 1625.]
Morley of truth of religion [by P. de Mornay.]
Attersons badges of Christianity
Downam Consolatrix [Jo. Downame: Consolations]
Elton on 7 Romans
A declaracon of Quintill. question
Byfeild on 3 of Peter [1637.]
7 p^rbleames against Antechrist [G. S.: Sacræ Heptades, or seaven problems concerning Antichrist. 1626.]
Dike upon Repent
Sibbs Soules Comfort [1625.]
Passions of the mynd
5 bookes of Sermons stichet together

Constitucons & Cannons of bb. of Cant.
Wittenhall discovery of abuses [Th. Whetenhall.]
Rollock on Thessal[onians]
Heauen opened by Coop [by Wm. Cowper.]
Treasury of Smiles [Rob. Cawdrey: A Treasurie or Store-House of Similies.]
Downefall of Popery [by Th. Bell.]
Saints by calling by Wilson
Udal on Lamentacons
Dyocean Tryall [P. Baynes: The Diocesans Tryall.]
Sparks ag^st Albin [Tho. Sparke: An Answere to J. de Albines notable Discourse against heresies.]
Wottons defence of Perkins Refor[med] Catholicke
Brinslow on Ezech [Ezekiel] [by J. Brinsley. 1622.]
Defence of Ministers reasons [by S. Hieron.]
Downam ag^st Bath & Wells [G. Downame: A Defence of the Sermon preached at the Consecration of the L. Bishop of Bath and Welles . . . .]
A discourse of troubles Chu. of Amster[dam]. [by G. Johnson.]
Mr. Smyths 3 treatises
Discourse of Equivocation [by H. Mason. 1634.]
Mr. Smyths paroliles [Jo. Smyth: Paralleles, Censvres, etc.]
A peticon for reformacōn
A primer of Chr. Relig.
A discourse of variance betweene pope & Venet. [Chr. Potter: A Sermon . . . . added an Advertisement touching . . . . the quarrels of Pope Paul 5, with the Venetians. 1629.]
Broughton on Lament[ations].
Perkins on Sat[ans]. Sophist[rie]
A discourse of Adoracōn of Reliq^us
A trew mark of Catholike Church [by T. Beza.]
A quodlibet to bewarr of preise
Iustifycacon of Sepācon [by J. Robinson.]
Storke answere to Campion [W. Charke: An Answere to . . . . a Jesuite (E. Campian) . . . .]
Dike on the heart
Perkins on 11 Hebrewes
Bayne on Ephes[ians]. [1643.]
Dike on repent[ance]. & ch[rists]. temtations

Bolton on true happynes
Downam ag[st] Beller [G. Downame: A Treatise . . . . against all the objections of R. Bellarmine . . . .]
Wotton on 1 Iohn
Gouge Armor of God
Plea for Infants [by R. Clyfton.]
Rollock on effectual calling
Calling of Iews by Finish [by H[y] Finch. 1621.]
Prin Antearminescence [Wm. Prynne: Anti-Arminianisme. 1630.]
Discouery by Barrow [H[y] Barrowe: A Brief Discouerie of the false Church.]
Ainsworths defence of Scripture
Admonition to Parli[nt] [by J. Field & T. Wilcox.]
Refutacon to Gifford [by H. Barrowe & J. Greenwood.]
Perth Assembly [by J. Forbes.]
Treatise of Ministery of England [by F. Johnson.]
Cassander Anglicañs [by J. Sprint.]
Downam's warfarr. [Probably another of the four parts of The Christian Warfare]
The meane of mourneing [by Th. Playfere.]
Hackhill History of Judges [?Geo. Hakewill: Scutum Regium, Id est, adversus omnes regicidas, etc.]
Sweeds Intelligencer [The Swedish Intelligencer. 1632.]
Comunion of Saints [by H. Ainsworth.]
Abridgment of Ministers of Lincolne
Jacob Attestation [H. Jacob: An Attestation . . . . that the Church government ought to bee . . . .]
Modest Defence [of the Petition for Reformation]
Exposicon of Canticles
Whitgifte answere to a libell
A reply to a libell
Duplesš of a Chur [P. Duplessis-Mornay: A notable Treatise of the Church . . . .]
Perkins on Iude
Downams 4 treatises
Deareing on Hebrews
A Collection of Englands Deliũanc[s] [G. Carleton: A Thankfull Remembrance of Gods Mercy, In an Historicall Collection

of the . . . . Deliverances of the Church and State of England . . . . 1627.]

1000 notable things [by Th. Lupton.]

Riches of elder ages

tymes turne coat [Turncoat of the Times. A Ballad. 1635.]

A continuacon of adventur of Don Sebastian [? J. Teixera: The strangest adventure . . . . A discourse concerning . . . . the King of Portugall Dom Sebastian . . . . *or* E. Allde: The Battell of Barbarie, between Sebastian King of Portugall, and Abdelmelec King of Morocco . . . . As . . . . plaid by the Lord High Admerall his seruants.]

Surveyor Dialougs [Jo. Norden: The Surveyors Dialogue.]

Apology Chur. of England ag^ts^ Brownists [by J. Hall.]

Kings declaracon about Parlia^ts^

Scyrge of Drunkerds [W. Hornby: The Scourge of Drunkennes.
(In verse.) 1619.]

Syons Plea [A. Leighton: An Appeal to the Parliament. 1628.]

Elton of Comandmts

Treatise of Chr. Religion [by Jo. Ball. 1620.]

A battaile of Palatinate

Treatise 122 Psalm [by Robt. Harrison. 1618.]

Concordance of yeares [by Ar. Hopton.]

Cesars Tryumphs

A dialogue concerning Ceremonies [by Saml. Gardiner.]

Essayes about a prisoner [Geffray Mynshul: Essayes and Characters of a Prison and Prisoners. 1618.]

Politike diseases

Exposicon of Liturgie [by Jo. Boys.]

Magnifycent Entertaynement of King Iames [by Th. Decker.]

Essex practise of treason [by Fr. Bacon.]

Prosopeia [?Prosopopœia, or a Conference . . . . between the Pope, the Emperor, and the King of Spaine. (a satire, in verse). *or* Prosopopoia, or Mother Hubberds Tale (in verse) by Ed. Spenser.]

Withers motto [by Geo. Wither. 1621.]

Standish for woods [Ar. Standish: New Directions . . . . for the increasing of Timber and Fire-wood. 1615.]

A recantacon of a Brownist [by P. Fairlambe.]

A supply to German History [? A suplement to the sixth part of the German History. 1634.]
Of the use of silk worms [by O. de Serres.]
Newes from Verginia [by R. Rich. A poem. 1610.]
News from Palatinate [1622.]
Hacklett [R. Haklyt: The principall Navigations . . . .]
Byfeild on the oracles of God [1620.]
Gods monarchy Deuells Kingdome [by I. Anwick.]
New shreds of old share
Discharg of 5 imputations [by Tho. Morton. 1633.]
Dauids Musick [by R. Allison.]
Horne sheild of the Rightous [by Rob. Horn. 1625.]
Ruine of Rome [by A. Dent. 1633.]
Downame on 15 Psalm
Pisca Evangelica [W. Symonds: Pisgah Evangelica.]
Virell on Lords prayer [by P. Viret.]
Answere to Cartwright
Broughton on Gods Diuinitie
Bayne tryall of Christ[ians] [e]state
Wheatley on Gods husbandry [by Wm. Whately. 1622.]
Exposicon on Reuelac
Perkins Reformed Catholik
Johnsons & Withers works [Rich. Johnson: The Golden Garland of Princely pleasures and delicate Delights. 1620. Geo. Wither: The Workes of . . . . 1620.]
10 sermons of the supper [by J. Dod & R. Cleaver. 1634.]
Ciuill Conuersacon Gnahzo [by Stef. Guazzo.]
Smyths plea for Infants
Bacons p~ficiency in Learning [F. Bacon: Advancement of Learning.]
Arguments ag[st] seinge
Theologicks
Eming on Iames [by N. Hemming.]
Catholike Judg.
The spirituall watch [T. Gataker. 1619.]
reasons for reformacon of Chur. of Eng[l] [by H. Jacob.]
A looking glass ag[st] Prelates [by W. Prynne. 1636.]
A sermon of Bishop of London
Resolucon for kneeling [by D. Lindesay. 1619.]

2 Exact discouery of Romish doctrine [by T. Morton.]
Warr was a blessing [?D. Digges: Foure paradoxes . . . . of the worthinesse of warre and warriors.]
Midland souldier [?M. Parker: The Maunding Soldier . . . . (a ballad.) 1629.]
Humillitie Christians life [?D. Cawdrey: Humilitie, the Saints liverie . . . . 1624]
Church Deliũance
Co̅ment on Ecclesiastic [? by J. Granger. 1621.]
Prerogative of Parlints [by Sir W. Raleigh. 1628.]
Temple on 20 Psalm
Abbott sermon
Soules Implantacon [by Tho. Hooker. 1637.]
A treatise of Stage pleas [by J. Rainolds: Th' overthrow of Stage-Playes.]
Apologue of Brownists [by F. Johnson & H. Ainsworth.]
State Mistery of Iesuits
Dike Schoole of affliccon
Sibbs Comfort [Rich. Sibbes: The Saints Comfort. 1638.]
Taylor on 32 psalm
Parable of the Vine by Rogers [N. Rogers: The Wild Vine. 1632.]
Apologeticall reply by Damfort [by J. Davenport. 1636.]
divers books sticht together[59]
Broughton of Lamentacons
A good wyfe [R. Brathwait: The Description of a Good Wife. (verse.) 1619.]
Northbrook against Images
The tryall of truth by Chibbald [1622.]
The paterne of true prayer
Household gouerment
Blackwells answers
Aristotles probleames
Symers Indictment [W. Ward: A Synners Indictament.]

[59] Identified by Dexter as a book which he owned containing: L. Chaderton: A Godly Sermon vpon . . . . 12. chapter of . . . . Romanes. A True, Modest, and just Defence of the Petition for Reformation. J. Robinson· The Peoples Plea for the exercise of Prophesie. R. Harrison: A Little Treatise vpon . . . . 122 Psalm. T. Dighton: Certain Reasons . . . . against Conformitie . . . . T. Dighton: The Second Part of a Plain discourse . . . . W. Euring: An Answer to the Ten Covnter Demands . . . .

Iohnsons psalmes in meeter
Mores discovery
A Sermon
Refutacon of tolleracon
Aphorismes of State [by the Colledge of Cardinalls. 1624.]
Of Union betweene England & Scotland [by Sir W. Cornwallis.]
Tales of Popes custome house [?W. Crashaw: Mittimus to the Ivbile at Rome: or the rates of the popes cvstome-hovse. 1625.]
Of Pope Ioane [by A. Cooke.]
A dialogue betweene a gent & a preist
Against kneeling
Perkins on fayth
Bacons Apologye [by Sir F. Bacon.]
A History of Mary Glouer [by J. Swan.]
A bundle of smale books & papers
Defyance of death [by Wm. Cowper.]
A Christians apparelling [by R. Jenison. 1625.]
Perkins on repentance
Essays by Cornwallis [Sir Wm.]
Spirituall stedfastnes [by J. Barlow. 1632.]
A manuell [? J. Usher: Immanuel. 1638.]
A breiffe of bible [by Henoch Clapham; in verse.]
Jacob on 2[d] Comand[nt]
A pill to purge popery
Withers
Cathologue of nobillyty of England [by R. Brooke. 1619.]
English Votaryes [by J. Bale.]
Sibbs Yea & Amen [1638.]
Sermons by Rollock
Kinges Bath [by Tho. Taylor: . . . . a Treatise on Matt. iii. 1620.]
Great Assise by Smyth [1625.]
Martin on Easter [?? N. Marten: The seventh voyage . . . . into East India . . . . 1625.]
Smyth on 6th of Hosea.
Discription of World [by G. Abbot. 1620.]
Cantelus Cannon of Masse [P. Viret: The Cauteles, Canon, and Ceremonies of the . . . . Masse.]

Gods mc̃y & Jurasā misery
Silū Watch bell [by T. Tymme.]
7 Sermons by W. B. [Ms. sermons by W. Brewster.]
Burton agst Cholmely [H. Burton: Babel no Bethel . . . . 1629.]
Sibbs Saints p^{r}viledges [1638.]
Sibbs Riches of mercy [1638.]
Regla Vite [Th. Taylor: Regula Vitæ. 1635.]
Pilgrimes p^{r}fession [by T. Taylor. 1622.]
Sermon at Pauls crosse
Nature & grace [Iohn Prime: A Treatise of . . . .]
Perkins of Predestinacon
Spirituall trumpett
Vox Regis [by Tho. Scott. 1623.]
Barrowes platforme
Exposicon of Lords prayer
Comon weale of England [by Sir Tho. Smith.]
Right way of peace [? R. Bruce: The Way to true Peace . . . .]
4th pt of true watch [J. Brinsley: The True Watch and Rule of Life: fourth Part . . . . 1624.]
Iohnson on Psalmes
Byfield paterne of [1627.]
Duke promises
A help to memorye [and discourse. 1621. (Partly in verse).]
p. posicons by Iohn Sprint
The morality of law
Cases of Conscience by Per[kins]
Discouery of famyly of love [by Io. Rogers.]
Sermon of repentance
Sermon at Paules Crosse
Sibbs spirituall maxims [1637.]
Memorable conceits [of Divers Noble and famous personages]
God & the Kinge [by R. Mockett.]
Smyth on Riddle of Nebuchudnez.
Estey on Comand^{nts} & 51st Psalm
Christians dayly walk [by Hy. Scudder. 1620.]
Exposicon of 11 & 12 Reuelacon [?by Th. Taylor. 1633.]
Treatise of English medicines [by T. Bedford. 1615.]
A dialogue of desiderias [Same as Barrowes platforme.]
A supplycacon to the King [? by H. Jacobs. 1609.]

Abba father [by Elnat. Parr. 1618.]
Abrahams tryall discourse [? by J. Calvin.]
Jacobbs ladder [by Hy. Smith.]
Perkins of Imagina[tions]
Burton Christī question
A toyle for 2 legged foxes [by J. Baxter.]
A cordiall for comfort [by Wm. Chibald. 1625.]
Zacheus conuersion [by Jo. Wilson. 1631.]
Spirituall touchstone [1621.]
Dearmies advantage
Englands summons [by Tho. Sutton.]
Burton wooing his Church
Goulden key [openinge the locke to Eternal Happynes.]
A remedy against famine & warr [by Jo. Udall.]
Treatise against popery [? by Tho. Stoughton.]
Treatise of Gods religion

Books Bequeathed to Harvard College by John Harvard.[60]

Ambrosij Dixionariū.
Antonius & Gralerus in Senecā.
Abernethyes physick for the soule.
Analysis Apocalypseōs.
Anglorū prælia.
Aquinatis Opa. Conclusiones.
Aynsworts workes. [Henry Ainsworth: Annotations upon the five bookes of Moses, the booke of the Psalms, and the Song of Songs, or Canticles.]
Amesij Theologiæ Medulla. De Consc: In Epistolas Petrj. contra Armin: Bellarminus Enervatus.

[60] Harvard Library, Bibliographical Contributions, No. 27, p. 7 ff. Explanations in brackets are from the same source. It should be noted that under one name several titles are sometimes given, often run together as one title. [This list has been revised from "Catalogue of John Harvard's Library" by Alfred C. Potter, Publications of the Colonial Society of Massachusetts, XXI. 190-230. Ed.]

Augustinj meditationes. Opa.
Alstedij Physica Harmonia. Compendiũ Thelogiæ.
Apeius in Nov. Testam[t].
Anatomy Arminianisme [by Pierre Du Moulin].
Anchorani porta linguarum.
Actus Synodi Nationalis.
Acta Synodalia.
Aschamj Epistolæ.
Arraingm[t] of the whole Creature.
Alicalj Emblemata.
Æsopi fabulæ.
Ægidius in Arist. Philos. & Metaph.
Academia Gallica.
Βασίλικον δῶρον.
Bezæ Test. N. cũ Annotat. Test. Græc. Lat. In Epist. ad Galat:. Ephe.
Baynes on Collos:. Ephes.
Bethneri Gram̄: Hebræa.
Berchetj Catechismus.
Buxtorfi. Dixionar. Hebr:. Gram̄: hebr:.
Beton displaying of ye popish Masse.
Bellarmin. de fælicitate sanctorũ. In Psalm. In 1[a] & 2[a] Epist: ad Thessalon. Conciones.
Bolton in 4 volumnes.
Ball on faith.
Bastingius on Palatines Catechisme.
Brerewood on the Sabbath.
Bacons advancem[t]. Essayes.
Bannes in Arist: de Gen: & Corrup.
Bovilij Adagia.
Bedæ Axiomata Philosophica.
Brentius de parabolis.
Beards theatre of Gods judgm[ts].
Brerewoods Tractatus Logicus.
Brentij Pericopæ &c.
Bullingerus in Isaj.
Biblia Tremelij & Junij.
Bucani Institutiones.
Bradshewes p[r]paration for the Sacram[t].

Broughton on the revelat: on Eccles. Positions on the Bible. On Daniel. texts of Script. chronol. pamphlets.

Baylyes directions for health.

Calvinus in Pent & Joshuā. Sermons vpon Job in English. p^{r}lectiones in Ezechiel. Institut. Religio. Christ. Tomus 4us ꝑpū Theologicorū. Harmonia. In Prophetas min: Homilia in Samuelem. In Epistolas Paulj. In Psalm.

Camamrarij meditationes histor.

Corradj Casus Consc.

Church his God & man. Good mans treasure.

Camdens remaines.

Cleonardi. [Entry almost illegible; trimmed off by binder.]

Chysostinj homilia. [Chrysostom.]

Castanej Distinctiones.

Calliopæia [or, a rich store-house of . . . . phrases].

Chrystopolitanj ꝑa.

Christianity.

Cornerj Psalteriū Lat:.

Curiel in Epist. Thomæ.

Chareus in Epist.

Cornelius de artibus & Scientijs. In Eccles:. Prophetas majores, & minores, in Pent. in Epist: Paulj. in Acta. In Prov. in 7 vol.

Clavis græc: Linguæ.

Com̄entariū in Horatiū in Fol.

Com̄ent: in 4 Euangel. & Acta Apost. On the Prov.

Cottons concordance.

Com̄ent in Arist. Phys. de anima.

Cartwright in Eccles. & Prov.

Collection of statutes.

Conradus in Apocalyp.

Carlton agst Pelag. & Armin.

Chytreus in Apocal. in Levit. in Genes. Numer. in Deut. Ester. Judices in 6 Tom.

Characciolus his life.

Catin. Phrases.

Danej ꝑa Theolog. Questiones. de salutaribus dej donis. in Math. his com̄on Ethicks.

Dickson on hebr.

Dictionariū Anglic. Historicū. Geograp. Poëticū. Lat. Græc.

Dounā his warfare.
Davenantius in Epist. ad Collos.
Duns Scotus in 8 Libros Arist. Phys.
Dove on the Cant.
Dike on the hart. his mischeife of Scandalls.
Death subdued.
Elton on the Cōmandm[ts].
Epictetj Enchyridion.
Eustachij Philosophia.
Euphoranius.
Erasmj Colloquia.
Elegant Phrases.
Garden of Eloquence.
Exon his meditations.
Essayes morall & Theol.
Francklin ὀρθοτονίας lib. [Tractatus de tonis in lingua græcanica.]
Funebres Conciones 15.
Fabritius in Hoseā.
Felthoms resolues.
Fuebernes lapidua Pasmaliensis.
Fayus in Epist. ad Timoth.
Feuardensius in Epist. ad Philemonem.
Gualterus in Marcū.
Golij Ethicæ.
Griners in Dan.
Goodwins Aggravation of sin.
Household Phys:
Haxions prælections.
The honest man.
Hunnius in Joh: Evangel.
Hindersham of fasting. On the Psal. on John 4. 2 Tom. [Hildersam.]
Hieronus in Haddanū in Isai.
Horatius cū Stephanj notis.
Hemmingius in 84 Psalm. in Epist. ad Collos:.
Homers workes in English. [Chapman's translation.]
History of the Church.
Haylins Geography.
H [One title trimmed off.]

Hutton agst Com̄on prayer booke.
Henshaws meditations.
Jackej Instit. Philos:
Juvenalis.
Isocratis Orat: Græc & Latin.
Judic: Synodi Nationalis.
Keckermannj Philos. Disput.
Keckermanj contemplat. de loco. et de terræ-motu.
Lutherus in Genesin. Tomus 1us, 2us, 3us, 4us, 5us, 6us, 7us.
Luke Angl.
Loscij Annotationes Scolasticæ.
Lightfoots Miscelanes.
Lucanus.
Lewes right vse of ꝑmises.
Lexicon Græco Lat:.
Lemnius medicus de complexione.
Londons complaint. [By Benjamin Spenser.]
Lamentations.
Lord Verul: Nat: History.
Livellj Vita & in Harding.
Leigh on ye ꝑmises.
Lumberds Justice.
Lycosthenjs Apophthegmata. Similia.
Loscij Questiones.
Laurentij oꝑa.
Mollerus in Psalmos.
Marloratj Thesaurus Scripturæ.
Musculus in Psalmos. Matthæū.
Mollinæus contra Arminios.
Marlotj Thesaurus Scripturæ.
Magirj Physica. Anthropologia.
Maxes Sermons.
Melanchj Logica.
Minshej Dictionariū.
A Manuduction to Divinity.
Martinij Gram̄: Hebr.
Micomius in Marcū.
Montanj in Psal. Prov^{r} Comt. & Hebr.
Moses Vayled.

N. Test. Catholicj Expositio Eccles:
Nichols mirrour for Magistrates.
N. Test. Lat.
Nonæ Novemb. æternitatj consecratæ.
Natales Comes. in 29 Tomis.
Osiandri Psalm.
Philosophers Banquet. [By Sir Michael Scott.]
Pfaltsgraues Church.
Polanj Syntagma Theologiæ. De Legendo cū fructu.
Piscator 17 Tomis.
Pelagius redivivus Prin.
Plin. Nat. Hist.
Plutarchj Vitæ Angl. Moralia Angl. [North's Plutarch.]
Philippi Homil: in Jonam.
Pike his worthy worthy com̄unicant.
Pareus de doctrina X^{iana}.
Phochenius. [Sebastian Pfochen.]
Plautus.
Porcensis orationes.
Pet. Martyr, in Epist. ad Rom. Loci Com̄unes.
Piccolominej Philos.
Patresius de Regin. & reg: Institutione.
Persij Satyræ.
Politianj Epist.
Passoris Lexicon. Græc. Lat.
Pellegronj Sylva. [Simon Pelegromius: Synonymorum sylva.]
Poetarū flores.
Pars Workes.
Pembles workes. de origine formarū.
Preston on ye Attributes. 4 Sermons.
Physick for ye Soule.
Pavenij Ethicæ. [Francesco Pavone: Summa ethicæ.]
Quirbj com̄ent: in Psalmos & Prophetas.
Quarles Poems.
Reinolds Vanity of ye Creature. Conference wth ye hart.
Rogers on Luke ye 15.
Rami Græca Gram̄: Lat. Logica cū Talæj Rhetorica, Molinej Log. vno volum:
Robinsons Essayes.

Royardus in Epist: Domin.
Rogers, his Divinity. On Loue.
Roxanæ Tragedia.
Reinoldi Liber de Idololatria.
Stola in Lucā.
Sculteti opa.
Schriblerj metaphoræ.
Schickardi gram. hæb.
Sibbs fountaine sealed.
Spongia contra Jesuit. Goloniū cū alijs opibus vno vol. compressis.
Sphinx Philosophy.
Speeds clowde of wittnesses.
Scalliger de subtilitate.
Scheibleri philosoph. compend.
Sebati Phys:
Setonj Dialectica.
Sarcerj Postilla.
Soules præparation.
Schenblerj sententiæ.
Salustius.
Smiths Logicke.
Scarfij Symphonia.
Saluthij Schola.
Sceiblerj Synopsis Philos.
Saints Legacyes.
Test. N. Græc.
Tossanj Diction. Hebr.
Terentius.
Touchstone of truth.
Thrapuntij rhetorica.
Thesaurus poeticus.
Textoris Epitheta. Epist.
Test. [Trimmed off.]
Twissus de gratia, potestate & Providentia.
Taylour on Titus. on Revel. 12.
Trunesse on X^an religion.
Turnerj Orationes.
Terus in Exod. Num. Deut. Josh. Jud.
Thesaurus linguæ rom: & Brittanicæ in fol.

Thomæ Aquinatis oꝑa.
Tullij oꝑa in 2 Tomis. de officijs.
Tyme well spent.
Treasury of God.
Vorsius de Deo.
Vdalls Heb^r Gram̄:.
Valerius Max:.
Vocatio Judæorū.
Warwicks Meditations.
Wall on Acts 18. V^s 28.
Withers.
Weames 4th Vol. of ye Image of God in man. on the Lawes morall, ceremoniall, Judiciall.
Willsons X^an Dictionary.
Watsonj animæ Gaudia. [Amintæ gaudia. A poem.]
Whakly his new birth. [William Whately: The new birth, or a treatise of regeneration.]
Wygandus de ꝑsec. piorū exilijs.
Wandelinj Contemplatio Phys. Tom 3.
Wardes Sermons.
Zanchij Oꝑa.

Selected Titles from the 1723 Catalogue of the Harvard Library.

Folio

Aristophanis	Comædiæ
Bacon	History of the Reign of K. Henry VII
Bacon	Instauratio Magna
Bacon	Natural History
Bacon	9 Books of the Advancement of Learning
Browne, Sir T.	Pseudodoxia Epidemica
Brahe, Tychonis	Historia Cælestis
Bertii	Theatri Geographiæ Veteris
Bullialdi	Astronomia Philolaica

Baudoin	Mythologie
Bochas	Tragedies translated into Englishe by John Lidgate, Monk of Burye
Burnet, Tho.	Theory of the Earth
Clarendon	History of the Rebellion
Chaucer	Works [title page missing]
Chapman, Geo.	English Homer
Cambden	Britannia
Cambden	History of Q. Elizabeth
Clark, Sam.	Lives of sundry eminent Persons
Collier, Jer.	Great Historical and Chronological Dictionary, and Supplement to same.
Cowley, Abrah.	Works
Danyel	Collection of the History of England
Demosthenes	Orationes
Dalton	Country Justice
Eadmeri	Historia Novorum
Euclid	Elements translated by H. Billingsley
Euripidis	Tragediæ
Fuller, Tho.	Church History of Britain
Fuller, Tho.	Pisgah sight of Palestine
Fuller, Tho.	History of the Holy War
Fuller, Tho.	Holy and Profane State
Fougasses, Tho. de	General History of Venice
Godwini	Rerum Anglican. Hen. 8. Edvar. 6. et Maria regantibus Annales
Guicciardines	History of the Wars of Italy, English'd by Fenton
Guicciardi.	La Description de tous les pais bas
Grymestone	Imperial History
	Godfrey of Bollogn [*sic*] or the Recovery of Jerusalem
Gassendi	Operum omnium, 6 vols.
Gassendi	Astronomia -
Galeni	Opera
Gerhard	Herbal
Grew	Catalogue and Description of the Rarities of the Royal Society
Guillims	Display of Heraldry

Hackluit	Voyages
Hyde, Tho.	Catalogus Librorum impressorum Bibliothecæ Bodleianæ in Academia Oxoniensi
Heylin	Cosmography
Hugo	Seige [*sic*] of Breda
Holingshed	Chronicle of England, Scotland, Ireland
	History of K. Charles
Harrington	Common-wealth of Oceana
Harris	Collection of Voyages & Travels
Hendy	Historia Mundi, or Mercator's Atlas rectified
Hormi	Geographia vetus Sacra et Profana
Hevellii	Machinæ Cœlestis
Hevellii	Cometographia
Hevellii	Selenographia
Hayes	Treatise of Fluxions
Hugenii	Horologium oscillatorum
Hill	Account of the Ottoman Empire
Harris	Lexicon Technicum
Herbert, Lord	Life of K. Henry VIII
Herbert, Lord	Compleat History of England
Hondius	Atlas
Howel	Institution of the General History of World
Josephus	Antiquities and Wars of the Jews, English'd by Lodge
Jonstoni	Hist. Naturalis de Piscibus, de Insectis, de Serpent., etc.
	Introductorium Astronomicum
Huygen	Itinerario, Voyage ofte Schipvært
Kircheri	Œdipus Ægyptiacus
Kircheri	De Arte magnetica opus tripart
	A Kalendar of the Statutes of England
Keeble	Statutes at large, 1684
Kersey	Algebra
Keckermann	Operum omnium
Lessii	Opuscula
Lessii	De Justitia et Jure
Liceti	De Intellectu
Liceti	De spontaneo viventium ortu

	The Lighting Colomne or Sea-Mirror
	Logarithmical Arithmetick
Longomontani	Astronomia Danica
Matchiavel	Florentine History
Montanus	Atlas Japannensis, English'd by Ogilby
Munsteri, Seb.	Cosmographiæ
Majoris, Joh.	Opera in Artes quas liberales vocant
More, Henry	Philosophical Writings
More, Henry	Operum omnium
Minshei	Ductor in Linguas
Minshei	Spanish and English Dictionary
Montaigne	Essays, London 1613
	Massachusett-Law-Book
Newton	Trigonometry
Ortelii	Theatrum Orbis Terrarum
	Ortus Sanitatis
Petiti	Leges Atticæ
Prideauxii	Marmora Oxoniensia; ex Arundelianis, etc.
Plutarch	North's Translation
Prynne	History of K. John, K. Henry 3. & K. Ed. 1.
Prynne	Canterbury's Doom
Purchase	Pilgrimes
Pulton	Collection of Statutes
Piccolominei	Universa Philosophia de moribus
Plinii	Historiæ Mundi
Plinii	Natural History, translated by Holland
Ptolomæi	Liber Geographiæ cum Tabulis
Pappi Alexandrini	Mathematicæ Collectiones, cum interpretatione et illustratione F. Commandini
Parkinson	Theatre of Plants
Parkinson	Garden of Flowers
Perrault	Treatise of the 5 Orders of Columns in Architecture
Riccioli	Chronologia Reformata
Riccioli	Astronomia Reformata
Riccioli	Almagestum Novum
Riccioli	Geograph. et Hydrograph. Reformatæ
Rushworth	Historical Collections 1618–1629
Richardson	State of Europe

Raleigh	History of World
Roberts	Map of Commerce
Rudolphinæ	Tabulæ, ex Editione Joan. Kepleri
Ricettario	Medicinale Fiorentino
Riolanus	Surest Guide to Physick and Surgery, English'd by Culpeper
A Soto	De Justitia et Jure Libri
De Serres	History of France, translated by Grymeston
Stuckii	Antiquitatum Convivialium
Schedel	De Historiis Ætatum Mundi ac Descriptione Urbium Collect.
Speed	History of Great Britain
	Statutes at large from the 35 of Q. Elizabeth to 4 of K. Charles
	Statutes at Large from Magna Charta to the 29th of Queen Elizabeth
Sandys, G.	His Travels
Socinatis	Quæstiones Metaphysicales
Seldeni	Liber de Successionibus in bona defuncti ad Leges Hebræorum
Seldeni	de Jure natural. et Gentium juxta Disciplinam Hebræorum
Scaligeri	Opus de Emendatione Temporum
Stephani, Carol	Dictionarium Historic. Geograph. Poetic.
Stapylton	English Juvenal
Suarez	Metaphysicarum Disputationum
Scharpii	Methodus Philosophiæ Peripateticæ
Spelmanni	Archæologus
Seller, J.	Sea Atlas
Seller, J.	Atlas Terrestris
Speed	Prospect of the most famous parts of the World
Schotii	Cursus Mathematicus
Sempilii Craigbataei	de Disciplinis Mathematicis
Sylvatici	Opus Pandectarum Medicinæ
Strype	Memorials of A.Bp. Cranmer
	Dr. Sacheverel's Tryal
Spotswood	History of the Church of Scotland
Thuani	Historiarum Sui Temporis

Tacqueti	Opera Mathematica
Tarvernier	Travels
Usserii	Annales
Virgilii, Poly.	Historiæ Anglicæ
Vincentio	Opus Geometricum Quadraturæ Circuli et Sectionum Coni
Victae	Opera Mathematica
Wing	Astronomia Brittanica
Wallis	Treatise of Algebra
Wirtzung	General Practice of Physic in English
Willis	Remaining Physical Works
Xenophon	Opera omnia
Xenophon	History of the Ascent of Cyrus English'd by Bingham
	Yearbook under K. Henry V. and K. Henry VI. From the 40 to the 50 of Edw. III.
	Young Students Library by the Athenian Society, 1692
Zuingeri	Theatri Humanæ Vitæ
Zabarella	Comment. in Aristot. Libros Physicorum
Zabarella	Opera Logica
Zabarella	De Rebus naturalibus
Zabarella	Comment. in Aristot. Libros de animâ

Quarto

Althusii	Politica
Alphonsinæ	Tabulæ, edente Paschasio Hamellio
Anderson	Of the Genuine use of the Gunne
	Acta Eruditorum Publicata Lipsiæ, from 1682 to 1698 inc.
	Ibid., Supplements for 1692 and 1696
Balduini	Tractat. de Casibus Conscientiæ
Butler	History of Bees
Boetii, Anselm	Gemmarum et Lapidum Historia
	Brittain's Busse, with a Discovery of New-foundland and a Discovery of Trade
Boyle	Philosophical Essays
Boyle	Tracts of the Admirable Rarefaction of the Air, &c.

Boyle	Experiments Physico-Mechanical touching the Air
Boyle	Natural Philosophy
Boyle	Of forms & Qualities
Bannes	Quæstiones et Comment. in Duos Lib. Aristot. de Generatione et Corruptione
Brathwait	English Gentleman
Brerewoodi	Tractatus quidam Logici
Buridani	Quæstiones in 10 Libros Ethicorum Arist.
Balfourii	Comment. in Organum Logicum Aristot.
Balfourii	In Aristotelis Philosophiam
Brinsly	Ludus literarius; or the Grammar School
Brahe, Tychon	Astronomiæ instauratæ
Brahe, Tycho	Operum omnium
Brahe, Tycho	De Mundi Ætherei recentioribus Phænomenis
Bariffe	Military Discipline
Barrow	Lectionis Opticæ et Geomet.
Barrow	Illustrat. in opera Archimedis, in Libros Conicorum Apollonii & in Spherica Theodosii
Brown's & Wottons	Mirror & Rules of Architecture
Branker	Introduction to Algebra
Bond	Longitude found
Blackborrow	Longitude not found
Binning	Light to the Art of Gunnery
Balloni	Conciliorum medicinalium
DuBartas	Poems
Cawdry	Storehouse of Similies
Cambden	Remains
Cambden	Britannia
Cambden	Britannia abridged
Cominoei	De Rebus Gestis Ludov. XI. Galliarum Regis
Contareno	Common-Wealth and Government of Venice
Contareno	Commentaries concerning Religion and the Common-Wealth of France
Carew	Survey of Cornwal
Camerarii	Meditationes Historicæ

Champlain	Voyages de la nouvelle France
Cognet	Politick Discourses of Truth & Lying
Cartesii	Meditationes de Primâ Philosophiâ
Cartesii	Principia Philosophiæ
Cartesii	Epistolæ Lat.
Cavallerii	Directorium Generale Uranometricum
Carpenter	Geography
Campanellæ	Medicinalium
Carpi	Anatomia
Cartesii	Geometria
Calovii	Encyclopædiæ Mathematicæ
Craig	Religionis Christianæ princip. Mathemat.
Chokieri	Thesaurus Aphorismorum Politicorum
Digby, K.	Treatise of Bodies
Digbei, E.	Theoria Analytica viam ad monarchiam
Dufortii	Gnomologia Homerica
Donelli	in Titulum de Usuris in Pandectis
Everarti	Ephemerides Novæ et Exactæ
	Essays of Natural Experiments made in the Academy del Cimento, translated by Waller
Fuente	Quæstiones Dialecticæ et Physicæ
Florio	First Fruits
Feltham	Resolves
Goodwin	Select Cases of Conscience
Gainsford	Glory of England
Gregorii XIII	Corpus Juris Canonici
Guicciardini	Historia d'Italia
Giles	Hist. Ecclesiastique des Eglises reformeés
Godwyn	Jewish and Roman Antiquities
Guevara	Dial of Princes. English'd by North
Guevara	Familiar Epistles
le Grand	Institutio Philosophiæ secundum Principia Renat. des Cartes
Golding	Translation of Ovid's Metamorphoses
Glanvil	Scepsis Scientifica
Galilæi	Dialogus de Systemate Mundi
Goclenii	Apologeticus pro astromantia Discursus
Gadbury	Ephemerides from 1672 to 1681

Hales	Golden Remains
	History of Italy
	History of Life of Philip de Mornay
Hottingeri	Historia Orientalis
Hanmer	View of Antiquity
Hackluit	History of the West Indies
Herodian of Alex.	History of the Roman Caesars
Husband	Exact Collections of Remarkables between the King and Parliament from 1641 to 1643
	History of the Reformation of the Church of Scotland
Hayward	Lives of the 3 Norman Kings of England
Heylin	Little Description of the Great World
Hugenii	Systema Saturnium
Hopton	Geodetical Staffe
Heurnii	Praxis Medicinæ
Hawksbee	Physico-Mechanical Experiments
Harry	Genealogy of K. James I
Jamesii	Catalogus Librorum in Bibliotheca Bodleiana
Lucy	Observations of Notorious Errors in Hobb's Leviatha
Lithgow	Voyages
Lorhardi	Theatrum Philosophicum
Lowthorp	Abridgement of the Philosophical Transactions & Collections to the end of 1700
Liceti	Controversiæ de Cometis
Lansbergii, P.	Commentationes in motum Terræ
Lansbergii, J.	Apologia pro Comment. Philip. Lansberg. in Motum Terræ, adversus Libert.
Leyburn	Geometrical Exercises for young Seamen
Langham	Garden of Health
Luytsii	Introduction ad Geographiam
Luytsii	Introd. ad Astronomiam
H-Mercurio Overo	Historia de' correnti tempi
Miltoni	Defensio pro populo Anglicano cont. Salmasium
Masii	In universam Aristotelis Philosophiam Comment.

M. Meurisse Royen.	Rerum Metaphysicarum
Martialis	Epigrammatum Libri Comment. Remirez de Prædo illustrati
Macchiavel.	Discours de L'Estat de paix et de Guerre
Macchiavel.	Art of War. English'd by P. Withorne
Moore	System of the Mathematicks
Molerii	Accurata descriptio Ecleipsium Solis et Lunæ 1505 & 1607
Moxon	Tutor to Astronomy & Geography
Moxon	Use of the Copernican Sphæres
Markham, G.	Masterpiece
Morisani	Apotelesma in Aristot. Logic. Physi. Ethic.
	Miscellanea Curiosa: sive Ephemeridum Medico-Physicarum Germanicarum, 1670 to 1694, inc., with Index, 1693
	Nomenclator autorum omnium quorum Libri extant in Bibliotheca Academ. Lugd. Batav.
Newton, Isaac	Opticks
Norwoods	Trigonometry
Origani, D.	Ephemerides Brandenburgica, 1595–1655, inc.
Oates, Titus	Picture of K. James
Pitsei, J.	de Rebus Anglicis
Pezelii	Mellificium Historicum
Perrin	History of the Waldenses & Albigenses
	Prelates Tyranny . . . . Prosecution of Prynne, Bastwick and Burton
	Parliaments Diurnal Occurrences, Nov. 1640–Nov. 1641
[Langland]	The Vision of Pierce Plowman, 1650
Platinæ	Historia de Vitis Pontificum
Prideaux	Introduction for Reading Histories
Prynne	Antipathy of Prelacy to Regal Monarchy and Civil Unity
Prynne	Sovereign Power of Parliaments and Kingdoms
Prynne	Histrio-mastix
Prolomæi, A.	Geographia, Interprete Pirckheimherio

	Philosophical Transactions, Savoy. 1665–1678, and Philosophical Collections to No. 7
Primaudaye	French Academy
Polluce	Onomasticon
Petisci	Trigonometria
Palmer	Catholick Planisphaere
	Philai, sive de vero Systemate Mundi
Plateri	Praxeos Medicæ
Phrygii	Comment. in Hist. Epidemicas Hippocratis
Paaw	De Ossibus Human. Corporis primitiæ Anatomicæ
Poeton	Chirurgeon's Closet
Puffendorfii	De Jure Naturæ & Gentium
Pisis	Pantheologiæ
Placæi	Opuscula Nonnulla
Robinson	Essays Moral and Divine
	Of Resisting the Lawful Magistrate
Robinson	Justification of the separation
	Reasons of the Necessity of the Reformation in England
Reineccii	Chronici Hierosolymitani
Ruvii	In 8 Lib. Aristot. de Physico Auditu Comment.
Ruvii	In universam Aristot. Dialectiam Comment.
Regii	Philosophia Naturalis
Raci	Clavis Philosophiæ . . . . seu introductio ad naturæ Contemplationem Aristotelico-Cartesiana
Rami	Arithmet.-Geometr.
Rami	Scholarum Mathemat.
Reinoldi	Prutenicæ Tabulæ cælestium motuum
Rossæi	Commentum de motu Terrae circulari refutatum
Smith	Essex Dove
Swinnock	Of the Dignity & Beauty of Magistracy and the Duty of the Magistrates
Seldeni	De Synedriis & Præfecturis Juridicis Vet. Hebra.

Stow	Annals of England
Simancæ	De Republica Lib. XI.
Soto	Quæst. in 8 Lib. Physicorum Aristot.
Sabatecii	Logica Pet. Rami florens
Scoti, J. Duns	in Isagogen Porphyrii et in Aristot.
Scoti, J. Duns	in 8 Lib. Physicorum Aristotelis
Suarez	Metaphysicarum Disputationum Syllabus
Sophoclis	Tragediæ 7
Sylvayn's	Orator in English
Street	Astronomia Carolina
Schooten	Exercitationes Mathematicæ
Scheineri	Fundamentum Opticum
Sennerti	De febribus
Senguerdii	Philosophia naturalis
Schroderi	Thesaurus Linguæ Aremenicæ
Tarich	Series Regum Persiæ cum Comment.
Toleti	Introductio in Universam Aristot. Logicam Comment. unà cum Quæst. in 3 libros Aristotelis de Animâ
Terrence	Andria Latin & English
Usserii	Veterum Epistolarum Hybernicarum Sylloge
Usserii	Brittanic. Ecclesiarum Antiquitates
Usserii	Quæstionis de Ecclesiarum Successione Historica Explicatio
Ubaldino	Vita de Carlo magno imperadore
Vossii	De Origine & Progressu Idololatriæ
Vossii	De Historicis Græcis
Vossii	De Historicis Latinis
Velagut	Practica Canonica Criminalis secund. Juris Communis ac Doctorum antiquorum et recentium Decreta
Vries	Exercitationes Rationales
Wickliff	Complaint to the King and Parliament
Waseri	De Antiquis numis Hebræorum, Chaldæorum & Syriorum
Wright	Errors in Navigation detected
Wallis	Mechanica, sive de motu Tractat. Geometric
Wing	Ephemerides from 1672 to 1681

Wardi	Idea Trigometriæ
Zanardi	Comment. cum Quæst. in Logicam Aristot.
Zanardi	Disputatio de Universo Elementari
Zanardi	Disputationes de triplici universo

Octavo, Etc.

Appiano	delle guerre Civili de Romani
Adami	Vitæ Germanorum. Theologorum
	Antiquitas Academ. Cantabrigens. & Oxoniens.
	An Abridgement of the Chronicles of Scotland
Angli	Euclides Metaphysicus
Angli	Euclides Physicus
Amama	Dissertationum Marinarum Decas.
Amyraldi	De Libero Arbitrio Disputatio
Alstedii	Logicæ Systema Harmonicum
Aristot.	de Moribus lib. 10
Alciati	Emblemata cum Comment.
Agrippæ, H. C.	De Incertitudine et Vanitate omnium Scientarum Liber
Aviani	Clavis Poeseos Sacræ
Aristot.	Artis Rhetorice
Aesopi	Fabulæ
	Apologies of Justin Martyr, Tertullian & Minutius Foelix, Englished by Reeves
	Ars Sciendi
Alchmariani	Instit. Astronom.
	Annals of King George, Vol. 1.
Boyle, R.	Of the Style of the Scriptures
Boyle, R.	His Seraphic Love
Boyle, R.	Occasional Reflections
Brooke	Of the Nature of Truth
Buchanani	Paraphrasis Poetica Psalmorum
Batei	Elenchi motuum nuperorum in Anglia
Benzonis	Novæ novi orbis Historiæ
Bembo	Letters
Bale, J.	Of Actes or Unchaste Exemples of the Englyshe Votaries

Bedæ	Venerabilis Historia Ecclesiastic. Gentis Anglorum
Baconis	Historia Henrici Septimi
Barclai, J.	Argenis
Boyle, R.	Tracts about Cosmical Qualities
Boyle, R.	New Experiments touching the Relation of Air and Flame
Boyle, R.	Experiments about Colours
Boyle, R.	Cogitationes de Sacræ Scripturæ Stylo
Boyle, R.	Paradoxa Hydrostatica
Boaysteau	Theatrum mundi translated into English
Burgersdicii	Collegium Physicum
Boehmen	Aurora, das ist Morgen Rothe
de Bosnay	Cosmopolite, ou nouvelle Lumiere de la Physique naturale avec une Traicté du Soulphre
Butleri	Rhetoricæ
Burgersdicii	Institutionum Logicarum
Baronii	Metaphysica
Baconis	Historia Ventorum
Baconis	Historia Vitæ & Mortis
Baconis	Essays, 1668
Buscheri	Harmoniæ Logicæ Philipporaneæ
Barclai	Satyricon
Beroaldi	Declamationes
Buchleri	Thesaurus Poeticus
Brown	Description & Use of Triangular Quadrant
Boehmen	Opera nonnulla Teutonic
Boehmen	De Signatura Rerum
Boehmen	Josephus Redivivus
Brodrick	Compleat History of the late War in the Netherlands
Becheri	Supplementum secundum in Physicam Subterraneam
Brome	Travels over England, Scotland, & Wales
	Chroniche Antiche d' Inglilterra
Casaubon	Treatise of Enthusiasm
Casaubon	Diatriba de Verborum Usu
Crantzii	Metropolis, sive Historia Ecclesiast. Saxoniæ

Caesar	Commentarii tradotti [into Italian] per Ortica
Caesarii, Joan	Rhetorica
Camdeni	Annales Rerum . . . . regnante Elizabethâ
	Constitucyons Provincialles; and of Otho & Octobone translated into English
Comine	Ses Memoires
Comitis	Mythologiæ
Casmanni	Marinarum Quæstionum tractatio Philosophica bipartita
Cujacii	Paratila in Libros 50 digestorum seu Pandectarum et in Libros 9. Codicis Justiniani
Comenii	Janua Linguar. Gr. & Lat.
Comenii	Janua Linguar. Trilinguis
Comenii	Janua Linguarum Referata
Camdeni	Institutis Grammatices Græcæ
Ceporini	Compendium Grammaticæ Græcæ
Celestina	Tragicomedia de Calisto y Melibea
Case, M. de la	Le Galateé ou des facons et maniers louables
Causini	Tragediæ Sacræ
Culpeper	English Physician enlarged
Craig	Scotland's Sovereignty asserted
Clarendon	History of the Rebellion
Cross	Taghmical Art
Donne	History of the Septuagint
Delrii	Disquisitionum Magicarum
	Doctrina Antiqua de Natura Animæ
Drax, Tho.	Calliepeia, or Rich store-house of Phrases
Donne	Essayes
Digby	Discours touchant la Guerison par la poudre de sympathie
	Disquisitiones Politicæ
Danaei	Aphorismorum Politicorum Sylva
Donaldsoni	Synopseos Philosoph. Moralis
Derham	Astrotheology
Eitzen	Ethicæ Doctrina
Eberi	Calendarium Historicum
Elenchus	Motuum Nuperorum in Anglia

	Elementa Jurisprudentiæ
Euripidis	Tragædiæ
Erasmi	Moriæ Encomium, cum Ludo Senecæ de Morte Claudii Cœsaris
Freigii	Quæstiones Instinianæ in Institut. Juris Civilis
Fells	Life of Dr. H. Hammond
Fasciculus	Præceptorum Logicorum, unà cum Crackanthorpii Introductione ad Metaphysicam
Fabri	Cursus Physicus et Metaphysicus
Frommen	Exercitationes Metaphysicæ
Fabritii	Poemata
Figon	Discours des Estats & des Offices tant de Gouvernement que de la Justice, & des Finances de France
Fichet	Arcana Studiorum Methodus
Fuchsii	Opera nonulla
Fuchsii	Institutiones Medicinæ
Fuchsii	Historia stirpium
Frambesarii	Scholæ medicæ Examen practicum
Fregii	Pædagogus
Grotii	De jure Belli ac Pacis
Grotii	In Cassandri Consultationem annotata
Grotii	De Imperio summarum Potestatum
Grotii	Apologeticus
Grotii	Votum pro pace Ecclesiast.
Grotii	Defensio fidei Catholicæ
Grotii	Animadversiones in Andr. Riveti
Grotii	Opera nonnulla Argumenti Theolog. Jurid. Politic
Grotii	Et Aliorum Dissertationes
Grotii	Epistolæ ad Gallos
Gaule	Distractions
Gaule	Practique Theories
Gale	Theophilie
Grotest	Tractatus de Cessatione Legalium
Greaves	Pyramidographia
Goodwin	Mystery of Dreams
Gumble	Life of General Monck

Guicciardini	Historiarum sui Temporis
Guicciardini	Fragmentum
Golii	Epitome Doctrinæ moralis ex 10 Lib. Ethic. Aristot.
Galei	Philosophia Generalis
	The Gentleman's Calling
Guillet, Dame du	Rithmes & Poesies
Galilæi	Nuncius Sydereus
Gilfusii	Opusculum Politicum
	Great Treaty of Peace
Hammond	Of Fundamentals in a Notion referring to Practise
Herodoti	Historiæ
Hayward	Life of K. Edw. 6. & Q. Elizabeth
	Historia Ecclesiastica del Scisma del Reyno de Inglaterra
	Historia Persecutionum Ecclesiæ Bohemicæ
Heerebordi	Collegium Ethicum
Harvei	Exercitationes de Generatione Animalium
Hotomani	J. C. Quæstionum illustrium
Hotomani	Partitiones Juris Civilis
Hesselbein	Theoria Logica
Hewis	Survey of English Tongue & Phrases
Horatii Flac.	Poemata
Hieroclis	Philosop. Comment. in Aurea Pythagoreorum Carmina
Holliband	Campo de Fior—flowery Field of four Languages
Herbert	Temple, or Sacred Poems
Jovii	Historiarum sui Temporis
Jure	Life of M. de Reuty Nobleman of France
Jamblicus	de Mysteriis Ægyptiorum
Jacchei	Primæ Philosophiæ Institutiones
Jacobi Regis	Dæmonologia
	Index Expurgatorius
King James	Apology for the Oath of Allegiance
Juvenalis et Persii	Satyræ
Junii	Vindiciæ contra Tyrannos
Johnson	Lexicon Chymicum

Josephus	Works
Johnstoni	Idea Universæ Medicinæ Practicæ
Kempisii	De Imitatione Christi
Keckermanni	Systema Logicæ
Keppleri	Epitomes Astron. Copernicanæ
Lawson	Examination of Hobbs Leviathan
	Lettre Escrite a Monsieur le Coq. Charenton
Lucani	de Bello Civili
Lightfoot	Miscellanies
	Letters between the Ld. George and Sr. Kenelme Digby
Laurentii	Historia Anatomica
Leoni	Ars Medendi
Langii	Elementare Mathematicum
Liddelii	Ars Medica
Lydii	Waldensia
Meisneri	Dissertatio de Legibus
Meisneri	Anthropologiæ Sacræ
Meisneri	Disputationes quinque
More	Chronology
Matchiavelli	Disputat. de Republica
Magiri	Physiologiæ Peripateticæ
Martini	Exercitationum Metaphysic.
Martini	Logicarum Institut.
Martini	Prælectiones extemporaneæ in Systema Logicum Keekermanni
Molinæi	Elementa Logica
Melanchthon	Epitomes Philosoph. moralis
Meurier	Magazin de Planté en Francoises & Flameng.
Moore	Modern Fortification
Mercatoris	Institut. Astronomicarum
Mead	De Imperio Solis ac Lunæ in Corpora humana
Moroni	Directorium medico-practicum
Manuiti	Epistolarum Lib. XII.
Mather, Inc.	Angelographia
Mather, Inc.	Remarkable Providences
Mather, Inc.	Cases of Conscience

Mather, Inc.	[Many more]
Mather, C.	Decennium Luctuosum
Mather, C.	[Many more]
Niem	Historiarum sui Temporis
Neandri	Physice
Neperi	Rabdologia
Nepair	Description of the Table of Logarithms
	Orationes ex historicis Latinis Excerptæ in Usum Scholarum Hollandiæ
Oughtred	Opuscula Mathematica
	Pseaumes mis en Rime Francoise par Marot & Beze
	Psalmi Davidis Hispanicè
Patavini	Defensor Pacis
Pleix	De L'Ethique, ou Philosophie Morale
Pavonii	Summa Ethicæ
Petrarchæ	de remediis utriusque Fortunæ
Petrarcha	nuovamente ridotto alla vera Lettione
Porta	Magia naturalis
Patricii	de Regno & Regis Institutione
Pelegromii	Synonymorum Silva
Politiani	Epistolæ
	Proverbs Espagnols traduit en Francois
Platti	Manuale, seu Flores Petrarchæ
Porphyrii	Philosophi Pythagorici de Abstinentia
Plinii	Secund. Epistolarum Lib. 9
Plauti	Comædiæ
Pisonis	de Cognoscendis & Curandis humani Corporis morbis
	Pharmacopæia Londinens. Colleg.
Phocylidis	Dissertatio Astronomica
Puteani	Statera Belli & Pacis
Purbachii	Dispositiones motuum Caelestium.
Purbachii	Theoriæ novæ Planetarum
Quinti Curtii	Historiarum Libri
Quinti Calabri	Poetæ derelictorum ab Homero
Rutherfoord	Letters
Robinson	Apology for the Brownists
Romani	Commentationes Physicæ & Metaphysicæ

Rami	Scholia in 3 primas liberales Artes
Rami	Schol. in Aristotelis Libros Acroamaticos
Rami	Grammaticæ Lib. 4
Richardson	Logician's School-master
[W. Alabaster]	Roxana Tragædia olim Cantabrig. acta, &c.
Record	Arithmetick
Raii	Catalogus Plantarum Angliæ
Rulandi	Medicinæ Practica
	Remarks on several parts of Italy in 1701, 1702, 1703.
Raleigh	History of the World abrig'd
Sallustii	Opera omnia
Stoughtonii	Fælicitas ultimi seculi
Stafford	Niobe
Stafford	Female Glory
Sulpicii Severi	Opera omnia
Stradæ	de bello Belgico
Selden	de Dis Syriis
Speed	Abridged Description of Britain & Ireland
Sleyden	Key of History
Scaligeri	Exotericarum Exercitationum de Subtilitate
Scaligeri	Poemata
Scaligeri	Epistolæ omnes
Schookii	Collegium Physicum
Sculteti	Ethicorum Libri
Sluteri	Anatomia Logicæ Aristotelicæ
Snellii	In Physicam Corn. Valerii Annotationes
Scheibleri	Metaphysicæ
Senecæ et aliorum	Tragædiae
Senecæ	Tragediae
Senecæ	Epistolæ quæ extant
	Speculum Anglicarum atque Politicarum Observationum
	Schollar's Companion
Smetii	Prosodia
Sennerti	Epitome Institut. Medicinæ
Sylvii	Methodus Medicamenta Componendi
Sutholt	Dissertationes quibus explicatur universum Jus Institutionum

Suetonius	Lives of the 12 Caesars
Shakespear	Plays, 6 vols. London, 1709
Trenchfield	Christian Chymistry
Taciti	Opera
Taciti	Annales
Turselline	Epitome Historiarum
Timpleri	Metaphysicæ Systema Methodicum
Tesmari	Exercitationum Rhetoricarum
Trapezuntii	Rhetoricarum
	A Treatise of Metalica
Trieu	Manuductio ad Logicam
Tullii	De Officio Libri Tres
Turneri	Orationes & Epistolæ
Terentii	Comædiæ Sex
Tacqueti	Arithmeticæ Theoria & Praxis
	Tractatus duo Mathematici; primus de Globis, a Rob. Hues
Timpii	Cynosura Professorum ac Studiosorum Eloquentiæ
Temple, Sir Wm.	Memoirs
Temple, Sir Wm.	Letters
Varenii	Descriptio Regni Japoniæ & Siam
Valerii Max.	De dictis et factis memorabilibus
Velcurionis	Comment. in Aristotel, Physicam Lib. 4
Verronis	Physicorum Libri 10
Valesii	de Sacra Philosophia Liber
Vosii et aliorum	De Studiorum Ratione opuscula
Valerii Ultraj	Grammatic. Institut.
Vallæ	Elegantiæ
Wilkinsoni	Conciones 6 ad Academicos Oxonienses
Walton	Lives
Wotton	Remains
Wendilini	Contemplat. Physicarum
Wallis	Grammatica Linguæ Anglicanæ
Wither	Abuses stript and whipt
Wither	Shepard's Hunting
Wardi	Astronomia Geometrica
Winshemii	Quæstiones Sphæricæ
Witteni	Memoria Jurisconsultorum justa

Witteni	Memoria medicorum semper vivens
Witteni	Memoria Philosophorum sempiterna
Witteni	Memoria Theologorum
Zahn	Ichnographia municipalis
Zuichemi	J. C. Comment. in 10 Titulos Institutionum Juris Civilis

Supplement

Grew	Cosmologia Sacra, or a Discourse of the Universe
Ortelius	Theatre de L'Universe
Milton	Poetical Works, 2 vols. 1720
	Cry from the Desert . . . . things lately come to pass in the Cevennes
Chamberlayne	Present State of Gt. Brittain, 1716
	Lives of the French Philosophers
Langii	Medicina Mentis
Neal	History of New-England
Parecbolæ	Universitatis Oxoniensis
Strada	Histoire de la guerre de Flandre

Selected Titles from the 1725 Supplement to the Catalogue of the Harvard Library.

Folio

Bayle	Dictionaire Historique et Critique
Brandt	History of the Reformation in the Low Countries Englished by John Chamberlayne
Du Pin	New Ecclesiastical History
Grævii	Thesaurus Antiquitatum Romanarum
Hooker	Laws of Ecclesiastical Polity
How, J.	Works
Highmori	Disquisitio Corporis Humani Anatomica

Lightfoot	Works
Lock, J.	Works, 3 vol. 1722
Montfaucon	Antiquity Explained . . . . in Sculptures; Englished by David Humphreys
Ogilby	Translation of Virgil, with Cuts
Robinsoni	Annales Mundi Universales
	Papal Usurpation . . . . with History of the old Waldenses
Sallengre	Novus Thesaurus Antiquitatum Romanarum
Tillotson	Works
Willughby	Ornithology with 3 Discourses of Mr. John Ray

Quarto

Rami	Opticæ Libri quatuor
Speckhan	Quaestionum et Decisionum Juris Caesarii, &c.
Stierii	Præcepta Logicæ, Ethicæ, &c.

Octavo, etc.

Boemi	Enchiridion Precum
Barlow	Exact Survey of the Tide
Burnet, T.	Essay upon Government
Cheselden	On the High Operation for the Stone, 1723
Clerici	Opera Philosophica
	Cromwell's Life, 1724
Cheyne	Essay of the Gout, 1723
Cheyne	Essay of Health & Long Life
	Critical History of England, Ecclesiastical and Civil
Echard	Ecclesiastical History
Fuchsii	Institutiones Medicinæ
Gordon	Geographical Grammar
	History of Virginia, 1722
	Miri-Weys, the Persian Cromwell, 1724
Mather, C.	Life of Increase Mather, London, 1724
Pliny	Panegyrick upon the Emperor Trajan, Englished by Geo. Smith

Potter	Greek Antiquities
Strother	On Sickness and Health, London, 1725
Vareni	Geographia Generalis
Wendelini	Institutiones Politicæ
Whiston	New Theory of Earth, 1722
Watts, I.	Lyrick Poems
Watts, I.	Versions of the Psalms
Watts, I.	Art of Reading & Writing English
Watts, I.	Songs for Children
Watts, I.	Hymns
Watts, I.	Logick

Bibliography.

THE following books have been the chief sources of material for this study. Use has also been made of several manuscripts not included in this list.

ALMANACS, Colonial. All copies from 1657 to 1722 in the possession of the Massachusetts Historical Society, including photostat copies of all in existence which belong to the seventeenth century.

ALMANACS, English. All between 1599 and 1707 in the possession of the Massachusetts Historical Society.

AMERICAN ANTIQUARIAN SOCIETY. Proceedings. Worcester, 1812-1880. New Series, 1881-1914. Continued.

AMERICAN ANTIQUARIAN SOCIETY. Archæologia Americana. Transactions and Collections. Worcester, 1820-1912. Continued.

ANDREWS, CHARLES MCLEAN, editor. Narratives of the Insurrections. New York, 1915.

ANDROS TRACTS: being a collection of pamphlets and official papers. William Henry Whitmore, editor. Boston, 1868-1874.

ARBER, EDWARD, editor. The story of the Pilgrim Fathers. Boston, 1897.

BAXTER, RICHARD. Poetical Fragments. London, 1699. 3d Edition.

BEERS, HENRY AUGUSTIN. An Outline Sketch of American Literature. New York, 1887.

BIGELOW, FRANCIS HILL. Historic Silver of the Colonies and its Makers. New York, 1917.

BLACKMORE, SIR RICHARD. Prince Arthur. An Heroick Poem. 2d Edition. London, 1695.

BLAKE, JAMES. Annals of the Town of Dorchester, 1750. Collections of the Dorchester Antiquarian and Historical Society. Boston, 1846.

BRADFORD, WILLIAM. A Dialogue, or the Sum of a Conference between some Young Men born in New England and sundry ancient men that came out of Holland and Old England. Anno Domini 1648. In Young's Chronicles of the Pilgrim Fathers, pp. 414 ff.

———— A Dialogue or 3[d] Conference, betweene some yonge-men borne in New-England: and some Ancient-men, which came out of Holand, and Old England concerning the church. Massachusetts Historical Society, Proceedings, 1st Series, Vol. 11, P. 405 ff.

———— History of Plymouth Plantation 1620-1647. Boston, 1912. Massachusetts Historical Society, Collections. 2 vols.

BRADSTREET, ANNE. The Works of Anne Bradstreet in Prose and Verse. Edited by John Harvard Ellis. Charlestown, 1867.

BRODRICK, G. C. A history of the University of Oxford. 2d Edition. London, 1891.

BUCKINGHAM, THOMAS. The Journals of Madam Knight, and Rev. Mr. Buckingham. From the Original Manuscripts, written in 1704 & 1710. New York, Wilder and Campbell, 1825.

BUNYAN, JOHN. The Pilgrim's Progress from this World to that which is to come. Temple Classics. London, 1904.

BURR, GEORGE LINCOLN, editor. Narratives of the Witchcraft Cases, 1648-1706. New York, 1914.

BURTON, ROBERT. The Anatomy of Melancholy. London, 1907.

CALEF, ROBERT. See FOWLER, SAMUEL P.

CALENDAR OF STATE PAPERS, Colonial Series, America and West Indies. 1661-1668. Edited by W. N. Sainsbury. London, 1880.

CAMBRIDGE HISTORY OF AMERICAN LITERATURE, THE. New York, 1917.

CHAPLIN, JEREMIAH. Life of Henry Dunster. Boston, 1872.

CHAUCER, GEOFFREY, The Complete Works of. Edited by Walter W. Skeat. 6 vols. Oxford, 1899.

CLAP, ROGER, Memoirs of. Collections of the Dorchester Antiquarian and Historical Society, Vol. 1. Boston, 1844.

CLAP, THOMAS. The Annals or History of Yale-College. New Haven, 1766.

CLARENDON, EDWARD, Earl of. The History of the Rebellion and Civil Wars in England. Edited by W. Dunn Macray. Oxford, 1888.

COLLIER, JEREMY. The Great Historical, Geographical, Genealogical and Poetical Dictionary.... 2d Edition. London, 1701.

COLONIAL SOCIETY OF MASSACHUSETTS. Publications. Boston, 1895-1915. Continued.

COOK, ELIZABETH CHRISTINE. Literary Influences in Colonial Newspapers, 1704-1750. New York, 1912.

CUNNINGHAM, W. English Influence on the United States. Cambridge, 1916.

DANCKAERTS, JASPER. The Journal of Jasper Danckaerts, 1679-1680. Edited by Bartlett B. James and J. Franklin Jameson. New York, 1913.

De MONTMORENCY, J. E. G. The Progress of Education in England. London, 1904.

DEXTER, FRANKLIN BOWDITCH. Biographical Sketches of the Graduates of Yale College with Annals of the College History. October, 1701, to May, 1745. New York, 1885.

———— Documentary History of Yale University under the original charter of the Collegiate School of Connecticut, 1701-1745. New Haven, 1916.

———— Estimates of Population in the American Colonies. Worcester, 1887.

DEXTER, HENRY MARTYN and his son, MORTON. The England and Holland of the Pilgrims. Boston, 1905.

DICTIONARY OF NATIONAL BIOGRAPHY. Leslie Stephen, editor. New York, 1885-1900.

DRAKE, SAMUEL GARDNER, editor. Increase Mather's The History of King Philip's War. 1862.

DUNIWAY, CLYDE A. The Development of Freedom of the Press in Massachusetts. New York, 1906.

DUNTON, JOHN. Letters from New-England. Edited by W. H. Whitmore. Boston,1867.

———— The Life and Errors of John Dunton. London, 1705.

EGGLESTON, EDWARD. The Transit of Civilization from England to America in the Seventeenth Century. New York, 1901.

ESSEX COUNTY, MASSACHUSETTS. Records and Files of the Quarterly Courts of Essex County, Massachusetts. 4 vols. Salem, 1911-1914.

ESSEX COUNTY, MASSACHUSETTS, The Probate Records of. Vol. 1. Salem, Mass., 1916.

EVANS, CHARLES. American Bibliography. Chicago, 1903.

EVEREST, CHARLES. Poets of Connecticut. Hartford, 1843.

FELT, J. B. Memoir of the Reverend Francis Higginson. Boston, 1852.

FITZ, REGINALD H., M.D. Zabdiel Boylston, Inoculator, and the Epidemic of Smallpox in Boston in 1721. Bulletin of the Johns Hopkins Hospital, xxii. 315.

FORD, WORTHINGTON CHAUNCEY. The Boston Book Market, 1679-1700. Boston, 1917.

FOWLER, SAMUEL P. Salem Witchcraft: comprising More Wonders of the Invisible World, collected by Robert Calef; and Wonders of the Invisible World, by Cotton Mather: together with notes and explanations by S. P. Fowler. Salem, 1861.

FRANKLIN, BENJAMIN. The Autobiography of. New York, no date.

———— Works of. Nurnberg and New York, no date.

FULLER, THOMAS. The Church-History of Britain. London, 1655.

———— The History of the University of Cambridge from the Conquest to the year 1634. Cambridge, 1640.

———— The History of the Worthies of England. Edited by P. A. Nuttall. 2d Edition. 3 vols. London, 1840.

GOOKIN, DANIEL. Historical Collections of the Indians in New England. In Massachusetts Historical Society, Collections, 1st Series, Vol. 1, pp. 141-226.

GOOKIN, FREDERICK WILLIAM. Daniel Gookin, 1612-1687...... his Life and Letters and some Account of his Ancestry. Chicago, 1912.

GREEN, SAMUEL ABBOTT. John Foster, the earliest American engraver and the first Boston printer. Boston, 1909.

GREEN, SAMUEL ABBOTT. History of Medicine in Massachusetts. Boston, 1881.

GRISWOLD, RUFUS W. Female Poets of America.

———— Poets and Poetry of America.

HARVARD UNIVERSITY. Library of. Bibliographical Contributions, No. 52. The Librarians of Harvard College, 1667-1877. By A. C. Potter and Charles K. Bolton. Cambridge, 1897.

HARVARD UNIVERSITY. College Books I, III, and IV. Harvard College Records: in manuscript, about to be published and examined in proof sheets.

———— Catalogus Librorum Bibliothecæ Collegij Harvardini Quod est Cantabrigiæ in Nova Anglia. Boston, 1723.

HERBERT, GEORGE. The Temple: Sacred Poems and Private Ejaculations. Fac-simile reprint of first edition of 1633. London, 1882.

HINCKLEY, THOMAS. The Hinckley Papers. Massachusetts Historical Society, Collections, 4th Series, Vol. 1.

HULL, JOHN. The Diaries of. In Archæologia Americana: Transactions of the American Antiquarian Society, iii. 109-318.

HUTCHINSON PAPERS. Massachusetts Historical Society, Collections, 3d Series, Vol. 1.

JOHNSON, EDWARD. Wonder-Working Providence. Edited by J. Franklin Jameson. New York, 1910.

———— Wonder-Working Providence. Edited by William F. Poole. Andover, 1867.

JOSSELYN, JOHN. An Account of two Voyages to New-England, etc. The Second Addition [*sic.*] London, 1675. Reprint in Massachusetts Historical Society, Collections, 3rd Series, Vol. 3, p. 211 ff.

———— New-England's Rarities Discovered. With an Introduction and Notes by Edward Tuckerman. In Archæologia Americana, iv. 105-238. Worcester, 1860.

KEEP, AUSTIN BAXTER. History of the New York Society Library with an Introductory Chapter on Libraries in Colonial New York, 1698-1776. New York, 1908.

KETTELL, SAMUEL. Specimens of American Poetry, with Critical and Biographical Notices. 3 vols. Boston, 1829.

KIMBALL, EVERETT. The Public Life of Joseph Dudley. A Study of the Colonial Policy of the Stuarts in New England 1660-1715. New York, 1911.

KNIGHT, SARAH KEMBLE. The Private Journal of. Being the Record of a Journey from Boston to New York in the year 1704. Norwich, Conn., 1901.

LAWSON, DEODAT. Christ's Fidelity the Only Shield against Satan's Malignity. Asserted in a Sermon Deliver'd at Salem-Village the 24th of March, 1692. Boston and London, 1704.

LECHFORD, THOMAS. Note-Book kept by Thomas Lechford, Esq., Lawyer in Boston, Massachusetts Bay, from June 27, 1638, to July 29, 1641. Cambridge, 1885.

LINCOLN, CHARLES H., editor. Narratives of the Indian Wars, 1675-1699. New York, 1913.

LITTLEFIELD, GEORGE EMERY. Early Boston Booksellers, 1642-1711. Boston, 1900.

——— The Early Massachusetts Press, 1638-1711. Boston, 1907.

——— Early Schools and School Books of New England. Boston, 1904.

MAINE HISTORICAL SOCIETY. Collections and Proceedings. Portland, 1890-1906.

MARVELL, ANDREW. Poems of. Muses Library. London, no date.

MASSACHUSETTS BAY. Records of the Governor and Company of the Massachusetts Bay in New England. Boston, 1854.

MASSACHUSETTS HISTORICAL SOCIETY. Collections. Boston or Cambridge, 1792-1914. Continued.

——— Lectures delivered in a course before the Lowell Institute, in Boston, by members of the Massachusetts Historical Society on subjects relating to the Early History of Massachusetts. Boston, 1869.

——— Proceedings. Boston, 1879-1916. Continued.

MASSON, DAVID. The Life of John Milton. 7 vols. London, 1881.

MATHER, COTTON. The Accomplished Singer. Boston, 1721.

——— A Brand Pluck'd out of the Burning. In G. L. Burr's Narratives of the Witchcraft Cases, pp. 259-286.

——— Diary. Massachusetts Historical Society, Collections, 7th Series, Vols. 7 and 8.

——— Magnalia Christi Americana; or the Ecclesiastical History of New-England. Edited by Thomas Robbins. 2 vols. Hartford, 1855.

Mather, Cotton. Memorable Providences, Relating to Witchcrafts and Possessions. In G. L. Burr's Narratives of the Witchcraft Cases, pp. 93-144.

——— A New Year Well Begun. New London, 1719.

——— Psalterium Americanum. The Book of Psalms. Boston, 1718.

——— Repeated Warnings. Another Essay, to warn young people. Page headings use title of *Children of Disobedience.* Boston, 1712.

——— The Right Way to Shake off a Viper. Boston, 1720.

——— Speedy Repentance Urged. Boston, 1690.

——— The Wonders of the Invisible World. To which is added A Farther Account of the Tryals of the New-England Witches by Increase Mather, D.D. London, 1862.

——— The World Alarm'd. Boston, 1721.

Mather, Increase. Diary. Massachusetts Historical Society, Proceedings, 2d Series, Vol. 13, p. 339 ff.

——— Early History of New England. Together with an Historical Discourse concerning the Prevalency of Prayer. Boston, 1677.

——— A Farther Account of the Tryals of the New-England Witches. Published with Cotton Mather's The Wonders of the Invisible World. London, 1862.

——— Life and Death of that Reverend Man of God Mr. Richard Mather. Cambridge, 1670.

——— Remarkable Providences Illustrative of the Earlier Days of American Colonisation. Edited by George Offor. London, 1890.

Mather, Richard, Journal of. 1635. His Life and Death, 1670. Collections of the Dorchester Antiquarian and Historical Society. Both in one volume, paged consecutively. Boston, 1850.

Mather Papers, The. Massachusetts Historical Society, Collections, 4th Series, Vol. 8. Boston, 1868.

Mayflower Descendant, The. A Quarterly Magazine of Pilgrim Genealogy and History. Boston, 1899-1916. Continued.

Milton, John, The Poetical Works of. Edited by David Masson. London and New York, 1903.

MILTON, JOHN. A Selection from the English Prose Works of. Boston, 1826.

MORTON, NATHANIEL. New England's Memorial. Boston, 1855.

MORTON, THOMAS. The New English Canaan. Edited by Charles Francis Adams, Jr., Boston, 1883.

MULLINGER, JAMES BASS. Cambridge Characteristics in the Seventeenth Century. London, 1867.

————A History of the University of Cambridge. London, 1888.

————The University of Cambridge. Vol. 3. Cambridge, 1911.

NEAL, DANIEL. The History of New England. 2d Edition. 2 vols. London, 1747.

NEW ENGLAND HISTORICAL AND GENEALOGICAL REGISTER, THE. Boston, 1847-1916. Continued.

NEW HAMPSHIRE HISTORICAL SOCIETY. Collections. Concord, 1824-1915. Continued.

NEW HAVEN COLONY HISTORICAL SOCIETY. Papers. New Haven, 1865-1914. Continued.

NORTH AMERICAN REVIEW. Vol. 107.

ONDERDONK, J. L. History of American Verse. 1610-1897. Chicago, 1901.

OTIS, WILLIAM BRADLEY. American Verse 1625-1807. A History. New York, 1909.

OVIATT, EDWIN. The Beginnings of Yale 1701-1726. New Haven, 1916.

PALFREY, JOHN GORHAM. History of New England during the Stuart Dynasty. 5 vols. Boston, 1858.

PATTERSON, S. W. The Spirit of the American Revolution as revealed in the poetry of the period. Boston, 1915.

PENHALLOW, SAMUEL. The History of the Wars of New-England with the Eastern Indians . . . Collections of the New Hampshire Historical Society for the Year 1824. Vol. 1 of the series.

PLYMOUTH COLONY, Records of. Wills. In manuscript.

PRIOR, MATTHEW, Selected Poems of. Edited by Austin Dobson. London, 1889.

QUINCY, JOSIAH. The History of Harvard University. 2 vols. Cambridge, 1840.

RICHARDSON, C. F. American Literature. 2 vols. New York, 1887, 1889.

RODEN, ROBERT F. The Cambridge Press 1638-1692. New York, 1905.

ROSSITER, WILLIAM S., editor. Days and Ways in Old Boston. Boston, 1915.

ROYAL SOCIETY. Philosophical Transactions. London, 1666-1916. Continued.

SANDYS, GEORGE. Ovid's Metamorphosis Englished, mythologiz'd and represented in figures. London, 1640.

SEWALL, SAMUEL. Diary of, 1674-1729. 3 vols. Massachusetts Historical Society, Collections, 5th Series, Vols. 5-7. Boston, 1878.

————Letter-Book of. 2 vols. Massachusetts Historical Society, Collections, 6th Series, Vols. 1-2. Boston, 1886.

————The Selling of Joseph. In George H. Moore's Notes on the History of Slavery in Massachusetts, pp. 83-87. New York, 1866.

SHEPARD, THOMAS. Autobiography. Manuscript volume in the Harvard Library.

SIBLEY, JOHN LANGDON. Biographical Sketches of Graduates of Harvard University. 3 vols. Cambridge, 1873.

SMALL, WALTER HERBERT. Early New England Schools. Boston, 1914.

STEINER, BERNARD C. A History of the Plantation of Menunkatuck . . . . comprising the present towns of Guilford and Madison. Baltimore, 1897.

THOMAS, ISAIAH. The History of Printing in America. 2d Edition. Transactions and Collections of the American Antiquarian Society, Vols. 5-6. Albany, 1874.

THOMPSON, E. N. S. Essays on Milton. New Haven, 1914.

TRUEBNER'S Bibliographical Guide to American Literature. London, 1855.

TURELL, EBENEZER. The Life and Character of the Reverend Benjamin Colman, D.D. Boston, 1749.

TUTTLE, JULIUS H. The Mather Libraries. American Antiquarian Society, Proceedings, New Series, Vol. 20, pp. 269-356.

TYLER, MOSES COIT. A History of American Literature, 1607-1765. 2 vols. New York, 1879.

VERSTEGAN, RICHARD. The Restitution of Decayed Intelligence in Antiquities, concerning the most Noble and Renowned English Nation. London, 1673.

WATERS, THOMAS FRANKLIN. Ipswich in the Massachusetts Bay Colony. Ipswich, 1905.

WEEDEN, WILLIAM B. Economic and Social History of New England, 1620-1789. 2 vols. Boston, 1890.

WEGELIN, OSCAR. Early American Poetry. A Compilation of the Titles of Volumes of Verse and Broadsides, Written by Writers Born or Residing in North America, and Issued during the Seventeenth and Eighteenth Centuries. New York, 1903.

——— Early American Poetry 1800–1820 with an Appendix containing the Titles of Volumes and Broadsides issued during the Seventeenth and Eighteenth Centuries which were omitted in the Volume containing the years 1650–1799. New York, 1907.

WENDELL, BARRETT. Cotton Mather, the Puritan Priest. New York, no date [1891].

——— A Literary History of America. New York, 1900.

WHEELWRIGHT, JOHN, Memoir of. Boston, 1876.

WIGGLESWORTH, MICHAEL. The Day of Doom . . . . . with other Poems. New York, 1867.

WILLIAMS, ROGER. The Bloudy Tenet of Persecution for Cause of Conscience discussed. Edited by E. B. Underhill, London, 1848.

WINSLOW, EDWARD. Good News from New England. Massachusetts Historical Society, Collections, 1st Series, Vol. 8, pp. 239–276.

——— New-England's Salamander, Discovered . . . . Massachusetts Historical Society, Collections, 3d Series, Vol. 2, pp. 110 ff.

WINSOR, JUSTIN, editor. The Memorial History of Boston, 1630–1880. 4 vols. Boston, 1880.

WINTHROP, JOHN, Journal of. [History of New England, 1630–1649.] Edited by James Kendall Hosmer. 2 vols. New York, 1908.

WINTHROP, ROBERT C. Life and Letters of John Winthrop. Boston, 1869.

WINTHROP PAPERS, THE. Massachusetts Historical Society, Collections, 3d Series, Vols. 9–10.

WOLCOTT, SAMUEL. Memorial of Henry Wolcott. New York, 1881.

Index.

THE *following Index includes names of individuals mentioned in the main text, authors of books listed or referred to, titles of unidentified books and of periodicals published before 1720. The Appendix has not been included. The editor is indexing the entire volume, including the Appendix, and will deposit the complete Index with Mr. Wright's manuscript in the Yale University Library.*

Quotations and book lists have been taken without change from the sources quoted, variations or errors in spelling having been retained. The Index, however, lists the name of each individual under one spelling only.

Index.

Why Do You Need This New Edition?

More and more people get their information from online sources, and they want their information in a clear, to-the-point style of writing. Even as methods of information delivery change, the need for good writing becomes more important. Writers and journalists will be successful only if they can gather information and present it accurately and concisely and in language that appeals to a specific audience—no matter what the medium used to display the information.

In today's media world, students need a book like *Reaching Audiences* to strengthen grammar, spelling, punctuation, and math skills, while at the same time to refine basic writing skills. The basics are often less important or even lost in high school and sometimes in college, but they are essential to clear writing. As more information is loaded online, students need to be able to assess the quality and accuracy of that information. They must be able to discern whether what they are reading and hearing is accurate and important enough to become part of their own writing.

The fifth edition of *Reaching Audiences*

1. Continues to stress the basic writing, editing, and reporting skills essential to all good communication, whether the product is a print or online article, a news release, a broadcast story, or an image-building advertisement.
2. Adds a new chapter on producing online content and strengthens the existing section on online editing.
3. Includes historical context for recent changes in transmission of information.
4. Contains updated examples from newspapers and news sites around the country and exercises to provide practice in writing.

PEARSON

Reaching Audiences

A Guide to Media Writing

FIFTH EDITION

Jan Johnson Yopp

University of North Carolina at Chapel Hill

Katherine C. McAdams

University of Maryland at College Park

Ryan M. Thornburg

University of North Carolina at Chapel Hill

Allyn & Bacon

Boston New York San Francisco
Mexico City Montreal Toronto London Madrid Munich Paris
Hong Kong Singapore Tokyo Cape Town Sydney

Acquisitions Editor: Jeanne Zalesky
Series Editorial Assistant: Megan Lentz
Marketing Manager: Blair Tuckman
Production Editor: Karen Mason
Editorial Production Service: Elm Street Publishing Services
Manufacturing Buyer: Debbie Rossi
Electronic Composition: Integra Software Services Pvt. Ltd.
Cover Administrator: Kristina Mose-Libon

Between the time website information is gathered and then published, it is not unusual for some sites to have closed. Also, the transcription of URLs can result in typographical errors. The publisher would appreciate notification where these errors occur so that they may be corrected in subsequent editions.

Library of Congress Cataloging-in-Publication Data

Yopp, Jan Johnson.
Reaching audiences : a guide to media writing/Jan Johnson Yopp, Katherine C. McAdams, Ryan M. Thornburg.—5th ed.
p. cm.
Includes bibliographical references and index.
ISBN-13: 978-0-205-69310-8
ISBN-10: 0-205-69310-5
1. Mass media—Authorship. 2. Mass media—Audiences. I. McAdams, Katherine C. II. Thornburg, Ryan. III. Title.

P96.A86M38 2010
808'.066302—dc22

2008048623

10 9 8 7 6 5 4 3 2 1—EB—13 12 11 10 09

Allyn & Bacon
is an imprint of

www.pearsonhighered.com

ISBN-13: 978-0-205-69310-8
ISBN-10: 0-205-69310-5

Contents

6 Beyond the Lead: Writing the Message 146

7 Producing Online Content 170

8 Beyond Breaking News 199

PART THREE ■ *Gathering Information*

Preface

More than 15 years ago, we had a great idea: We wanted to create a book about the core skills needed for all media writing—the skills writers need so they can reach audiences anywhere, in any medium, on any topic. Today, the convergence of media predicted in the early 1990s has become a reality, making our little book more valuable than ever. In editing the fifth edition, we have focused again on teaching writers to reach active audiences in a vibrant, fast-changing world by applying age-old principles of good communication. To keep us on the cutting edge of new technologies, we have added a co-author, Ryan Thornburg, who has extensive experience as an editor in today's online environment.

Information-age media offer a multitude of ways to send and receive information. Audiences are drawn to today's dazzling array of sources for news and entertainment: News reaches audiences now by cable, Web, iPod, and iPhone, as well as by magazines, newspapers, radio, and TV. Wave after wave of invention adds to the growing list of available media. Each new medium invites attention, analysis, and adoption. Developments seem to appear faster than they can be mastered and offer more interactivity for audiences.

Technology allows communicators to produce messages efficiently and quickly, just as it allows users to access information faster, more selectively, and in greater quantities. Technology has also broadened the field for communicators. Students graduating from journalism and mass communication programs have many career possibilities, including but extending far beyond traditional jobs in newspapers, magazines, public relations, advertising, radio, television, and multimedia. Recent graduates have found themselves with such titles as Web developer, Web master, content editor, and media products coordinator.

Professors of journalism and mass communication still teach specific styles of writing. Students interested in journalism first learn the inverted pyramid style of writing, then more complicated formats. Broadcast students follow a shorter and more casual electronic format. Advertising students learn copywriting. Public relations students practice writing news releases and brochures. Photojournalism students write cutlines. Online editors write blurbs. Multimedia producers create multilevel infrastructure. Graphic designers write legends. Each format has its prescribed guidelines, and fields frequently overlap. Some print journalists write versions of their stories for online sites or for distribution via individual email addresses. Advertising and public relations at times blend into integrated marketing. Broadcasters stream video to Web sites and pop stories to podcasts.

Regardless of format or medium, today's students must meet the demand for writing that is clear, accurate, relevant, and appealing. They must think constantly about their audiences. They must know their audiences and their specific language uses and interests. Students need to understand the importance of good writing and be willing to take on the task of reaching audiences.

At the same time, professors must push students harder to pay attention to their writing and editing skills. The key ingredient for success in any communication job is good writing. Today's students are the communicators of tomorrow—regardless of how portable or accessible their writing becomes.

In today's world, writing often suffers. The proliferation of technology has diverted many communicators from their main task: clear, concise, complete writing. Communicators can be charmed by the medium of delivery—so much so that they are distracted from thinking about the content and structure of the message. In the rush to produce and send information, people often overlook the critical need for accuracy and proper spelling and grammar. Too many communicators believe the first draft is good enough and do not spend time editing and rewriting, a critical issue with online postings. Working quick and dirty is a habit that can erode informative, entertaining, accurate, well-crafted writing. Technology allows anyone with information to put it out for public view. As a result, much published information is poorly written and irrelevant to audiences.

Students need to learn the skills required to become exceptional communicators, to rise above the mire of quick-but-sloppy writing so often seen in today's media. Students must be committed to the craft of writing. They cannot rely more on computer spell-checkers and grammar-checkers than on their own knowledge. They must know the basics of proper sentence construction. They must know how to gather information, sort it, and put it in a format audiences will notice. They must be willing to check for accuracy. All along, they must use critical thinking skills to connect the message with their audiences. Otherwise, communication will not happen. Remember: Communication must get through to the audience.

The 14 chapters in this book stress the basic writing skills essential to any student in any mass communication field, including news-editorial, advertising, public relations, strategic communication, broadcast and online communication, photography, graphic design, and multimedia presentation. The essentials of good writing apply to all writers, regardless of format or medium.

Part One of the book presents the basic components of the writing process and the critical role of audiences. Students will learn the fundamentals of print journalism, how to write text for different media, and the value of the inverted pyramid style of writing in all media. Any informative writing must be grounded in the tenets of basic newswriting and reporting, and it must be checked and rechecked for precision and clarity. Chapter 2 speaks to the need for accuracy and provides diagnostic spelling, grammar, and math tests. Specific tips are given to improve writing—from word selection and sentence length to grammar and usage. Students also will learn the steps of editing, a crucial part of the writing process for any delivery system.

Part Two of the book shows students how to write leads and organize different story formats.

Part Three discusses how to gather information through three principal methods: research, observation, and interviewing. Students also are introduced to online searches and resources as well as the dangers of libel and unethical conduct in newsgathering and how to avoid bias in writing.

Part Four discusses other media writing: broadcasting and strategic communication, often referred to as public relations and advertising. These types of messages also must be formatted to reach particular audiences.

The appendices to the text contain the answer keys to the self-guided spelling, grammar, and math tests.

Mass communication at all levels demands writing that is accurate, complete, fair, and concise. Writers must constantly consider their audiences; they must create messages that are well written and that will reach the intended individuals.

We clearly embrace technology with all of its changes and challenges. Without it, we would not have been able to produce our writing in this text efficiently and easily. Technology will not disappear, and no one would wish it away. But technology changes. The importance of good writing does not.

Acknowledgments

Writing a book is never the work of just the individuals whose names are under the title, and so it is with this book and its fifth edition. A number of colleagues and friends have provided invaluable contributions.

The core of the book would not have been done without Kevin Davis of Macmillan, who many years ago saw the potential in our initial concept and encouraged us to write, and Karon Bowers, Jeanne Zalesky, Karen Mason, and Megan Lentz at Allyn and Bacon and Amanda Zagnoli at Elm Street Publishing Services, who guided and assisted on the fifth edition.

For the fifth edition, we thank at the University of North Carolina at Chapel Hill, Associate Professor Rhonda Gibson, Associate Professor Michael Hoefges, Assistant Professor David Cupp, and Assistant Professor Barbara Friedman. We also thank researchers Alissa Weinberger and Meg Elliott. In addition, we gratefully acknowledge the following reviewers of this fifth edition: J. Linn Allen, University of Illinois at Chicago; Scott Brown, California State University at Northridge; Deborah Petersen-Perlman, University of Minnesota; J. Frazier Smith, University of Dayton; and Gale A. Workman, Ph.D., Florida A&M University.

Beyond our professional colleagues, we also acknowledge the contributions of our families and their support.

—J.J.Y.

—K.C.M.

—R.M.T.

CHAPTER 1

Understanding Today's Audiences

Each morning, Tom Adams rises at 6 a.m. and turns on his TV to check the weather and last night's sport scores. After he showers and dresses, he checks his BlackBerry for e-mail that would alert him to any emergencies he might have to deal with at work or traffic jams on his personalized commute route. At 7 a.m., he pours a traveling cup full to the brim and heads for his car, stooping carefully to pick up *The Washington Post* on his doorstep. Today's *Post*—all 127 pages of it—rides shotgun for the 15-mile trip to the environmental consulting firm where Adams works.

While driving, Adams plugs in his iPod to listen to a podcast of highlights from his favorite sports talk show from the town where he grew up. His phone buzzes with a text message from his friend—their softball game for tonight may be cancelled because of rain.

Once in the office, Adams flips on his computer. He logs in to his account on Facebook to track his friends throughout the day and quickly browses a few blogs that round up the latest news on environmental science and regulation. At lunch, he scans a few national news sites and then sorts through the day's postal mail: two brochures on upcoming seminars, along with current copies of the *Environmental Reporter* and the *Federal Register*.

It is noon in the Washington, D.C., area, and Adams already has processed hundreds of media messages—and ignored or missed thousands more. By the time he returns home at 6:30 p.m., he will have processed hundreds more before he ever sits down to order an "on-demand" movie or play video games online with his brother in Miami.

Several hundred miles away, Lorayne Oglesbee begins her day with a televised morning show, complete with news, weather, and tips for entertainment, cooking, and fashion. As she dresses and packs her briefcase, she pauses from time to time for a look at the TV screen or to attend to one of her two school-aged daughters.

She says her goodbyes when the kids board their bus, then picks up her regional newspaper—*The News & Observer*—from the driveway. She relaxes with the paper over breakfast for a few minutes before her three-mile drive to work. As she drives, she listens to XM Radio, a gift from her husband intended to help with the morning's transition to her hectic life at work. She is an attorney for a large regional hospital.

Oglesbee spends most of her days at work reading, researching, and meeting with legal staff and other attorneys. At the end of a day filled with complex information, she likes to spend leisure time watching television drama or mystery shows with her family. Some evenings, by necessity, are devoted to working on her laptop computer or responding to e-mail messages that arrived late in the day.

Mass communicators have trouble reaching active audiences because of heavy competition from various media and from busy lifestyles. Think about your day so far. How did you get information as you moved through the day? You, like Adams and Oglesbee and other people in the 21st century, are bombarded by an overabundance of media messages. You are faced with many choices about what to read, view, and access.

As a result, only a select few messages actually reach the average person, who is blocking or tossing out messages judged irrelevant, unclear, or uninteresting. Messages must be carefully structured to reach an intended audience. The fate of any message lies in good writing that is streamlined to reach a busy and active person. This chapter discusses

- a historical context to understand the evolution of today's media and audiences,
- how writers can understand and serve audiences,
- how writers can overcome roadblocks to reaching audiences, and
- why the writing process is important for communicators.

Reaching Audiences

Heavy competition from various media and from busy lifestyles vie for people's attention today. Children and adults—including you—have developed the skills to sort constantly what will and will not be read, watched, or heard in the limited time available.

People today have a nearly insatiable desire to be informed about breaking news, such as devastating floods in the Midwest, entertainment figures, or how athletes fared in the Olympic Games. How people sought information was clearly evident in the terrorist attacks on the United States in September 2001, in the aftermath of Hurricane Katrina in 2005, and in the presidential elections of 2008. They went to live audio and video on television and online news services and used e-mail and text messages to connect with relatives and friends. Newspapers—even if they were morning newspapers—rushed to put out special editions or updated their news sites.

People in an uncertain and changing world are looking for information that keeps them safe and saves them money. Today's audiences also seek relief from economic and military tensions around the world, turning to media for entertainment and information about leisure activities. Some people enjoy the analysis and discussion of events found on online independent sites and blogs. Overall, audiences want and need information that will help them cope with—or escape from—everyday life.

How do writers get through the clutter of today's lifestyles and multimedia? How do they reach waiting audiences? They can do it with good writing. They write messages that are simple, clear, and accurate. Audiences will not stick with messages that are confusing, incoherent, or unbelievable. Writers today must craft messages that attract and hold people with their content and structure and that are relevant and emotionally compelling.

Most writers today have a purpose in writing. They want to tell of a family's trauma after massive earthquakes or other natural disasters. They want to inform voters about candidates. They want to entertain viewers of a late-night talk show. They want to highlight a product's usefulness. They want to sell a client's services. These writers want their messages to reach a destination, and they want audiences to pay attention.

Writing Is the Basic Task

Before they are printed, broadcast, aired, or distributed, messages are written. Communicators have to write first, regardless of what medium or technology they use. Consider these examples:

- A school principal writes the monthly calendar of activities before posting it on the school's Web page.
- A radio reporter types stories before she reads them on the 6 a.m. news show.

- A working mother sends her teenage son a text message, asking him to prepare dinner.
- An advertising copywriter creates a direct mail letter for customers of a sporting goods company.
- Three television journalists write their scripts before the weekly Sunday morning news program.
- The editor of the campus newspaper writes two editorials for each edition.
- An advocate of stringent controls on auto emissions adds his opinion to a clean-air blog.
- A student carefully words the subject line of an e-mail to a state senator.
- A Web site developer maps the story flow for an animated guide to holiday performances.

All communicators—whether journalism or mass communication students, newspaper reporters, advertising copywriters, school principals, or even colleagues—must write a message before it is sent to its intended audience. Once writers let go of the message, that is, after the message is aired or distributed, they have little control over whether the audience absorbs the message. Although the message might have arrived, it might be crowded out, deleted, or ignored.

For audiences to pay attention, writers must create messages that are accurate, appealing, organized, readable, relevant, compelling, clear, complete, and simple. Audiences today require good writing.

Roadblocks to Reaching Audiences

A variety of obstacles exist between writers and their audiences:

- **Media and information glut.** More kinds of information delivery systems become available almost daily. Each memo, article, text message, or news brief has infinitely more competition for an individual's attention than could have been imagined a decade ago. People use interactive and on-demand media in addition to traditional magazines and newspapers. They are hungry for information of all kinds and can choose from an array of media most relevant to their lifestyles.

- **Taxing lifestyles.** Despite labor-saving devices, audiences today are busier than ever with multiple commitments to work, family, and recreation. People are spending more of their leisure time on family activities and household chores and less on media consumption.
- **Diversity of audiences.** U.S. society and the media are becoming increasingly diverse in many ways: racial, ethnic, sexual orientation, family structure, and so on. Media writers constantly must work to keep up with changes in audience makeup as well as audience needs and interests. No longer is the average media consumer a white, middle-class man.
- **Unfriendly messages.** Poor writing interferes with message comprehension, just as commuting, working, children, and too many media choices do. A message that bores or taxes or takes too long to understand can be the greatest roadblock to complete communication.

Media Glut

Writers must remember that today's world offers more to read, watch, and listen to than anyone could possibly consume. In the early 1960s, Marshall McLuhan predicted today's trends, suggesting that new media would alter society in dramatic, unanticipated ways:

> *Electronic technology is reshaping and restructuring social patterns of interdependence and every aspect of our personal life. It is forcing us to reconsider and reevaluate practically every thought, every action and every institution formerly taken for granted. Everything is changing—you, your family, your neighborhood, your education, your government, your relation to "the others."*

He was right: Society has changed. McLuhan could hardly have envisioned the information explosion today. Blog search engine Technorati reported that between 2003 and 2007 more than 72 million blogs were created, and that the blogosphere continued to grow at a rate of 1.4 new blogs every second.

No one can possibly read or see the tiniest fraction of information available today. Media pervade daily life. Technology has overcome the barriers of geography and cost—almost anyone can buy the equipment to be in touch with anyone anywhere in the world. People in remote areas can tune in to events via satellite dishes; a sailboat captain in the Caribbean can view an online copy of the latest *Wall Street Journal*; a vacationing executive can send or receive messages via a BlackBerry or iPod; viewers can watch live Web cam broadcasts from Iraq.

Changes in Media and Audiences

Although the preferred media have changed, the need for information and entertainment is constant. The changes, however, have not been so good for traditional media, such as newspapers. Research has shown that fickle audiences may not return to a medium once they have abandoned it for another.

Newspapers have been hard hit by change as audiences have moved to other technologies to get information and entertainment faster. Since the 1980s, the circulation of daily newspapers has dropped, and hundreds of daily newspapers have closed. Critics of the newspaper industry have said that newspapers have not kept up with technology and have not changed enough to attract readers. Some newspapers have taken steps to reach out to readers by distributing news via online social networks or encouraging the creation of "user-generated content." Others have launched special reporting projects targeted to community interests.

Watching television news is still a daily activity for most Americans. Although television still appears to be the main source of news, it also has dealt with declining ratings and increased competition from other news sources. ComScore, a company that tracks and analyzes media usage, reports that 11 billion online videos are viewed each month in the United States. Apple's iTunes Store has more than "100,000 podcast episodes from independent creators and big names like HBO, NPR, ESPN, *The Onion*, CBS Sports, and *The New York Times*." Awards that traditionally recognize excellence in broadcast news are now awarded to newspapers like *The Washington Post*.

Media forms continue to evolve, taking audiences on a rollercoaster ride into an unimagined future of interactive and virtual reality. More specialized media, more ethnic media, and more electronic media—in fact, more media of all kinds—are on the market. And all these media, old and new, compete fiercely for audience share and attention.

You saw in the Adams and Oglesbee examples that people do not accept or assimilate every message that comes their way. They sift through messages and choose which ones they will hear and read. Successful communicators know they must compete for audience attention. Writers must understand an audience's lifestyles, media preferences, interests, and languages. That knowledge will aid in selecting topics and polishing any message so that it fits an audience's needs and interests. Audiences change, just as society changes, and successful communicators take into account the impact of these changes on their audiences.

The latest census shows that most people in the United States live in households but less than half of those household groups are what was once considered a stereotypical family. Single-occupant, single-parent, and blended families are more common than the so-called typical family household. Neighborhoods and communities that were once homogeneous are now home to many racial and cultural groups.

New media directly affect audiences. New technologies give them greater access to information, entertainment, shopping, bill paying, and even online dating and meditation.

Today's media audiences are filled with people accustomed to fast food, fast travel, and fast information. Today, hundreds of millions of people worldwide have Internet access via desktop PCs and an ever-increasing array of mobile phones, and many of them regularly use the Internet for daily tasks such as banking and shopping. Increasingly sophisticated audiences expect immediate, accurate, high-quality information.

Lifestyles and Diversity

Life today is complex with more sources of news from all directions. Media have proliferated, but no new hours have been added in the day to give audiences more time to use more media. So media choices change and shift.

Even though some audience members use new media to search for information, others are more resistant. Caught in the demands of daily living, they still rely on the more traditional media for information. Perhaps they do not have the financial means to buy computers and software to go online. Writers must be aware, therefore, of how to communicate in both old and new media.

At the same time, people's lifestyles are changing in the United States, and the country is witnessing another trend affecting media use: cultural diversity. Demographic experts predict increasing shifts. The latest U.S. Census data show that minorities make up the fastest-growing one-third of the U.S. population. The traditional categories—African Americans, Asian Americans, Hispanic Americans, and Native Americans—lose meaning as new groups, such as Caribbean and Pacific Islanders, immigrate and as intercultural families become commonplace. Some young people of mixed heritage will no longer classify themselves in a single ethnic category.

Although ethnic- and gender-specific media have long had a role in this country, the changing complexion of the United States has meant an increase in media that address specific groups and individuals. The changes have meant new topics, new discussions, new themes, and new services. Media, particularly general-interest newspapers, cover issues that for many years were carried only in specialized media, such as the black or Hispanic press.

Changing diversity means media are also working to hire employees who represent different groups so that newsrooms will more accurately reflect the makeup of the population in general. This evolution has not been easy. African American, Asian American, and Hispanic American reporters, for example, are still few in number. They are not represented in newsrooms in the same percentages as they are in the population overall.

To attract and retain audiences, media executives consider constraints such as money, lifestyles, increasing demands on time, and the lure of other media. Smart media managers realize they must adjust and be flexible to reach specific audiences. They recognize that often they need to create a profile of their audience members, by research and other means, to find out exactly who they are and what they need. Armed with knowledge about audiences, media leaders—and writers—can aim messages more specifically at their targeted destinations.

Knowing Audiences

People who write tend to read more than the average person. They are likely more educated, have a larger vocabulary, and exhibit a greater interest in various topics. They may write to please themselves or to satisfy what they think audiences want to know. As lifestyles and diversity change, these writers might be out of touch with their audiences and not know who their audiences truly are.

Such ignorance is dangerous. Writers are at risk if they do not know their audiences or if they assume they know their audiences. They also cannot assume that all audiences can grasp complicated, technical messages. Successful writers make an effort to know and get in touch with their audiences.

Identifying Audiences

This explosion of media choices means it is more important than ever to know your audience. A survey of online journalists indicates that analysis of how people are using their Web sites is one of the most common and time consuming parts of their job.

Few writers have a single audience, although many mistakenly write for what they call a mass audience. In today's world, mass audience is only a rough term used to describe a conglomeration of many smaller, specific audiences. Some may consider CNN, for example, to have a mass viewing audience. But even its audience can be broken into subgroups.

Members of small audiences have much in common. Some typical smaller audiences are veterans, working mothers, union members, and power company customers. An audience may be tiny (members of Temple Sinai) or huge (Americans interested in better health care).

Regardless of size, every audience may be subdivided. For example, members of the congregation at Temple Sinai will include smaller audiences of children, teens, young adults, singles, marrieds, new parents, empty nesters, maintenance staff, grounds workers, and so on. Even a smaller audience in the congregation, such as immigrants from other countries, could be further divided into those from specific countries, such as Poland, Germany, or Israel.

Breaking an audience into its composite groups is an important activity for people who need to communicate essential messages. Each subgroup may have specific needs for information and a particular way of getting it. A university, for example, has many audiences, including students, faculty, staff, alumni, potential students, governing bodies, the press, and potential donors. No single message will effectively reach all of these audiences. Most universities spend a great deal of time and money developing specific messages targeted to their many audiences, such as the alumni newsletter for alumni, direct mail for potential donors, and news conferences for the media.

Writers must identify their audiences. A shortcut is to ask the question, "Who cares?" The answer will be a list of groups or audiences that are potential consumers of the message.

Let's try the "Who cares?" method for listing audiences for a message. You are writing an article for your company newsletter on a new policy that provides preventive health care benefits to employees with children. "Who cares?" yields this list:

- married employees with children,
- single employees with children,
- employees thinking about having or adopting children, and
- part-time employees who have no children but wish they had health care benefits.

Listing audiences is important because once writers have at least listed them, they may change their writing approach. For the employee newsletter, your initial attempt at an introduction might have read:

> A new company policy will provide health care benefits for preventive medicine.

But after you list audiences, your introduction becomes more personal:

> As a single parent, staff geologist John Payne has worried about the extra expense of annual medical exams for his three children and a doctor's visit if the children were only mildly ill.
>
> But Mega Oil's new health benefits program will ease those worries. The plan will reimburse employees with children for preventive health expenses such as well-child checkups.

As audiences are subdivided and defined, so are writing tasks. When writers take time to identify specific audiences, such as single parents, messages can be targeted for those audiences. The approach, structure, and language can be chosen to suit the audience, and communication becomes possible—and even likely.

The Writing Process Explained

E. B. White, in the introduction to *The Elements of Style*, explains that good writing is a writer's responsibility to the audience. He tells how his professor and coauthor, William "Will" Strunk, taught rules to writers out of sympathy for readers:

> *All through* The Elements of Style *one finds evidences of the author's deep sympathy for the reader. Will felt that the reader was in serious trouble most of*

> *the time, a man floundering in a swamp, and that it was the duty of anyone attempting to write English to drain this swamp quickly and get this man up on dry ground or at least throw him a rope.... I have tried to hold steadily in mind this belief of his, this concern for the bewildered reader.*

It is time to return to Strunk's wisdom. As a teacher in the early 20th century, Strunk knew that audiences were hindered by poor type quality and low levels of literacy. Today, writers contend with new distractions Strunk could never have imagined. But the remedy in either era is the same: clear messages that show consideration for audiences.

Many people believe that good, skillful writing springs not from teaching and learning but from inborn talent that eludes most ordinary people.

Nonsense.

Writing a straightforward message requires no more inherent talent than following a road map. Author Joel Saltzman compares learning to write with learning to make salad dressing:

> *This is the only way I know to make a terrific salad dressing: Mix up a batch. Taste it. Mix again.*
>
> *The secret ingredient is the patience to keep trying—to keep working at it till you get it just right.*
>
> *Do most people have the talent to make a terrific salad dressing? Absolutely.*
>
> *Are they willing to make the effort to develop that skill? That's a different question.*

Good writing, like good salad dressing, can make even dry material palatable and can make good subject matter great. Like ingredients in a recipe, each word, sentence, and paragraph is selected carefully with one goal in mind: pleasing the consumer. The first bite will determine whether the diner eats more; good writing will sell a piece beyond the first paragraph. Like cooking, not every writing session will produce a masterpiece, but the end product must be palatable.

Writers today work in the same way as writers have worked throughout time—by following a regimen called the writing process. Once writers have identified their topics, they follow seven stages of the writing process presented here: information gathering, thinking and planning, listing, drafting, rewriting, sharing, and polishing.

All writers—whether producing a dissertation or a birth announcement—follow these steps. Even students writing under deadline pressure in class can go through the process in an abbreviated way: thinking, organizing, drafting, and revising.

Stages of the Writing Process

The same sequence of steps outlined here occurs in good writing of all kinds. Once they have a topic, all communicators must gather information, think about and plan the message, list key information, draft the message, rewrite the draft, share the message, and polish by checking and editing. Together, these separate stages of activity form the writing process: a set of behaviors common to all writers. The order of stages may vary, and some stages may be repeated, but each stage is essential to producing a good message.

Critical thinking is essential at each stage as well. In selecting a topic, writers have to assess the value of the idea, whether it will appeal to audiences, whether information is available, and how to approach the research and information gathering. At the actual writing stages, writers again think carefully about how to communicate the information clearly in such a way that the audience gets the message. If readers or listeners cannot understand the relevance of the message because the language is convoluted, full of jargon, or unappealing, then the writer has failed. For communication to be successful, audiences have to understand and react or act. Often for inexperienced reporters or writers, knowing the broader context within which an event or situation lives is the greatest challenge to understanding and presenting information to audiences.

Each stage in the writing process is briefly explained here. As you read through them, consider the critical thinking skills needed in each. Later chapters in this book will explain writing tasks in greater detail. You will be referred to relevant chapters as each stage is discussed. Following these stages will produce successful writing in business, education, advertising, public relations, the new media and news media, and daily life. Throughout this text, you will learn what professional writers know: Writing is a skill that can be learned like other skills, one stage at a time. And the first stage is to go beyond yourself to gather information. Good writers are seekers.

Stage One: Information Gathering. Gathering information or reporting on your topic is the first stage of the writing process. To begin the search for information, you must answer questions that all people are prone to ask: Who? What? When? Where? Why? How? How much? Then what?

New technologies put many answers at our fingertips. Basic facts and figures are easy to obtain online, but every writer needs to go beyond superficial statistics. The Internet is just one tool.

Never begin to write without talking to other people or reading their work. Good writing requires basic external information or reporting. Once you know the questions, go beyond your own knowledge to find the answers. Even if you are an expert on the topic, you must find other reliable authorities as quotable sources.

In writing an announcement of an art exhibit at a local art gallery, for example, a writer might begin the questioning by talking with obvious experts—perhaps the curator and an art professor—who can provide answers and lead the writer to additional sources. For the exhibit announcement, aside from the basic *when* and *where* questions, the audience still needs to know the following: What types of artwork will be shown? Will prizes be awarded? Will any special guests appear at a reception? The additional questions will guide the next steps in the information-gathering search:

1. **Interviews.** Writers talk, in person or by phone or e-mail, to authorities or to people when initial sources suggest. (Interviewing is discussed in Chapter 10.)
2. **Library and online research.** Any kind of writing can require research in libraries, Web sites, or databases. For example, if the art on display at the art gallery celebrates Impressionism, the writer needs to find out about the Impressionists and their art. (Basic research skills are included in Chapter 9.)
3. **Other sources.** Brochures, publications, or archives can provide helpful information. For example, an article or brochure about last year's art exhibit could be located through a newspaper index or online archive. (Chapter 9 explains how to use traditional and innovative reference sources.)

It is important to gather information from a variety of sources. Ideally, a writer compiles more information than actually needed so that he or she can be selective about which information to use.

A writer takes notes on every source used in the information-gathering stage. He or she never knows when an important fact or statistic will emerge or when a quotable statement will be uttered. It is best to have a notepad always ready. In addition, careful notes enable writers to attribute interesting or unusual information to sources and to be accurate in what they have written.

Some writers refer to the information-gathering stage as "immersion" in the topic or reporting. Whatever it is called, this first stage of writing turns the writer into an informal expert on the subject matter.

Stage Two: Thinking and Planning. Once information is gathered, the writer studies the notes taken in Stage One, scanning the material for what information that seems most important and most interesting, and then determines the angle and focus.

A good writer always makes decisions about priorities, keeping in mind the audience that will receive the message. Successful writers actually picture the probable audience, hold that image in mind, and plan the message for that imaginary group. Some writers say they write for a specific person, such as a truck driver in Toledo or Aunt Mary in Hartford. Sometimes the thinking stage will allow the writer to see possibilities for creative approaches to writing.

In this stage of the writing process, the writer may realize that more reporting is needed before listing and writing can begin. Once the writer has gathered enough information, he or she will begin to evaluate and set priorities, asking, "What does my audience need to know first? What next?" and so on. If no further gaps in information become apparent at this stage, the writer takes pen and notepad in hand and moves on to Stage Three.

Stage Three: Listing. Listing requires writers to list the facts and ideas that must be included in the message. Some writers note key words; others write detailed outlines. Initial lists should be made by brainstorming, jotting down each important message element, and perhaps scratching out, adding, or combining items in the lists. The lists incorporate the decisions the writer made in Stage Two.

Once lists are committed to paper, the writer reviews them and attempts to rank the information. Imagine, for example, the top priority item on the list is "student art in the show." Another item is "students outside the arts," and another is "Impressionism is the theme." Isolating these items guides the writer to structure a message that will feature student art, mention Impressionism, and appeal to students in majors other than the arts.

In this stage, the writer imposes order and organization on the information, and the text begins to take shape.

Stage Four: Drafting the Message—As You Would Tell It. For most people, even experienced writers, writing seems somewhat unnatural. In contrast, conversational speech always seems to flow. So the efficient writer drafts a message by writing it as it might be told to a friend, thinking about the language that will appeal and resonate.

Checking the lists made in Stage Three, the writer would begin by "talking" about the first and most important element in the message, perhaps like this:

> A student art show that displays the talents of 27 of the University's young Impressionists will open at 7 p.m. Wednesday in the Parents' Association Gallery in Stamp Student Union.

Once this telling process has begun, it continues easily. The writer will move smoothly through interesting aspects of the message to a stopping point after the listed priorities have been included.

By the end of this stage, the writer has created a draft, rather than a message. The term *draft* distinguishes this version from a finished product. It is different from a polished message, and purposely so. Think of the draft as a raw lump of clay, in which substance is what counts. The stages that follow will shape the clay, giving form to the finished message. Drafting messages is discussed in Chapters 5, 6, 7, and 8.

Stage Five: Rewriting. In this stage, conventions of the written language are imposed on the draft. Writers must look at their work with the eye of an editor, critically assessing how to improve the earlier draft. Sentences are checked for completeness and coherence, paragraphs are formed and organized, and transitions and stylistic flourishes are added.

A good portion of this book is devoted to the skills involved in rewriting or content editing. Only through rewriting—sometimes repeated rewriting—can a message be streamlined to reach its intended audience. All good writers rewrite; great writers pride themselves on the painstaking reworking of their original phrases. Author E. B. White labored for three years over his slim classic *Charlotte's Web*, and he willingly revised much of his other work as many as 14 times.

Of course, writers on deadline cannot afford the luxury of spending years, or even hours, rewriting a draft. But they can carefully edit the content and check the accuracy of their work even in a few minutes, determining if all facts are included and supported in effectively organized language. At this stage, every writer is a tough editor of his or her work.

Writers develop shortcuts to rewriting as they become familiar with print formats, as described in Chapters 6 and 8. But no good writer ever skips the rewriting or content editing stage.

Rewriting is separate from polishing (Stage Seven), in which fine points of style, such as capitalization, are debated. If a writer stops in mid-draft to debate a style point, the train of thought is interrupted, and the writing process stops. Small decisions are left for the last stage—a stage that may be conducted by someone other than the writer.

Rewriting or content editing a draft is the bulk of the writing process. It is hard, time-consuming work; factors to consider in the process are discussed in Chapters 2 and 3. A rewritten draft is far from a finished work, however.

Stage Six: Sharing. The revised draft should go to another reader—almost any other reader. By this stage, most writers have lost perspective on the message. They have become knowledgeable about the topic, and they may no longer be able to judge how the message would be received by an average member of the audience.

Sharing your work at this stage gives you a much better idea of how an audience member may react. Outside readers will quickly let you know whether the information is confusing or unclear or whether any important details are missing.

It is a good idea to share your work with a naive reader—someone who knows far less about your topic than you. Sometimes a colleague at work or a family member is an excellent choice for sharing because of that person's distance from your topic. In class, your instructor might allow peer editing of stories.

In large offices, outside review of your revised draft might be built in. For example, in big companies, drafts usually are reviewed by one or more editors and often by top management. Such an editing process is helpful in many ways, and certainly it saves the time and trouble of finding someone with whom to share your writing.

Regardless of who is sharing and commenting on your work, you as a writer must never forget that you did the initial research. You have expertise on your topic that your colleagues, family members, or even top managers may not have. Be sure to get feedback from your outside readers in a setting where you both can talk. You may need to explain why certain parts of your message are written as they are. Good editing is negotiation; no editor is an absolute dictator. You as a writer need to work with, and not for, editors and outside reviewers. Together, you can produce clear, correct writing.

Stage Seven: Polishing. The final stage in the writing process is one that many people ignore or abhor. This stage ensures the mechanical aspects are accurate and clear. A misplaced comma can confuse a reader.

Here's where writers consider: Is there an apostrophe after "Parents"? Is the "the" capitalized in "The Parents Gallery"? Finding the answers to such polishing questions is an essential and critical part of the writing process, and it is appropriately the last stage. Many young writers feel that all capitalization, punctuation, grammar, usage, and spelling must be perfect, even in an initial draft. Concentrating on perfection in all those areas is unimportant in the early stages of writing. You might spend 10 minutes looking in the dictionary for a word you eventually decide not to use!

Working on word-by-word perfection at the early stages of writing is wasteful and even paralyzing. Writers who worry about every comma will find it difficult to get through the stages of drafting and revising. Writing becomes a much more comfortable and speedy task when polishing is put off until its proper place at the end of the process. After the important substance and form of the message have been established, writers should spend time with style books, dictionaries, and thesauruses.

All writers should polish their work, even when they pass the message to someone else to edit. An editor or editorial assistant may make the final checks for correctness and consistency and put a message in final form. Confident writers welcome assistance with this final, cosmetic touch, knowing that letter-perfect writing will add to the credibility and clarity of their message.

Getting across messages to people in today's society is an unparalleled challenge. Writers have to accept that they cannot do much to change an individual consumer's lifestyle. They cannot reduce the number of media.

They cannot modify society's diversity. They cannot alter the fact that audiences pay attention to only a few messages amid the daily clutter.

But they can control one aspect: the structure of the message. Good writers have context for today's media world. They know which techniques and which structures best fit their audiences. They use their critical thinking skills to select topics and the approach to developing a story, and they follow the stages of writing to ensure messages are concise, complete, and correct.

Exercises

1. Keep a media log for a 24-hour period between today and the next class. Make a chart showing how you got information, how you communicated information, and which media you used. Indicate how long you viewed or read, a summary of messages, and what else you were doing while using each medium. Indicate whether you had interferences or distractions. Be prepared to compare your media-use patterns with those of others in the class.

2. Interview a relative about his or her media use, formulating questions based on your log. Explore how his or her media use has changed during the last five years, 10 years. Where does the person get most news? entertainment? information that is dependable? in-depth information? Does your relative use new media or more traditional media? What is his or her age?

3. Write a few paragraphs describing the characteristics of the audience for your student newspaper. Then explain how you could follow Strunk and White's advice to help the audience use and better understand the student paper.

4. Choose a news event that occurred today. Select several sources from different media that reported the event. Compare the way each introduced and developed the story. Look at writing style, language, length of story, anecdotes, and quotations. Does the format for presenting the news fit the medium's audiences? How?

5. Interview a classmate. Follow the stages of writing in producing a 30-line story about the person. Explain what you did in each stage. For example, in listing, you might list the person's accomplishments or extracurricular activities. In sharing, you might have another classmate read your draft.

References

Apples iTunes homepage, accessed at http://www.apple.com/itunes/store/podcasts.html.

Associated Press Managing Editors Home Page. Available: www.apme.org.

"11 Billion Videos Viewed Online in the U.S. in April 2008," comScore, accessed at http://www.comscore.com/press/release.asp?press=2268.

Marshall McLuhan and Q. Fiore, *The Medium Is the Message: An Inventory of Effects*. New York: Bantam Books, 1967.

The Poynter Institute Media Diversity Beyond 2000 Home Page. Available: www.poynter.org/dsurvey.

Joel Saltzman, *If You Can Talk, You Can Write*. New York: Ballantine Books, 1993.

William Strunk, Jr., and E. B. White, *The Elements of Style*. New York: Macmillan, 1979.

"The State of the Blogosphere," Sifry's Alerts, April 5, 2007, accessed at http://www.sifry.com/alerts/archives/000"493.html.

U.S. Census Bureau Home Page. Available: www.census.gov/population.

CHAPTER

2

Tools for Writers
Spelling, Grammar, and Math

> An ad for used cars states that many more comparible cars are available.
>
> A morning television news show posts a headline that the U.S. secretary of state is meeting with NATO officials in Brussles.
>
> A company's annual report notes that revenues rose from 80 million to 90 million, or a 10 percent increase.
>
> A student blog says, "John Peter Zinger established free speech in America."

A close check of all the above statements shows that more *comparable* cars are available; the meeting is in *Brussels*; the revenues actually rose 12 percent; and it was *John Peter Zenger* who made his mark as a Colonial journalist.

Writers can take care as they gather information and write stories. But if they are not careful in checking their grammar, punctuation, spelling, numbers, or facts, they can damage their credibility—as well as their company's credibility. With the Internet, inaccuracies can be captured and spread indefinitely. Readers might not see posted corrections.

Errors need not be dramatic to cause audiences pause or dismay. In announcing the university's hiring of a prominent journalist, a campus newspaper headline billed him as a "Pultizer Prize winner." Did you catch the typo? CBS reported on shark attacks along the North Carolina coast, and the map identified the location as Monteo, rather than Manteo. Often, such errors are caused by haste or carelessness.

Research has shown that when messages are perceived to be error free, they also are thought to be credible and well written. The perception of quality carries over to the writer and to the medium, be it newspaper, television, or online. In other words, messages free of errors are perceived to be of high quality and produced by professionals.

Students often argue that they do not need spelling, grammar, or punctuation skills. They believe an editor—somewhere—will fix any errors or errors will be caught by spell-checkers or grammar-checkers. Wrong. As a communicator, you must be both writer and editor, particularly if you are writing for an online site or blog. Spell-checkers don't always catch the difference between *principal* and *principle*. Any number of synonyms and homonyms can present problems, so it's up to you to know the difference.

Communicators who pay attention to their audiences know they must also pay attention to detail. That means attending to spelling, grammar, punctuation, and style. Most media have style rules. They follow Associated Press style, or they have developed style guidelines of their own. Adopting a specific style ensures consistency in all articles, regardless of who writes them or where they appear. Even in short text messages, writers follow a certain style of known abbreviations; otherwise, recipients would have difficulty translating the meaning. (Style is covered in Chapter 3.)

Writers today are expected to know basic math and elementary statistics. They need to know how to compute percentages, figure out square footage, determine whether poll data are representative, and analyze budget figures.

In this chapter, you will learn

- typical spelling errors to watch for,
- common adult grammar problems, and
- bottom-line math skills.

Spelling in the Computer Age

Writers, BEWARE: Spelling skills are essential in the computer age. This warning might sound exaggerated because, as we all know, computers can check spellings of thousands of words in minutes. But take heed.

What Spell-Checkers Will (and Won't) Do

Checking systems embedded in computers are a great invention, virtually eliminating senseless typographical errors, such as "scuh" and "typograpical," as well as common spelling problems such as "seperate" and "mispell." Unfortunately, however, spell-checkers merely highlight many potential problems without correcting them. You, the writer, are expected to check the highlighted words or phrases and to approve them or provide correction.

Here's an example: If a computer merely finds a word in its dictionary, it "checks" that word, assuring the writer that the spelling is correct. Say, for example, the computer encounters this sentence: "Robin was going too the fare." The sentence checks. The words "too" and "fare" exist in the dictionary, so they pass muster. And if "Robin" happens to be spelled correctly as "Robyn," that error will go unchecked because "robin" would be found in the computer's dictionary. Or perhaps the typo is an actual word, such as "count" instead of "court." The error would slip by as correct, and the writer would have created an immediate audience-stopper and confusion.

So spell-checkers aid writers in only some spelling instances, not all of them. Some of the most challenging spelling tasks (listed in the next section) are still the writer's responsibility.

A Do-It-Yourself List. By now, it should be clear that spell-checkers will not do everything. The writer has the hands-on, do-it-yourself responsibility of checking the following problems that spell-checkers do not correct.

Homonyms. Writers must distinguish among homonyms, or words that sound alike but have different meanings and are spelled differently. Any writer's credibility would drop if his or her readers saw these sentences:

> Mrs. Margolis consulted two professional piers before suspending the student.
> (Readers will see Mrs. Margolis conferring in a lakeside setting.)

> Barnes said he didn't want to altar his plans.
> (Will Barnes offer his plan during religious services?)

> All navel movements will be approved by the commanding officer.
> (Whose belly buttons?)

> Investigators found millions of land mines sewn into the earth.
> (Did someone use a needle and thread?)

Such homonyms as "pier" and "peer," "alter" and "altar," and "sewn" and "sown" escape highlighting by the spell-checker, which recognizes each as a dictionary word. Writers overconfident in the ability of spell-checkers will undoubtedly leave simple errors in their writing. Some words writers should watch for include the following:

to, two, too	aid, aide
their, they're, there	it's, its
no, know	whose, who's

Some subtle and damaging errors are made when writers confuse other commonly occurring homonyms, such as those listed below. Good writers distinguish between or among homonyms.

affect (verb)
effect (noun, meaning result, verb meaning bring about)

a lot (colloquial expression substituted for "many" or "much")
allot (to distribute)

allude (refer to)
elude (escape)

altar (in a church)
alter (change)

altogether (adverb meaning entirely)
all together (adjective meaning in a group)

bare (naked, uncovered)
bear (animal, to support)

baring (showing)
bearing (supporting)

bore (to drill, to be dull)
boar (pig)

canvas (cloth)
canvass (to poll)

capitol (building)
capital (city)

compliment (flattering statement)
complement (fills up or completes)

counsel (to advise, legal adviser)
council (assembly)
consul (diplomatic officer)

dual (two)
duel (combat between two people)

flair (style; panache)
flare (torch)

guerrilla (person who engages in warfare)
gorilla (ape)

immigrate (come to a new country)
emigrate (leave one's country)

legislature (body)
legislator (individual official)

miner (in a mine)
minor (under age)

naval (of the navy)
navel (belly button)

pore (small opening; to examine closely)
pour (to cause to flow)

pier (water walkway)
peer (social equal)

principal (head, first)
principle (lesson, belief)

role (in a play)
roll (list)

stare (regard intensely)
stair (step in a staircase)

stationery (paper)
stationary (permanent)

vein (blood vessel)
vain (conceited)
vane (wind detector)

Similar Words with Different Uses. Spell-checkers will highlight commonly confused pairs of words, such as "conscience" and "conscious," "affect" and "effect," "flout" and "flaunt," "loose" and "lose," "lead" and "led," "read" and "red," "border" and "boarder," or "populace" and "populous." Keeping a good dictionary, stylebook, or grammar guide on your desk is the best way to make distinctions between similar words. Again, the writer or editor must catch the error, even though his or her computer includes a spell-checker.

Compound Words. Some compound words, such as "speedboat" and "bookkeeper," will pass spell-checkers as two words, even though they are correctly spelled as single words. The reason? The spell-checker recognizes the separate words—"speed," "boat," "book," and "keeper"—as valid entries, leaving the writer appearing not to know the correct spelling.

Proper Names. As noted earlier, proper names—unlike most units of language—may be spelled any way an individual desires. The infinite variety of name spellings makes it essential to check and doublecheck all names, regardless of what spell-checking approves. Many names, such as Robin and Lily, are also common nouns listed in computer dictionaries. Often the correct spelling for the proper name is different from that offered by a spell-checker. For example, Robin may be "Robyn," and Lily may spell her name "Lillie." Double-check names in any document.

Both spell-checking and manual, word-by-word editing are essential parts of the writing process. No software can replace the complex decision-making an editor provides. In the information age, good writers and editors ensure accurate writing.

BOX 2.1 Useful Tools for Writers

Professional writers and editors have their favorite resources. Despite their age, some reference books have timeless value vis-a-vis more modern Web sites.

Books

Theodore M. Bernstein, *Dos, Don'ts and Maybes of the English Language*. New York: The Times Book Co., 1977.

John Bremner, *Words on Words*. New York: Columbia University Press, 1980.

Claire Kehrwald Cook, *Line by Line: How to Improve Your Own Writing*. Boston: Houghton Mifflin, 1985.

Norm Goldstein, ed., *The Associated Press Stylebook 2005 and Briefing on Media Law*. New York: The Associated Press, 2005.

Lauren Kessler and Duncan McDonald, *When Words Collide*. Belmont, CA: Wadsworth, 2004.

Purdue University's Online Writing Lab. Available: http://owl.english.purdue.edu/handouts/grammar/index.html.

William Strunk, Jr., and E. B. White, *The Elements of Style, 3rd ed.* New York: Macmillan, 1979.

Kathleen Woodruff Wickham, *Math Tools for Journalists*. Oak Park, IL: Marion Street Press, January 2002.

Web Sites

www.editteach.org, with resources for language, editing, teaching.
www.newsu.org, the site for News University with access to a range of reporting and writing courses that require user registration.
www.poynter.org, the site for the Poynter Institute.

Grammar to the Rescue

Our world is fast-paced and fast-changing—hardly the kind of place you would expect to need something as tedious as a lesson on grammar. But today's communicator cannot afford to slow down audiences, and faulty grammar does just that. Just as writers are cautioned about relying too much on spell-checking systems in computers, they should be aware that grammar-checking programs also have flaws.

Consider the reader who encounters "its" where "it's" should be. For a split second, the reader will pause and wonder about the error, the writer, and the site. Sometimes the musing reader will stop reading entirely because of the slowdown or because of the reduced credibility or appeal of the flawed message.

People do not have to be grammar experts to stop and wonder about correctness. For example, any unusual use of "whom" or "who" may cause a reader to reflect rather than read on. "Now, what was it I learned about whom?" the reader muses, and the tempo of reading is lost.

Television viewers may cringe when the news announcer says, "The committee will reconvene their meeting tomorrow morning." They know a committee is referred to with an "its," not a "their." As they pause to correct the sentence, they lose the remainder of the announcer's message.

But My Grammar Is Good…

Most of us who pursue writing as a career consider ourselves to be language experts, and in general, our grammar and language use are far above average. Even educated people have problems, however. Evidence of grammar problems is found in mistakes made daily by adults in business letters, memos, and reports, as well as in newspapers and on the airways. An ad proclaims, "There's no down payment and no service charge!" To be grammatically correct, it should say, "There are no down payment and no service charge." A newsletter states, "Children will be grouped by age, irregardless of grade in school." There is no such word as "irregardless"—it simply is an aberration of "regardless."

Educated people regularly make grammar mistakes that other educated people will recognize. Writers need to identify their most frequent grammar errors and learn how to correct them. A first step in checking your grammar is to know what errors you are most likely to make.

Grammar Problems

Author Katherine C. McAdams, associate professor at the University of Maryland, developed "The Grammar Slammer," a workshop on grammar problems that identifies five areas in which real-life errors are most likely to occur:

- punctuation, especially commas, semicolons, colons, apostrophes, dashes, and hyphens
- subject and verb agreement
- correct pronoun choices that provide agreement and avoid gender bias, such as "Each student has his or her book" rather than the more common and erroneous "Each student has their book"
- correct sentence structures, especially when sentences use modifiers or require parallel structure
- word use—that is, using words (such as "regardless") correctly; this area often involves spelling problems and confusing words that sound alike (such as "affect" and "effect," or "vain" and "vein").

This section follows the format of the Grammar Slammer workshop, giving a short lesson on each of the problem areas and following that lesson with some exercises. The approach is designed for writers who are bright, motivated, and capable of learning quickly.

The lessons provide a quick fix rather than an in-depth lecture. They are designed to refresh and renew rather than to re-educate. Going through the grammar lessons will help you identify your grammar deficiencies. You can then be on guard for your particular problems when writing and editing. You may find you have many weaknesses in language skills and understanding. If so, you will want to study the books recommended at the end of this chapter or take a grammar course.

Test Yourself

To determine your grammar problem areas, take the following diagnostic quiz. Record your answers on a sheet of paper.

Grammar Slammer Diagnostic Quiz

The following sentences contain errors in grammar and punctuation. No sentence contains more than one error. Read each sentence. Circle the error, and in the margin note how the sentence should be written correctly. Sentence 1 is corrected for you as an example.

1. If past performance is any indication, Maryland should be considered a top challenger for the championship; having downed defending regional champion Duke twice in the regular season. (*Correction*: Use a comma in place of the semicolon because the second half of the sentence is not an independent clause.)
2. The list of candidates being considered as successors for the university chancellor have been trimmed to approximately 50 names, including four university officials.
3. The computer did not seem to be working today, it kept rejecting the operator's instructions.
4. The following afternoon, Wednesday, October 25 a Royal Indian Air Force DC-3 landed in the abandoned dirt strip of Srinagar Airport.
5. Traditionally expected to be in control of their surroundings, the insecurity makes students uncomfortable in their new situation.
6. The president's body will lay in state until services are held at the chapel.
7. Hopefully, the council will pass a new noise ordinance before the students return to campus in September.
8. Among those who attended services for the coach were Ralph Brooks, head football coach at Eastern, Mary Barnes, chancellor; Michael Thomas, former chancellor; and Paul Wells, former athletic director.
9. She predicted that neither the speaker or the minority whip would receive the Republican nomination.
10. In its advertising, the Acme Company claims that they are in business only to do good works for the community.
11. Millie Rosefield, chair of the Cityville Historic Preservation Committee ran fifth in the Nov. 6 race for four council seats.
12. One of every five of the state's residents live in the sort of poverty that drove Erskine Caldwell to write.

13. Three-fourths of the business district in Long Beach, N.C. was destroyed by Hurricane Hugo, which struck the coast in 1989.
14. Many a boy use to believe that he could acquire practically super human strength by eating the right cereal.
15. The mayor said the parade would feature the homecoming queen, the marching band will play, and as many floats as possible.
16. Several people, all of them eager to give their opinions and all of them pressing forward to meet the governor, who was conducting interviews with voters in the area.
17. I like ice cream and cookies, I don't like cakes with icing.
18. Rosalie complained, and she had no heat.
19. Being a weight lifter, his muscles were well developed.
20. The alligator is hunted for their skin.

Several of the following words are misspelled. Circle the misspelled words and write the correct spelling for each in the space provided.

1. principal (of a school) ______________________
2. waiver (permission slip) ______________________
3. bore (a wild pig) ______________________
4. naval (belly button) ______________________
5. stationery (you write on it) ______________________
6. role (a list) ______________________
7. roommate ______________________
8. canvass (cloth) ______________________
9. complement (flattering statement) ______________________
10. cite (reference or footnote) ______________________

Answers for the diagnostic quiz are included in Appendix A at the end of the book.

Grammar Problems Up Close

Examine the items you missed on the diagnostic quiz. You should have an idea of which grammar problems you need to review. The discussion of each problem is presented here, followed by exercises. Test your proficiency and move on. Record your answers on a sheet of paper. To check your work, look at the answers in Appendix A.

Problem 1: Punctuation

Perhaps no problem looms larger than punctuation. Few people actually know the rules and regulations of punctuation use. Most of us, much of the time, use the "feel good" school of punctuation, saying, "I just feel like I need a comma here" or "A semicolon just felt right."

Professional communicators must give up their "feel good" philosophy of punctuating. The first rule of punctuating professionally is this: **Do not punctuate unless you know a rule.** When you even think of adding a mark of punctuation, stop and think about whether it is justified by the rules in this chapter. If not, you probably do not need to punctuate at all.

If you find you are punctuating excessively—that is, using more than three punctuation marks within any given sentence—it is probably time to rewrite that sentence. Sentences requiring many punctuation marks, even if they are all correct, usually are too long and complex to be easily understood. So another rule of punctuating professionally is this: Less is better. Less punctuation leads to clearer, more readable copy. When in doubt, leave the comma out.

Commas. Literally hundreds of comma rules exist. But the nine listed here, distilled by high school English teacher Mary Penny in the 1940s, have been found over the years to take care of most everyday comma problems.

Rule 1. Use commas in compound sentences when clauses are separated by a conjunction such as "and," "but," "for," "nor," or "yet."

- She managed the restaurant, but he did the cooking.

Note: In such sentences, leaving out the conjunction leads to an error known as a comma splice, whereby a comma is left to do the work of joining two sentences: "She managed the restaurant, he did the cooking." Like weak splices in a rope, commas are not strong enough for this task. A period or semicolon is needed to make a correct sentence:

- She managed the restaurant. He did the cooking.
- She managed the restaurant; he did the cooking.

Rule 2. Use commas to separate elements in a series. Such elements usually are adjectives, verbs, or nouns.

Note: Journalism departs from traditional rules of punctuation by leaving the comma out before a conjunction in a series of elements, following this rule in *The Associated Press Stylebook*. The text in this book follows the comma in a series rule, but the journalism examples do not—as you may have already noticed in reading this text.

English composition version:

- The tall, dark, handsome man hailed, lauded, and applauded Ben, George, Maude, and Rebecca.

Journalism version:

- The tall, dark, handsome man hailed, lauded and applauded Ben, George, Maude and Rebecca.

Rule 3. Use commas when attributing from quoted material. Commas set off words of attribution from the words of a one-sentence quotation unless a question mark or exclamation mark is preferred. Use them also in greetings:

- He said, "Hello." "Good-bye," she replied. "The fair has been canceled," she said.

Rule 4. Commas follow introductory matter, such as after an introductory adverbial clause:

- When the team was forced to kick, the coach sent in his best players.

Commas also follow two or more introductory prepositional phrases:

- In the spring she returned to College Park. (no comma)
- In the spring of 2008, she returned to College Park. (comma needed because "in" and "of" are two prepositional phrases)

Also use a comma with a phrase that contains a verbal (i.e., a verb form used as a modifier):

- Singing as she worked, Mary answered her phone.
- Kicked by a horse, Don was more than stunned.
- To cure hiccups, drink from the far side of a glass.

Rule 5. Commas follow the salutation of a friendly letter and capitalized elements, such as the complimentary close (e.g., Sincerely, Very truly yours). A colon follows the salutation of a business letter:

- Dear James,
- Dear Dean Smith:
- Sincerely, Dean Smith

Rule 6. Commas follow all items in a date or full address:

- July 16, 1992, is his date of birth.
- She has lived in Lake City, Fla., all her life.

Rule 7. Commas surround nonessential words or phrases:

- Well, we will just have to walk home.

Commas also set off appositives, which are words or phrases that rename a noun. Appositives amplify a subject:

- Betty Brown, his mother-in-law, has been married four times.

Also use a comma to set off nonessential modifying clauses and phrases:

- The president-elect, suffering from laryngitis, canceled his speech.

Rule 8. Commas surround words of direct address:

- Maria, please pass the butter.
- I can see, Fred, that you are lazy.

Rule 9. Commas indicate omitted verbs, usually expressed in another part of the sentence:

- Talent often is inherited; genius, never.

This rule is an old one and is rarely used today except in headlines. It would be rare to find a comma indicating an omitted verb in contemporary writing, but far from surprising to see such headlines as:

- Pilots Ask for Guns; Airlines, for Marshals
- Coach Smith Has Much to Gain This Season; His Team, Even More

Semicolons and Colons. Miss Penny added three more rules to her list to take care of another widespread punctuation problem: the correct use of semicolons and colons. Miss Penny's rules 10 and 11 explain the two uses of the semicolon—the only two uses. Rule 12 explains the use of colons.

Rule 10. Semicolons connect two complete sentences if sentences have a related thought. Use of a semicolon usually creates a sense of drama:

- The brown-eyed, dark-haired, vivacious model, at age 18, seemed destined for quick success; on Sept. 11, 2001, her apparent destiny was altered.

Rule 11. Semicolons are used in a list separating items that require significant internal punctuation:

- He lived six years in Richmond, Va.; four years in Raleigh, N.C.; one year in Greenville, S.C.; and six months in Baton Rouge, La.

Rule 12. Colons precede formal lists, illustrations, multisentence quotes, and enumerations:

- The following students received scholarships: Jim Johnson, Juanita Lopez, Martha Taylor, Tiffany Eldridge, and Courtney Sampson.
- He answered her with a parable: "A man once had six sons. Five of them. . . ."

- The senator listed the steps in her economic recovery program: first, to raise interest rates; second, to reduce spending....

Do not use a colon after "include" or forms of "to be," such as "was" or "were." Example: Her best friends were Sally, Marisa, and Claire.

Slammer for Commas, Semicolons, and Colons

Now, using Miss Penny's list of 12 rules as your reference, complete the following exercise. Remember, the most important rule is that you do not punctuate unless you know a rule. Defend each mark of punctuation you use by citing one of the Penny rules on a sheet of paper and listing the rule next to the sentence.

Rule or Rules

1. Although we watched the Super Bowl we don't know who won.
2. John Blimpo an egocentric man dropped his hat in the fruit salad.
3. Guitars have six strings basses four.
4. The tall dark handsome man listed his hobbies as reading fishing painting and writing.
5. To Whom It May Concern.

   The spelling and grammar test will be given on March 2 3 and 4 2009 in Room 502 of Knight Hall.

   Grammatically yours

   Dean Sarah Jones
6. Dad go ahead and send the money now.
7. The women's basketball team was down by four points at halftime however it came back to crush the opponent.
8. Congress passed the bill but the debate took several weeks.
9. Well just be in by daybreak.
10. Her blind date was a real disappointment he talked loudly and constantly about his pet snake.

11. She was elected on Nov. 4 2008 in Baltimore Md. the city of her birth.
12. She named her courses for the fall semester journalism English political science history and French.

Check your answers by looking at the answers in Appendix A. Then go on to tackle some other troublesome marks of punctuation.

Hyphens and Dashes. Remember that hyphens and dashes, although often confused, are different. The hyphen differs from a dash in both use and appearance. The hyphen is shorter (- as opposed to —), and it comes, without additional spaces, between two words combined to express some new concept, such as polka-dot and part-time. Hyphens are useful joiners that bring some creativity to language.

Rather than joining phrases, dashes are useful in separating them—usually where that separation can be heard. Dashes are sometimes used to replace commas to ensure that a pause is audible and even dramatic (e.g., "Although charming, he was—on the other hand—a thief").

Here is a list of guidelines for using hyphens and dashes correctly:

1. Never use a hyphen after a word ending in "ly."
   - The newly elected president stepped to the podium.
2. Use a hyphen to connect two or more related modifying words that do not function independently.
   - Kim always ordered the blue-plate special.
   - Todd dreaded any face-to-face confrontations.
3. The dash is a punctuation mark one "hears." It is a noticeable pause. Choose a dash instead of a comma so the audience can "hear" the pause.
4. Dashes work where commas would also work. The only difference is the dash adds drama—and an audible break in the text. Because dashes may substitute for commas, they are used to set off nonessential material.
   - The murderer was—if you can believe it—a priest.
5. Too many dashes in any text may be distracting and even irritating to readers. Limit dashes to only the most dramatic of pauses. In most cases, such as this example, commas will suffice.
   - She is—as most of you know—a punctuation expert.

Other marks of punctuation, especially apostrophes, can be troublesome. Correct use may vary from time to time and publication to publication. Always check your stylebook, and keep a current grammar reference book handy.

Problem 2: Subject and Verb Agreement

Few writers make obvious errors in subject and verb agreement, such as "I is interested in cars" or "The class know it's time to go to lunch." But most people struggle with the following subject–verb agreement problems:

1. Collective subjects can be confusing. Some nouns that appear to be plural are treated as singular units:
   - The *Girl Scouts* is a fine organization.
   - *Checkers* is an ancient game.
   - *Economics* is a difficult subject.

   Some collective subjects, however, have Latinate endings and remain plural, although spoken language tends to make them singular. In formal writing, these plurals require plural verbs:
   - The *media* have raised the issue of the senator's competency.
   - The *alumni* are funding a new building.
2. The pronouns "each," "either," "neither," "anyone," "everyone," and "anybody" are always singular, regardless of what follows them in a phrase. Take, for example, this sentence:
   - Either of the girls is an excellent choice for president.

   The phrase "of the girls" does not change the singular number of the true subject of this sentence: the pronoun "either." Following are some other examples of correct usage:
   - Neither has my vote.
   - Either is fine with me.
   - Each has an excellent option.
   - Anyone is capable of helping the homeless.
   - Everyone is fond of Jerry.
3. A fraction or percentage of a whole is considered a singular subject.
   - Three-quarters of the pie is gone.
   - Sixty-seven percent of the voters is needed to withhold a veto.

4. Compound subjects, in which two or more nouns function as the subject of a sentence, can lead to agreement problems. To solve such problems, substitute a single pronoun, such as "they" or "it," for the sentence's subject or subjects. For example, transform this problem sentence: "The students and the teacher is/are waiting for the bus." By substituting, the subject becomes "they": They are waiting for the bus. The following are some other examples:
   - The opening number and the grand finale thrill the audience. (they thrill)
   - There are no down payment and no service charge. (they are not charged)
   - The Eagles, a classic rock band, is my dad's favorite group. (it is favorite)
5. When subjects are structured with either/or and neither/nor, use the verb tense that corresponds to the subject closest to the verb, as in the following cases:
   - Either the leader or the scouts pitch the tent.
   - Either the scouts or the leader pitches the tent.
   - Neither the parents nor the students win when rules are broken.

Slammer for Subject–Verb Agreement

Check your knowledge of subject–verb agreement by taking the following quiz. Select the verb that agrees.

1. He did say he would look at the sheet of names, which includes/include the owners of two apartment buildings.
2. Their number and influence appears/appear greatest in West Germany.
3. Experience in the backfield and the line gives/give the coach a good feeling on the eve of any opening game.
4. A first offense for having fewer than 25 cartons of untaxed cigarettes results/result in a $500 fine.
5. Before you make a final judgment on this student's story, consider the time and effort that has/have gone into it.

6. Who does the teaching? Full professors. But so does/do associates, assistants, and instructors.
7. She said they would visit Peaks of Otter, which is/are near Lynchburg, Va.
8. The news media is/are calling for a peace treaty that is fair to everyone.
9. The United Mine Workers exhibit/exhibits solidarity during elections.
10. There is/are 10 million bricks in this building.
11. The president said that students today are too job-oriented and neglect the broader areas of study that constitutes/constitute a true education.
12. Five fire companies fought the blaze, which the firefighters said was/were the longest this year.
13. Each of the 100 people believes/believe in God.
14. It is/are the boats, not the swimmers, that stir up the dirt in the lake.
15. The editor told the staff there was a shortage of money for the newsroom, a shortage she said she would explain to the board of directors, which decides/decide all matters on the budget.
16. One of my classmates typifies/typify student apathy.
17. Drinking beer and sleeping is/are the most important things in my life.
18. Dillon said he has insurance for everything except the buildings, which is/are owned by Thomas F. Williams.
19. Approximately 51 percent of the U.S. population is/are female.
20. There is/are only one way to beat taxes.
21. Neither the professor nor her two assistants teaches/teach this course in a style students like.
22. Each student is/are responsible for getting the work done on time.
23. All students considers/consider that an imposition.
24. The General Assembly and the governor disagrees/disagree on the solution.

Check your answers against those in Appendix A.

Problem 3: Correct Use of Pronouns

Pronouns are little words—"he," "she," "you," "they," "I," "it"—that stand for proper nouns. Look at this sentence:

- International Trucking is hiring 20 new drivers because it is expanding in the Southeast.

In this sentence, the word "it" is used to substitute for International Trucking. Pronouns help avoid needless repetition in language by doing the work of the larger nouns, called antecedents. In the previous example, "International Trucking" is the antecedent for the pronoun "it."

Pronouns must agree with their antecedents, as in the following examples:

- Marianne said she (Marianne) would never color her (Marianne's) hair.
- Baltimore became a model city after it (Baltimore) successfully restored the waterfront.
- Journalism is a popular major, and now it (journalism) prepares students for many careers.

Following are guidelines to ensure correct pronoun choices:

1. Watch for collective subjects—groups treated as single units—and use the correct pronoun.
   - The committee gave its report.
   - The United Mine Workers gave out a list of its legislative goals.
2. When using singular pronouns, use singular verbs.
   - Each of the rose bushes was at its peak.
   - Everyone in the audience rose to his or her feet and chanted.
3. Use correct pronouns to handle issues of sexism in language. The generic person is no longer "he."
   - Each of the students had his or her book.
   - The students had their books.
4. Be attentive to stray phrases or clauses that come between pronouns and antecedents and cause agreement problems.

- He presented the list of candidates being considered for the office and told the committee members to choose from it. (antecedent agreement; it refers to the list)
- He posted the list of candidates for the position and read it aloud. (antecedent agreement; "it" refers to the list)

5. Use reflexive pronouns, such as himself or herself, only when a subject is doing something to herself or himself or themselves.
   - Jan introduced herself to the new chancellor.
   - Henry never could forgive himself.
   - The relatives had the chalet to themselves.

Slammer for Pronouns

To ensure you understand agreement of pronoun and antecedent, select the appropriate pronoun for each of the following sentences.

1. Each student had (his or her/their) assignment completed before class.
2. General Foods plans to change (its/their) approach to marketing baked goods.
3. Larry introduced me and (him/himself) to the governor.
4. The jury took (their/its) deliberations seriously.
5. The board of directors set a date for (their/its) annual retreat.
6. The Orioles (is/are) my favorite team.
7. Neither the Terps nor the Crimson Tide (was/were) having a winning season.
8. Neither of the teams (was/were) victorious.
9. The alumni voted to charge $1 an issue for (their/its) magazine.
10. Any of the three finalists (is/are) an excellent choice.
11. The six-member committee voted to reverse (its/their) decision.
12. The librarian's collection fascinated him, and he asked to borrow from (her/it).
13. The media (is/are) ignoring the mayor's speeches.
14. Each of the students could handle the job by (himself or herself/ themselves).
15. Everyone in the audience rose to (his or her/their) feet for the ovation.

Check your work against the answers in Appendix A, and prepare to tackle the biggest pronoun problem of all: the *who/whom* dilemma.

Who and Whom. The word "whom" has all but disappeared from spoken English, so it is little wonder that few of us know how to use it correctly. Even though usage is changing, writers of published materials still need to know the rules that govern the distinction between "who" and "whom":

1. "Who" is a substitute for subjects referring to "he," "we," or "she," or the nominative pronoun.
   - Who saw the meteor?

   The statement, "He saw the meteor," as a question becomes, "Who saw the meteor?" "Who" is substituted for the subject "he." Relative clauses work the same way when "who" is substituted for a subject. In the sentence, "He questioned the man who saw the meteor," "who" substitutes for the subject of the clause, "He saw the meteor." The entire clause serves as an object of the verb "questioned." But the function of the clause does not change the role of a pronoun; in this sentence, the role of "who" is as the subject of the verb "saw."
2. "Whom" is a substitute for objective pronouns, such as "him," "her," or "them."
   - Whom did he question for hours?

   The statement, "He questioned her for hours," as a question becomes, "Whom did he question for hours?" "Whom" is substituted for "her" as the object of the verb "questioned." Substitution works the same way in relative clauses. In the sentence, "Marcella was the one whom he questioned for hours," "whom" substitutes for the object "her" in the clause, "He questioned her for hours." Again, it is the role of the pronoun within its subject–verb structure that determines whether it is the subject or the object and therefore "who" or "whom."

That and Which. Another fine distinction between pronouns is the difference between "that" and "which." Again, the spoken language no longer follows strict rules regarding these subordinate conjunctions, but careful writers need to observe the following guidelines:

1. "That" is a restrictive pronoun, indicating that the information it precedes is essential for correct understanding of the sentence.
   - Dogs prefer bones that improve their dental health.
   - The use of "that" tells us that dogs prefer only this specific kind of bone.
2. "Which" precedes nonessential material; therefore, it typically appears with commas (the ones used to set off nonessential information).
   - Dogs prefer bones, which improve their dental health.

   The use of "which" tells us that all bones improve dogs' teeth.
3. "That" and "which" are not interchangeable. As you can see in the example sentences, the meaning of the sentence is affected when the comma is added in the second sentence and "that" becomes "which." In the first sentence, dogs like only bones that are good for them; in the second, dogs like bones better than other things, and bones just happen to be good for dental health. The second sentence is far more logical.

Slammer for Who/Whom and That/Which

Select the appropriate pronoun in the following sentences:

1. Alvin, (who/whom) everyone adored, absconded with the family fortune.
2. Betty, (who/whom) was the apple of his eye, followed him to Mexico.
3. The FBI agents (who/whom) Alvin had avoided for several months finally arrested him.
4. Veronica, Alvin's sister, (who/whom) needed the money desperately, refused to post bond.
5. Alvin, (who's/whose) health was delicate, wasted away in prison.

Select the appropriate pronoun, then note the proper punctuation as needed in the following sentences:

1. Betty bought a gun (that/which) was on sale and set out to free Alvin.
2. She headed north from Mexico in a stolen car (that/which) had more than 130,000 miles showing on its odometer.

3. The car (that/which) had New Jersey license plates was quickly spotted by police in Texas.
4. The Texans (that/which/who/whom) spoke in a slow drawl told her she was wanted in New Jersey for conspiring with Alvin.
5. She pulled out the gun (that/which) she had in her glove compartment and started shooting.
6. The police officer (that/which/who/whom) was standing closest to her car died after he was struck by a bullet.
7. Other officers took Betty's gun (that/which) now was empty of bullets.
8. They also arrested Betty and placed her in a local jail (that/which) overlooked the Rio Grande.

Check your answers against those in Appendix A and move on to the next grammar problem.

Problem 4: Sentence Structure

Aside from fragments and run-on sentences, two other categories cause most adults problems with sentence structure: faulty parallelism and modifier placement.

Journalists often struggle with giving sentences parallel structure—that is, making sure that series or lists of phrases are parallel in form. Rather than, "He enjoys reading and to go skiing," use the parallel form, saying, "He enjoys reading and skiing." Writers must always remember to check lists within sentences as well as bulleted lists to see that phrases are stated in parallel form, as shown in these examples:

- Marvelene listed steps in planning a successful party: sending invitations early, greeting guests personally, and supplying abundant food and drink. (parallel gerunds: sending, greeting, supplying)
- A successful host always is sure
  —to send invitations early,
  —to greet guests personally, and
  —to supply abundant food and drink. (infinitives are parallel)

Other sentence errors might occur when modifiers are placed incorrectly and give readers an inaccurate, sometimes humorous, picture as, for example, in these sentences:

Wrong: Swinging from an overhead wire, we saw a kite.
Better: We saw a kite swinging from an overhead wire.

Wrong: When wheeled into the operating room, the nurse placed a mask over my face.
Better: The nurse placed a mask over my face after I was wheeled into the operating room.

Wrong: The jury found him guilty of killing his wife after deliberating for three days.
Better: After deliberating for three days, the jury found him guilty of killing his wife.

To solve modifier placement problems, place modifying clauses and phrases closest to what they modify.

Slammer for Modifiers

Rewrite these sentences to correct misplaced modifiers. Some sentences are correct as written.

1. The waiter served ice cream in glass bowls which started melting immediately.
2. The Simpsons gave a toy robot with flashing eyes to one of their sons.
3. We saw a herd of sheep on the way to our hotel.
4. Most people have strawberry shortcake topped with mounds of whipped cream.
5. The house is one of the oldest in Rockville, where Mrs. Rooks taught ballet.
6. Flying at an altitude of several thousand feet, the paratroopers could see for miles.

7. I could not convince the child to stop running into the street without yelling.
8. After the first act of the play, Brooke's performance improves, the critic said.
9. While watching the ball game, Sue's horse ran away.
10. The museum director showed me a spider with the orange diamond on its belly.
11. The bank approves loans to reliable individuals of any size.
12. After being wheeled into the operating room, the nurse placed a mask over my face.
13. Riding in a glass-bottom boat, we saw thousands of colorful fish.
14. Aunt Helen asked us before we left to call on her.
15. Do it yourself: Make up a sentence suffering from modifier malady. Then correct it.

Check your work against the answers in Appendix A, and prepare for the final grammar problem: word usage.

Problem 5: Word Usage

English is a language enriched by words borrowed from other languages, resulting in a rich vocabulary—but also, in many cases, in unorthodox spelling and idiosyncratic usage. It makes little sense to have both "affect" and "effect" in the same language, functioning so similarly but not identically. And why do we distinguish between "pore" and "pour," or "flair" and "flare"? Who cares?

Careful writers have to care because subtle usage errors can cause big misunderstandings. Correct usage leads to credibility; readers have confidence in error-free reading.

Slammer for Troublesome Words

Use a dictionary to help identify correct usage for each of the following troublesome words.

Hopefully
Affect versus effect
Less versus fewer

Lie versus lay
Sit versus set
Comprise versus compose

Math for Journalists

All professional communicators must be able to handle routine computations such as adding, subtracting, multiplying, dividing, figuring ratios and percentages, and rounding off numbers. Such simple calculations routinely are used in daily journalism, and any error would make a story inaccurate.

Professor Emeritus Phil Meyer at the University of North Carolina at Chapel Hill advised mass communication students that if they chose the field because they thought they could escape math, they were wrong. Basic math is necessary.

Here's a typical example of statistical writing that misses the mark: An advertisement tells audiences that computer prices have dropped 200 percent. This news would appeal to someone shopping for a new computer. But what's wrong here? When the price drops 100 percent, the item is free. Below 100 percent means stores are paying customers to take away computers. The writer needs a few quick lessons on math.

Here's another example of a writer in need of math skills: A news story reports that police chased a suspect for 90 minutes from Town X to Town Y, a distance of 300 miles. Possible? Hardly. The cars would be traveling 200 miles per hour to cover that distance in 90 minutes. Something is wrong with the information—unless the cars were literally flying.

Basic Math

Basic math errors show up continually in writing, usually because writers are careless. But a reader somewhere is going to see the error and doubt the writer's and the medium's credibility. Mass communicators need to know some simple math, or at the very least, they need to recognize when data are misrepresented and find someone who can do correct calculations.

Percent. A lead reports that the president's popularity dropped from 85 to 75 percent, a decrease of 10 percent. Correct? No. The decrease is 10 percentage points, but not 10 percent. That's the first lesson to learn in writing about percent. If you subtract 75 percent from 85 percent, you get a 10 percentage point difference. To calculate the percent difference, you need to find the difference and divide that by the base or original figure: % = d/b (i.e., percent = difference/base). Here, that would be 10/85, a change of 12 percent. It works the same way with increases. If the popularity goes up from 70 percent to 80 percent, the difference is 10 percentage points, which yields 10/70, or a 14 percent increase.

For another example, let's look at a financial story on company revenues. Suppose Midland Trucking Company had revenues last fiscal year of $535,000 and revenues this year of $635,000. The difference is $100,000. If you follow the formula d/b = percent difference, you would divide $100,000 by $535,000. The percent change is 18.6 percent, or rounded off, 19 percent.

If you made an error and divided the difference by the new amount of $635,000, you would get an increase of 16 percent, a significant difference from 19 percent—and one that could affect stockholders' perception of company management. The writer for the company's annual report must be careful in calculating numbers that could influence investments or stockholder confidence.

Rates. Often, writers will state numbers as a rate—1 in 10 or 3 in 100—so that complicated figures are easier to understand. For example, a writer finds a health department report saying that 0.0021 percent of teens aged 13 to 19 in the county became pregnant last year. The writer decides to translate the percentage into a figure that people can visualize.

One way to calculate the rate is to multiply the percent figure by 100 or 1,000 so that decimals no longer appear. In this case, multiplying 0.0021 × 1,000 gives a rate of 2.1 per 1,000. Rates can be stated by hundreds, thousands, tens of thousands, and on up. More clearly stated, the rate of teen pregnancy is 2.1 per 1,000, or about two teens out of every 1,000 teens aged 13 to 19 living in the county got pregnant last year.

Probability. Writers need to have an appreciation for probability theory and an understanding of the likelihood that a predicted event will actually occur. If there is a 40 percent chance of rain, how likely is it that we will get wet? Should we write or broadcast the news that rain is on the way? We hear probability each time we listen to a weather report. But if the probability of rain is 40 percent, it's important to remember there's also a 60 percent probability that the weather will be clear.

Writers often make errors when they combine one probability with another, such as "The football coach predicts a 50 percent chance of thunderstorms and a 50 percent chance the game could be delayed." Does that mean a 100 percent chance the game will be delayed? No. To calculate the probability in this case, you must multiply one probability with another. The probability of thunderstorms and a game postponement is .5 × .5 = .25, or a 25 percent chance both will occur.

Reporting Poll Data

Many numbers are reported in poll stories every day in the media. An article notes that the president has a 63 percent approval rating. What does 63 percent mean to the average reader or listener? Translated, the 63 percent means more than six out of 10 people (remember your percentage calculations from earlier in this section) approve of his performance—and four of every 10 do not. You can break that down even further to say simply that three out of five (divide 6 and 10 by 2 to bring to their lowest common denominator) people approve of the president.

When reporting poll data, it is important to make the statistics as clear and understandable as possible. Readers need to grasp what the numbers mean. To report poll numbers correctly, writers must be able to read the charts to determine what the poll figures mean. The following table presents poll results, divided into categories by income. These responses came from people queried at a local mall about whether they support Proposition Y, a proposal for a new city entertainment tax:

	Yes	*No*	*Total*
Earn $50,000 or less a year			
Count	148	152	300
Percent	49.3%	50.7%	100%
Percent of total	26%	27%	
Earn $50,001 or more a year			
Count	159	109	268
Percent	59.2%	40.8%	100%
Percent of total	28%	19%	

A writer notes that almost 50 percent of respondents who earn under $50,000 a year support Proposition Y on the ballot. He or she can even translate that 49.3 number to one out of two people interviewed in that income bracket and still be fairly accurate.

But then the writer notes that 59 percent of respondents earn more than $50,000 and support Proposition Y. Is the writer correct? No. The 59 percent figure represents what percentage of those people who earn that amount of money favor the proposition. The total number of people who earn $50,001 a year or more is 159 plus 109 (268). Of the 268 people in that income bracket, 59 percent favor the proposition.

To find out the percentage who actually earn more than $50,000 a year, go back to the actual counts and recalculate from there. If you add all the counts in each box, you will find 568 respondents to the survey. To find out how many earn more than $50,000 a year, divide difference by base, or 268 divided by 568, or 47 percent of those surveyed earn more money—much less than 59 percent.

It is extremely important when reading poll results to read the information correctly and calculate differences correctly. Also, be sure to translate your information to tangible language.

Margin of Error

A necessary part of poll reporting is reporting margin of error. In a poll on the safety of the nation, 87 percent report feeling safe, "plus or minus 3 percent." That "plus or minus" figure is the margin of error.

In simple terms, the error figure, usually from 1 to 5 percent, represents the accuracy of the poll results. Researchers know that in any survey they must allow room for error. Common sense and statistics tell us that the more respondents polled, the more accurately the poll results reflect the opinions of the public at large. Statistically, once the number of people polled reaches a certain level, the margin of error doesn't change or improve much. With several hundred respondents, the margin of error stays around plus or minus 4 to 5 percent. If careful sampling methods are used, poll results will allow researchers to interview 1,200 U.S. residents and then estimate what 280 million people believe. Most pollsters strive for a margin of error around 3 percent. Let's see how that works.

A poll says 45 percent of Americans believe the tax burden is too great on middle-income people. Another 42 percent believe it is just about right, and 13 percent have no opinion. The pollster reports a plus or minus 3 percent margin of error. Here's how the results look in chart form:

Reported results (with error = ± 3%)	
Too great	45%
Just about right	42%
No opinion	13%

The margin of error indicates the 45 percent who believe the tax burden is too great may, in reality, be 42 percent (minus 3 percent). Or it may be as high as 48 percent (plus 3 percent). Likewise, for those who think the tax burden is just about right, the range in reality could be as much as 45 percent to as little as 39 percent. So it's likely neither group can claim a clear majority. With such close percentages, a writer cannot say, "Most Americans said they think the tax burden on the middle class is too great." It would be more accurate to report that many Americans believe the tax burden is fairly distributed.

The Associated Press Stylebook has a separate entry for polls and surveys and lists items that should be included in any poll story. This entry discusses margin of error and urges writers to take care, especially when reporting that one candidate is leading another. According to the stylebook, only when the difference between the candidates is more than twice the margin of error can you say one candidate is leading. The same rule applies to the tax burden survey results presented here: The difference between the two groups is 3 percentage points, not the 6 required to be twice the margin of error of plus or minus 3 percent. So it's clear that in the case of individual opinions about tax burdens—and in many political poll results—a writer would have to say that opinion is just about even.

Tips

Many schools and departments of journalism and mass communication require their students to have basic competencies in math. At the University of North Carolina at Chapel Hill, faculty members in the School of Journalism and Mass Communication have considered adding a math competency requirement for journalism and mass communication majors.

Students who want to test their skills can take a math test online at www.unc.edu/~pmeyer/carstat/. Professor Emeritus Phil Meyer and Associate Professor Bill Cloud at UNC-Chapel Hill produced the test, along with partner *USA Today*.

The Associated Press Stylebook recommends rounding numbers because readers have little use for numbers such as $1,463,729. In this case, the writer needs to round the number to two decimal places, which would convert the number to $1.46 million. Rounding numbers makes it easier for readers to digest numbers and helps avoid inaccuracies.

The Associated Press Stylebook has other entries that relate to numbers, such as those on decimals, fractions, percentages, median, average, norm, and the metric system. Another section explains business terms. All these entries help writers when math is an issue—often the case in communications professions.

Slammer for Math

The following exercises will test your basic math skills. Please use a calculator. Answers are found in Appendix B.

1. The jury has 13 members. There are four members who are women. There are two African American jurors, and only one of them is a man. There also is one Hispanic American man on the jury. (Round percentages to the nearest tenth.)

- **a.** What is the ratio of men to women on the jury?
- **b.** What percentage of the jury is female?
- **c.** What percentage of Hispanic American men makes up the jury?
- **d.** What percentage of African American men makes up the jury?

2. The town manager tells the town council that he is proposing that the town build a new recreation center. The center would be 15,000 square feet. He has an estimate that the cost to build would be $85 per square foot plus an additional $25 per square foot for furnishings.

- **a.** What is the cost to build the center?
- **b.** What is the cost to furnish the center?
- **c.** What is the total cost for building and furnishing the center?
- **d.** Round the total cost to the nearest $100,000.

3. A local advertising company is sponsoring a community-wide yard sale in a local middle school parking lot. Each booth space is equivalent to two parking spaces. Each parking space measures 12 feet by 8 feet. The parking lot has 240 spaces.

- **a.** What is the square footage of one booth?
- **b.** How many booths can the advertising company rent?
- **c.** At $30 a booth, how much revenue will the company earn?
- **d.** You decide to rent two booths to get rid of your old furniture. How much space do you get?

4. Sarah Lamb owns a condominium valued for tax purposes at $175,000. The town's tax rate is 85 cents per $100 valuation, but the City Council is proposing to raise the tax rate by 3 cents for next year.

   a. How much in taxes did Sarah pay this year?
   b. How much will she pay under the proposed tax rate?
   c. What percentage increase will that be in her tax bill?
   d. If her property increases in value 5 percent by next year, how much will her tax bill be under the proposed tax rate?

5. Look at the following chart about support for three candidates for mayor.

	Smith	*Small*	*Tucker*
Female			
Count	107	137	31
Percentage	38.9%	49.7%	11.4%
Male			
Count	192	137	23
Percentage	54.4%	39.0%	6.5%

   a. How many respondents were women?
   b. What percentage of the total respondents were women?
   c. What percentage of the total respondents favored Tucker?
   d. What percentage of the total respondents favored Small?

6. Christine wants to go to the state fair Friday night. Her mother said there is a 50 percent probability that she will be able to take Christine to the fair. But Christine's band director said there is a 75 percent chance that he will schedule band practice on Friday night. What is the probability that Christine will actually get to the fair?

7. Jonathan works 40 hours a week at a local hardware store. He earns $7.50 an hour. The manager said he will give Jonathan a 25-cent per hour pay raise. How much will Jonathan earn a week with the raise?

   a. $340
   b. $10
   c. $310
   d. $260

8. Mr. Tennyson is teaching his class how to convert to the metric system. If the average weight for the class members is 135 pounds, what is that in kilograms? (Note: 0.454 kilograms is equal to one pound.)

a. 61.29
b. 50.3
c. 792
d. 297
e. 74.2

References

Katherine C. McAdams, *The Grammar Slammer*. College of Journalism, University of Maryland, 1991.

Mary Penny, Class handouts, Needham Broughton High School, Raleigh, NC, 1974.

Web site of Professor Phil Meyer, University of North Carolina at Chapel Hill, at www.unc.edu/~pmeyer/carstat/.

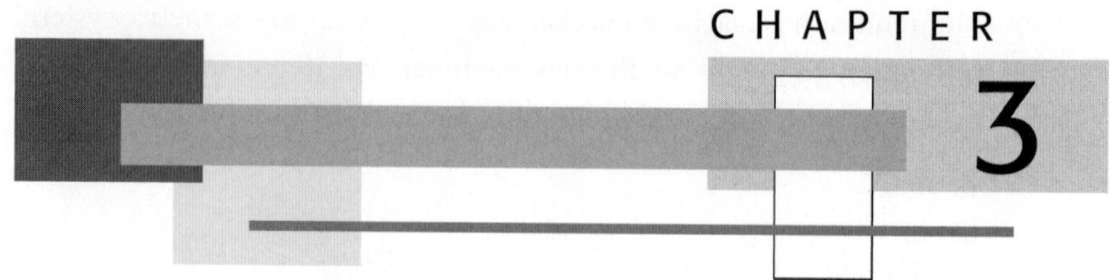

CHAPTER 3

Editing for Audiences

Good writing depends on good editing. Many student or beginning writers assume a writing job is finished once they get a message written. But that's exactly when editing must begin, even in a short text message. With your final reading of any draft, ideas for improving the message begin to flow: How can the message be more focused? Streamlined? Intriguing? What kinds of fine-tuning can send the message on its way, with clarity and accuracy, to target audiences?

While some people choose editing as their job, every writer must be an editor. Self-editing has become even more critical as more and more content is posted online without being edited first. While three or four editors might read a story before it is printed in a newspaper or magazine, a story posted online might not be read by any editor before it is posted. So the burden for editing falls more squarely on the writer.

You already have learned some ways to improve your writing through strategic planning and correct use of language and numbers. These same techniques are applied in the editing process, along with many other guidelines. Hundreds of books have been written about editing (Amazon.com lists more than 1,500), all filled with advice and rules on style and correctness. No writer can remember all the rules while writing a first or even a second or third draft.

Between the first draft and the finished product come polishing and editing. The first draft should be as good as possible; then, self-editing and the editing of others will refine and improve it. Novelist and teacher Doris Betts tells her students: "Handing in your first draft is like passing around your spittle." In other words, an unedited message is unprofessional and offensive.

Editing is more than just a courtesy to readers. It is a necessity because a single set of facts may be edited to produce several messages. For example, a newspaper article on car maintenance may also be edited to appear in the

"Living" section of a Web site, on the "Hot Tips" page of a weekly magazine, or in another writer's automotive blog. Editing is more than just checking for correctness: Today's editor sculpts and reformats information for many presentations to many different audiences.

But first things first: When all is said and done, editors must be sure that messages conform to correct style. In this chapter, you will learn

- basic style and editing rules,
- how different media sometimes require different kinds of editing, and
- steps to guide the editing process.

Watching Style

Part of good editing is ensuring consistency throughout writing. Using a consistent style guarantees a certain pattern persists in word usage, titles, punctuation, abbreviations, grammar, and spelling. If "Dr." means doctor in the first paragraph of an online story, it will not mean "Drive" as part of someone's address later in the piece. Consistent usage builds credibility and reduces chances of audience confusion.

Media organizations follow a style that guarantees consistency. Most newspapers and public relations firms follow the style in *The Associated Press Stylebook and Briefing on Media Law*, updated annually as usage evolves. Others, including *The Washington Post* and *The New York Times*, have their own style manuals. Many universities and publishing houses use *The Chicago Manual of Style* or the style manual of the Modern Language Association.

Online news sites don't yet have an industry standard for style on things such as verb tenses, link text, and site navigation. Media professionals also have to learn the "folk styles" that exist more as tradition than anything else and that change from newsroom to newsroom. But even in a world in which the rules are not yet written, editors will be well served if they remember the reason that style rules exist in the first place—to help the audience more easily understand the message.

The text in this book uses a style that differs from the Associated Press style, so you will notice discrepancies between usage in the text and in examples and exercises.

No one is ever expected to memorize stylebooks, but writers and editors must be familiar with their content. When a question arises, they need to know where to find the answer. Writers will find that certain rules are used so often that they become second nature. For example, most writers become familiar with the capitalization rule for titles: Professional titles are capitalized before a person's name but never after a name. Here's an example, "University President Bill Sandler said classes would end early Tuesday because of the threat of a blizzard." After his name, the title would read, "Bill Sandler, university president, said . . . ."

Basic Style Rules

The most broadly accepted style rules for professional communicators are those set out by *The Associated Press Stylebook*, which covers subjects as diverse as correct abbreviations for military titles, to spellings for Hanukkah and Santa Claus, to capitalization of Kleenex. But several categories in the stylebook are indispensable to media writers. Summaries of those entries that apply to news and online writing are included here. Because the general style rules differ for broadcast writing, they are included in Chapter 13.

Titles. Long titles should go after an individual's name. William McCorkle's name is not lost if a short title is used before it, such as "University President William McCorkle." But his name would be hard to find if his title were "University Associate Vice Chancellor for Student Affairs and Services." When an individual has a long title, put the title after the name: "William McCorkle, university associate vice chancellor for student affairs and services."

When titles precede names, they generally are capitalized. After names, they are not.

Most titles are written out. The only time some are abbreviated is when they precede a name. *The Associated Press Stylebook* indicates which titles can be abbreviated. For example, "governor" may be shortened to "Gov. Sheila Aycock" and "lieutenant governor" as "Lt. Gov. James Ramsey." Titles that are never abbreviated include "president," "attorney general," "professor," and "superintendent." Most military titles can be abbreviated, and those abbreviations are listed in *The Associated Press Stylebook*.

Stand-alone titles are always written out, and they are never abbreviated or capitalized. Examples are "The vice president said he would turn over the files to the Justice Department" and "The pope will visit the United States in May." Note that "vice president" is not hyphenated.

Capitalization. The general rule is to capitalize proper nouns that refer to a person, place, or thing. Examples include "Sacramento is the capital of California" and "Mayor Harmon Bowles agreed to lead the town's Independence Day parade."

Abbreviations. Abbreviate only what your style manual permits. Abbreviate states' names when they are used with the name of a town or city; otherwise, write them out. Note that the Associated Press does not use postal abbreviations in text, except when the complete address is used with a zip code, as in "124 E. Main St., Lakeland, FL 33801." In other instances the Associated Press uses the following abbreviations: Ala., Ariz., Ark., Calif., Colo., Conn., Del., Fla., Ga., Ill., Ind., Kan., Ky., La., Md., Mass., Mich., Minn., Miss., Mo., Mont., Neb., Nev., N.H., N.J., N.M., N.Y., N.C., N.D., Okla., Ore., Pa., R.I., S.C., S.D., Tenn., Vt., Va., Wash., W.Va., Wis., and Wyo. Eight states' names are never abbreviated: Alaska, Hawaii, Idaho, Iowa, Maine, Ohio, Texas, and Utah. You can abbreviate months when they are used with a specific date: "Nov. 12, 1948." Write out "November 1948," however. Never abbreviate March, April, May, June, or July.

Don't abbreviate the days of the week or the words "assistant" and "association."

The Associated Press allows some abbreviations on first reference because people are familiar with them, such as FBI, CIA, UFO, and IBM. But that does not mean to use only the abbreviation. The context of the story may require that the full title be used somewhere in the text. On second reference, use the abbreviation or substitute words such as "the bureau," "the agency," "the object," or "the company."

Acronyms. Acronyms are abbreviations that can be pronounced as words, such as "AIDS" for "acquired immune deficiency syndrome" or "UNESCO" for "United Nations Educational, Scientific and Cultural Organization." See style manuals for the correct first and second references for acronyms, just as with other abbreviations.

Numbers. The general rule according to AP style is to write out numbers zero through nine and use numerals for numbers 10 and higher. Always spell out numbers at the beginning of a sentence, however. In writing numbers above 999,999, write out the words "million" and "billion" rather than using all those zeroes. For example: "To clear the site, the construction crew moved 1.2 million cubic yards of dirt" and "Congressional aides discovered the budget would require an additional $1.4 billion in revenues."

AP style lists two dozen or so exceptions to the rule, but the main ones are these:

Age. Always use a numeral for age: "She has a 3-year-old daughter and an 85-year-old mother."

Percent. Always use a numeral: "He estimated 9 percent of employees are truly satisfied with their jobs."

Time. Always use a numeral: "The guests will arrive at 9 p.m."

Dates. Again, use numerals: "He was born Jan. 3, 1926."

Temperatures. Use numerals for all temperatures except zero: "The weather service predicted the coldest weather in 15 years for the weekend, noting that temperatures would drop to 2 to 3 degrees below zero."

Dimensions. Always write height and weight as numerals: "The average height of the team's basketball players is 6 feet 4 inches." "The record-breaking carrot weighed 5 pounds."

Money. Write dollars and cents as numerals: "The price of an egg is about 18 cents." "Hemming the dress will cost $9."

Editing Responsibilities

As a writer, you are responsible for editing and revising your own work, even if you work in a newsroom with a separate copy desk or in a large corporate communications office where others ultimately will edit your work. You are the originator, the one who must shape and streamline the initial draft of the message. Your copy must be clear, fair, accurate, complete, and in correct style when it leaves your hands.

Many resources are available to help develop your editing skills, such as those listed in Box 2.1 in Chapter 2. One easily accessible guide is EditTeach.org (www.editteach.org), launched under a grant from the John S. and James L. Knight Foundation. Its Web site is geared "for editing professors, students and working professionals to help strengthen the craft of editing and support the work of editors."

As you gain experience as a writer, you also will be asked to revise the work of others. You might be promoted to an editing position or asked for help by others who know less than you do about good writing skills. When you edit others' work, you must apply both editorial and personal skills, coaching and negotiating respectfully with writers. Editing is hard work, and it is time consuming. It can be creative and satisfying. But in any case, it has to be done. Editing is a crucial part of all writing. And like other writing, it proceeds in steps.

The Steps of Editing

Writers should consider editing as a process. Specific tasks allow writers-turned-editors to be focused and thorough in the editing process. Of course, writer-editors approach a news brief differently from a long feature. Sometimes, on first reading, an editor will decide the story needs substantial revisions; other times, only minor changes will be needed. That decision is made in the first step of the editing process and will determine how much time needs to be devoted to editing.

Today's writers learn to edit at the computer. They may not have time to print out a draft and edit on paper. Editing on screen saves time and allows the writer to use computer tools, such as the grammar-checker and Web resources for fact-checking, to help in the editing process.

Editing follows basic steps focusing on these elements in this order: content, completeness, accuracy, language, and final read-through.

Reading the Copy for Content. The first step is to check for content. Read the written piece from start to finish to get a sense of what has been written. You may fix any minor errors, but at this point, determine whether substantial changes are needed. Underline sections that need attention.

In this step, the ideal scenario is to put away a piece of writing for a few days and come back to it. Then you can look at it with a fresh eye—with the eye of an editor rather than the eye of the writer. But you might not have that luxury. If you are pressed for time, get up, walk around, have a snack, and get some fresh air. Then return to your writing. You will see it from a new perspective.

Read aloud to slow down and "hear" what you have actually written—not what you think is there. The most common errors detected by reading aloud are awkward language, inadequate explanations that confuse the meaning, and too much prose on a particular topic.

As you read and detect weaknesses, you can make simple notes in the margin, such as "fix," "delete," or "explain." If your piece needs substantial revisions, you might need to consider the audience again and ask yourself: "Does the message attract audience attention and meet audience needs? Does the introduction adequately set up the article? Are all the questions raised answered in subsequent paragraphs? Are opening sentences interesting and written to attract an audience to the message?"

To hold the audience to the message, a writer must look at the overall organization and ask the following questions:

- Is the message developed logically? Do facts follow in a clear sequence?
- Is the transition from one point to another effective? Each paragraph should be tied to the previous one.
- Are paragraphs organized so each contains one thought or idea? Readers will be confused if too many thoughts are packaged into one paragraph. Start a new paragraph—basically a unit of organization—with a new quote or a new idea.
- Are there statements or sentences that stop you because they are out of context?
- Do all the quotes add to the message? Would it be better to paraphrase or omit some?

The answers to these questions might require rewriting.

Checking for Completeness. To determine if you need more information, ask the following questions:

- Is the message current? Are the latest statistics used? For example, a television news story on accidental deaths attributed to alcohol must have this year's figures on reported cases, not figures from two years ago, or even last year. Your audience wants to know how serious the situation is today. If those numbers aren't available, you need to say so, and why.

- Are any questions raised left unanswered? Are all essential elements of the message present, including meaningful context? Each message must be complete. A news release that says a company is privately held must define what privately held means.

Answering these questions as you check your content will show how much reporting and rewriting must be done so that copy is complete and flows smoothly and logically.

Checking for Accuracy. Once the content is okay, writers and editors must check for accuracy—an intense, time-consuming job. No aspect of writing is more important than accuracy. Employees might ridicule an executive who includes inaccurate information in memos. Readers turn away from publications and advertisements where they repeatedly find errors. Students lose faith in textbooks when they uncover wrong data.

The bottom line is trust: If your audience doesn't trust the validity of any part of your message, it will question the accuracy of the entire message. Once it loses trust, the audience will be less willing to believe in future communications from you and might move to other media, never to return.

Research has shown that even one error in a newspaper can cause readers to doubt the rest of the paper and to have less faith in the reporter's abilities. Accuracy, therefore, can build or break your reputation, not just the reputation of the medium that carries the message. Use the following steps to check for accuracy:

- Check name spellings. Review your notes. Double-check with the researcher or another writer. Use a telephone book, city directory, or other printed reference. Correct names are essential to avoid confusion—and even legal trouble—when people have the same or similar names. For example, in writing about a nightclub singer named Delsie Harper, a reporter inadvertently left off the D, and the newspaper immediately got a call from a church deacon named Elsie Harper.
- Use reputable sources to confirm information. For example, the city budget director will have more knowledge on changes in the next fiscal year budget than will an anonymous city employee who calls a newspaper to complain.

- Make sure quotes that contain opinion or outrageous claims are attributed, such as this one: "Abused women get what they deserve," a self-proclaimed antifeminist said today. The quote has some credibility with the attribution but would have more if the antifeminist were named.
- If quotes are libelous—that is, damaging to a person's reputation—either make sure they can be defended or cut them. A person's barroom allegation about his next-door neighbor's drug use is not protected by law and should never be published. You could quote a witness's remark in a trial, however, because what occurs in court proceedings is protected. See more about libel in Chapter 12.
- Question statistics. For example, a story reports the president received positive approval from "more than half" of the nation. The actual statistic was 53 percent. The margin of error, or accuracy of the poll, was plus or minus 3 percent. Adding 3 percent to 53 percent means as many as 56 percent of the country support the president. But subtracting 3 percent from 53 percent also means that as little as 50 percent of the nation approve of him. And 50 percent is not more than half. More about math is discussed in Chapter 2.
- Recalculate percentages. Your boss may tell you the company CEO will get only a 7.6 percent pay increase. Check it. A raise from $150,000 to $172,500 is a 15 percent pay increase, not 7.6 percent. The inaccuracy would hardly make other employees confident in the public relations department and its message.
- On technical subjects, when there is doubt about an explanation, call an expert source, and read your material to that person for comment.

Getting information right is also important because inaccuracies are audience-stoppers. When radio listeners hear statistics that they question, they puzzle over the error and no longer hear what you have to say. The best-constructed message framed in the finest form means nothing if your information is wrong or even confusing.

What if you cannot check a fact? Enlist someone else, such as a reference librarian, to verify what is in question. If you cannot verify information and you are working on a deadline, leave it out. If the information is vital to the message and it can't be checked, the message will have to wait. Never publish information if you have doubts about its accuracy. In a professional office, writers have help from editors or fact-checkers. But regardless of who helps, writers ultimately are responsible for the accuracy of their work.

Using Clear Language. In this step, you are looking at word usage that will improve your writing. Consider these questions:

- Is the copy clear and easy to read?
- Are words simple, direct, and easy to understand?
- Are jargon and institutional language eliminated?
- Is redundancy gone?
- Are sentences short and to the point?

This step includes spelling, grammar, and punctuation. In the technological age, many writers use computers with spelling and grammar checking systems. Few spell-checkers adequately check troublesome homonyms, such as "affect" and "effect," "red" and "read," "naval" and "navel," "stationary" and "stationery," "trustee" and "trusty," "lead" and "led," and so on. Chapter 2 contains a guide to spelling in the computer age.

Just as you have to check spelling, you have to review grammar. Chapter 2 discusses common grammar problems; consult the reference books listed in that chapter for additional help.

Writers must be on the lookout for jargon. Such language should be replaced immediately with clearer terms, so that, for example, "organizational inputs" becomes "suggestions from parent groups" and "facilitation of new methodologies" becomes "trying a new survey."

In this step of editing, you also should pay careful attention to word choice. Do you want to refer to a hit man as "specializing in conflict resolution"? Remember: The right word enhances audience understanding and willingness to pay attention, whether the message is read or heard. "Let your conscious be your guide" might not affect listeners. And some readers might not even notice the confused choice of "conscious" for "conscience." Those who do notice will not be impressed. If necessary, review the discussion of word usage in Chapter 4.

If you need to shorten your article, do so by looking at phrases, groups of words, titles, and word usage for shorter ways to state the same idea. For example, the statement "He decided to take part in the debate" could be rewritten "He joined in the debate." Or "The banners that were blue and white fluttered in the breeze" could be changed to "The blue and white banners fluttered in the breeze." More on word usage is found in Chapter 4.

Giving the Piece the Last Once-Over: After revisions are complete, read the entire piece again. At this point, no major reworking should be needed. Check, however, for any editing errors that might have crept in during earlier steps. Check carefully any sections that have been changed. Often, writers make new errors when they revise. The last stage is a final read-through for overall quality and reader appeal. This stage is what some people equate with the term editing. It is the final cosmetic once-over where the writer-editor is pleased with the story. If the writer-editor is not satisfied, then the editing steps should be repeated.

If you have been editing on the computer, you should do one final step: Consult the computer's spelling and grammar checker. It will catch spelling errors and flag repeated words, possible grammar problems, and missing spaces. Such errors often are overlooked.

Some writers may question the sequence in editing. But the reasoning is quite simple: It is efficient. If reviewing for language came first, sentences that had been fine-tuned could be deleted during later content editing. It's far better that the sentences go first. More important, the most critical tasks are done first in case the writer-editor runs out of time. For example, it is more important to write a compelling lead than to smooth out a transition. And it is more important for the piece to be complete and accurate than free of style errors.

Note: Editors should be flexible as they edit. If they see a problem that needs to be fixed, regardless of the step, they should address it then. Editors who wait may forget to make the repair.

Now you might send your copy to your editor or to a corporate executive for review, if you are in an organization or business. If you are an advertising copywriter, the message will go to the account executive and then to the client. In print media, the story will go to an editor and in broadcast, to a news director. If you are a high school principal, your memo might be reviewed by the school system's superintendent before it is sent to parents. If you are a student, you turn the article in to a professor or instructor.

Even if your copy is posted online without ever being edited, your readers will see it, and they won't be shy about letting you know about the errors in your story. Or, even if the grammar is perfect and the facts are correct, the story might change and require you to keep revising the piece with new information.

But do not think that turning in your piece ends the editing process. The copy could come back for another round of editing and changes before publication.

Editing for Online and Other Formats

Online news sites have presented new opportunities for professional communicators. Online news can be published quickly to alert your audience to a breaking news story. But online news—unlimited by the physical space of a print publication or time constraints of a broadcast—can be more in-depth. And, once published, online news often stays online forever and remains findable by anyone with a search engine.

Editors who work online, often called "producers," are often required to work quickly to post stories. But they are also required to be more comprehensive as they enhance the story with photos, audio, and video, and insert links to archive stories or to connect to material on other sites.

Online editors sometimes need to tailor the language of the news for the online audience. People who read news online often are more interested in what is happening now, rather than what is delayed or expected. Online readers often spend no more than a few seconds scanning a story before moving on. This perusal places emphasis on brevity and action.

When working online, editors must remember that their headlines, short descriptions, and key phrases will also function as live links. A click takes the reader to the full story or to a photo essay. So in addition to bearing information, these words must move the reader easily to the related story.

Online news also means more than just Web sites. More and more news is distributed via e-mail or RSS feeds—and is shared by readers on social network sites such as Facebook. Editors should be aware of all the places their words will appear. In some cases—most search engines, for example—only a small portion of the words will appear to the audience. Editors need to stay abreast of continuous changes in tools the audience uses to find your copy.

Regardless of the medium, the same basic editing process is important to a writer's ability to craft a relevant and memorable message.

Well-edited Web sites exploit all the benefits of online communication: brighter pictures, links to original documents or sound, and the potential for instant feedback from an active audience. Readers expect to move quickly among media when they are online—from photos to text to sound to e-mail and back again, many times over in a single seating. Audiences appreciate the extras that come with online stories: more choices, more control, interaction, and variety. Writers and editors must deliver these benefits and remember that one story on a given topic could end up being the only story a reader might see. Editors must check to be sure each story is self-sufficient and fully connected to related materials and sites.

When it comes to feeding content to any Web site, editors function as part of a team that includes artists, writers, photographers, videographers, and others. Even archivists and museum curators get involved when original documents become part of online news. The entire team is important because audiences gravitate toward sites that have strong design and are easily navigated. Content is important, but so is the packaging.

Putting the Editing Rules into Practice

With your knowledge of guidelines for good editing in mind, read the following story:

> A Grove City–area woman has been accused of rigging her ex-husband's washing machine in hopes of torching him and his trailer for the insurance money.
>
> State police at Mercer last week arrested Valerie Norine Lagun, claiming the 43-year-old had hoped to kill semidisabled Thomas Lagun in May when he turned on his washer. She was charged with attempted murder, attempted arson and recklessly endangering another person.
>
> Free on $10,000 bond, Mrs. Lagun is again living with her 57-year-old ex-husband at her home at 458 Blacktown Road, Pine Township, detective Robert Lewis said Tuesday.
>
> "They're still using the washing machine," Lewis said.
>
> According to court papers at District Justice Larry Silvis' Worth Township office, Mrs. Lagun told police she conspired with another man in the plot. She agreed to pay him half of the $5,000 from Lagun's life insurance policy and $10,000 from their renter's insurance.
>
> Police didn't name the man—described as an acquaintance of Mrs. Lagun—because he hasn't been charged, Lewis said. Police know of his whereabouts but are still gathering evidence in hopes of charging him, Lewis said.

According to court papers:

Mrs. Lagun told police she took the man to Lagun's trailer at 169 Jamison Road, Worth Township, after dark.

Once inside, the man wired three bottles containing gasoline to the washing machine. A flip of the washer's switch should have ignited the fire.

"It could've exploded and probably killed him if it blew up. The potential was there," Lewis said.

Lagun discovered the gasoline after an electrical breaker tripped when he attempted to use the machine, according to court papers. He reported the incident to police, and Mrs. Lagun confessed July 24.

She told police she was surprised the explosive didn't work, but happy that her ex-husband wasn't killed, according to court papers.

Mrs. Lagun has a preliminary hearing at 1 p.m. Jan. 8 before Silvis.*

*Reprinted with permission of The Sharon Herald Co.

The story has compelling interest: potential death, oddity in an alleged method of killing someone, human interest because the ex-husband and wife are still living together despite the charges, and the twist about the washing machine.

Consider this edited version of the story that includes most of the original information. But it is rewritten to apply good writing rules and reorganized in a format to pull readers through the story and reward them at the end:

A Grove City–area woman has been accused of rigging her ex-husband's washing machine to explode, killing him and destroying his trailer so she could collect the insurance money. But that's not where the story ends.

Valerie Norine Lagun, 43, was arrested last week by police who claim she had hoped to kill semidisabled Thomas Lagun in May when he turned on his washer. She was charged with attempted murder, attempted arson and recklessly endangering another person.

Mrs. Lagun is free on $10,000 bond and has a preliminary hearing at 1 p.m. Jan. 8 before District Justice Larry Silvis.

According to court papers, Mrs. Lagun told police she conspired with another man and agreed to pay him half of the $5,000 from Lagun's life insurance policy and $10,000 from their renter's insurance.

The man—described as an acquaintance of Mrs. Lagun—hasn't been charged, detective Robert Lewis said Tuesday. Police know of his whereabouts but are still gathering evidence and hope to charge him.

Mrs. Lagun told police she took the man to Lagun's trailer at 169 Jamison Road, Worth Township, after dark. The man wired three bottles containing gasoline to the washing machine. A flip of the washer's switch should have ignited the fire, according to court papers.

Lagun discovered the gasoline after an electrical breaker tripped when he attempted to use the machine, according to court papers. He reported the incident to police, and Mrs. Lagun confessed July 24.

"It could've exploded and probably killed him if it blew up. The potential was there," Lewis said.

Mrs. Lagun told police she was surprised the explosive didn't work, but happy that her ex-husband wasn't killed, according to court papers.

Despite the charges, Mrs. Lagun is again living with her 57-year-old ex-husband at her home at 458 Blacktown Road, Pine Township.

And, noted detective Lewis, "They're still using the washing machine."

The following exercises will require you to apply the guidelines in this chapter. When you have completed them, take a message you constructed during the last week and rewrite it to be clearer and simpler.

Exercises

1. Check your ability to apply the rules you have learned so far. On a separate sheet of paper, copyedit the following sentences according to Associated Press style. Also check for any grammar, spelling, or punctuation errors. Use proper copyediting symbols to save time.

   1. Lieutenant Governor Stanley Greene was stripped of his powers by the N.C. Senate.
   2. William Williams, Dean of the Graduate School of Journalism, will speak to students about graduation requirements on Wed. afternoon.

3. The students are expected to begin the test at 9:00 a.m. Tuesday.
4. The President lives at 1600 Pennsylvania Avenue, but his mail is delivered to the U.S. Post Office on Twenty-second Street.
5. The state Senate is expected to enact a bill to require polio vaccinations for children under the age of two.
6. The airport in Medford, Oregon was closed yesterday after an Alaskan airlines jet made an emergency landing on the runway.
7. The Atty. Gen. has a B.A. in history from American University.
8. The then-Soviet block countries sponsored the Friendship Games rather than attend the 1984 olympics in Los Angeles.
9. The city and county used thirteen busses to transport the children to the July Fourth picnic.
10. Water freezes at 0 degrees Centigrade.
11. Three houses on Sims street were destroyed by the fire, which began at 112 Sims Street.
12. Following the Federal Reserve action, three banks announced a one percent increase in the prime rate, putting it at six percent.
13. The late Senator Jesse A. Helms (R-North Carolina) used to be city editor of The Raleigh Times.
14. John L. Harris, 48 years old, of 1632 Winding Way Road was charged Tuesday with cocaine possession.
15. The champion wrestler measured six feet six inches tall and won 4/5 of his fights.
16. Army Sergeant Willie York was charged with misappropriating $1,000,000 dollars in construction equipment.
17. Hurricane Diana, blowing from the East, caused millions of dollars in damages to the east coast of the United States.
18. Colonel Max Shaw, who has served as a national guardsman for more than 20 years, is Ed's commanding officer.
19. Ability with a frisbee is not a valid measure of IQ.
20. We heard the kickoff announced over the radio at the Laundromat.
21. The stockings were hanged by the chimney with care, in hopes that Kirs Kringle soon would be there.
22. Travelling the 48 miles, or 60 kilometers, to Kansas City, we got 32 miles per gallon in our new minivan.

23. The five-year-old boy got on the wrong bus and was missing for two hours.
24. Sarah sold two hundred and two boxes of Girl Scout cookies to her neighbors on Sweetbriar Pkwy. and Pantego Ave.

2. Read the following message. Assume the audience for this information is readers of the campus newspaper. Using only the available information, edit this message according to Associated Press style, and use proper spelling and grammar. Watch out for usage errors and redundancies.

> All of the faculty members from the School of Journalism and Mass Communication will be attending on Thursday of this week a regional meeting of the Association for Education in Journalism and Mass Communication at the Holiday Inn in the state capitol.
>
> The meeting will commence at 10 a.m. in the morning and conclude at 2 p.m. in the afternoon following a noon luncheon.
>
> In the morning, sessions will offer journalism educators the opportunity to have discussions on current issues addressing journalism and mass communication.
>
> At a luncheon program, professor Walter Blayless will be speaking on the topic of cigarette advertising and the effect on the nation's young people of today.
>
> The meeting sponsored by AEJMC is exemplary of the several regional meetings the organization holds across the country each year. The National meeting is always held in August each year at different locations around the country.

As you edit, make a list of questions you would like to ask about information that would improve the message. Also make a list of the steps you followed in editing. Take these two lists and your edited story to your next class where you can meet with a group of other students to discuss the strengths and weaknesses of various approaches to this editing task.

3. Look at the story you edited in Exercise 2. Now edit it as an online story that will be posted to the campus news Web site on Thursday morning, the day of the meeting. Which elements of the story are now most important to your audience? Is your lead the same? Or did it change? Also, add three links to related content on the Web and determine which words in the story should be linked.

References

Clair Kehrwald Cook, *Line by Line: How to Improve Your Own Writing*. Boston: Houghton Mifflin, 1985.

Norm Goldstein, ed. *The Associated Press Stylebook and Briefing on Media Law*. New York: The Associated Press, 2005.

CHAPTER

4

Guidelines for Good Writing

For years, writing coaches have worked to distill a set of qualities in writing that will catch and hold readers. Many people, such as Roy Peter Clark at the Poynter Institute in St. Petersburg, Florida, have spent a great deal of their professional careers analyzing the qualities of good writing. Authors such as William Zinsser, best known for his book *On Writing Well*, offer advice on how to strengthen and improve prose. Even communication researchers, charged with finding out what makes publications sell, have considered which qualities are valued in messages. The research shows the most effective writing is simple and forceful; that is, it says it straight without flourishes and pomp.

In this chapter, you will learn

- four essential qualities in writing: accuracy, clarity, completeness, and fairness,
- five broad rules for good writing, and
- specific tips to improve writing.

Watchwords of Writing

No message will succeed if it does not have four essential qualities: accuracy, clarity, completeness, and fairness. We know from the discussion in Chapter 1 that audiences can be fickle; once lost, they may not return. Writing that is accurate, clear, complete, and fair has a better chance of holding audiences, particularly those who might be clicking through a Web site or leafing through a magazine.

Accuracy ensures the credibility of all writing. When the audience catches a misspelled name or an erroneous date, it doubts the accuracy of the information that follows. An audience will abandon a communicator it cannot trust.

Clarity means the writer uses language an audience understands. Simple language is preferred over complicated words. Jargon and technical language are avoided. The message comes through.

Completeness anticipates and answers an audience's questions. A complete message satisfies the audience and does so quickly.

Fairness occurs when the writer uses a variety of sources to keep an article balanced, excises any editorial opinion, and is as objective as possible.

Let's look at each element more closely.

Accuracy

Good communication of any kind always contains accurate information. Accuracy is comforting to audiences, who depend on information. Errors can occur at any stage in writing: gathering information through research and interviewing, transcribing notes, calculating figures, and creating the copy (when typos can occur). To ensure accuracy, writers must use good information-gathering techniques. They must obtain information only from reliable sources, then check and recheck it against other sources. If they find a discrepancy or an error but don't have time to check it, they should follow the adage, "When in doubt, leave it out."

We are all prone to committing errors on occasion. Just because a well-known person recites a fact or the fact is found in a computer database does not mean it is correct. The potentate might be wrong, and humans type information into databases. Name spellings, middle initials, street numbers, birth dates—seemingly trivial details—become monumentally important once they become part of a message. Such details might be accurate in notes but then could be transcribed erroneously into copy.

Today's information environment constantly tests accuracy. Deadlines, competition, and 24/7 news cycles push reporters and editors to publish and air the news quickly—sometimes, too quickly. In their hurry to produce copy, writers run a greater risk of getting information wrong.

Errors have always been a danger to a communicator's credibility, but the Internet has made it even more treacherous for writers who don't take the time to get it right. Once incorrect information is cached on the Web, it often remains there for others to pick up and reuse. Always available from search engines, this incorrect information can then be found and repeated by other writers who may also fail to double-check for accuracy.

The ease of publishing information online has made it easier for malicious or lazy writers to spread inaccurate information, but at the same time it has also increased accountability for professional communicators. Some bloggers closely monitor professional news sites, standing ready to criticize inaccuracies. Two of the most prominent sites dedicated to correcting inaccurate information are Snopes.com, a semi-professional site run by a California couple, and Factcheck.org, funded by the Annenberg Public Policy Center of the University of Pennsylvania.

If messages are wrong, people are misled. Writers and audiences rarely forget the mishap when a name is misspelled or an address is wrong. Inaccuracies in messages lead to distrust among audiences—and they can lead to libel suits. Once audience members are misled by a source, they have difficulty trusting it again. Even the venerable *New York Times* has struggled with lost credibility because of inaccuracies. Recently, bloggers have recalled information they posted too quickly, such as reporting that political candidates were dropping out of races or that certain individuals were vice presidential nominees—and none of the information was true.

Clarity

A message will have impact if it is clear and straightforward and everyone in its audience can understand it. "Send a check for $75 by February 1 if you want to ski with the Seniors Club in February" makes the requirement clear. The writing is direct and uses simple, to-the-point language.

A message needs to be so clear that no misunderstanding or confusion can possibly result. People rely on media for information on where to vote, get flu shots, take vacations, enroll their children in school, and find cheap gasoline. If the directions to a polling site are unclear, such as "the church on Capitol Square," people will be unhappy when they arrive and discover a church on each corner of Capitol Square.

Completeness

Useful messages also are complete, giving sufficient information for real understanding and guidance. A news story that omits an important fact can be misleading and even harmful.

When an important highway intersection outside Washington, D.C., was under construction, traffic was rerouted for a 12-hour period. News reports warned drivers about the detour, but some neglected to mention the additional 45 minutes of drive time required to navigate the detour. This problem with completeness caused headaches for the many travelers who missed important appointments.

Fairness

Messages will be more believable if audiences sense the stories are fair. Readers or viewers will turn away from reports they feel are skewed or one-sided.

For a story to be fair or balanced, it must have a variety of sources. That doesn't mean that every story must present each side of an issue in the same detail and the same number of words. Such balance is not possible in most writing. A reporter might not be able to get in touch with sources on one side of an issue, but in the story, the reporter should let readers know that he or she tried.

Writers must be careful about the language they use so audiences don't ascribe any specific leaning or viewpoint to the story. Language should be neutral. Quotes can be inflammatory or weighty—but such language should be reserved to quotes attributed to specific sources, not to the writer.

Keys to Good Writing

Researchers, language professionals, and experienced writers agree on five basic tenets of good writing: (1) use short sentences, (2) use short words, (3) eliminate wordiness, (4) avoid jargon, and (5) come to the point quickly. Anyone can apply the rules while writing and editing.

Good Writing Uses Short Sentences

Most readability experts argue that regardless of age, education, or economic status, people prefer and understand writing that uses short sentences. Humans have little patience with long, complicated sentences that tax their brain power. Of course, not all sentences should be short; sentence length should vary. A short sentence can have impact. A long, complex sentence can set up an idea for the audience or create a mood, and a short sentence can follow immediately—almost as a punch line. Get the point?

A study at the American Press Institute showed that reader understanding drops off dramatically if sentences exceed 20 words, and comprehension continues to drop as sentences grow longer. Only about one of 20 people studied could clearly comprehend 50-word sentences, a common length in newspapers and in academic writing. Short sentences are critical in broadcast writing or descriptive links on Web sites. People tend to skim online news stories more quickly than print stories, and search engines have difficulty classifying Web pages containing more than about 1,000 words.

Short-term memory rarely exceeds 15 seconds, which might not be enough time to read one of the many 50-word sentences in traditional magazines and newspapers. Consider this lead:

> LAS CRUCES—James McDonough has withdrawn his acceptance of New Mexico State University's interim presidency, and the president of the board of regents said he plans to nominate Waded Cruzado, the university's executive vice president and provost, in McDonough's place.

By the time many readers reach the end of this 38-word sentence, they have forgotten whom the Board of Regents named as interim president.

The English language is based on a pattern of simple, subject–verb–object constructions. Most are short. Because people learn and use English this way in everyday life, they prefer this pattern in messages.

Readers would be more likely to warm up to a straightforward approach to the news, such as:

> LAS CRUCES—James McDonough has decided to turn down the offer as interim president of New Mexico State University, citing personal reasons.
>
> A successor has already been identified. Waded Cruzado, the university's executive vice president and provost, will be nominated for the position, said the president of the board of regents.

Retired journalism Professor Fred Fedler of the University of Central Florida said that simplicity makes stories more interesting and forceful. He cites as an example a prize-winning story by World War II journalist Ernie Pyle; the average sentence length was 10.6 words.

Good Writing Uses Short Words

Perhaps your high school English teacher praised you for using "penurious" rather than "stingy," or "inebriated" rather than "drunk." Then you were expanding your vocabulary, but now your audience will thank you for choosing the simpler word.

Just as with long sentences, readers and listeners become tired and discouraged when faced with too many complex words—usually those exceeding three syllables. To be sure, you can use commonly known, longer words, such as "responsibility," "establishment," "participate," and "governmental." Be sure, however, that the longer words are a better choice than a shorter version, such as "duty," "founding," "join in," or "federal" or "state."

When writing, select the simplest word possible to convey the meaning. For example, in a police story, a writer said, "The contents of the suspicious package were innocuous." Some readers might wonder if the contents were dangerous or not. Use "fight" instead of altercation. Replace "finalize" with a word such as "conclude" or "finish." Rather than "exasperate," use "annoy" or "bother." Instead of "terminating" this paragraph, we will "end" it.

Good Writing Eliminates Wordiness

"You can almost detect a wordy sentence by looking at it—at least if you can recognize weak verbs, ponderous nouns, and strings of prepositional phrases," Claire Kehrwald Cook writes in her book, *Line by Line: How to Improve Your Own Writing*. Her advice gives writers clues about where to find wordiness and where to improve sentence structure.

Author William Zinsser notes that the secret to good writing is to strip every sentence to its cleanest components. Writers must detach themselves from the information and chisel it to the bare essentials. Writers must throw out extra words and phrases—even extra sentences and paragraphs. Remember this adage: "Two words are never as good as one." Consider the simple word "new." When used in the following sentence, it is unnecessary: "Crews expect the new building to be completed within two months." All buildings under construction are new. Leave the word out.

Audiences can find the facts only when excess is trimmed. Sparse writing is more professional, more informative, more objective, and more likely to be read. In Saltzman's *If You Can Talk, You Can Write*, writer Stanley Elkin describes the process of eliminating excess in writing: "[It's] a kind of whittling, a honing to the bone, until you finally get whatever the hell you're looking for. It's an exercise in sculpture, chipping away at the rock until you find the nose."

Wordy writing is likely redundant. No writer needs to say a fire "completely destroyed" a downtown block; if it was destroyed, the destruction was complete. This classic often appears: "Jones is currently the manager of consumer services." "Is" means "now," and "now" means "currently." Kill the word "currently." Think about other phrases such as "past history," "acres of land," "4 p.m. in the afternoon," "at 12 midnight," "dead body," and "totally incomprehensible."

In seeking wordiness, look specifically for unnecessary adjectives and qualifiers. For example, a project cannot be the "most" unique. "Unique" means one of a kind. Qualifiers such as "very," "truly," and "really" can generally be cut without damage to copy.

Sometimes a statement or entire paragraph that repeats a speaker's direct quotes can be deleted:

> Jones said he was delighted the school would receive $40,000 to use for purchasing audiovisual equipment materials for the library.
>
> "I am just delighted that we will have the $40,000 to buy audiovisual equipment for the library," Jones said.

Delete the first paragraph. It does more than serve as a transition to the direct quote—it steals it.

As in art, too much embellishment in writing only detracts and distracts. Consider the effectiveness of the following message before and after its extra words are deleted:

> More than 100 years ago, the Tung Wah Dispensary attempted to cure the ailments and afflictions of the San Francisco Chinatown community from its humble outpost at 828 Sacramento Street. When the institution realized that its cramped quarters were counterproductive to the logistics of health care, it expanded its services and relocated to 845 Jackson Street, eventually being renamed the Chinese Hospital.

Simplified, the history looks like this:

> A century ago, the Tung Wah Dispensary treated sickness in San Francisco's Chinatown from its humble outpost at 828 Sacramento Street. Cramped quarters and expanded services led to a new location at 845 Jackson Street, the building that eventually was named the Chinese Hospital.

Without its embellishments—"ailments and afflictions," "institution," and "counterproductive"—this message is much more readable and just as informative.

Good Writing Avoids Jargon or Technical Language

In our high-tech society, so much jargon exists that it is difficult to tell what is jargon and what is plain English. Few people recall that "input" and "output" originated in computer jargon. The same is true of the terms "bottom line," "24/7," and "in the red." The Internet has introduced "google" to mean "look for" and "blog" for weblog as part of common language.

Jargon abounds in everyday life. For example, in listing its objectives for the year, an annual report from an elementary school stated:

> Objective Three: The mean score for the kindergarten program will increase from 5.1 to 5.4 as measured by the FPG Assessment Report. The lead teacher for developmentally appropriate practice coordinated the efforts of our kindergarten teachers to enable our program to meet this objective.

For parents, what does this say? Not much. What is a mean score? What is the FPG Assessment Report? What is developmentally appropriate practice? When people see or hear such words, they stop. Confusion sets in. Parents just want to know how their children are doing in school.

Why Is Jargon Such a No-No? Jargon should be avoided for several reasons. First, it makes too many assumptions about audiences. Technical language reserves a message for insiders: those who are familiar with the lingo. "Outsiders" who could benefit from the information might be put off. For example, an art exhibit notice that contains artistic jargon might scare away potential visitors to the gallery. Technical terms might create a feeling that the gallery is reserved for an elite group. As a result, town residents might feel excluded or perceive the message as exclusive. For the same reason, it is also wise to avoid foreign words and phrases in published writing—unless those words are commonly used, such as *voila*!

Second, jargon is precise only to the insiders who use it. Once again, consider the word "input," which may be anything from telephone conversations to cash contributions. A more specific term is better.

Third, jargon usually is ambiguous. The "bottom line" mentioned in a school newsletter could mean many things: expenditures, income, or both; parent satisfaction; student learning outcomes—or almost anything. Skilled writers avoid vagueness by avoiding jargon.

Of course, whether writers use jargon or technical language depends on the audience. If they are writing for a medical publication whose audience is nurses and doctors, the language can be more specific to that profession.

Too often, though, messages for general audiences or laypeople are filled with educational, legal, economic, or medical jargon. Some technical language has become more understood by the general public, such as "SAT" scores for "Scholastic Assessment Tests" and "AIDS" for "acquired immune deficiency syndrome." But language too often goes unexplained.

Institutional Language. Another problem related to jargon is the use of institutional language: abstract terms and phrases that might communicate well in a specific workplace or institution but that lose meaning for a general audience. For example, medical professionals use the term "treatment modalities." That terminology is nonspecific and lacks meaning and interest, even to a well-educated general audience. Treatment modalities should be named in terms an audience can understand: a series of shots, an antibiotic for 10 days, physical therapy for several months, and so on. It is easy to find words to substitute for institutional terms, and the simpler words are always more specific.

A professor wrote, "Shrinking and unstable sources of funding lead to short-term dislocations." What he meant was a lack of funding interrupts research. Some terms cannot be avoided such as the nation's "gross domestic product (GDP)." Writers must explain such words adequately when they use them. As *The Associated Press Stylebook* explains it, "The gross domestic product is the sum of all the goods and services produced within U.S. borders."

Although institutional language may be the conversational standard at work, it rarely works in writing. When you are talking, you can be sure how much your audience knows about your topic; you can supplement messages with hand gestures, facial expressions, and other visual aids; and you can clarify or define confusing terms if your audience looks puzzled or asks questions.

But when you are writing, your text stands alone and must be absolutely clear. Your goal as a writer is to eliminate misunderstanding, and omitting jargon and technical language is a giant step toward that goal.

Good Writing Comes to the Point Quickly

Chapter 5 will focus on the need for writers to come to the point quickly, perhaps the most problematic of writing challenges. A writer might not want to come to the point because the point is unpleasant: A company has lost money or laid off employees, or a popular program has been discontinued. But audiences see through attempts to delay bad news and interpret them as sneaky ways to hide information. However unwelcome the message, direct communication conveys a feeling of openness and honesty.

Some writers fail to come to the point because they are in "writer's mode," self-indulgently crafting a long introduction to the main points rather than getting to those points. Readers of nonfiction want information rather than art, and they consider the most direct messages to be the greatest masterpieces.

Still other writers have trouble coming to the point because they do not know what the point is. Critical thinking—deciding on the main goal in communicating—precedes every writing task. To come to the point, writers must know their audiences and analyze information carefully enough to know the point audiences will want to know.

Writer and filmmaker Nora Ephron tells a story about her high school journalism teacher. In one lesson, he taught his class to recognize main points by telling them their faculty members would be attending a major conference the next day. He asked them to write a news story about it. In the students' articles, the introductory paragraphs summarized the facts: All teachers would travel to a nearby city and hear famous speakers. After collecting the papers, the teacher threw them away and told the students, "The point is that there will be no school tomorrow." Ephron says she never forgot the point:

> *It was an electrifying moment. So that's it, I realized. It's about the point. The classic newspaper lead of who-what-when-where-how and why is utterly meaningless if you haven't figured out the significance of the facts. What is the point? What does it mean? He planted those questions in my head. And for the first year he taught me journalism, every day was like the first; every set of facts had a point buried in it if we looked hard enough. He turned the class into a gorgeous intellectual exercise, and he gave me enthusiasm for the profession I never lost. Also, of course, he taught me something that works just as well in life as it does in journalism.*

Words

Three of the five keys to good writing just given—using short words, avoiding wordiness, and eliminating jargon—focus on words, the basic unit of any oral or written message. A good writer also needs knowledge of language, a good vocabulary, and the sense to know when a word is inappropriate or unnecessary.

The Power of Little Words

Most of the little words in our language come from the original language spoken in England before Roman and French invaders added their vocabulary to the mix. The English common folk retained their own words for everyday things, and they borrowed from Latin and French only when they had to.

As a result, the things nearest and dearest to us still are called by their original English names—home, fire, food, and mother, for example. And it is these words to which English-speaking people still respond emotionally. The word "home" has much stronger emotional appeal than the cooler, more technical word "domicile," which is borrowed from Latin. Likewise, "food" sounds good; "nutrients," a Latin-based word, is another matter.

How Little Words Are Successful

Professor and writing coach Carl Sessions Stepp says people respond to small words because they usually are "first-degree" words, or words that are immediately understood. Everyone has a single, readily available mental picture of "home," along with a host of meanings and feelings associated with that mental picture. But few people can respond so completely to "domicile." The writer who uses "mother" taps the audience's rich reserves of emotion and information.

Stepp points out that larger, multisyllabic words, many of which have origins in other languages, are "second-degree" words. Such words are abstract rather than concrete. They produce no immediate images in the minds of readers or listeners and are often ambiguous when other information is given. Take, for example, the word "nutrition." Does it mean food substances, or measures of vitamins and minerals? It is a second-degree word because the audience needs more information for full understanding.

Consider other second-degree words, such as "facility" and "output." Compare them with these first-degree words: "school" and "grades."

Stepp argues that writers are more likely to appeal to audiences if they choose first-degree words and avoid second-degree words. In writing, we deal with many second-degree words that are part of science, technology, education, and almost every other field. Writers need to remember to define such words in first-degree terms whenever possible, as in this sentence:

> Nutrition—the kinds of foods patients eat every day—is the topic of a workshop for nurses at Sibley Hospital on Saturday.

Little words are more heart-warming and more easily understood. They also save space, time, and the reader's energy. They are more readable. In an Associated Press article about a Dallas drug bust, the language could not be much simpler (see Box 4.1). Most fifth graders could read the story with very little trouble.

BOX 4.1 Crime, Fear, Poverty—All Part of Life in America

Young Woman's Eyes Reflect Despair of Violent Nation

BY JULIA PRODIS
Associated Press

DALLAS—Her eyes are the color of earth, and as vacant as the lot next door.

She's sitting on a concrete step holding a baby that's not hers. Her 16-year-old friend is lying face down on the sizzling sidewalk beside her, his arms arched awkwardly behind him, his hands cuffed in plastic police ties. A girlfriend is similarly contorted at her feet.

"What's your name?" a policewoman asks this hot August day in Dallas.

In a low, slow whisper, she answers, "Latasha."

"La-what?"

"La-Tasha," the thin, moonfaced 19-year-old says with slightly more effort, her blank gaze never looking higher than the holster holding the officer's 9 mm semiautomatic.

Minutes ago, eight muscular members of the Dallas drug enforcement squad, wearing black boots and bulletproof vests, had stormed the faded yellow bungalow behind her. It took two heaves of "the slammer" to break down the door, blocked only by an empty bookcase.

Shrieks from inside, then blurs of motion as the young man bolted out the rear and the woman ran toward the back fence. Latasha

Smith never said a word, and the baby didn't cry.

She has the dull look of someone who had seen this rerun too many times. Her look of despair, so deep it turns everything gray, is the same look that flattens the faces of the young and hopeless in poor, violent American neighborhoods everywhere.

Neighborhoods where crack heads fear friends and neighbors more than the cops. Where homes are so filthy detectives can't pickup evidence without something crawling on it. Where neighbors scatter when someone screams for help.

For Americans who say crime is their gravest concern, these calloused Latashas and their criminal friends stir angry fear. But for Latasha, it's just another day.

The baby with cocoa skin and wavy brown hair spits up on Latasha's chest as she rocks negligibly back and forth. Indifferently, she wipes his face with her droopy white tank top.

"Who's payin' for that baby?" the policewoman asks.

"It ain't MY baby," she retorts.

"It's my baby," says the 16-year-old boy, squirming awkwardly on the sidewalk. As he strains to lift his head to speak, the pebbles clinging to his cheek dribble to the ground.

Latasha tells the officer she has three children of her own and she's on welfare. She quit the last job she had washing dishes because she didn't like it. Her children are scattered with relatives and friends today.

"Did you grow up like this baby is growing up?" the reporter asks.

"My daddy shot my momma dead when I was 2." She speaks flatly, like a kid bored with homework. She was raised by her grandfather.

She doesn't explain why she is at this house that isn't hers holding somebody else's baby.

An undercover officer recently bought drugs at this house. The police had come back to clean it up and close it down—one of nearly 400 Dallas dope houses stormed this year.

After running background checks on the three, the sergeant in charge decides to arrest the handcuffed youths on drug charges and ticket Latasha for failing to appear in court after being cited for driving without insurance.

"Do you ever dream of a better life?" the reporter asks.

She shrugs.

She doesn't watch the van carry her two friends away. She just sits in front of the house with the For Rent sign and the broken door, holding someone else's baby, and stares blankly at the vacant lot next door.

The Right Word

Wordsmiths such as the late Theodore Bernstein and the late John Bremner have long decried the lack of precision in language. Bremner lamented what he called "the surge of literary barbarism" in English usage. Both stressed the importance of knowing language and definitions. To language lovers like

Bremner, writing is a love affair with language. In his book, *Words on Words*, Bremner wrote,

> *To love words, you must first know what they are. Yes, words are symbols of ideas. But many words have lives of their own. They have their own historical and etymological associations, their own romantic and environmental dalliances, their own sonic and visual delights.*

A careless writer describes a basketball player as "an intricate part of the team." Perhaps his footwork is intricate, but what the writer really meant to say was "an integral part of the team."

A letter from a university provost to a newspaper columnist thanked her for "the prospective" she gave to a local issue. The provost meant "perspective."

In a news story, a student quoted a speaker as saying the decision "reaped haddock" on the school's admissions procedures—a fishy end to "wreaked havoc." Language needs to be specific and correct. When writers misuse or misspell words, such as "brew ha-ha" for "brouhaha," we laugh. As writers, we do not want our audiences laughing at us—unless we mean for them to chuckle.

Similar Words

Words that sound alike are troublesome for writers. Among the most common homonyms are "principal" and "principle," "affect" and "effect," and "its" and "it's." Such words are particularly troublesome today when writers depend heavily on computer spell-checkers. Few programs will know the difference between "naval" and "navel" or "stationary" and "stationery," as we discussed in Chapter 2. The resulting confusion can be misleading and embarrassing. Writers must be comfortable in reaching for a good dictionary or other reference books to check correct spelling and usage. Other references, such as those listed at the end of this chapter, are valuable for writers who are choosy about words. Refer to Chapter 2 for help with spelling in the computer age.

Writers should pay heed to synonyms. Many writers haul out the thesaurus when they are weary of using a word too often. But a synonym might not be specific. One editing teacher advises against using a thesaurus and prefers a dictionary. Remember that repetition of a word or words throughout a message is acceptable. Repetition can unify a message. For instance, use the phrase "online news site" throughout a story about the launch of a television station's Web site. It unifies the story and is more specific than "media product."

Word Choice

While taking care with word usage, writers should strive to choose words that are universally accepted and understood. If they are unsure about a word or its use, they should consult a stylebook or a dictionary. *The Associated Press Stylebook*, for example, adds cautionary notes about how specific words in its entries should be used. The note might warn that the word is offensive or derogatory. Dictionaries will include in the definition whether the word is below the normal standard for literate writing. Dictionaries also will indicate spellings of words and correct usage, as in the case of homonyms.

If a dictionary or a stylebook warns against usage of a word, as profanity perhaps, writers should use it only if they have a compelling reason. They might also have to explain in a note at the beginning of the article or the broadcast that the message contains offensive language. Using profanities and vulgarities is discussed more fully in Chapter 10 on quotes and attribution.

Sentences

Sentences should be complete. Each must have a subject and a verb and must state one complete idea, thought, or meaning. Granted, some writers use short but incomplete sentences for emphasis, such as "The day he left was cold and in the dead of winter. January 22, to be exact." Sentence fragments or stray phrases generally have little place in straight writing, and beginning writers should avoid using them.

This is a fragment: "January 22, to be exact."
This is a sentence: "The day he left was cold and in the dead of winter."
This is a sentence: "That day was January 22, to be exact."

Sentence Types

Grammarians define different types of sentences on the basis of structure.

- A simple sentence is one independent or main clause. It can have more than one subject and verb, object, and modifying phrase.

The tanker ran aground, spilling 11 million gallons of crude oil into the bay.

Six seniors and two juniors are on the University's debate team.

- A compound sentence has two or more simple sentences that may be joined by a conjunction such as "and" or "but" or by punctuation such as a semicolon.

  Homer used his share of the settlement to buy a fishing boat, but within two years his business was bankrupt.

  Many people have changed their diets to cut out high-fat foods; others have ignored warnings that a high-fat diet might cause heart disease.

- A complex sentence has at least one independent or main clause and other clauses dependent on the main clause.

  Downloading applications on a social networking site might open your private information to third parties, despite your belief those details are locked away from public view.

- A compound-complex sentence is a compound sentence with at least two independent clauses and one or more dependent clauses.

  When the album was released in May, investors expected it to do well, but it zoomed to No. 2 on the charts, exceeding all their hopes.

Vary Sentence Types

Good writers use a variety of sentence types, but they prefer the simple sentence. A good guideline is to use many simple sentences and to use compound sentences formed from short simple sentences.

Writers use complex sentences because of the need for attribution, amplification, and identification. But they work hard to avoid compound-complex sentences, saving them to express ideas difficult to state any other way.

Studies show that people of all ages and levels of education prefer simple sentences, in which subjects come before verbs and verbs before the remainder of the sentence. A series of simple sentences relaxes your readers or listeners and prepares them to encounter something more complex when it occurs in your text, as it inevitably will.

Look at the sentence variety in the story by Alison Delsite of *The Patriot-News* in Harrisburg, Pa., in Box 4.2. She uses a mix of complex sentences and simple sentences. Paragraph 5 is one complex sentence. But in the next paragraph a series of short, simple sentences carries the action.

BOX 4.2 Life-Saving Tickets Win Fame, but No Fortune

BY ALISON DELSITE
The Patriot-News

Patrick Gayle's lottery tickets weren't losers after all.

Not only did they help deflect a bullet and possibly save the Harrisburg man's life, they brought him a few days of fame and, maybe, a little extra cash.

Gayle was interviewed on CNN. Crews from TV's "Hard Copy" taped a segment outside the Allison Hill convenience store where he was shot.

He was interviewed for publications nationwide, including The National Enquirer and a lottery magazine in Florida. He did radio shows. "I told them, 'I feel blessed,'" Gayle says.

On April 23, Gayle was walking into a Regina Street store to play the Daily Number when he was struck by a bullet during a shooting that police say was a continuation of the longstanding Allison Hill-Uptown rivalry.

The bullet was deflected by a cigarette lighter and a wad of tickets in his shirt pocket. The lighter shattered. The tickets were tattered. The shirt had a hole in it. He wasn't injured.

The Patriot-News story about the shooting made the Associated Press' wire. Since then Gayle's phone has been ringing.

Edward Meyer, vice president for exhibits at Ripley's Believe It or Not, said Ripley's intends to do a cartoon on Gayle and hopes to purchase his tickets. For now, they are evidence, in the custody of Harrisburg police.

Meyer wouldn't say how much Ripley's would pay. "Probably a couple hundred dollars. Stories like this are right up our alley," he said. "We'll make it worth his while, but not make him rich." Gayle, a forklift driver, said he spends $40 a day on the lottery.

Meanwhile, the phone in Patrick Gaylor's home in Swatara Twp. also has been ringing.

It seems callers—including ones from TV's Montel Williams and Maury Povich shows—unable to find Gayle's number, have called Gaylor's instead.

"They ask, 'Are you the person who was shot and saved by a pack of lottery tickets?'" said Gaylor. "No," he laughs. "But I hope he makes a lot money off it anyway."

Common Sentence Errors

In constructing sentences, some writers forget the rule of parallel structure, noted as a grammar problem in Chapter 2. In writing, all parts of any list or series must be parallel—that is, if the first element in the list starts with a noun, all others must be nouns as well. For example, the structure of this sentence is not parallel:

> Plaintiffs reacted to the court's decision with sorrow, rage, surprise, and vowing to appeal the ruling.

Nouns in the list, "sorrow, "rage" and "surprise," are not parallel with the verb form "vowing." The sentence should be rewritten to read:

> Plaintiffs reacted to the court's decision with sorrow, rage, surprise, and vows to appeal the ruling.

When writers start with a specific verb form, such as an infinitive with "to," they must keep the same format. The structure of the following sentence is not parallel:

> In the new budget, the county will have funds to expand social services, to hire five police officers, and for adding bike lanes to Main Street.

It should be rewritten to read:

> In the new budget, the county will have funds to expand social services, to hire five police officers, and to add bike lanes to Main Street.

Another common sentence error is the incorrect placement of modifying phrases or clauses. Such misplaced elements can lead to humorous and misleading sentences, such as the following:

> After wheeling me into the operating room, a mask was placed over my face.

> The bank makes low-interest loans to individuals of any size.

> Mrs. Rogers was arrested shortly after 3 p.m. at the home where the couple lived without incident.

Once spotted, modifier problems are easy to repair. Good writers train themselves to check modifier placement: Did the mask really wheel me into the operating room? Does the bank make loans based on height and weight? Did the couple really live in the house without incident? The questions can be cleared up by quick rewriting:

> After I was wheeled into the operating room, a mask was placed over my face.

> The bank makes low-interest loans of any size to individuals.

> Mrs. Rogers was arrested without incident shortly after 3 p.m. at the home where the couple lived.

A good sentence can never be interpreted to mean more than one thing. Linguists say it has a "single reading"—meaning the reader never needs to go back and read it again to understand it. If the reader goes back, it should be to savor the quality of the writing. Good writing aims for a single reading, so readers move unobstructed through messages to meaning. Once they understand the message, then readers can act or react—and communication is complete.

Paragraphs—Short Paragraphs

Words become sentences, and sentences become paragraphs. English composition books devote entire chapters to the topic of writing good paragraphs. When writers are concerned with transmitting information quickly, their ideas about paragraphing change. A paragraph is a whole presentation or argument on a topic in an essay for an English composition or literature class, whereas in mass communication, a paragraph is a single fact, thought, or "sound byte." That single thought or idea might take several sentences to explain. In newswriting, paragraphs often are short to break up blocks of gray copy. Journalists talk about "graphs," a shortened version of "paragraphs." One thought or idea is in a graph, and graphs are one sentence on occasion.

Effective use of three graphs of varying lengths is shown in the opening of this story written by *St. Pete Times* reporter Michael Kruse to describe damage from Hurricane Katrina:

> WAVELAND, Miss.—City Hall is gone.
>
> The post office is gone.
>
> The restaurants, the condos, the houses. Gone, gone, gone.
>
> In this coastal town of about 7,000 people, on a wide swath of land that stretches about a mile up from the Gulf of Mexico, almost everything south of the railroad tracks is gone.

Newspaper and magazine writers start a new graph to signal a new fact or a change of speaker—and sometimes just to give the reader a break. Readers appreciate white space in a publication, and frequent "graffing," as it is called, gives such visual relief by making space—literal and figurative—between ideas.

New Speaker Equals New Paragraph

One of the most useful functions of frequent graffing is that it effectively signals a change of speakers. Notice how Associated Press writer Timberly Ross moves smoothly from one quote to another, just by starting new graphs and giving background in between. The story focused on a tornado that hit a Boy Scout camp:

> Taylor Willoughby, 13, said several scouts were getting ready to watch a movie when someone screamed that there was a tornado. Everyone hunkered down, he said, and windows shattered.
>
> "It sounded like a jet that was flying by really close," Taylor told NBC's "Today" on Thursday. "I was hoping that we all made it out OK. I was afraid for my life."
>
> Ethan Hession, also 13, said he crawled under a table with his friend.
>
> "I just remember looking over at my friend, and all of a sudden he just says to me, 'Dear God, save us,'" he told "Today."
>
> "Then I just closed my eyes and all of a sudden it's (the tornado) gone."

With quotations, the short graph adds a lively, conversational air to newswriting and holds the audience's attention. "New speaker, new graph" is a writer's rule that can add clarity to all writing.

Most writing can benefit from shorter paragraphs. Bite-sized paragraphs may not be appropriate in all settings, but leaner paragraphs tend to streamline messages of all kinds, saving time and space—the most precious resources in any medium.

The Way to Clearer Writing

Writing often moves from the general to the specific, and this chapter is following such a path. At the outset, we discussed broad principles of accuracy, clarity, completeness, and fairness. We then looked at the basic tenets of good writing and the components of any piece of writing—words, sentences, and paragraphs—as summarized in Box 4.3. When listed, the rules seem more manageable.

Now for the specifics. Additional guidelines can help you say it straight. Keep the guidelines in mind as you write, but do not be so tied to them that you stop after every sentence to analyze whether it meets the standards of good writing. Go ahead and write, then go back and apply the guidelines.

BOX 4.3 Good Writing Rules

1. Good writing uses short sentences.
2. Good writing uses short words.
3. Good writing eliminates wordiness.
4. Good writing clears away redundancy, jargon, and institutional language.
5. Good writing comes to the point quickly.
6. Good writing has a mix of sentence types.
7. Good writing has short paragraphs.

Write the First Draft as You Would Say It

Writing coach Robert Gunning said writers should write the way they talk. He argued that all writing would improve if people simply talked and wrote down what they said. Gunning was onto a great idea: First drafts are most effective when a writer puts down on paper what he or she would tell someone about a topic. Most people talk in subject–verb–object order that is easy to understand. The result is text that is conversational, uses simple language, and is easy to revise into a well-organized written message.

Colorful Description

Author Tom Wolfe made his mark among fiction writers by writing the way he talks—frankly, and with rich description. In his bestseller, *The Bonfire of the Vanities*, Wolfe describes Maria, the girlfriend of his anti-hero, Sherman McCoy:

> *Now Maria pushed the door all the way open, but instead of ushering him inside, she leaned up against the doorjamb and crossed her legs and folded her arms underneath her breasts and kept staring at him and chuckling. She was wearing high-heeled pumps with a black-and-white checkerboard pattern worked into the leather. Sherman knew little about shoe designs, but it registered on him that this one was of the moment. She wore a tailored white gabardine skirt, very short, a good four inches above the knees, revealing her legs, which to Sherman's eyes were like a dancer's, and emphasizing her tiny waist. She wore a white silk blouse, open down to the top of her breasts. The light in the tiny entryway was such that it threw her entire ensemble into high relief: her dark hair, those cheekbones, the fine features of her face, the swollen curve of her lips, her creamy blouse, those creamy flan breasts, her shimmering shanks, so insouciantly crossed.*

In this passage, all parts of speech become part of the description. The verbs are active: pushed, leaned, folded, worked, and threw. The nouns—doorjamb, pumps, flan, shanks—are concrete and tangible, and the adjectives appeal to the senses: high-heeled, black-and-white, checkerboard, tailored, fine, swollen, creamy, and shimmering. All writers can learn from Wolfe's gift for conversational, dense description that leaves readers with strong sensory images.

Don't Begin at the Beginning

After seeing a four-car collision, the typical observer arrives home and blurts out: "I saw an incredible wreck on Highway 501. Four cars collided; all the drivers were injured, and one car burned." Only then will the observer back up and give background: "I was in the left lane, coming home from the mall," and so on.

Like urgent conversation, writing needs to jump straight to the point, then fill the reader in—just as we will discuss in Chapter 5 on writing leads. This technique gives writing a conversational tone and at the same time gets to the ever-so-important point of the message.

Starting with salient facts is a natural way to tell about important information. Unfortunately, it is a form that most people forget after years of reading stories and writing essays, both of which usually start with formal introductions. If your goal is to say it straight, say it—your main point—soon in your message. Suspenseful beginnings work best in drama.

Writing and Editing: Two Compatible Tasks

When you spill out your conversational first draft, write it without stopping to edit. Mixing writing and editing wastes time and effort. If you edit as you go (and most amateurs do), you might fuss over a sentence you eventually cut. At the very least, you will interrupt your own thought processes and conversational flow. So write first. If you pause to ponder sentence structure or information, that's okay. But do not wander or stray from the effort.

Some beginning writers lack the confidence to sit down and write. But author Joel Saltzman points out that we all are more competent wordsmiths than we think:

> *When you're talking, odds are that 98 percent of the time you don't even think about grammar. You're doing fine and it's just not an issue.... I am suggesting that you don't worry about it right now; because the more you worry about grammar, the less you're going to write.*

Stick with Subject–Verb Order

Most human languages prefer to place subjects before verbs, and English is no exception. Curious people want to know who did something, then what they did (and to whom or what). Keep these audience interests and preferences in mind when you write. Subject–verb–object order generally gives the sentence action.

> Soldiers of the People's Liberation Army cleared rocks the size of houses from blocked roads.

> A massive earthquake registering 6.8 on the Richter scale rocked Japan early Tuesday morning.

Readers get confused if subjects and verbs are scrambled, regardless of how artistic the result may be:

> Came he swiftly to her bower?

Not in the information age.

Choose Active Verbs

Verbs are action words, but not all verbs are active. Some show no action at all, such as the verb "to be" in all its forms (is, am, are, was, were, be, being). Such verbs are less interesting and harder to picture than active verbs.

Writers prefer active verbs because they contain more information and sensory detail. "He was president" is vague compared with "He dominated the country as president." "Lightner whacked the ball with such force that it sailed over the right outfield wall" evokes the sound of the bat striking the ball. Good writing is filled with active verbs that evoke images in the mind of the reader or listener. In the following lead, the writer uses active verbs in a weather story:

> MOSCOW, Ind. (AP)—Tornadoes ripped through this central Indiana community and skipped over National Guard barracks full of sleeping soldiers as thunderstorms battered the Ohio Valley, authorities said Wednesday.

Choose the Active Voice

When writers use active verbs, they write in active voice.

"Lightner whacked the ball." The subject, Lightner, performs the action. The object, the ball, receives action. This sentence format is called *active voice*, and it is the natural order of English. "A man wearing a stocking mask robbed the university dining hall" carries more action than "the university dining hall was robbed by a man."

Every now and then, a sentence has no obvious subject and must be written in another format, called the *passive voice*. Take, for example, this sentence: "The law was changed several years ago." It is in passive voice. The recipient of the action, the law, has been moved into the subject position—probably because a long legislative process kept the writer from isolating a single person or session responsible for changing the law.

Research shows that people prefer active sentences over passive ones. The sentence "Congress passed the bill" is easier to read and comprehend than its passive equivalent, "The bill was passed by Congress." Skilled writers prefer the active voice and use passive sentences only when necessary. In our example about Lightner, a passive structure would hardly have the same effect: "The ball was whacked by Lightner."

Sometimes writers use passive sentences for emphasis: "The anticrime bill that will give police departments more powers was passed by Congress." Here the writer wants to focus on the provisions of the bill rather than on congressional action and writes the lead accordingly.

Generally Put Time Elements after the Verb

Because verbs are stimulating to readers, they should come before less interesting elements. Audiences need to know when something happened, but they can wait to find out. The time element, a necessary but often dull part of a message, can be relegated to a place after the verb. Some writers prefer to put it immediately after the verb. Here are a few examples:

> The second annual Wiener Festival, featuring dachshunds of all sizes and breeds, will be held Saturday in Laurel.

> Grant applications requesting up to $100,000 for research on learning disabilities may be submitted through June 15 to the National Institutes of Health.

Sometimes, however, the time element carries importance and needs to go elsewhere—even first in the sentence:

> On Wednesday, a 14-year-old youth collected $125,000 he found in a paper bag a year ago. No one claimed the money.

In the above example, the beginning and end of the sentence set up the time span: On Wednesday, the youth cashed in after waiting a year.

> Beginning July 1, North Carolina residents will need to show their Social Security cards or verify their numbers when getting new or replacement driver's licenses.

Right away, people know the laws will change.

Be Specific

Always give the most specific information you can. Significant details enlighten and delight readers and pack information into a few words. Instead of saying singer Mariah Carey went shopping, tell what she bought: cosmetics. What kind? Inquiring minds want to know! Instead of saying a reporter had a messy desk, try:

> On his desk, Howard had a can of unsharpened pencils and two potted ferns, both of them dead.

Watch out for words that have almost a generic quality, such as "facility." Be specific: bank, gymnasium, recreation center, high school. Use the specific noun.

Author Tom Wolfe has a marvelous talent for combining simple words into colorful, entertaining description. In *The Bonfire of the Vanities* excerpt we discussed earlier, Wolfe creates pictures with his prose. Like other excellent writers, he uses language to appeal to the senses. Wolfe gives specific details, such as the skirt riding "a good four inches above the knees" and the "checkerboard pattern worked into the leather." His technique is one that all good writers use, regardless of the medium.

Appeal to the Senses

Whether reading or listening, an audience still can use the full range of senses as it absorbs information. That means writers must pay attention to their senses when gathering information. Writers can report the facts or describe the scene without being subjective—a fear that keeps many beginning writers from using descriptive writing.

Through writing that appeals to the senses, *New York Times* reporter Mark Landler takes readers inside an Austrian monastery:

> HEILIGENKREUZ, Austria—As noon draws near, the monks glide into the church, their white cowls billowing behind them. They line up in silence, facing each other in long choir stalls. Wood carvings of saints peer down on them from the austere Romanesque nave.
>
> Bells peal and the chant begins—low at first, then swelling as all the monks join in. Their soft voices wash over the ancient stones, replacing the empty clatter of the day with something like the sound of eternity.
>
> Except, that is, for the clicks of a camera held by a photographer lurking behind a stone pillar.
>
> It has been like this since last spring, when word got out that the Cistercian monks of the Stift Heiligenkreuz, deep in the Vienna woods, had been signed by Universal Music to record an album of Gregorian chants.

The reader sees the monks and senses the stillness that precedes the bells and chanting. Writing that creates mental pictures, aromas, and sensations is more memorable and more appealing because it transports the audience to the scene of the message. Once captured, the audience is likely to remain in the writer's world long enough to get the message.

You don't need to be a feature writer to use sensory appeal. It works well in everyday forms of communication, such as directions to the company picnic. Instead of "turn right two blocks after the fork in the road and proceed to 1511," how about:

> Look for a grove of tall pines two blocks after the fork in the road; turn right and go to the red mailbox marked 1511. You'll smell pungent smoke from Marvin's famous barbequed ribs.

With such sensory appeal, it is doubtful anyone will get lost.

Use Statistics Sparingly and Powerfully

We live in an era where numbers make powerful messages: A basketball arena will cost $121 million. A pharmaceutical company will lay off 1,600 workers.

Audiences become desensitized if bombarded by alarming numbers, regardless of how striking those numbers may be. Statistics of any kind should be delivered one at a time. Never let two numbers touch in written copy; avoid putting numbers close to one another except in direct comparisons:

> The report assumes oil prices ranging from a low of $113 a barrel to as high as $186 a barrel by 2030; a barrel was trading above $133 on Wednesday.

Another good rule of thumb is to limit yourself to no more than three numbers in any paragraph to avoid overwhelming your reader or listener. In a business story, for example, numbers can be confusing, so spread them out and keep them simple. Consider the following lead packed with numbers:

> Dr. Marcy LePique, a Flagstaff obstetrician and gynecologist since 2003, has delivered more than 10,000 babies and about 20 litters of puppies in her 25-year career as a physician and 30-year career as a breeder of golden retrievers.

Professor Emeritus Philip Meyer, a former consultant at *USA Today*, suggests that in any statistical report one or two numbers stand out as crucial. The important numbers should appear early in your message, and others may be summarized in lists or tables outside the written text.

Translate Statistics into Everyday, Tangible Terms

People have little intuitive understanding of large numbers. The citizen who learns that a sports arena will cost $121 million is left with many questions: Is that a good price for an arena? How many new schools would that buy? How much will my county taxes increase?

Good writers provide an understanding of big numbers in several ways. One way is to compare one number with another:

> The $121 million price tag compares with the $58.2 million cost of an arena built in 1989 in Springfield.

Another way to present numbers is to give them in terms the average person deals with each day. Few of us can visualize $121 million, but many people can understand a 3.5 percent tax increase to fund the stadium.

The clearest way to present costs is to use an individual citizen as an example:

> A person owning a home with a tax value of $154,000 will pay about $200 more each year in taxes to finance the arena.

Such writing allows the audience to understand personal gains or losses that may be obscured in reports of large numbers.

Double-Check Your Math

Many writers jokingly say they went into communications because they could not do math. But any writer needs to use numbers and must be sure they are correct. Errors can be embarrassing.

In a news story about salary increases at city hall, a reporter looked at the current year's salary for the city attorney: $130,000. The proposed salary for the next fiscal year was $138,000. The city attorney would get a 5 percent pay increase, she wrote. The actual increase was 6 percent. The reporter erroneously divided the difference of $8,000 by the new salary rather than the current salary. Other city employees were upset that the city attorney was getting 5 percent compared with their 2 percent. When the real difference eventually was published, the unhappiness grew. (And the city attorney expressed his anger that the figures were published at all, forgetting that the salaries of public officials are public record.)

When in Doubt, Leave It Out

Unless you check the accuracy of a number, spelling, or surprising fact, leave it out or hold publication until you can verify it. Accuracy is linked, in the minds of audience members, with quality—with media quality and writer quality. Your reputation is riding on what you write.

Some errors are painful to people in the community. A university magazine noted offhandedly that a famous scientist had discovered a new kind of plant. His research assistant, who in fact had made the discovery and received credit for it in scientific journals, called the reporter to correct the error. Few people will ever see a small correction notice, but people such as the offended research assistant will remember the slight for years.

Mistakes, no matter where they appear, also may lead to legal problems. Chapter 12 discusses libel.

Rewrite Long Introductory Phrases

Audiences are eager to get to the point, and long introductory phrases slow them down. Long phrases also interrupt the subject–verb–object pattern that readers and listeners prefer.

Avoid:

Because the Cardinals had been waiting all season for a victory and had received what they considered to be negative media attention, several players refused to be interviewed.

Prefer:

Several Cardinals players refused to be interviewed after a winless season amid negative media coverage.

Eliminate Long Strings of Prepositional Phrases

Any group of two or more prepositional phrases makes a sentence meander rather than flow. Too many prepositional phrases strung together within a sentence are undesirable but easy to fix. Prepositional phrases are among the movable parts of any sentence; they also can be placed in new (short) sentences.

Avoid:

The school's marching band will appear in a series of performances on three consecutive Tuesday afternoons on the athletic field near the gymnasium on the school campus beginning this Tuesday.

Prefer:

The school's marching band will present a series of Tuesday afternoon performances beginning this week. The band will play on the athletic field near the gymnasium.

Look for unnecessary prepositional phrases everywhere in writing. Take

> Marilyn Jacobs, one of the writers of the letter, said the group wants action immediately.

and edit it to read

> Marilyn Jacobs, who helped write the letter, said the group wants action immediately.

Avoid Making Everything Look IMPORTANT

Some writers like to add emphasis by underlining text or using capital letters, exclamation marks, bold type, and even quotation marks. Frequent use of such elements detracts from professional polish. Once in a while, everyone needs to add emphasis. Save it for when it really counts. In some messages, such emphasis can be interpreted as anger, exasperation, and even sarcasm.

Avoid a message that looks like this sentence:

> If you don't get your information sheet in today, you WON'T be in the new directory AT ALL.

Try:

> If you don't get your information sheet in today, you won't be in the new directory.

Clear Out Euphemisms

Most of us were taught to use euphemisms in polite conversation—to say "expecting" rather than "pregnant," "plump" rather than "fat," and "passed away" rather than "died." Most euphemisms are designed to be imprecise—to mislead or give false comfort. In fact, we like euphemisms because they are handy substitutes for embarrassing words. In media, straight talk is preferred.

Avoid:

The guard said two residents of the correctional facility had gone to "their just reward."

Prefer:

The guard said that two prisoners had died.

Using the straightforward "prisoners" and "died" instead of the longer euphemisms keeps the sentence short and the reading easy. Once euphemisms are removed, the meaning is clear and timeless.

Watch Out for Language Trends

Writers should avoid popular trends in writing that substitute a myriad of words and phrases for ones that had been part of common language. In many cases, the new language is wordy and less precise.

The use of such "pop" language excludes segments of the audience that might not be cued to the lingo. Certainly language evolves. Each time a new edition of *Webster's Dictionary* comes out, new words are included. Many of us can remember when "ain't" was not in the dictionary. Dictionaries list and define words common in the English language, but a dictionary is just one of many sources writers use.

One trend that has caused extreme pain to language experts is the conversion of nouns to verbs. Host has become "to host," and conference has become "to conference." An advertising director notified clients: "We will deadline ad copy for Friday's paper on Wednesday." Many computer terms already are accepted usage, but some writers still cringe when they hear nouns such as "text" used as a verb for the act of contacting someone via the short messaging service on a mobile phone or "fiend" as a verb for the act of connecting with another user's profile on a social networking site.

Another trend that offends many writers is the addition of "-ize" to create new words: "prioritize," "finalize," "maximize," "accessorize." Again, although the words have found their way into everyday usage, language professionals try to find better and more accurate verbs.

Keep Writing Readable

Readability is defined most simply as the level of difficulty of a given message. Readable, or high-readability, writing is easy to understand. Several ways to measure readability have been found, most of which are based on (1) sentence length and (2) concentration or number of multisyllable words.

One common readability measure is the Fog Index, developed in the 1940s by Robert Gunning for United Press International wire service. Despite its age, the Fog Index is still used as a measure of readability. To compute a Fog Index, (1) calculate the average number of words per sentence in a given message and (2) count the number of difficult words, or those with three syllables or more, in a 100-word sample from the message. Add these two figures together and multiply by 0.4.

The resulting number—the Fog Index—corresponds to the number of years of education a reader would need to read and understand the copy. For example, a publication with an average of 22 words per sentence and 15 difficult words in the 100-word sample would have a Fog Index of 14.8. That means its readers would require some college education to read the piece comfortably.

Most readability experts agree that clear writing is geared to the 11th- and 12th-grade levels. Even people with a great deal more education seem most comfortable reading at this level. Many grammar-check software packages have readability measures that automatically tell writers the readability of any piece. *The Wall Street Journal's* Fog Index routinely falls into the 11th- to 12th-grade range, despite the complicated nature of financial reporting. A clever marketing strategy is operating here: Dow Jones knows that to make business reports palatable, they must be readable.

Exercises

1. Change the words used incorrectly in the following sentences:
   - The perspective budget for the coming year will include raises for the city's fire fighters.
   - An incoming ice storm will effect whether we can drive to work tomorrow.
   - The state historical society will reenact signing the state constitution in the Capital.
   - The country's navel force has been reduced.
   - His desire for money is his principle guiding force in business.
   - The coach said the team ignored his advise to make it a passing game.

- Jiminy Cricket said Pinocchio should let his conscious be his guide.
- The engineer eliminated the High Road sight because it sloped to much.
- Returning the stolen car to it's owner is the best decision.
- The most affective writing follows good writing principals.

2. Edit the following sentences to make them shorter and to the point:

- In order to expedite the delivery, the company will add a third delivery truck for its routes on Monday.
- We will have pizza for dinner whether or not you choose to come.
- She is presently employed as the assistant to the president, but she expects to make a decision whether or not to change jobs by the end of the year.
- If they are willing to pay the difference between the economy pack and the family pack, customers will learn that the family pack will save them more money in the long run.
- Students voted Thursday to conduct a poll to determine the status of living conditions in dormitories.
- Clarendon Park residents will march Saturday to protest the city council's decision to annex the neighborhood over residents' objections.
- If the school maintains lines of communication and makes the alumni feel as if they are still a part of the school even though they have already graduated, the school should have no problem reaching its fund-raising goal.
- The residents of the neighborhood said they would petition the city council to reconsider again the decision to allow beer sales before 11 a.m. on Sunday morning, which would be against the wishes of many church-going citizens.
- Fifteen scholarship winners, who were chosen because of their high academic achievement, will be given $15,000 in scholarship money to use at the college of their choice after they graduate from high school.
- Child-care experts disagree over whether or not children should be spanked as part of a parent's disciplinary techniques or whether or not putting children in a time-out away from activities is punishment enough.

3. Edit the following to eliminate redundancy:

- Susan is currently director of marketing sales.
- He served as past president of the Rotary club.

- The elementary school will need twenty-five acres of land for a multipurpose building, playground, and ball fields.
- Fire completely destroyed the town hall in the month of June.
- The future outlook for the economy indicates interest rates may rise slightly.
- The circus will be at 3 p.m. Sunday afternoon and 7 p.m. Sunday night.
- Due to the fact that more than two-thirds of the people did not respond, the picnic will be canceled.
- She climbed up the tree in order to get a better look at the defendant.
- John went on to say that any student's effort should be recognized.
- The Broadway show will close down six months after it first began.

4. Look through newspapers, magazines, and Web sites and select an article or blog that shows five or more of the characteristics of good writing mentioned in this chapter. Clip or print out the piece you selected and write a short paper, listing the guidelines for good writing that are followed. For each guideline you mention, quote a passage or paragraph that shows how the writer used the good writing rules or techniques.

References

Henry Beard and Christopher Cerf, *The Official Politically Correct Dictionary and Handbook.* New York: Villard Books, 1992.

Theodore M. Bernstein, *Dos, Don'ts and Maybes of the English Language.* New York: The Times Book Co., 1977.

John Bremner, *Words on Words.* New York: Columbia University Press, 1980.

Nora Ephron, "Writers' Workshop," video series produced by South Carolina Educational Television, 1980.

Robert Gunning, *The Technique of Clear Writing.* New York: McGraw-Hill, 1954.

Ernie Pyle, *Here Is Your War.* New York: Pocket Books, 1945.

Joel Saltzman, *If You Can Talk, You Can Write.* New York: Ballantine Books, 1993.

Carl Sessions Stepp, excerpt from videotape, "Taking Charge of Your Local Paper," National Rural Electric Cooperatives Association, Washington, D.C., March 1993.

William Strunk, Jr., and E. B. White, *The Elements of Style, 3rd ed.* New York: Macmillan, 1979.

Tom Wolfe, excerpt from *The Bonfire of the Vanities.* New York: Farrar, Straus & Giroux, 1987.

William Zinsser, *On Writing Well.* New York: Harper & Row, 1976.

CHAPTER 5

Getting to the Point

When the president of a university spoke at her installation ceremony, she discussed the broad issue of improving undergraduate education and specific points to achieve that goal. Media began their respective stories from different angles. The student newspaper focused on greater rigor in classroom teaching. A television station with a broad viewing audience began its 6 p.m. report with her call for accountability to state legislators, then posted video and the text of her speech on its Web site. A business publication examined her challenge for a more aggressive investment policy to increase the school's endowment. The university's alumni publication looked at the outcome: the continued strength of the university's reputation and the value of its degree. A donor newsletter picked up her request for additional funds for scholarships and teaching excellence awards.

Because audiences are information-seeking, writers have to let them know right away what is in the message. Writers familiar with their audiences know which information will be relevant and appealing. Writers must alert audiences to important messages. They know what will attract the attention of the individual who juggles time for job, home, spouse, children, hobbies, and friends.

Messages must therefore hook the audience. The hook must be set in the first few sentences or paragraphs, the *lead* of the message. That is where writers must show the relevance of the message and attract, entertain, and inform. Readers or listeners then will decide whether the message is compelling, entertaining, or informative enough to warrant their attention.

Leads must fit the medium's style and format. While a longer descriptive lead might work in the print edition of a newspaper, a shorter version with important elements that can also help index the story's content would appear on the online site. Writers today need to know how to write all types of leads.

This chapter will discuss lead writing, specifically

- the role of leads in capturing audiences,
- elements in lead writing,
- news values, and
- types of leads.

What's the Point?

To hook a particular audience, writers must know why they are writing. It sounds simple enough. But many people regard writing as an artistic endeavor, not as a craft. They avoid thinking about the substance of what they are going to say. Instead, these writers sit down to write with a broad purpose or goal in mind, such as informing an audience about government waste. Their copy might ramble because they have not figured out the main point of the specific message, an essential element in hooking the active audience.

Determining the point requires critical thinking. Writers must look at the components of the message and weigh each as it pertains to audiences. They must lay out the facts and evaluate their importance and relevance. The steps are part of the stages of writing discussed in Chapter 1.

What does a rural community need to know about issues in a state legislative session? How about a professional association of school board members? These two audiences will need different hooks when a bill is introduced in the state House. As writers consider information and audiences, they get closer to the point of the message, establishing where they want to start.

Getting to the point is like opening a package: As you open the carton, you get closer to the real heart of your search. You might toss out styrofoam popcorn, then layers of tissue paper. Finally, you uncover the gift—the point of your search.

Finding the point of your story is essential to writing. Along the way, writers will discover facts and pieces that relate to the main point, surrounding and supporting it like the tissue paper. Other pieces could be discarded. But the examining process must be completed first.

Consider the advertising copywriter who says, "I want to write an ad that will get more business for my client." He or she is still handling the whole package—a big and unworkable problem. Thinking and planning—a stage of writing—will help in moving from the broad idea of producing an ad to the task of communicating the benefit of the service or product. The writer will get to the point.

If the client makes hand lotion, the advertiser's point might be beautiful hands or healthier skin or convenient packaging. If the client owns a tax service, the point might be customer peace of mind and the accountant's knowledge of tax laws. Once that benefit—the point—has been identified, the writer's job is to select precise words that will emphasize that point and grab a consumer's attention. And once writers have established where to start, they will know the direction to go.

In crafting messages, writers focus on the point, the hook, the lead, and the copy.

- The *point* is crucial information that justifies creating a message in the first place: A bill is passed. New funds are available. A road is closed.
- The *hook* is an enticing opening phrase or sentence that draws audiences into a message.
- The *lead* is the opening few sentences of a media message. Typically, it contains the hook and the point.
- The *copy* is the entire body of a media message, including a lead and all supporting information, such as new facts, background, quotes, and statistics.

In the Beginning Comes the Lead

In journalism, the first sentences or paragraphs of a story are called a *lead.* The lead has a heavy responsibility: It is the bait to hook the reader. By educating, entertaining, or enlightening, it stimulates the reader to pay attention. The lead shows relevance and is relevant to the audience. It also entraps. A publisher once wrote that a lead must be provocative, vigorous, and even at times startling to the reader.

Every piece of writing has a beginning or opening statement; every piece of writing has a lead. Long-time syndicated columnist James J. Kilpatrick once wrote:

> *The lead is vital to any writing, whether one is writing a novel, a short story, a book review, a term paper, a newspaper editorial, or a homily to be read in church on Sunday morning.*

A lead needs to establish relevance for readers:

> If you plan to have a summer internship next year, be aware that editors often begin their searches in October and November and make offers in December.

The lead contains the stimulus for reading, sets out the message's relevance, and gives readers the most important information first. As the stimulus, the lead entertains, enlightens, and educates. As it sets out the relevance, it whets the reader's appetite to stay with the message. In giving the most important information first, the lead ensures that readers get the point quickly. They can stick with the story or even move to other messages.

The lead must also set up the story. After reading or hearing the lead, audiences should know the main points of the message that follows. If not, the lead has misled them, and the writer's credibility is damaged. How does a writer know whether the lead sets up the story? When the story is complete, a writer must consider the main points in the body of the message and ensure they are noted in the lead. The lead sets up the story; the story backs up the lead. For example, a story reports a robbery at the campus dining hall and includes details about the robber locking the dining hall manager in a closet. That fact should be noted in the lead, along with the information about how the robbery occurred and how much money was taken. The chronological details of the robbery appear in the body of the story.

Journalists, primarily print journalists, have recognized for decades that getting to the point is essential to attract and retain readers. Media writers have found they immediately must set out the critical aspects of the message for their readers, listeners, consumers, or other audience members. Writing a lead is a crucial assignment for any writer.

Leads and Audience

Different audiences will react differently to leads. That makes sense. The audience of a local newspaper expects writing and prose that differ from what readers of a campus newspaper want. In a campus newspaper, leads will be focused for a university audience and its interests. The local newspaper has to attract an audience that includes students and university staff as well as people with no connection to the campus. The local newspaper might consider the language in a campus newspaper inappropriate for its audience.

Writers, whether for newspapers, Web sites, television stations, or magazines, have to structure their leads and stories to suit their audiences. When Republican presidential nominee John McCain announced Alaska Gov. Sarah Palin as his running mate, the media covered the story with an angle that would relate to readers. Many noted her relative obscurity on the national political scene. Consider these leads from *The New York Times* and the *Anchorage Daily News*, respectively:

> DAYTON, Ohio—Senator John McCain astonished the political world on Friday by naming Sarah Palin, a little-known governor of Alaska and self-described "hockey mom" with almost no foreign policy experience to be his running mate on the Republican presidential ticket.

> Alaskans woke to a new kind of earthquake Friday.
>
> So did the other 49 states.
>
> Instead of making a scheduled appearance at the Alaska State Fair, Gov. Sarah Palin stepped onto a stage in Ohio as Sen. John McCain's running mate on the Republican presidential ticket.

In each lead, the writer focused on Palin's selection. The Anchorage paper, however, brought the story closer to home with references to earthquakes and the state fair.

How to Get Started

Before constructing a lead, writers must know their information thoroughly. They must look at information collected via research or interviewing, then evaluate it, using judgment and experience, to determine what is most relevant to their audiences. As a prewriting activity, some writers go through their notes and add priority numbers next to information.

For example, before writing the lead that tells readers they should plan in the fall for the next summer's internship, a writer should list information to be included: students want internships; editors plan eight to ten months ahead; offers are made in December; don't wait. Next to each fact, the writer should put a number corresponding to its importance to the audience.

In writing the lead, the writer determines that the audience does not need to know the specific date that editors begin to interview or how many editors interview in the fall. Priority No. 1 is that editors will start looking soon and readers can avoid missing out on an internship if they plan ahead. The writer sets out the main part of the story—getting ready for internships—and then the relevance—students can miss the opportunity to apply if they wait until spring.

Writers can try another prewriting approach to evaluating information. They can simply ask, "What must my audience know?" and then list three to five things in order of importance. In the case of internships, the list would look something like this:

1. It is almost time to start planning for next summer's internship.
2. If students want to have an internship, they need to be prepared now.
3. Editors make hires in December for next year's interns.

The main point would become the lead. Other main points would be fashioned into the rest of the copy. Writers then have followed the format many journalists use—the inverted pyramid, which ranks information in descending order of importance. That format is discussed in Chapter 6.

Writers who struggle with ranking information and its relevance should remember that most people want to know the personal angle first. It all comes down to the audience's automatic question, "How does this message affect me?" The audience immediately looks for the explanation.

Sometimes stories or messages don't have that simple, personal component. Then writers must look beyond the "what about me?" question or relevance rule to other factors that make some pieces of information more important than others. Such factors are also guides to the selection of information for the lead. Those elements are called *news elements* and *news values* and are discussed next in this chapter.

News Elements

Certain elements are of interest in all writing. Journalists over the years have spelled out the elements that must appear in news stories: who, what, when, where, how, and why. This list is a basic starting point for any writer in determining what will go first.

These news components can form a question: "Who did what to whom, how, when, where, and why?" Every letter, news story, news release, or advertisement will answer this question.

Why are these elements important? Because people are most interested in other people, who they are, what they say and do, where they live and work, what happens to them, why they make certain choices, and how they deal with those choices. They are interested in conflict, competition, and achievements. People want to know about other people who overcome adversity, who are defeated, and who do the unusual. Look at this example:

> A Hollywood, Fla., man and woman exchanged wedding vows at 1,300 feet as they plummeted to earth hand-in-hand under silver parachutes five miles west of here Wednesday afternoon.
>
> Grace Mason and John Kempner met while skydiving at a local club and decided it would be the most significant way to start their married life together.

The elements are there:

Who:	Grace and John
What:	Got married
When:	Wednesday
Where:	Near Hollywood, Fla.
How:	By parachutes
Why:	Because they wanted to start married life in a manner meaningful to their courtship and to them

The two-paragraph lead summarizes what happened. Readers can decide whether they want to read further to learn more about Grace and John. The author has also set it up so that after two paragraphs, the reader knows the most important information and can turn to another message.

Where to Put *Who* and *What*

Putting all the elements in the first sentence can result in a long, convoluted sentence. Consider the following lead and its clearer rewrite:

> Sam Atwood, an associate professor of political science at the University, told students in a speech Thursday in MacPherson Hall that they should be more concerned about world events that more and more directly affect their lives and their future.

Rewritten:

> Students should be concerned about world events that more and more directly affect their lives and their future, an associate professor of political science at the University said Thursday.

In the rewrite, students get the content first. Rather than the professor's complete name, a descriptive phrase or identifying label describes him. The location of the speech and why he was giving it can be included in a subsequent paragraph.

Writers must decide which elements deserve emphasis and are most relevant before they write a lead. All elements will be included somewhere in the story. As a general rule, *who* and *what* will be included in the first sentence. *Where* and *when* will also appear here because they take up little space. This formula also follows the natural order of the English language: subject, verb, object. *Who, what, when*, and *where* set up an active structure: "A masked man robbed the university dining hall of $3,000 Wednesday night and locked the dining hall manager in a closet." *How* and *why* can be included in the first sentence if they are unusual. A full explanation usually will require several sentences or paragraphs.

Consider this lead from the *Great Falls Tribune* that focuses on *who, what, when*, and *where.*

> A man who witnesses say was driving erratically and clutching his chest drove through a fence and into the fairgrounds Tuesday morning, hitting a woman who was on a riding lawn mower, police said.

Again, the elements are there:

Who:	A man driving erratically
What:	Drove through a fence and hit a woman
When:	Tuesday
Where:	The fairgrounds

A Closer Look at the Elements

Let's define the lead elements and what role they play in the copy.

Who defines the person carrying out the action or affected by the story. *Who* may not be a specific name, such as Grace or John, but rather an identification or label. For example, a news release may say in the first sentence that two marketing employees have been promoted and in the second sentence give their names and titles. But if the president is retiring, his name will be given first because it has recognition among company employees and in the community, as in the following:

> Charles Southwick, chief executive officer of Englewood Mills, who began his career sweeping floors, will retire April 1 after 42 years with the company.

The *who* is Charles Southwick, specifically named because of the role he plays in the local business community. *What* represents the action: will retire. Usually, *what* can be simply stated in a verb. Consider this news lead:

> CAPE CANAVERAL, Fla. (AP)—To everybody's relief, astronauts fixed the toilet at the international space station on Wednesday and opened up a grand new science lab.

The phrases "fixed the toilet" and "opened a science lab" tells *what.* Similarly, in a letter to a high school's alumni, the verb "donate" tells *what:*

> Southeast High School's PTA is asking alumni to donate money to put at least two computers in every classroom by the end of the year.

What in the example is asking alumni for money.

When tells the audience the timeliness of the event or the time frame of specific actions. Often it is one word. In most writing, *when* will go after the verb because the time element rarely is the most interesting information. Few leads begin with *when*. In the space station example above, "Wednesday" tells when the events occurred. In the lead on the alumni letter, the time frame is less specific. But an alumnus reading the letter will know the goal for installing the computers is December 31, so contributions should be made between receipt of the letter and well before December 31.

When can also be used to set up a longer time frame, as in this *San Antonio Express News* lead:

> NATCHEZ, Miss.—Fifty years ago today, the civil rights movement began when racist thugs butchered Emmett Till, a Chicago youth visiting relatives in Money, 150 miles from here.
>
> And for 50 years, nobody has been punished for the crime, or for many other racially motivated killings.
>
> It's taken decades, but America is finally bringing justice to the Old South, with an unprecedented campaign to reopen unresolved civil rights murders such as Till's.

The writer sets up the time frame between what happened 50 years ago and today.

Where gives the reader the geographic context of the story. In many cases, this information will pique audience interest because readers want to know about events that affect them. The closer the story is to the reader's backyard, the greater the interest will be.

Wire service and other stories in newspapers often start with *where* by using a dateline—the name of the city in capital letters—to let readers know immediately where the event occurred.

> BLENCOE, Iowa—Frightened Boy Scouts huddled in a shelter as a tornado tore through their western Iowa campground, killing four teens and injuring 48 others who had little warning of the approaching twister.

In stories without a dateline, the exact location would be the first word or words in the lead only when it offers some unusual aspect to the story. Usually, the *where* is tucked elsewhere into the lead.

> A slice of history awaits you at the Tastee Diner in Silver Spring.

How expands on the what aspect. Look at the following lead from the *Wyoming Star-Tribune:*

> Power Resources, Inc., will pay $900,000 in penalties to the state to settle a long list of violations at its Smith-Highland Ranch in-situ leach uranium mine in Carbon County.

The lead tells *who, what, when,* and *where* but also talks about *how:* how the company will settle the violations.

Why gives the audience the reason a decision or a change was made or is pending or the cause of an event. In the Boy Scout example, the audience knows why the youngsters died: because tornadoes destroyed shelter in their campground. In the alumni letter, alumni are asked to give money. Why? So the school can buy computers. *Why* is often oversimplified or overlooked. Writers should go beyond superficial explanations.

Remember: *How* and *why* should appear in the first sentence or lead if there is some unusual aspect or if they are essential to understanding the message. Consider this lead from the *Reno Gazette-Journal:*

> Unable to cope with soaring fuel costs, Texas-based ExpressJet will cease all flights under that brand name, including five daily flights out of Reno, on Sept. 2.

Why and *how* ExpressJet is handling higher costs are immediately clear to the reader.

Watch Out for Too Much

Sometimes all elements fit concisely into a lead, as in the ExpressJet example. But because all elements do not have to appear in every first sentence, a writer can set up the point of the story using a few elements in the first sentence and explain the other elements in later paragraphs. Consider this lead:

> A major housing development that preservationists believed had died last year has been resurrected by developers who say local planning officials are much more receptive to the revised version.

Are *who, what, when, where, how,* and *why* all answered in this first sentence? No.

Who:	Developers
What:	Are resurrecting a housing development plan
When:	Implied now, but not stated
Where:	Implied in the county, but not specifically stated
How:	Not stated
Why:	Because planning officials seem more receptive

The lead would have been complex if the writer had included more elements, such as adding that preservationists will fight the renewed development with a door-to-door campaign before a planning board hearing next month and the exact location of the 300-acre site. With complicated material, the writer should consider a lead that sets out the new information in the first paragraph followed by some context or an explanatory quote in the second graph.

A lead attracts readers to the story because it has other elements—not just *who, what, when, where, how,* and *why*—that must be considered when the writer is structuring the first sentence. These other elements are called *news values.*

News Values

In structuring leads, writers are guided by what journalists traditionally have called *news values,* or aspects of an event that the audience might want to know about. The more writers know about their audience, the easier it is to predict the news values that will interest people or satisfy them in some way. These values or qualities carry over into any type of writing.

The traditional news values taught by journalism professors become second nature to reporters: *prominence, timeliness, proximity, impact, magnitude, conflict, oddity,* and *emotional impact.* News values are important in any media writing because they guide writers in identifying and listing crucial information. Let's look at each of the news values and how they affect lead writing. Several are closely allied to the elements *who, what, when, where, how,* and *why.*

Prominence

When the main characters in your story are well known, that is a signal to put those names in the lead. Readers recognize those names and are drawn into the story.

When well-known figures die, the obituaries become front-page news. When celebrities end up in divorce court or have custody battles, again, their lives make headlines. When prominent people have a medical issue, their names draw attention to treatments, such as actress Christina Applegate who opted to have radical mastectomies when she learned she had the breast cancer gene. Even people who are merely related to famous people are lead-worthy, such as Jamie Lynn Spears, Britney's sister. Prominence extends even to pets, such as Paris Hilton's Chihuahua, Tinkerbell.

Timeliness

One adage in journalism is "old news ain't news." People want to know what is happening as soon as it happens. They want newness in the news. They want to know information they did not know yesterday. They want timely, up-to-date news and depend increasingly on television, radio, and online services as initial sources of information. Therefore, *when* an event happened is almost always included in the first sentence of a story so that people will have a context for that event.

> The official ceremony for east Montgomery's latest new school took place this morning, which is named in honor of an icon of Montgomery's civil rights movement.

> ISTANBUL, Turkey (AP)—Turkish authorities captured a gunman Thursday wanted in the deadly attack on the U.S. consulate after rounding up suspects who had communicated with three other assailants killed by police, local media reports said.

Proximity

People are most interested about news that happens close to them. Audiences easily identify with stories with a geographic proximity—that is, those in their own community, town, county, or state. They like to read stories about their neighbors' successes and even defeats.

Audiences are also interested in what happens to people from their communities in other locations. For example, people in Cleveland would want to know about an airplane crash in Washington state that kills residents from their city. A Cleveland newspaper might run this lead:

> SEATTLE, Wash.—Two Cleveland businessmen were among 19 people killed early this morning when a jet struck a radio tower just outside Seattle.

The lead emphasizes Cleveland's loss while reporting that the plane crash occurred. Writers call this *localizing a message*, or putting a local angle on a story that originated miles away so that audiences can see how the message relates to them and their community.

News reports might also have an emotional or nonspatial proximity, whereby readers identify with a certain group of people. People who have suffered heart attacks are interested in articles about how other heart-attack victims have coped. People who live in a college town may be more inclined to read about stories originating from other cities with campuses, even if the cities are far away. Parents anywhere could relate to the following *Ames* (Iowa) *Tribune* lead about the return to school:

> The kids arrived by the busload and carload, on foot and on bikes, toting backpacks and dragging parents behind them.
>
> The first day of school was upon Ames.

Impact

Audiences always want to know how they will be affected, whether by a road closing while a sewer line is being laid or by a sale at the local supermarket. Reporters often hear people ask, "But how does this affect me? What does this have to do with me?" High in any message should be an explanation of how an event affects individuals' daily lives or why they should be concerned.

When possible, the impact should be translated into tangible terms. For example, a water and sewer rate increase approved by the Cityville Town Council Tuesday night will mean that the average resident will pay $3.52 a month more for service, bringing the average monthly bill to $31.96.

Sometimes impact is harder to detect. In such cases, it may be even more important for the writer to point out effects on ordinary individuals. Many stories will begin with anecdotal leads that give an example of how an event, decision, or medical breakthrough will affect specific individuals. Readers often can identify their own family and friends who would fit in the scenario. Using the example brings impact close to home.

In natural disasters, the impact might be stated in terms of how people are affected. When a hurricane, earthquake, wildfire, or tornado occurs, thousands of residents will probably be without electricity and potentially hundreds of houses damaged.

Consider the impact clearly outlined in this lead from *The Associated Press:*

> NEW YORK (AP)—Floods that have inundated the Midwest could reduce world corn supplies and drive food prices higher at a time when Americans are already stretching their grocery budgets and people in poor countries have rioted over rising food costs.

Impact can be positive, such as free bus service:

> Residents can ride the town's buses for free, beginning Monday, the first time the transit service has been offered at no charge to riders.
>
> University students, staff, and faculty will also benefit from the free bus service, made possible by a $200,000 grant from the university to the town.

Magnitude

Some folks like to distinguish between impact and magnitude in defining news values. *Magnitude* is defined as the size of the event. Death, injury, or loss of property are all elements of magnitude that attract audience attention. Large amounts of money, such as lottery winnings, as well as disasters, such as earthquakes, carry magnitude and are always big news. When wildfires ravage the California hills, the acreage burned as well as the speed and intensity of the flames are part of the magnitude.

Consider this lead, which has magnitude and an understood impact:

> Tuesday morning 54 school buses will drive more than 1,000 miles as they pick up 2,500 school children for the first day of classes this year.

The magnitude is represented in part by the 2,500 students, the 1,000 miles traveled, and the 54 school buses. The understood impact of the first day of school is much broader, affecting any household in the county that has school-age children, an employee of the school system, or an early morning commuter.

Conflict

Most news reports contain some kind of conflict: contract disputes with striking workers, continuing struggles in African countries and in the Middle East, the battles between neighbors in rezoning issues, or a grievance filed by an employee against a supervisor. People like to read about conflict. The extent of the conflict, either its size or its duration, will determine whether conflict is included in the lead of the message.

Conflict permeates the news. For example, when a devastating cyclone hit Myanmar, the country's leaders prevented the entry of much-needed aid, as noted in this lead:

> YANGON, Myanmar (AP)—U.S. Navy ships laden with relief supplies will steam away from Myanmar's coast Thursday, their helicopters barred by the ruling junta even though millions of cyclone survivors need food, shelter or medical care.

Or as shown in this lead by Susana Hayward of the *Miami Herald:*

> FORT SAM HOUSTON, Texas—Clutching their children, siblings, spouses and parents amid tears and applause, three former American hostages held captive for more than five years by Colombian guerrillas denounced their captors Monday as terrorists who kept them chained by their necks.

Oddity

Editors often encourage writers to look for oddity or some unusual twist to a story, such as a police officer who responds to the accident call and discovers that one of the injured people is his son. When a doctor used a claw hammer to pull a nail out of a 60-year-old man's skull, the man survived—except for some lingering headaches—and kept the nail as a souvenir. This *Miami Herald* lead sets up an unusual story:

> A shopper looking for a deal in the garden department of a South Florida Wal-Mart found more than he bargained for when he startled a poisonous pygmy rattlesnake hiding in some plants.

The article tells readers that emergency medical services crew gave the man an antidote and explains the risks of a pygmy rattler bite.

Consider this lead from the *Detroit Free Press:*

> Nothing wrong with teaching your kid your trade. But when your line of work is shoplifting, well. . . .

Or this lead from the *Bismarck Tribune:*

> Riding a bike while intoxicated is still considered driving drunk, police say.

Whenever a writer is working on a message that has an element of oddity, care must be taken to ensure that people are not portrayed as freakish or unnatural. For example, a story on the largest baby born in the county in 30 years might not need to be written at all.

Emotional Impact

Writers are recognizing more and more that people like stories that affect them emotionally and that have emotional impact. This news value is also called *human interest* and *universal appeal.* It is the quality that draws audiences to children, young people, and pets, as well as stories tied to love and romance. Emotional events are important elements in stories and generally should be included in the first paragraph, as in this example:

> MADDOCK (AP)—Most 3-year-olds don't have much of a story to tell. Barkley is an exception, though he's not much of a talker.
>
> Barkley is a handsome, 98-pound golden retriever who has just found a new home at the Maddock Memorial Home, nestled next to a rolling prairie in the small central North Dakota community of Maddock.

The story continues, revealing that Barkley is a refugee of Hurricane Katrina who eventually finds a new home at a retirement community.

Think about your own interests. In looking at a page of a company newsletter, the photo of children and balloons at the company picnic will probably have more appeal than the picture of the president presenting a $5,000 check to the local PTA president. Death and injury convey emotional impact. A spousal murder also captures audience attention, from the arrests through the trial.

Remember the Audience

In applying news values, writers must think about what is important to their audience. Knowing the audience determines what's in the lead and affects how the writer will rank information. For example, a college community audience hears the mayor speak in a lecture series. What he says looks like this in the college newspaper's lead:

> Students play a vital role in boosting the town's economy when they shop at downtown businesses, Mayor Leo Ryan said Wednesday.

The primary audience for the college newspaper is students. What the mayor said has a different focus for the lead in the town's general-circulation newspaper:

> Town and college administrators need to develop a joint long-range plan that will address growth, particularly along the campus perimeter, during the next 20 years, Mayor Leo Ryan said Wednesday night.

A general-interest audience, primarily made up of town residents, would be more interested in what the mayor said that affected them directly.

News with a local angle will have more appeal to audiences. Think of interest in concentric circles: People are interested first in what happens in their neighborhoods, then their towns, their counties, their states, their countries, and the world. Leads should be written to focus on the local angle, such as this one for readers in Annapolis, Maryland:

> If you are planning to drive to Ocean City for the weekend, avoid Maryland Highway 113 near Dagsboro where highway crews are working and traffic is slowed to one lane.

Television satirist Jon Stewart often makes fun of reporters who introduce news that they say is "the story everyone is talking about." The humor of this phrase, as Stewart points out, is that the audience isn't talking about the story—it's only the reporters and TV anchors. Apparently, "everyone" doesn't include the audience. The serious point that Stewart makes is that writers, if they aren't careful, can easily mistake their own interests with the interests of the audience.

And just because everyone is talking about a story doesn't necessarily mean it is true. One day in late June 2008, people using the online messaging service Twitter helped spread a false rumor that Subway spokesman Jared Fogel had died. The rumor spread so quickly that his name became one of the hottest search terms on Google that day. People who had heard the rumor were apparently hunting for news of Fogel's demise. Even though traditional news sources like CNN or the Associated Press didn't report on it, this item was "the story everyone is talking about."

Sorting It Out

At this point, you are educated about the elements of a lead, but you still may be unclear about the sorting process. Let's walk through it.

Suppose you are a business writer for a local newspaper. In three months, a major employer in town will open a fitness center for employees. The center will be in the old YMCA building next door to the bank's corporate headquarters. You have collected the needed information. Your list of elements looks like this:

Who: Amana Savings and Loan
What: Will open a fitness center
Where: Next door to corporate headquarters in the old YMCA
When: In three months
Why: To improve employee health and to provide a benefit to employees
How: By renovating the old YMCA

Now make a list of news values as they relate to the story. Ask whether each applies and if so, how:

Prominence: No
Timeliness: Yes, within three months

Proximity:	Yes, in downtown
Impact:	Yes, the renovation will mean local jobs and other economic benefits to the town. It will affect the lives of the company's 275 employees and the townspeople who have been wondering what will happen to the old YMCA.
Magnitude:	Yes, the acquisition and renovation will cost the company almost $1 million.
Conflict:	None internally—shareholders approved the expenditure at the annual meeting. None externally—town residents want the building saved.
Emotional impact:	Possibly, for people who remember using the old YMCA

In writing the lead, you as the writer must consider the newspaper's audience—the townspeople, including employees of the bank—and ask, "What will they want to know first?" The answer is the timeliness of the renovation. The renovation is new news. A first draft of the lead might read like this:

> Amana Savings and Loan will spend $1 million to renovate the vacant YMCA downtown on Sycamore Street to create an employee fitness center that will open within three months.

Here, you have answered *who*, *what*, *when*, and *where*. You also have addressed the *magnitude* of the project. The second paragraph will answer *why* and *how*, and the third paragraph will explain *impact:*

> The bank will renovate the old YMCA building to provide a convenient way for employees to remain physically fit, said employee manager Kay Barnes. The bank will use the existing layout and install new equipment and furnishings.
>
> The project will mean additional jobs during the renovation and later when the center opens, Barnes noted.

The story can continue with information on the actual renovation, such as the construction company that will do the job, types of equipment and furnishings, how many jobs created, among other facts.

General Rules for Leads

No matter what type of lead you choose to write, all leads have common features.

Leads should be short. As a guide, some writers use no more than 30 words. Many wire service stories have leads no longer than 20 words in the first sentence or paragraph. This *Bismarck Tribune* lead sets up the story in nine words:

> He lost his home, but saved a wedding dress.

Readers know what happened, but will continue to find out exactly how he lost his home.

Leads should be concise and to the point. Writers must eliminate unnecessary words. Look at the following lead and see what has been eliminated in the rewrite and how the focus has changed:

> A local daycare center was broken into Wednesday night and property vandalized, toys overturned and a pet rabbit, named Ray, killed with a broom.

Rewritten:

> Vandals broke into a local daycare center Wednesday night, killed the center's pet rabbit with a broom, overturned toys, and damaged property.

Words in the lead should be precise and in general vocabulary. The words in the following Associated Press lead are precise and show the impact:

> LAND O'LAKES, Fla.—When 3-year-old Mikey Spoul took his father's car for a joyride last month and explained "I go zoom," the act grabbed national attention and even became fodder for late-night show monologue jokes.
>
> But nobody's laughing now. Mikey torched his bedroom curtains with a cigarette lighter and burned down his family's home, authorities said.

Leads should use active verbs. Consider the verbs in the preceding lead example: "grabbed," "torched," and "burned down," or the verbs in this lead:

> A Cityville man smashed the glass door on a Laundromat washing machine and yanked a 3-year-old child from the swirling waters Saturday morning.

Leads should be simple, not rambling, convoluted sentences. No one wants to work too hard at understanding most communication. The writer has lost if the "huh?" factor enters in. That's when a person has to stop and reread a lead to understand what the writer is saying. Compare the simple lead about the Cityville man in the Laundromat with this more convoluted lead:

> Under a handgun-control plan, announced by state and county grassroots organizations Monday, a person who sells a handgun to an unlicensed customer would be liable to a victim for three times his losses if that handgun is used to commit a crime.

Apply what you have learned about leads so far to untangle this report on controlling handguns. What's the point? Some grassroots organizations have come up with an idea for making handgun salespeople more responsible for crime. What does the audience have to know? How about this lead:

> If a local citizens group gets its way, people who sell guns will help pay for the lives and property lost in handgun crimes.

Writers base the structure of their leads on the type of story and the audience. Some information, such as police reports, lend themselves to summary leads. Other material works better in a descriptive or anecdotal lead. The next section looks at leads and where each works best.

Summary Leads

The most common lead format is a summary lead that tells or summarizes the most important information:

> Four Cityville teens will receive all-expenses-paid trips to the U.S. city of their choice, their prize in a local essay contest.

> To reduce attrition, Telstar Corp. will build an on-site day-care center that will enroll 125 children of its employees in May.

> World leaders meeting at the G-8 Summit endorsed a plan Tuesday to halve the world emissions of greenhouse gasses by the year 2050.

The summary lead serves the audience members who skim newspaper stories, online articles, company newsletters, or handouts from school; who listen with one ear to radio news reports and one ear to the kids in the backseat of the car; or who casually tune into the morning television news while getting dressed. Because of the crowded field of communication today, summary leads are used often to give people information quickly.

Summary leads are useful. They can be the introduction of a letter, the hook of an online story, the beginning of a news release, the headline of a broadcast story, or the homepage link to the complete story.

Beyond One Paragraph

Although most summary leads consist of one sentence or one paragraph, they may be longer to provide adequate information and context. Leads must be clear and easy to understand. Look at this Associated Press lead:

> BELLEVILLE, Ill.—James Dowdy has gone to prison three times, and may go there again, for the same crime: burglarizing homes and stealing women's socks.
>
> Dowdy had been free on bond in one alleged sock caper when police say he was caught with socks that had been taken from someone's laundry room Monday morning in Belleville, a St. Louis suburb. The 36-year-old remained jailed Wednesday on a felony burglary count filed the previous day.

The writer needs the second graph to set up the context and bring readers up-to-date.

A writer in a company's corporate communications department needs to tell employees about payroll changes. She must do so in a way that is informative, pertinent, and clear:

> Long Branch Entertainment employees will see in their paychecks next month some changes that represent good news and bad news.

> The good news is the company's across-the-board 3 percent pay raise.
>
> The bad news is each employee with a family plan will pay $52.22 more a month in health insurance premiums and employees with individual plans $26.32 more a month.

The three-paragraph summary lead contains information essential to employees: how the company's health insurance plan will change and how much their raises will be. The writer wanted employees to know right away they were about to be hit in the pocketbook and why. Employees who want to know more about how and why the changes occurred will continue to read the message.

Multiple-Element Leads

The Long Branch lead on health care also illustrates how a writer presents more than one aspect to a message. Often, a lead has multiple elements or more than one point it must convey to readers. A *multiple-element lead* summarizes information for readers and sets up what will be covered in the rest of the copy. It presents a challenge to the writer, who must be wary of complex or convoluted sentences. The best approach is to rank the elements, put the most important in the first sentence, and then create a second or third paragraph to present the other points:

> A group of university students has presented a list of concerns to Chancellor Paula Walls, asking foremost that the university put a moratorium on tuition increases.
>
> The letter, hand-delivered to Walls on Wednesday, also asks the administration to name more students to campus-wide committees, to recruit minority faculty members, and to renovate the Student Union.

From this lead, readers have the most important information first: the list of demands and the high-priority demand. And they know the content and structure of the message. For writers, the lead sets up how to organize the story: in order of the points listed in the lead.

Delayed-Identification Leads

Another type of summary lead is the *delayed-identification lead.* When individuals in a news story carry no prominence, their proper names are not given in the first paragraph. Rather, they are identified by a generic label: "An Orange County woman died when..." or "A Lockwood High School student has been named a National Merit Scholarship winner...." Immediately, in the next paragraph, the individual is named. If more than one person is in the lead or first paragraph, the individuals are renamed in that order in the next paragraph. Consider this:

> WOBURN, Mass. (AP)—A British man convicted of shooting to death his 9-month-old baby and wife as they cuddled together in bed showed no reaction Thursday as he was sentenced to two life prison terms without the opportunity for parole.
>
> Neil Entwistle was found guilty Wednesday of two counts of first-degree murder in the 2006 deaths of his wife Rachel and their baby, Lillian Rose, in their rented home in Hopkinton. He fled to his native England afterward.

Other Lead Formats

Although the summary lead is the most useful, writers sometimes find other lead formats better suited to the kind of message they need to send. Some types of leads, such as anecdotal or descriptive, are popular in media today. They can be risky because they don't hook readers soon enough. They must therefore be well written to entice readers to stay long enough to find out what the message is about.

In general, when using other lead formats, make sure you get to the point by the fourth paragraph. Otherwise, you might lose your reader. If you are writing for a newspaper, the story might have jumped to another page before the reader ever gets to the point. Let's evaluate some types of alternative leads.

Anecdotal or Affective Leads

Many newspapers have developed a lead style that uses an anecdote to illustrate how one person is or has been affected by a social, health, political, or economic problem. The lead makes readers feel the abstract on an interpersonal and even emotional level. The abstract then becomes real. McClatchy reporter Tim

Johnson used the following lead to get into the broader story of China's security sweeps prior to the 2008 Summer Games:

> BEIJING—When Dechen Pemba, a British citizen, walked out of her Beijing apartment at 8:55 one morning this week, she found seven to eight security agents milling about waiting for her.
>
> They allowed her to throw some clothes in a rucksack, then took her in a whizzing convoy to the airport, ordering her deportation on a flight to London.
>
> The expulsion of Pemba, who's of Tibetan descent, is part of a broader campaign to sweep away anyone deemed a potential troublemaker before the Aug. 8–24 Olympic Games.

In the story, Johnson uses sources to explain to audiences how China's fears of any embarrassment have affected people, such as Pemba. Her experience opens and closes the article.

The key to using the anecdotal or affective lead is to keep it short and get to the point right away. Writers must quickly reveal the message's social or economic issue. Writers must use the anecdotal example throughout the story, not solely as a hook dropped after the lead. Consider this *Associated Press* lead:

> WINONA, Minn.—On the morning after the house party on Johnson Street, Jenna Foellmi and several other twentysomethings lay sprawled on the beds and couches. When a friend reached out to wake her, Foellmi was cold to the touch.
>
> The friend's screams woke up the others still asleep in the house.
>
> Foellmi, a 20-year-old biochemistry major at Winona State University, died of alcohol poisoning on Dec. 14, one day after she had finished her last exam of the semester. According to police reports, she had three beers during the day, then played beer pong—a drinking game—in the evening, and downed some vodka, too.
>
> Foellmi's death was tragic but typical in many ways.
>
> An Associated Press analysis of federal records found that 157 college-age people, 18–23, drank themselves to death from 1999 through 2005, the most recent year for which figures are available. The number of alcohol-poisoning deaths per year rose from 18 in 1999 to 35 in 2005.

The writer sets up the subject through an anecdote as a way to get to the point in paragraph 5: The numbers of college-age individuals dying from alcohol poisoning is on the rise. The reporter interviewed Foellmi's mother, who is quoted throughout the story.

Descriptive Leads

Like an anecdotal lead, a descriptive lead puts emotion or a human element into a message. It sets the scene for the reader. Consider *The New York Times* lead in this story:

> HEILIGENKREUZ, Austria—As noon draws near, the monks glide into the church, their white cowls billowing behind them. They line up in silence, facing each other in long choir stalls. Wood carvings of saints peer down on them from the austere Romanesque nave.
>
> Bells peal and the chant begins—low at first, then swelling as all the monks join in. Their soft voices wash over the ancient stones, replacing the empty clatter of the day with something like the sound of eternity.
>
> Except, that is, for the clicks of a camera held by a photographer lurking behind a stone pillar.
>
> It has been like this since last spring, when word got out that the Cistercian monks of the Stift Heiligenkreuz, deep in the Vienna woods, had been signed by Universal Music to record an album of Gregorian chants.

The writer, Mark Landler, uses the description to launch a story about the monks and their profitable music.

Consider this *Associated Press* lead:

> SAN FRANCISCO—Serenaded by a gay men's chorus, showered with rose petals and toasted with champagne, hundreds of tearful same-sex couples got married across the state Tuesday in what some are calling California's new Summer of Love.
>
> Wearing everything from T-shirts to tuxedos and lavish gowns, they rushed down to county clerks' offices to obtain marriage licenses and exchange vows on the first full day that gay marriage became legal in California by order of the state's highest court. They were joined by jubilant crowds that came to witness the event.

In the following descriptive lead from the *Seattle Times*, a human element is ascribed to a machine. Writer Lisa Heyamoto has taken a subject that affects Seattle residents—drilling under Queen Anne Hill—and presented it in a readable, interesting manner.

> She weighs 305 tons, is 27 feet long and creeps forward in four-foot intervals, her teeth gnashing through clay and rocks like corn nuts in a blender.
>
> You can call her Cassandra, and she's been burrowing her way 150 feet beneath Queen Anne Hill all summer.
>
> Cassandra isn't a Tolkien-esque subterranean monster. She's basically a drill—a giant one—carving a tunnel beneath Seattle that will store storm-water runoff until it can be treated and piped into Puget Sound.

Question Leads

Question leads should be avoided. They rarely are successful. In most cases, they are the lazy writer's way out, and they turn off audiences. In almost every case, they give the audience the option to turn elsewhere.

> Who will pay to build the county's new schools?

The reader might say, "Not me, and I don't care who pays." Think of another angle such as:

> The average Cityville resident will end up paying the cost for building new schools, a local watchdog group stated today.

On rare occasions, a question lead can work, as in this one from the *Arkansas Democrat Gazette:*

> What's a prairie dog worth?
>
> Two to six years, Little Rock police say.

The reader at first mentally guesses a dollar figure, but then is surprised immediately that the correct answer is a prison term. The reader is hooked into the story on prairie dog-napping.

Quote Leads

Quote leads should be used sparingly because rarely does someone sum an entire speech or premise for a decision in one simple quote. A quote can be used if it is short, is relevant to the rest of the message, and does not need any explanation. It must be clear within itself. Look at this newsletter lead:

> "Taking advantage of the different opportunities available in the Scholars program is what made a difference in my academic career," said a University of Maryland senior who will attend Georgetown Law School next year.

The lead here is empty and nonspecific. It fails to point out that the senior is a semifinalist for a Rhodes scholarship, is the Student Government Association vice president, and was an intern at the FBI. A stronger lead would have focused on his accomplishments and linked them to his involvement in the Scholars program:

> Randy Cates, a senior at the University of Maryland, is a semifinalist for a Rhodes scholarship, one of the most prestigious international academic awards; an FBI intern; and vice president of the student government association.
>
> He is also a College Park Scholar, and he says that award "is what made a difference in my academic career."

A partial quote is used effectively in this example from the Associated Press:

> Smoking and drug use among U.S. teenagers are increasing after a decade of decline, a study showed Monday, and its author warned that "the stage is set for a potential resurgence of cocaine and crack use."

Direct Address Leads

The direct address lead talks straight to the reader or consumer. It usually gives advice or has a "hey, you" aspect to it. Consider Shauna Stephenson's lead in the *Wyoming News:*

> If you've been to the national parks during the height of tourist season, you know how grandeur can suddenly become a grand headache.
>
> So if you're looking for a bit of solitude, go to a place so quiet that the National Park Service won't speak above a whisper about it: the Laurance S. Rockefeller Preserve.

Writing Leads for Online Media

Sometimes the medium can dictate the type of lead. The more time you anticipate a reader will spend with a story, the longer you can make your lead. Anecdotal leads, for example, are particularly well-suited for longer stories often found in magazines or in the Sunday editions of newspapers. However, online readers often quickly skim stories, or they may only see the headline and first paragraph before deciding whether to click and read the whole piece.

Writers who work for online publications must balance two influences that sometimes compete with each other. On one hand, many readers turn to the Web for breaking news. This usage suggests that online writers should put an emphasis on immediacy by clearly and prominently telling readers *when* something is happening.

On the other hand, online readers use search engines to find old stories relevant to an area of interest. Search engines use the first dozen or so words of a Web page to deliver the pages that are most relevant to a person's search terms. This process suggests that online writers should make an effort to use in their leads keywords that potential readers might search. People tend to search for nouns more than verbs or adjectives, so writers concerned about search engine optimization will emphasize the *who*, *what*, and *where* in their leads. This lead was written for a story published by WebMD Health News:

> Intense control of blood glucose levels in type 2 diabetes helps reduce the risk of kidney and eye complications, but not cardiovascular risks such as heart attacks and strokes, researchers said at a news briefing during the annual meeting of the American Diabetes Association in San Francisco.

Count the number of nouns that someone with Type 2 diabetes might use to look for information about treating the disease, and the potential side effects of the treatment: "blood glucose," "type 2 diabetes," "kidney," "eye," "complications," "cardiovascular," "heart attacks," "strokes," and "American Diabetes Association." Now, look where those keywords are located in the paragraph. "Blood glucose" and "type 2 diabetes" are the most widely used keywords, and they appear high in the lead. The writer emphasizes the results of the study, saving the attribution information until the end of the paragraph.

You may also have noticed other nouns, such as "San Francisco," that are popular search terms—probably even more popular than "diabetes." But someone looking for this information probably doesn't care where the meeting was held. And someone planning a vacation in San Francisco probably isn't interested in attending a meeting of the American Diabetes Association. Remember: only the relevant keywords are important.

Now, compare this lead from a *New York Times* article on the same topic:

> Two large studies involving more than 21,000 people found that people with Type 2 diabetes had no reduction in their risk of heart attacks and strokes and no reduction in their death rate if they rigorously controlled their blood sugar levels.

This story has some keywords—"type 2 diabetes," "heart attacks," "strokes," and "blood sugar"—but not nearly as many as the Web MD article, and they aren't as high in the lead. This lead puts the attribution of the news—"two large studies"—and even some details about the scope of the studies—"involving more than 21,000 people"—ahead of the findings. While a study's size is important, people with diabetes probably are less interested in "two large studies involving more than 21,000 people" than in information about "intense control of blood glucose levels in type 2 diabetes."

Google has two tools to help online writers learn which search terms people are most likely to use. To find these tools, do a Web search for "Google keywords tool" or "Google trends." For example, using the Google Keyword Tool, a writer would have seen in 2008 that "presidential election" was a far more popular search term than "presidential campaign," even though journalists often use those terms interchangeably. And using Google Trends, we can see that the number of searches for information about the "presidential election" spiked in February 2008 and then declined throughout the summer.

Before writing their lead, online writers should ask themselves a few questions:

- Is this story valuable to readers because of its immediacy or because of its in-depth and relatively timeless account of a subject in which people will be interested for some time to come?
- What are the key search words most likely to be used by people interested in my story?

Choosing a Lead Type

In many cases, the information will dictate the type of lead. A crime story, for example, generally will use a summary lead. A story on a city council meeting will need a multiple-element lead to cover the council's different actions. Lack of prominence will dictate a delayed-identification lead. But sometimes a writer must ponder and decide which lead will set up the story best. Look at this Associated Press lead about a 911 operator:

> NEW YORK—"You want the police to your house because your mother didn't come home?"
>
> It's nearly 7 p.m. on a Wednesday in the weeks before Christmas and somewhere in New York City, two scared young girls watch the clock, more frightened by the minute. They call 911 and reach Ivey Bruce.
>
> Her voice is soothing and steady. "OK, what apartment are you in? And what's the telephone number? And how old are you and your sister?"
>
> As she speaks Bruce types on a battered gray computer. The figures 10 and 11 appear on her screen, then "HOME ALONE." Another tap of a key speeds the girls' telephonic SOS to a police dispatcher in a nearby room.
>
> Bruce, a 45-year-old mother of two sons, nods as if to reassure the unseen child and then tells her police will be there soon.
>
> Like a novel half read, a mystery never solved, this story has no end for Bruce. After 14 years on the job, she knows that's as it must be.
>
> It's only suppertime in New York, and by the end of her 3:30 p.m. to 11:30 p.m. shift, this 911 operator will have heard accounts of panic and terror by the score.

The writer chose a long, anecdotal lead to set up a story about 911 operators. The story specifically follows one operator, Ivey Bruce, before it gives information about 911 services. By focusing on one typical call, the writer lets readers know how a 911 operator reacts to a call and interacts with the caller. The writer could have written this lead:

> NEW YORK—The hectic and gargantuan New York City 911 service will field more than 10 million calls this year.
>
> The system represents a lifeline found in 89 percent of the country. The operation rests largely with the 911 operators, who answer scores of accounts of panic and terror during their shifts.

Which lead works? The one with the human element referring to children and their missing mother will draw more people into the story than one that tosses out numbers. The faces behind the digits set up the story, and readers know by the end of the second paragraph that the key elements are 911, operators, Ivey Bruce, and calls.

Does It Work?

Once you have written a lead, scrutinize it, keeping in mind the guidelines in the leads checklist at the end of the chapter. Consider this lead from a daily newspaper:

> Ten-month-old Betssie Martinez-Oidor's fever soared to 105 degrees Monday. Her mother, Isabel Oidor, called York Hospital. Oidor and her husband, Gabriel Martinez, told a Spanish interpreter they had never seen their baby this ill.
>
> "They both got scared," interpreter Carmen Bones said. She told them to bring the baby to the hospital. They stayed until late Monday so the baby could be observed because of her fever. Betssie also had a runny nose, mild cough, and little appetite for her formula.

As the reader, what do you think the story is about? The lead says that the baby is ill with a high fever. Is the story about the effects of fevers on infants? No. See how far you have to read before you know what the story is really about.

> Periodic doses of Tylenol® helped bring the fever down to 100.6 degrees by the time they returned Tuesday for a follow-up exam by Dr. Mary Barnes in the Mother/Child Clinic.
>
> Applying her stethoscope to the baby's back and chest, Barnes ruled out bronchitis and pneumonia.
>
> "I think the baby has the flu and an ear infection," Barnes said. "It's out there. There's so much of it around."
>
> "Maybe she got it through me," the baby's father said to Barnes in Spanish.
>
> Betssie's parents have been ill with flu-like symptoms. They're far from alone. Pennsylvania is one of about 20 states experiencing an earlier-than-usual start to the flu season. The state's physician general, Dr. Wanda Filer, issued a statement that some flu cases of a Type A strain known as A/Nanchang have been confirmed in residents of several counties.

By paragraph 7, the story is clear: Pennsylvania is having a flu epidemic. All the discussion about the baby's illness makes readers wonder about fevers, immunizations, colds, or perhaps care for children. The example of the sick baby could be used, but readers need to know sooner what the actual topic is. Consider the rewrite:

> Ten-month-old Betssie Martinez-Oidor's fever soared to 105 degrees Monday, scaring her parents who took her to the hospital. Betssie has the flu. She is among the latest and youngest victims of this year's flu season. Pennsylvania is one of about 20 states experiencing an earlier-than-usual start to the flu season.

Then the writer can proceed with quotes from the parents and other details of the flu, its symptoms, and treatment.

Leads Should Do the Job

Remember to read through your stories carefully and ensure your leads are honest and set up for the reader what the story covers. Review the checklist in Box 5.1. In addition, remember that deaths, injuries, or substantial loss of property are other items that should be included in leads. All relate to news values that capture audience attention.

Readers will be disappointed if they believe that a story is about one topic only to discover that it is about another. Writers will lose credibility if they make false promises in their leads.

You can become a good lead writer, whatever the copy, by focusing on what is important to your audience, learning the guidelines of good writing, and reading good leads that are specific and present information accurately, clearly, and concisely. Look for such leads in everything you read.

BOX 5.1 Leads Checklist

Essential Lead Elements

1. I have looked at the facts and decided which are the most important.
2. My initial sentence is simple and complete.
3. My lead is accurate.

4. My lead is relevant to my audience, and includes keywords they might use to find the story online.
5. My lead comes to the point, is well edited, and makes sense.
6. I have used understandable, fresh words and strong, active verbs.
7. My lead sets up the story.

Desirable Elements

1. I have emphasized the latest information.
2. I have included unusual aspects of the message.
3. If possible, I have used a local angle to show how the information relates to readers.
4. I have kept my lead short and readable—no longer than 30 words.
5. My lead attracts the audience's attention.
6. My lead summarizes the message.

Exercises

1. Read the following lead. Identify the elements and the news values present:

    A third elementary school in Johnston County will be delayed for a year because school officials have asked architects to revise the plans to include more space for computer labs, the school board chairman announced Monday.

    The school will be a model for schools across the state and will take about 14 months to build.

    Elements

    Who:

    What:

    When:

    Where:

    Why:

    How:

News Values (identify only those present; not all will be)

Conflict:

Timeliness:

Proximity:

Prominence:

Magnitude:

Impact:

Oddity:

Emotion:

2. Read the following lead. Identify the elements and the news values present:

Two fishermen whose boat capsized in the Atlantic Ocean were rescued Sunday after spending 24 hours floating in life preservers.

George Blackburn and Brian Livengood, both of Wilmington, Del., went fishing off the coast early Saturday. Their boat capsized about 2 p.m. that day after a fire burned a hole in their boat. The Coast Guard rescued them about noon.

Elements

Who:

What:

When:

Where:

Why:

How:

News Values (identify only those present; not all will be)

Conflict:

Timeliness:

Proximity:

Prominence:

Magnitude:

Impact:

Oddity:

Emotion:

3. Read the following lead. Identify the elements and the news values present:

WASHINGTON—Hospital leaders told members of Congress Tuesday that reductions in Medicare and Medicaid could have great impact on the people they care for.

The federal budget calls for $115 billion less for Medicare and $21.6 billion less for Medicaid. More than 1,000 hospitals across the country depend heavily on the two federal programs for about two-thirds of their annual revenues.

Elements

Who:

What:

When:

Where:

Why:

How:

News Values (identify only those present; not all will be)

Conflict:

Timeliness:

Proximity:

Prominence:

Magnitude:

Impact:

Oddity:

Emotion:

4. Read the following lead. Identify the elements and the news values present:

The Cityville Town Council approved a 3-cent property tax rate increase for the coming fiscal year budget and more programs to assist in low-income housing.

The tax rate increase means a person who owns a home valued at $100,000 will pay $30 more a year.

Elements

Who:

What:

When:

Where:

Why:

How:

News Values (identify only those present; not all will be)

Conflict:

Timeliness:

Proximity:

Prominence:

Magnitude:

Impact:

Oddity:

Emotion:

5. You are a reporter for the Cityville Chronicle. Write leads for the following information. List for each exercise *who, what, when, where, how,* and *why.* You may want to list the news values to help you determine what information should go into the lead. Think about the local audience. Write just the lead, not the entire story, for each.

   - A Johnston Community College student died yesterday. He was working at a construction site at Town Hall. The construction company he worked for was building an addition to the Town Hall. He was dead on arrival at Cityville Hospital. He died when scaffolding he was standing on collapsed and he fell three stories to the ground. One of the cables holding the scaffolding broke and he slipped off the scaffolding. A board from the scaffolding, which came apart, fell on his head as he lay on the ground. He worked part time for the construction company while he was in school.
   - The Natural Resources Defense Council had a news conference today in Washington. The NRDC is a national environmental lobbying group. It said that smog is getting worse in metropolitan areas across the country and is reaching the stage of "a public health emergency." The group also said the government is seriously understating the problem. Smog is the polluted air that irritates eyes and lungs

and causes long-term health problems. The Council said unsafe levels of smog occur in many large cities twice as often as the federal Environmental Protection Agency says it does.

- The Cityville Planetarium has regularly scheduled programs at 7 p.m. and 8 p.m. on weekdays and 10 a.m. Saturdays. This weekend, the planetarium will expand its offerings to the afternoon. "Sam, Space Cat" will be at 1 p.m. and 3 p.m. on Saturday and Sunday. The film "Beyond the Earth" will be shown at 2 p.m. each day. The planetarium director said the additional showings will allow more people, particularly those who work during the week, to see the special offerings.
- Workforce.com, a local company in the Cityville Research Park, employs 85 people. Company officials have announced a restructuring that will layoff 60 employees and that they hope will allow them to save the company. Profits have dropped 40 percent in the last six months. Workforce.com was founded five years ago. It is an online employment company that had targeted a national clientele, but company officials said the number of clients did not reach expectations.

CHAPTER 6

Beyond the Lead
Writing the Message

Once writers have fashioned the lead, they face the task of organizing the rest of the message. They must decide what will come after the first sentences or paragraphs that hook the audience. The ranking decisions discussed in Chapter 5 that help them write the lead are invaluable in helping them develop the body of the message. Again, with audience needs and interests in mind, the writer outlines how the message will evolve.

As mentioned in Chapter 5, journalists have traditionally used the inverted pyramid form of writing to get to the point quickly and to set priorities for basic news stories. The principle behind the inverted pyramid style—to order information according to its value to the audience—is valuable in much writing today and is becoming more valuable as audiences read more news online and spend less time with each story they read there. The process of ordering information for the inverted pyramid involves critical thinking, an important skill for all writers.

Different styles of writing might be more suitable for other audiences or for a particular medium. Students will find various organizational styles in print and online publications: newspapers, magazines, company newsletters, and so on. If you find yourself reading a story from start to end, study it to identify the elements that pulled you into and through the message. Save it. Some day you may want to adopt the style for a piece of your own.

This chapter discusses

- the inverted pyramid form of writing,
- news peg and nut graph,
- other organizational formats, and
- how to unify writing.

The Inverted Pyramid

Leads must get to the point quickly, and messages must provide important information right behind the lead. Newspaper editors have recognized that need for decades. Henry A. Stokes, as an assistant managing editor for projects at the *Commercial Appeal* in Memphis, Tennessee, once wrote in a staff memo that reporters had to ensure stories attracted reader attention.

Stokes told staff writers they were to "tell the news in an identifiable, functional format that guarantees the reader will receive the best information we can provide, written in a way that the reader can quickly and easily understand."

As a result, the newspaper adopted the four-paragraph rule: Tell the essential message in the first four paragraphs of the story. Details that could be cut would follow.

The format Stokes advocated was the inverted pyramid style of writing, long a standard in journalism. With the inverted pyramid, information in a message is organized in descending order of importance. The most important and compelling information comes first and is followed by information of lesser value. His advice years ago still applies in today's electronic and online media world where important information must be stated immediately.

To be successful at using the inverted pyramid, writers must be able to evaluate and rank information, and they must know what is most important to their audiences. This simple model shows how the inverted pyramid works:

Lead summarizes information. Next few paragraphs back up the lead.

Next section provides background and additional important information.

Next section has information of lesser importance about the topics introduced in the lead.

Final section contains least important information, which could be cut.

In the inverted pyramid, the lead paragraph or paragraphs summarize the most important news values and elements and hook the audience.

The next paragraphs usually give additional crucial information that would not fit into the lead. Background information to provide context comes next. From there, subsequent paragraphs develop the topics presented in the lead, introduce other important information, expand the significance of the information, and give details.

Each section will vary in length, depending on what the writer has introduced in the lead and whether he or she is building the message with quotes. A local government reporter might devote four or five paragraphs to dialogue from a meeting before moving on to other city council actions set forth in the lead paragraph.

The inverted pyramid format helps a writer organize information logically, whether the topic is a single subject or has multiple subjects or elements. If the writer plans to develop several issues in the message, the summary multiple-element lead would set up the organization in the following way:

> The Cityville City Council voted unanimously Tuesday night to renew the city manager's contract for three years with a raise each year and to annex 325 acres south of town and just west of the Newtar River.

Through the inverted pyramid, the writer sets up the order of importance in the lead and how the message will be organized. The most important item is the city manager's contract, which includes a pay raise. Because no one objected to the annexation of acreage, it carries less importance because it is not controversial. It can be discussed second. The important point, the action of annexation, is contained in the lead. The rest of the story follows the lead like this:

> In discussing City Manager Larry Morgan's new contract, council members agreed that Morgan had done an exemplary job in his six years as manager.
>
> "We couldn't find anyone better," said Council Member Dick Haynes, who made the motion to give Morgan a 10 percent pay raise in the first year of the contract and 5 percent in the second and third years.
>
> "We have maintained quality town services with only modest tax increases while Larry has been here," added Council Member Loretta Manson.
>
> The council voted to annex the Heather Hills subdivision following a public hearing in which no one objected to the annexation plan. Residents who spoke said they wanted to come under the town's water and sewer services and to gain improved fire and police protection.

The inverted pyramid is more than just an organizational tool. It has been identified traditionally as a writing style that uses simple words, short sentences, and one idea to a paragraph. It also represents critical thinking: It forces writers to evaluate information and rank it in order of importance. Some critics have said the inverted pyramid puts pressure on reporters to craft an attention-getting, information-packed lead, leaving them little time to follow through with a well-organized message. To be successful, writers must do both: write a compelling lead and organize a story logically. In reality, time constraints or deadline pressure may interfere with both functions.

Why Use the Inverted Pyramid for Media Writing?

Newspapers traditionally have used the inverted pyramid format for two primary reasons: to give readers the most critical material quickly so they can move to other stories if they wish and to allow a story to be cut easily from the bottom, leaving important information intact at the top of the story.

Newspapers have a limited news hole, or space, to fit editorial content, so story lengths can change at the last minute, depending on where a story is placed on a page. For online sites, the story length is potentially limitless, but online writers and editors know audiences have limited time and their work must capture and retain readers.

Many beginning writers question why they should follow the inverted pyramid style of writing when they plan careers in public relations, advertising, or marketing. They object to what they see as a rigid way of writing or formula writing—a basic format devoid of creativity.

At first glance, the objections seem valid. But as students use the inverted pyramid, they will discover plenty of opportunities for description and for their own style to develop. They will also learn that their audiences expect upfront delivery of essential information and that critical thinking goes along with the inverted pyramid style. For the inverted pyramid, writers must gather information, list or rank information, write a draft, and rewrite, as outlined in Chapter 1.

John Sweeney, professor in the School of Journalism and Mass Communication at the University of North Carolina at Chapel Hill, teaches advertising courses. He advises all students, no matter their major, on the value of learning the inverted pyramid structure.

"Before you can develop your own style, you have to master the basics," he tells introductory writing students. "You have to be taught to be meticulous. To say it succinctly, concisely, precisely. You have to be able to distill information, whether it's a 30-second TV spot, or a piece of newswriting, or an ad distilled from a 100-page document on product data.

"Writing also has to have access: Anyone can read it and understand it," Sweeney advises. "You have to focus on what's key, get to the heart of the matter, and put the issue in perspective."

Communicators first must be able to master the traditional before they can be avant-garde. Mastering the inverted pyramid style of writing gives any student journalist or communicator the basic plan for writing messages that focus on what is important and emotionally compelling for the audience. Whether writing for print or online, the inverted pyramid style organizes information so that it is accessible, appealing, simply stated, and easy to understand.

The Inverted Pyramid for Other Media

Research supports the belief that the inverted pyramid retains value today, when the majority of messages are becoming shorter and more direct. Consider broadcast messages, which usually begin with a short, catchy headline to grab the viewer's attention and then summarize the main points. Because broadcast news stories are short, it is imperative for TV and radio reporters to fit in as many compelling facts as possible in the few seconds allotted. The inverted pyramid allows for the speedy, information-rich writing that broadcast demands.

Corporate communication offices and nonprofit agencies, whether staffed by professionals or volunteers, more and more follow the traditional inverted pyramid style. It puts their agenda where readers and editors can see it. Even advertising depends on the inverted pyramid style, communicating to consumers in an abbreviated way a product's qualities and the reasons for buying it.

Although it works best in shorter pieces, the inverted pyramid style can be adapted for longer, more complex pieces, many of which use the inverted pyramid format early and then other organizational patterns later. For example, nondeadline pieces, such as feature stories and documentaries, attract readers best by getting to the point and summarizing first. Simple pyramiding in nondeadline writing can attract readers by creating a mood, setting the stage for more detailed information, or providing a memorable image.

The growth in online news consumption has made the inverted pyramid more important than ever. Many online news readers are quickly skimming the Web or their mobile phones for the latest headlines. Bombarded with an increasing array of news sources, online readers want to know quickly what is the point of a story.

In one sense, news Web sites themselves are one giant inverted pyramid. News sites put the most important information on their homepage, often in the form of brief one-paragraph story summaries called "blurbs." If the blurb entices a reader, he or she may click deeper in the site to get the full news story. And from that news story, the reader may have the option of reading original source documents, archival material, or other news stories related to the original article. Because the online reader with each click can exercise the choice to go deeper in to the material, online writers don't have to cram tangential information in to every story, but they do need to think about ways they can construct an inverted pyramid of links that will make it easer for the reader to read more information if he or she desires.

Organizing a Story

The basic work of organizing a message in inverted pyramid style is done when you use the steps outlined in Chapter 5 for writing leads. The writer first identifies news values and the elements needed to structure a lead. News values and elements introduced in the lead will be developed in greater detail within the message. The writer will use the remaining news values and elements in subsequent paragraphs based on ranking information important to audiences.

In summer 2008, a sailboat operated by a student crew from Texas A&M University capsized in the Gulf of Mexico. The initial stories reported the boat missing after the crew failed to check in by radio at a specific time. Updated stories followed the 26-hour search, then the rescue efforts.

Broadcast media and online sites continually updated the leads and information at the top of their stories as the ordeal unfolded. Reporters had basic information to consider:

Who:	Four student crew members and two coaches
What:	Capsized, then were found after drifting
When:	26 hours Friday to Sunday
Where:	Gulf of Mexico
How:	Boat rolled on its side
Why:	Boat lost its keel

Look at the news values we discussed in Chapter 5 and determine which ones apply here. The human interest angle is crucial as is the timeliness as the news is updated. Conflict and oddity could be relevant in man versus the sea and the rarity of a student crew floating in the Gulf of Mexico for more than a day. Other news values such as impact, prominence, or magnitude may not exist.

Consider the lead from MSNBC after the crew was found:

> Four student crew members and the captain of a capsized Texas A&M University sailboat are alive after 26 hours in the Gulf of Mexico without a life raft–thanks to a heroic coach who gave his life to save two students, as well as their own survival training.

The lead identifies the elements *who*, *what*, and *how* with the elements *when* and *where* understood. A second paragraph—a direct quote—expands on how they survived.

> "The students are here today because they did a great job. They were positive, they didn't panic. They kept working as a team and taking care of each other," Steve Conway, skipper of the "Cynthia Woods," told TODAY's Matt Lauer Monday from Galveston, Texas. "We pretty much did a textbook drill. We held onto each other very tightly, and we used our belts and our rigging to lash ourselves together."

Later graphs answer why the accident happened.

For any natural disaster or breaking news event, reporters will update information continuously. Story angles will focus on what readers and viewers need to know to prepare for storms and protect themselves and their property, or the details as police search for suspects.

Applying News Elements and News Values

A news value, such as oddity, may be referred to in a lead but then be developed fully later in the message. Remember the lead in Chapter 5 about the wedding dress? Although readers have the basics from the lead that something was lost, they may want more information about how the house was lost. The body of the message answers that question.

FARGO (AP)—He lost his home, but saved a wedding dress.

Joe Westbrock dashed back into his burning apartment building Saturday afternoon in south Fargo after alerting others to the blaze.

Westbrock, who lives on the third floor with his girlfriend, said there was little smoke or fire on the floor when he rescued his girlfriend's wedding dress. He said he also grabbed a laptop computer.

"She said her wedding dress was up there, and without even thinking, I just ran back in," Westbrock told Fargo's KFGO radio.

No one was injured in the fire.

Westbrock said he saw the fire after hearing a loud banging noise. When he realized the danger, he pulled the fire alarm and knocked on doors to alert others.

"My dad was a volunteer firefighter, so I've seen all the videos growing up," he said. "I've gone through all the drills with him. I used to be a lifeguard in high school...everything just kicks in to be calm, collected and try to be levelheaded. Some type of instinct told me to run and grab the fire alarm and knock on people's doors."

He has not been able to get back into the building to see if anything else is left.

The wedding is set for early next year.

Damage to the apartment building has been estimated at more than $750,000. Dozens of people were displaced by the blaze.

Fire officials say they cannot determine the cause of the fire, but Fire Department Capt. Dan Freeman said officials do not consider it suspicious.

In this story, the writer uses a short lead that focuses on *who* and *what.* Graph 2 gives readers information about *where* and *when* and answers how he lost his home and saved the dress. Readers reach paragraph 5 before they learn no one was injured.

Beyond the news value of oddity, the story has impact because of the dozens of people displaced, human interest because of the dress and Westbrock potentially saving lives by pulling the alarm, and magnitude in the damage estimate. Conflict and prominence are not relevant.

Instead of writing a straight news story about a fire that caused $750,000 in damage and displaced dozen of residents, the reporter chose to emphasize one aspect to attract readers and make them pay attention.

You also might have noticed in the organization of the story that the information came in paragraphs of varying lengths. Paragraphs in an essay for an English composition or literature class differ from paragraphs in all forms of media writing. In an essay or composition, a paragraph can be a whole presentation or argument on a topic. But in mass communication, a paragraph is identified as a single unit of timely information and usually is one to three sentences long. It conveys a solitary fact, thought, or "sound bite" from the larger message. When a writer is concerned with transmitting information quickly, his or her ideas about paragraphing change.

As mentioned in Chapter 4, journalists rarely use the word "paragraph." In the newsroom, a paragraph is a "graph." This abbreviated word symbolizes the abbreviated form that paragraphs take in news stories. A graph generally will have several sentences, but on occasion it may be one sentence long and transmit a single news element or news value.

News Peg and Nut Graph

Newspaper reporters talk about the *news peg* when developing stories. The peg, just like a peg on the wall where you hang a coat, is what a writer hangs the story on. It is the reason for writing the message. In the sailboat story, the news peg comes in the lead: The crew has been rescued.

Every piece of writing—whether it appears in print or is aired or shared—has a news peg. Writers, no matter their skill or medium, have a reason for composing a message. That reason is spelled out in the *nut graph:* the paragraph that defines the point the writer is making. The rest of the message expands and clarifies the singular idea in the nut graph.

In some cases, the lead serves as the nut graph, particularly if it is a summary lead, and sometimes the nut graph is more than a paragraph long. The nut graph should be in the first four to five paragraphs or writers risk losing audiences who want the point quickly. In today's writing of shorter paragraphs, the nut graph might be lower because audiences don't have to wade through long copy. When writers use anecdotal or descriptive leads, as described in Chapter 5, they must summarize and focus the message for audiences after drawing them in.

Look for the nut graph in this *Washington Post* story by Dan Morse:

> We could all use one from time to time: a dog that can find the darn cellphone.
>
> Maryland has three. Their job is to sniff out phones smuggled into prisons.

> "Seek," Sgt. David Brosky told his dog Alba yesterday, offering a public demonstration at the former Maryland House of Correction in Jessup.
>
> Alba made her way through an unoccupied prison cell until she came upon a rolled-up pair of jeans on a bed. She sat, a signal she had found something.
>
> "Good girrrrrrrrrl," said Brosky, a corrections officer, handing the dog a ball, a reward for finding the black cellphone tucked in the pants.
>
> The state's trained dogs—Tazz and Rudd, along with Alba—could be the solution to a problem facing prison administrators nationwide, a solution taking hold in the Washington region.
>
> Smuggled cellphones allow inmates to run criminal enterprises, threaten witnesses and warn fellow inmates about the movements of correctional officers, state officials said.

By the second paragraph, readers have a clue to the story: dogs sniffing phones in prison. In graph 7, the actual nut graph, readers learn the point: Smuggled cellphones allow inmates to continue criminal activities from within prison walls.

Remember *The New York Times*' descriptive lead about the Austrian monks from Chapter 5:

> HEILIGENKREUZ, Austria—As noon draws near, the monks glide into the church, their white cowls billowing behind them. They line up in silence, facing each other in long choir stalls. Wood carvings of saints peer down on them from the austere Romanesque nave.
>
> Bells peal and the chant begins—low at first, then swelling as all the monks join in. Their soft voices wash over the ancient stones, replacing the empty clatter of the day with something like the sound of eternity.
>
> Except, that is, for the clicks of a camera held by a photographer lurking behind a stone pillar.
>
> It has been like this since last spring, when word got out that the Cistercian monks of the Stift Heiligenkreuz, deep in the Vienna woods, had been signed by Universal Music to record an album of Gregorian chants.

> When the album, "Chat: Music for Paradise," was released in Europe in May—and shot to No. 7 in the British pop charts, at one point outselling releases from Amy Winehouse and Madonna—the trickle of press attention turned into a torrent. (The CD will be released in the United States on Tuesday.)

By graph 5, readers learn the news peg that is included in the nut graph: The CD will be released within days in the United States, hence coverage by U.S. press.

Other Organizational Styles

Although the inverted pyramid works for much writing, other formats might seem better for a particular message because of the event reported. Some formats use the inverted pyramid format to introduce material, then move into another organizational pattern.

Chronological Format

In some cases, making the decision about how to organize the body of a message is easy. Chronology—telling events in the same order in which they occurred—often can meet audience needs. A breaking news story about a bank robbery, for example, would have a summary lead telling that the robbery occurred, where, and when. Then, after the nut of the news is clear, events would be revealed chronologically. The writer would organize the rest of the story by using time elements, as in the following article:

> A masked woman robbed the First Guaranty Savings and Loan on Main Street shortly after 9 a.m. today and escaped into a thickly wooded area nearby. Police have made no arrests.
>
> The robbery occurred when the woman entered the bank and approached a teller. She handed her a note asking for money and saying she had a gun in the sleeve of her sweatshirt.
>
> Although the teller did not actually see a gun, she gave the woman an undisclosed amount of cash. The woman put the money into a purple sack, ran from the Savings and Loan, and disappeared in the woods behind the bank's parking lot.

At 6 p.m., police were still looking for the suspect, who was described as a white woman in her mid-20s. She weighs about 150 pounds and stands about 5 feet 6 inches. She has shoulder-length blonde hair. She wore a purple sweat-suit and had pulled a stocking as a mask over her face. Bank employees could not describe her facial features.

Here, the lead, or the first paragraph, states *who* did *what*, *where*, and *when* and the latest information. Graph 2 starts *how* events unfolded. The last time element tells readers the status of the investigation at the newspaper's deadline.

In breaking news stories that are continually updated, such as those online, chronology works well as a format. New information can be added in the lead and first few paragraphs. All the details that have unfolded chronologically can remain. Any additional information that adds to the timeline can be inserted easily.

While some messages can be developed chronologically, organization generally is not that simple. Not all messages involve action that evolves over time. For example, a high school principal writing in the school newsletter cannot use chronology to inform teachers about changes in ordering classroom supplies. Although teachers may be interested in the events that led up to the changes, they want to know the specific changes immediately. That is when another format, such as inverted pyramid, is needed.

Hourglass Format

Some writers have adapted chronological development to longer stories in what they call the *hourglass format* of writing. A summary lead followed by the inverted pyramid style gives readers the most important information in four to six paragraphs, allowing them to stop at the end of the inverted pyramid segment. Then the writer sets up more information with a simple statement by a source, such as "The police chief described the events this way."

Beyond the transition statement, the message unfolds chronologically. Writers can use the style for many kinds of stories, such as telling of the search for a lost child, recounting a day in the life of a popular singer, or bringing out the details of a baseball game. Electronic media writers often use the hourglass format. For example, a local television station aired a story about a crime that police had been unable to solve. After noting the latest information, the reporter said, "Here's how police have recreated the sequence of events." The details that followed were a chronological account of the crime. The story ended with the reporter showing the local telephone number for Crimestoppers.

Mapped Format

Assistant Professor Jacqueline Farnan and newspaper copy editor David Hedley discussed another variation on the inverted pyramid style called the *mapped format.* They noted that the inverted pyramid becomes confusing for longer pieces, but they believed it served as a way to introduce the most important elements of the message.

Mapped format is a technique to indicate points of interest within the message, just as a map includes highlights for its readers. The mapped format benefits topics, such as business and government, that are of interest to readers. It also aids readers in finding information of particular interest to them in longer stories.

A mapped message is organized into sections. The first is the inverted pyramid lead. Following the lead, a series of subheads in a subject–verb–object form define categories of information. Readers can quickly find the segments of information that most benefit or appeal to them.

Subheads for an expanded story on the bank robbery would look like this:

Robber Approaches Teller
Escape into Woods
Police Still Searching

The mapped format can also help the writer organize. Assume you are writing a story on the cost of funerals and the alternatives to traditional burial. Your research finds categories of information: reasons why funerals are expensive, caskets and their costs, funeral home expenses, cost of burial plots, cost of cremation versus burial, memorial services, and how to cut costs. After drafting the lead, you can group categories of information under subheads, which help organize the story and readily identify parts of the story for readers.

Newspapers are not the only medium to use mapped formats. For example, CNN.com uses subheads in its full stories. This style helps readers quickly find information and helps search engines better understand the key topics on each page.

Numerical Format

A writer might organize a message numerically or by points. For example, a city council votes on three issues: water and sewer rates, a rezoning application, and the town manager's contract. The writer would list in the multiple-element lead the actions taken and the votes, thereby setting up the three points to be expanded, in that order, in the body of the story.

Writers covering a speech will often use a numeral or point-by-point format that follows the organizational structure of the speech. For example, a speaker discusses three major risk factors in heart disease. The writer notes the three risk factors in the lead: smoking, lack of exercise, and lack of a well-balanced diet. The points serve as transitions from the lead to the sections of the message. The reporter's story might read:

> Cardiovascular disease is the No. 1 cause of death in the United States, but it can be reduced with lifestyle changes such as no smoking, regular exercise, and a well-balanced diet, the chairman of the American Heart Association's Wayne County chapter said Tuesday.
>
> Gus Rivas said Americans should pay attention to the risk factors at an early age and get children to be aware of healthy lifestyles.
>
> More than 3,000 children smoke their first cigarette every day. This number will translate into more adults who are at risk for cardiovascular disease.
>
> "Children consume more than 947 million packs of cigarettes in this country per year," Rivas said. "More than 25 percent of high school students who smoke tried their first cigarette while in the sixth grade."
>
> Youngsters need to exercise, he noted. Studies show that today's youth do not get enough regular exercise.
>
> "Riding a bike, walking, even doing household chores can establish fitness patterns," Rivas said.
>
> A well-balanced diet low in fat is essential to reduce the risk of heart disease, Rivas said. About one out of four children is obese, and obese children are at a risk for obesity as adults.

The writer followed the lead, using the three points or risk factors as a way to organize and unify the story.

Unifying Writing

Any story, memo, news release, or online message needs unity to be a coherent and complete piece. Each paragraph in a written piece must follow the preceding paragraph logically and build on previous information. Each section of the piece must fit the subject or theme. Unifying writing takes careful thought and planning, and it requires rewriting or reorganizing after a draft is done.

Transitions and repetition of certain words are ways to unify writing and to get readers from the beginning to the end. The first two or three paragraphs set up many of the unifying elements—for example, people, places, things, controversy, or chronology.

Repetition of Words

Some writers are uncomfortable repeating words in their writing. They pore over the thesaurus or dictionary, looking for synonyms that might not be as good as repeating the word itself. Repetition is okay; it offers unity in a message and gives readers familiarity. Repetition is also clearer; readers are not stopping to match synonyms and words.

The topic will determine the words repeated. A memo that covers changes in employee benefits should use the word "employee" throughout rather than switching from "worker" to "staff" to "professional." The same applies in writing about an organization; "organization" or the organization's name can be used throughout rather than "group," "agency," or "company."

Transitions

Transitions are cues for readers. They set up changes in location, time, and mood, and they keep readers from getting lost or confused.

A simple sentence or word might be needed as a logical bridge from one section of the message to the next. Any transition should wrap up the previous thought and introduce the next one.

> "We must continue our efforts to reduce teenage pregnancy, and our programs are aimed to do that," the governor said.
>
> While the governor defended his policies, others in state government cited lack of action on welfare issues for his dwindling popularity.

The second sentence uses "while" and "others" to indicate a shift from the governor's words to those of state government officials.

Most writers are accustomed to simple words or phrases as transitions. Look at some of the following words and phrases that give readers certain information about where a story is going:

A change in opinion:	but, on the other hand, however
Clarification:	in other words, for example, that is, to illustrate, to demonstrate, specifically, to clarify
Comparison:	also, in comparison, like, similarly, on the same note, a related point
Contrast:	but, in contrast, despite, on the contrary, unlike, yet, however, instead of
Expanded information:	in addition, an additional, moreover, in other action, another, further, furthermore, too, as well as, also
A change in place:	above, higher, beneath, nearby, beside, between, across, after, around, below
Time:	while, meanwhile, past, afterward, during, soon, next, subsequently, until then, future, before, at the same time

Look at how a few transitions work. In developing a story chronologically, time serves as a transition. Refer to the First Guaranty bank robbery story earlier in this chapter. The time elements pull the reader from shortly after 9 a.m., when the robbery occurred, until 6 p.m., when the woman still had not been caught. In other stories, time-oriented words and phrases could be "at the same time," "later that day," "Tuesday," and "last week."

A story about voter reaction on election day uses polling sites around town as geographic transitions: "Voters at Precinct 35 (Town Hall) said...," "Those voting at Precinct 15 (Main Street Presbyterian Church) said...," "Precinct 2 voters (Blackwell Elementary School) said...." Other geographical phrases would be "on the other side of town," "at his father's 25-acre farm," "next door," and "at the White House."

Tone to Unify a Message

Familiarity with your audiences will help determine what tone to set in organizing and writing a message. The tone of a story can act as a unifying device. A PTA newsletter editor knows that her audience is busy, fast-moving, and distracted by children, work, day-to-day routine, and a deluge of information. She knows her audience is in need of quick tips about kids and school. She must write lively copy with short, pithy sentences and paragraphs. Active parents need newsletter copy that looks like this:

> Spring cleaning may leave you with trash and treasures. Please donate them to Southview School's Trash and Treasure sale! This year's sale is planned for May 9.
>
> Jennifer Chen will begin receiving donations April 26 at her home, 322 Dale Drive. For more information, call 499-2342.

In contrast, a lead in *The New York Times* on a story about a Supreme Court ruling has a more formal, serious, thoughtful tone that will carry into the story:

> WASHINGTON—The Supreme Court on Thursday embraced the long-disputed view that the Second Amendment protects an individual right to own a gun for personal use, ruling 5 to 4 that there is a constitutional right to keep a loaded handgun at home for self-defense.

A writer's knowledge of audiences will determine the mood or tone that will best maintain interest and retain it throughout the message.

Quotes to Unify Stories

Quotes can be effective transitions throughout writing. They add liveliness and allow people to speak directly to readers and listeners, helping them feel more connected to personalities and events. They can supplement facts and add detail. News stories and news releases should have a good balance between direct and indirect quotes. Information on direct and indirect quotes, attribution, and punctuation of quotes is given in Chapter 10.

In a profile story about boxer Tony Thompson, writer Zach Berman of *The Washington Post* uses quotes to pace the story and allow Thompson to explain why he fights.

> Thompson doesn't love boxing. He derives no joy from training. He fights for the reward, not the act.
>
> "I really don't like getting hit," he said. "I really don't like to train for boxing. I'm just good at it. It's what I do to make a living. If I had my choices of making a living, I'm not one of those people who would say boxing…Boxing was so far down the list for me."

Quotes can refer to the lead and wrap up a piece, they can leave the reader looking to the future, or they can add a touch of humor. But sometimes writers have to be careful in using a quote at the end. If the story is cut from the bottom, readers should miss only a chuckle, not important information.

Unifying Devices in Practice

Let's go back and look at the short article on the wedding dress and the fire. What are the unifying devices? First, see what the lead set up.

> He lost his home, but saved a wedding dress.

Throughout the story the writer refers to wedding and dress.

The second paragraph identifies Joe Westbrock and makes it clear that a fire is the cause for Westbrock losing his home and identifies the home as an apartment building.

> Joe Westbrock dashed back into his burning apartment building Saturday afternoon in south Fargo after alerting others to the blaze.

Graph 3 uses an indirect quote from Westbrock as reasoning why he went back into the burning building. Repeated are the themes of smoke, fire, and the wedding dress.

> Westbrock, who lives on the third floor with his girlfriend, said there was little smoke or fire on the floor when he rescued his girlfriend's wedding dress. He said he also grabbed a laptop computer.

Graph 4 alerts readers that although he went back into the building, no one was injured.

> No one was injured in the fire.

Graph 5 gives readers more information about Westbrock and his actions. The word "wedding dress" is repeated.

> "She said her wedding dress was up there, and without even thinking, I just ran back in," Westbrock told Fargo's KFGO radio.

Graph 6 continues explanation about Westbrock's actions to save neighbors, which was introduced in Graph 2.

> Westbrock said he saw the fire after hearing a loud banging noise. When he realized the danger, he pulled the fire alarm and knocked on doors to alert others.

Graph 7 adds insight into Westbrock's thinking and repeats terms of "fire" and the theme of alerting residents.

> "My dad was a volunteer firefighter, so I've seen all the videos growing up," he said. "I've gone through all the drills with him. I used to be a lifeguard in high school…everything just kicks in to be calm, collected and try to be levelheaded. Some type of instinct told me to run and grab the fire alarm and knock on people's doors."

The short graph 8 gives readers more information: The building has not been cleared for residents to return.

> He has not been able to get back into the building to see if anything else is left.

Graph 9, also short, returns to the wedding theme.

> The wedding is set for early next year.

Graphs 10 and 11 broaden the story to the fire and its impact on others besides Westbrock. Similar language appears: blaze, fire, apartment building, people.

> Damage to the apartment building has been estimated at more than $750,000. Dozens of people were displaced by the blaze.
>
> Fire officials say they cannot determine the cause of the fire, but Fire Department Capt. Dan Freeman said officials do not consider it suspicious.

Writing is a series of choices—choice of language, pertinent facts, introductions, organizational pattern, tone, quotes, and topics—to unify copy. All need to be made in an informed way, based on what writers know about their audiences.

Books and other writers can give you tips on how to organize your writing. The best way to learn is to apply the techniques through your own efforts. Do not let organization just happen. Remember the stages of writing. Make an outline. Consciously apply a certain organizational style to your writing. Let someone else read your piece to see whether it makes sense.

Good organization helps you reach your audience. Return to the Associated Press drug bust story on page 83 in Chapter 4. The reporter uses all the strengths of simple writing, repetition for unity, and quotes as transitions to pull readers through an emotionally compelling story that could have been just another routine drug bust story. The following chapters will guide you further in knowing your audience and writing for it.

Exercises

1. You are a reporter for *The Cityville Chronicle*. You have picked up the following police report—written last night—from the town police department. Write a message with a summary lead, then develop the message in chronological order.

> Report: Tony's Restaurant Robbery
>
> Investigating Officer: Sgt. Rodney Carter
>
> At 10 p.m. a robbery at Tony's Restaurant was reported. Owner Tony Hardy said he was working late preparing the payroll when a man wearing a stocking mask entered the back door of the kitchen at about 8:40.

Hardy said the man told him to go into the office and open up the safe. Hardy took almost $3,000 out of the safe and put it into a blue, waterproof sack.

The restaurant closes at 9 p.m. Hardy said he thought the robber knew he was there alone, but he didn't think the robber was a Cityville resident.

Hardy said he got a good look at the man: a stocky white man, about 5'6", and round-faced. He estimated the man's age to be 24. Hardy said the man's shoulders were so broad that he might have been a weight lifter. Hardy suggested that if the thief wanted to lock him up somewhere, the storage closet off the kitchen was as good a place as any. The thief agreed and locked him up there. The thief wrapped a clothes hanger around the door. He told Hardy he had a partner, and that Hardy wouldn't live to see his family and relatives if he came out of the closet before 15 minutes had passed.

Hardy said he waited the 15 minutes even though he didn't believe the story about the partner, or at least a partner who would be stupid enough to hang around for 15 minutes. He had no trouble getting out and then called the Cityville police.

We have some leads on the suspect and the investigation is continuing.

2. From the following information, write a summary lead for *The Cityville Chronicle* that focuses on *who, what, when,* and *where,* plus human interest. Then develop the message in hourglass format.

   From the Cityville police chief, Alston Powers, you learn the following:

   Two sisters were playing at a Laundromat about 5 p.m. yesterday. The girls are the daughters of Nancy and Phillip Childs of Cityville. The girls were with their aunt, Janice Childs. The 3-year-old, Jennifer, climbed into one of the washing machines. Her sister, Elizabeth, 7, closed the door. The machine started filling up with water. When she realized the washer was running, Elizabeth ran to get her aunt. Ms. Childs tried to open the washer door but could not, because the washers are equipped with automatic locks on the doors.

Powers said the girl was trapped in the washer for more than five minutes before she was rescued. He said a customer had put coins into the machine before the little girl crawled inside, but the customer hadn't used the machine because he thought it wasn't working.

On the telephone you talk to Chris Gibson, of 124 Basketball Lane, Cityville. He was on his way home from work and stopped at the Glen Rock Shopping Center to buy groceries. He heard screams coming from the Glen Rock Laundry and Dry Cleaner. He ran inside the Laundromat to see what was going on. Ms. Childs ran up to him and asked him to save the child. She asked if he had any tools, so he ran back to his toolbox in the back of his truck and got a hammer. Gibson said he took the hammer back inside and smashed the glass in the washing machine door. He then reached in and pulled her out.

A Cityville Hospital spokesperson said Jennifer was admitted yesterday afternoon and was listed in good condition. Her parents could not be reached for comment.

3. You are a reporter for *The Cityville Chronicle.* You are to write a story from the following information. Focus on a summary lead with a local angle. Organize the story in inverted pyramid.

A group of 55 cyclists from the United States arrived in Ho Chi Minh City in Vietnam yesterday. They ended a 1,200-mile course through Vietnam. The trip took them 20 days. The course was fairly grueling through some of the country's mountainous areas as well as flat parts. The group camped and stayed in villages along the way.

The U.S. Cycling Federation, which arranged the tour, said it planned to organize another event next year. Officials said the tours are a way to allow U.S. residents to get a close-up look at the country and their people.

When the group arrived it was greeted by firecrackers, flower necklaces, and cold towels. Bob Lester, 33, of Cressett, was one of the cyclists on the trip. He said, "This trip was the most amazing thing I have ever done in my life. I would recommend the experience to anyone who can pedal a bike." The cyclists are expected to return to the United States in two weeks.

The tour was part of an effort to open up Vietnam to outsiders and to present a different picture of the country than people had come to expect from the Vietnam War.

Among the cyclists were seven Vietnam veterans and three Vietnamese Americans, all from the United States. The 55 cyclists were from 23 states.

Several of the Americans said the journey had erased any doubts they might have held about Vietnam and its people.

4. You are to write a story for the next issue of *The Cityville Chronicle*. Write a summary lead, then organize the story point by point. Make sure to unify your writing. Your audience is Cityville residents.

LuAnne Neal, director of public affairs for the state Department of Commerce, tells you today the state is launching a three-part train safety program. The state has had its share of train crossing accidents, one recently in Johnston County where a man was injured when his car was hit at a crossing. The worst accident occurred five years ago when an engineer was killed and more than 350 people injured when a train derailed after hitting a truck near Haysville.

First, the state is asking that state highway crews work in cooperation with the Department of Commerce to inspect train crossings in the state. Engineers who ride the trains will spend the next month noting intersections that don't have lights or warning signals that possibly might need them. Highway workers can do the same in their jobs.

Second, the state is compiling statistics on the most dangerous railroad crossings in the state, that is, the ones with the most accidents. That way officials will know where to focus state and federal monies in improving the most dangerous crossings.

Third, a public education program will caution drivers on crossing railroad intersections. Too many times an accident was caused because a driver tried to beat the train to the intersection. That kind of action endangers not only the driver but everyone on the train, whether it is a passenger train or a freight train. The state will put flyers at drivers' license offices and in license renewal tag offices around the state. The flyers will be distributed to all students taking drivers education. Notices will be sent to all people who are renewing their automobile or truck license tags.

References

Jacqueline Farnan and David Hedley, "The Mapped Format: A Variation on the Inverted-Pyramid Appeals to Readers." Paper presented at the Association for Education in Journalism and Mass Communication Conference, Atlanta, GA, August 1993.

Fred Fedler, *Reporting for the Print Media.* New York: Harcourt Brace Jovanovich, 1989.

"Newswriting for the Commercial Appeal," produced by Lionel Linder, editor, and Colleen Conant, managing editor, 1989.

William Zinsser, *On Writing Well.* New York: Harper & Row, 1976.

CHAPTER

7

Producing Online Content

Most writers who work for media today produce copy with an eye and ear toward their companies' online sites. As the audience for online news continues to grow, traditional print and broadcast news sources are moving more breaking news coverage and other features to their Web sites. Technology companies like Yahoo!, AOL, and Microsoft dominate online news consumption in the United States. And millions of people who could never afford to print a newspaper of their own have become amateur reporters or commentators with their own blogs that cost nothing to publish online.

Increasingly, editors expect entry-level reporters as well as experienced staff to be more than just writers or photographers. Reporters today must be able to choose the right medium to tell each story, and they must be able to use the tools necessary to collect and edit information whether it is text, still images, video, audio, or animated and interactive graphics. You might have a job as a reporter who gathers audio and video along with notes. An editor might re-edit your story for multiple media, or you might do it yourself.

Professional communicators are trying to reach audiences in new ways. They are distributing news headlines via e-mail, mobile phones, and online social networks. Even in a multimedia world, writing remains the critical skill. Understanding and knowing audiences is also crucial, particularly in a media environment where newspapers, television stations, and Internet sites are competing for readers' and viewers' attention. Information that is relevant, concise, accurate, and complete is just as important for online content as for any other medium.

In this chapter you will learn

- how historical and other developments have led to a world of online information,
- the components of a news Web site,

- specific writing formats for online news stories,
- the effect of online audiences on news values,
- how to integrate a written story with multimedia elements, and
- challenges and opportunities facing future professional communicators.

The World Goes Online

The growth of the Internet as a communication tool ranks as one of the most important revolutions in publishing. Like the revolution set off by Johannes Gutenberg's invention of the printing press in the early 15th century, the growth of the Internet in the final decade of the 20th century made the publication and distribution of the written word much cheaper for publishers.

But the Internet, which has distribution methods from e-mail to instant messaging to the World Wide Web, has become more than a tool for cheap publishing. Its multimedia capabilities allow for video, audio, photos, and animations to be distributed without the expense of broadcast towers or government licenses and even without the delay of mailing a videotape. More revolutionary than the Internet's multimedia capabilities is its reliance on "hypertext" that links one page to another in an endless trail of footnotes and citations. Hypertext changes the way people consume and evaluate information. It has also led to changes in the relationship between publisher and reader.

Before the Internet, consuming a news medium such as a newspaper, magazine, or television newscast generally was the same for every member of the audience. A subscriber to the local paper received basically the same content at basically the same time of day as every other subscriber. Viewers of a television newscast saw the same program at the same time of day as every other viewer of that newscast. But with the advent of the Internet and other digital technologies, readers now have much more control over what news they read and the time and place they read it.

Although the explosion of the Internet as a news source in the United States dates only to about 1996, the concepts behind the Internet go back to about 1945 when Vannevar Bush, the director of the Office of Scientific Research and Development under presidents Franklin Roosevelt and Harry Truman, wrote an article called "As We May Think" in the July 1945 issue of *The Atlantic Monthly*.

In the article, Bush suggested that scientists whose ingenuity had been focused on war efforts turn their attention to the organization of the vast and rapidly growing collection of human knowledge. Bush proposed a tool called the "memex" to aid in the organization of the world's information. He described it as "a device in which an individual stores all his books, records, and communications, and which is mechanized so that it may be consulted with exceeding speed and flexibility." He said that its "essential feature" would be the ability of its users to connect information through a series of "trails."

Twenty years later Theodor Nelson, a sociology professor at Vassar College, began widely using the term "hypertext" to describe the information trails imagined by Bush. A reporter covering one of Nelson's lectures that year described hypertext as a "non-linear presentation of material on a particular subject." Just a few years after that, the U.S. Department of Defense began building a network of computers that would become the precursor to the Internet.

The networking technology that underpins the Internet remained the domain of the government for the next two decades. Internet didn't become widely available to the public until late 1990 when computer scientist Tim Berners-Lee created a new system for physicists around the world to share data. Berners-Lee called his set of computer programs "the WorldWideWeb project," and he made the code generally available for others to use for free.

In 1993 a group of professors and students at the National Center for Supercomputing Applications at the University of Illinois at Urbana-Champaign developed Mosaic, the first Web browser. The Mosaic computer program made it easy for a person who didn't know computer programming to read text and view images stored on a remote computer that connected to the Internet. Unlike many computer programs, Mosaic was also available for free to most users.

Newspapers made their first foray into online publishing by posting stories to gated online services, such as CompuServ and America Online. They began migrating to the Web in the mid-1990s, and visits to newspaper Web sites quickly increased for the first time as people stormed the Web looking for election returns in November 1996.

The Internet exploded as a source for news during the last decade of the 20th century. In 1996, 12 percent of Americans went online to get information on current events, public issues, and politics. News events such as the Clinton-Lewinsky scandal, the Super Bowl, and the terrorist attacks of September 2001 each led to a higher plateau in the numbers among the online news audience. By 2000, one in three Americans went online for news at least once a week. In late 2007, more than seven in 10 Americans said they went online for news. During the same time period, audiences declined for daily newspapers, television news, and radio news.

Electronic Media Then and Now

New media always bring about new ways to reach audiences. In preparation for discussing online communication, significant developments in electronic media, as shown in Box 7.1, deserve some attention: the telegraph, the telephone, radio, television, and the Internet.

BOX 7.1 Highlights in Electronic Media History

1844	Samuel Morse introduces first U.S. telegraph line
1861	Telegraph used, along with Pony Express, to report news from Civil War battlefronts
1877	Alexander Graham Bell patents the telephone
1878	First telephone exchange installed, allows one telephone subscriber to call another
1906	First experimental broadcast of AM radio
1912	RMS Titanic sinks; distress signal and news of disaster is transmitted worldwide via telegraph
1920	KDKA in Pittsburgh broadcasts the results of the presidential election
1922	First radio advertisement broadcast on WEAF in New York, lasts 10 minutes
1927	Radio Act provides government with authority to issue licenses and assign frequencies to radio stations
1933	President Franklin D. Roosevelt addresses the public via radio in a "fireside chat" meant to alleviate anxiety during the Great Depression
1933	"War of the Worlds" broadcast results in mass hysteria
1940	FM radio is introduced
1948	Demand for television increases; 975,000 televisions manufactured, up from 179,000 in 1947
1950	CBS gives the first demonstration of color television
1964	First television correspondent arrives in Vietnam to cover war

1971	First e-mail sent by computer engineer Ray Tomlinson
1973	First call made on a handheld mobile telephone
1983	FCC approves the first mobile phone for civilian use in the U.S.
1991	British scientist Tim Berners-Lee introduces the World Wide Web, the system of hyperlinked documents held on the Internet
1995	First web-based mail software released to public
1999	Google launched by Stanford University classmates Larry Page and Sergey Brin
2001	XM Satellite Radio launched
2006	Western Union sends its last telegram

Telegraph: Quick, Short, and Sweet

Introduced by Samuel Morse in 1844, the telegraph provided a solution for East Coast to West Coast communication. This new technology allowed an operator to transmit written messages as signals (Morse code) across wires so news could travel from city-to-city, then state-to-state, and eventually across the country at a faster rate than ever before.

The telegraph played a key role in the Civil War, as newspaper editors in the North and South sought to gather and report news as quickly as possible. By 1912, messages could be sent by wireless, and distress signals were telegraphed to nearby ships when the Titanic sank after striking an iceberg. Distant wireless operators reported rescue operations to news organizations, and by early morning, the entire world grieved simultaneously the loss of more than 1,500 passengers. Such instant communication paved the way for a consolidation of news organizations now known as the Associated Press, formed by U.S. newspapers in hopes of pooling resources and saving expenses through telegraphic news delivery. Consolidation provided for a standardization of the news. *The AP Stylebook*, a staple in today's newsrooms, emphasizes uniform styles of punctuation, spelling and language use.

Telephone: "Talking with Electricity"

In 1877 Alexander Graham Bell patented the telephone, a result of efforts to improve the telegraph. The telephone represented a dramatic change in communications, permitting voice transmission or "talking with electricity" and not requiring an operator skilled in Morse code.

In the early 1900s, about one in every 250 people in the United States had a home telephone. But by 1970, more than 90 percent of U.S. households and virtually all businesses subscribed to telephone service. In the 1990s, fixed-line phones gave way to today's cellular phones. The ability of handheld computers to play music and video and to store text has led many people to favor phones that combine computing and telecommunications with data storage capabilities.

Radio: Communicating through a Box of Wires

Radio at first was the purview of boys who built crude crystal sets so they could listen to a blend of talk, music, and, inevitably, static. By the late 1920s, people could purchase bulky receivers for their homes, and by the 1930s, radios were in 50 percent of U.S. households. Eventually, the radio became a household fixture, much as home computers did in the 1990s.

One of the first radio stations, KDKA, broadcast the results of the 1920 presidential election, and in 1925 news and special events became a regular part of programming. The number of radio stations grew rapidly, and by 1930 radios came installed in automobiles.

As the influence of radio increased, a single broadcast demonstrated the profound effect the new medium could have on public attitude. On October 31, 1938, Orson Welles broadcast an adaptation of H. G. Wells' *The War of the Worlds*. The program used simulated news flashes to suggest that Martians had invaded Earth. Despite frequent announcements that the Halloween program was fictional, mass hysteria resulted. In the aftermath, politicians called for more oversight of radio programming.

During the Great Depression, President Franklin Roosevelt broadcast a series of "fireside chats" in which he reassured an anxious public. Until television displaced it, radio was the dominant medium for information and entertainment in U.S. households and automobiles.

Television: Communication Heard and Seen

The technology required for radio paved the way for the introduction of television. Reporting a 1927 demonstration of television by Bell Laboratories, *The New York Times* said it was "as if a photograph had suddenly come to life and begun to talk, smile, nod its head and look this way and that." The development of television was suspended during World War II. In 1947 manufacturers produced 179,000 televisions; in 1948, the number jumped to 975,000. By the 1960s, 87 percent of American households had at least one television set and in 2003, 98 percent.

Subscription-based cable television introduced more choices and "premium channels" starting in 1972. Not until the 1990s did 24-hour broadcasts become common. Today, more than half of U.S. households receive their television signal via broadband, a form of high-speed Internet access. While television long ago replaced newspapers and radio as the dominant source of news and entertainment, TV viewership appears to have stabilized even as more young Americans turn to the Internet.

Internet: High(est)-Speed Communications

The Internet has perhaps had the greatest influence on modern lives, from the way people conduct business, participate in the political process, shop, and learn about distant people and places. Using the Internet, people all over the globe can communicate via e-mail, instant messaging, blogs, and even in real time, transcending the boundaries of time and geography.

The Internet represents a media environment combining text, video, and audio. News organizations can edit and update stories instantly and augment traditional print/text stories with digitized video interviews or photo galleries for which the print edition would not have adequate space.

Internet technologies allow for "citizen-journalists" who can report or post items they believe to be interesting or newsworthy. The Internet requires users to exercise news judgment or editorial skills because they often must determine the reliability of information found online. Today, going online is a routine activity for Americans in search of news, information, entertainment, and social networking.

Technological innovations affect how you reach your audiences. The access and depth of the Internet allow a diverse audience to watch or read the content you generate, perhaps well beyond the group for which your information is intended. Prospective employers assume today's college graduates will be comfortable creating content in multiple forms—and using new technologies to send it.

The Audience Begins to Participate

Beyond growing as a source for news, the Internet also brought about changes to the types of people who published news. Technology companies, such as Yahoo! and Microsoft, became major sources of news while the audience itself began publishing all sorts of information on the Web. Using hypertext technology, individuals no longer passively consumed news—they shared it, commented on it, and added new information to it. With access to the World Wide Web, anyone could become a publisher.

Perhaps the biggest contributor to the rise in amateur journalism has been the advent of blogging tools that made it easy for people who didn't know hypertext markup language (or HTML) to create Web pages for themselves. The first widely used blogging service was created in 1999, accompanied by other self-publishing tools that made it easier for someone without technical expertise to publish photos, videos, audio, or just about any combination of media online—often for free. Technorati, a company that tracks blogs, keeps an eye on more than 112 million bloggers.

Most bloggers don't consider themselves journalists who report facts to a broad audience. Most blogs are a type of personal diary that mixes opinion and first-person accounts for a small audience of friends and family. Others, however, are tied to media companies and contain news tidbits or staff observations.

As Internet access becomes faster and more pervasive, media consumption habits will continue to change. Many news organizations in the United States are beginning to think about how people will read news and information on mobile phones and other portable devices connected wirelessly to the Internet. The boom in unedited and unverified content that appears alongside accurate information online has made it even more challenging for people to organize, sift through, and validate vast amounts of information.

Online News Is Always On

Online news values are pretty much the same as for any other medium, but the continuous nature of online news can create a new struggle between the value of immediacy and other news values, such as prominence and proximity. Newspaper writers must stop collecting and organizing information at some point so the paper can be printed and delivered. And when it's time to go on the air, even live broadcasters are forced to stop writing and editing so they can present the information to their viewers. But the Internet never goes to press, and the cameras are always rolling.

While continuous news has been around since the advent of CNN, the nature of news is a bit different online than on broadcast. Because broadcast is a linear medium—meaning its delivery of the news moves continuously and in one direction through time—currency or timeliness almost completely trumps all other news values. Small developments in a story line are given exaggerated importance—whether the time horizon of the story is one day, like a refinery fire, or more than a year, like a presidential campaign. Broadcasters who always have air to fill often fill it with repetition, speculation, and analysis. They emphasize immediacy. And they have no choice but to keep talking—about something.

Online writers, however, have a choice about whether and when to move the story forward rather than the obligation imposed by broadcasting. Most online news sites (with the notable exceptions of sites with a blog format) do not emphasize immediacy to the detriment of all other news values. Online news readers choose which stories to read, at what time of day, and in what order. This advent of on-demand news puts a larger burden on the online news writer to balance currency with proximity, prominence, and impact.

Imagine, for example, you are the daytime editor for a news Web site. It's 10 a.m., and the president has just announced a new economic stimulus package. Or the mayor has just announced she won't run for re-election. Certainly both are news, but so is the investigative piece you posted at 6 a.m. about the landfill's contamination of the local watershed. And so is the analysis piece you did of the increasing political importance of Latinos in the upcoming local election.

The two in-depth pieces had been leading the site. But what do you do now? And if you decide to lead with the breaking news, when—if ever—do you put the in-depth pieces back atop the site?

This kind of tension doesn't just happen at the macro, site-wide level. It happens at the story level as well. Do we add the latest news from the campaign trail to the lead, or do we lead with the most prominent?

These decisions have always been a challenge to some extent for wire services, but the additional uncertainty of writing for online is that editors don't know when a reader is going to come back. Newspaper editors know they will get a chance to talk to their newspaper readers tomorrow morning, at a fairly certain time. The broadcast audience will tune in at the top of the next hour. But how often is the online audience coming back? Without the answer to this question, it's tough for online writers to know whether the audience seeks incremental updates or in-depth analysis. Surveys by the Pew Internet and American Life Project indicate that members of the online news audience are slightly more likely to say they read news online for its immediacy than to say they read online news for its depth or breadth.

Online News Is On-Demand

While writers use news values in structuring content, online editors use news values to determine where to place content. Editors of a news site may place one set of stories on the homepage in the morning because they think those are the stories that are the most important for readers to see. By the end of the day, computer records often show the stories that received the most audience attention were completely different stories scattered deeper in the site. Audiences are using their news judgment to decide what to view—often in conflict with what editors think.

Readers have more tools than ever before to disregard the news judgment of editors. They use e-mail, RSS feeds, blogs, and social networking sites to "re-mix" stories from a variety of sources into a news site made just for them and perhaps a group of friends or colleagues.

Readers use their own news values to search for information, and those might differ from what journalism students learn in newswriting classes. Searching is second only to e-mailing in its frequency among all online pursuits. For example, on a day when snow threatened the suburbs near Washington, D.C., "Fairfax county public schools" was one of the most popular search terms on Google Trends. And on the day Lindsey Paulat was arrested for firing a gun in the home of Pittsburgh Steelers wideout Cedrick Wilson, her name quickly appeared as one of the most popular search terms on the Web.

With the Internet, audiences can choose what information they consume and when they consume it. TiVo and other digital video recorders have made "time-shifting" more prevalent among television audiences who literally move programs from the time a broadcaster sends it to another time that is more convenient for them to watch it.

Apple's iPod and other portable digital audio players have done the same thing for "place-shifting" news reports. National Public Radio's news reports, once available to an audience only at the top of the hour, are available anytime via NPR's podcast.

Audience behavior is affecting news judgment in at least one way. News outlets from Yahoo! to *The Washington Post* to *The News & Observer* display lists of the most read, most e-mailed, most discussed, or highest-rated news stories.

Prominently featured, these stories become self-fulfilling prophecies, driving still more readers to them.

For the editors of many sites, watching real-time consumption of news is becoming a factor that determines which stories they cover further, play higher, and explain more deeply. Popularity is becoming a more predictable element of news judgment among professional journalists.

A quick glance at social news sites such as Digg.com shows that the stories most likely to be shared by readers are stories that are remarkably original—some even too good to be true, no doubt. This fact means that, in a world where more people are reading news online, writers must work much harder to differentiate their stories from all the other similar reports across the Web. With so many choices for readers, news writers need to seek unique angles, target specific audiences, and dig deeper for uncovered facts. News values of impact, magnitude, and human interest are just as important online as in traditional media.

What's Different about Online Content

Writers have three primary advantages when they publish online.

1. Online news can be multimedia, incorporating not just text and still images, but audio, video, animation, and audience interactivity.
2. Online writing can be made more relevant, either by publishing news faster or by customizing the content of the story for specific audiences.
3. On the Web, space is virtually unlimited, so writers can explain many more details than in print. Online writers must remember, however, that the audience still has limited time, so long-format writing must be compelling from the first paragraph to the last.

Although online writers can enjoy these three benefits of the medium, professionals know that not every storytelling technique is suitable for every story. For example, a piece about new enrollment figures at the local college might include many numbers, making it appropriate for a long, explanatory text story but not necessarily video. A human interest story about a local personality, however, might warrant using video to show readers the face and behaviors of the story's subject. More and more, professional writers need to practice not just news judgment, but also media judgment—the ability to know which storytelling techniques to use for a particular story.

Multimedia Aspects

In 2007, *Washington Post* columnist Gene Weingarten won a Pulitzer Prize for a piece he wrote about the reaction of subway riders to violin virtuoso Joshua Bell. Weingarten's words won him journalism's most coveted award, but he also used *The Post's* Web site to tell the story with video—a technique that worked well because the audience could see and experience the scene Weingarten artfully described with his words. Without the words, the video would have been curious, and it would have lacked context. The words without the video would have left much to the readers' imaginations.

Just as photographs enhance stories in print, video and audio can make human subjects more compelling, and they can help readers visualize unusual scenes. Video often works well for stories dominated by the *who*, *what* or *how* news elements.

Weingarten's use of video allowed audiences to experience Bell playing in a subway station at any time—they didn't have to be there when it happened. Audiences could view the video on demand. But many online communicators are also streaming live video over the Internet. The White House streams its daily press briefings, and many local newspapers stream high school football games on Friday nights. Both take advantage of the medium's ability to provide immediate information.

Relevance of Online News

Online writers can also use the medium to make their stories more relevant to individual members of their audience. Perhaps one of the biggest challenges for writers in traditional media is the choice of which facts to include in the lead of a story. They must choose facts that are most compelling to a broad general audience. Online writers with some computer programming skills are beginning to look at new ways of telling stories that allow individuals to begin with information most relevant to themselves.

One example might be a story about the local housing market. In print, the lead of such a story might focus on a statistic—perhaps the average sales price or the aggregate sales volume in a market—that characterizes a broad area. But within those broad statistics are often outlying neighborhoods where home sales are bucking the trend. Online, a writer might be able to create a database so that each member of the audience could look up home sales in a specific neighborhood or the sales of homes of a certain size.

Even with this ability to customize information, the writer's job is to put the numbers in context. Understanding data without historical background, or information about an overall trend, requires more effort from the audience. Professional writers know how to make data relevant, help readers process that information, and put it in some usable form.

Another way online writers make their stories more relevant is engaging the audience in online conversation. This dialogue can take the form of a live chat, a list of reader comments on articles, or discussion boards on a general topic.

Writing in these interactive conversations with the audience can have its own style or drawbacks. On one hand, they can take a more conversational tone that inherits some style from broadcast media, such as call-in radio talk shows. Or, because the text lives forever, an awkwardly phrased sentence or inaccurate statement by a writer might give the audience the impression that the writer might not have a strong grasp of the subject or of written language. Writers in online chats must be able to think quickly and clearly on their feet.

The Components of a News Site

To understand how to produce online content, writers must know the structure and organization of Web sites. News Web sites are organized differently than a newspaper, although they have some important similarities. First, Web sites are comprised of two types of pages: index pages that guide viewers to content and the content pages. Newspapers, on the other hand, have only one kind of page that serves both purposes. The headlines that help readers find a story are found on the same page as the body of the story.

Among printed media, the structure of magazines most closely resembles the structure of news Web sites. At the front of most magazines—and on the covers of many—an index catalogues the stories found deeper in the magazine. In a print magazine, the content indexes provide some enticing information about the story and tell readers on which page the story can be found. On news Web sites, index pages also contain enticing information about stories deeper on the site. But the information about where the audience can find the story also contains the computer code the audience doesn't see to link to the specific content.

For example, the contents page of a print magazine might have this summary:

> 62 Parents Battle High Costs of College
>
> This year's freshman class will take out more college loans than any group of college students in history.

The "62" before the text of the headline tells readers that the story can be found on page 62.

On the magazine's Web site, readers might see the same words but without the number 62. Instead, readers would click on the headline and activate the computer code that makes the story appear.

It is important for writers to understand how audiences use index pages differently than content pages so they can use the language (see Box 7.2) and style appropriate to each purpose. Audiences use index pages to skim quickly for information relevant to them. They often spend just a few seconds on an index page, and they rarely click on every piece of content to which items on the index page link. Writing on an index page needs to be brief and informative.

BOX 7.2 Glossary of Web Terms

Home page: the page typically encountered first at a World Wide Web site that usually contains links to the other pages of the site

Web site: a group of World Wide Web pages usually containing hyperlinks to each other and made available online by an individual, company, educational institution, government, or organization

Web page: a single page of data within a Web site, often written in HTML and ending with either ".htm" or "html"

Tag: Identifiers that go around each type of text on a page. The tags may identify links or even text as a headline, such as: <h1>News Alert: Airplane Crashes on Freeway</h1>.

Cascading Style Sheets or CSS: Another type of code that tells a computer how to display items on a screen

Homepages are a type of index page, although not all index pages are homepages. A homepage is the "top" or "front page" or the "cover" of a news Web site, and there editors place the information they most want readers to see. The homepage often is the single most-read page on a Web site.

Other kinds of index pages may be found deeper in the site and often are indexes of only one particular category of information. They can be thought of as "section front" pages or "topic" pages because they contain links to content that is all on the same topic – for example, sports, politics, or entertainment. Some index pages are very broad in their scope while some are incredibly narrow, even down to the point where they are only about a single person.

If the information shown on the index page is relevant to the audience member's needs and if it is presented well, the reader will click on the link for that story. Then he or she arrives at content pages or destination pages for the audience. There the reader will likely spend more time delving deeper into the story. Many content pages on news Web sites follow the format and style of a news story in any other medium.

Leads and Blurbs

From earlier chapters in the text, you are already familiar with the characteristics of a good lead: short, to the point, attention-getting. Such leads are essential when writing for an online audience. Online leads should be brief and full of information for several reasons:

1. Online audiences often quickly skim information and are unlikely to have the patience for any type of lead that delays presentation of the essential *who*, *what*, *when*, *where*, and *why* of the story.
2. Web publishing systems used by many professional news and information organizations often extract the lead and distribute it to index pages or even to other Web sites as a stand-alone piece of content. Leads that don't contain the essential information often seem like heads without a body.
3. Search engines scan Web pages by starting with the text at the top of the page. Online leads should contain any key words a potential reader might use to find the story. Sometimes search engines display the first few words of a story on the search results page.

When writing leads for the Web, writers should emphasize nouns over verbs and especially nouns over adjectives because people are much more likely to include nouns in their search terms. They are more likely to search for the *who*, *what*, or *where* of a story than for the *when*, *why*, or *how*.

Search engines also emphasize the traditional value of tight leads. While the average lead in a newspaper or wire service story is between 20 and 40 words, search engines often display on their results pages only the first 20 to 25 words in an article.

Writers and editors must remember that leads should be written primarily to be read by humans and only secondarily to be read by computer programs, such as search engines. But very often good techniques for search engine optimization are also good techniques for writing a more clear and concise story.

While summary leads are popular online and well-suited to the Web, they are not the only kind of summaries a writer or editor might need to write for an online story. The summary information found on index pages are called "blurbs," and they require a slightly different writing style from the style used in a summary lead.

Remember, index pages are collections of stories, and the audience quickly skims these pages. Blurbs, therefore, need to be very brief and full of information. But they should also be more evocative—or even promotional—in their tone.

For example, compare the headline and blurb on the washingtonpost.com homepage to the headline and lead on the associated story. The homepage blurb had this text:

> **After Iraq, the Battles Continue**
>
> Mixed martial arts star Brian Stann has a story that sells and an undefeated fighting record.

The story had this headline and lead:

> **The War Is Over for Stann, but the Battles Continue**
>
> Before each fight, Brian Stann walks into the cage knowing that whatever happens, nothing will compare to the hell he survived in Iraq.

While both the blurb and the lead are written to tease the reader deeper into the story, the blurb on the homepage conveys more information and has about

30 percent fewer words. The lead on the actual story doesn't tell the reader why Brian Stann is walking into a cage for a fight, but the blurb tells readers right up front that he is a mixed martial arts star. On the homepage, the word "Iraq"—a popular news topic among readers in mid-2008 when the story appeared—is prominent in the blurb's headline. In the story's lead, Iraq is saved until the end for dramatic effect. The blurb aims to draw the reader in by directly promising "a story that sells," while the lead hints at cage fights and a portrait of "hell."

Because they usually appear directly below a headline for the story, it is important that headlines and blurbs are written to work well together, avoiding redundant information where possible. Look at this headline and blurb from the homepage of NYTimes.com:

> McCain Camp Says Obama Is 'Playing the Race Card'
>
> The statement was in response to remarks Barack Obama made warning that Republicans would try to scare voters.

In this blurb, "the statement" is ambiguous without the headline. But alongside the headline, it clearly refers to the comments from McCain's presidential campaign.

Updates to Breaking News

Because of the "always on" nature of online news, information updates must be made quickly when new facts are available. When filing breaking news for the Web, it's important for writers to write a story quickly with as much information as they can verify, even if it is clear that more is coming. This pattern follows on the long tradition of broadcast news, when networks would interrupt their regularly scheduled entertainment program with short news briefs in the event of big news.

For example, a local newspaper might receive word about a shooting at a local high school. Reporters know that concerned parents who can't get through the jammed phone lines on campus will likely turn to the newspaper's or TV station's Web site for updates. It's possible that no one was injured, but it's also possible that several students were killed. A reporter working on this story for the next day's paper would want to wait to obtain the essential information before writing the lead or determining how much prominence it should be given in the next day's paper. But the interest of public safety demands that a journalist post even this cursory information online as fast as possible.

An early version of the story might be a single paragraph that includes only the *what*—that a shooting has occurred. And it may directly acknowledge which important news elements remain unknown. It might read something like this:

> Shots were fired at Central High School shortly after 11:30 a.m., according to police reports. It's unknown whether anyone was injured in the shooting or exactly where on campus it took place.

While the reporter is still waiting for more news, the story could then be fleshed out with background about Central High School or school shootings across the country. A second paragraph may look like this:

> Central High School is no stranger to violence. Last year, two students were sent to the hospital after they were stabbed in a gang-related brawl.

Later, the reporter might hear that a former student is in police custody in the shooting. Where should that information be placed in the story? Rather than add it as a third paragraph, that important information could be worked in to the lead.

> Following a shooting at Central High School this morning, police are holding a former student in custody in connection with the incident. It's unclear whether the student is a suspect, and it is also unclear whether anyone was hurt. Police reported that shots had been fired on the campus shortly after 11:30 a.m.

The story now has some information about *what*, *where*, *when* and *who* was involved. But it's far from complete. The most important information to the news site's audience will be whether anyone was injured. When the reporter receives this news, the lead will need to be rewritten entirely, perhaps like this:

> Three students were killed this morning in a shooting at Central High School. The names of the victims have not been released, but police identified them as two girls and one boy. Police are holding a former student in custody in connection with the shooting that took place shortly after 11:30 a.m.

The lead news element shifted from the *where* and the *when* used in the original lead to the *who*—albeit an incomplete version—in the latest variation of the lead.

Each of the new versions of the story replaces the previous one at the same Web address. This technique is important so that readers who found the initial story can easily come back to the same place to find updates. If each version were published at its own unique address, the audience might never know the story had changed. Most news organizations also print at the top of the page the time the story was updated so readers can gauge the currency of the information.

Each of the changes to the story has been an update. In other words, new information prompted a change in the story. This process would also follow if the death toll increased from three to four, for example. Because the Web allows for information to be changed, it is okay to publish facts that may eventually change.

Structuring Messages

Today, the limitation that writers must grapple with is the time of the reader. The online audience tends to skim news at a much faster pace than the print news audience. A reader not quickly hooked with a compelling and complete lead is a reader likely to click on to the next site.

The Inverted Pyramid Online

On the Internet, which was designed for reliability and where the space is practically unlimited, the inverted pyramid remains one of the best-suited story forms. The inverted pyramid has even become a metaphor for the structure of news sites themselves. The homepage of a news site contains the essential information about a broad range of stories, and as visitors to a site delve deeper, they gain more and more details. From the home page, a reader is likely to click to a news story. From that news story, a reader might click on one or more links to related stories from the archives, primary source documents, or other in-depth information on the topic.

Links are an important tool of online news writing, but they must be used with care. Done well, they can improve the transparency of the reporting and build the audience's trust. Done poorly, they can erode confidence in the reporting as much as any misplaced comma or misspelled word.

Incorporating links into a story allows a writer to omit nonessential details that might interest only some readers. Links can be especially helpful to readers who might be skeptical about the information in the article or to readers with immediate or deep interest in the topic.

A writer might add different types of links to a news story online:

1. Primary source documents, such as town budgets or long government reports cited in the story.
2. Audio or video of full interviews with a source quoted in the story.
3. Older news stories on the same topic.
4. Other sites that contain detailed biographical or historical material related to the story.
5. Other sites where a source may make a longer or more nuanced argument in support of a position noted briefly in the news story with a quote or paraphrase.

Any link that allows readers to examine a writer's reporting methods is a good link because it builds trust with the audience. But writers can also erode trust if they don't use links correctly. Writers who include links in their stories must be aware of two pitfalls:

1. While links to other Web sites are not explicit endorsements of the information found on those sites, they imply a level of validity from the writer to the reader. Linking to another Web site that contains false or defamatory information can tarnish the writer's reputation.
2. Broken links that lead nowhere or to the wrong page can also erode trust. If possible, writers should check their links before they are published. If that's not possible, they must verify their links as soon as possible. Such checks are part of the online editing process and are as important as checking for spelling and grammar.

Editors use two ways to link from a story. "Inline" links are made from words inside the body of the story. "Sidebar" links stand alone, often in a bulleted list, in a separate space adjacent to the story.

Inside the story, editors must choose which words to link so the audience understands where they will go when they click on the link. Here are some guidelines:

1. Link no more than three words in a row. Longer links often are difficult to read on a computer screen.
2. Choose nouns or verbs that describe the destination of the link. For example, if linking to a police report, look for the words "police report" to choose as the linked text.
3. If multiple places in the story reference the destination page, place a link only on the first reference.

When placing links adjacent to the story, here are some guidelines:

1. Write three to five descriptive words as the text of the link. Emphasize nouns and verbs, such as "action unfolds at Olympic venues."
2. Use single word descriptions to tell the reader important information about the medium or style of the destination link. For example, if the link goes to a video of the high school football game, good link text might be "Video: Friday's Game Highlights."
3. Readers have a difficult time choosing from more than three to five links. If your news organization has thousands of archival stories on a topic, don't link to all of them from the space adjacent to the story. It is better to place a long collection of links on a separate page.

The Blog Format

Starting in 1999 with the widespread adoption of the first Web-based, free publishing system called Blogger, the Web has exploded with sites laid out in the blog format. Blogs—short for "Web logs"—grew in popularity first as a tool for amateur diarists to publish text to the Web without the need to know HTML code.

Since then, some of those bloggers have become semi-professional or full-time professionals as diarists, commentators, or even news-breaking reporters in every niche category imaginable. Blogs are now stand-alone columns or even attached to local news. Thus the format has become widely adopted at traditional news organizations like *The Washington Post* and *The New York Times*, where editors once shunned it. Most bloggers, however, are amateurs who do not consider themselves journalists, do not adhere to a tradition of professional ethics, and do not write for a general audience.

Blogs generally have these characteristics:

1. A blog consists of "posts," which can be of varying length. Posts, like news stories or articles, are about a single topic or event. But unlike articles or news stories, they do not necessarily follow the same inverted pyramid structure.
2. Posts are laid out vertically on a blog's homepage in reverse chronological order. The most recent post is at the top of the page and the oldest at the bottom.
3. Professional news blogs are almost always on a single topic. In newsrooms, those topics often are called "beats." Music, schools, parenting, technology, politics, a certain sports team, or a specific television show are all common topics for a blog.

From these basic similarities, blogs can take on all sorts of optional forms. They can be filled with straight news or pure commentary and often are a mixture of both. They might contain dozens of participants' views on an event, such as the hometown supporters who attended the 2008 Olympics. Many allow their readers to comment on each post. Most are written by a single author, but many news blogs have several reporters who post to them. Most bloggers make prolific use of links within their posts to footnote their commentary or to demonstrate transparency by allowing readers to view original source material.

Because of their layout that places the most recent post at the top of the page, blogs are good tools to use for breaking news situations. When a gunman killed 32 people and himself at Virginia Tech University in Blacksburg, Virginia, in 2007, student journalists on that campus and professional reporters at the nearby *Roanoke Times* both turned to a blog format to publish breaking news updates to the Web.

Here are the first four updates on the shooting from *The Roanoke Times.* Note how the newer posts at the top avoid repeating information in older posts—this aspect of the blog format makes it different from updating a breaking news story written in a traditional, inverted pyramid style.

11:53 a.m.

Scott Hendricks, an associate professor of engineering science and mechanics, said he was on Norris Hall's third floor this morning around 9:45. "I started hearing some banging and some shots, then I saw a student crawling on the ground."

Hendricks said he was not sure if he saw any of the casualties, but "I saw a bloody T-shirt."

Hendricks said he went into a classroom with students, closed the door and waited until things were quiet before leaving the building.

11:49 a.m.

The Associated Press is reporting eight to nine casualties, attributing the information to an unnamed official source.

Virginia Tech's Newman Library became a shelter as university staff urged students and passersby to come in from the sidewalk. Library staff estimated that hundreds of people are in the building now, far more than would be usual at this time of day.

Sarah Ulmer, a freshman from Covington, sat on the floor and recounted how she'd been walking between buildings this morning when she saw police officers near McBryde and Norris halls.

"The police said, 'Get out of the way, get out of the way,' and then they said 'Run,'" Ulmer said. She couldn't return to her dorm room in East Ambler Johnson hall because it was near one of the shooting sites, so she headed toward Newman.

"I figured it was safe," she said. "It was the library."

Watching police from the library's fourth-floor windows, David Russell, a sophomore from Montgomery County, Md., echoed a common sentiment, comparing today's events to last year's manhunt for accused murderer William Morva.

"This year with Morva, the bomb threats and this now, it's crazy. It's not really what you'd expect from a small farm school."

Updated: 11:06 a.m.

The Associated Press is reporting there is at least one person dead as a result of multiple shootings on the Virginia Tech campus this morning. Wounded have been removed from buildings. Tech student Steve Hanson was working in a lab in Norris Hall at 10:15 a.m. when he heard what he thought was loud banging from construction. Hanson was soon scrambling out of the building and he said he saw one person who was shot in the arm. At Pritchard Hall, a dormitory near one of the shooting sites, students were being pulled into the buildings and told to stay away from windows and off the phone.

Updated: 10:17 a.m.

Multiple shootings have occurred at Virginia Tech this morning involving multiple victims. The second shooting happened in Norris Hall, the engineering building near Burruss Hall. Police are on the scene and rescue workers have set up a temporary treatment facility. The campus is on lock down. All classes and activities have been cancelled for the day.

Montgomery County public schools are all on lock down. In Blacksburg, no one is being allowed in any school building without approval by the school administrators, said Superintendent Tiffany Anderson.

The university has posted a notice of the incident on its Web site and is urging the university community to be cautious and contact Virginia Tech police at 231-6411 if they notice anything suspicious. No further details were available. The Roanoke Times will update with new information as it becomes available.

Ryan Teague Beckwith, a political reporter who writes the "Under the Dome" blog for *The News & Observer* in Raleigh, North Carolina, also uses this format to update fast-moving stories. But his writing style is more similar to the style audiences might find commonly used by news or sports columnists in a newspaper. In a word, the style is more "conversational" and less formal in its adherence to grammar and more likely to include subjective adjectives like "finally" or "only." Despite these differences in style, verified factual reporting remains the driving force behind his posts. An example of how he covered a tussle in 2008 between the John Edwards presidential campaign and a journalism student at the University of North Carolina can be found at http://projects.newsobserver.com/tags/carla_babb.

It is important for professional communicators to remember that blogging is merely a format, just as the inverted pyramid is just a format. Blogs can be filled with any sort of content—truth, lies, opinion, gossip. Anyone who wants his or her blog to be broadly read and respected must adhere to high standards of accuracy, but writers who are considering using a blog as a source in a news story must remember that many people do not adhere to those standards.

Correcting Online Copy

Because the stories live online long past the time when the story is news, it is also important to correct quickly, permanently, and transparently any error of fact that might make its way into publication. What happens if a reporter has to change a story because a fact is wrong? That is when it is essential to print a correction.

Perhaps the reporter misunderstood the police department spokesman who told her the gender of the victims. Or perhaps the spokesman got it wrong himself. The story of the text must be corrected, and the correction must be clearly described elsewhere on the page. Without a description of the correction, a reader who returns to the story might see the changed information and become confused about whether the old information or the new information is accurate.

Both *The Washington Post* and ESPN, among other news sites, keep collections of the corrections they run in all media. For current examples of the wording of online corrections, you can type either "washingtonpost.com corrections" or "ESPN corrections" into a search engine.

Corrections need not always be formal. Some opinion columnists and bloggers use a more informal tone to alert readers to their errors. For example, *U.S. News & World Report* columnist Michael Barone posted this correction to his blog in 2005:

> In my August 25 post I made a mistake.
>
> *Austin Bay, syndicated columnist, novelist, blogger, and reserve Army colonel who has served in Iraq, is always worth reading. Here, in response to a challenge by blogger Jeff Jarvis, he argues that the Bush administration should try to engage the mainstream media, despite its bias and hostility, rather than engage in what he and Jarvis agree is a policy of "rollback."*
>
> The blogger I cited was not Jeff Jarvis, of www.buzzmachine.com, but Jay Rosen, of New York University. Since I linked to the correct post, many readers

> may well have caught the error and therefore were not materially misled. Still, I'm sorry for the sloppiness, and I apologize to Jay Rosen and to Jeff Jarvis. In his courteous E-mail pointing out my mistake, Rosen notes that many people confuse him and Jarvis and wonders why. My reply was that both have first names starting with J and both seem (to me anyway) to specialize in intelligent press criticism not from a right-of-center perspective–a small category, I think.

Regardless of the tone, placement, or content of corrections, professional writers aim to make them rare. Errors of style, grammar, or fact compromise the trust a writer has established with the audience.

Professional writers should never report information that has not been vetted and verified as fact. Unconfirmed rumors—even those from a usually reliable source—have no place in news writing in any medium.

Challenges and Opportunities

The Internet—and other emerging digital and networked communication tools—are changing the way we share stories about the world in which we live. Writers in all media must be aware of the threats and opportunities that new media present to traditional formats and rules of news.

Perhaps one of the biggest changes is the rush of new publishers to the Internet, from personal diarists to technology companies that have no tradition of journalistic ethics or values. In a world where publishing information is easy, a writer's message must be heard among the chatter and clutter.

Influences to Monitor

Because of the proliferation challenge, news writers might begin to cater their efforts to the audiences' behavior in an attempt to predict the audiences' interests and tell stories that meet those interests. But audiences will always have a need for unexpected news and information. After all, oddity is an important news value. Good writers will need to find ways to bring new information before audience members who increasingly filter out information they consider irrelevant or uninteresting. New information, new ideas, and new voices are needed to provide democracy with constant rejuvenation.

Some professional communicators are also concerned about an emerging "digital divide" between people who use new communication technologies and people who continue to rely on traditional media. While home computers, broadband Internet access, and mobile phone use has exploded over the last decade, many Americans cannot afford the latest gadgets. When considering their audiences, writers need to decide whether they want to reach a broad audience or only the most sophisticated and affluent people.

As technology develops and use expands, today's media world remains somewhat of a Wild West in terms of ethics and values. Writers must proceed with caution in adopting each new information format so they don't unwittingly violate audience trust. Standards and expectations—and sometimes the laws—of privacy, transparency, and professionalism continue to change not only in the United States, but in cultures around the world that have the same access to a small-town newspaper Web site as town residents. Most immediately, news writers today face increased pressure to publish information quickly, sometimes at the potential expense of accuracy.

Media companies have had to consider their liability when readers post story comments directly to the news site. Some postings contain language considered by some to be offensive, vulgar, or profane. While federal law protects online sites from libel in such postings and readers are encouraged to respond, media managers on occasion have opted to shut down and prevent postings, but more for ethical than for legal considerations.

The way writing reaches audiences—literally—through new delivery outlets is also changing. While newsstands and street-corner vendors or living room television sets and cinema newsreels might have been familiar forms of media distribution in the past, the future may be dominated by search engines like Google, online service portals like Yahoo! and MSN, or even hybrid content delivery companies like Apple's iTunes or Amazon.com.

This change in the distribution system of news and information is also changing the business models of many traditional news media companies that behaved according to a long-established standard of ethics and values. Will writers pay to have their articles displayed on popular locations? Will Web sites or mobile phones pay to make unique news and information available exclusively to their audiences? Will telecommunications companies that provide Internet access begin to sell advertising? Will advertisers that used to pay for placement in newspapers and on broadcast stations start paying for placement across a network of amateur blogs? Will readers who want high quality information start paying premium prices for immediate or customized news alerts? All of these changes to the media economy may affect writing styles of future news professionals.

Audience Consumers and Producers

New media provide many new opportunities for writers to make their work relevant and memorable to audiences. As more and more Americans work at desks with computers connected to the Internet, the daytime audience for news has grown remarkably over the last decade. Newspapers and broadcast shows that could reach audiences only once a day now can deliver important information to people all day long.

Breaking news throughout the day is training the news audience to demand more relevant information. They are using databases, search engines, and complex algorithms to find only the stories most relevant to them. For example, people suffering from a rare disease don't need to wait for a new study or drug trial to put that disease in the news. They now can quickly turn to specialty Web sites at any time to see the latest information from the Centers for Disease Control and Prevention or from the American Medical Association.

And it's not just official government or industry sources from which people are seeking on-demand information. They are also turning to each other, and professional communicators are just now learning how to engage with their audience in a conversation that leads to more relevant and enlightening news.

In some cases, news writers are turning to their audience to help them find new information and write more complete reports. As professional news organizations employ fewer reporters, the reporters are asking the audience for help sorting through vast amounts of data—such as campaign finance reports—and helping them be their eyes and ears, watching for everything from potholes on neighborhood streets to drink specials at the local bar.

Many of the best opportunities for writers are probably yet to be imagined, but professional communicators of the future will need to remain alert for new ways to reach audiences with the same high standards of accuracy, completeness, transparency, and relevancy that have won audience trust in traditional media. The rapid changes in communication technology seem likely to increase the pace and broaden the scope of these challenges. However, if history is any guide, writers who remain committed to providing precise and concise information to their audiences will surf the waves of change most successfully.

Exercises

1. Compare the news articles on the front page of a national newspaper's Web site with the news articles on the front page of Digg.com and the front page of a national television news site. Which news values are most commonly reflected in each site's story choices? Why might that be the case?

2. As a writer with a story to share with the world, how would you use social news sites?

3. Look at search trends and social news sites. Compare the stories to those found on a traditional news site. Write a story proposal for your editor about a potential article you could write. Base the idea on your survey of the search and social sites. What news values are found in your story pitch?

4. You are an online editor for your newspaper's Web site. You have the following lead from the print edition. Write a blurb for the home page. Then rewrite the lead so the important keywords would appear in the first 20–25 words in the online story.

> When Carmen Alvarez planned her Christmas decorating, she knew she wanted to string lights across the front of her two-story house. She bought icicle-type lights on sale, then last Saturday morning she hauled the family's ladder out of the garage, set it against the wall by the front porch and began to climb. As she reached the fifth step, the ladder collapsed. Alvarez fell on the concrete front porch steps, broke her collar bone and suffered an upper-back injury. Her 12-year-old son heard her scream and called 911.
>
> Alvarez's accident is quite common. More than 500,000 ladder-related injuries are reported each year, and about 500 people die. Organizations, such as the American Academy of Orthopaedic Surgeons, publish information about how to inspect ladders and do home chores without injury. They sponsor a program called "Climb It Safe."

CHAPTER 8

Beyond Breaking News

Media messages are written for many reasons: Some messages break urgent news stories or give consumer information; some explore newsworthy personalities or places; others present opinion, analysis, or criticism. The reason or purpose of a message can determine the format. A story about a hotel fire, for example, will use a different format and tone from a profile of an award-winning teacher.

Each day audiences find a range of stories in their favorite newspapers, magazines, online sites, or television shows. Writers might follow one of the organizational formats outlined in Chapter 6 or develop a combination that works for the specific piece they are writing. For example, a breaking news story will have a summary lead, background, and chronology. Consumer stories might use an anecdotal lead followed by specific tips. What works for a bank robbery will be inadequate for longer pieces that must communicate more complex information.

Entire textbooks have been written on how to research and construct specific story types, such as features. Web sites such as www.poynter.com and publications of journalism organizations also give tips. No basic text can cover in depth all story types and how to write them. Beyond breaking news, among the more common story types that writers develop are features, obituaries, and speech stories.

In this chapter, you will learn

- the difference between features and news,
- feature leads and organizational formats,
- the parts and style of obituaries, and
- the basics of writing speech stories.

News versus Feature

Apart from breaking news, most articles today are news-features or features. Features can be developed on any subject for any reason and inform or entertain audiences. A writer might be curious about the craft of making a basket he bought while on vacation in Charleston, South Carolina, or the sudden sound of cicadas around his home at night.

Increased reports of domestic violence might prompt a reporter to write a lengthy article on one woman's recovery. Just as with any story, features must be complete, clear, accurate, and fair. Some features will be more concise than others. Features use quotes and adequate attribution, and they mix indirect with direct quotes. Features carry the same news values as news stories—prominence, conflict, oddity, proximity, and especially human interest.

Traditionally, writers have used one value to distinguish news from features: timeliness. Features have a timeless quality. They can be published at any time and remain useful and entertaining. News, however, must be printed immediately. The death of a nationally known fashion designer is news; a story about fashions is a feature. In sum, *news tells*, a *feature shows.*

Some features, however, are linked to news stories. When actor Heath Ledger died, related or sidebar stories focused on abuse of prescription sedatives and antidepressants and the dangers of combining such drugs in potentially lethal quantities. Such sidebar stories can stand alone, that is, they are complete stories themselves but have been written because of a news event.

Adding the Visual

To the traditional distinction of timeliness, writers must add another consideration: How much did the reader see? In other words, did the story take the reader to the scene? Did the writer make the reader feel he or she was there? It has been said that journalism becomes literature when it tells the reader not just what happened but what it was like. Erik Lawson wrote in *Isaac's Storm*, his book on the hurricane that struck Galveston, Texas, in 1900:

> *The wind neatly sliced off the top floor of a bank, leaving the rest of the building intact. It stripped slate shingles from houses and turned them into scimitars that disemboweled men where they stood. Atmospheric pressure fell so low, a visiting British cotton official was sucked from his apartment trailing a slipstream of screams from his wife.*

More than 100 years later, feature writing must still carry the visual impact. Because electronic media more and more have assumed the role of breaking news, newspapers and magazines have taken on a visual aspect seen in more description, in analogies and metaphors, and in more explanation or analysis. The feature story's job is to flesh out the headline and to provide the substance and follow-up—even with the magnitude of a news story like Hurricane Katrina.

Feature stories that appear in a newspaper might also appear on the newspaper's Web site. Because of the multimedia capability of the Internet, an editor could add to the text a slide show with a voiceover or a video where readers see the person and hear her voice during the interview. Additional information might list, for example, agencies that work with battered spouses or the phone numbers for the state's Congressional delegation. Television stations also refer viewers to their Web sites for more detailed information on feature spots.

At the heart of today's feature writing is what Gene Roberts, retired executive editor of *The Philadelphia Inquirer* and managing editor of *The New York Times*, expected of his writers. His expectations are aptly described in the text for the Eugene L. Roberts Prize awarded to qualifying students at the School of Journalism and Mass Communication at the University of North Carolina at Chapel Hill:

> The Eugene L. Roberts Prize is meant to encourage and is dedicated to the story of the untold event that oozes instead of breaks; to the story that reveals, not repeats; to the reporter who zigs instead of zags; to the truth as opposed to the facts; to the forest, not just the trees; to the story they'll be talking about in the coffee shop on Main Street; to the story that answers not just who, what, where, when and why, but also "So what?"; to efforts at portraying real life itself; to journalism that "wakes me up and makes me see"; to the revival of the disappearing storyteller.

The "so what" aspect that Roberts notes is critical for any feature writing. Just as in news stories, many features have a nut graph or news peg. Readers need to know why the story has been written. As noted in Chapter 6, the nut graph might be found after five or six graphs. In a feature story, readers might have to look a little longer, but the nut graph should be clear. Consider this lead from *The Seattle Times:*

> Sally Garcia, a 53-year-old lawyer disabled by multiple sclerosis, was torn.
>
> A new-generation medication, Copaxone, was really working for her. After two decades of being in and out of hospitals, Garcia was taking steps to work again.
>
> Her wallet, though, was in severe distress. Under her Medicare prescription plan, Garcia's share of the expensive drug was $330 per month. All together, medications were taking a third of her disability payments—her only income—and she couldn't swing it.
>
> Copaxone, Enbrel, Remicade: For some patients, such new-generation drugs, often called "biologicals" or "bioengineered" when they are created by genetically modified living cells, have performed magic. In some cases, they work when other drugs have failed, or for diseases that previously had no drug treatments at all.
>
> But they cost a lot—often $2,000 to $3,000 per month.
>
> And in a double whammy, some insured patients who previously paid a fixed amount—likely $30 to $50 even for the most expensive, brand-name drugs—are suddenly finding the rules have changed.

Health reporter Carol M. Ostrom uses an anecdotal lead to set up the story. The fourth graph is the nut graph where readers begin to learn the point of the story: Bioengineered drugs are helping many people. But then graphs 5 and 6 complete the point: These wonder drugs are also priced beyond what many people can afford and what insurance companies will pay.

Writing the Feature Lead

Lead types covered in Chapter 5 apply to writing features. Writers have the freedom to use direct address, descriptive, question, or other leads to attract readers to stories. For example, reporters writing stories in advance of the state fair might lead with:

> Come one, come all, to this year's state fair.

Or:

> Food. Rides. Ribbons. Pigs.
>
> That's what brings Martha Bryson to the state fair each year.

Or:

> For Matt Rutger, vacation is 10 days at the state fair where he has operated his family's foot-long hot dog stand for 20 years.

Whether topics are light or serious, most features do not use summary leads in the same way news stories do. A summary lead might be used in a side-bar or supplementary story in a package of feature stories. Rather than the straightforward *who-what-when-where* news summary format, the summary feature lead might tally reaction in an informal poll or synthesize data. For example, a story that uses an anecdotal lead to introduce an economic story about downsizing of the furniture-building industry in the state might have a sidebar story giving the latest unemployment figures and trend data. The lead might read:

> The state's unemployment rate reached 6.2 percent in June, its highest since August 2004, according to statistics released today by the state office that tracks such data.

The lead summarizes other economic woes in the state.

Probably the most common leads for feature stories are descriptive and anecdotal. Many news-features use those lead types to set up stories grounded in a news event. When reporters use an anecdotal lead, they must remember to carry that example throughout the story. For example, if a campus reporter writes a news-feature about the increased cost of textbooks, she might use one student's experience as a lead into the story. The body of the feature would cover the increased costs, why textbook prices are going up, what percentage the campus bookstore gets, and comments from the student in the lead, as well as from other students. The end of the story would use a quote from the student introduced in the lead.

The Wall Street Journal has utilized this approach to the point that it is often called *Wall Street Journal* style. It takes the reader through the hard facts of the story—the background, analysis, and details that form its hard core—but focuses on an individual, a project, or a family. Look for the features on the *Journal's* front page to study this writing style.

Feature Formats

No single format defines a feature story. A feature might be as simple as the local reaction to a well-known high school athlete's death: A summary lead followed by a unified telling of family members' and school friends' recollections. Or, some reporters might spend months investigating and writing a series of articles to run in a one-day package or be spread out over several days.

Most writers agree that a feature has a beginning, a middle, and an end. Within that framework, a writer uses description, quotes, unifying elements, and tone to pull readers through the story. Narrative devices, such as suspense and action, can also capture readers.

The purpose and content of a feature story might dictate a format. For example, a how-to feature on improving study habits will describe why study habits are important, then outline where to study, when to study, how to organize notes, how to review, and how to gauge success. A feature on reducing the risk of heart attack might begin with an anecdotal lead, focusing on a heart attack survivor, then outline in a mapped format three criteria—lack of exercise, poor diet, and smoking. A story on a retiring faculty member might use chronology as a primary format for chronicling the teacher's career.

Feature Organization

Writers often look for fresh ways to portray a subject covered time and time again. At the retirement of a living-legend baseball star, a writer assigned to the story with a horde of other reporters noticed the star's wife standing several feet behind him, and to the side. The writer told the story through her reaction to the tributes offered to her husband and his farewell words. At a routine story of children going off to camp, a writer noticed that one child's parents had a hard time saying goodbye; they'd kiss the child, send him off toward the bus, then call him back... again... and again... and again. The writer told the story from that family's perspective.

Writing formats change. Newspaper reporters, for example, have adopted more narrative styles of writing, using anecdotal and descriptive approaches. Some editors believe that style attracts more readers; others say the style will pass. Time will be the test of whether new formats attract and retain audiences.

Types of Features

As noted earlier, feature stories are written simply to entertain or inform, standing on their own or complementing news stories. While feature stories contain similar elements, such as description and quotes, they sometimes can be classified by type.

- **How-to** features are included among consumer features that instruct readers or viewers. Experts give tips on topics ranging from how to build a coffee table, make strawberry jelly, find day care, or get a date. Stories should include additional resources and step-by-step guidelines. The story might use bullets to list information, such as specific ingredients and where to buy them for a specialty recipe.
- **Personality** stories can be two- to three-page pieces that focus on one aspect of an individual's life or a 60-inch profile that gives an in-depth look at a person. For example, when the president presents a Cabinet or U.S. Supreme Court nominee, the media will write extensive profiles on the individual's professional—and sometimes personal—career.
- **Historical** features recount events in an earlier time. Often, the anniversaries of events, such as the Battle of Gettysburg, generate such features. When the Discovery shuttle was launched after more than a two-year hiatus, historical features gave an overview of the U.S. space program. Researching these stories might mean looking at archives and other historical records as well as getting oral histories from people who remember.
- **Place or travel** features tell readers or viewers what they will find at a particular destination. Such stories can also be how-to articles, containing information about where to stay or eat and what to see. Detailed description sets the scene so audiences can see the place in their minds—beyond the accompanying photos or other visuals—and be enticed to visit. As a note, most publications will not publish a travel feature if the writer has had his or her expenses paid by a business or group.

- **Color** features are just that: They describe in great detail a colorful event. For example, a reporter assigned to cover a street festival would use language and description that relate to all the senses: sound, taste, smell, touch, and sight. Writers must be careful to use original and fresh description and avoid clichés or superficial language.
- **Brights** are often news stories that can be a short news-feature, generally no longer than six to seven paragraphs and with a twist at the end. Such stories must be well crafted and succinct. Consider this bright, including the end quote, from the Associated Press:

> SHANGHAI, China—These pigs run, jump and swim—almost anything but fly. Thousands of Shanghai residents turned out to a city park to watch a herd of pigs compete in what organizers are calling the Pig Olympics.
>
> They run over hurdles, jump through hoops, dive and swim in shows twice a day, according to the Shanghai Daily newspaper.
>
> The pigs, a midget species from Thailand, begin training soon after birth and can start performing after they are 12 months old.
>
> "These lovely pigs are a special species that is good at sports by nature," said Yang Ying, a manager with promoters Bluesea Broadway Co. Ltd.
>
> Pig races are common in many places, but heavily urban Shanghai offers few opportunities to see farm animals in action.
>
> "It's incredible," said 8-year-old Tan Yizhou, who presented a gold medal to one of the winning pigs. "I never thought that a pig could be so clever."*

Putting It Together

Look at this feature by Associated Press writer Kathleen Hennessey. Her story has all the attributes of good feature writing: quotes, description, prominent characters, suspense, and humor. She uses simple language and varies sentence types.

> LAS VEGAS—Tempest Storm is fuming. Her fingers tremble with frustration. They are aged, knotted by arthritis and speckled with purple spots under paper-thin skin.

But the manicure of orange polish is flawless and matches her signature tousled mane.

She brushes orange curls out of her face as she explains how she's been slighted.

She is the headliner, you know. She is a star. She is classy.

"I don't just get up there and rip my clothes off," she says.

Indeed, the 80-year-old burlesque queen takes her clothes off very slowly.

More than 50 years ago, she was dubbed the "Girl with the Fabulous Front" and told by famous men she had the "Best Two Props in Hollywood." Since then, Storm saw the art that made her famous on the brink of extinction. Her contemporaries—Blaze Starr, Bettie Page, Lili St. Cyr—have died or hung up the pasties.

But not Storm. She kept performing. Las Vegas, Reno, Palm Springs, Miami, Carnegie Hall.

Her act is a time capsule. She knows nothing of poles. She would never put her derriere in some man's face. Her prop of choice is a boa, perhaps the occasional divan.

It takes four numbers, she says adamantly, four numbers to get it all off. To do it classy.

But the producers of tonight's show, just kids, they want her to go faster. She gets just seven minutes.

They gave her trouble last year, too. They even cut her music before she finished.

There may not be a next time for this show, she says. The threat lasts just minutes.

"No, no. I'm not ready to hang up my G-string, yet. I've got too many fans that would be disappointed."

Famous friends

Stardom and fandom feature prominently in Tempest Storm's life—and in her neat, two-bedroom Las Vegas apartment.

Visitors are greeted by photos of a young Elvis, her favorite rock 'n' roller and, she says, a former lover.

The relationship ended after about a year because Elvis' manager didn't approve of him dating a stripper, she says.

But she could not change who she was. Stripping already had made her famous.

It put her in the room with Hollywood's heavyweights. Frank Sinatra, Dean Martin, Mickey Rooney, Nat King Cole.

She dated some, just danced for others. The evidence is framed and displayed on tables and the living room wall.

That's Storm and Vic Damone. Storm teaching Walter Cronkite to dance. Storm and her fourth and last husband, Herb Jefferies, a star of black cowboy films who swept her off her feet in 1957 when such unions were instant scandals. They divorced in 1970.

"When I look at this picture I say, 'What…happened between this gorgeous couple?'" she says.

Storm is rarely wistful. She has no doubt she still is what she once was. Although she performs just a handful of times a year, she would do more, if asked. She chides those who think age takes a toll on sex appeal.

"Ridiculous," she says.

There are just as many recent photos in the room: Storm and her daughter, a nurse in Indiana. Storm and her fiance, who died a few years ago. Storm and a beaming older gentlemen, just a fan who approached her for a photograph.

"That stage saved me," she says as she leaves a sound check hours before the night's performance.

She had been expecting a much smaller space, and she is relieved. She's a "walker," she explains. She needs room to move.

It is a direct and once-racy style, the signature work of Lillian Hunt, the choreographer at the Follies Theater in Los Angeles where Storm became a star.

She was Annie Blanche Banks then. The 22-year-old sharecropper's daughter had fled sexual abuse, two loveless marriages and poverty in small-town Georgia, she says.

She was working as a cocktail waitress but wanted to be a showgirl. First, she needed her teeth fixed.

"Do you think my bust is too big for this business?" she asked Hunt at her audition.

Hunt put her in the chorus line, told her not to gain a pound and called a dentist.

In Storm's telling, she didn't stay long in the background. She got a new name. ("I really don't feel like a Sunny Day.") She took to the spotlight quickly.

No reason to stop

On Sundays, Storm tunes in to a televangelist who tells her anyone can overcome odds. It's the only religion she's ever taken to.

She believes this is the lesson of her life. Be a survivor. Never stop doing what you love; it makes you who you are.

"If you want to get old, you'll get old," she says.

There have been men who disappointed her, financial strain, brain surgery.

After it all, she sits on her couch and exercises in front of the television on a small stationary bike. She doesn't smoke or drink or eat much.

"I'm just blessed, I think. And I know when to push myself away from the table."

If some might see all this as chasing after lost youth, she says she cares little. Younger dancers tell her she is an inspiration to them, and she has no reason not to believe them.

"I feel good about myself. And I enjoy it," she says. "I have fun when I'm on-stage, and the audience loves it. Nobody ever said it's time to give it up. Why stop?"*

Obituaries

When people die, reports of their deaths usually appear in local media. Those stories, called obituaries, often are among the most-read articles in the paper. They chronicle an individual's life and follow a specific format set by the particular medium. Obituaries generally are two types: news obituaries or paid death notices. The news obituary is written by a member of the news staff and published in a news section. The paid death notice is handled by the advertising department, might appear in a smaller type size than news columns, and can be written by a family member. Media publish obituaries, whether news or paid, in specific locations familiar to audiences.

Major media, such as *The New York Times*, have obituary files on prominent individuals as do the major news wire services, such as the Associated Press. Background information, photos, and even articles are stored, ready if the person dies unexpectedly—or not. When U.S. Sen. Jesse Helms died in 2008, the media were prepared. They had known he was ailing and had compiled extensive material. Along with the main news story reporting his death and funeral services, media included articles on his political career, a history of his votes in Congress that earned him the nickname "Senator No," and stories on his family. Biographical material was ready even for younger celebrities, such as actor Bernie Mac who died at age 50 and songwriter-singer Isaac Hayes at age 65. Media were able to produce complete reports of each man's careers within hours of the news he had died.

Basic Information

Obituaries contain the news elements and the résumé of an individual. Each obituary should note the complete name of who died, when he or she died, where, how, and why. (The "what" is that the individual died.) "How" someone died, such as unusual or tragic circumstances, might make that death a news story, such as a teen mauled by a tiger. Often why a person died will not be revealed based on the family's request. In the 1990s, media grappled with reporting that a person died from complications of AIDS. That cause of death is now included. Many media do not include the cause of violent death unless it can be attributed to a medical examiner, particularly in the case of a suicide.

Obituaries also outline a person's life, particularly career details, accomplishments, contributions, volunteer work, organizational membership, or other personal information. For a prominent individual, a reporter might interview coworkers, family members, or others to have quotes in the obituary. Clips from speeches or other appearances might be included. The notice will also list funeral arrangements, visitations, survivors, and where to send memorials or contributions.

For survivors, immediate family members are included. Ex-husbands and ex-wives are not, unless you are writing an obituary of someone who has had a number of spouses. Their names would be part of that person's life story.

Funeral homes provide most information for obituaries. Some media will not accept obituary information from family members. People have played practical jokes on friends by placing a death notice when the person turned 40 or 50 years old. Reporters who are writing news obituaries will get information from résumés, place of employment, interviews, biographical sources, the Internet, and government documents. For obituaries written in advance of a person's death, an interview with the individual might make up part of the file.

Accuracy is critical in obituaries. Often families cut out obituaries and keep them with family records or in a family Bible. In a time of mourning, a family's sadness and stress increase when an obituary reports the wrong age or misspells a name. In compiling information, reporters must ensure the information is correct. They should get the birth date and calculate the person's age. Pitfalls of research are discussed in Chapter 9.

Format and Structure

Each media outlet has a format it uses for writing obituaries. For example, the obit might simply state:

> Kevin D. Smith, 33, New Orleans, Saturday. Funeral: 10 a.m., Tuesday, Jones Funeral Home. Surviving: wife, Katherine; children, Thomas, Renee, Gretchen of the home.

In paid death notices, the family pays according to the length, generally measured in column inches. The family can write the notice as long as it wants, including such detail as the person's parents and grandparents, career path, organizational membership, even personal information, and where to send memorials.

In a news obituary lead, a writer would focus on *who*, *what*, *when*, and *where*, along with *what* the individual is known for, such as a professional career or volunteer efforts. Consider this Associated Press lead when Isaac Hayes died:

> Isaac Hayes, the baldheaded, baritone-voiced soul crooner who laid the groundwork for disco and whose "Theme From Shaft" won both Academy and Grammy awards, died Sunday afternoon after he collapsed near a treadmill, authorities said. He was 65.

A dateline would tell where the person died, but where the person lives should be included as in this lead from *The New York Times:*

> Dr. Michael E. DeBakey, whose innovative heart and blood vessel operations made him one of the most influential doctors in the United States, died Friday night in Houston, where he lived. He was 99.

From the leads, readers learn *who* died, *when*, *where*, and *why* they will be remembered. The body of the obituary will put the events of the person's life in order, usually chronologically. The general format for obituaries is the lead, contributions, career and life, survivors, funeral services, and memorials or donations. Norma Sosa, a former obituary writer for *The New York Times*, notes that the *Times* follows a specific format that has a kicker, when appropriate, as the last paragraph. She says:

> *Use a quote or anecdote that you feel reflects a stand-out aspect of a person's life, views, work, or contribution. It's the thought that remains in the reader's mind—what you, the researcher and writer, felt was the single most important or interesting thing you learned about the person. It could be something counter-intuitive, funny, sad, surprising, or poignant.*

Sometimes quotes from the individual as well as others can tell the story, as in the CNN obituary on former press secretary Tony Snow, who died as a result of colon cancer in 2008. Snow told reporters shortly after he was diagnosed: "Not everybody will survive cancer, but on the other hand, you have got to realize you've got the gift of life, so make the most of it. That is my view, and I'm going to make the most of my time with you."

The CNN obituary quoted President Bush: "The Snow family has lost a beloved husband and father. And America has lost a devoted public servant and a man of character."

The CNN story on Snow's death exhibited the depth the online format has in reporting. Links throughout the article took readers to gallery comments from politicians and journalists, to information about cancer, to video clips of Snow, and to a page where people could leave remembrances.

Speech Stories

Writing speech stories presents challenges to note taking and organization. Taking notes during a speech is much more difficult than during an interview. In an interview, you can ask an interviewee to wait a few seconds while you fill in your notes. During a speech, you cannot stop the speaker; you have to keep up with what he or she is saying.

Taking notes during a speech, however, is somewhat like taking notes for a professor's lecture: You want to have as much material to study as possible, and you may have the opportunity to ask a clarifying question after the lecture is over. You may find that developing a shorthand is the easiest and fastest way to get complete notes.

Also, when the speaker is telling a joke or an anecdote, use this time to review your notes and to complete sentences. Put quotation marks around remarks you know can be used as direct quotes—this tip helps when writing the story.

Good note taking means listening carefully to what speakers say. Ears can deceive. Consider the following errors made when writers did not listen carefully and then did not think when writing the story.

> "Bureaucrats are never seizing in their efforts to keep information from the public," he said.

The speaker actually said "ceasing" not "seizing."

> "Having a big hearth has nothing to do with how big your wallet is," said Mrs. Bush.

She actually said "heart" not "hearth."

> "The creation of new toxic dumb sites has all but been eliminated," Browner said.

She really said "dump," not "dumb" sites.

> She saluted American industry, small business, schools, and American citizens for banning together to solve the country's environmental problems.

The speaker said "banding" not "banning."

> People in countries have "the need to create extinct, stable governments," he said.

The speaker said "distinct," not "extinct."

> "Canada stepped outside its democratic laws to get the treaty written," she said.

The speaker actually said "diplomatic," not "democratic."

Sometimes writers hear the right word but misspell it. This error damages their credibility and can be embarrassing. For example, one writer called a school's lecture series the "Wheel" lecture when it is named the "Weil" lecture. Another referred to a river as the "Noose" River when it is spelled "Neuse." Consider these:

> "Investigators found millions of land mines sewn into the earth," Williams said.

The writer should have written "sown."

> "Our commitment cannot waiver," she said.

She said "waver."

> "Congress is trying to role back the progress of 25 years of environmental legislation."

It's "roll" not "role."

> "America should be neither a claste nor a classified society."

The speaker said "classed" not "claste."

> "Ronald Reagan was applicable with the press during his presidency."

The speaker said "affable."

> "After belaying a question about tithing, [Ronald] Reagan whispered to me, 'I should have taken your advice,'" journalist Helen Thomas said.

Thomas said "belaboring" a question.

> "The accident does not pose any immediate treat to nearby residents."

The writer made a typographical error. The speaker said "threat" not "treat."

Tips for Writing about Speeches

- When you start to write the story, always look for the theme. Ask yourself: What does the speaker want us to know? In one speech the theme may be the importance of democracy, in another the value of higher education, and in yet another public service. It may be in the speech title, or the speaker may deviate and pick out a pet subject on which to elaborate. The theme will be a clue to the lead for your story. Generally, in the lead, a summary of what the speaker said will go first, and then attribution will end the first sentence. An exception is made for a prominent speaker, such as the president or a local government official. Then the name goes first.
- Rarely will the first paragraph be a direct quote. Few speakers summarize their comments in 20 words or less. The lead may use a partial quote.
- Write a lead that states what the speaker said. Use attribution verbs such as "said" or "told."
- Do not write a label lead that simply identifies the topic or theme of the speech. That means do not use attribution words such as "discussed," "talked about," "spoke about," or "expressed concern about." See the difference:

Label Lead:

Three members of the Broadcasting Board of Governors held a panel discussion on the future of international broadcasting on the university campus last Wednesday.

Summary Lead:

U.S. government broadcasts to regions all over the world can explain democratic values to people living in countries that have repressive governments, according to a panel of experienced broadcasters and journalists who spoke at the university last Wednesday.

- Have a second graph that follows and supports the lead.
- Do not have a second graph that burdens readers with background on the speakers. See the difference:

Graph 2:

The panelists were David Burke, chairman of the Broadcasting Board; Evelyn Lieberman, director of Voice of America; and Kevin Klose, director of the International Broadcasting Bureau, which oversees Voice of America, Radio and TV Marti, and Worldnet Television.

Better Second Graph to Follow the Summary Lead:

"By providing news and public affairs broadcasting, we can help them establish stable democracies," said Kevin Klose, a panelist and director of the International Broadcasting Bureau, which oversees Voice of America, Radio and TV Marti, and Worldnet Television.

The third graph would note the other two panelists and the qualifications that speak to their credibility. You do not have to include a complete résumé. If the panel had a discussion title, it would be included in graph 3. Writers would also summarize here the topics covered, such as

The panelists primarily focused on the role of U.S. broadcasts since the fall of the Berlin Wall, but they also discussed new technology and how to bring their organizations into the 21st century.

- Have a balance of direct and indirect quotes.
- Look for a direct quote as a good way to end a story. Or end the story with more background about the speaker.
- Make sure your story has adequate attribution, even if you cover only one speaker.

Writing the Actual Story

With the 2008 presidential campaign, people throughout the United States had many months of reading or listening to speeches or media coverage of speeches. The availability of speech texts online through campaign offices allowed voters to read the complete comments, no matter what the specific stories said.

Reporters today often do not write stories solely off the speech content itself, but they will include others' reactions to the speaker's comments, background information to give the speech topic some context, and sometimes references to previous speeches. The availability of transcripts allows reporters to double-check speakers' quotes and determine whether a speech is more of the same rhetoric or a departure. The posting of transcripts also means that reporters today must be especially careful in quoting speakers accurately because a vigilant readership will certainly check behind them.

Exercises

1. Find a news story that also carries a sidebar or companion story that is a news-feature or feature. Compare the language between the two stories. Identify how the sidebar story carries more description by highlighting the words. Look at the organization of both stories. How do they differ?

2. Based on the stories in Exercise 1, look at the publication's Web site for the same stories. How are the stories presented visually, such as photos or video? Can readers find additional information? What do these elements add to the stories' information or entertainment value?

3. Go to today's *New York Times* Web site, and click on obituaries. Look at a lead and how the writer has focused on the individual's life. Look at the last graph. How did the end (usually a quote) wrap up the individual's life? Compare *The New York Times*' obituary to an obituary on the same individual in your local or regional newspaper. How did the obituaries differ?

4. Prepare an advance obituary for a national figure, either in politics or the media. Using a search engine, find at least five online sources, for example, the state Web site for a governor, a campaign Web site for another politician, or a news station's Web site that includes employee biographies. Try to find an article by or about the individual so that you can use quotes. Write the obituary with all the information; leave the lead blank where date, time, place, and cause would be included.

5. Go to a political site, such as the home page for the Republican National Committee or Democratic National Committee. Check for transcripts from major speeches. Then do a search for news stories to compare how media covered the speeches. How were the leads different? The quotes used? Background? Additional information?

6. Check CSPAN's latest offerings of videotaped speeches. Select one and play the speech. Write a news story of 500 words, then do an online search to compare your story to coverage in media.

References

Norma Sosa, Lecture on how to write obituaries, Midweek Special, School of Journalism and Mass Communication, University of North Carolina at Chapel Hill, Spring 2001.

"Former White House spokesman Tony Snow dies," CNN, July 12, 2008, accessed Aug. 19, 2008 at http://www.cnn.com/2008/POLITICS/07/12/obit.snow/.

CHAPTER 9

Research and Observation

Writing begins with an idea. During a trip to the ocean, a writer is fascinated with the porpoises that periodically surface and roll as they travel offshore. She wants to write about porpoises. But she needs more than just her observations to write a factual, accurate, complete, and entertaining article. She must learn more.

Gathering information is like detective work. As a sleuth, you start with a clue. Step by step you add pieces until you have enough information to reconstruct events and solve the case. As a writer, you add to your knowledge until you can create an accurate and complete summary of the topic.

Writers, like detectives, gather information from research, interviews, and observations. Also, like detectives, writers gather a broad array of information to ensure their searches are objective. Such work is called reporting. Research—or reporting—allows writers to study what others have already found out. That information might be in books, magazines, letters, statistical abstracts, encyclopedias, databases, blogs, or any number of other print or electronic sources. Writers can access thousands of documents using online Web search engines or commercial databases. More and more information is added to the free, easy-to-use Web every day. But it's important to remember that much of the best information in databases can't be found on the Web. Reporters often team with news librarians who have information-tracking skills to develop breaking news and long investigative pieces.

Armed with facts retrieved in research, writers can continue reporting by interviewing expert and relevant sources who add personal comment on the topic. Personal reflections give context and interest to facts, and interviews can confirm or verify online or library research. Interviewing, quotes, and attribution are discussed in Chapter 10.

Writers also take time to note their observations as part of their reporting. Student writers are sometimes reluctant to include their impressions for fear they will appear too subjective. They must overcome that fear. In the porpoise story, the writer would be remiss not to describe the rolling action of the sleek, gray mammals as they break water a hundred yards off the beach. Audiences want to know what the animals look like and how thrilled the author is at seeing a school of several dozen porpoises dotting the waves as they surface for air.

In this chapter, you will learn

- how to develop search strategies that will mine print and online resources,
- what specific sources to consider,
- the plusses and minuses in online and other research, and
- how observation is a part of gathering information.

Getting Started

Writers start out as generalists; they know a little about a lot of subjects. Some develop specialties or subject areas they prefer. Whether they are newspaper or electronic media reporters, public relations practitioners, or advertising copywriters—whether they cover general assignment topics or special beats, such as business, medicine, sports, or environment—writers need to do research as the first step in reporting. A medical writer may know medical terminology, but if he wants to write about autism he must become knowledgeable about the topic. A government reporter must learn about the newly elected members of Congress before she goes to the opening session.

Writers need to find information that is accurate, relevant, and up to date. Time is their greatest enemy. Most writers have deadlines and limited time to devote to research, particularly if they write for daily publications. So they need to find information quickly and efficiently.

Librarians can save you time, develop search strategies, and expand source lists. As the librarian at the School of Journalism and Mass Communication at the University of North Carolina at Chapel Hill, Barbara Semonche developed a dozen guides for students in the quest to find information. She notes:

> *You can be certain of two things: either you will find useful information efficiently or you will not. You will find too much information or too little. Your success will depend, to a certain extent, upon the quality of your search strategies. The other part is finding the best reference sources.*

For UNC–Chapel Hill students, Semonche wrote a "first steps in basic research" handout that cautions:

> The resources available to students, scholars, journalists, and the general public are staggering in variety and amount. Nevertheless, not every question has a simple, direct, fast, comprehensive and/or accurate answer. Further, different reference books and resources offer differing responses, accounts, and statistics for the same or similar queries.... It is essential that students develop a growing and diverse repertoire of reference/research sources and information strategies.

She recommends that students build their own personal set of reference materials. On her list are a dictionary ("the best you can afford"); a thesaurus; several style and usage manuals; the current year of *Statistical Abstract of the United States;* the current year of *The World Almanac of Facts*; the current year of *The Almanac of American Politics*; several books of quotations; a good atlas or gazetteer; and a good math textbook, "preferably one that does math the 'old' way." Students should also get into what she calls the "browse habit" and seek new, unfamiliar references.

Developing a Strategy

To be successful in research, you need a strategy to find information. Once you have defined your topic, you must make a list of questions, identify obvious sources, conduct searches for additional sources, review those sources for additional leads, refine your questions, and then interview.

Let's say you are a medical reporter and want to write a story on childhood immunizations. You first must make a list of the information you need to know, such as the following questions:

Initial Question List for Story on Childhood Immunizations

Who has to be immunized?
What are the state laws?
What shots do children have to have?
At what ages do children get which shots?
Are there any reactions to the shots?
How much do the shots cost at a doctor's office?
Can children get shots at public health clinics? How much do they cost?

Where are the clinics here? What are the hours for immunizations?
How many local children register for school and aren't immunized?
Is this a problem locally?
Have any other diseases surfaced locally?
Why are children not immunized?

Additional Questions after Research

What are the risks to children who aren't immunized?
Do children ever die from immunizations?
What are the reactions parents can expect after a child gets a shot?
How many children in the state aren't immunized properly when they start school?
How many immunizations are given each year in the state? In our county?
What childhood diseases are appearing again?
How much of the cost of immunizations does the government pay?
Do we consider some diseases eradicated?
Fifty years ago, children suffered from mumps, measles, and even polio. Now children can be protected against even chicken pox. Are we too complacent about a resurgence of diseases?
Are there any diseases left that children need to be protected from?
If a certain number of children are immunized, does that protect other children, as in the herd effect?
What factors prevent parents from having children immunized at the proper time?
What immunizations do college students need?

The obvious sources for answers to these questions would be newspaper and journal indexes, articles and information at online health sites, pediatricians, and local health department and school officials. You would also interview experts and agency officials.

Eventually your source list grows to include state health officials, state statutes that stipulate which immunizations children must have to enter school, officials at the Centers for Disease Control, legislators who allocate funds for immunizations, parents, and even children. You refine your list of questions for each source and prepare to interview your sources.

Your search strategy is similar if you are writing a story for your alumni magazine on a graduate whose first novel has been published. She is an assistant professor at a college in another state. Before the interview, you need to find information on the author. Most students and writers today go to the Internet first and use a search engine to find information. Such a search might reveal biographical information on her publisher's Web site. Check your library for *Contemporary Authors*, a biographical guide to current writers in fiction, journalism, film, television, and other fields.

If you can find no accessible biographical history, you will have to rely on a strategy that includes interviewing former professors, roommates, colleagues, friends, and family members. You might have to call the English department where she teaches and have someone fax her curriculum vitae. You might have to consult newspaper indexes in public libraries in her home state to find specific articles about her. If one source indicates an organization to which she belongs, you might need to look for references with that organization. Articles about the organization could include material about your up-and-coming author.

Basic References

As you search for information, your journey might include online searching as well as a trip to a special collections library to pore through historical documents. Many basic print sources are available online. You can find out which ones by exploring virtual libraries, such as the Librarians' Internet Index at http://lii.org. Librarian Barbara Semonche's basic reference list mentioned earlier in this chapter is an excellent starting point. Writers should always remember basic sources such as telephone books, city directories, and collections of people by occupation, political affiliation, or other activities. From there, more specialized references can tell you the meaning of certain acronyms, such as MASH for Mobile Army Surgical Hospital, or even real estate terms, such as escrow.

Today's researchers and writers use hundreds of sources and always must be sure sources are credible and updated. Listed here are some types of publications that writers traditionally have relied on for information. Remember: Most publications have Web sites.

Biographical Sources. Biographical references contain information about well-known people. Some are specific, such as *Who's Who in American Politics.* The information will include date of birth, parents' names, education, career, awards and achievements, and family data. Among other biographical sources are *Who's Who*, *Webster's Biographical Dictionary*, *Current Biography*, *Who's Who* *among African Americans*, and *Who's Who among Hispanic Americans.* More than 100 biographical dictionaries exist, each focusing on a special group or profession.

Statistical Information. *Statistical Abstract of the United States* is one of the most widely used reference books and is online. It provides information from the number of police officers in Albuquerque, New Mexico, to the number of houses with indoor plumbing in Lincoln, Nebraska. Data are based on information collected by the federal government and other sources. *The Census of Population of the United States* is published every 10 years. Census information is available on the Internet at www.census.gov. *Editor and Publisher Market Guide* contains data on cities, such as a city's shopping malls and whether its water is fluoridated. Most states compile statistical books, particularly those dealing with vital statistics: births, deaths, marriages, and divorces. Writers can find information on states, counties, cities, and even sections within cities that is especially helpful if they are looking for the local angle on a story. For international information, writers can consult the *United Nations Demographic Yearbook.*

Political and Government Information. *The U.S. Government Manual* contains information on departments and agencies in the executive branch. *Congressional Quarterly* publishes a weekly report that catalogues the voting records of Congress and major political speeches. States annually publish manuals that contain information about branches of government and legislatures, summaries of the state history, the state constitution, and biographies of major state officials. Information on foreign governments and leaders can be found in reference books, such as *The Statesman's Yearbook 2008: Politics, Cultures and Economies of the World* and other publications that focus on world leaders. Remember to check for online sites, too.

Geographic Data. Writers might need to check on the locations of cities, towns, and countries. They can refer to local maps or the *Times Atlas of the World* and *Rand McNally Commercial Atlas and Marketing Guide.* Online sites, such as mapquest.com, will guide writers to locations and even provide maps and directions to get there. Writers can find up-to-date maps of continents and regions at sites such as World Sites Atlas at www.sitesatlas.com or National Geographic at www.nationalgeographic.com.

Business Information. Writers might need data on a company or an industry, and students might need information on a potential employer. Today's competitive companies usually have extensive and interactive Web sites. Research on companies could also be found in annual reports, on file in many libraries.

Information on thousands of companies can be found at the Securities Exchange Commission Web site at www.sec.gov. Incorporation records must list officers, addresses, and company descriptions, and these documents are filed with states' secretary of state offices. Many businesses fall under the purview of state regulatory agencies, such as the state insurance commissioner. Information on companies can also be found in reference books, such as *Standard & Poor's Index*. Also, for company information that can lead reporters to sources, check out the American Press Institute's site for business writers at www.businessjournalism.org.

Professional Sources. In any search for information sources, writers should consider professional organizations such as societies, guilds, and associations. These sources often have links or references to other depositories of information and can provide updates on media issues, contact names, and historical background and serve as a means to verify facts. Before writing about trends in real estate, reporters will want to look at NationalAssociationOfRealtors.com and at related sites for local and regional Realtors. Similar sites are available on thousands of organizations that serve particular interests such as medicine, law, construction, government workers, architects, and others.

For background on professional issues in journalism and mass communication, some sites worth checking are the Poynter Institute at www.poynter.org; the American Society of Newspaper Editors at www.asne.org; the Inter American Press Association at www.sipiapa.org; Nieman Reports at www.nieman.harvard.edu; Public Relations Society of America at www.prsa.org; American Advertising Federation at www.aaf.org; Association of Electronic Journalists at www.rtnda.org; Investigative Reporters and Editors at www.ire.org; and Society of Professional Journalists at www.spj.org. Journalism organizations and issues also are a focus of UNITY: Journalists of Color at www.unityjournalists.org.

Pitfalls in Research

The hunt for information can be complex. Librarian Barbara Semonche warns that not all information comes in a compact, convenient form. At the start of a search, students may discover people who share the same names as celebrities, such as basketball star Michael Jordan, television personality David Letterman, or even McDonald's mascot Ronald McDonald. Researchers must check to be sure that the person named on records or documents is in fact the same person they seek.

Information may be dated or incomplete. For example, early biographies of actor Brad Pitt would fail to include the correct number and names of his children. Students and other researchers must remember that not every reference includes every individual, and those that do may not have all the facts. Researchers must look at many sources, both print and online, to find complete information. Searching for information is rarely one-stop shopping. Using many sources helps uncover discrepancies and inconsistencies about information and ensure that information is as accurate as possible.

Writers should look continually for additional and alternative sources. The research game is a detective hunt. Names or sources mentioned in an article or in references can lead to nuggets of information elsewhere. The only constraints will be time and deadline pressure.

Government Sources

Local, state, and federal governments produce millions of pages of documents every year, ranging from official findings, such as federal Food and Drug Administration studies, to county tax records and the disposition of local traffic cases. Most government documents are open and accessible to the public. Many are free by mail on request, and others are available at the city hall, the county courthouse, a regional federal repository, online, or the Library of Congress. They provide a wealth of information for writers and curious citizens.

Government officials and others have taken advantage of the information age to put reams of material online. Agencies maintain their own Web sites that provide history, facts about elected officials, agendas and minutes of meetings, and other relevant data. For information on legislation, try THOMAS, a congressional online system; Congressional Record; congressional legislation digests; and directories of congressional members' e-mail addresses. Even the White House has its own Web site featuring news releases of the day, speech transcripts, and access to federal agencies.

Public Records

Routine government documents are considered public. The documents have been created by the government, which is supported by taxpayers' money. Researchers, writers, and anyone who wants the documents can request to see them or to have copies made. All states have laws that pertain to what is and what is not a public record. The general rule most journalists follow is that any document is considered a public record unless the agency or individual who has the document can cite the section of state or federal law that prevents its disclosure. If the agency cannot, it must relinquish the information.

Media writers should know the open records laws for their particular state. State press associations can provide the law and its exceptions. Publications such as *The News Media and the Law*, published by the Reporters Committee for Freedom of the Press, can be consulted. The Electronic Frontier Foundation is a valuable resource and can be accessed via the Internet.

Agencies can charge a reasonable fee for photocopying documents. Most states have regulations pertaining to computer storage of public documents and reasonable charges for making copies or providing access to electronic information.

Freedom of Information Act

In 1966, the U.S. Congress passed the federal Freedom of Information Act (FOIA). The act became law in 1967 and has been amended five times. The law is much like state laws regarding public records. Anyone is allowed to make a written request for information from any federal agency, but not all information is available. The act provides broad exemptions, such as information relating to national defense or foreign policy, internal personnel rules and practices of an agency, personnel and medical files that would constitute an invasion of privacy, information compiled for law enforcement purposes, and geophysical information such as that related to oil well locations.

In 1996 the Electronic Freedom of Information Act Amendments required federal agencies to release electronic files of certain types of records created after November 1, 1996. Because of the time needed to respond to requests for electronic data, the amendments extended the agencies' required response time from 10 to 20 days. In 2002 amendments to the FOIA affected requests from foreign governments or any requester acting on behalf of a foreign government to any agency considered part of the government's intelligence community. Changes under the "Open Government Act of 2007" further clarified government agencies' duties in regard to FOIA requests.

The media have worked continually to reduce the number of exemptions to FOIA. Michael Gartner, former president of the American Society of Newspaper Editors, once lamented in a speech on national Freedom of Information Day that the name "Freedom of Information" implies the government is holding information hostage. He objected to many of the restrictions, particularly those that prevent publication of what the United States broadcasts to developing countries over the Voice of America. Homeland security concerns have added to difficulties in accessing information in some settings. To help with access, George Washington University houses the National Security Archive, a repository of government documents and declassified material at www.nsarchive.org. Its Web site notes that it "is also a leading advocate and user of the Freedom of Information Act."

FOIA sets out the procedure for requesting information, the time required for an agency to respond, appeals procedures, and fees. Individuals must pay the cost of photocopying the information but can request a waiver of that cost if the release of the information is in the public interest. Writers or individuals seeking information under the act might be frustrated—delays can occur even when procedures are followed. The request must be specific and must be sent to the proper agency. When the information is uncovered, a reporter may receive a desired document, but with sections or entire pages inked out to protect exempted information. The reporter pays the cost of photocopying all pages—even the blackened ones.

FOIA searches can be time consuming and costly, but many journalists and researchers have used them to find information for fact-filled articles. For example, a student in an advanced reporting class filed an FOIA request with the Federal Communications Commission (FCC) to find out what kinds of complaints and how many had been lodged with the agency after singer Janet Jackson's breast was exposed during the Super Bowl 2004 halftime performance. The student's request was broad and asked for copies of the complaints. An FCC representative responded, asking for clarification and letting the student know that to provide copies of all the complaints—500,000 plus—would cost more than $125,000. Needless to say, the student amended the request and asked for a sampling of the complaints, a request that cost her $100.

Investigative Reporters and Editors presents awards each year to media that produce stories using public record searches and requests. Background on the award and award-winning stories are available at www.ire.org/foi/.

Online Research

Technology has changed the way writers collect, transmit, and share information. Distance from sources has become irrelevant. A public relations practitioner in Detroit can search online for background information on the success of drugs to treat acid reflux disease and e-mail it to a company official in Switzerland. Photographs and other color visuals can be e-mailed anywhere. Using a laptop, a reporter can write a breaking-news story and transmit it in a matter of seconds to the city desk 30 miles away.

A major change in recent years is how information is stored. People who began writing careers in the mid-1980s and earlier have seen phenomenal changes in the ways they seek information. In the "old days" before 1985, most searches for information centered on treks to libraries at a newspaper, city or county, university—wherever resource books were housed. People had to handle paper to get information.

Computers have allowed anyone who produces information to store it online so others can access it. When people get online, they search for information; download data, photos, or text to their computers; send e-mail, blog, or IM; or chat. Writers can call up information in a matter of seconds while sitting at computers in the office, at home, in the dorm, or in the library. Newspapers, books, magazines, library holdings, company profiles, and even job banks are online. Electronic indexes and databases offer citations, abstracts, and even full text records, and the number of databases available online grows daily in diversity and ease of access.

The ease of using the Internet and the breadth of information found there can lull novice reporters into a false sense of security in regard to accuracy. As much as students and professional writers have come to depend on the Internet, they must still have some skepticism about what they find there. All Web sites are not created alike. With the proliferation of information has come discussion of issues on privacy, legal uses, copyright, and ethics (discussed in detail in Chapter 12). A helpful publication is *Nora Paul's Computer Assisted Research*, published by the Poynter Institute in St. Petersburg, Florida. Updates are available online.

Pitfalls of Online Research

Convenience is one of the advantages of online research, but some important concerns persist. Online, identities may be cloaked, expertise exaggerated, and content tweaked in such a way that critical errors go undetected. Because blogging and social network tools have made it easy for anyone to publish, writers must realize that not everything they read online is true, just like not everything they hear on the street is true. Writers must take specific measures to establish the accuracy and credibility of sources and sites. In *Web Search Savvy: Strategies and Shortcuts for Online Research*, author Barbara Friedman suggests Web-based content be evaluated with the following five criteria:

- **Accuracy.** Impossible facts are a giveaway that a Web site is bogus, although some errors may simply be clerical. Yet if a site is riddled with spelling or grammar errors, it's a safe bet the author has been careless with overall content, and the researcher should be wary of using the material. The quickest way to spot inaccurate information is to check Web-based content against traditional or nondigital sources.
- **Authority.** What individual or organization claims responsibility for the site's content, and does it have the proper credentials to speak authoritatively on this particular subject? Use a site's contact information or a domain lookup, such as WHOIS or InterNic, to verify who's behind a site.
- **Currency.** Web sites may linger online long after their authors have stopped maintaining the content. Check the site for dates that indicate when the content was posted and last revised.
- **Audience.** Determining the intended audience for a Web site will help you evaluate the usefulness of the information. A site about political campaigns designed for an audience of elected officials may be too complicated if you are writing for elementary school students.
- **Agenda.** Whereas journalists are urged to remain impartial, in the online world everyone has an opinion. Bloggers, for example, publish views on a range of topics using personalized language that would be discouraged in traditional journalism. That bias is not intended to make you doubt a site, but rather understand its purpose. Knowing whether a Web site's author is motivated by a personal or professional agenda helps you find a context for the information.

Online research may be the first and most convenient choice for writers, but it is just one step in the research process. Taking the time to evaluate the integrity of Web-based content will go a long way in establishing your credibility as a researcher and writer.

Additional Online Search Strategies

Writers can find information quickly by typing key words into search engines, the very basis of an online search strategy. But search engines still miss a lot of information. A 2001 study estimated that 400 to 550 times the amount of information existed on the "hidden" Web compared to the amount found with search engines. Some of the information not easily found is on commercial or fee-based sites or is stored in data formats that Web search engines cannot easily crawl.

When searching online, reporters should remember that most search engines have advanced search functions. Google, for example, offers a step-by-step guide on how to look more precisely for information on a topic by typing in appropriate search requirements.

Writers should also be aware of the growing number of virtual library consortia, which offer a state's residents access to online library catalogues, reference materials, and commercial online databases. Librarian Barbara Semonche notes that the consortia "are a rich resource for freelance writers, reporters, students, and researchers who need free or very low cost access to extensive, sophisticated information and data."

For example, NCLIVE, the North Carolina Library link to the world at www.nclive.org, offers online access to complete articles from more than 4,000 newspapers, journals, and magazines, as well as indexing for more than 10,000 periodical titles. Galileo, Georgia's virtual library at http://www.galileo.usg.edu/welcome/, provides secured access to licensed products. Some states' virtual libraries are open only to educational institutions, including students, faculty, and staff, so writers need to find out the privileges for their particular states' digital libraries.

What You Can't Find Online

Writers today must remember that online information is a recent phenomenon. Most history is buried in letters, memos, newspapers, magazines, and other written material not catalogued in online databases. When writer

Nadine Cohodas began researching her book, *Spinning Blues into Gold: The Chess Brothers and the Legendary Chess Records*, she went hunting. Her research included visits to the Chicago neighborhoods where brothers Phil and Leonard Chess had offices and where the great blues singers performed.

Cohodas produced a book that brought information to readers they would not have gotten on their own. Finding the details required hours and hours of reading trade journals, such as *Billboard* and *Cash Box*, to understand the evolution of the record company; poring over Chicago newspapers; and scouring public records, such as old liquor licenses to trace the brothers' business beginnings, city phone books and directories to confirm relevant addresses, and the Federal Communications Commission archive for details about their radio stations. "You have to love the hunt," she said.

Every now and then, Cohodas had "eureka" moments when she found something that provided the telling detail for a piece of the story. For example, she needed information about the history of the Macomba Lounge, owned by the Chess brothers. She explains how she found it:

> *To find out what the Macomba Lounge had been, I photocopied about 30 pages of the Chicago Yellow Pages in the tavern listings, then read them one by one to find the same address. Lo and behold, the Congress Buffet showed up at 3905 S. Cottage. I used that name to request the liquor license for that venue so I could trace the history further.*
>
> *Meanwhile, I found the only ad anyone knows of for the Macomba Lounge by going through the now defunct* Chicago Bee *week by week in the first or second year Leonard and Phil were in the club and that's when I saw the ad—a sweet moment.*

The result of nearly three years' work was a fascinating account of two Polish immigrants who built a company promoting black singers, such as Muddy Waters, Chuck Berry, Bo Diddley, and Etta James. *The New York Times Book Review* named it one of the notable nonfiction books of 2000, and the book won the 2001 Blues Foundation "Keeping the Blues Alive" Award.

Observation

Observation—an old method of research—still is a key tool in gathering information. At the same time reporters note what speakers are saying, they should notice how speakers deliver their remarks, how they move their bodies, what they are wearing, and how the crowd reacts to their comments. Such details are part of the reporting process.

Many students and inexperienced writers, however, are reluctant to include too many details. They fear that audiences will doubt their descriptions. They believe using description borders on being subjective when, in fact, leaving out description might distort an event. For example, a story might reveal a speaker's eloquence and pointed remarks on U.S. trade with China, but the reporter might not mention that only 22 people were seated in an auditorium that holds 550 people. Although the speaker might have been eloquent, the speech's title failed to attract a sizable audience.

Seeing Isn't Enough

Many people notice their surroundings or the events happening around them in one dimension. They see. Rarely do people consciously smell, taste, hear, or touch their environment. Even using only sight, most people miss much of what goes on. So do writers. They have not trained themselves to observe events that happen simultaneously. At the state fair, a reporter might notice the lines in front of concessions but not see the child wailing for more cotton candy, the youth loaded with three bright green teddy bears, the overflowing garbage at a nearby trash can, and the cigarette hanging from the hawker's lips. The unobservant writer does not smell the odor of fried dough, taste the grease in the air near the ferris wheel, hear the ping-ping from the shooting gallery, or feel the slap of heat from the barbecue cookers.

To be skillful observers, writers must hone all their senses. To be complete and successful writers, they must describe scenes to absent audiences. Even when viewers see events on television, they still need the reporter's or news anchor's observations. When television covers the annual Thanksgiving Day parade in New York City, for example, reporters must identify floats and provide background on performers. Viewers need the information to understand what they are seeing.

General Observation

Many people exist on autopilot. They drive the same route to work, live in the same house or apartment for years, and work in the same office. They become less and less observant. What about you?

Any person or writer can sharpen observation skills. Try this experiment: Take a piece of paper. Describe what your roommate or friend wore to school or work today. Note colors and types of fabric, if possible. What did you eat for breakfast? Can you remember the smell as well as the taste? What about the color or feel? What sounds do you hear in this room? Can you name more than three?

Keep a notebook in your car, backpack, or pocket. Start recording what you see and hear in multidimensional ways. Use your cell phone to capture the visual and even audio. Although most people can note different sounds, it is harder to catch and record events happening simultaneously. The oft-told adage is that two people on a street corner would give two different accounts of an accident both witnessed. Think of ways to compare what you see with events or items that are common knowledge.

Remember the story on the burlesque queen? Writer Kathleen Hennessey uses simple language to describe Tempest Storm's physical attributes from the color of her hair to her fingernail polish. She notes her fingers "tremble with frustration. They are aged, knotted by arthritis and speckled with purple spots under paper-thin skin." Hennessey describes Storm's apartment, including her exercise bike and the photos that catalogue her relationships. Readers get a sense of Storm's physical surroundings as well as her philosophy of life.

How Observation Changes the Action. The act of reporting, of being an observer, might have the unintended effect of changing the behavior of an individual you are observing. Think about a friend who would rush to pick up living room clutter when you pull out your cell phone and take a picture. Your presence can change the way events unfold.

The same tendency holds true when reporters attend a meeting or a rally or when they participate in an online discussion. Their presence affects how people behave. The town council members sit up straighter and look busy when the public access television channel is airing the meeting. Rally organizers look efficient and engaged when reporters approach. Store managers beam smiles of success on the first day of business.

The trick to accurate observing is to observe over time. Most people can maintain a facade for some time, but they cannot keep it up forever—even when they know a reporter is in the room. You might have to observe for more than a few minutes, taking notes or photographs unobtrusively. Two hours into a meeting, the mayor might forget the unobtrusive camera and rail against the accusations of an unhappy citizen.

With advanced technology, people can be observed and recorded when they don't know it. Those images can appear on video or photo-sharing Web sites, social networking sites, or other Internet venues—much to a person's surprise. As a reporter, you must be careful not to invade an individual's privacy, discussed in Chapter 12, as you record your observations. When people are involved in events considered public, such as a rally or a plane crash, they do lose their right to privacy. But if they are partying in the privacy of their apartment, then those actions cannot become visuals for a story taken surreptitiously with your cell phone.

Participant Observation

Social scientists have long used observation as a means of getting information about groups. They join a group as participants to observe individual behavior within a group and the individuals' interactions. Journalists also have adopted the practice, gaining admission and recording the interactions of the group. Such intrusion by journalists affects the way people interact. Over time, however, reporters become accepted, and other members might forget their role.

Because their presence does affect how members relate, some journalists have opted to become members of groups and not to identify themselves as reporters. In the 1890s, reporter Nellie Bly pretended to be a mental patient to get a true picture of how the insane were treated at Blackwell's Island, New York's asylum for the mentally ill. Some have joined cults, followed the Hell's Angels, or gotten jobs in nursing homes. One reporter in her mid-20s enrolled in a Philadelphia high school to observe it firsthand—and was invited to the senior prom. Before resorting to undercover work, reporters and their editors must determine that a change of identity is the only way to get the story.

In either case, problems can arise when it is time to write. Reporters might feel a kinship to the group and have difficulty setting themselves apart. Journalists who become group members put their impartiality at risk in writing a story. Writers might become too emotional or too attached to sources and not be able to distance themselves. They also run the risk of not knowing completely whether their presence altered the group in any way. They can double-check their reactions and observations, however, by interviewing a balanced mix of sources. Reporters might also get complaints from group members who feel betrayed when the article appears.

Nonverbal Communication

Although writers get the bulk of their information from sources and from interviewing, they can add details from nonverbal communication. Such cues come from the way people move or act when they say something. A politician might raise her eyebrows at a constituent's question. A child might shift his hands behind his back when leaving the kitchen. A teacher might frown while correcting student essays. Each action implies a thought or behavior to the observer. The politician might be surprised. The child might be guilty of swiping a cookie. The teacher might be unhappy about a good student's low grade.

When recording nonverbal cues either in note taking or with a camera, reporters must be careful. They must think beyond the obvious because the same cue could carry different meanings for different observers. Furrowed eyebrows might indicate puzzlement or anger. Waving hands can mean agitation or enthusiasm. A smile might be sincere or forced. Generally, one action alone is not sufficient to indicate how an individual is feeling. The gestures must be catalogued in addition to words and other body movements. A reporter might have to go so far as to ask an individual what a particular posture meant. For example, pacing during an interview may not be a result of nervousness; the interviewee may suffer from restless legs syndrome, but no reporter could tell that simply by observing.

In addition, nonverbal actions have different meanings across cultures. In some cultures or ethnic groups, individuals do not make eye contact while speaking. An ignorant or inexperienced reporter might be suspicious of such behavior, thereby including a cultural bias. When U.S. business leaders engage in negotiations with Japanese officials, they have to learn etiquette and protocol. For example, the Japanese consider it offensive to write on a business card, while in the United States, executives and others make notations or add home telephone numbers to business cards. The good reporter learns about cultural differences or asks questions to clarify behavior. Such sensitivity and awareness is essential to accurate reporting.

Dangers in Observation

John Salvi was charged with murdering two people and injuring five others in shootings at two abortion clinics in Boston. When Salvi was arraigned on weapons charges in conjunction with the shootings, Gary Tuchman of CNN gave a live report and description for audiences who were not in the courtroom.

Tuchman described Salvi as wearing a blue blazer, white shirt, white socks, loafers, and nice pants. The description implied that Salvi had dressed conservatively and neatly. A print news account reported that Salvi was wearing "an ill-fitting blazer." The implication here contradicted the neat appearance of Tuchman's report. Which account was right? Audiences who heard and read the two accounts might have noticed the discrepancy and been puzzled. Or maybe it just added to their belief that you cannot trust the media to be right.

Tuchman also took his reported observation one step further. He noted to viewers that if they had a stereotype of someone who would be charged with committing murder, Salvi did not look like that stereotype—that is, Salvi did not look like someone who would commit murder. Viewers may have wondered: "What does the stereotypical murderer look like? Why didn't Tuchman give us a description of that stereotype?"

Observation plays a major role in writing, but we must be circumspect about the descriptions we use. As will be discussed in Chapter 11, we as writers carry our prejudices and biases with us as we collect information and write. We must be careful. Think about Tuchman's reference to a stereotypical murderer. Can you describe one? Of course not. If murderers were readily identifiable, people who have been killed would have had some warning. But murderers vary in shape, size, age, gender, skin tone, hair color, and clothing preference. They do not all have greasy hair and shifty, beady eyes and act furtively or in a suspicious manner.

The Importance of Accuracy

As noted, Tuchman's observations might have been distorted by his experiences. He might have a stereotypical idea of what a murderer looks like. Writers can bring biases to observation, just as they can to any aspect of reporting.

Just as you double-check facts, you should be circumspect about your observations. Take emotions into account. If you covered an anti-abortion rally, you might have found your emotions surging if you are pro-choice. Despite your role as a journalist, your feelings might not be neutral. Your feelings could influence your description. Be aware.

To ensure accuracy, you should record impressions in your notebook or on your electronic equipment at the scene and then review to add context as soon as possible afterward. The longer you wait, the fewer details you will remember accurately. Memory fades over time.

Like other kinds of research, observation leads to a more complete message. Description that is simple, clear, fair, and complete also will aid accuracy. Writers should lay out description alongside other facts and allow audiences to judge for themselves. Audiences invariably will apply their own biases to the description and form their own opinions, but writers' choices of words should not be the deciding factor.

Exercises

1. Condoleezza Rice, former Secretary of State, is coming to campus to give a lecture. Before the lecture, she will have a news conference, which you will attend for the campus newspaper. First, you need to find out more information. Using three biographical sources, answer the following questions. Cite the reference used. One reference should be online.

    a. When and where was Rice born?
    b. Where did she go to college?
    c. What jobs did she hold before joining the Bush administration?
    d. What has she done since she left the State Department?
    e. Has she won any awards? If so, list them.

2. Identify a reporter in your college community or in your hometown by reading bylines and articles in the respective paper. Call the reporter and ask what sources he or she uses in researching stories. Note whether the reporter uses online sources to retrieve information. Find out how the reporter ensures accuracy in using sources. Share the information with your class.

3. You are the state desk researcher for the local newspaper. The state editor wants to do a story on parents charged with killing their children. Before making the assignment to a reporter, the editor asks you to do an online search of national newspapers and magazines to find accounts of such crimes. Your task is to prepare a memo to the state editor that lists six references to substantial articles on parents charged with killing their children. The references need to be annotated; that is, they should be accompanied by explanatory notes as well as enough information to enable the reporter to find the articles.

4. You discover that many adult day care facilities exist in your area, and you want to make a case to your editor that a feature story about these facilities would be a good one. Search online for information on these facilities and identify at least three in your area. Compare the completeness and the credibility—as well as the limitations—of the Web pages you use as you find information on adult day care.

5. Pick a place on campus or attend a town government meeting as an observer along with another student. Use your senses to take notes on what transpires outside the actions of passersby or officials. Write a description of the meeting, using aspects such as the room, the mood, the speakers' attitudes, the officials' attitudes, the tone of the meeting, and how many people attended. Then compare your account with the other student's accounts. See what each of you chose to include and chose to ignore. Compare the ways you described aspects of the meeting. Then discuss what made your observations different.

References

Nadine Cohodas, Using documents. Interview via e-mail, October 2001.

Barbara Friedman, *Web Search Savvy: Strategies and Shortcuts for Online Research.* Mahwah, NJ: Erlbaum, 2004.

Freedom of Information Act, 5 U.S.C. 552, 1966. Amended in 1974, 1976, 1986, 1996, 2002.

"FOIA Legislative History," National Security Archives, at http://www.gwu.edu/~nsarchiv/nsa/foialeghistory/legistfoia.htm.

Michael Gartner, Speech in honor of national Freedom of Information Day. Washington, DC, National Press Club, March 1989.

Mary McGuire, Linda Stilborne, Melinda McAdams, and Laurel Hyatt, *The Internet Handbook for Writers, Researchers, and Journalists.* New York: Guilford Press, 1997.

Nora Paul, *Computer Assisted Research: A Guide to Tapping Online Information, 4th ed.* St. Petersburg, FL: The Poynter Institute for Media Studies, 2001.

Barbara Semonche, Personal interview. Chapel Hill, NC, School of Journalism and Mass Communication, University of North Carolina at Chapel Hill, 1995, 2005.

CHAPTER 10

Interviewing, Quotes, and Attribution

Asking questions and collecting answers—interviewing—is an essential skill for all media writers. Becoming a skilled interviewer takes practice; it is not something someone does naturally.

Most of us interview in a casual way when introduced to someone new. We ask questions: Where are you from? Are you a student? What year are you in school? What is your major? We hope to get responses that help us learn more about the person.

But if you are going to write about that individual, your questions must be much more specific. You hardly have enough for a story if you know that Steve Monroe is a junior from Lake Geneva, New York, majoring in information and library science. You need more detailed information, perhaps his career objective and his views on information storage and retrieval.

So, good interviewing is more than just carrying on a casual conversation. It takes skill, and it takes practice. This chapter will start you on the road to becoming a good interviewer.

In this chapter, you will learn

- how to prepare for an interview,
- how to conduct an interview, including use of audio and video recorders,
- how to handle off-the-record information,
- how to use quotes, and
- the importance of accuracy, attribution, and punctuation in quotes.

Interviewing as a Challenge

Writers do interviews in different ways. The medium they work for, deadline pressures, the accessibility of sources, and people's willingness to talk affect how well a writer can plan and do interviews. More and more, reporters are mobile journalists, or mojos, capturing quotes and filing stories from cars or coffee shops. They need to plan whether a pad and pencil are adequate or if they need audio and video equipment to record sound and visuals for online postings. In today's media world, stories can be multidimensional, as noted in Chapter 7 on online content.

Writers face challenges as they work diligently to reach as many sources as possible before a deadline. They become detectives as they figure out just whom they should interview and how. Like anyone else, writers feel nervous and even excited when they have the chance to interview a well-known newsmaker or celebrity. And they feel great satisfaction and accomplishment when a source answers their questions and gives them something extra.

Reporters usually interview multiple sources to get the information they need for a story. See how many sources Mark Landler used to get the variety of opinions and description for the following story:

> HEILIGENKREUZ, Austria—As noon draws near, the monks glide into the church, their white cowls billowing behind them. They line up in silence, facing each other in long choir stalls. Wood carvings of saints peer down on them from the austere Romanesque nave.
>
> Bells peal and the chant begins—low at first, then swelling as all the monks join in. Their soft voices wash over the ancient stones, replacing the empty clatter of the day with something like the sound of eternity.
>
> Except, that is, for the clicks of a camera held by a photographer lurking behind a stone pillar.
>
> It has been like this since last spring, when word got out that the Cistercian monks of the Stift Heiligenkreuz, deep in the Vienna woods, had been signed by Universal Music to record an album of Gregorian chants.
>
> When the album, "Chant: Music for Paradise," was released in Europe in May—and shot to No. 7 in the British pop charts, at one point outselling releases from Amy Winehouse and Madonna—the trickle of press attention turned into a torrent. (The CD will be released in the United States on Tuesday.)

Now this monastery, where the daily rituals of prayer and work have guided life for 875 years, finds itself in a media whirligig at once exhilarating and unsettling for its 77 brothers.

"We're monks," said Johannes Paul Chavanne, 25, a Viennese who entered the monastery after studying law and is training to be a priest. "We're not pop stars, and we don't want to be pop stars."

Too late: the album has made the monks of Heiligenkreuz a crossover hit, the latest example of how Gregorian chant, a once-neglected 1,000-year-old part of the Roman Catholic liturgy, can be repackaged for a secular society that savors its soothing, otherworldly cadences.

Heiligenkreuz—the name means Holy Cross—has put one of its more worldly monks, Karl Wallner, in charge of public relations. When not in prayer, he spends his days fielding calls from reporters as far away as New Zealand. His cellphone, its ring tone set to chant, sings constantly.

"I'm like a shield around my community," said Father Wallner, who has been a monk for 26 years. "There was a lot of concern at first that this would destroy the serenity of the monastery."

Some monks also worried that putting chants, which are, after all, prayers, into a commercial product amounted to a kind of profanity—"like using Leonardo da Vinci as wallpaper," in the words of one. For most, those risks are outweighed by what they believe is the music's great potential: to stir feelings of faith in a society that has drifted far from religion.

Still, the making of these latest monastic stars may say more about the way the secular world, thanks to the power of the Internet, can penetrate even the most secluded of cloisters.

In 1994, the Benedictines of Santo Domingo de Silos in Spain prompted the last big revival of Gregorian chant with an album that became a phenomenon. More recently, the use of chant on the popular video game Halo has piqued interest.

Eager to get in on the trend, Universal's classical music label took out an advertisement in Catholic publications, inviting chant groups to submit their work. Finding another ensemble like the Benedictines was going to be a long shot, the label's executives figured.

"Not all monks want to enter into a commercial relationship because that's not what they spend their days doing," said Tom Lewis, the artist development manager in London for Universal Classics & Jazz.

But the advertisement was spotted by the grandson of a monk from here. He tipped off Father Wallner, who, in addition to his public-relations duties, runs the monastery's theological academy and its Web site.

"An Austrian monk would never know what Universal Music is," Father Wallner said. "We were chosen by divine providence to show that it is possible to have a healthy religious life today."

Divine providence may have less to do with it than one monk's resourcefulness. Father Wallner sent Mr. Lewis a short e-mail message with a link to a video of chants that the monks had uploaded to YouTube after Pope Benedict XVI visited the monastery last September.

While monks in many monasteries chant, Heiligenkreuz is particularly proud of its singing, which has been honed over years by one of the monks, who used to direct choirs in Germany.

Mr. Lewis was entranced, recalling that the video eclipsed the more than 100 other submissions. "There was a smoothness and softness to the voices that you associate with younger people," he said.

Universal negotiated a contract with the monks, who proved to be anything but naïve in the ways of business. It helped that the abbot, Gregor Henckel Donnersmark, has an M.B.A. and ran the Spanish outpost of a German shipping company before he entered the monastery in 1977.

Among the clauses he sought: Universal cannot use the chanting in video games or pop music. The monks will never tour or perform on stage. And Heiligenkreuz will earn a royalty based on the sales of the album, which the abbot said worked out to roughly 1 euro per CD sold.

The monastery's share, Father Henckel Donnersmark figures optimistically, could be between $1.5 million and $3.1 million, which it will use to help finance the theological studies of young men from developing countries. So far, Universal has sold nearly 200,000 copies.

"Money is not a source of fulfillment," the abbot said, though he pointed out that it would defray the monastery's expenses, which are high, partly because of its success in attracting novices.

Even before the album, these monks had encountered the world of show business. The abbot's nephew, Florian Henckel von Donnersmark, wrote the screenplay for "The Lives of Others," an Academy Award-winning film about East Germany, while holed up in a monk's cell at Heiligenkreuz. He brought his Oscar back to the monastery, where the monks took turns holding it.

"A place like that can recalibrate your moral compass," Mr. Henckel von Donnersmark said by telephone from Los Angeles. "These people do nothing but think about how to love and serve God."

For now, the monks seem sanguine that they can balance this solitary vocation with the glare of celebrity.

"If the problem becomes too big," the abbot said, "I'll take a plane down to Santo Domingo de Silos and ask the abbot there for advice."

Landler did not rely on just one monk or monastery representative or just one person on the outside world. In his own words, each told his perspective about why the monks would produce an album of Gregorian chants for public sale—and how they will benefit from the profits. Solid reporting requires multiple interviews and viewpoints. The space allotted to detailed interviews shows what print and online media can offer above broadcast media.

Research before Interviewing

The first step in interviewing, of course, is to know your topic, and that requires research. Before any interview, you should have knowledge of your topic and the people you will interview. The general rule is not to go into an interview cold. You will have more success if your source quickly sees you are prepared. Preparation shows that you are serious about the interview, and it flatters the source.

With deadline pressure, however, some journalists might find that they do not have time to do research before they have to be on site to cover an event. On some occasions, you might go into an interview unprepared. Experienced writers or reporters will tell you that such an experience is uncomfortable and often embarrassing. No one wants to walk up to the newest

Nobel Prize winner for medicine and ask, "Now just what was your work that caused you to win?"

With the advantages of technology today, a reporter can be on his or her way to an interview while a researcher searches files for background information. The reporter can get data from the researcher and arrive somewhat prepared. Or the reporter can stop and do some quick online research via his cell phone.

Writers—whether print or broadcast reporters, online journalists, freelancers, public relations practitioners, graphic designers, or advertising copywriters—look in their own files first for information, then move to the company's or community's library. They might find other articles or broadcasts about their topic, or they may consult research materials such as government sites. Specific sources are noted in Chapter 9.

Sometimes as part of research, media will do an informal survey of people's opinions; for example, reporters may ask for residents' views on changes in Social Security or on plans to widen Main Street. Those stories require meaningful questions to get good quotes and complete identification of respondents. Such stories are a way to get readers or viewers into the newspaper, on an online site, or on radio or television. Media, as well as public officials or professional pollsters, can uncover public sentiment.

Considering more formal poll results could also be part of your research before setting up an interview. Polling firms spend millions of dollars each year interviewing voters about their favorite candidates and consumers about their favorite products and services. Marketers use the results to promote everything from a specific politician to toothpaste. Their questions have to be worded carefully to avoid bias and to obtain relevant, pertinent, and accurate information. Such firms have professionals who draft questions, oversee interviews, and compile results.

Getting the Interview

Once you have sufficient knowledge, you must determine whom it is you want to interview. For a story on credit card fraud, a local bank president might be a primary interview. But you must also talk to experts in the financial services industry, consumers, and whoever is knowledgeable about the subject. Some names might appear during research, and some could come as referrals in other interviews.

Setting Up the Interview

When you know whom you want to interview, you need to determine the best method of interviewing and make an appointment, whether the interview is by telephone or in person. Some interviews can be conducted by e-mail. Online questions and answers are fast and convenient, but remember: They have serious limitations. The source might not be known to the writer. The writer who interviews only via e-mail loses the candid spontaneity that comes with live interviews, as well as any sense of the source's surroundings and personal characteristics. A low chuckle or a timely grin are impossible to detect in an e-mail.

In setting up any interview, you may have to go through a secretary or a public relations person who maintains the source's schedule, and that process can be time consuming. Or you may be able to call the person directly.

Make sure that a source has firsthand information. If you are working on a story that requires expert opinion, for example, be sure your source is an appropriate one. The primary surgeon for a lung transplant is a much better source than a hospital public information officer or a physician who assisted during the operation. People who have never been involved in a child abuse case and are just giving you secondhand or hearsay information are not good sources for a story on that subject. A few filter questions upfront can eliminate unnecessary interviews: "I am looking for people who tried to break into the country-western music market. Did you ever sing professionally? Or perhaps prepare a demonstration tape for an agent?"

In setting up an interview, be sure to specify the amount of time you will need. Don't underestimate, or you will lack time to ask all your questions. Some people may be willing to be interviewed on the spot when you call, so be ready with your questions. Others will want to set a specific time at a later date. Ask for more time than you will need.

Select a comfortable place for an interview. The source's terrain is best because he or she is usually more relaxed in a familiar environment. The reporter also has the opportunity to observe personal items, such as family photographs or collected memorabilia, that can add to the story.

Avoid doing interviews during meals. People have difficulty talking while eating, and a discussion over who should pay for food—source or writer—can be uncomfortable. If the individual is from out of town and staying at the local hotel, you may choose to do an interview over coffee—a fairly inexpensive way of meeting and talking.

Dress appropriately for the interview. If you are interviewing the chief executive officer of a Fortune 500 company, wear a suit. If you are meeting a peanut grower in his fields, shuck the cashmere coat. And, if you are meeting with teenagers at the local hangout, jeans are okay.

What to Work Out in Advance

Do not agree to pay for an interview. Only in very rare situations should you consider paying for information. A news organization may agree to pay because the source's information is newsworthy, but any payment should be worked out ahead of time and be consistent with company policy. If you are a freelancer, you should not agree to pay for information; publications might not buy your work if sources were lured by profit.

Work out arrangements if you plan to use an audio or video recorder. Do not just show up with the equipment. Sources might want to be prepared, particularly in regard to their physical appearance if they are to be filmed. A tape recorder is advisable if you are planning a long interview or one that might contain controversial or important information. You might want a tape as a backup if you suspect a source might question your quotes in the printed article. One good way to have a source agree to be taped is to stress your need for accuracy in getting quotes right. Few people will argue.

Of course, you will need audio equipment if you know you will be writing an online version of the story and sound will be part of the package an editor will prepare. The same applies if the online editor wants video clips. Be sure to reserve equipment in advance, make sure it is working and has batteries before you leave the office, and review any operations so you can use it comfortably.

If you are doing an interview by e-mail or telephone, establish a time period for questions and answers so you will get responses by your deadline. You also might want to agree on a code word that the source will include at the end of responses so you know the source answered the questions and not someone who had access—whether legally or illegally—to the e-mail account. Some writers use e-mail only as a follow-up to a telephone or face-to-face interview. Be sure to note in the story which quotes came from e-mail interviews, just as you would note "in a telephone interview."

Some people will want to see a list of questions before they agree to an interview. Such a request can be honored if sources need to collect specific information, such as statistics. People who are not used to being interviewed may want some time to formulate responses. Or, if you are getting an actuality to use in a broadcast, a source may want a few minutes to prepare a response so he or she will have a script to follow. In many cases, your deadline will determine whether you have the luxury of submitting questions and waiting for responses. In any case, don't give up the right to ask a question that is not on the list.

Some sources will ask if they can see the article before it is printed or listen to the tape before it is aired. Of course, if you are a public relations practitioner or an ad copywriter, your source—who may be your client—will have final approval. But in the news business, the answer is *no.* Deadline pressure generally precludes allowing time for a source to review the message. Sources can become editors, wanting to change more than what applies to them.

If a source insists on previewing the piece, check it out with an editor or producer. You might want to find someone else to interview. Be clear if the answer is no. One inexperienced reporter caused herself and her newspaper some unpleasantness because a source thought he would have the right to edit a story citing him before it was printed. The reporter did not flatly say no, and the source misunderstood, believing he could review the story in advance. When the story appeared, the source felt deceived.

Writing the Questions

Interviewers, no matter how skilled or practiced, should write a list of questions before an interview. The list can be typed and printed or scribbled on an envelope. The questions ensure that all important aspects are covered during an interview. A reporter can review the list before ending an interview to make sure all points were asked. Questions also serve to keep an interview on track. For example, a minister might divert an interview to a discussion of the writer's religious beliefs. The writer can refer to the list and remind the minister that she is there to interview him. The list can also fill in lags in the conversation.

Covering the Basics

Obviously, when you are planning questions, you want to ask the basics: *who, what, when, where, how*, and *why*. But you need to ask other questions to get more information and to make the message complete. One formula for interviewing is called *GOSS*, an acronym for *Goals–Obstacles–Solutions–Start*, devised by Professor LaRue Gilleland of the University of Nevada. It can be applied to many interviews and is based on the assumption that people have goals, obstacles loom before goals, and solutions can be found to obstacles. Talking about goals, obstacles, and solutions gives the source plenty to discuss. During the interview, you may discover that you need to "start"—to go back to the beginning of an event or topic to get a more complete understanding.

For example, you might interview a chemist who does research on polymers. Using GOSS, you would ask about the goals of the research, the obstacles to discovering new uses, and the solutions to overcome the obstacles. "Start" would lead you to ask more broadly about the field of polymer research and what is happening in this particular laboratory compared with others.

Ken Metzler, author of *Creative Interviewing*, has suggested two more letters to Gilleland's GOSS: *E* for *evaluation* and *Y* for *why*. Evaluation suggests a need for an overall assessment of the situation—seeking meaning beyond the facts. To get such information, the writer asks for the source's interpretation: What does all this (polymers and research) mean to you? The *Y* is a reminder not to forget to ask why a situation has occurred and why particular research is important.

Think about quantitative questions. How many times has the baseball star struck out? How many ounces of marijuana were confiscated, and what is its street value? How many tons of concrete are needed for the runway, and is that equal to filling the high school football stadium to the top row 15 times?

When formulating questions, think of the unusual aspects. Don't hesitate to include questions you and your audience would like answered. You might even ask friends or colleagues what questions they would include if given the chance to interview a particular source.

Conducting an Interview

Always be punctual for an interview. Making a source wait is rude and could cost you the interview. Call to let the individual know if you will be late.

If you are interviewing a celebrity or high-ranking official, avoid appearing to be a fan or worshiper, nervous or excited. Few people would be calm the first time they interviewed an Oscar winner or a country's head of state. Butterflies are to be expected, but you should show respect rather than adulation.

Getting Started

When you introduce yourself, always give your name and identify yourself as a reporter. Also state your employer or where you expect to have the story appear, and a summary of what you need from the interviewee. That introduction puts the interviewee on notice that anything he or she says is on the record or for publication in some format.

After you introduce yourself, start an interview with some questions that will set a relaxed mood. For example, if you are in the person's home, comment about trophies, collections, or decor. Show you are interested. Don't ask weighty questions right away.

Avoid starting an interview by asking people what they do or routine information. They will know you haven't done your homework, and they could be insulted. You might need to verify information, however. A student who interviewed author Barbara Victor discovered in a biographical source that she was born in 1944. A question revealed that Victor actually was born a year later, in 1945.

Before beginning an interview, ask yourself the questions in the checklist shown in Box 10.1.

Using Recording Equipment

Even if they don't edit the stories, reporters have to collect raw video that online editors can scan to find relevant images to the story being told. Most reporters can learn to use recording equipment in a few lessons and through trial and error.

BOX 10.1 Checklist for Interviews

- Have I researched thoroughly my subject and source?
- Have I selected the right people to interview?
- Have I set up the interview in a place conducive to the interviewee?
- Have I allotted adequate time?
- Have I worked out using a tape recorder? A video camera? Is the equipment in good working order?
- Have I written a thorough list of questions?
- Do I feel prepared and confident?

If you are using a voice recorder, hold the microphone about six inches below your interviewee's chin to get good audio free of distortions from your interviewee's breath.

Be sure you let sources know when the tape recorder is on. Most states require that you notify people if they are being recorded. If you are doing a telephone interview and plan to record it, you must ask the individual's permission before you turn the recorder on. Rarely, if ever, will you need to hide a tape recorder in your briefcase or under your clothing.

If you are using video equipment and doing the recording yourself, get cover or overall shots first so that you can then focus on the interview. If a videographer is doing the shooting, use the time he or she is setting up the equipment to ask questions to put the person at ease and distract them away from the equipment. Many recorded interviews are done in offices where the lighting can be enhanced and little outside noise detracts or interferes with the sound.

Remember, when recording outside, any noises can interfere with the quality of the recorded interview. Stay away from streets, try to avoid wind, and watch the person's head position so he or she doesn't turn away from the recorder. Visually, what's going on in the background might distract viewers from the interview subject as they watch the action behind.

Remember to think of your microphone as if it were a camera lens. If you want the sounds of an event, move back to capture the jumble of noises as well as the panorama. Then move in close for the more specific.

Asking the Questions

Ask the easy questions first. This technique allows the person to relax and feel comfortable when responding. How to ask the tough questions is covered in the next section.

Be straightforward and specific in questioning. "So, Mr. Rich, you have investments and your construction business. And you have inherited money from your uncle and aunt. I imagine there are lots of people out there who are wondering how much you are worth." Of course, you can preface a question with a statement, but don't talk around a question—ask it. "Mr. Rich, you have investments and inheritance that have many people asking the question: Just how much are you worth?"

As you take notes, be sure to read back any confusing quotes to ensure you have complete and accurate statements. Sometimes a person will talk quickly or start a sentence, stop midway, and begin again. You might need to repeat part of a quote and ask the speaker to confirm or clarify what he or she said.

Maintain control. Don't let the person lead you. Keeping an interview on track might be difficult for a student writer or inexperienced reporter. Someone accustomed to being interviewed could have an agenda or might have what seem like canned responses. A politician, for example, might ignore a question about changes in tax laws and answer instead about his or her plan for economic development. If the person digresses, wait for a suitable pause, then steer the person back to the subject. Use your list of questions as a reference. If you interrupt, you could be cutting off some valuable comments.

Try to keep yourself out of an interview. Often a person will throw questions at the interviewer. Be polite and firm, and remember that you are there to do an interview, not to be interviewed.

Watch your body language. Avoid any behavior, such as nodding your head, that could subtly indicate you agree with comments. If the source believes you are sympathetic and empathetic, he or she might expect a positive story.

Maintain a friendly but professional distance. Do not become the source's friend. Writers who get too chummy with their sources can create tension when the article is published. The source might believe the writer betrayed confidences.

Leave all preconceptions and misconceptions at home. You might be a single working journalist with no children, and your interview is with a stay-at-home mother with five children. Mask any feelings of envy of her domestic life or notions that her job is not as fulfilling as yours. Do not be antagonistic if you disagree with a person's philosophy. Some people will open up, however, if they sense that you do not agree with them.

Listen to the source. Be aware of inconsistencies. Be willing to divert the conversation from the prescribed list of questions if you hear a tidbit that should be developed through another line of questioning. If you do not understand a response, ask for clarification. Remember: If you aren't clear about information, you'll never convey it clearly to audiences.

The Tough Questions

Save all embarrassing and controversial questions for the end of the interview, such as those dealing with a person's gambling debts or reports that a presidential candidate has had an extramarital affair. Of course, if a suitable occasion to ask such a question occurs during an interview, ask it. Be aware that you run the risk of having an interview terminated if you ask a particularly sensitive question. When asking these questions, be straightforward. If you act embarrassed, you will transmit that feeling and possibly not get a response.

The fact that a person does not answer a tough question is often noteworthy in a story. A former foreign service diplomat who settled in a small town was arrested on charges of shoplifting. When he refused to answer reporters' questions after his trial, one reporter noted his refusal in the story. His silence supported statements that he was close-mouthed about his current life. But don't fail to ask a question in the expectation a person might not answer it. You might get a response.

Many times writers must interview people who have suffered trauma or witnessed a traumatic event. An individual might have endured years of repeated physical abuse, survived a plane crash, been a hostage in a domestic dispute, or been wounded. A person might have witnessed a friend's drowning, seen a fiery truck crash, or found a house full of diseased and starving animals.

Writers must understand that people who have suffered trauma or an atrocity recover from those events in different ways and at different times, depending on the particular trauma and their personalities. Judith Lewis Herman notes in her book, *Trauma and Recovery*, that part of the healing process is remembering and telling the event. People seeking quotes and information might find individuals quite willing to talk and others who refuse to be interviewed. Herman writes:

> *People who have survived atrocities often tell their stories in a highly emotional, contradictory, and fragmented manner, which undermines their credibility. . . . It is difficult for an observer to remain clearheaded and calm, to see more than a few fragments of the picture at one time, to retain all the pieces, and to fit them together. It is even more difficult to find a language that conveys fully and persuasively what one has seen. Those who attempt to describe the atrocities that they have witnessed also risk their own credibility.*

Reporters must be aware of the psychological state of people who have just experienced a tragedy or atrocity, such as a subway bombing. Interviewers should ask the questions but understand when they do not get complete or even accurate responses. Interviewing more than one source might be required to get a full picture of what actually happened. Reporters might have to come back for follow-up interviews well after a traumatic event occurs.

Just as it is difficult to approach victims and witnesses, it is hard to interview victims' families. The media, particularly the electronic media, have drawn criticism for asking family members of victims "How do you feel?" only minutes or hours after a relative's death. Although some view such questioning as aggressive, others regard it as heartless. In some instances, reporters might find that a family member is willing to talk and is helped by remembering the individual. Reporters must use judgment and good taste in how far they should go in trying to get information. Reporters must try to ask the questions, but they must respect a person's right not to answer.

Interviewing during traumatic situations takes special care. The Dart Center for Journalism & Trauma at the University of Washington has an informative Web site—www.dartcenter.org—that defines trauma, gives specific advice on interviewing trauma victims or witnesses, and outlines what clues reporters should recognize if they are adding to the stress through interviewing.

Off-the-Record Information

In the middle of an interview, a public official says, "The following information needs to be off the record." Stop the official. Don't let him or her talk any longer. Off the record means you cannot use the information. As a writer you don't want information you cannot use. Politely refuse the information. Then you can proceed to clarify what the official means. People have different definitions of what off the record means: Don't use the information at all; use it but don't attribute it to me; or use it to ask questions of others, but I never said it.

A source might want to go off the record because he fears retribution if certain comments can be attributed to him. Sources also might have an ulterior motive in sharing what they imply is a secret, so reporters must be sure the information is valid and can't be learned any other way.

If you refuse to accept off-the-record information, the source might open up. People who have juicy information usually feel important and want to show they know something you don't. Think about it. Has a friend told you some gossip about someone else and sworn you to secrecy? Within 24 hours, had you shared it with someone else, despite your promise? Few secrets exist that are known only by one person.

As an interviewer, you must remember that many people who have information want to share it but may not want to take responsibility for making it public. They will let you as the writer do it anonymously, or let you find someone else to confirm it and become the public source. Be careful. Audiences do not necessarily believe information attributed to "a source close to the president" or "a high-level State Department official."

Some people will want to do interviews for background or just to educate you about a situation or to give you context. That means they are giving you information not to be attributed to them. For example, a bank executive might give you background on lenders and home mortgages. The information helps you in explaining the process to your readers or in asking questions of executives at other banks.

A final warning: Make sure you and the source are clear on how the information can be used before you accept it. If you agree to use the information but not the individual's name, you can use the information but not for attribution. If you agree the tidbit is confidential, you must not publish it. You might want that person as a source again. If you act unethically and violate the agreement, you can write that person off your source list, and you might attract unflattering attention to yourself and your employer.

Note-Taking Tips for Interviews

Most people talk faster than an interviewer can write. If you are not using a tape recorder and if you have trouble keeping up, politely stop the source and ask for a moment to catch up on notes. You could preface it by saying, "I want to make sure I record this correctly, so I need a moment to complete your last comment." Few sources would respond: "I don't care if you get it right. I want to keep talking."

Be sure when you are writing comments that you get them completely rather than in bits and pieces that might not fit together when you write the article. Complete notes help you avoid taking quotes out of context or misinterpreting quotes later.

If you have a quote that is complete, put it within quotation marks in your notebook. Then you will know you have the speaker's exact words when you review your notes and are ready to write. If you are using a tape recorder and hear a quote that you know you want to use, you can quickly check the counter on the recorder and write the time next to the quote in your notebook.

You might find it handy to flag your notes as you take them. Put a word or two in the margin to indicate where certain information occurs. For example, you may have a wide-ranging interview with the incoming Democratic speaker of the state legislature. "Welfare," "tax cuts," "power," and "education" would remind you where each topic was discussed. If you're using a tape recorder, it might also be useful to write down the "timestamp"—the number of minutes and seconds after the start of the recording—of each interesting statement by the source. That can help you write not only the correct words in a text report, but it will also reduce the amount of time you spend on editing audio if you are doing a multimedia report.

At the end of an interview, take a few moments to ensure you have asked all your questions. Most sources won't mind waiting while you double-check. If a quote is not clear, ask the source to repeat it. "You said earlier, Mr. Speaker, that changing the rules will help the House pass legislation faster. Could you clarify the parliamentary procedure a little more?" You also might want to ask if you can telephone or e-mail if any clarification is needed when you are producing the story.

After an Interview

Take time soon after you leave an interview to review your notes. Fill in any blanks that might appear confusing later. Note your feelings, the qualities of the source, any additional description, and other details while they are fresh in your mind. You should transcribe your notes as soon as possible to retain important details or impressions. If you store your notes on your computer, you can call them up easily when it is time to create the piece.

After an interview, you might want to write the person a thank-you note.

Selecting and Using Quotes

You have pages of notes from your interview. How do you determine which quotes to use? The same rules for using quotes from interviews apply to selecting quotes from speeches, presentations, or even published works. Selected quotes should be vivid, show opinion, reflect the speaker's personality, support the speaker's thesis, and unify a piece of writing.

When to Use Quotes

In organizing material, writers have to decide whether to quote an individual, then whether to use that information in an indirect or direct quote.

Direct quotes give the exact words of the speaker. The quotation marks signify to readers "here's exactly what was said." Direct quotes are used for colorful statements, opinion, and emotions. Direct quotes can convey an individual's personality and manner of speaking. Here's one rule to follow: Use a direct quote if it is better than any paraphrase.

Direct quotes can be either complete quotes or partial quotes. Here is a complete direct quote:

> "Russia needs to honor the agreement and withdraw its forces and, of course, end military operations," the president said.

Or:

> "If Speaker Pelosi and her Democratic colleagues were truly serious about increasing production of American energy and lowering the price of gasoline, they would call Congress back into session immediately to vote on our 'all of the above' energy plan," said Rep. John A. Boehner of Ohio, the Republican leader.

A partial direct quote would be written as:

> House Speaker Nancy Pelosi said legislation being assembled by Democrats "will consider opening portions of the Outer Continental Shelf for drilling, with appropriate safeguards and without taxpayer subsidies to big oil."

Or:

> A 27-year-old Egyptian woman gave birth to septuplets in what one of her doctors called "a very rare pregnancy—something I have never witnessed over my past 33 years in this profession."

Be careful not to switch person even in a partial quote—for example, switching from third person ("the senator") to the first person ("my influence"), as in the following sentence:

> The senator vowed to "use every last little bit of my influence" to block the bill increasing military spending.

A grammatical sentence would use the words "his influence," but then the quote would be inaccurate. In such cases, as in this example, rewrite as:

> The senator vowed "to use every last little bit" of his influence to block the bill increasing military spending.

As a note, most writers avoid using what are called orphan quotes—that is, quotation marks used for emphasis on a single word.

> The special envoy said the cease-fire represented a "monumental" effort.

Why use quotations? "Monumental" is hardly an inflammatory phrase or an unusual adjective.

To Paraphrase or Not

Indirect quotes are used to summarize or paraphrase what individuals say, particularly if they have rambled about an issue or topic. They do not use a speaker's exact words and are not set off with quotation marks. Writers use indirect quotes to keep quotes relevant and precise.

Many writers find indirect quotes particularly valuable when speakers have digressed from the main topic or when they inject jokes or anecdotal material that cannot be used. After deciding that Connecticut was unfairly burdened by the No Child Left Behind education act, Attorney General Richard Blumenthal announced that the state would sue the federal government. Part of his comments needed to be paraphrased. Here is an excerpt from his comments:

> *Give up your unfunded mandates or give us the money . . . if I believed that the $8 million cost of adding additional tests in grades, three, five and seven was educationally beneficial to Connecticut's students, I'd be the first one in line advocating for the expense. The cost, however, is not worth the questionable educational benefit. After multiple failed attempts to attain a mutually agreeable resolution to our reasonable, research-based requests, it is time to see resolution in another forum—the courts.*

Good media writing summed up Blumenthal's position in this lead from *The New York Times:*

> The State of Connecticut will sue the federal government over President Bush's signature education law, arguing that it forces Connecticut to spend millions on new tests without providing sufficient additional aid, the state attorney general announced yesterday.

Correcting Speakers' Grammar and Other Slips

Reporters who covered a high-level state official quickly learned that the man was not a good speaker. He had a vernacular accent for that region of the state, used incorrect grammar, and stated goals that seemed out of reach. How to quote him?

Early in the official's tenure, some print journalists chose to paraphrase his remarks so they could clean up the grammar errors. But others chose to clean up the grammar in direct quotes, making the official sound well schooled. But they soon discovered that cleaning up the official's language was not good practice. Audiences who also watched local television broadcasts saw and heard the official as he really was. The image they read in the newspaper did not match.

Journalists are faced continually with deciding how to use quotes. If a speaker uses improper subject–verb agreement, should the writer correct it in a direct quote? How far should writers go in cleaning up quotes? In the case of the state official, print journalists figured out they had to be true to the quotes or else paraphrase. They could not dramatically clean up the quotes, put them in direct quotations, and tell audiences, "Here's exactly what the man said." He didn't.

The Associated Press Stylebook advises writers:

> *Never alter quotations even to correct minor grammatical errors or word usage. Casual minor tongue slips may be removed by using ellipses but even that should be done with extreme caution. If there is a question about a quote, either don't use it or ask the speaker to clarify.*

Are Profanities and Obscenities Acceptable?

The Associated Press Stylebook also advises writers not to use profanity, obscenities, or vulgarities unless they are part of direct quotations and there is a compelling reason for them. Writers are cautioned to warn editors of writing that contains such language. The language should be confined to a single paragraph so that it can be easily deleted. Writers should not modify profanity, such as changing "damn" to "darn." Editors may change the word to "d—" to indicate that profanity was used by the speaker if no compelling reason exists to spell it out in the story.

Writers need to check with their publications and media organizations to determine their particular rules on profanity, obscenities, and vulgarities. Some specialized publications, listservs, blogs, or television shows allow such language. Audiences who subscribe to or view such programs are familiar with the language and either do not find it offensive or overlook it.

Sometimes a reporter will not include profanity in the news story on which the interview is based, but they will when it is part of an associated full transcript of the interview. Writers who link to the transcript from the online news story may want to consider ways to warn the reader that the transcript contains language that some readers may consider vulgar.

General Rules about Quotes

- Never make up a quote. Quotes must be accurate.
- Don't take a question answered "yes" or "no" and turn it into a direct quote. For example, if an interviewer asks a high school basketball coach if he believed many students bet on the outcome of games and the coach answered, "No," the quotation in the newspaper should not read:

  Coach Lyman Jones said, "I don't think many students bet on the outcome of our basketball games."

  All you can really say is this: When asked whether he thought many students bet on the outcomes of games, Coach Lyman Jones replied, "No."
- Watch out for redundancies when setting up quotes. Use the direct quotes to expand or add to the information in the indirect quote.

  Avoid:

  She said she was surprised at being chosen the school's outstanding senior. "I was so surprised when they called my name," Gonzalez said.

Prefer:

Melissa said she was surprised when the principal called her name. "I couldn't move or react," she added. "I felt glued to my chair in shock."

- Set up situations before using the quote so readers will have a context for quotes, as in the following Associated Press story:

An exercise program supported by the federal government and the trucking industry is aimed at eliminating spare tires on the truckers.

The goal is to make interstate drivers slimmer, healthier—and safer.

The Rolling Strong Gym has opened at a truck stop in North Little Rock, Ark., and others are planned elsewhere along Interstate 40. The president of the Richardson, Texas, health club company, as well as government and industry officials, are watching to see if the truckers will work out.

"It's been long overdue," said Paul Todorovich of Myrtle Beach, S.C., an independent driver. "I'm hoping it catches on and they flourish."

Transportation Department officials also hope so. "Research shows that drivers who are physically fit are safe drivers and that exercise is key to getting people into healthier lifestyles," said Transportation Secretary Rodney E. Slater in a statement endorsing the concept.

- Use "according to" only with printed or factual information. Do not use it as an attribution to a person.

Avoid:

The state's prison system is 3,456 inmates above the legally allowed level, according to the secretary of correction.

Prefer:

The state's prison system is 3,456 inmates above the legally allowed level, said the secretary of correction. According to prison documents, the level has exceeded capacity for the past seven years.

- Use attribution in the middle of a sentence only if it occurs at a natural break. Otherwise, put it at the beginning or the end so that you don't interrupt the flow of the person's statement.

  Avoid:

  "We can always," he said, "commission a new statue for the college commons."

  Prefer:

  "We can always commission a new statue for the college commons," he said.

  Acceptable:

  "The marine sciences lab is vital to the state's economy," he said, "and we must persuade the legislature to allocate more funds this year."

- Always use attribution for statements that use "hope," "feel," or "believes." You as a writer are not inside another person's head; you know how he or she feels, thinks, or believes because you were told.

  The district attorney said she believes the verdict fell short of what she expected the jury to do. She said she believes the community will be angered that Ammons was not found guilty of first-degree murder.

More on Attribution

Quotes, whether direct or indirect, must be attributed completely and adequately. Readers or listeners must know who is talking and who is making each statement. They need to know the proper sources of information. The general rule is that attribution should go at the beginning of each new quote or at the end of the first sentence, whether the quote is one sentence or more than one sentence.

If the quote goes on for several paragraphs, attribution usually is placed at least once in every paragraph, and most writers follow the rule of attribution somewhere in the first sentence. Some writers will omit attribution in a middle paragraph if they have several short paragraphs of quotes by the same speaker. The key is to ensure that readers know who is talking.

If paragraphs contain strong statements of opinion, however, the writer must use attribution for every sentence.

For many writers, particularly news writers, "said" is the attribution word of choice. "Said" carries no underlying connotation as to a speaker's emphasis or meaning; it is neutral. "Added" and "told" are also fairly neutral. Attribution words that contain subtle meanings include "emphasized," "stressed," "declared," "demanded," "ordered," "stated," "criticized," and "contended." Writers avoid many of these words.

Do not use words such as "smiled," "laughed," "grimaced," "chuckled," and so on as attribution words. They are descriptive words that tell how a person was behaving when she or he said something. Rather than writing "'Hello,' he smiled," use "he said with a smile." Phrases such as "she said, and frowned," "he said, and grimaced," and "she said, then laughed" are preferred.

When using attribution that includes a person's title, do not place the title between the person's name and the attribution verb.

Avoid:

The University will accept 3,475 freshmen for the incoming class, Polly Wilson, director of undergraduate admissions, said.

Prefer:

The University will accept 3,475 freshmen for the incoming class, said Polly Wilson, director of undergraduate admissions.

Punctuating Quotes

General punctuation rules are discussed in Chapter 2. Here are the basic rules for punctuating quotes:

- Attribution at the end of a quote—whether direct or indirect—must be set off with punctuation. In most cases, the punctuation will be a comma.

Fifteen barrels of sardines will be delivered Wednesday, he said.

"Fifteen stinking, dripping barrels of sardines will be delivered Wednesday," he said.

"Will you deliver the barrels of sardines before noon?" he asked.

- Attribution at the beginning of an indirect quote is not set off with punctuation.

He said 15 barrels of sardines will be delivered Wednesday.

- Attribution at the beginning of a direct quote requires punctuation. If the quote is only one sentence long, use a comma. If the quote is two or more sentences long, use a colon.

Johnson said, "We have spent three days examining the department's accounts and have found no evidence of impropriety."

Johnson said: "We have spent three days examining the department's accounts and have found no evidence of impropriety. We will recommend that no further action be taken."

- Quotes within a direct quote are set off with single quotation marks.

"He said, 'Go ahead and throw it away, just like you have done every game,' and he walked out and slammed the door," Smithers said.

"I think 'War of the Worlds' was a frightening movie," she said.

- Commas and periods go inside quotation marks in direct quotes.

"Fifteen stinking, dripping barrels of sardines will be delivered Wednesday," he said.

Matthews said, "This race should be the test of every man's and every woman's physical and mental stamina."

- When placing the attribution at the end of the first sentence in a direct quote, the attribution is closed with a period. It marks the end of a sentence.

Wrong:

"The new gymnasium is fantastic and humungous," said basketball player Brad Jones, "We're proud to play there. We really feel important playing our games now."

Right:

"The new gymnasium is fantastic and humungous," said basketball player Brad Jones. "We're proud to play there. We really feel important playing our games now."

- Question marks go inside or outside quotation marks depending on whether they are part of the quote.

Mark said, "Are you asking me whether I cheated on the exam?"

One of Dionne Warwick's popular renditions included "Do You Know the Way to San Jose?"

- Consider what may be slightly confusing but correct punctuation here:

Sara asked Kate, "Have you ever seen the movie 'Gone With the Wind'?"

Here, the writer has a movie title that must be set off with quotation marks within a direct quote plus a question mark that is not part of the title.

- If the attribution breaks up a direct quote, it must be set off with commas and the quotation marks continued.

"Go ahead and throw it away," said Smithers, "just like you have done every game."

- If a speaker is quoted for several continuing paragraphs, the quotation marks are closed only at the final paragraph. Each paragraph must open with quotation marks to indicate the person is still speaking.

> Resident John Loftis of Hollowell Road said, "We have been waiting two years for the southeast area to be annexed, and we are getting annoyed that the town council has further delayed a decision.
>
> "I have written and my neighbors have written all the council members to say we want town services and are willing to pay for them.
>
> "We just don't understand what the holdup is," Loftis said. "If a decision doesn't come after the next public hearing, I plan to picket city hall."

Not closing the quotation marks at the end of the first and second paragraphs tells the reader that Loftis has not finished talking. The quotation marks at the beginning of graphs 2 and 3 reopen the continuous quote from Loftis.

Writers must ensure that readers know who is speaking and when a person stops speaking. Attributing a quote to the wrong person because punctuation is incorrect could cause problems, ranging from jeopardizing a writer's relationships with sources to more serious issues of damaging credibility or even leading to defamation lawsuits. Careful writers pay attention to detail and accuracy, down to every quotation mark.

Remember:

- Be circumspect in your use of quotations. Just because you have a quote doesn't mean you have to use it.
- Look for variety in quotes when writing, and use a mix of indirect and direct quotes.
- Check *The Associated Press Stylebook* rule about correcting quotes.
- If you are not sure about a quote, follow this rule: When in doubt, leave it out. Don't try to reconstruct it as a direct quote. And be sure you have the gist of the remarks if you convert the comments to an indirect quote.
- Develop recording skills so you can use electronic equipment to add visuals and sound or to assist in long or complicated interviews.

Exercises

1. Interview a friend or classmate about political life on your campus. Consider using a tape recorder to practice taking notes and listening to the tape again to double-check accuracy. Take careful notes. Then list five quotes, with correct attribution, that you might use in a finished story about political life at your school. Focus on correct attribution and use of both indirect and direct quotes.

2. Identify a campus leader who has been in the news recently. Select a specific topic related to the leader's expertise. Set up an interview and prepare questions as outlined in the chapter. If possible, take a video camera to record the interview. While interviewing, take notes on the surroundings to add description. When the interview is over, compare your notes to the tape. Write a story that focuses on the campus leader's view. Use a mix of direct and indirect quotes. Select 30 seconds of video to use as well.

3. You are a reporter for the campus newspaper. Your editor has asked you to come up with a story based on money, specific to the campus. Ideas might be the cost of tuition or books, lack of enough financial aid, lack of funds to maintain classrooms, cost of getting settled in a job after graduation, increased student fees. Think of a story that would interest your audience: students. Stick to the campus for interviews. You must use more than one source. If the story relates to campus funding, you will need to talk to an administrator. You would also want to talk with a student who is affected. Be sure to have enough sources. After the interviews, write a story showing all sides of the issue.

4. Many publications reveal how average citizens feel about or react to an event. Editors will select a current topic and assign a reporter to get public reactions. Scan today's daily newspaper and select a current topic, such as an ongoing international conflict, national legislation, a campus issue, or another major event that students and staff would have read or heard about. Interview 10 people. Ask each one the same question. If you have to ask a question that is answered yes or no, you will need the follow-up question—"Why?"—or your responses will be skimpy. Get each individual's name (check the spelling) and two other identifying labels: year in school, academic major, hometown, age, and residence. Your attribution would look like this: Jane Smith, a senior chemistry major; or Alex Jones, 19, of Whiteville.

Write the story. The first paragraph should have a summary lead, giving the results of your informal poll, such as "Five of 10 university students interviewed Thursday at the student union said they believed the presidency is a tough job that receives little credit, and not one student would want the job." The second paragraph gives the question: "The students were asked, 'What is your assessment of the job of president, and would you want the job?'" Then you can proceed with each person's response.

5. Find a story in your local newspaper and the same story on the newspaper's Web site but with audio and video components added. Listen and view the recorded pieces. How do audio and visual elements add to the story? What can they tell that print alone cannot? E-mail or call the reporter and find out whether he or she was trained to use broadcast equipment and how such skills were learned. What advice does the reporter offer in extending interviewing beyond just pad and pencil?

References

John Brady, *The Craft of Interviewing.* Cincinnati: Writer's Digest, 1976.

Rene J. Cappon, *The Word: An Associated Press Guide to Good News Writing.* New York: Associated Press, 1991.

Norm Goldstein, ed. *The Associated Press Stylebook 2005 and Briefing on Media Law.* New York: Associated Press, 2005.

Mark Landler, "Heiligenkreuz Journal: Sacred Songs Sell, Drawing Attention to Their Source," *The New York Times,* June 26, 2008, accessed at http://www.nytimes.com/2008/06/26/world/europe/26monk.html?_r=1&oref=slogin&ref=world&pagewanted=print, accessed July 1, 2008.

Judith Lewis Herman, *Trauma and Recovery.* New York: Basic Books, 1992.

Ken Metzler, *Creative Interviewing, 2nd ed.* Englewood Cliffs, NJ: Prentice-Hall, 1989.

CHAPTER 11

Recognizing Bias and Stereotypes

Understanding bias means considering your own background as well as the backgrounds of others. Many people believe they can write about other people without allowing any personal bias to creep into their stories, news spots, or news releases. But few people can step outside personal bias because most people are unaware of how ingrained their beliefs and attitudes can be. All of us have biases or preconceived notions about others. Bias is not just overt, as racial prejudice or political beliefs are. It is subtle—and it comes from who you are.

Consider your background. Did you come from a suburban middle-class home where you attended a school with little ethnic diversity? Did you speak a language other than English at home? What is your family's ethnic or racial background? Did you grow up in an urban ethnic neighborhood—Italian, African American, or Laotian?

Did you live in a subsidized housing project, in an inner city, or in a small town of 5,000 people or fewer? Maybe you grew up on a farm or ranch, and your nearest neighbor was a half mile away. Did your grandparents or another relative live near you? Did you attend private or public schools?

What is your gender? Do you or does someone in your family have a physical or mental disability? What is your religion? What political party do you claim?

All these aspects of your background and many others helped to build your attitudes and beliefs. As a communicator, you must become aware of your attitudes and beliefs to curb the bias still evident in many stories produced by the media today—and the bias that keeps many stories from appearing.

Bias often surfaces in stereotypes that show up in adjectives or nouns used to describe certain groups. People form stereotypes from their perceptions of individuals' or groups' behavior and from their experiences and those of friends and relatives. Think about the label in the sentence "Jane is a typical college student who wants to have a good time and study as little as possible." As a student, you would not want people to ignore your full array of attributes and view you only as a lazy, party animal. The generalization is not fair to you or most other students. As a writer, you must learn to confront such stereotypes and avoid perpetuating negative overgeneralizations about groups.

In this chapter, you will learn

- how writers can begin to recognize bias,
- how bias in writing affects specific individuals and groups, and
- specific tips on how to avoid bias in writing about individuals and groups.

The Bias Habit

Journalists' cultural values can affect their ability to be truly fair. Because of the way the brain processes information, people must categorize and label people and events. Walter Lippmann referred to this phenomenon in 1922:

> *The real environment is altogether too big, too complex and too fleeting for direct acquaintance. We are not equipped to deal with so much subtlety, so much variety, so many permutations and combinations. And although we have to act in that environment, we have to reconstruct it on a simpler model before we can manage it.*

The *adaptive process* means people do not consider as many perspectives as possible, or they develop a view that does not accurately reflect reality. Most important, in this adaptive process, people often will select the information that confirms their existing attitudes and beliefs, say journalism researchers Holly Stocking and Paget Gross, who add that people may not even be aware they process information with a cognitive bias. They do not have to make a conscious effort to be biased; in fact, they may be trying to be unbiased, as journalists do in attempting objectivity.

It is important to remember that bias surfaces in many arenas. Adjectives and nouns are ascribed to people because of where they live, their political beliefs, their sexual orientation, and their religion. Bias attributes certain characteristics to women, men, people with disabilities, children, older people, and members of ethnic and racial groups. Labels are dangerous. They often are offensive and usually imply inferiority. They can exclude or oppress. Labels do not accurately describe individuals nor do they accurately apply to groups. Writers who do not think beyond labels perpetuate negative stereotypes and myths.

Not all stereotypes necessarily appear negative, however. For example, a majority-culture stereotype has been exhibited in several kinds of traditionally American stories such as cowboy stories, soap operas, or musicals where the heroes usually are depicted as tall, broad-shouldered, white, and handsome and where women most frequently play minor roles.

Another example of a positive stereotype is the "model minority" in the Asian American community, where people are depicted as geniuses in music, math, and science. That generalization, although it seems complimentary, is not true and affects the majority of Asian Americans who might not have aptitudes in these particular fields.

Usage also changes as perception and bias changes. Writers who rely on *The Associated Press Stylebook* for guidance on word choice notice the changes in each annual edition. For example, the 2008 edition notes "mentally disabled" as the preferred term, replacing "mentally retarded."

Bias in Writing

Groups such as journalists can construct a shared view of "reality" because of the similarities in the way they view the world. Timothy Crouse in his book, *The Boys on the Bus*, explained the close working relationship among political reporters on the campaign trail:

> *It was just these womblike conditions that gave rise to the notorious phenomenon called "pack journalism" (also known as "herd journalism" and "fuselage journalism"). A group of reporters were assigned to follow a single candidate for weeks or months at a time, like a pack of hounds sicked on a fox. Trapped on the same bus or plane, they ate, drank, gambled, and compared notes with the same bunch of colleagues week after week.*

As early as 1950, one famous study showed how wire editors relied on their own values to select the news. David Manning White reported that "as 'gatekeeper' the newspaper editor sees to it (even though he may never be consciously aware of it) that the community shall hear as a fact only those events which the newsman, as representative of his culture, believes to be true."

Almost half a century after the Civil Rights Movement became a force in the United States, inequities based on race and ethnic background persist. Mass media have both helped and hindered the effort for equal rights in this country. On the one hand, they give voice to various social movements and allow the message of equality to reach a mass audience. On the other hand, they perpetuate misinformation and ignore a myriad of other ethnic groups.

Although the complexion of management is changing, most people who run the media are of Western European descent, and a large majority are male. They have little context, therefore, to help them know what it is like to be an African American, Native American, Asian American, Hispanic American, or other person of color in the United States. (Only about 13 percent of journalists nationwide are from these groups. Journalists as a group are educated, and few grew up in poverty.) Too often, stories about those communities are reported with an outsider's perspective, resulting in misinformation or stereotypes. In other cases, the stories might not be reported; the group might be invisible to the journalist.

The issue of race and the media—both how the media cover race and the racial makeup of newsrooms—surfaced in the 1968 Kerner Commission Report. The report was commissioned by President Lyndon Johnson's administration after the race riots in Los Angeles in August 1965. As part of the report, the committee looked at media and race. Ten years later, another study, *Window Dressing on the Set: Women and Minorities in Television: A Report of the United States Commission on Civil Rights*, noted the token roles played by women and minorities in TV news and sitcoms. The two are considered classic cases that started media managers looking at racial issues and prompted news organizations, such as the American Society of Newspaper Editors, to launch diversity committees.

Consider some of these other overt problems of bias in coverage:

- *The New Yorker* cover that depicted then-presidential candidate Barack Obama in a turban fist-bumping his wife, Michelle, who had a rifle slung over her shoulder.
- The rush to believe that even Muslims who were U.S. citizens were affiliated with the radical fringe accused of the World Trade Center and Pentagon attacks in 2001.
- The belief that teens with dyed, spiky hair and black leather jackets are drug users.

- The use of black or Hispanic women as the subject of photos about welfare when the majority of welfare recipients are white, not black or Hispanic.
- The use of photographs of gay men in ballet tutus to illustrate a story about gay civil rights.

Breaking the Bias Habit

Today, writers and reporters are trying, through better awareness, to overcome their own biases in addition to cultural bias implanted in the news. But old habits die hard. A first step is for writers to be aware of their own biases and how easily biases can slip into communication. Take religion as an example. Our religious beliefs may contain opinions about others that we should not include in our writing, even though we firmly believe them. Some writers may have Biblical or "sacred text" attitudes and opinions about homosexuals, Jews, gentiles, African Americans, and women. In other words, religion may teach us things about those who don't believe as we do.

Another important way to break the bias habit is to know your own biases. You can check yourself by taking the Implicit Association Test, a University of Washington and Yale University test that measures biases regarding race, age, gender, and ethnicity. You can find it online at https://implicit.harvard.edu/implicit/. What's important in the real world is that communicators do not convey these preconceived notions in their communication, even if they believe them.

Writers also must not fall into the habit of ascribing tired adjectives to certain groups, as noted earlier in the chapter. Writers unconsciously tend to write on traditional stereotyped templates, such as "rural–urban or inner city," "black–white," "rich–poor/tale of two cities," "old–young," or "rags to riches/Cinderella." Writers need original and accurate language to describe individuals.

Society itself helps writers. Today a multicultural approach is being integrated into numerous aspects of society, from school textbooks to television advertisements. All types of cultures in the United States are gaining a voice. Coverage of the 2008 Olympics in Beijing gave many reporters and people around the world a look into a communist country that is emerging as a world economic force. As someone disseminating information, you can learn to tap into these cultures for stories and diverse insights.

Media can have an impact in breaking the bias habit. As newsrooms become more diverse, the types of stories aired or printed will continue to become diverse.

Reporters can describe people as individuals, not cast them in broad terms ascribed to a group. Reporters can also become circumspect when using language and learn which terminology individuals and groups prefer. Diverse groups should be covered year-round, not just on holidays or in certain months.

Many organizations have developed guidelines on language use. Professional journalism organizations have Web sites that often include examples of stereotyping or negative portrayals. For example, the National Association of Black Journalists has posted on its Web site "NABJ Style" under its "Newsroom" link. The committee that spent three years compiling the entries notes that the style guide is "a first draft, an evolving document." Anyone, from journalists to students, can find definition and preferred usage for terms listed alphabetically at http://www.nabj.org/newsroom/stylebook/index.php.

Students can become more familiar with groups, their goals, their membership, and current issues by accessing Web sites for organizations that support those groups, such as the American Association of Retired Persons at www.aarp.org. Professional media organizations are also good sources. The Asian American Journalists Association can be found at www.aaja.org; National Association of Black Journalists at www.nabj.org; Native American Journalists Association at www.naja.org; National Association of Hispanic Journalists at www.nahj.org; and the National Lesbian & Gay Journalists Association at NLGJA.org. Most sites have links to related organizations. Other helpful Web sites are listed in Box 11.1.

BOX 11.1 Helpful Web Sites with Cross-Links to Other Informative Sites

www.ciij.org—Center for Integration and Improvement of Journalism's comprehensive site with links to major associations of minority journalists and the National Lesbian and Gay Journalists Association, among others. It includes diversity news and media sites.

www.unityjournalists.org—The UNITY Web Site, self-described as "a strategic alliance advocating news coverage about people of color." It includes a link to the National Association of Black Journalists' style guide.

www.mosaicweb.com/index2.htm—A multicultural site that is constantly updated. It includes links to "Filipino-American," "Caribbean," "women," and "multicultural."

www.spj.org/diversity.asp—The Society of Professional Journalists' guide to diversity with links to other articles as well as to its "Guidelines for Countering Racial, Ethnic and Religious Profiling."

Considering Specific Groups

John Mitrano, executive director of the National Organization of Italian Students and Educators, noted the following in a survey:

> *While there is usually a grain of truth to stereotypes, over time, these become no longer salient. With the twilight of ethnicity upon us in third and fourth generation families, new portrayals must be used to depict groups accurately. Television shows, movies, and advertisements must emphasize the qualities that we see ourselves as having. We must also become vocal and mobilized when we do not like the way we are portrayed.*

Many words and images applied to specific groups have historically negative and derogatory connotations. Writers must be aware of them and avoid them.

Race or ethnicity often has relevance for stories and should be used only when pertinent. Writers should avoid racial identifiers that imprecisely identify someone as black, Latino, or Asian American, particularly in crime stories. Keith Woods, dean at the Poynter Institute, in using the example of describing a man solely as Hispanic, writes:

> *Think about it this way: In order for everyone reading, watching, or listening to the story to conjure up the same image in their mind's eye, they must all share a common understanding of what a Latino person looks like. In other words, people who are Latino would have to look alike.*
>
> *What does a Hispanic man look like? Is his skin dark brown? Reddish brown? Pale? Is his hair straight? Curly? Coarse? Fine? Does he have a flat, curved nose or is it narrow and straight?*

Woods advises journalists to "challenge the presence of racial identifiers" and to "demand more from the people who give vague, meaningless descriptions, just as you do whenever a politician gives you vague or meaningless information."

Writers should also avoid descriptive words that strengthen stereotypes, such as "oil-rich" and "nomadic" to characterize Arab Americans, says former newspaper editor Fernando Dovalina. He notes the problems surrounding the terms “illegal alien” and “illegal immigrant,” which for many have become synonymous with Hispanic, particularly Mexican Americans. Dovalina writes:

> *“Illegal aliens” and “illegal immigrants” were created because of the need to have short and handy phrases to describe people who cross the border illegally.... We have no perfect alternative, but the other choices, “undocumented immigrants” or “undocumented workers” are slightly better, even though they are awkward and unwieldy and smack of political correctness.*

Racial and Ethnic Groups

Writers must avoid terminology perpetuating beliefs that all members of any group look alike, talk alike, think alike, or belong to the same political party. Having the first black candidate for U.S. president in 2008 brought attention to race, culture, and language. Some discussions proved positive and others negative, as evidenced in the fallout from the Rev. Jeremiah Wright’s comments and Barack Obama distancing himself from his former pastor.

Some language, although it may seem biased, can be appropriate when used in a historical context or with cultural sensitivity, noted Pale Moon Rose, president of the American Indian Heritage Foundation. Terms such as “redskin” and “brave” are acceptable if used appropriately and in a historical context.

The use of Native American names as sports team mascots, such as the Florida State Seminoles and the Washington Redskins, has generated criticism. In another article, Poynter’s Keith Woods writes,

> *The harm here is not that all Native American nicknames are insults on the order of Washington’s Redskins. It’s that nearly all of them freeze Native Americans in an all-encompassing, one-dimensional pose: the raging, spear-wielding, bareback-riding, cowboy-killing, woo-woo-wooing warriors this country has caricatured, demonized, and tried mightily to exterminate.*

Dovalina, retired assistant managing editor for international coverage of *The Houston Chronicle*, developed a list of diversity questions for a national copy editors’ workshop. The questions came from his 37-year career and the experiences of other journalist colleagues. The following were among Dovalina’s questions:

- Do you absolutely have to say that a black person or Hispanic or Asian or Native American is the first of his or her race to have attained the distinction in question? . . . Sometimes the news is that it took so long for a black female or a Hispanic male to be named the first head of a city or college department.

- Do you assume that all blacks are African Americans or Africans? Remember that culturally some blacks are Jamaicans and Haitians and Brazilians. . . . Some Latin Americans are more German and Italian than Spanish. . . . To people south of the Rio Grande, the term "America" does not refer to the United States alone. It refers to the hemisphere, and they too are Americans.

Use of the term "minority" is problematic in an international sense because people of color make up the majority of the world's population, and population changes in the United States mean that some ethnic groups are the majority in certain locations. Remember also that "minority" always refers to a group rather than to certain individuals; it is best to use the term "members of minority groups" rather than "minorities." Always look for a diversity of sources when writing. A Native American might be interviewed about political struggles instead of the meaning of a ceremonial dance. Dovalina reminds us, "Just as there are no Anglo leaders who speak for all Anglos, there are no black leaders or Hispanic leaders who speak for all blacks or all Hispanics." Keith Woods of Poynter has guidelines for racial identification in the form of five questions (Box 11.2). He notes that delicate material can be handled better "if we flag every racial reference and ask these questions." His questions should be considered when writing about any underrepresented group in society; just substitute the name of the group for "race."

Sexism

Women have risen to powerful jobs in both the public and private sectors, but they have not gained enough power to transform their image fully in the media. Many writers thoughtlessly use language that treats women as inferior or that is demeaning or insulting. They are sometimes referred to as girls or mothers and are described by their physical attributes such as "attractive" or "brunette" or "shapely."

Writers should use description when it is complete and adds to the understanding of an individual's personality. Feature writers must be especially careful when creating a mood. Often what looks like interesting detail might come

BOX 11.2 Guidelines for Racial Identification

1. **Is it relevant?** Race is relevant when the story is about race. Just because people in conflict are of different races does not mean that race is the source of their dispute. A story about interracial dating, however, is a story about race.
2. **Have I explained the relevance?** Journalists too frequently assume that readers will know the significance of race in stories. The result is often radically different interpretations. This is imprecise journalism, and its harm may be magnified by the lens of race.
3. **Is it free of codes?** Be careful not to use "welfare," "inner-city," "underprivileged," "blue collar," "conservative," "suburban," "exotic," "middle-class" "Uptown," "South Side" or "wealthy" as euphemisms for racial groups. By definition, the White House is in the inner-city. Say what you mean.
4. **Are racial identifiers used evenly?** If the race of a person charging discrimination is important, then so is the race of the person being charged.
5. **Should I consult someone of another race/ethnicity?** Consider another question: Do I have expertise on other races/cultures? If not, broaden your perspective by asking someone who knows something more about your subject. Why should we treat reporting on racial issues any differently from reporting on an area of science or religion that we do not know well?

Reprinted with permission of the Poynter Institute.

across as sexism in disguise. Writers should guard against describing women in terms of their physical appearance and men in terms of wealth and power.

Issues of sexism in coverage came to the fore in Sen. Hillary Clinton's bid for the Democratic presidential nomination in 2008. An example was the hundreds of column inches and hours of air time spent on Clinton's laugh, which became labeled as the "Clinton Cackle." One *New York Times* writer wrote an entire column on her laugh. Clinton defenders charged that coverage of male candidates didn't characterize their laughs in such a demeaning way and that it was irrelevant to presidential coverage. Dee Dee Myers, a former presidential press secretary, noted: "Have we had more male candidates with funny laughs? Almost certainly. Have they gotten as much attention? Certainly not. But it just reflects a sexist strain in society that certain things are not acceptable in women."

The laugh characterization proved fairly mild compared to other pundits' use of language to describe Clinton, ranging from the debate over whether the word "bitch" applied to *Washington Post* columnist Maureen Dowd's note that Clinton had moved from "nag to wag." Having the first woman presidential candidate offered new fodder for political writers and plowed new ground in coverage. Clinton supporter Susan Estrich, who had been involved in other presidential campaigns, noted in a National Public Radio report that the role of a woman as the nation's leader had not been defined when Clinton ran for office. "I think that's why there's been so much attention to Hillary's clothes and to Hillary's cleavage and to Hillary's husband and to Hillary's marriage and her motherhood and her own daughter," Estrich says.

On the other political side, many stories on Cindy McCain, wife of Republican candidate John McCain, mentioned the size of her jeans. She was also described as a "blond, blue-eyed former rodeo queen and cheerleader" as opposed to her philanthropy and work in third-world countries. During the campaign, both she and Michelle Obama, a Harvard-educated lawyer, received praise for their fashion style more than for their accomplishments. After McCain announced Alaska Gov. Sarah Palin as his vice presidential running mate, debate erupted on blogs and elsewhere about media characterizations that were deemed sexist. Among them, discussions of whether Palin, a mother of five and former beauty queen, would have time or talents to be vice president. Such questions are not asked of male candidates, they said.

Words such as "chairman" have a male bias. *The Associated Press Stylebook* says to avoid "chairperson" unless an organization uses it as a formal title. When possible, use "firefighter," "flight attendant," "postal service worker," or "letter carrier." Writers should also know their publication's policy about courtesy titles. Many organizations have eliminated courtesy titles, such as Mrs., Miss, and Ms., before women's names. Only the last name is used on second reference.

Sexual Orientation

Writers should also avoid perpetuating negative images based on sexual orientation. Gay and lesbian rights movements since the mid-1950s have worked diligently to recast gay and lesbian portrayals in society. Until the mid-1970s, most news stories that referred to gays and lesbians did so only in the context of police reports or mental illness. Gay and lesbian issues have been addressed in the schools, in the workplace, and in the military. Despite increased coverage, some editors and reporters still produce stories that present homosexuality as deviant, and negative stereotypes continue.

Writers and broadcasters must be careful not to make value judgments when a source is gay or lesbian or when the subject deals with homosexuality. Saying, for example, that a source "confessed" to being gay communicates negative, secretive feelings about homosexuality that your openly gay source will resent.

A person's gender or sexual orientation should be ignored in a message unless it is relevant. People's sexual orientation might be part of the fabric of the message but should be woven in as part of who they are, not presented as their complete identity.

Associated Press writer Kristen Gelineau wrote a piece about openly gay Southern legislators, focusing on Adam Ebbin, a Democrat from Alexandria, Virginia. The story primarily examined how Ebbin and others handled and felt about anti-gay legislation and the resulting debates as state legislators. Such stories must be written accurately and without bias. Gelineau let her sources tell the story, as evidenced in this quote from Rep. Ebbin: "I know that any time that people are gonna tell lies about gays and lesbians on the House floor, that I can grab my mike and speak—and that's really empowering. . . ." Or in this statement from New York Assemblywoman Deborah Glick: ". . . It is rare that my colleagues who are straight get to hear directly some of the incredibly mean-spirited attitudes so clearly enunciated."

Writers should never make assumptions about people's sexual orientation or people's sentiments toward gay and lesbian issues. Some people favor equality for all people. Remember that many people who are not gay or lesbian support gay and lesbian rights, just as many white people support civil rights for people of color. Writers should also not feel the need to balance every story that initiates from a gay rights source or event. In covering any group, sometimes balance is not appropriate, adds a shallow reporting element, or reduces the impact of the event.

Disabilities

Unless you or someone in your family has a physical or mental disability, as a writer you may tend to forget people with disabilities exist. Among the derogatory labels applied to disabled people are "crippled," "deformed," and "invalid."

The Disabilities Committee of the American Society of Newspaper Editors noted a list of terms to avoid, including "special," which is considered as patronizing; "stricken with or suffers from" instead of "a person who has" a specific disability; "victim of" rather than "a person who has" AIDS or cerebral palsy.

Unlike other groups that are discriminated against because of social norms, people with disabilities face discrimination from attitudes and actual barriers created by society's architectural and communication designs. Maybe you have never seen a person who uses a wheelchair in your local grocery store because there is no curb cut in the sidewalk in front of the store or no ramp at the door of the store. Maybe you have had little interaction with a profoundly deaf person because you do not know where to find a Telecommunications Device for the Deaf (TDD), which would allow you to call the person on the phone.

Many people, including writers, forget that people with disabilities constitute a vital, and numerous, part of our society. Under the New Freedom Initiative for Persons with Disabilities, the federal government has taken steps to remove barriers that people with disabilities still face. DisabilityInfo.gov is a Web portal that provides information about federal programs.

According to the American Community Survey, about 15 percent of the U.S. population not living in an institution reports some type of disability. That's more than 41 million people. Therefore, a significant number of today's audiences either has a disability or knows someone who does. Civil rights violations, new technology, legislation, and changes in business practices are possible story topics that are of interest to these audiences.

The late John Clogston, a journalism professor at Northern Illinois University, said that writers often portray people with disabilities in one of three demeaning ways: They imply that people who have a disability are somehow less human than other people; they present them as medically defective or somehow deviant or different in society; or they go overboard in trying to portray them positively, thus making them superhuman or "supercrips," as Clogston called them. Writers have a tendency to focus stories on the individual rather than the issues surrounding a disability, and they tend to wrap people with disabilities in pity and sympathy.

The Associated Press Stylebook cautions writers not to describe a person as disabled or handicapped "unless it is clearly pertinent to a story. . . . Avoid such euphemisms as mentally challenged and descriptions that connote pity, such as afflicted with or suffers from multiple sclerosis. Rather, has multiple sclerosis."

Such language carries negative connotations and can exclude people with disabilities. The focus should be on the person, not on the physical impairment.

Be careful about writing that someone succeeded "in spite of" a disability—a phrase often viewed by people with disabilities as extremely patronizing. Some writers may contend that a disability implies that individuals are not able, and if they succeed, then the news value of emotional impact and conflict is there to attract readers. Never assume an accomplishment by a person with a disability is unusual.

At one time, leaders' disabilities often were not a visible part of reporting. When the late Sen. John East ran for election in North Carolina, all photographs showed him sitting. Few voters realized he used a wheelchair. President Franklin D. Roosevelt conducted business from a wheelchair, and controversy arose when one panel in the FDR Memorial in Washington, D.C., showed him seated in a wheelchair. A Kennedy family book and documentary film footage released several decades after his death showed President John F. Kennedy unable to lift his children or to bend deeply.

In general, people specializing in coverage of disability issues recommend two easy rules in writing about people with disabilities. First, avoid clichés and clichéd constructions. Use value-neutral terms—that is, words that do not stereotype. Avoid saying someone is confined. The person gets out of the wheelchair to sleep and to bathe. To that individual, the wheelchair is liberating. It is more accurate to say the individual uses a wheelchair. Second, never inject pity or a condescending tone into copy.

Ageism

Older people may also face stigmatization by society, and the mass media play a role in that process. In some instances, older people are labeled as forgetful, senile, rigid, meddlesome, childlike, feeble, fragile, frail, gray, inactive, withered, or doddering. Such adjectives might describe older people at some point in their lives or may be medically appropriate. But if such words are used indiscriminately, they demean older people and perpetuate inaccurate stereotypes. With the repeal of mandatory retirement, older people continue to work into their 70s and even 80s if they choose. They do most things that younger people do.

The Associated Press Stylebook cautions to use terms such as "elderly" and "senior citizen" sparingly and carefully. "If the intent is to show that an individual's faculties have deteriorated, cite a graphic example and give attribution for it," the stylebook notes.

The older population is growing in the United States; the latest census predicts the 65- to 74-year-old age group to grow 16 percent by 2010. The numbers will be even greater after that date as baby boomers turn 65. Many journalists and others focused on Republican John McCain's age during the 2008 presidential campaign and his ability to lead as a septagenarian.

Syndicated columnist Lucille deView, who writes on aging, suggests that writers avoid these myths about older people:

- Older people can participate in a variety of activities, so do not adopt a "gee whiz" attitude toward their abilities. Most people over the age of 50 continue the physical activities they enjoyed when younger, whether swimming, hiking, or playing tennis.
- People are continuing to work well into their 60s, 70s, and even 80s. The American Association of Retired Persons produces a list of the Best Employers for Workers over 50.
- Older people should be seen as individuals, not as members of a senior age group in which people are believed to have the same interests and abilities. Older people's interests are just as varied as those of individuals in other groups.
- Older people are not stereotyped in appearance. They dress in numerous fashions, and not all older people have physical problems or even gray hair.
- Age does not mean loneliness or loss of sexual interest. According to a 2005 AARP study, two-thirds of the individuals polled said they lived with a spouse or a partner or that they had a regular sexual partner.

DeView says writers should focus on realistic presentations of older people. Some older people have no financial problems, whereas others struggle financially in later life. Not all older people have ill health or are unable to cope with poor health. Serious medical conditions may not severely limit their participation in society. Only about 5 percent of older people live in nursing homes.

Children also should not be portrayed in an unpleasant light. Not all children are immature, naive, whining, sneaky, dishonest, or lazy. Children mature and develop at different paces. Some are responsible, creative, athletically gifted, loving, aggravating, and mean. Each must be considered individually and be allowed to ascribe traits to himself or herself, as did one 5-foot teenager, who described herself as being "vertically challenged."

Poverty

One societal group cuts across all racial, ethnic, and other groups: the people who live at or below the poverty level. In 2005, that level was defined as a family of four earning less than $20,000.

Although the United States is a leading world power, the number of Americans who live in poverty is 36.5 million, according to the U.S. Census. Household income has not increased in recent years. Even though people living in poverty may be limited media consumers, they still are part of U.S. society. Poverty, often not breaking news, affects every city in the United States. How the less-fortunate subsist should be part of regular, ongoing coverage—not just at holiday times when their plight stirs a need to give or during recessionary times when more people suffer economically.

Poverty overlaps many areas of coverage: health, religion, social services, local government, nonprofit sector, and education. Many school systems provide poor children with free or reduced-cost breakfasts and lunches. Lack of health insurance forces many people to use emergency rooms for medical care. Almost any story touches poorer segments of society. Reporters can find sources among nonprofit organizations, such as poverty assistance programs; community resources, including government officials; and churches that operate shelters and kitchens. When stories of less-fortunate residents appear, they help agencies and the needy get a boost.

When reporters write about lower-income people, they must watch their language. The word "poor" implies "disadvantaged" and often is ascribed to people of color, as are "welfare recipient" and "public housing resident." Editor Dovalina points out that a larger percentage of blacks and Hispanics are poor compared with whites, but most poor people are white.

Religion

Religion news, which has grown in importance and visibility since the terrorist attacks on September 11, 2001, showed U.S. audiences and media how little was known about different forms of Islam. The intricacies and differences among religions can lead to writers unknowingly conveying biased and misleading information.

Maha ElGenaidi, executive director of the Islamic Networks Group, an educational outreach organization, was quoted in *The San Jose Mercury News*:

> *In all religious traditions, people tend to blame the religion for what a few people have done in misapplying the religion or using it for political ends.*

Her quote could apply to Islam and to U.S. politicians who have invoked religion as a basis for their positions or votes on public policy or law.

In writing about religion, reporters must be aware that religion stories often involve other issues, such as politics, medicine, or community services. While some might see cloning as a medical or scientific story, the topic generates strong opinions from religious organizations. Same-sex marriage stories include politics, religion, and sexual orientation issues and cause people to consider "What is marriage?" Even the Harry Potter children's book series stirred discussions of witchcraft and whether the stories were anti-Christian.

Anyone who covers religion must also examine his or her own religious beliefs before developing questions and interviewing sources. Because the United States is dominated by Judeo-Christian traditions, many writers might be unaware of non-Christian faiths. While most of us grew up with some exposure to religion, whether within our families or our communities, that does not automatically make us tolerant of other people's views and beliefs.

Writers can do research to increase their knowledge and understanding of religions and denominations. Web sites provide information on denominations, beliefs, and practices and even positions on social, political, and ethical issues. One such site—www.beliefnet.com—has information on different religions.

Overcoming Bias in Writing

Even after a discussion of bias such as the one in this chapter, traces of insensitivity can still creep into writing. You need to be constantly aware of your own background and attitudes to understand when and how bias might surface in writing, to recognize it, and to exorcise it.

Writers, reporters, and broadcasters today must be trained to avoid the flaws of their predecessors in the mass media. They must learn to question their own beliefs and assumptions to understand better the diverse ethnic groups within society.

Today's writers, through greater awareness, are trying to overcome cultural bias by sifting through information and presenting the least stereotypical and biased picture possible. Messages—from school textbooks to television advertisements—use a multicultural approach that presents all kinds of people. But despite education, old biases die hard for many; every time a bias is confirmed by a writer, it is strengthened for readers.

Beginning and even experienced writers sometimes pass along stereotypes, such as the ditzy blonde or dishonest politician, because they think people like and understand such shorthand portrayals, just as they like cartoons. Therein lies the danger. Because mass media professionals present distinctive images of people and groups, they can determine how consumers view people and groups who are not like themselves. Thus, writers must work responsibly in disseminating information rather than misinformation.

Stereotypes communicate inaccurate information and can undermine the quality of your work. Make sure what you write or broadcast does not perpetuate stereotypes. Use anecdotes rather than adjectives to show people's attitudes and behaviors. Sensing stereotypes and avoiding them is a critical step on the path to better writing.

Exercises

1. Describe yourself culturally and ethnically. List any physical disabilities or other pertinent differences. Make a list of words or phrases, both negative and positive, that you have seen used in reference to your special traits. Compare your list with those of others in your class, and compile a directory of words you should avoid when writing—and why. Explain the connotation of each word. Make a list of acceptable words or phrases.

2. What is the ethnic makeup of your college or university? The town or city where your school is located? Do a five-day content analysis of your local or student newspaper. Count the number of stories each day in the news, sports, and features sections. Count the number that focuses on an ethnic group or an issue related to an ethnic group. At the end of the five days, calculate the percentage of newspaper stories related to ethnic groups. Do the percentages match the groups' makeup in the university's or town's population? Was coverage positive, negative, or neutral? What types of stories do you believe are missing?

3. Do a similar content analysis of the evening news broadcast, locally and for a national network. Count the total stories and the number concerning

ethnic groups. Give your impressions about whether the general coverage was positive, negative, or neutral.

4. You have the opportunity to interview the incoming student government president, a son of two Uzbek refugees. List five objective questions you could use to begin the interview, then list two effective questions you could ask to determine his experiences with cultural differences in the United States.

5. Examine your local or student newspaper. Find examples of stories about various ethnic communities or societal groups that do a good job of unbiased writing. Bring examples to class to share and indicate why the stories could be models for writing.

References

Caren Bohan, "Michelle Obama, Cindy McCain are study in contrast." *Reuter News*, at http://www.reuters.com/article/idUSN2937505020080610, accessed June 10, 2008.

Matthew Brault, "Disability Status and the Characteristics of People in Group Quarters: A Brief Analysis of Disability Prevalence Among the Civilian Noninstitutionalized and Total Populations in the American Community Survey." February 2008. Accessed at http://www.census.gov/hhes/www/disability/disability.html on August 12, 2008.

Timothy Crouse, *The Boys on the Bus.* New York: Random House, 1993.

Ashleigh Crowther, "Sexist Language in Media Coverage of Hillary Clinton," on Media Crit, posted December 12, 2007 at http://mediacrit.wetpaint.com/page/Sexist+Language+in+Media+Coverage+of+Hillary+Clinton, accessed June 10, 2008.

Lucille deView, "Regardless of age: Toward communication sensitive to older people and children," in *Without Bias: A Guidebook for Nondiscriminatory Communication.* New York: John Wiley & Sons, 1982.

Fernando Dovalina, Presentation for the Institute for Midcareer Copy Editors, Chapel Hill, North Carolina, Summer 2005, accessed at www.ibiblio.org/copyed/diversity.html.

David Folkenflik, "Clinton Coverage Reflects Tensions of Historic Bid," National Public Radio, "Morning Edition," May 28, 2008 at http://www.npr.org/templates/story/story.php?storyId=90880203, accessed June 10, 2008.

Walter Lippmann, *Public Opinion.* New York: Harcourt, Brace and Co., 1922.

Julie Patel, "Countering Stereotypes," *San Jose Mercury News*, May 30, 2005.

J. Pickens, ed., *Without Bias.* New York: John Wiley & Sons, 1982.

Taylor Marsh, "We Have Not Come a Long Way, Baby," accessed at www.huffingtonpost.com/taylor-marsh/we-have-not-come-a-long-w_b_123242.html, on Sept. 4, 2008.

Pale Moon Rose and John Mitrano, Comments, in Surveys of Ethnic and Racial Groups, by Jan Johnson Elliott, associate professor, University of North Carolina at Chapel Hill, Fall 1993.

Poverty 2006 Highlights. U.S. Census Bureau at http://www.census.gov/hhes/www/poverty/poverty06/pov06hi.html, accessed August 12, 2008.

Holly Stocking and Paget Gross, *How Do Journalists Think? A Proposal for the Study of Cognitive Bias in Newsmaking*. Bloomington, IN: Eric Clearinghouse on Reading and Communication Skills, 1989.

The Associated Press 2008 Stylebook and Briefing on Media Law. New York: The Associated Press, 2008.

"The News Media and the Disorders," Chapter 15 of Report of the National Advisory Commission on Civil Disorders, Kerner Commission Report, 1968.

David Manning White, "The 'gatekeeper,'" *Journalism Quarterly*, Vol. 27, No. 3, Fall 1950, p. 383.

Window Dressing on the Set: Women and Minorities in Television: A Report of the United States Commission on Civil Rights, 1977.

Keith M. Woods, "The Language of Race," Poynter Online at www.poynter.org/special/tipsheets2/diversity.htm, accessed September 28, 2005.

Keith M. Woods, "Nicknames & Mascots: Complicity in Bigotry," Poynter Institute at www.poynter.org/column.asp?id558&aid587263, accessed September 4, 2005.

CHAPTER

12

Legal and Ethical Issues

A newspaper intern is fired after editors discover that he has plagiarized parts of several stories from other publications.

A major broadcast network is sued after it airs a story criticizing a grocery store chain's meat packaging. One problem is that two reporters who worked in a meat department didn't state on their job applications that they were members of the news media.

An actor sues a tabloid for libel after it reports she was drunk and disorderly in a Washington, D.C., restaurant. The magazine had not a single reliable source for the story.

A reporter writes a story about a company's alleged bad business practices, using information from executives' voice mails he accessed without their permission. The newspaper renounced the articles and removed them from its Web site, paid a huge out-of-court settlement, and fired its reporter.

These scenarios may sound improbable, but each is true. Each story and the newsgathering methods used to produce it had consequences for the reporter and the media outlet that printed or aired the story. In gathering and using information, writers often face a mix of legal and ethical issues. Decisions are not always easy because laws and ethics constantly change.

In many cases, state and federal laws aid reporters in their quest for information. For example, shield laws protect reporters from revealing their sources in court. Libel laws outline the conditions under which individuals can sue when they feel falsely defamed. Although state laws protect citizens and public figures in regard to privacy, implied consent may protect a reporter who goes on private property to get a story. Many laws have been around for years and have evolved through the courts. Others, such as shield laws, are more recent.

Over the last decade, the media law battlefront has moved from libel cases to disputes over how media gather information. Subjects of news coverage have sued the media for misrepresenting who they are or the type of story they are working on, for trespassing on private property, and for using hidden cameras or hidden tape recorders. Some media observers say the methods represent unethical behavior by reporters, and some courts have begun to rule that such actions violate the law.

Other issues for writers in the information age have been plagiarism and copyright violations. Information gathering today via the Internet makes it easy to commandeer information and claim it as the writer's own work—whether unintentionally or purposefully. Sometimes the writer stores information and later inadvertently uses it without attributing the original source. In other cases, the material is stolen outright. In any case, the writer may have plagiarized and possibly infringed on another's copyright.

Copyright violations occur when writers use another's work and don't get permission. It is not sufficient simply to credit the original author, unless the material falls under a category known as fair use, explained later in the chapter.

In this chapter, you will learn

- what libel is,
- the issues of privacy and the relationship between sources and writers,
- the dangers of plagiarism and what constitutes copyrighted material,
- how ethics policies guide writers, and
- when writers cross the line in gathering information.

Libel

Writers can unknowingly or carelessly damage an individual's reputation by publishing false and defamatory statements about that individual. Even if a slip is unintentional, if the libel is in print or is aired, the writer can be sued, as can a newspaper, a television station, a church administration, or a non-profit group.

Libel can occur in any written form: a news article, a news release, a public service announcement, annual reports, corporate financial statements, a television talk show, a student's Web site, or a church bulletin. If a news release that has a false and defamatory statement about a person is mailed but not printed by any of the newspapers that receive it, the writer of the news release might still be sued successfully. Mailing the release to others who read it can be considered "publication" under defamation law. A radio or television station that broadcasts slander (oral defamation) or libelous statements can be sued under the state's libel laws.

Libel often occurs when people write about topics they do not really understand. Inexperienced reporters, student writers, and occasional writers are most at risk. They need to evaluate critically information they uncover. They can be held legally liable for accurately republishing a false and defamatory statement that someone else made. Good data collection, complete identification, and good writing techniques can prevent many libel problems, however. Mass communication professors advise their students to be accurate, thorough, and scrupulously fair in what they write. The legal system generally will protect writers who do a good job of investigating and who use many sources. Innocent mistakes that are not negligent or malicious are not usually actionable in a defamation lawsuit.

A huge body of law exists on libel. Thousands of libel cases have been filed. Although most editors, writers, and copy editors do not need to be lawyers, they do need to know the basics of libel law. A writer may be the only member of a nonprofit organization's communication staff; he or she needs to know what might cause trouble. Libel laws differ from state to state. For example, the statute of limitations—the time within which a person can file a libel suit—varies; it is usually from one to two years. Writers should be familiar with the libel laws in their states or in the states in which the material will be disseminated. Writers can stay current on freedom of the press issues through the First Amendment Center at Vanderbilt University. Information can be accessed online at www.firstamendmentcenter.org.

Elements of Libel

Writers who know about libel law do not have to be afraid to write negative information. If they know the essential elements of libel, they won't be chilled into self-censorship.

An individual—the person written about—has to prove six essential elements to win a libel case:

1. **Defamatory content.** The individual has to show the information was defamatory or bad enough to cause him or her to be held up to hatred, ridicule, or contempt.

2. **Identification.** The story clearly identifies the individual by name, in a recognizable photo, or through description from which others can reasonably identify the individual. In rare cases, courts have allowed individuals to recover when a false and defamatory statement has been made about a group to which they belong even though the statement does not single out anyone by name.
3. **Publication.** The memo was circulated, the story printed, the news release received, the report aired, or the message communicated to at least one person other than the person defamed.
4. **Falsity.** The information published was not true. In a few cases, the burden of proof falls on the media, which attempt to prove the information was true.
5. **Harm or injury.** The individual has to show harm to his or her reputation or emotional well-being. Proof of monetary loss can increase the amount of money the media will have to pay if they lose.
6. **Fault.** The individual has to prove that the newspaper, radio station, or other party was at fault in presenting the libel.

To win a case, most plaintiffs have to prove all six elements. On the sixth item, court decisions have set different criteria for private citizens and public figures. In most cases, ordinary folks usually have to prove a standard of fault, called *negligence*, to win a libel suit. They must show that the writer failed to follow professional standards or acted unreasonably in carrying out his or her research and in writing.

Public officials including politicians, public figures including many celebrities and prominent business executives, and otherwise private individuals who prominently involve themselves in public controversies often must prove more than negligence in establishing fault when suing for libel. In most cases, they must prove the writer knew the information was false or showed reckless disregard as to whether the information was true or false. That is called *actual malice*. That element came about through the 1964 *New York Times v. Sullivan* case, in which the U.S. Supreme Court ruled that a public official cannot recover damages for a defamatory falsehood relating to his or her official conduct unless he or she proves the statement was made with actual malice. Actual malice is extremely difficult to prove and is the major hurdle for most plaintiffs.

Let's say you are writing a story about your town's mayor. During interviews, an unreliable source tells you the mayor leaves town twice a year to meet his childhood sweetheart—not his wife—at a mountain cabin. If you were to write that bit of information without further investigation, you would be setting yourself up for a libel suit. Your reliance on a single, unreliable source would be reckless disregard for whether the information was true.

People are defamed, perhaps falsely, every day. Just think about the hundreds of police reports naming people who have been arrested. They can prove many of the six elements, such as publication, identification, and defamation. But would they win a libel suit? Rarely.

A Writer's Defenses in a Libel Suit

Nothing can prevent someone from filing a libel claim. But, within the legal system are defenses and privileges writers can use to avoid liability or to reduce damages. The major defenses are these:

1. **Truth.** The writer can prove the information was substantially true through reliable witnesses and documentary evidence.
2. **Qualified privilege.** Writers are protected when they report fairly and accurately matters of public concern from official government proceedings or reports, such as meetings, trials, or a sheriff's news conference. This defense is one reason why news media rely so heavily on government meetings and sessions. A witness in court can falsely accuse someone of committing murder, and you as a reporter can print the accusation. Your reporting must be accurate, fair, and complete; attributed to the government meeting or record; and not motivated by spite or ill will.
3. **Wire service defense.** Some states have adopted what is known as the wire service defense. Newspapers and other media organizations are protected if they get and reprint a story from the wire services or other reputable news agencies, such as the Associated Press. They would not be protected if they knew or had reason to know the story contained falsities or if they altered the story substantially. It would be impossible for writers to verify every fact in a wire service story. Wire service clients have to trust that the information sent to them is true.

4. **Statute of limitations.** Individuals cannot sue after a specific number of years has passed from the date of publication. The statute of limitations in libel cases varies from state to state, and in some rare instances, a plaintiff might be entitled to extend the statute of limitations in his or her case, depending on the circumstances.
5. **Opinion defense.** The opinion defense protects two kinds of statements. Writers are protected if they are critiquing a performance or service as long as they give a general assessment that cannot be proved true or false. For example, a restaurant critic could probably write that the restaurant food did not taste good to her without much fear of being convicted of defamation. The critic could not say that the chef stole the high-quality meats for his family, leaving lesser meats for the restaurant dishes—unless that were true, of course.

In addition, many courts consider humor, satire, parody, and rhetorical hyperbole to be privileged under defamation law if the statements are so exaggerated and outlandish that reasonable people would not believe they are true. For example, the Supreme Court ruled *Hustler* magazine had a First Amendment right to publish an outrageous insult directed at television evangelist Jerry Falwell who sued the magazine after it published a cartoon parody of Campari liqueur's "first time" advertising campaign. The cartoon depicted the Rev. Falwell as having his "first time"—his first sexual encounter—while drunk with his mother in an outhouse. The jury at trial ruled against Falwell on his libel claim and found that the ad parody could not be reasonably believed as "describing actual events…or facts." Although the case proceeded to the U.S. Supreme Court on other issues, the jury's verdict on the libel claim was not overturned on appeal.

In a case in 2004, the Texas Supreme Court concluded that a satirical and humorous—but totally false—column about a local district attorney and judge could not be the subject of a defamation lawsuit because the content was not reasonably believable.

Writers should know they cannot be sued successfully for libel by the government—state, local, or federal. Writers can say the federal government or some part of it is an overgrown, bumbling bureaucratic mess without fear of being sued. But, they cannot falsely accuse the director of a government agency of misspending public funds without risking a lawsuit by the director individually.

Minimizing the Risk of Being Sued

Writers do not want to be sued for libel—even if they win. Libel suits are costly, time consuming, and emotionally draining. They can go on for years, then be dismissed. People do win libel cases against media. For example, CapCities Communications lost $11.5 million in a libel suit when one of its New York television stations incorrectly identified a restaurant owner as having ties with organized crime. In 1994, an attorney won a $24 million judgment against *The Philadelphia Inquirer*, which had reported he quashed a homicide investigation when he was an assistant district attorney because it involved the son of a police officer. The case took more than 10 years to conclude.

Ninety percent of libel cases filed never make it to court. Some are dropped, and some end up in out-of-court settlements, which cost media actual payouts and attorneys' fees. Libel suits are to be avoided. The following are some recommendations:

- Don't write lies and publish them.
- Use credible, reliable, multiple sources.
- Recognize the importance of fairness.
- Be accurate.
- Be complete.

Also, be polite if someone complains about inaccuracy. One study showed that most people who sued decided to do so after they were treated rudely when they pointed out the mistake.

Corrections

Most publications have a policy on writing corrections when errors have been made and run corrections because they believe they should correct their mistakes and not lie. Lawyers might caution against widespread use of corrections because they could be used as an admission of guilt: The correction states that the media outlet made a mistake. In most cases, the correction includes the correct title, statistic, address, or whatever was wrong and does not repeat the erroneous information. Many states have retraction or correction statutes that specify ways individuals or media can reduce or avoid damages.

Some editors say that any correction should be as prominently displayed as the error; that is, if the error is in a front-page headline, then the correction needs to be large and on the front page, not buried on page 22. Policies might require requests to be referred to editors and even lawyers. Ignoring a request could have legal consequences.

When to Publish or Not

Media often take criticism when they publish too much information. For example, critics charge that the public doesn't have a right to know the name of a crime victim, such as a rape victim. They contend that the public needs to know when and where such crimes occur, but not the victim's name or address.

Most newspapers do not publish names of rape victims. Some states have laws that allow police to withhold the names of any crime victim if they believe publication will put the person in danger or cause him or her more harm. Some media will publish or broadcast victims' names only with their permission. Others note that the names are part of public record and if a person is charged, the name of the victim or accuser should also be included.

Media can get into trouble if they republish defamatory information not protected under the wire service defense. They must ensure that any story used is accurate. Media also can get into trouble when they publish quotes they believe are relevant but in reality are libelous. For example, a newspaper reporter is covering the trial of a woman charged with involuntary manslaughter in the death of her 6-month-old daughter. The reporter walks a litigious tightrope if he or she includes a family member's quote that implies the woman's guilt and that was said outside the courtroom. If the family member makes the comment as part of court testimony, the reporter generally is protected against a libel suit. But if the remark is said in a parking lot while the trial is underway, the reporter and the editor must be careful not to republish any of the libelous statements. If they do, they can be sued for libel.

Most newspapers follow the policy of publishing private information if it relates to or affects public officials' or public figures' civic duties. For example, when Washington, D.C., intern Chandra Levy disappeared, attention eventually focused on the private life of Congressman Gary Condit. His relationship with Levy emerged, as did his relationships with other women outside his marriage. Many voters questioned Condit's judgment and even called for his resignation after learning more about his personal life. The media believed they had a responsibility to publish the personal information.

Privacy

Reporters frequently face privacy dilemmas in their quest to gather and report the news. These dilemmas are both legal and ethical and provoke loud protests when the public believes the media are trampling the privacy rights of individuals in the news.

Right of Privacy

The doctrine of the right to privacy has evolved to protect individuals and to give them the right to be left alone, particularly from unwarranted publicity. Decisions from lower courts up to the U.S. Supreme Court have involved individuals' right to privacy.

Privacy law varies considerably from state to state, and writers should know what constitutes invasion of privacy in their states or in the state where articles will be published or stories aired, and whether certain torts or injuries are recognized. Generally, however, writers sometimes invade individuals' privacy in four ways while gathering and writing information.

First, a journalist might go on private property without permission to get a story. The writer then could be sued for intruding on the property owner's privacy. But people could still sue for *intrusion* in a public place, even though people in public places have less expectation of privacy than when they are in private places. For example, some news-gathering techniques, such as secretly recording someone with high-powered audio or video equipment, could be considered highly offensive to reasonable people—even if it occurred in a public venue. A reporter, for example, could be cited for intruding either physically or with electronic equipment. In such cases, the journalist is sued for his or her means of gathering information, not for the content of what he or she wrote. The writer could be sued successfully even if no story resulted.

Second, a writer might disclose private and embarrassing but true facts about an individual, who could claim the facts should not have been published. Winning such suits could be difficult, however, because of the qualified First Amendment privilege to publicize lawfully obtained information that is truthful and involves a legitimate matter of public concern. Also, courts have recognized a common law defense in such cases when information published is considered newsworthy. Also, express or implied consent from an individual allows media to publish *embarrassing or private facts* about him or her and is a defense. But that protection might not extend to people giving their consent for media to publish embarrassing facts about others or, depending on the circumstances, when minors reveal private facts about themselves to reporters.

Third, *The Associated Press Stylebook* notes that the news media "may be liable for invasion of privacy if the facts of a story are changed deliberately or recklessly, or 'fictionalized.'" An individual can sue in such *false-light* privacy cases even if the publicity seems to be positive. The bottom line is that the publicity is considered false and objectionable, even if it is not defamatory. Plaintiffs in false privacy cases have to prove that the language would be highly offensive to a reasonable person and that the writer acted in reckless disregard to the falsity and the image it would create. These privacy cases closely resemble defamation cases, and just as with libel considerations, writers must be careful to be accurate and thorough.

Media can be sued for a fourth privacy injury or tort: *appropriation.* Most of these types of cases involve the unauthorized use of a person's image or likeness for commercial purposes, such as advertising a product or service to consumers. Appropriation cases can also arise when the content is news-editorial and not commercial, although in such non-commercial cases, courts have required plaintiffs to prove actual malice. Actor Dustin Hoffman sued *The Los Angeles Times* for a digitized photograph of himself that appeared in *The Los Angeles Times* magazine: a head shot from his role in the movie *Tootsie* superimposed on the body of a model. Hoffman won $1.5 million in damages, but the verdict was overturned on appeal. In that case, the image was used in editorial—not commercial—content, and the evidence was insufficient for Hoffman to prove actual malice.

In some states, privacy law is so protective of the media that privacy is more of an ethical problem than a legal one. In dealing with the ethics of privacy, many media outlets have categories of individuals and treat them differently. For example, compared with private citizens, politicians and public officials are held to a higher standard of behavior in what journalists will or will not pursue.

Media also hold to a high standard public figures who trade on their public image or who are briefly prominent in the news. Reporters may assume a higher standard means such figures have less privacy. Other people, like you and me, garner more privacy from the media.

Public versus Private Property

Some privacy disputes hinge on whether the news took place on public or private property. For example, a Christmas parade on city streets is considered a public event in a public place, and reporters—whether print or broadcast—would have access to people viewing or participating in the parade. Furthermore, people in public places should expect their actions to be public—and those actions can be reported in the media legally. In other venues, individuals have a reasonable expectation of privacy. A grandmother who attends the parade and whose photo is printed in the local newspaper probably cannot sue successfully for invasion of privacy. However, if a reporter used a microphone to record secretly the conversation of the woman and her daughter at the parade, that action would probably exceed a reasonable expectation of privacy.

Courts consider people's homes to be the most private places, so reporters need to be especially cautious when they gather news in people's homes. Places between private homes and the Christmas parade sometimes are more difficult to locate on the public/private property continuum. Shopping centers and restaurants are quasi-public places. Working reporters asked to leave shopping centers must do so, no matter what the news event, or face a trespassing charge.

In all court cases concerning privacy violations, consent might be a useful media defense. The best consent defense results when a reporter is invited onto private property or told explicitly that she or he has permission to be there. Next best is implied consent, which occurs when media are on the property and are not asked to leave. The media might not be protected if a property owner says okay but the tenant feels his zone of privacy was invaded, or they might not be protected if a police officer gives the okay for media to be on private property. The Supreme Court has ruled that police violate the Fourth Amendment rights of homeowners when they give permission.

At the same time, reporters must heed a police officer's order to leave property and can be charged with trespassing if they don't. Consider the Reporters Committee on Freedom of the Press's guidelines on access:

> *Regardless of whether news occurs on public or private property, if you ignore police orders regarding access, you risk arrest and prosecution. Case law makes clear that police can limit media access when they believe such restrictions are needed for public safety or to prevent interference with an investigation, and that the First Amendment does not provide immunity from criminal sanctions for disobeying police orders.*

Copyright and Plagiarism

Copyright and plagiarism become concerns when writers take original work they did not create and use it without permission. A copyright is a right granted to the creator of an original work to control copies and reproductions of his or her work, derivatives of his or her work, and the rights to perform and display his or her work. Others who want to use the creator's work—such as reproducing copyrighted photos on a personal Web site—must either receive permission in writing (and usually pay for that use) or agree to a license that specifies terms of the use, such as using a computer program.

Plagiarism is an ethical issue; it occurs when a writer takes original material and claims it as his or her own. A writer can violate copyright law without plagiarizing, and a writer can plagiarize without violating laws. In both instances, however, the penalties can be severe.

Copyright: A Definition

Copyright is the legal ownership of a story, publication, book, song, online article—anything produced as original work and fixed in any tangible medium, such as a newspaper or CD-ROM. When a work is copyrighted, the owner has exclusive legal rights to its use for a limited time. Anyone can copyright material by applying to the Copyright Office in the Library of Congress. Anyone can claim a working copyright as soon as a piece is created. But without registration, an individual is limited from seeking certain damages under the federal copyright statute. Generally, an individual has ownership of the work for his or her lifetime plus 70 years for work produced after January 1, 1978. For corporations, the time is longer: 95 years from publication or 120 years from creation, whichever is shorter.

People, such as authors or songwriters, copyright their work so they can benefit solely from royalties or the money it earns. Newspaper companies copyright each issue of the newspaper, a series, or longer articles. Online sites are also copyrighted. Copyright is designed to encourage the creation of more works and to benefit the public. If authors are given exclusive rights to their works for a period of time, the assumption is that they will create more.

In most cases, anyone who wants to use any portion of copyrighted material has to get permission—and often must pay a fee to use the material. For example, a writer who is doing a book on authors of horror stories cannot quote extensively from author Stephen King's work without permission. An advertising copywriter who wants to use the music from an Andrew Lloyd Webber song must get permission. In both cases, the writers would probably pay a fee based on how much is used and in what context.

Some material can be used without permission or payment of fees. Anything produced by the federal government is considered public domain and can be used. If a private organization does a report for the government, however, that material might be copyrighted.

Generally, copyright law does not protect facts, ideas, procedures, processes, or methods of operation that might be protected under patent law. That means the fact that the United States was a British colony or the text of Einstein's theory of relativity can be used. But a historian's analysis of the British impact on the colonies or a researcher's interpretation of Einstein's work may be copyright protected.

The Copyright Act of 1976, Section 107, allows *fair use* of copyrighted material for "criticism, comment, news reporting, teaching, scholarship, or research." Fair use of material is not an infringement of copyright and does not require the permission of the copyright holder. For example, a book reviewer who wants to quote from Stephen King's novel in his review would not have to get permission to use the excerpt so long as the amount excerpted is reasonable. Because a fair or reasonable amount is debatable, a judge or jury might ultimately resolve a specific use. The factors to consider for fair use are:

1. purpose and character of the use, including whether such use is of a commercial nature or is for nonprofit educational purposes;
2. nature of the copyrighted work;
3. amount and substantiality of the portion used in relation to the copyrighted work as a whole; and
4. effect of the use on the potential market for or value of the copyrighted work.

Translated, a writer cannot use a major portion of the material without permission, particularly if its use could violate the copyright owner's rights. The individual also cannot use a major portion of the material. Some people follow a 5 percent rule; that is, no more than 5 percent of the copyrighted work can be used without permission. Some follow a 50-word rule. To avoid any question over how much is acceptable use, get permission or check out a copyright holder's stipulations. For example, some newspapers do not require permission to use 30 words or less of a story. You can find out through their permissions offices.

Getting into Trouble

With the development of the Internet and the proliferation of computers, more and more material, including software, is illegally copied. Copyright holders sue for copyright infringement and hope to collect monetary damages, including an amount for lost royalties.

Writers get into trouble with copyrights when they believe the material they are using is fair use. Sometimes they believe they are not using a substantial part or that their use is somehow exempt for educational reasons. Or they believe the work has been quoted so much that it has become part of the public domain and can be used. Some also erroneously assume that citing the author or source and giving credit protects against copyright suits.

If writers have questions about copyright infringement, they should consult an attorney familiar with copyright law. The discussion here is not to frighten students or media writers away from using material; however, all writers must be aware of laws and penalties for using others' work without proper credit or authorization.

Recent Copyright Conflicts

A major issue in copyright in recent years has been the unauthorized copying of songs and movies. Artists who made money, or royalties, from the sale and use of their CDs, DVDs, or videos began suing to keep from losing income. One issue in this conflict is who owns the rights to a piece: the artist, the company that distributed the work, or the individual who bought a copy. Ownership is important in any litigation and in determining lost revenue.

To address copyright infringement of digital media, Congress passed the Digital Millennium Copyright Act, signed into law in 1998. Among other items, the act amended copyright law to provide limits on the liability of service providers, or sites that stored information online, from the conduct of their users who might violate copyrights. If service providers are aware of violations and do nothing, they, too, can be liable.

In one case, a group of freelancers sued several publishers because they contended that the distribution of their work to online databases like LexisNexis was not part of the rights they transferred and sold to these publications. The freelancers won. However, after the case, many publishing companies altered their freelance contracts to include these rights specifically.

Copyright will always be an issue for people who want to ensure they receive credit for and earn income from the work they produce. You as a writer must be aware of copyright laws and ensure that whatever material you use falls under fair use. If you are not sure, consult a lawyer—or find out who owns the copyright, secure permission, and pay any requested fees.

If the fee is expensive, then you will have to determine whether the material justifies the cost. Don't try to get around copyright law by paraphrasing—it will not protect you. If the paraphrase can be readily identifiable as the author's words or if the work is substantially similar, you can get into trouble.

Plagiarism: A Definition

Plagiarism occurs when people take information, copyrighted or not, and use it as their own without crediting the original source. With the growth of the Internet, plagiarism occurs more often, intentionally and unintentionally. Attribution of sources can help mitigate plagiarism, but it is not always a protection against charges of plagiarism.

An intern at *The San Jose Mercury News* was fired after editors found he had plagiarized articles from *The Washington Post* and other publications. A reporter for *The San Francisco Chronicle* saw similarities between articles the intern wrote and stories that appeared in *The Post*. When editors investigated, they found that information had been copied from other publications, too.

The Indianapolis Star and *The Indianapolis News* suspended their television columnist when editors discovered he had plagiarized a column by a TV writer at another newspaper. The columnist admitted he had lifted the column, which editors discovered before it was published.

A sports columnist for a college newspaper was fired after the editor learned that sections of his column were taken from a *Sports Illustrated* columnist's work. The editor wrote an open letter to the newspaper's readers to explain how the plagiarism occurred and the resulting action.

Student and novice reporters often get themselves in trouble by using information and not properly crediting the source. Sometimes the error occurs out of ignorance rather than deliberately stealing material and using it as their own. In other cases, reporters may take material because of pressures of meeting deadlines, the lack of ideas, or inadequate information through their own research.

Whatever the reason, the consequences are dire. The owners of copyrighted material can sue for copyright infringement. In most cases of plagiarism, however, writers who steal will be suspended or fired—and their credibility will be severely impaired.

How to Avoid Plagiarism

The easiest way to avoid plagiarism is to be honest. Honesty covers how reporters gather information, store it, and use it. When reporters gather material, they need to be meticulous in their note taking and in citations. If they download a story from the Internet, they must ensure they have included the source and date. If they copy information from a book, newspaper, or magazine, they must include a citation. Noting sources completely is necessary for proper attribution, that is, giving the original source credit. (Attribution is discussed in Chapter 10.)

If writers are working on a project that takes days or even months of investigation, they must be exceedingly careful when they return to notes they have not viewed in a while. When fashioning the story, they must be aware of which notes were their own and which ones came from another source. Remember from the discussion earlier in the chapter that even material that is condensed, summarized, and rewritten from another source should be attributed, as should any material used verbatim.

Of course, you should never take another person's work and claim it as your own, regardless of deadline pressure. A professor in a reporting class became suspicious when a student turned in a final project story that was much better than her other work throughout the semester. A quick check on the Internet pulled up dozens of stories on the student's topic—and blocks of copy pulled from three or four articles. The student had submitted the work as her own and violated the university's honor code, punishable by suspension. The outcome proved more severe than the penalty of not writing the story at all.

Ethics in Gathering Information

What is ethical in writing? Just as in any profession, ethics in journalism is a set of moral guidelines regarding what writers should and should not do when gathering and disseminating information. Journalists' ethical decisions determine their behavior.

Communicators must behave ethically. In most cases, you can't be sued for ethical violations. States don't have ethics laws, like libel laws. You can't go to jail for revealing the source of your story even after you promised you wouldn't, but you could be sued for breach of contract.

You might not be sued for libel, but you could be sued for the method you used in getting information. You won't get disbarred like a lawyer or lose your license like a physician, but if you violate your code of ethics or that of your publication, you lose your credibility or your source—and possibly your job. The bottom line is your professional reputation.

When it comes to ethics, mass communicators often are criticized for publishing certain information and for violating individuals' privacy, as discussed earlier in the chapter. They are criticized for failing to remain objective and for stepping over the line from reporting to commenting. They are criticized for violent or sexual content. They are also criticized for the way they collect information, from stealing to deceiving to harassing unwilling sources.

Former newspaper editor and ABC News president Michael Gartner notes that communicators have an ethical responsibility in the age of technology. "Readers don't know what is fact or fiction, what is an enhanced photo, what is slanted or straight, or what is the docu in docudrama," he cautions. "What comes out of a computer can be just as biased as what comes from a pulpit."

Communicators must be just as careful with their language and how it is interpreted as they are with their news-gathering techniques. In some situations, writers have ethics policies to guide them; in other instances, they have to use gut instinct.

Ethics Policies

Most news organizations, advertising agencies, public relations firms, online sites, and other mass communication businesses have ethics guidelines. Some policies come from parent companies, such as Gannett, which rewrote its ethics policy in 1999 and then conducted in-house training at its more than

80 newspapers and media outlets. Other media rely on professional organizations for guidance, such as the American Advertising Federation.

Most ethics policies establish an environment in which employees are to work. Some companies use ethics contracts, and employees agree to them when they are hired. Policies outline areas where ethical considerations arise, such as conflict of interest, confidentiality of sources, impartiality of reporting, accuracy, acceptance of gifts or honoraria, and community or political involvement. Policies may be extensive, such as Gannett's policy (accessed at www.gannett.org), or they can be as short as one page.

In addition to written ethics policies as guides, journalists should have their own ethical standards. In some cases, reporters have to use what their gut says, rather than refer to the company policy. For example, an editor learns that the son of a popular, local minister has become an out-of-wedlock father. The editor wants you—the reporter—to write a story because the minister has attracted a large following because of his views on teen abstinence. What does your ethical compass say about pursuing this story?

Deception. In recent years, the media have been criticized more and more for using deception to get their information. Deception occurs in everything from posing as other people to giving false promises of confidentiality to using hidden cameras or tape recorders to gather news. When is deception acceptable? Most editors would agree to deception if the information cannot be obtained any other way. The information would have to be of such importance that knowingly deceiving sources is acceptable. And editors and lawyers would have to be part of the decision to resort to such news-gathering techniques.

Deceptive news gathering is not new. One of the most well-known cases occurred in the late 1970s when *The Chicago Sun Times* set up a bar called the Mirage. Reporters posed as bartenders and waiters and used hidden cameras and tape recorders to secure evidence that building inspectors, police officers, and other city officials were soliciting bribes to allow the bar to operate. The series won several awards and was nominated for a Pulitzer Prize, the highest award in journalism. The Pulitzer Prize board rejected the series, however, because it felt that the *Sun Times'* methods were deceptive and unethical.

Students in an advanced reporting class were investigating whether citizens treated homeless people differently from others on downtown streets. As part of the story, students approached residents and asked for directions. Some students were well dressed and neat in appearance; others wore disheveled clothes and had not shaved or combed their hair. The students found significant differences in residents' demeanor and interaction toward students who were neat and those who were not. They incorporated the reactions into their stories.

Such investigation, sometimes called participant observation, can produce information that adds to a story. However, reporters should not inject themselves into a situation in a way that could change the outcome of the story.

Deception was at the heart of the highly visible ABC/Food Lion case in 1992 in which ABC reporters applied for jobs at a Food Lion store to check out complaints about how Food Lion repackaged meats for sale. The reporters used false résumés that omitted the fact that they were journalists. They used hidden cameras to film their work that subsequently was aired on ABC's "Prime Time Live."

The reports alleged that Food Lion workers repackaged outdated meats, bleached meats, and committed other offenses. Food Lion executives sued, not for libel or falsity in the reports themselves, but for fraud, trespassing, and breach of loyalty. Initially, a North Carolina jury awarded Food Lion $5.5 million, but on appeal, the amount was cut to only $2. Despite the ultimate reduction in a monetary settlement, reporters' credibility had been damaged and their behavior hanged in the public eye.

Reporters should always consult their editors when they plan to use deception or any other method to get information. They should determine that they have exhausted all other means and that the benefit of going undercover outweighs any negative impact. When the stories are published, editors should be forthcoming in letting audiences know how the information was gathered and why such methods were used.

The San Jose Mercury News fired a reporter who used his status as a graduate student at the University of Iowa to obtain information from the university archives and use it in a story. The article revealed that university researchers had used children from an orphanage in a project on stuttering—actually turning the children into stutterers. The archives are open only to students, staff, and faculty members, and anyone using the archives must sign a form that the use is for research only. The reporter got the information a month before he began his internship at the newspaper—and wrote on the form that he was a graduate student in psychology when he really was a student in journalism.

Such cases show that the legal battlefield for media is shifting from individuals or companies suing for libel to acting on their concerns with methods used to gather information.

Fabrication. The bottom line: Reporters do not make up information or people or attribute made-up quotes to individuals. Some journalism teachers boil that even more simply: Don't lie. But in some cases, a tiny alteration in a quote or description that makes it through the editing process can lead writers of any experience level to even greater fabrication.

Trying to save time required to do a weekly poll that posed a single question to a local resident cost two young reporters at *The Reidsville* (N.C.) *Review* their jobs. The reporters shared the responsibility for asking a citizen each day a single-topic question, such as name your favorite singer and why. But rather than actually asking the question, the reporters used mug shots of college friends posted on Facebook. Then they made up quotes.

The fabrication surfaced when a sister publication owned by the same media group reported the story. The *Review* editor wrote a letter to the paper's readers to explain how the fabrication occurred and why it went unnoticed. The two reporters were fired, and the editor resigned.

The Associated Press fired a reporter after it reviewed several of his stories and could not find the people quoted. Although the reporter claimed the people were real, editors could not. He also cited an organization in Chicago that editors could not locate.

Any journalist can cite the cases of Jayson Blair of *The New York Times* and Jack Kelley of *USA Today*—and the outcome—after editors discovered parts of their stories had been fabricated. In another case, the U.S. Supreme Court upheld a false light invasion of privacy verdict against a newspaper whose reporter made up portions of a story about a woman whose husband had been killed in a bridge collapse. The court concluded that the evidence was sufficient to establish actual malice in the case.

Confidential Sources. When gathering information, sometimes reporters are asked to protect the identity of a source. Some media do not allow unnamed sources to be quoted in stories; others require editors to know the source's name. The Associated Press and the Associated Press Managing Editors Association jointly surveyed U.S. newspapers about their policies on anonymous sources and learned that one in four of the 419 newspapers that responded never allowed reporters to quote anonymous sources. Others had specific policies.

Journalists know that if they promise confidentiality to a source and then break it, they damage their reputation. In one case, the U.S. Supreme Court concluded that the First Amendment did not prevent a source from recovering damages from newspapers that had breached promises of confidentiality to the source. The source had lost his job after the newspapers published articles identifying him as having notified the newspapers about negative court documents regarding a political candidate. This type of action might not be available to confidential sources when reporters are compelled by a court to identify their sources in a criminal or civil proceeding, even though many journalists refuse to testify under such circumstances and instead face possible contempt sanctions, including fines and even jail time.

The most visible case in recent years of a journalist going to jail to protect a source occurred when *New York Times* reporter Judith Miller refused to name who revealed to her the identity of a CIA agent. Miller never wrote a story, but she still refused to identify her source. After months of legal sparring, a judge sentenced her to four months in prison. After spending 85 days in jail, Miller was released when her source, I. Lewis "Scooter" Libby, former chief of staff for then Vice President Dick Cheney, signed a waiver of confidentiality. Miller then testified before a grand jury investigating who leaked the identity of the undercover CIA operative, Valerie Plame.

While judges invoke the Sixth Amendment as the reason journalists must comply with their orders to testify or to turn over notes and other materials, journalists contend that the free flow of information will be jeopardized if they cannot offer sources anonymity. Thirty states have shield laws that protect journalists from naming sources in a criminal case or judicial proceeding. Laws also establish who is defined as a journalist, what kinds of information the privilege protects, and when the privilege is waived. Reporters should always know their state laws as well as the policy of their publications or employers. No federal shield law exists, although bills have been introduced before Congress.

More recently, journalists have been concerned about how to protect sources' confidentiality when the reporters have kept their notes on their computers. The computer notes can be subpoenaed and the computers confiscated. Even if the notes are deleted, they could be recoverable. Even a reporter's phone records could be subpoenaed and checked to determine whom the reporter had called, as were Judith Miller's phone records. The advantages of technology can also affect a reporter's ability to get information from confidential sources, who might not feel so protected.

Other Dilemmas. Other ethical issues arise in information gathering, particularly in reporters' and editors' discussions about whether a story warrants media attention. You suspect a public official is having extramarital relations, so you stake out his house and discover he spent the night in an apartment of a woman, not his wife. Do you write the story? You learn an anti-abortion rights activist had an abortion as a 15-year-old. Do you include that information in a story when she leads an anti-abortion protest?

Public officials' behavior has been the focus of many news stories since *The Miami Herald* staked out the apartment of Democratic presidential contender Gary Hart in Washington, D.C. The news media published photos of Hart with a woman, not his wife. Although Hart never admitted his relationship with model Donna Rice was sexual, he withdrew from the race. Former President Bill Clinton went through an impeachment trial on charges that he committed perjury and obstructed justice in denying a relationship with intern Monica Lewinsky.

Is reporting such behavior unethical? Journalists would cry no; they are reporting the news. The public outcry comes when the stories report and re-report lurid and seemingly minor details of such relationships. Audiences become saturated. The answers to such publication issues have to be reached case by case, medium by medium. What one publication decides to print, another may refuse to air.

In addition, reporters must use their judgment when gathering information. Their behavior might prove illegal and could generate ethical questions. Such questioning occurred when *The Miami Herald* fired long-time metro columnist Jim DeFede for tape-recording a conversation with Arthur E. Teele Jr., a former city commissioner, shortly before he committed suicide. The local state's attorney charged DeFede with violating the state law making it illegal to tape record individuals without their knowledge. The case was later dismissed.

DeFede lost his job for breaking the law and because the paper's editors felt the reporter had acted unethically by not telling Teele he was being recorded. Editors said the taping could damage sources' trust in reporters. Despite management's position, DeFede's firing became the topic of other media articles and generated criticism and unhappiness among *Herald* staff. Some might question whether DeFede should have intervened upon hearing the emotion in Teele's voice, which he later said was unusual in a man he had covered for 14 years. Reporters generally are observers rather than participants in events. They should choose not to become part of the story.

In the days following Hurricane Katrina's assault on the Gulf Coast, many reporters showed their sadness at the plight of those who could not evacuate and their anger and frustration at the response of government officials. In some instances, reporters controlled their feelings while others did not. Reporters are human beings and must be aware that their emotions could influence readers and viewers.

A good policy is to gather news in a manner that allows the public focus to go where it should—to the wrongdoing you are reporting, advises Associate Professor Cathy Packer at the University of North Carolina at Chapel Hill. Unethical and illegal news-gathering techniques shift the public focus to the media, and the bad guys walk away looking like victims, she notes.

Without circumspect decision making and honesty with audiences, any medium—and the reporter—will lose credibility. When credibility is lost, so are audiences.

Aspiring journalists should be honest, ethical, and legal in information gathering. Methods should be unquestionable. Information should be accurate. Editors should always know a reporter's source and serve as backup in the event someone has doubts about a source's or the reporter's credibility.

Exercises

1. Can you lawfully use the following information in a story? Explain your reasoning and any defenses you could use if you were sued for libel.

   a. You are doing a story on drug use in the county. A police source tells you that a certain spot on Main Street, a bench outside Walton's restaurant, is a known place for drug deals.

   b. You are covering a case about a man charged with involuntary manslaughter in a car accident that killed two teenagers. You do a search using public records of prior convictions and find he has two for careless and reckless driving in another state.

   c. A state senator running for re-election tells you that her opponent is a tax evader who has not paid any state income taxes in the last five years.

   d. You are covering the performance of Alice Batar, a local resident who has begun a successful acting career. You have been assigned to write a review of her performance in the community theater's production of "Who's Afraid of Virginia Woolf?" Prior to the performance, you overhear two people next to you talking about Batar's latest divorce and what one called "a really pathetic settlement on her part."

   e. You are to write a story about the chancellor of your university. You interview a faculty member who says the chancellor "runs off at the mouth and doesn't pay enough attention to faculty members' needs."

2. Write a two-page report on plagiarism, using at least three sources. Include a fellow classmate's views on plagiarism. Include at least one example other than what is in this chapter. Include your views on plagiarism as an ethical issue and what the consequences should be for a reporter who plagiarizes.

3. Go online and find the site for your hometown newspaper. See if you can find on the site the newspaper's code of ethics. If not, e-mail the editor and find out if the newspaper has a written code or how ethical behavior is conveyed to the staff. Bring in the code or information to share with class members.

4. Look at codes of ethics from professional organizations such as the American Society of Newspaper Editors, the American Advertising Federation, Public Relations Society of America, and others. Compare the issues that each covers as ethical considerations.

5. Consider the following scenarios. Discuss in class how you would behave in each situation and whether you would use the information gathered.

   a. You are a state legislative reporter. A number of legislators meet every Thursday night for dinner at a local restaurant. One of the legislators whom you cover on a regular basis invites you to come along one night. Do you go?
   b. You are interviewing the director of the local community theater for a story on the upcoming season. You are having lunch together at a local restaurant. At the end of the meal and interview, the director picks up the tab and goes to pay for both of you. Your portion of the bill is $6.50. What do you do?
   c. You suspect a local real estate company is discriminating against Hispanic tenants when it comes to rental housing. Your editor suggests that you and another reporter, who is Hispanic, pose as a couple and try to rent a house from the company. What should you do?

d. You cover the financial industry as a business reporter. At the end of an interview on mortgage rates, the banker says to contact him whenever you are ready to buy a house and he'll make sure you get a really good interest rate. Do you call him when you are mortgage hunting?

References

"AP Fires Reporter after Source Query," Yahoo! News, accessed September 17, 2002, at http://story.news.yahoo.com/news?tmpl5story2&cid1519&u5ap2002916/ap_on_re_us/reporter_dismis.

"Appeals Court Sides with ABC in Food Lion Lawsuit," ABCNews.com, October 20, 1999, at http://abcnews.go.com/sections/us/DailyNews/foodlion 991020.html.

"California Paper Fires Intern for Plagiarism," *Publishers' Auxiliary*, January 22, 2001, Vol. 147, No. 2, p. 20.

Cantrell v. Forest City Publishing Co., 419 U.S. 245 (1974).

Chuck Strouse, "The Agony of DeFede," Newtimes.com, accessed September 18, 2005, at www.newtimesbpb.com/Issues/2005-09-15/ news/news2.html.

Cohen v. Cowles Media Co., 501 U.S. 693 (1991).

Copyright Act of 1976, Section 107, at http://www.loc.gov/copyright/title17/.

"Ex-commissioner kills self in newspaper lobby," CNN.com, accessed July 28, 2005, at www.cnn.com/2005/US/07/28/miami.teele.ap/index.html.

Don Fost, "Mercury News Case Stirs Debate over Ethics of Deception," *San Francisco Chronicle*, August 8, 2001.

Michael Gartner, keynote address, Association for Education in Journalism and Mass Communication, Washington, DC, August 5, 2001.

Hustler Magazine, Inc. v. Falwell, 485 U.S. 46 (1988).

New Times, Inc. v. Isaaks, 146. W. 3d 144 (Texas 2004).

New York Times Co. v. Tasini, 535 U.S. 483 (2001).

Cathy Packer, interview, School of Journalism and Mass Communication, September 4, 2008.

"Poll finds many newspapers bar anonymous sourcing," The Associated Press, as reported on the Web site of The First Amendment Center, at www.firstamendmentcenter.org/news.aspx?id515417, accessed September 23, 2005.

Reporters Committee for Freedom of the Press, at www.rcfp.org.

Joe Strupp, "TV Columnist Canned," *Editor and Publisher*, September 11, 1999, at www.archives.editorandpublisher.com.

The Associated Press 2008 Stylebook and Briefing on Media Law. New York: The Associated Press, 2008.

CHAPTER

13

Broadcast Media

WHEN YOU WRITE FOR BROADCAST MEDIA, YOUR COPY WILL LOOK LIKE THIS: A SCRIPT FORMAT THAT OCCUPIES HALF THE WIDTH OF THE PAGE. BUT THE CONTENT WILL REMAIN ACCURATE, CONCISE, AND COMPLETE, JUST AS IN ANY WRITING YOU DO.

Writing for radio and television requires the basic writing skills discussed in earlier chapters. Broadcast messages must be concise, clear, and simple so that audiences can understand the information.

Broadcast news writing differs in some respects from writing news for print. First, it differs in what it requires of the audience. Tuning in to radio, for example, audiences have to rely on careful listening. Radio writing has to be simple and specific. Fashioned after radio, television news also captures attention quickly, as TV messages breeze by passive audiences who cannot rewind or re-read items of interest. That has changed for more and more Americans who are watching video online, or with DVR devices, such as TiVo. Watching the saved broadcasts later, viewers of on-demand video can bypass ads or replay news. But typically, broadcast writers, whether for radio or television, have only one chance to get audience attention.

While broadcast reporters must use good writing skills, they must also look beyond the written word. They must find audio and video content that will attract audiences and enhance the message.

In this chapter, you will learn

- how print, broadcast, and online writing are alike and how they differ,
- the essential qualities of effective broadcast writing, and
- basic writing techniques for radio and television.

The Medium Changes the Style

Print journalists think in terms of a story or article because these items fit best in the pages of print media, such as newspapers, magazines, and newsletters. But broadcast journalists learned early that just reading news over the airways was dull. They realized that newer media required sound, voices, and visuals. As a result, formats for producing radio and television programming have become distinct from other media in several important ways.

While print media use photographs to enhance their stories, broadcast messages are best when voices accompany sounds and images from real life. For example, a radio reporter on the campaign trail can use actual comments from politicians along with the sounds of a cheering crowd. The sounds serve two purposes: They attract audience attention, and they add depth to the report. Audio and visual content complement writing and make any report come alive by appealing to the audience's senses.

Behind every newspaper reporter are editors and production staff to get the story from the computer to the printed page. In broadcast, the supporting cast is more visible. For a newscast, a central anchorperson or people serve as moderators for the newscast. They introduce the work of individual reporters. A producer determines the story order, edits the writing, and puts the show together.

Also, rather than typing stories in news article formats, broadcast reporters create a story with a careful mix of recordings: interviews with experts or bystanders, background or scenic information (usually with a "voiceover" of the reporter relating information), and a reporter standing and relaying information. The reporter's identity and location close out the piece. For TV reporters, their story might be a package; in radio, a wrap, short for "wraparound."

Print versus Broadcast Copy

A well-written broadcast story has much in common with any good print or online story. In all three types, writers work to focus the audience's attention on news values. All insist on accuracy and clarity; however, differences in technologies and audiences result in different formats and approaches.

Similarities

The Writing Process. The skills learned in the writing process discussed in Chapter 1 apply to broadcast writers. Broadcast reporters start with an idea for a news package, then work with a producer. They do research and interviews, then produce copy that is well written and relevant to their audiences. Outlining is critical for broadcast writers, who must write and shoot or record package materials before they leave the scene of an event. They must collect a variety of sounds or images to illustrate the news, as well as quotes. Once in editing, they usually don't have time to go back and catch additional sources or visuals before deadline.

News Values. All mass communication writing must include some news values from among those discussed in Chapter 5: prominence, timeliness, proximity, impact, magnitude, conflict, oddity, and emotional impact. Broadcast writing is no exception. Timeliness is the most defining news value for broadcast media, which makes broadcast more similar to online than print in this regard. Radio and television, because of their ability to broadcast live, can get information out to audiences in real time, as news events actually occur. Online news coverage can also be done live and in real time. Immediacy is a key factor in the success of broadcast news. In radio and television, news that happened in the morning may be revised, refreshed, or even replaced in the afternoon. Consider how immediate and up-to-date information, such as the approach of a hurricane, can be updated by the minute on broadcast media, while print outlets are limited to overall summaries of the previous day's events. In weather disasters, both print and broadcast would focus on the news values of impact, magnitude, and emotion.

Clear, Concise Writing. Particularly critical in broadcast writing are the rules of using short sentences, active voice, and short words; avoiding jargon and technical language; cutting wordiness; and getting to the point quickly. Broadcast stories generally are shorter than those in print. A print news story may use 250 to 500 words to tell about an event. A broadcast report might have

15 to 30 seconds or 30 to 75 words. Every word takes time away from other reports. In addition, listeners and viewers who don't understand jargon or complicated language usually don't have the chance to go back and hear the word again. Broadcast stories must be clear to the entire audience on the first pass.

Research. Like print reporters, broadcast reporters develop sources and do research and interviews. Research can be difficult when time is limited. Broadcast reporters must be generalists and cover a variety of topics even within a single day. Many reporters have multiple beats. They might attend the governor's news conference in the morning and cover a hotel fire that same afternoon. In trying to stay informed, broadcast reporters use the same library and online resources as their print colleagues. Some broadcast reporters have the opportunity for in-depth research when they specialize in a particular area or beat, such as medicine or business.

Differences

Deadlines. Broadcast reporters often work under multiple, tight deadlines. Print reporters generally have one or two deadlines each day, usually in the evening for the next morning's newspaper. For broadcasts, deadlines come early and often. Newscasts appear at morning, noon, evening, and late night, with updates in between. A single reporter may be developing several stories for any single broadcast. Once a story is aired, it may need to be reviewed and refreshed prior to the next news show. Deadlines might be more frequent for both print and broadcast reporters if they are also writing news for the company's online site or for a 24-hour television news service.

Writing Structure. Because radio and television reports are shorter than print versions, they must be understood immediately. Broadcast messages have only one chance to be heard, so they must make it through clutter. Effective communicators know that radio and television audiences are doing other things: driving, working, caring for kids, cooking, cleaning, and commuting.

To meet their special challenges with active audiences, broadcast writers use a slight variation of the inverted pyramid style. They typically begin any news item with a hook or headline that will grab listeners or viewers. Then they give the actual lead to the story, setting up some context and giving essential information. Next comes a more detailed explanation, followed by a wrap-up that may mention impact or future possibilities.

Broadcast writers also use a *diamond structure*, in which they start with a specific person or example, then broaden the story to explore the bigger picture. Then they return to the original person or example to close out the story. The example is similar to the use of anecdotal leads discussed in Chapter 5.

Style. Broadcast writers, like many online writers, use a more conversational style. Often the style is narrative, focusing on people and events—more like telling a story to a friend. Words and phrases are less formal and more colloquial, similar to the style found in many blogs. A reporter might use contractions or colloquialisms in sentences or follow specific style, such as writing out numbers smaller than two digits or larger than three, explained later in this chapter.

Format. Because broadcast media require sounds and images, they use a specific format that differs from how print reporters type their stories. All journalists, both print and broadcast, double-space their copy, but broadcast reporters must leave space for cues and instructions indicating when audio and visual elements are to be added.

Radio reports are typed across the page, just as print journalism stories are, but they include notes on what pre-recorded elements are to be inserted between blocks of copy that will be read aloud. In television reports, copy that will be heard fills the right-hand side of the page; cues for the technical members of the crew appear in the left-hand column. Some broadcast journalists type their copy all in capital letters, but others prefer upper and lower case. In broadcast writing, paragraphs are not split between pages, and each new story begins on a new page. Specific broadcast style rules on how to use abbreviations, numbers, and attributions are explained later in this chapter.

The Differences in Practice

A radio reporter and a print journalist are rewriting wire service copy for their respective media. How would their leads look, based on the differences between broadcast and print writing? Let's see. The print journalist writes:

> NEW ORLEANS—Mayor Ray Nagin has plans to begin moving New Orleans' residents back into the city, although federal officials want to hold off on citizens' return to the hurricane-ravaged city.

The broadcast journalist writes:

> IF THE NEW ORLEANS MAYOR HAS HIS WAY, RESIDENTS MAY RETURN TO THE CITY AS EARLY AS NEXT WEEK.

The broadcast writer does not use a dateline, uses the present tense, avoids a proper name, and establishes the location—New Orleans—as context for listeners and viewers. Consider two other examples:

> A SURVEY REPORTS THAT ALL WOMEN HAVE SIMILAR CONCERNS.

> WOMEN ARE MOST CONCERNED ABOUT BALANCING HOME AND JOB, HEALTH INSURANCE, AND STRESS, ACCORDING TO A SURVEY RELEASED TODAY.

Which is the broadcast lead? The first one is. It is short and uses attribution at the beginning to establish the source immediately. It also establishes a context for the story to follow.

Leads and Structure

No matter where an electronic journalist works, the need for clear, concise writing is essential. Sabrina Smith Davis began her career as a radio reporter and then made the transition from radio to television as a reporter for KOAT-TV in Albuquerque, New Mexico, the ABC affiliate. She summarized the need for good writing:

> *You have to be able to write. In radio, all audiences have is your voice and what they hear. As a reporter, you have to write the story colorfully and to visualize for audiences what they only can hear. If you can do that, you are ahead of the game. In television, good writing is also essential. So many people in television write in a boring way because they rely on visuals. Do this test: To see if the video matches, turn down the volume and just watch the video to see if you know what the story is about. As a viewer, you should have some idea. If you can write well and integrate visuals well, then you will do well as an electronic media journalist.*

Writing for radio and television means writing for the ear by using short sentences, conversational speech, subject–verb–object sentence order, clear and understandable copy, and smooth, clear transitions between thoughts. Let's look at producing broadcast copy, following these guidelines.

Broadcast Leads

A broadcast lead is short and gives basic information. It should be written in present or future tense to set the tone of breaking news. The lead may be catchy and even entertaining. It causes the audience to stop and listen to the story. As noted earlier, the lead generally establishes a context for the story. Such leads ensure specific information will follow:

> THIRTEEN PEOPLE GET RICH IN INDIANA.
>
> TOMORROW THE MAYOR WILL ANNOUNCE THAT NEW JOBS ARE COMING TO THE AREA.

The context is clear in each example. The first story will be about Powerball lottery winners. The second lead sets up audiences for a story on economics, with information about how many and what kinds of jobs and the name of the company. In both instances, the leads are much shorter than in print.

Broadcast writers who cover continuing or recurring stories try to find leads that will pique audience attention and interest in just a few words:

> RIGHT NOW UNION WORKERS ARE WALKING A PICKET LINE AT BALTIMORE HARBOR.
>
> A SURPRISE WITNESS MAY TESTIFY BEFORE CONGRESS TODAY IN THE ENRON INVESTIGATION.
>
> WHAT'S UP IN THE STOCK MARKET TODAY?

Broadcast Structure in the Message

Again, the structure of any electronic message must appeal to the audience's ear. The message must be clear and direct. Sentences are short and written primarily in subject–verb–object order. Language must be simple. The writer develops the story using the three-part format: context, explanation, and effect. It sets out the context or the reason why the story is being written. It may focus on a particular news value or the latest information—that is, timeliness. The second part is explanation, in which listeners or viewers get more information, whether it is background, a historical perspective, or more details of the current situation. Then the writer wraps up with the effect, generally with a look to the future or the impact of the event. Look at this story:

> IN ESPANOLA STUDENTS WILL RETURN TO FAIRVIEW ELEMENTARY SCHOOL TOMORROW AFTER ALMOST TWO WEEKS OF NO SCHOOL.
>
> THE SCHOOL CLOSED MONDAY OF LAST WEEK AFTER A PLUMBER DOING ROUTINE MAINTENANCE WORK DISCOVERED A GAS LEAK. THE SCHOOL WAS BUILT IN 1966, AND ADMINISTRATORS SAY EXTENSIVE REPAIRS WERE NEEDED.
>
> SCHOOL OFFICIALS PRICED THE REPAIRS AT MORE THAN 40 THOUSAND DOLLARS. THEY SAY THE SYSTEM'S OTHER SCHOOLS WILL BE CHECKED FOR LEAKS, TOO.

The message clearly lets parents in the audience know that children will go back to school, and it gives other general-interest members an update on a story that has been in the news. The writer follows the lead with context by giving background on why the school was closed. The next sentence explains why the school was closed for so long. Listeners then learn the repairs were expensive. The effect, or impact, is an investigation of other schools' plumbing.

As for language, all words are simple. According to the readability formula discussed in Chapter 4, this story is easy for viewers to understand. The most complicated words are "maintenance" and "extensive."

Writing Guidelines

Basic writing principles apply for broadcast stories. Because timeliness is crucial to electronic media, writers should open their stories in the present tense, explaining the latest developments. Even if they have to shift to past tense later in the story, present tense is preferable in the lead.

Avoid:

A CONVICTED RAPIST WAS EXECUTED TODAY AFTER MONTHS OF APPEALS FAILED.

Prefer:

A CONVICTED RAPIST DIES AFTER MONTHS OF APPEALS.

Avoid:

SIXTEEN WINNERS WERE DECLARED IN THE LONG-AWAITED STATE LOTTERY.

Prefer:

SIXTEEN PEOPLE ARE WINNERS IN THE LONG-AWAITED STATE LOTTERY.

Some other writing rules to follow:

- Introduce unfamiliar people before using their names. Describe people in terms of employment, life's work, or relevance to the story. Then name them, as in "sprinter John Jones" or "angry ticketholder Billy Cupp." Only the instantly recognizable names of widely known people should be used without prior explanation.

  A ROCKLAND SECOND-GRADE TEACHER IS THE NATION'S TEACHER OF THE YEAR.

  RONNIE MILLER,...

  Or

  ROCKLAND MAYOR JOAN TILLIS IS IN GOOD CONDITION AFTER BACK SURGERY.

- Avoid tongue twisters that can cause problems when reports are read on air. Always read copy aloud before it is broadcast. "The clandestine clan committed continual crimes" or "the player's black plastic pants" may look clever on paper, but it may be difficult for an announcer to enunciate.
- Use action verbs. Remember that verbs can paint pictures, an especially important aspect of radio reports. "Race car driver Rusty Wallace roared to victory" has more life than "Race car driver Rusty Wallace won."
- Use quotes sparingly. Paraphrased statements are more easily understood. If a quote is particularly good, use it live from the source. Make sure the writing does not imply the statement is from the reporter or newscaster. Direct quotes that use "I" or "we" can cause such confusion. Consider this quote: "Chamber of Commerce president David Fall says, 'I have doubts about the town's development practices.'" Listeners who miss the attribution may infer the reporter is doubtful. Instead, write: "Chamber of Commerce President David Fall says he has doubts about the town's development practices."

- Put attribution at the beginning of a quotation: "Medical experts say the new treatment may cause cancer cells to die." If you must use a direct quote, try "Johnson said in his own words, 'The new treatment may cause cancer cells to die.'"
- Avoid writing that uses a lot of punctuation. Punctuation—even a question mark—cannot be heard. Listeners may miss the inflection.
- Avoid long introductory clauses with participles, like this one: "While doing a routine maintenance check at the school, a plumber found. . . ." The story example used earlier puts that information at the end of the sentence.
- Avoid separating subjects and verbs, particularly with phrases in apposition. "Marian Johnson, a director for the Rockland Little Theater, will leave her job in two weeks" becomes "Rockland's Little Theater director will leave her job within two weeks. Marian Johnson. . . ." Don't leave verbs at the end of the sentence. Follow subject–verb–object order as much as possible.
- Break up lengthy series of modifiers and adjectives, such as this one: "Police described the man as blond, long-haired, blue-eyed, and five-feet, six-inches tall." Rather, write: "Police say the suspect has long blond hair and blue eyes. They also say he is about five feet, six inches tall."
- Avoid negatives. A listener may miss the negative words "no" and "not" in a broadcast and thereby be misinformed. Use alternatives: "Police could find no motive for the shootings" can be translated "Police say the motive for the shootings is unknown."
- If your report runs long, say more than 30 seconds, look for ways to unify the story. Repetition of key words is one way to help listeners and viewers follow along.

Style in Copy

In Chapter 3, we looked at copyediting style for print. Broadcast writers also follow style rules for preparing copy:

- In the case of a word that might be mispronounced, spell it phonetically, just as you would with complicated names. For example, if you are reporting about lead content in paint, write it "led." Even though it is misspelled for the usage, you don't have to worry about an anchor reading "lead" as "leed" paint.

- If a name is difficult, write it out phonetically. Anchors and reporters can stumble in stating people's names. Sound it out. For example, names with "ei" or "ie" can be confusing, such as Janice Weinberger. Write out "Wine Burger" so the anchor will use a long "i" pronunciation. For former Iraqi leader Saddam Hussein, the pronunciation spelling is "Who Sayn."
- Put titles before names and keep them short. Use "former Florida Governor Jeb Bush" rather than "Jeb Bush, the former governor of Florida." A university vice chancellor for institutional research services becomes "a university administrator." You can use a descriptive title if audiences easily identify a person that way, such as "evangelist Billy Graham" or "singer Sheryl Crow."
- Use people's names the way they are commonly cited. Former President Clinton is known as Bill Clinton, not William Clinton. Former Vice President Al Gore is rarely called Albert Gore, Jr.
- Write out single-digit numbers. Use numerals for two- and three-digit numbers. Return to words for thousand, million, etc; write out numbers between zero and nine. Use numerals for 10 through 999. Above 999, you can combine numerals and words. For example, write "nine thousand 45," "10 thousand 200," and "22 billion."
- Round off numbers. Say "more than 10 thousand" rather than "10 thousand 232 subscribers."
- Write out amounts for dollars and cents, percent, and fractions:

GASOLINE PRICES ARE THREE TO FOUR CENTS A GALLON HIGHER.

THREE-FOURTHS OF TOWN RESIDENTS SAY THEY ARE PLEASED WITH THE MAYOR'S PERFORMANCE.

ABOUT FIFTY-FIVE PERCENT OF WHAT YOU READ, YOU REMEMBER.

- Use numerals for phone numbers and years: 919-555-1212, 1999, or 1865.
- Keep statistics to a minimum. Put them in a format people will understand. If a poll says 67 percent of the state's residents support NASA's plan for a lunar space station, report that "two out of three state residents say they favor NASA's plan for a lunar station."

- Write out Roman numerals. Write out "Harry Holland the third" rather than "Harry Holland III," or "Queen Elizabeth the second," not "Queen Elizabeth II."
- Avoid acronyms on first reference unless an organization is better known by its initials than by its full name, such as E-S-P-N, F-B-I, and N-C-A-A. Insert hyphens between letters if they are to be read individually. Omit hyphens if the acronym is to be read as a word, such as in FEMA. For local or state law enforcement, it is better just to say police or law officials on subsequent references.

Broadcast Formats

A major difference between print and broadcast media is the format for the final message, as noted earlier. Broadcast media use a script format that indicates the text along with the sound bites or visuals. Time is critical in broadcast writing. Scripts indicate how long the total story runs plus the length of specific segments within the story. Radio reports are typed across the page, much like a print story, with audio cues. Following is an example of a radio news script:

7/30 MK Road Construction

SPEEDING ALONG HIGHWAY 86 IN NORTH CHAPEL HILL COULD COST YOU AS MUCH AS 165 DOLLARS. THAT'S THE WARNING FROM THE CHAPEL HILL POLICE TRAFFIC UNIT. OFFICER CHUCK QUINLAN SAYS A CONSTRUCTION WORK ZONE WILL STRETCH FROM ASHLEY FOREST TO INTERSTATE 40 FOR THE NEXT YEAR-AND-A HALF. QUINLAN SAYS THE WORK ZONE WILL HAVE A UNIFORM 35-MILE-PER-HOUR SPEED LIMIT WITHIN WEEKS. THAT MEANS DRIVERS NEED TO PAY ATTENTION.*

#145 QUINLAN:21 A:....ROAD, ETC.

QUINLAN SAYS HE AND HIS COLLEAGUES HAVE BEEN DEALING WITH REAR END COLLISIONS IN THE WORK AREA. AND HE SAYS THE SITUATION COULD GET WORSE, AS CREWS CONTINUE MOVING DIRT NEAR THE ROADWAY.*

*Reprinted with permission from Mitch Kokai, WCHL-AM radio, Chapel Hill, NC.

In television reports, the cues on the left-hand side of the page give such information as the title or slug of the story, what newscast it will appear on, the tape number, the length of the story, the name of the anchor, and any graphics to be used, as shown earlier in the chapter. After the story text begins, cues will tell whether the story has a voiceover that is read by the anchor along with the visuals. Cues also indicate who is speaking—for example, a source interviewed for the story, the reporter, or the anchor.

When the story text is typed, sometimes all capital letters are used. That helps clarify writing where a lowercase "l" might resemble a capital "I" and create problems for announcers. Capital letters are also easier to read from a distance. But some writers are moving to using upper- and lower-case letters, as in print journalism.

When students study broadcast journalism, they learn the codes and copy preparation style early on. A complete radio story, such as the script shown earlier, may seem longer than a story typed for print because cues take up space on the left-hand side of the page. The goal is to make the copy legible for the anchor and the reporter who read from the copy.

Trends in Broadcast Media

Television is a regulated and competitive medium that depends heavily on technology. And in the past decade, it has been on a rollercoaster of change. Audiences use television primarily as an entertainment medium but also for news. Almost every household in the United States has a television set, and about three out of four homes have more than one.

In the last quarter of the 20th century, the television industry went from a handful of networks and few cable or satellite services to almost a dozen major networks and to cable and satellite distribution companies that increased the U.S. media buffet to hundreds of channels. The broad reach of television is extended now by connections to Internet sites and other media. This coming together of powerful media formats is known as convergence.

As one of the latest trends evolving, particularly in broadcast media, convergence can take several forms, such as shared information or shared staffs. In shared information, a news reporter for a television station might give information about an event to a reporter from a sister newspaper with which it has a sharing agreement. A television station might do a promotion for a story in a sister newspaper. With shared staffs, a television reporter may write a story and then rewrite it for the station's Web site. Or a newspaper reporter may write versions of a story for the newspaper and for the online site.

Some see convergence as a permanent fixture in U.S. media; others see it as just an experiment. Some media observers say newspapers and their sister online sites and TV and radio stations already represent convergence, which is getting support from publishers and media owners who see shared staffs as a way to reduce newsroom expenses. A plus for the business side is the ability to sell advertising packages that include ads for all media in a certain market: newspaper, radio, television, and online. Advertisers get a reduced rate to advertise in more than one medium. Supporters say each medium—newspaper, radio, television, online—can maintain its values and basic structure but have the benefit of broader resources and expanded reach among audiences.

The trend toward convergence has prompted some schools of journalism and mass communication to teach students to write across platforms or different media styles. At the very least, those hiring students want them to know how writing styles differ and how to be comfortable with different media. Phil Currie, vice president of news for Gannett, commented at a journalism educators' meeting that he wanted newspaper reporters to be comfortable being interviewed on television even if they were not trained specifically to write television copy.

The television industry is also moving to HDTV, or high-definition television, that changes the way television signals are transmitted. The picture viewers see on HDTV screens is much crisper and more detailed, giving the feeling of seeing images in a three-dimensional form. All full-power television stations nationwide were expected to move to DTV transmission in February 2009, ending analog broadcasts. Television viewers had several options to allow their television sets to receive the HDTV broadcasts if they could not afford to buy a new television set.

While the federally mandated changes affect the visual aspect of television programming, they do not affect how writers produce content. Writing styles and structures remain the same, and news videographers have learned that their pictures air on a wider format with greater clarity.

Mobile digital television, which uses a Mobile Pedestrian Handheld (MPH) system, is in early development and allows broadcasters to deliver DTV to mobile devices, including cellular phones, laptops, and personal media players.

Exercises

1. Write a broadcast lead for each of the following stories:
   - Sam Snyder, president of the Chamber of Commerce, has been elected to the board of directors of the National Chamber of Commerce.
   - The Federal Reserve Board raised interest rates one-quarter percent, which means consumers will be paying higher rates on their adjustable-rate home mortgages if they are seeking mortgages.
   - David Parkinson of Waverly County won first place at the county fair yesterday for the largest squash. It weighed 6 and 1/2 pounds. David is 6 years old.
   - Competition begins Thursday for the National Collegiate Athletic Association title. The tough competition in basketball has been dubbed March Madness.

2. Using the formula that a 60-space typed line equals 4 seconds of air time, write a 20-second radio script for the following information:

   A masked man robbed the university dining hall of $3,000 and escaped after locking the dining hall manager in a closet.

   Tony Jones, the manager, escaped unharmed. Police are looking for a heavy-set white man about 5-feet, 5 inches, and weighing about 175 pounds. He has a round face and broad shoulders. Jones could give no description of the man's facial features because he had a stocking pulled over his face.

   Jones was preparing the payroll when he heard a noise in the kitchen. When he went to investigate, he said, the man came charging at him. The man ordered him to open the safe and put money in a blue sack. Jones complied, and the robber locked him in a closet before leaving.

3. Write a 20-second radio script for the following information and indicate an audio you could use to illustrate the spot:

   The legal age for minors to buy cigarettes in most states is 18. Studies show that underage youth or minors still buy up to 500 million packs of cigarettes a year, despite the states' laws. About 25 states have agreed there should be stricter laws on tobacco products, and even tobacco industry officials claim their advertising is not geared to teenagers.

4. Write a 30-second television script for the following information. Type the copy in the right-hand column and indicate on the left what visuals you would use.

 A coalition of child-care advocates marched on the state legislature today. They distributed flyers encouraging legislators to approve monies during the current session that would subsidize the cost of day care for families earning below $16,000 a year. They claim that day-care costs in the state have skyrocketed, and even working families are finding it hard to pay for quality day care out of their salaries. The coalition estimated 15 percent of the state's population fell below the federal poverty level guidelines last year. The coalition officials said that last year it had to turn away almost 400 families who needed financial assistance because funds just were not available.

5. Watch the local evening news. Do a tally that covers the number of stories, story topics, whether they were local or based on a national event, the length of each, and numbers and types of sources used. Write several paragraphs on whether you felt adequately informed about news items from the television account.

6. Based on the information collected in Exercise 5, look at the local or regional newspaper the following day. See how many stories from your evening television newscast were covered in the newspaper. Look at the length of those stories and what new information you learned.

References

Felicity Barringer, "Growing Audience Is Turning to Established News Media Online," *The New York Times*, August 27, 2001.

Phil Currie, panel on convergence, Association for Education in Journalism and Mass Communication, Washington, DC, August 6, 2001.

Seth Finn, *Broadcast Writing as a Liberal Art*. Englewood Cliffs, NJ: Prentice-Hall, 1991.

Cecilia Friend, Don Challenger, and Katherine C. McAdams, *Contemporary Editing*. Chicago: NTC/Contemporary Publishing Group, 2000.

Radio-Television News Directors Association Web site. Available at: www.rtnda.org.

C. A. Tuggle, Forrest Carr, and Suzanne Hoffman, *Broadcast News Handbook: Writing, Reporting, and Producing in a Converged Media World*. New York: McGraw-Hill, 2006.

Leslie Walker, "Web-Page Collection Preserves the Online Response to Horror," *The Washington Post*, September 26, 2001.

CHAPTER

14

Strategic Communication

The president of a national company that operates health clubs and sells exercise equipment wants to improve its corporate image. In addition, he wants to increase the company's name recognition in the fitness market. He needs to develop a plan for advertising in a variety of media, including online, with public relations efforts in the community around each health club. But he doesn't know how.

That's when he seeks the talents of professionals who can develop a strategic plan to target specific audiences and develop the communications tools to reach them. The plan will use public relations and advertising in an integrated marketing program that might include news releases, pop-up Internet ads, sponsorship in a community bike race, and local appearances of well-known athletes at company gyms.

This book has focused on producing factual, non-opinionated content for audiences. Many writers, editors, multimedia producers, and others in advertising and public relations jobs perform the same tasks. But in addition to factual information, they usually have a specific, persuasive message to share. The goal is to influence people to buy their products and services or to take some other sort of action.

Most journalism and mass communication programs separate public relations and advertising as courses of study, but many students take one or two courses in the other subject. Some jobs specifically require PR skills, others just advertising, and others knowledge of both. Public relations practitioners who work for nonprofit organizations, for example, might write news releases, the annual report, and all advertising copy. As the PR director for your town's historical society, you might write the advertising copy to promote the society's annual Christmas tour of homes, then possibly solicit a local company to underwrite the cost and give the company credit within the ad.

Many advertising and PR professionals are joined in what the industry is calling integrated marketing communications—and what we will refer to in this chapter as strategic communication. This type of communication requires strategy developed from input and planning for all aspects of message delivery from advertising to direct marketing to news releases—whatever is necessary to get a client's message to the audience.

This chapter looks at the importance of

- good writing in strategic communication,
- the practice of public relations,
- public relations communications tools,
- advertising strategies, including branding and product placement,
- guidelines for effective ad writing, and
- strategic communication in an online world.

The Importance of Good Writing

Within strategic communication, good writing is at the heart of every successful and effective campaign and event. Strategic communicators must send news releases and buy ad space so audiences, including media, know their organizations or businesses exist and what they do. The reporter must receive the media advisory before writing a story. The mother must read the brochure on a community's child-care offerings before calling for more details. The college student must peruse the company's home page to learn about its internship program.

Practitioners of strategic communication must identify audiences to determine the best methods to reach them, then conduct research, plan and carry out communication strategy, develop specific tools, and evaluate plans. Writing is crucial at each stage, but particularly in crafting the messages to important audiences.

As writers, strategic communicators must be able to adopt different styles and tones because they have many more audiences than the writer for a newspaper or specialized publication. In the morning, they might write a general-interest news release and in the afternoon a speech in the language style of the company president. Or they might write an article for the employee newsletter, proofread ads in a statewide magazine, and later consult with a production company on a video script for an upcoming stockholders meeting.

PR and advertising students often take media-writing courses to learn the inverted pyramid and other formats. The courses also teach the fundamentals of grammar, punctuation, and style, and they stress the need for clear, concise, and accurate writing that interests and attracts targeted audiences. Students are also trained in building and maintaining Web sites for specific audiences.

Strategic communicators generally divide writing into two categories: informational and persuasive. The organization's or company's objective will determine the type and tone of the writing.

Informational writing is just what it says: It presents materials in a straightforward, factual manner—just as in journalistic writing. A brochure can be informational, simply listing an organization's history, services, address, and telephone number. A brochure might give specifics about an upcoming program or new service.

A brochure can also be persuasive. Persuasive writing clearly pitches a particular point of view and reflects a specific attitude and behavior. Some types of communication are deliberately persuasive. A direct mail letter to university alumni will try to persuade them to donate to endowed professorships. A public service announcement on radio will encourage listeners to donate canned goods to the local food bank.

Persuasive writing follows the tenets of good writing: accuracy, clarity, and conciseness. A brochure can be persuasive and still be informational, using facts and graphics to portray positively the company's position.

Such writing adheres to journalistic standards of fairness and impartiality. Experienced practitioners know that arguments explained factually will have more impact than those that are biased and long-winded.

Public Relations in Practice

Professor James Grunig at the University of Maryland defines public relations as the management of communication between an organization and its publics, or audiences: employees, clients, customers, investors, or alumni. Grunig emphasizes the importance of strategy and analysis in approaching those relationships.

Successful public relations builds and maintains good relationships between an organization and its publics through balanced, open communication. Public relations may be as simple as an announcement by the local literacy council about its success rate for the past year. Or it may be a complicated integrated marketing program that incorporates public relations with advertising, investor relations, and market research.

Diverse organizations use public relations: local, state, and national nonprofit organizations, such as the American Heart Association; schools and universities; small companies; multinational corporations; and local, state, and federal government, including the president and the armed services. Public relations practitioners share information with the public to help the organization achieve its objectives. The objective of PR efforts may be to announce new products or to show how a company works as a good corporate citizen or as a leader in its field. The objective may be public service, as in broadcast messages to reduce teenage pregnancy or to warn smokers about the risks of heart attacks.

Some people erroneously think of public relations as free publicity, believing there is no cost. But real public relations—ongoing programs of communication with various publics—is expensive. Organizations must pay salaries and production costs, buy supplies and equipment, and cover additional overhead expenses, such as office space, computer support, and utilities. Most are hidden costs the public does not see or consider.

Public Relations Stages

In the late 1960s, Scott Cutlip and Allen Center identified four stages of a PR campaign: research, planning, communication, and evaluation. Public relations practitioners still follow those stages today.

For example, a bank plans to change its checking account service in three months. The PR department is charged with informing the bank's publics of the change. Look at how the PR practitioner would use each stage.

Research. Research is essential to enable the bank to state public relations goals, identify relevant publics, describe the service, and identify its strengths and weaknesses. For example, the bank's reputation would be a strength; competition from other banks' services would be a weakness. Research could use focus groups or surveys to determine what the bank's customers would like in a checking account.

Planning. In planning, the practitioner devises a communications plan or strategy. The practitioner determines what communications tools will be used during the next three months and sets deadlines for each one. For example, dates for news releases to trade publications differ from those for statewide media. Magazines usually need copy two months before publication dates; broadcast media, online sites, and newspapers can print information within 24 hours of receiving it.

Communication. In the communication stage, the practitioner carries out the plan. Information is written and distributed via the communications tools: news releases, brochures, fact sheets, annual reports and other publications, Web sites, and speeches, just to name a few. Although writing is important in developing the plan, good skills are critical in the communication stage.

Evaluation. In evaluation, the practitioner uses qualitative and quantitative ways to evaluate the success of the communications plan and strategy and change in audience attitudes or behavior. For example, the bank can use focus groups of customers to determine how well they understood communication about the service. After the news release is distributed, the public relations staff can count how many times the news release information appeared in local media or the number of hits to the company's Web site link to the news release.

Public Relations Tools

Public relations practitioners often use the term "public relations tools" or "communications tools" to describe the techniques or methods they use to reach audiences. All require solid writing skills. Among the more common communications tools, which are usually online, are these:

News releases. Articles that describe newsworthy events and are sent to media outlets. They are written in a style ready to be used.

Feature releases. More in-depth, less timely articles about organization employees, projects, or services. These releases generally are targeted to a specific publication.

Media kits. Folders that contain relevant information on the organization or company or a special event. Included are fact sheets, photographs, reprints, biographies, and other material.

Direct mail letters. Letters written to targeted publics, generally to solicit support for a project or event.

Brochures. Booklets or folders that include general information or targeted information about an organization or a special project. These pieces are designed to be easily mailed or distributed at events or in racks.

Web sites. Full-service Web sites that give information about an organization, invite the public to interact in a multitude of ways from e-mail to games, and link to other sites.

Face-to-face contact. Speeches or appearances at meetings, conventions, or other programs.

Multimedia presentations. Productions that incorporate text, audio, photography, graphics, and video to supplement information and to depict more visually an organization or its services. Such presentations can be posted online or distributed on CDs.

Specialized publications. Newsletters, annual reports, and magazines produced for internal audiences, such as employees, or for external audiences, such as customers and the general public. In some corporate settings, annual reports are produced by the investor relations department, and the PR practitioner may help with some writing. Many specialized publications are online and linked to Web sites.

Video and audio news releases. Actual film footage with or without sound, especially voiceover, to give radio and television stations ready-to-use material. Some organizations have broadcast footage or other images that can be downloaded from their Web sites.

Public service announcements (PSAs). Short announcements, generally sent ready-to-read to radio stations or in video format for television use or posted on Web sites.

Blogs. Short for Web logs. These online diaries are managed usually by one person, but companies are also using them for conversations among internal and external audiences.

Image advertising. Attempts by an organization to improve an audience's perception of it. Such advertising is often done in conjunction with marketing departments.

Communications tools are incorporated into strategic plans that serve as guides for PR activities or campaigns. Corporate communications departments, for example, begin work in the fall on the next year's plan to support goals, specific actions, and target dates.

Of course, not all public relations is planned. A reporter might call the corporate communications department about a story idea, and the PR practitioner will respond or arrange for a company executive to reply. The practitioner might send the reporter a media kit that contains a mix of communications tools, often called collateral materials, such as a news release, a fact sheet, a CD with a multimedia show, and a brochure.

Considering Audiences or Publics

Just as in any other mass communication field, PR practitioners must consider their audiences, or what they call *publics.* The publics are the people who will be reading news releases or viewing video news releases. They may be employees, customers, other business people, town residents, lawmakers, reporters, or officials in local, state, or federal government agencies. Public relations practitioners must identify and know which publics are important to their organizations.

Imagine you are the public information director for a university system that is planning a capital campaign to raise funds for new buildings. The university administration has set a goal of $500 million. In planning a public relations campaign, you would have to consider the university's publics: alumni, faculty members, staff members, students, students' parents, potential students, donors, legislators (if the university is public or state supported), the general public, and the media. From that list, you might identify five key or important publics.

Practitioners use research, such as informal surveys or focus groups, to learn about their publics. Specifically, practitioners need to know how their publics get information. Then they can decide which media, or communications tools, are most effective in reaching them. And they can decide the tone and style of the messages.

As part of targeting publics, PR practitioners must be aware of the growing diversity of U.S. society and how to reach specific audiences. Specialized publications and Web sites are geared to individual interests, and

PR professionals should monitor a diverse array of media to stay up-to-date. For example, a range of news pertinent to African American audiences can be found on Black PR Wire at www.blackprwire.com and for Hispanics on Hispanic PR Wire at www.hispanicprwire.com. More on considering diverse audiences is discussed in Chapter 11.

The Media as a Public

An important public for any public relations practitioner is the media. The media learn about an organization through standard communications tools, such as news releases and media advisories. But they also use annual reports, Web sites, investor publications, executive speeches, brochures, and other means to find out information about companies. In turn, practitioners must know the media. They must know the media's audiences, formats, and content. They must convince the media to use PR information. Media are essential audiences because through newspapers, magazines, radio and television, specialty publications, online sites, and others, the practitioner reaches many other publics. Among the primary tools for PR practitioners to reach their publics through the media are news releases, fact sheets, brochures, and public service announcements, many posted on company Web sites.

News Releases

News releases provide timely information to media. They might announce a promotion or staff change; a service or product; new information, such as the effects of legislation or the results of a survey; financial earnings; an upcoming event; or community service, such as a new scholarship program. Some news releases, especially those concerning events, are presented in the form of media advisories, or short notices that tell media in advance about an event or issues and that focus on *who*, *what*, *when*, *where*, *how*, and *why*.

News releases must contain some of the news values discussed in Chapter 5: prominence, timeliness, proximity, impact, and magnitude. They may also include conflict, oddity, or emotional impact. The lead should summarize the relevant information. The rest of the release should be organized in the inverted pyramid style of writing discussed in Chapter 6 and follow Associated Press style, which most news outlets use.

The practitioner's goal in sending a news release is to get publicity. But the practitioner must remember that news releases are uncontrolled; the final story is up to the reporter's and editor's discretion. Reporters might use the release as a basis for an expanded story, or they might take the news release as is and even give the PR writer a byline. Reporters, editors, and producers need news releases that are complete, accurate, newsworthy, and appropriate for their audiences. They will favor news releases in a ready-to-use format.

News releases should contain the PR contact name, organization, organization address, organization phone number, fax number, e-mail address, and even the PR contact's home phone number. The information goes above the headline. (If the organization's address is readily visible on letterhead, it can be omitted.) The date and the headline follow, setting up the contents of the news release.

Often PR practitioners will include a contact name and telephone number within the text of the news release, usually at the end, to ensure that further information is available to interested publics if the news release is run verbatim. Online news releases, such as those posted on PR Newswire or other online news services, often contain a link so readers can give feedback on whether the information was useful and understandable.

Fact Sheets

Fact sheets generally are one page long—or the front and back of one sheet—and are designed to be read quickly. Information about the organization, a service, a product, or a special activity is highlighted in short segments.

An easy way to develop a fact sheet is to follow the news elements discussed in Chapter 5: *who*, *what*, *when*, *where*, *how*, and *why*. A statewide children's forum is planning its annual fund-raiser. The fact sheet would be organized:

Who:	The Children's Forum
What:	Annual fund-raiser—a black-tie dinner and dance
When:	June 14
Where:	Downtowner Hotel
How:	Ticket prices $75 per individual for the dance and $150 for dinner and dance through the institute offices at 444–1234
Why:	To raise money for administrative and program costs

Fact sheets should also contain the contact name, organization, and phone numbers if reporters and others want additional information. When fact sheets are produced or updated, the date should be placed at the bottom of the fact sheet to indicate how current the information is. Fact sheets are also uncontrolled. Media can use the information any way they wish.

Brochures

In writing and designing brochures, PR practitioners are limited only by their talent, creativity, and budget. With desktop publishing and multimedia technology, many more organizations can produce high-quality, good-looking brochures for little cost. They can also publish brochure content online. The more work that is done in-house, the more money saved. Here are some questions to answer when writing a brochure:

- Is the brochure persuasive or informative? If the brochure's primary role is to persuade, it will be written with emotional language, comparisons, and familiar concepts. If informative, material will be to the point and language straightforward.
- Who is the audience? Whether the audience is specialized or general will determine the level of language used.
- Will the brochure be read and thrown away or saved? Deciding how it will be used will affect the cost and design.
- Will the brochure be a stand-alone piece, such as those in a display rack at a state's welcome station, or a collateral piece in a media kit or with a related Web site? A stand-alone brochure must be complete because it cannot rely on information in other pieces or online links.
- What is the appropriate format? If the brochure is a self-mailer, it will need to have an address space. Information has to be arranged logically, and decisions have to be made on artwork, such as photographs, and on graphic elements and white space, the size, the number of folds or pages, and how the brochure will open. How will the brochure copy be formatted for a Web site?

Brochure copy should be short. Publics are looking for a quick read. Each panel should stand alone, and copy shouldn't jump from one panel to the next.

Brochures, whether printed or online, are appealing to PR practitioners because they are controlled messages. The practitioner has the final say on copy and design. No one can change the content or wording; the only uncontrolled aspect is placement—for example, whether brochures are left at a doctor's office to be displayed or given to volunteers to distribute. The concerns are visibility of the brochure rack and whether all brochures are handed out.

Public Service Announcements

Public service announcements, or PSAs, are generally short pieces that give information of value to a specific audience. Traditionally, media have accepted the briefs from nonprofit organizations or government agencies and run them for free. Most PSAs range from 30 to 60 seconds in length, though some produced by individuals and posted on YouTube or MySpace can run as long as the person thinks people will watch.

Public service announcements must get basic information into as few words as possible. When they include audio, writers must grab listener attention and write clearly so that the message is understood. Increasingly, the audio and transcripts of PSAs can be downloaded off Web sites, and running PSAs is part of broadcast outlets' community service programming.

You probably have seen numerous PSAs on television, online, or in print, pointing out the dangers of drinking. International advertising firm Saatchi & Saatchi did a series of posters using images of cars, bottles, and keychains to form a noose or a firearm with the simple message: "It's like killing yourself. Don't drink and drive."

Any online search can produce hundreds of PSAs on any topic, produced by anyone from individuals to government agencies and on topics ranging from healthy behaviors to public services. For example, other PSAs on drinking and driving use images from simulated accidents to the bar scene from *Star Wars Episode IV, A New Hope* to catch attention and drive home the message. PSAs are free for the taking because the creators want the message widely distributed.

Advertising's Role in Strategic Communication

Advertising is probably the first form of media writing that children notice. Kids respond to ads, often before they can talk. Toddlers excitedly point at Ronald McDonald and "read" the golden arches as a sign for food even before they know their ABCs. By combining color, sound, movement, symbols, and language, advertising creates some of the most powerful messages in our world today.

Like all media presentations, good advertising depends on good writing. "Good advertising writers are writers first. They are personal writers—people who bring their own feelings and reactions to the product," observes Professor John Sweeney, former creative director for a major U.S. advertising agency. "Good advertising slogans are some of the most effective communication available today. They have a concise, pithy, sensory quality that other writers would do well to study and adopt."

Volney Palmer is generally credited with being the first advertising "agent." In 1841, he began selling newspaper advertising space for a profit. Advertisers prepared their ads; Palmer and other agents placed the ads for them. Such advertising agents became concerned with copy and artwork for the ads several years later. In 1869, F. W. Ayer started N. W. Ayer & Son, an advertising agency that provided writing, art, and media placement to its clients.

Advertising agencies have changed throughout the years, but the seeds of the modern agency planted with N. W. Ayer & Son and other early agencies still exist today. Advertisers also have myriad ways to reach consumers, not just newspapers or billboards. A company might advertise in newspapers, on radio and television, and on the Internet. New media and the changing media habits of audiences allow advertisers to funnel product information directly to specific and special audiences.

The goals of ad writers, regardless of medium, have remained constant over the years:

- To communicate availability of products to audiences.
- To communicate product benefits to audiences.
- To provide accessible information about products in a few words.
- To communicate reasons why the product can deliver benefits.

Other goals include corporate image building, when a company wants consumers to view it as a good corporate citizen; response to a disaster, such as a utility company telling customers how soon power will be restored after massive hurricane damage; or public service messages, such as alerting audiences to the dangers of unprotected sex or the benefits of low-fat diets.

Some people think of advertising as propaganda—distorted information designed to lead, or mislead, its audience. Propaganda is manipulative, and so is advertising, some people say.

Unlike most other forms of published writing, advertising is one-sided by its very nature; no one wants to spend his or her advertising budget extolling the benefits of a competitor's product. But the absence of other products from ads does not have to mean that an ad is unfairly biased if the information presented is accurate.

Presenting your best to the public, Sweeney explains, is a core value of advertising culture. Advertising that is less than ethical is not advertising; it is propaganda or huckstering or manipulation. Professional advertising writing is an accepted form of argument—a fair argument—and it abides by an ethical code.

Advertisers are subject to many government rules and regulations. The Capital Council of Better Business Bureaus advises that all advertisers stay abreast of regulations through subscription services, such as Do's and Don'ts in Advertising or the National Advertising Case Reports. Such subscription services are quite expensive and typically are used by large agencies or companies. The industry has self-regulators, such as the National Advertising Review Council (NARC). The Federal Trade Commission has information on how advertisers should behave, whether advertising in print or online.

Advertising and Today's Audiences

The environment for advertising has changed tremendously in the past decade. New media and new products compete for audience attention, and advertisers may no longer assume that mere publicity will lead to success or consumers using services and buying products. Today's advertisers must understand how audiences think, feel, and behave. Only through selecting likely audiences and streamlining ads for those groups can advertisers reach consumers.

Ad production is seldom the work of just the writer. In most cases, the copywriter is part of a team. For an advertising agency, the team could include account planners, who determine audience interest and product competition; an account executive, who oversees the account and serves as the liaison with the client; the copywriter, who takes the research and theme and creates text; the art director, who designs ads and other collateral pieces for the client; the creative director, who oversees the concept and production; media planners, who develop strategy for placing ads; and the media buyer, who places ads. All members of the team must know the others' roles. The copywriter often works most closely with the art designer on aspects such as typeface, length of copy, size of the ad, and graphic elements.

Newspapers still design ads for advertisers who cannot afford to pay agencies to do the work. The newspaper ad staff could include an ad sales representative, art director, and copywriter—all working as a team to produce and place ads that appeal to audiences.

Advertising Strategy

When a copywriter and an art director sit down to design an ad, they are guided by a creative brief that presents the advertising strategy. The advertising strategy is made up of the media strategy (where the ads should be placed and when to place them) plus the creative strategy (what should be in the ads and how they should look). Generally, the ad strategy lists marketing or business goals, such as more sales or improved corporate image; target audience; positioning, or how consumers perceive the service or product vis-à-vis competitors; benefits; creative approach, such as tone of the advertising message; and appropriate media to reach audiences.

The plan will enable the copywriter to know what structure will have the greatest appeal to the target audience. The creative approach is affected by the goals—selling a product, providing general information about a company, positioning a product as superior among its competitors, or boosting a corporate image. Target audiences will determine the tone of language and whether the ad must be serious or can have humor. Even corporate image will affect how a copywriter pitches an ad.

One of the copywriter's first responsibilities to support the advertising strategy will be to come up with a theme or the "big idea." Philip Ward Burton notes in *Advertising Copywriting* that the theme "is the central idea—the imaginative spark plug—that will give your advertisements continuity, recall value, and thus, extra selling power. Your theme is the lifeline of your campaign."

Targeting Audiences

The process of identifying and communicating with specific audiences is often called *targeting*. Clinique might target girls aged 13 to 15 as a likely audience for messages about a new tinted lip gloss. With the target group in mind, Clinique's ad writers design messages that will appeal to young teens and place these ads in locations where teens go. Clinique, for example, might place an ad for its new lip gloss in *Teen People* magazine and between scenes on the TV show "The O. C."

Targeting is a necessity in an era of budget consciousness and the rise of cable TV and audience fragmentation that have limited advertisers' ability to reach mass audiences. To get maximum benefit from advertising dollars, advertisers select target audiences for specific products. Beer, tires, and trucks are advertised in sports sections and broadcasts; toys and sweet cereals are advertised with children's programming; and pain relievers, laxatives, and investments are sold with financial news.

Professional market research is used by major corporations to identify the best possible markets for particular ads. Cluster marketing attempts to impose some order on the new media-and-audience mix, dividing Americans into subgroups and predicting specific media behaviors, as well as products and services that each group is likely to use. Companies, such as Claritas, offer their clients detailed information about consumers. Through its Prizm feature, anyone—individual or business—can type in a zip code and learn what types of people live in an area. Advertisers can use the information to target audiences. For example, a community might be made up of "Boomtown Singles," "Up-and-Comers," and "Young Influentials." On its Web site, Claritas defines for each group characteristics, such as median income, housing type, and lifestyle traits.

Product Placement

You are watching television, and the scene moves to the kitchen. On the counter are cereal boxes, diet soda, and cans of spaghetti. All the product names are clearly visible. Having real products in movies and on TV shows is called *product placement*. The benefits of product placement seem obvious: product reinforcement and possible recall when consumers shop.

Product placement has been around for years and is a fairly well-accepted advertising tool. When product placement first came into vogue in movies, skeptical viewers wondered about the effects of certain products on younger viewers. For example, the war on tobacco and on smoking among teens included criticism of tobacco product use in movies.

Most product placements are the result of a business deal, and some companies make product placement their business. Popular television game shows, such as "The Price Is Right," award specific products to participants. The product names and logos are repeated during each broadcast. Companies have sponsored events, such as bicycle races, and have their products and logos included with promotional materials.

Advertisers use the word "integration" to describe incorporating specific products into movies, television shows, and elsewhere. Most agree that integration needs to make sense, that the product needs to fit with the show's theme or message. Product placement is less common in magazines or newspapers.

Whether product placement actually works is still debated. Research has shown that in some instances, cross-cultural differences prevent audiences from connecting with the products they see. As more and more products are included within television programming, some observers are concerned about consumers' reactions to their top picks becoming more commercial-laden. Most companies, however, like the idea of product placement as yet another way to create brand recognition. But researchers are still assessing whether product placement does increase brand recognition and sales. Seeing a product for a fleeting second on a movie screen or in the hands of a celebrity might not be enough to put it in a consumer's shopping cart.

Branding

Branding has become a primary factor in advertising strategies. Consumers are part of the branding process every day as they walk around with the apple on their MacBooks, Lexus logos on cars, Gap on baby overalls, Starbucks on coffee cups, and L.L. Bean on backpacks. Meaningful branding can inspire depths of customer loyalty, and companies rely on such loyalty to maintain sales and market share.

When a product is branded, it has a brand identity immediately recognizable to consumers. Part of the immediate recognition is an icon, a slogan, a jingle, and even colors that can trigger in consumers' minds the product—McDonald's golden arches, Nike's "Just Do It," or Ben & Jerry's black-and-white cow colors. Some slogans change, such as the U.S. Army's more recent slogan "Army Strong" instead of "An Army of One" used a few years ago. But the identity and association are still clear. Once consumers recognize the product, they ascribe certain feelings or values that create brand loyalty.

Companies have determined that brand loyalty is a combination of overall satisfaction and confidence or trust. Another component is emotional attachment. Think about brands you use and why you use them. You may use a certain deodorant soap because that's the one you always found in the shower's soapdish at home. Whoever did the grocery shopping in your family had a loyalty to that particular brand. Perhaps you prefer a certain type of fast-food pizza because of the crust, the toppings, the service, or the group of friends you usually eat pizza with. People develop a familiarity with a product, and they may oppose any changes to it. Companies bank on consumers and their ties to certain products.

When assessing what makes consumers become attached to a product, companies use criteria that represent loyalty factors. Looking at the soap example above, you may have loyalty to Soap X because it brings back good feelings about home—the emotional attachment—plus you like the way it cleans your skin. In the quest for determining customer loyalty, researchers have gone so far as to develop indexes that rate customer satisfaction. Gallup, known for its polling, has developed a measure of what it calls customer engagement. A list of questions measures customer loyalty as well as emotional attachment.

More and more in the last decade, companies have considered branding as a key to retaining customers and profits. Research has shown that the cost of attracting new customers is five times the cost of keeping current ones. As a result, companies are investing more research dollars into understanding what makes customers stick with certain products or brands. Businesses have adopted practices so they can determine which products and services customers buy and why. They can even track individual customers to find out more about their habits and needs. Such information is invaluable in focusing advertising—and in developing other areas that provide customer service.

Branding is important for anyone writing or designing ads. Armed with customer research, a copywriter might develop an ad that shows the product's character and appeal. Part of branding may be the slogan for the product, its name, or its logo that creates recognition and positive feelings. Consistency in the message across all media strengthens the brand identity. The brand elements add value and differentiate the product from similar products.

Another aspect may be choosing spokespeople to represent the brands. For example, at the 2008 Olympic Summer Games in Beijing, swimmer Michael Phelps surpassed his own 2004 Olympic medal total and that of Mark Spitz who won seven gold medals in 1976. Before competing in Beijing, Phelps already had done endorsements, particularly for Speedo. Others followed after his 2008 victories. His success evokes qualities of determination, stamina, down-homeness, and just an average American who wins big.

Tips for Ad Copy That Sells

No matter the medium, copywriters have to produce ads: strategic messages that move products and services. Advertising Professor Jim Plumb gave the following broad tips to both student and professional copywriters:

1. **Identify selling points.** Focus on concrete reasons for purchase. An abstract reason to buy a Subaru wagon is safety, but a concrete selling point is that buying a Subaru keeps the driver from shoveling snow or paying a tow truck.
2. **List the benefits.** Find and list the benefits of your product that are important to your audience. Build your ad writing around these benefits. Make sure they are unique from competitors' products. List them in the ad if you can, but be sure to mention them in some way. Don't forget to look for intangible benefits. Sometimes the most powerful benefits are intangibles, such as the mood a perfume creates or a feeling of belonging that comes from a health club. Again, the viewer or reader should experience the product.
3. **Identify the single greatest benefit of your product.** Research should identify the quality of your product that is most meaningful to your intended audience. Then create a headline or slogan that will convey this benefit to your audience. With "Just Do It," Nike sells discipline, an intangible benefit, as its star quality. A slogan in ads for *The Washington Post* reads, "If you don't get it, you don't get it." That is, if you don't take the *Post* regularly, you'll be left out. By communicating benefits in a few words, ad writing has the power to modify attitudes and behaviors. The same technique, among others used by copywriters, can work in all forms of writing.

Other experts in the field remind copywriters of other specifics. In their book, *The New How to Advertise*, advertising executives Kenneth Roman and Jane Maas list elements of good advertising strategy. They note that a good ad will show solutions to a problem; effective ads will aim for target audiences; and every good ad projects the tone, manner, and personality of the product. Other experts also recommend that ad copy should note details; use well-chosen language; have strong, clear words; have one unifying idea or theme; contain a beginning, a middle, and an end; and, for the most part, use correct grammar.

But some contend if such rules are followed, the result will be well-produced but boring ads. Other techniques are needed for fun or zany, truly creative advertisements. George Felton in his book, *Advertising Concepts*, discusses reversal as an approach to writing ads. He notes:

> *All great ads employ reversal: Something significant has been put in, left out, inverted, photographed oddly, colored wrong, talked about differently, or in some way had violence done to its ordinariness. Otherwise, if our preconceptions have been fulfilled instead of violated, we'll be looking at clichés.*

He gives as an example the classic Volkswagen ad that took the maxim "Think big" and reversed it to "Think small." The print advertisement used exceptional white space and put a small Volkswagen near the upper left-hand corner. "The ad reversed our expectations twice: once as user of clichés and once as viewers of ads," Felton notes.

Strategic Communication Online

Since the mid-1990s, any organization that wants to reach audiences quickly and provide in-depth information has moved internal and external communications online. Corporate newsrooms on Web sites post the latest news releases as well as archives of past releases and visuals that can be downloaded. Inhouse Web sites, e-mail lists, and message boards help employees stay in touch, whether they are in the same building or scattered across the world. Established companies have found they can expand their marketing efforts through the Internet and even hook into the Federal Trade Commission's advice for advertising on the Internet found at http://www.ftc.gov/bcp/edu/pubs/business/ecommerce/bus28.shtm. Web sites also provide information about the company to potential investors and customers.

Public relations practitioners use online software to track how many people access information online. Instead of sorting through clips of print stories, a media manager can count clicks on Web links. Software can also help build media lists and generate more media coverage.

Companies that once relied on banner ads or pop-up ads on Web sites have moved into more innovative ways to reach customers, even though pop-ups are still a strong part of Internet advertising. Such innovation has been necessary to catch a visual audience with a short attention span and also to counteract software that can block advertising. Some companies advertise online by buying space next to editorial content on Web sites and using animation and video to attract attention—the more traditional advertising choice on the Internet. Or they have their own Web sites where they can advertise their products and offer troubleshooting advice.

As a result, e-commerce has prospered fairly well, allowing people to shop online. Shoppers can pick out products, change colors and styles, and buy online—then play virtual games. The shipment arrives on their doorsteps in a few days. Convenience sells products, and the more customers use credit cards securely to order online, the more willing they are to spend via the Internet. People who want to avoid having their e-commerce use tracked can install adware and spyware software to identify and quarantine cookies they might be downloading.

Any communicator must be creative and proactive in thinking about how the Internet can increase an organization's reach with its audience. Communication can be as targeted as podcasts and as broad as streaming video on a Web site. With the Internet, any company's information is available 24 hours a day. Web sites must be constantly monitored and updated, information has to be accurate and complete, and sites must be easily navigable.

For college students, the specifics that make up strategic communication online could be wildly different at graduation day from what you see in today's media landscape. Any changes are likely to offer more diverse career opportunities for those who have the skills to use words effectively and correctly and to add visually rich elements to online content.

Exercises

1. You are the public relations officer for the Campus Literacy Program. You want to recruit more volunteers to serve as readers to children in the community.

    a. Identify the audience(s) you are trying to reach as potential volunteers.
    b. Knowing your audience interests and media usage, identify three communications tools you would use to reach each audience.
    c. What information would your audience(s) need to make a decision whether to volunteer? Make a list.
    d. How could you evaluate the success of your communications effort?

2. You are the public relations director for Bicycle World Equipment Co. You are to write a news release for the local newspaper based on the following information:

> Bicycle World is planning to sponsor bicycle safety clinics in the public schools located in Wayne County, the company headquarters. The clinics will be held on two consecutive Saturdays from 10 a.m. to noon. Each of the county's six elementary schools will house the clinics. People who want to attend must call 555–3456 to register. The clinic is open to children 6–12 years of age. Each child must have a helmet.
>
> Bicycle World staff members will check each child's bicycle for safe operation and indicate on a check-off list any equipment that needs repair. Children will be advised of good bicycle safety, such as wearing helmets, riding in bike lanes, and using proper hand signals. Then each will be allowed to enter an obstacle course, which will test their riding proficiency. For example, as they ride down a "road," a dog may run out from between two cars. Children's reactions and reaction times will be monitored. After the road test, they will be briefed on what they did well and what they need to improve. At the end of the course, they will receive a certificate of accomplishment.
>
> "We believe bicycle safety is crucial for children," said company president Dennis Lester. "With just a little guidance, children can learn habits and rules that could save their lives. Those of us in the bicycle business want to ensure that children who use our products do so competently and safely. We want them to enjoy bicycling as a sport they can continue into adulthood."
>
> The clinics are free.
>
> Bicycle World is a three-year-old company that produces bike frames, components, bike helmets, clothing, and road guides to bicycle routes. Company President Dennis Lester is a master rider and formed the company to provide quality equipment to bicycle enthusiasts.

3. From the above information, write a one-page fact sheet based on the bicycle clinics sponsored by Bicycle World Equipment Co. You would be the contact, 555-2345. The company's address is 67 W. Lane Blvd., Your town, Your zip code.

4. President Dennis Lester at Bicycle World wants to implement a comprehensive advertising and public relations plan that will help sell more bicycles in your community. Develop a strategy that identifies target audiences and then include at least three types of advertising and PR activities that could reach each target audience.

5. Based on Exercise 4, you are to create an advertisement for Bicycle World to reach parents of children who ride bicycles. Make a list of the words that would appeal to parents looking for children's bikes, focusing on the prominent characteristics of bikes. Write at least three possible headlines for your ad, focusing on a characteristic in each.

6. Invite a professional who specializes in strategic communication to visit your class. Ask this person to talk briefly about advertising and public relations as part of strategic communication in today's competitive media environment. Have him or her talk about the importance of good writing and the influence of the Internet in strategic planning.

References

American Advertising Federation Web Site. Available at www.aaf.com.

"Auto Giants Push Harder for Magazine Product Placement," www.adage.com/news.cms? newsId545807, accessed August 19, 2005.

American Society of Newspaper Editors at www.magazine.org/Editorial/Guidelines/Editorial_and_Advertising_Pages/, accessed September 3, 2005.

Bruce Bendiger et al., *Advertising: The Business of Brands.* Chicago: The Copy Workshop, 1999.

Philip Ward Burton, *Advertising Copywriting, 6th ed.* Lincolnwood, IL: NTC Business Books, 1990.

Scott M. Cutlip, Allen H. Center, and Glen H. Broom, *Effective Public Relations, 7th ed.* Englewood Cliffs, NJ: Prentice-Hall, 1994.

George Felton, *Advertising Concepts and Copy.* Englewood Cliffs, NJ: Prentice-Hall, 1994.

Medialink Web Site. Available at www.medialink.com.

"Marketing beyond the Pop-Up," *Advertising Age*, March 10, 2003.

PR Newswire Web Site. Available at www.prnewswire.com.

Public Relations Society of America Web Site. Available at http://www.prsa.org.

Kenneth Roman and Jane Maas, *The New How to Advertise.* New York: St. Martin's Press, 1992.

Dennis L. Wilcox and Lawrence W. Nolte, *Public Relations Writing and Media Techniques, 2nd ed.* New York: HarperCollins College Publishers, 1995.

Appendix A

Keys to Grammar Quizzes

After years of working with these exercises, we recognize that no single answer exists for any exercise item. Each answer we provide is what we consider to be the best or preferred answer, rather than the only answer.

Grammar Slammer Diagnostic Quiz (pages 28–29)

1. Punctuation error. A comma replaces the semicolon because clauses on either side of a semicolon must be independent.
2. Subject–verb agreement error. The subject of the sentence is list, so the verb must agree. It is the LIST that HAS BEEN TRIMMED.
3. Punctuation error. A period or semicolon replaces the comma because commas may not separate independent clauses. Some would label this a comma splice; others, a run-on sentence.
4. Punctuation error. A comma is needed after OCTOBER 25 because commas follow all elements in a complete date and the phrase is a nonessential clause.
5. Sentence structure error. The modifying phrase, TRADITIONALLY EXPECTED TO BE IN CONTROL OF THEIR SURROUNDINGS is misplaced and needs to follow the word STUDENTS. In its present position, the phrase modifies THE INSECURITY.
6. Word use error. LIE instead of LAY when no action is taken.
7. Word use error. Modifying the word COUNCIL with the word HOPEFULLY leaves the council filled with hope. It is preferable to say, "We hope the council…."

8. Punctuation error. Semicolons are used to separate all punctuated items in a list. A semicolon is needed after EASTERN.
9. Word use error. Use neither and nor as a matched pair. The same goes for either and or.
10. Pronoun error. Use the pronoun IT to agree with the noun COMPANY, a singular thing.
11. Punctuation error. Phrases that rename subjects (appositives) are non-essential and therefore set off by commas. Place a comma after COMMITTEE.
12. Subject–verb agreement error. LIVES is the verb that agrees with the true subject of the sentence, which is ONE.
13. Punctuation error. Commas follow both elements of a city and state combination that occurs in mid-sentence, even if the state abbreviation ends in a period.
14. Word use error. The past tense, USED, is correct usage in this idiom.
15. Sentence structure error. Including WILL PLAY in this list of parade items makes for faulty parallelism. Delete WILL PLAY.
16. Sentence structure error. This sentence is incomplete. It is a sentence fragment. Even though it is lengthy, it has no verb. Add the word CAME after SEVERAL PEOPLE.
17. Comma error. Semicolon or period needed after COOKIES.
18. The coordinate conjunction AND is used where a subordinate conjunction, such as BECAUSE or THAT, is needed and delete the comma.
19. Modifier problem. His muscles are not being a weight lifter.
20. Agreement. ITS SKIN.

1. Correct. Your principAL is your PAL. PrincipLES are LESSONS.
2. Correct. A waiver is a document of permission; a waver is a person who waves.
3. Incorrect. A bore is a dull person or event. A boar is a wild pig.
4. Incorrect. A navel is a belly button. Naval means pertaining to the navy.
5. Correct. StationERy is sold by stationERs.
6. Incorrect. A role is a part in a play. A roll is something rolled up, even a class list.
7. Correct. Note also bookkeeper and withholding.
8. Incorrect. Canvas is cloth. To canvaSS is to cover thoroughly, as in a canvass of the neighborhood.

9. Incorrect. Complement is a verb that means to complete. A compliment is a flattering statement.
10. Correct. Cite is correct in this case.

Slammer for Commas, Semicolons, and Colons (pages 34–35) (Rule numbers are noted before each answer)

1. Rule 4, comma after Bowl.
2. Rule 7, commas after Blimpo and man.
3. Rule 10, semicolon after strings; Rule 9, comma after basses.
4. Rule 2, comma after tall, after dark, after reading, and after fishing.
5. Rule 5, colon after concern; Rule 2, comma after 2 and 4; Rule 5, comma after 2009 and after yours.
6. Rule 8, comma after Dad.
7. Rule 10, semicolon after halftime; Rule 4, comma after however.
8. Rule 1, comma after bill.
9. Rule 7, comma after well.
10. Rule 10, semicolon after disappointment.
11. Rule 6, comma after 4, after 2008, after Baltimore, and after Md.
12. Rule 12, colon after semester; Rule 2, comma after journalism, after English, and after political science.

Slammer for Subject–Verb Agreement (pages 37–38)

1. include
2. appear
3. gives
4. results
5. have
6. do
7. is
8. are
9. exhibits
10. are
11. constitute
12. was
13. believes
14. is
15. decides
16. typifies
17. are
18. are
19. is
20. is
21. teach
22. is
23. consider
24. disagree

Slammer for Pronouns (page 40)

1. his or her
2. its
3. himself
4. its
5. its
6. is
7. was
8. was
9. their
10. is
11. its
12. it
13. are
14. himself or herself
15. his or her

Slammer for Who/Whom and That/Which (pages 42–43)

1. whom (everyone adored whom/him, the object of the sentence)
2. who (who/she was, the subject)
3. whom (Alvin avoided whom/them, the object)
4. who (who/she needed, the subject)
5. whose (not who's or who is health)

1. which, commas after gun and sale (the fact that the gun was on sale is additional, nonessential information)
2. which, comma after car (the mileage is additional, nonessential information)
3. that, no commas (the Jersey plates helped police identify the car, so essential information)
4. who, commas after Texans and drawl (Texans are people so who or whom; who is subject of spoke; how they spoke is nonessential information)
5. which, commas after gun and compartment (where she kept the gun is nonessential information)
6. who, no commas (again, person takes who or whom; who/he is subject of was; phrase tells which officer was shot so it is essential)
7. that, no commas (the lack of bullets allowed the officers to get the gun, so the phrase is essential)
8. which, comma after jail (the view from the jail cell is nonessential)

Slammer for Modifiers (pages 44–45)

1. The waiter served ice cream, which started melting immediately, in glass bowls.
2. Correct.
3. On the way to our hotel, we saw a herd of sheep.
4. Correct.
5. The house where Mrs. Rooks taught ballet is one of the oldest in Rockville.
6. Correct.
7. Without yelling, I could not convince the child to stop running into the street.
8. The critic said that after the first act of the play, Brooke's performance improves.
9. While we were watching the ball game, Sue's horse ran away.
10. Correct.
11. The bank approves loans of any size to reliable individuals.
12. After I was wheeled into the operating room, the nurse placed a mask over my face.
13. Correct.
14. Aunt Helen asked us to call on her before we left.

Appendix B

Key to Math Test

Slammer for Math (pages 51–53)

1. **a.** The ratio of men to women is 9:4. Subtract the number of women from the total to get the number of men.
   b. To get percentage, divide the difference by the base. In this case, 4 (the number of women) is divided by 13 for a percentage of 30.8 percent (the actual number is .3076 but is to be rounded to the nearest tenth for 30.8).
   c. The same process is used to figure the percentage of Hispanic men on the jury: Divide 1 by 13 for an answer of 7.7 percent.
   d. Again, divide the number of African American men (1) by the base of 13 and you get the same answer as 1c: 7.7 percent.

2. **a.** To get the cost for the center alone, multiply the number of square feet by the cost per square foot, or 15,000 by $85 for a cost of $1,275,000.
   b. The cost follows the same formula: Multiply 15,000 square feet by $25 for a cost of $375,000.
   c. To get the total cost, add the cost of the building to the cost of the furnishings for a total $1,650,000.
   d. To round off, remember that you round up after 5, 50, 500, 5,000, etc. So rounded to the nearest 100,000 would be $1.7 million.

3. **a.** To get the size, multiply 12 by 8 to get the size of one booth (96 square feet) then double it because each booth is two parking spaces. The answer is 192 square feet. Note: You can't double both measurements then multiply because the booth will grow only in width, not in depth. So the booth actually measures 16 by 12, which is 192 square feet.
   b. The company can rent 120 booths. Divide the number of spaces in the parking lot by 2 because each booth is two spaces.

c. Multiply the number of booths (120) by $30 to get $3,600.
d. Go back to 3a. One booth is 192 square feet. If you get two booths, you get 384 square feet.

4. a. First you have to calculate how many units per $100. So divide the house value of $175,000 by 100 and you get $1,750. Then multiply by the tax rate of 85 cents (.85) to get a tax bill of $1,487.50.
   b. Under the new tax rate of 88 cents, Sarah will pay 1,750 times .88 or $1,540.
   c. To calculate the increase in her tax bill, you need the difference between the old bill and the new bill. So subtract $1,487.50 from $1,540 to get $52.50. To find the percentage increase, remember difference divided by base or $52.50 divided by $1,487.50, or a 3.5 percent increase in value.
   d. To find out how much her property would increase, multiply $175,000 by 5 percent (0.05) to get $8,750. Add that amount to $175,000 to get the new value of $183,500. To find the tax bill, follow the steps in 4a. Remember to use the new tax rate of 88 cents per $100 to get the answer: $1,617.

5. a. The total female respondents was 275. Add the female counts of 107, 137, and 31.
   b. Total respondents is 627. (Add all the individual counts for male and female.) Divide the total number of women respondents, 275, by 627 and the percentage is 44.
   c. You cannot add rows of percentages to get this answer. You have to go back to your counts. Fifty-four respondents (male and female) supported Tucker. Divide by total 627 and the percentage is 8.6.
   d. The same rule for 5c applies here. A total of 274 supported Small, divided by the total respondents of 627, and you get 43.7 percent.

6. The key here is that if she has a 75 percent chance of band practice, she has only a 25 percent chance of going to the fair. Multiply the two probabilities, 50 percent (.5) and 25 percent (.25). The likelihood she will get to the fair is 12.5 percent.

7. The answer is C; $310. If he earns $7.50 an hour, 25 cents more means $7.75 an hour. Multiply by the number of hours, 40.

8. The answer is 61.29. You multiply the number of pounds by 0.454 to get the number of kilograms.

Index

G

H

I

P

Q

R

S